The Cambridge Companion to

European Criminal Law

European Criminal Law has developed into a complex, jagged subject matter, which at the same time has become increasingly important for everyday criminal law practice. On the one hand, this work aims to do comprehensive justice to the complexity of the matter without sacrificing readability. In order to achieve this, the book's structure enables legal scholars and experienced practitioners to access the information relevant to them in a targeted manner and, at the same time, enables less-oriented readers to gain access to European Criminal Law. Thus, the volume both answers basic questions and offers discussion in more specialised areas. Written by experts in the field, the book offers discussions that are both of the highest academic standards and accessibly readable.

Kai Ambos is Chair for Criminal Law, Criminal Procedure, Comparative Law, International Criminal Law and Public International Law at the Faculty of Law, University of Göttingen, Germany. He is also Judge at the Kosovo Specialist Chambers, The Hague, Netherlands as well as Director of the Centro de Estudios de Derecho Penal y Procesal Penal Latinoamericano (CEDPAL), and Advisor (amicus curiae) of the Colombian Special Jurisdiction for Peace.

Peter Rackow is Associate Professor at the Institute for Criminal Law and Criminal Justice and the Department of Foreign and International Criminal Law, Faculty of Law, University of Göttingen, Germany.

Cambridge Companions to Law

Cambridge Companions to Law offers thought-provoking introductions to different legal disciplines, invaluable to both the student and the scholar. Edited by world-leading academics, each offers a collection of essays which both map out the subject and allow the reader to delve deeper. Critical and enlightening, the Companions library represents legal scholarship at its best.

The Cambridge Companion to European Union Private Law
Edited by Christian Twigg-Flesner

The Cambridge Companion to International Law
Edited by James Crawford and Martti Koskenniemi

The Cambridge Companion to Comparative Law
Edited by Mauro Bussani and Ugo Mattei

The Cambridge Companion to Human Rights Law
Edited by Conor Gearty and Costas Douzinas

The Cambridge Companion to Public Law
Edited by Mark Elliott and David Feldman

The Cambridge Companion to International Criminal Law
Edited by William A. Schabas

The Cambridge Companion to Natural Law Jurisprudence
Edited by George Duke and Robert P. George

The Cambridge Companion to Comparative Family Law
Edited by Shazia Choudhry and Jonathan Herring

The Cambridge Companion to Comparative Constitutional Law
Edited by Roger Masterman and Robert Schütze

The Cambridge Companion to the First Amendment and Religious Liberty
Edited by Michael D. Breidenbach and Owen Anderson

The Cambridge Companion to the Philosophy of Law
Edited by John Tasioulas

The Cambridge Companion to Legal Positivism
Edited by Torben Spaak and Patricia Mindus

The Cambridge Companion to Hugo Grotius
Edited by Randall Lesaffer and Janne E. Nijman

The Cambridge Companion to International Arbitration
Edited by Chin Leng Lim

The Cambridge Companion to Business & Human Rights Law
Edited by Ilias Bantekas and Michael Stein

The Cambridge Companion to International Organizations Law
Edited by Jan Klabbers

The Cambridge Companion to Gender and the Law
Edited by Stéphanie Hennette Vauchez and Ruth Rubio-Marín

The Cambridge Companion to the International Court of Justice
Edited by Carlos Espósito and Kate Parlett

The Cambridge Companion to

European Criminal Law

Edited by

Kai Ambos
University of Göttingen

Peter Rackow
University of Göttingen

CAMBRIDGE
UNIVERSITY PRESS

CAMBRIDGE
UNIVERSITY PRESS

Shaftesbury Road, Cambridge CB2 8EA, United Kingdom

One Liberty Plaza, 20th Floor, New York, NY 10006, USA

477 Williamstown Road, Port Melbourne, VIC 3207, Australia

314–321, 3rd Floor, Plot 3, Splendor Forum, Jasola District Centre, New Delhi – 110025, India

103 Penang Road, #05–06/07, Visioncrest Commercial, Singapore 238467

Cambridge University Press is part of Cambridge University Press & Assessment, a department of the University of Cambridge.

We share the University's mission to contribute to society through the pursuit of education, learning and research at the highest international levels of excellence.

www.cambridge.org
Information on this title: www.cambridge.org/9781108835190

DOI: 10.1017/9781108891875

First published 2023

A catalogue record for this publication is available from the British Library

ISBN 978-1-108-83519-0 Hardback
ISBN 978-1-108-79979-9 Paperback

Contents

Notes on Contributors

Silvia Allegrezza is Associate Professor of Criminal Law and criminal procedure at the University of Luxembourg. She is Principal Investigator in several research projects founded by the EU Commission and by the Luxembourg Fond National de la Recherche. Since 2022, she is a member of the EU Commission Experts Group for Criminal Justice and special expert on anti-money laundering for the EU Parliament. Her research focuses on Cryptocurrencies and crime; on anti-money laundering and banking regulations; on appeals proceedings and other judicial remedies in criminal matters and on forensic genetic investigations.

Kai Ambos is Chair for Criminal Law, Criminal Procedure, Comparative Law, International Criminal Law and Public International Law at the Faculty of Law, University of Göttingen, Germany. He is also Judge at the Kosovo Specialist Chambers, The Hague, Netherlands as well as Director of the Centro de Estudios de Derecho Penal y Procesal Penal Latinoamericano (CEDPAL), and Advisor (amicus curiae) of the Colombian Special Jurisdiction for Peace. He is the author of the three volumes Treatise on International Criminal Law (OUP, 2013 ff.) and publishes widely in the areas of criminal law, criminal procedure, international (criminal) law and comparative criminal justice

Lorena Bachmaier Winter is Full Professor at the Law School of Complutense University of Madrid, where she teaches Justice Systems and Procedure. She also teaches in Saint Louis University, Missouri. Her research focuses mainly on comparative law, rule of law, human rights and criminal procedure, and the building up of the European area of freedom, security and justice. She has written extensively in the field of criminal justice as well as on topics related to civil procedure and arbitration. She is a member of the editorial board of numerous legal journals and of the most important academic associations. She regularly cooperates as international expert with the Council of Europe, the European Commission and other international organisations in improving human rights standards and the rule of law in transitional democracies. She is also member of the *Expert Group on Criminal Policy* of the EU Commission.

Stefanie Bock is Professor for Criminal Law, Criminal Procedure, International Criminal Law and Comparative Law at the Philipps-Universität Marburg, Germany, and Director of the International Research and Documentation Centre for War Crimes Trials. Her main fields of research are international criminal law, European criminal law and comparative criminal law.

Martin Böse is Professor of Criminal Law, Criminal Procedure, and International and European Criminal Law, and Director of the Institute of Criminal Law at the University of Bonn. His main research interests lie in the fields of European criminal law, international cooperation in criminal matters and economic criminal law.

Pedro Caeiro is Associate Professor of Criminal Law in the Faculty of Law of the University of Coimbra. He is a member of the European Commission's Expert Group on EU Criminal Policy since 2012 and of the management committee of the European Criminal Law Academic Network. He is also a member of the editorial board of several publications, including the *New Journal of European Criminal Law* and Brill Research Perspectives in Transnational Crime. His research focuses on jurisdiction, European criminal law and international judicial cooperation in criminal matters.

Olivier Cahn is Professor of Criminal Law at CY Cergy Paris University in France, Director of the master in business criminal law and a researcher at the Center for Sociological Research on Law and Penal Institutions (CESDIP) (CNRS-UMR 8183). His research focuses on political violence, police law, economic and financial crime, and police and judicial cooperation in criminal matters.

Miguel João Costa is an advisor at the Portuguese Constitutional Court and teaches Criminal Law and Procedure at the University of Coimbra, where he obtained his LLB (2008) and LLM (2011). He holds a PhD from Maastricht University (2019) on the subject matter of extradition: *Extradition Law: Reviewing Grounds for Refusal from the Classic*

Paradigm to Mutual Recognition and Beyond (Brill, 2019). Since 2021, he is a member of the European Commission's Expert Group on the European Arrest Warrant.

Emanuela Fronza is Professor of Criminal Law at the Department of Legal Sciences at the University of Bologna. Her research interests span from national to international and comparative criminal law. She has been a Fellow of the Humboldt Foundation and Principal Investigator of the Memory Laws in International and Comparative Perspective – MELA Project. She has edited several books and published extensively in the field of international, European and comparative criminal law. She is the author of *Memory and Punishment: Historical Denialism, Free Speech and the Limits of Criminal Law* (Springer, 2018).

Fabio Giuffrida (PhD, Queen Mary University of London) worked as a postdoctoral researcher in EU Criminal Law at the Faculty of Law, Economics and Finance of the University of Luxembourg and is currently Policy Officer at the European Commission. He has authored several articles and studies concerning different aspects of EU Criminal Law, including a recent book on the fight against environmental crime at EU level, and co-edited a volume on the establishment of the European Public Prosecutor's Office.

Liz Heffernan is an associate professor and Fellow of Trinity College Dublin where she teaches in the fields of evidence and criminal law. She taught previously at Washington and Lee University School of Law, Lexington, Virginia, and worked as a law clerk at the US Court of Appeals for the Seventh Circuit. Her research focuses primarily on Criminal Evidence in the Irish courts and includes analysis of the impact of EU law and the ECHR on common law systems.

Alejandro Hernández López is postdoctoral researcher "Margarita Salas" at the Universities of Valladolid and Burgos. He teaches and writes on European Union criminal law and justice and national and comparative criminal procedure law. His main research focuses on the development and challenges of judicial cooperation in criminal matters in the European Union, including the role of Eurojust in the settlement of conflicts of criminal jurisdiction.

Francisco Jiménez-Villarejo Fernández has been Vice President of Eurojust and National Member for Spain. He is currently Deputy Supreme Court Prosecutor of the Kingdom of Spain and Head of the International Cooperation Unit at the General Prosecutor's Office. In addition to his extensive practical experience, he is the author of numerous contributions on the Area of Freedom, Security and Justice and the judicial cooperation in criminal matters between Member States of the European Union.

Krisztina Karsai is full professor in criminal law at the University of Szeged (Hungary) and is specialised in European and international criminal law, and criminal policy. Her position as an independent expert of the European Commission (DG Justice; Fields of justice, freedom and security; criminal justice, prevent and combat criminality) allowed her to take part also in evaluation procedures of tenders (since 2013). She is also working for the EUROJUST EUROMED project as a key expert. She has been granted with Jean Monnet Chair (2016–2019) for her project "Legal Innovation for Citizens, the Area of Freedom, Security and Justice". Krisztina Karsai is the author of many books and articles on Hungarian and European criminal law and policy; she is the editor and co-author of the Commentary on the Hungarian Criminal Code.

Katalin Ligeti is a full professor of European and international criminal law at the University of Luxembourg. Professor Ligeti plays a leading role in several transnational research networks: she is Vice President in Charge of Scientific Coordination of the AIDP and Co-coordinator of the ECLAN. Her research focuses primarily on police and judicial co-operation in criminal matters, EU criminal law, comparative criminal procedure and information technology and criminal justice. She has widely published on the European Public Prosecutor and other European criminal justice bodies and agencies.

Frank Meyer, LLM (Yale), Dr. iur. (Hamburg), Dr. iur. habil (Bonn), is Professor of Law at Heidelberg University where he holds the Chair for Criminal Law and Criminal Procedure with particular consideration of its relations to European law and international law. His research interests are in European criminal law, transnational cooperation and enforcement, comparative criminal law and human rights law. He has published in those areas and is the author of leading texts on the criminal law: chapters of the TFEU (von der Groeben/Schwarze/Hatje, Europäisches Unionsrecht, 7th ed., Nomos 2015) and Article 6 of ECHR (Karpenstein/Mayer, EGMR, 3rd ed., Beck 2021).

Valsamis Mitsilegas is Professor of European and Global Law and Dean of the School of Law and Social Justice, University of Liverpool. He is Co-Coordinator of ECLAN and is currently serving for a fourth term as a member of the European Commission Expert Group on Criminal Policy. Professor Mitsilegas is the founding General Editor of the Hart Studies in European Criminal Law, of the Queen Mary-Renmin Series on Comparative Criminal Justice Issues in China and Europe and of the Brill Research Perspectives in Transnational Crime. He is also General Editor of the *New Journal of European Criminal Law* and the Brill series on Immigration and Asylum Law and Policy in Europe. He is the author of 9 books and over 150 articles and chapters in academic volumes. The second edition of his monograph on EU Criminal Law is published by Hart in May 2022.

Kimmo Nuotio is Professor of criminal law and Director of the Institute of Criminology and Legal Policy at the University of Helsinki. He is former Jean Monnet Fellow of the European University Institute in Florence and he has held a visiting professorship or equivalent at the Australian National University, University of Leuven, Peking University and the University of Toronto. He has published widely in different areas of criminal law.

Noreen O'Meara is Associate Professor (Reader) in Human Rights, European and Environmental Law at the University of Surrey. She studied at Cambridge (MA), UCL (LLM) and Queen Mary, University of London (PhD), and worked at the European Commission, Court of Justice of the European Union and the British Institute of International and Comparative Law (BIICL) before starting her academic career. She teaches and researches in the areas of human rights and EU law, with particular expertise in the areas of procedural justice, fundamental rights and environmental law.

Peter Rackow is Associate Professor at the Institute for Criminal Law and Criminal Justice and the Department of Foreign and International Criminal Law, Faculty of Law, University of Göttingen, Germany.

Philipp Ronsfeld is Legal Advisor at the Ministry of Social Affairs of the state of Baden-Wuerttemberg in Stuttgart, Germany. He studied law at the University of Freiburg. In 2015, he obtained his Dr iur from the University of Kiel. He completed his doctorate on European penal law. His research was focused on reducing delays in legal assistance by promoting mutual recognition and trust, on the example of the new European Investigation Order. Currently, since the beginning of 2022, he has been temporarily seconded to the German Federal Foreign Office (Europe Department) in Berlin.

Miha Šepec is an associate professor and Head of the Institute for Criminal Law and Minor Offences at the University of Maribor, Faculty of Law. He is the sole editor of the Commentary on the General Part of the Slovene Criminal Code, released in 2021, and the sole editor of the Commentary of the Criminal Procedural Act, which will be released in 2022. He has experience in coordinating national as well as international projects related to European criminal law. He was voted amongst top ten most influential lawyers in Slovenia in 2018, 2019, 2020 and 2021.

Jan Stajnko is an academic assistant at Faculty of Law, University of Maribor, Chair for Criminal law, and a PhD student at the University of Ljubljana, Faculty of Law. He is a co-author of the Commentary on the General Part of Slovene Criminal Code, the Great Scientific Commentary of the Special Part of Slovene Criminal Code and the Commentary of the Slovene Criminal Procedural Act. He has cooperated in core research teams of national as well as EU and UNODC-funded projects.

Marianne L. Wade is Reader in Criminal Justice, Birmingham Law School (University of Birmingham, Birmingham, UK). She is a Fellow of the UoB Institute of Global Innovation, heading the Transnational Crime Stream within the 21st Century Crime Theme. Dr Wade's activities currently focus on European criminal law and criminal justice as well as prosecutors and terrorism. She has provided expert advice i.a. the international prosecutor's office of the ECCC, the UNDP's POGAR conference, the President of the German Prosecutor-Generals' working group, the Dutch Ministry of Justice, the LIBE Committee of the European Parliament and the EU Presidency. She is a member of the legal expert advisory board of the NGO Fair Trials International and a criminal justice expert for the European Commission.

Petra Weingerl is an assistant professor at the Faculty of Law, University of Maribor. Petra completed her doctorate and Magister Juris at the Faculty of Law of the University of Oxford. She is an adjunct professor at the University of Trieste. She is a holder of the Jean Monnet Module on Fundamental Rights in EU Business Law and Policy.

Liane Wörner, LLM (UW Madison), Dr. iur., Dr. iur. habil. (JLU Gießen), is Full Professor for Criminal Law, Criminal Procedure, Comparative Criminal Law, Medical Criminal Law and Legal Theory and Director of the Centre for Human | Data | Society at the University of Konstanz, Germany. She is a member of the scientific committee of the AIDP and a member of the Global Diplomacy Lab (GDL). Her main fields of research are comparative criminal law, European criminal law, digitalization and criminal law, medical criminal law and legal theory.

Preface

The Cambridge Companion to European Criminal Law is intended as a foundation for deeper studies. It aims to provide a structured overview of the field in six sections dealing with the foundations of European Criminal Law, its purposes and principles, the European substantive and criminal procedure law, and the relevant institutions. The volume concludes with a section on the perspectives of European Criminal Law. Each chapter explores key academic debates and provides guidelines for further reading.

In view of the dynamic development of European Criminal Law, a number of chapters focus on more recent developments such as the European Investigation Order (EIO) and the European Public Prosecutor's Office (EPPO) and the impact of Brexit. The discussion of specific, current, and dynamic issues is based on a thematically comprehensive presentation of the foundations of European Criminal Law and its practically relevant principles, such as the principle of mutual recognition, across various chapters. It is attempted in the last chapter, to rethink and reassess the foundations, institutional design, and aims of European Criminal Law and the EU criminal policy.

We are grateful to all authors for having submitted their papers and to the publisher to have taken up this project.

Kai Ambos
Peter Rackow
Göttingen, November 2022

Table of Cases

Civil Service Tribunal (CST)

Giraudy v. Commission, No. F-23/05, Judgment, ECLI:EU:F:2007:75, 2 May 2007, 348

Court of First Instance (CFI)

Camós Grau v. Commission, No. T-309/03, Order, ECLI:EU:T:2006:110, 6 April 2006, 347

Comunidad Autónoma de Andalucía v. Commission, No. T-29/03, Order, ECLI:EU:T:2004:235, 13 July 2004, T-29/03, 345

Dalli v. Commission, No. T-399/17, Judgment, ECLI:EU:T:2019:384, 6 June 2019, 333, 339

De Esteban Alonso v. Commission, No. T-138-18, Judgment, ECLI:EU:T:2019:398, 11 June 2019, 347

EKETA v. Commission, No. T-166/17, Judgment, ECLI:EU:T:2019:26, 22 January 2019, 344

Franchet and Byk v. Commission, No. T-48/05, Judgment, ECLI:EU:T:2008:257, 8 July 2008, 335, 340, 348

Inox Mare v. Commission, No. T-289/16, Order, ECLI:EU:T:2017:414, 21 June 2017, 344, 345, 346

International Management Group v. Commission, No. T110/15, Judgment, ECLI:EU:T:2016:322, 26 May 2016, 344

Le Pen v. Parliament, No. T-161/17, Judgment, ECLI:EU:T:2018:848, 28 November 2018, 337

Le Pen v. Parliament, No. T86/17, Judgment, 19 June 2018, 337, 348

Nikolaou v. Commission, No. T-259/03, Judgment, ECLI:EU:T:2007:254, 12 September 2007, 347

Oikonomopoulos v. Commission, No. T-483/13, Judgment, ECLI:EU:T:2016:421, 20 July 2016, 337, 339, 342, 347, 348

Panzeri v. Parliament, No. T-166/16, Judgment, ECLI:EU:T:2017:347, 18 May 2017, 337, 340

Planet AE Anonymi Etaireia Parochis Symvouleftikon Ypiresion v. Commission, No. T-320/09, Judgment, ECLI:EU:T:2015:223, 22 April 2015, 349

Court of Justice of the European Union (CJEU)

Garlsson Real Estate and Others, No. C-537/16, Judgment, ECLI:EU:C:2018:193, 20 March 2018, 107

Gasparini and Others, No. C-467/04, Opinion of Advocate General Sharpston, ECLI:EU:C:2006:406, 15 June 2006, 137

Gasparini, No. C-467/04, Judgment, ECLI:EU:C:2006:610, 28 September 2006, 53, 236, 238

Generalbundesanwalt beim Bundesgerichtshof, No. C-195/20 PPU, ECLI:EU:C:2020:828, 14. October 2020, 256

Generalstaatsanwalt Berlin (Extradition vers l'Ukraine), No. C-398/19, Judgment, ECLI:EU:C:2020:1032, 17 December 2020, 280

Gerado Ruiz Zambrano, No. C-34/09, Opinion of AG Sharpston, ECLI:EU:C:2010:560, 30 September 2010, 69, 70

Germany v. Commission of the European Communities, No. C-240/90, Judgment, ECLI:EU:C:1992:408, 27 October 1992, 170

Goetz v. Comité des Régions, No. F-89/11, Judgment, 19 June 2013, 339

Gözütok and Brügge, Joined Cases Nos. C-187/01 and C-385/01, Judgment, ECLI:EU:C:2003:87, ECR I-1345, 11 February 2003, 53, 235, 241, 268

Gözütök and Brügge, Joined Cases Nos. C-187/01 and C-385/01, Opinion of Advocate General Ruiz-Jarabo Colomer, ECLI:EU:C:2002:516, 19 September 2002, 234

Grand Duchy of Luxembourg v. European Parliament, No. 230/81, Judgment, ECLI:EU:C:1983:32, 10 February 1983, 93

Hansen, No. C-326/88, Judgment, ECLI:EU:C:1990:291, 10 July 1990, 39

Imm, Zwartveld and others, No. C-2/88, Judgment, ECLI:EU:C:1990:440, 6 December 1990, 207

Internationale Handelsgesellschaft mbH v. Einfuhr- und Vorratsstelle für Getreide und Futtermittel, No. C-11/70, Judgment, ECLI:EU:C:1970:114, 17 December 1970, 62

IR, No. C-649/19, Judgment, ECLI:EU:C:2021:75, 28 January 2021, 248

Ivan Gavanozov, No. C-324/17, Judgment, ECLI:EU:C:2019:892, 24 October 2019, 303

J. J. Zwartveld and Others, No. C-2/88, Order of the Court, ECLI:EU:C:1990:440, 6 December 1990, 93

J. Nold, Kohlen- und Baustoffgroßhandlung v. Commission of the European Communities, No. C-4/73, Judgment, ECLI:EU:C:1974:51, 14 May 1974, 62

Jeremy F, No. C-168/13 PPU, Judgment, ECLI:EU:C:2013:358, 30 May 2013, 50

JR and YC, Joined cases Nos. C-556/19 PPU and C-626/19 PPU, Judgment, ECLI:EU:C:2019:1077, 265, 394

Kadi and Al Barakaat International Foundation v. Council and Commission, Joined Cases Nos. C–402/05 P and C–415/05 P, Judgment, EU:C:2008:461 ('*Kadi I*'), 3 September 2008, 63, 68

Käserei Champignon Hofmeister GmbH & Co. KG v. Hauptzollamt Hamburg-Jonas, No. C-210/00, Judgment, ECLI:EU:C:2002:440, 11 July 2002, 170, 227

Kjell Karlssson and others, No. C-292/97, ECLI:EU:C:2000:202, 13 April 2000, 71

European Court of Human Rights (ECtHR)

Supreme Court of Canada

Abbreviations

Adelaide L. Rev.	*Adelaide Law Review*
AFSJ	Area of Freedom, Security and Justice
AG	Attorney General
AI	Artificial intelligence
AJCL	*American Journal of Comparative Law*
AJIL	*American Journal of International Law*
AML	Anti-money laundering
AP	Additional protocol
Art.	Article
B.C. Int'l & Comp. L. Rev.	*Boston College International and Comparative Law Review*
BJCFCL	*Brooklyn Journal of Corporate, Financial & Commercial Law*
BKA	Bundeskriminalamt (German Federal Police Bureau)
BPolG	Gesetz über die Bundespolizei (Federal Police Act)
BRP Trans.'l Crime	*Brill Research Perspectives in Transnational Crime*
BT-Drs	Bundestags-Drucksache (Official Printed Matter of the German Parliament)
BVerfGE	Entscheidungen des Bundesverfassungsgerichts
CahDroitEur	Cahiers de Droit Européen
CECE	Comité d'études pour la constitution européenne
CEPS	Research Report Centre for European Policy Studies Research Report
CFI	Court of First Instance
CFR	Charter of Fundamental Rights

Charter	Charter of Fundamental Rights of the European Union
CISA	Convention Implementing the Schengen Agreement
CFREU	Charter of Fundamental Rights of the European Union
CJELP	*Croatian Yearbook of European Law and Policy*
CJEU	Court of Justice of the European Union
CJEUS	Statute of the Court of Justice of the European Union
CML Rev.	*Common Market Law Review*
CLF	*Criminal Law Forum*
CLJ	*Cambridge Law Journal*
CLR	*Criminal Law Review*
CLSR	*Computer Law & Security Review*
CoE	Council of Europe
CSDPE	Centro Studi di Diritto Penale Europeo
CST	Civil Service Tribunal
CVM	Cooperation and Verification Mechanism
CYELS	*Cambridge Yearbook of European Legal Studies*
DPC	Diritto Penale Contemporaneo
EAW	European Arrest Warrant
ECE	European Convention on Extradition
ECCL	*European Journal of Crime, Criminal Law and Criminal Justice*
ECHR	European Convention on Human Rights
ECJ	European Court of Justice
ECL	European Criminal Law
ECs	European Communities
ECSC	European Coal and Steel Community
ECtHR	European Court of Human Rights
ed.	editor
edn.	edition
eds.	editors
EEC	European Economic Community
EHRLR	*European Human Rights Law Review*

EIO	European Investigation Order
EJIL	*European Journal of International Law*
ELJ	*European Law Journal*
ETS	European Treaty Series
EU	European Union
EuCLR	*European Criminal Law Review*
EuCMACM	European Convention on Mutual Assistance in Criminal Matters of 1959
EUMAC	European Convention on Mutual Assistance in Criminal Matters of 2000
EuR	*Europarecht*
Eur. Const. L. Rev.	*European Constitutional Law Review*
Eur. J. Crim. Policy Res.	*European Journal on Criminal Policy and Research*
Eur. J. Migr. Law	*European Journal of Migration and Law*
Eur. L. Rev.	*European Law Review*
EPPO	European Public Prosecutor's Office
ETIAS	European Travel Information and Authorization System
FD	Framework decision
FD EAW	Framework Decision on the European Arrest Warrant
Fordham ILJ	*Fordham International Law Journal*
GA	*Goltdammer's Archiv für Strafrecht*
GC	General Court
GoeJIL	*Goettingen Journal of International Law*
Harvard ILJ	*Harvard International Law Journal*
HJRL	*Hague Journal on the Rule of Law*
Howard JCJ	*The Howard Journal of Crime and Justice*
HRLR	*Human Rights Law Review*
HRRS	*Onlinezeitschrift für Höchstrichterliche Rechtsprechung zum Strafrecht*
Hung. J. Leg. Stud.	*Hungarian Journal of Legal Studies*
ICL Journal	*The Vienna Journal on International Constitutional Law ICLQ International & Comparative Law Quarterly*
ICON	*International Journal of Constitutional Law*

ICPC	International Criminal Police Commission
IJEL	*Irish Journal of European Law*
IJHR	*International Journal of Human Rights*
Int. J. Disrim. Law	*International Journal of Discrimination and the Law*
JEA	*The Journal of Egyptian Archaeology*
JEPP	*Journal of European Public Policy*
JHA	Justice and Home Affairs
JIT	Joint Investigation Team
JICJ	*Journal of International Criminal Justice*
JICL	*Journal of International and Comparative Law*
JSIJ	*Judicial Studies Institute Journal*
JZ	*Juristenzeitung*
KritV	*Kritische Vierteljahreszeitschrift für Gesetzgebung und Rechtswissenschaft*
KriPoZ	*Kriminalpolitische Zeitung*
LGTB	lesbian, gay, bisexual, and transgender
LJIL	*Leiden Journal on International Law*
L. Q. Rev.	*Law Quarterly Review*
Maastricht J. Eur. Comp. L.	*Maastricht Journal of European and Comparative Law*
mn.	marginal number
MLR	*The Modern Law Review*
MS	Member State(s)
N.C. J. Int'l L.	*North Carolina Journal of International Law* (formerly North Carolina Journal of International Law and Commercial Regulation)
Neth. Q. Hum. Rts.	*Netherlands Quarterly on Human Rights*
NGO	non-governmental organisation
NJECL	*New Journal of European Criminal Law*
Nordic J. Int'l L.	*Nordic Journal of International Law*
OJ	*Official Journal of the European Union*
OLAF	L'Office europeén de lutte coordination de la lutte anti-fraude (European Anti-Fraud Office)

p.	page
para.	paragraph
PIF	protection des intérêts financiers
PIF-Directive	Directive 2017/1371/EU of the European Parliament and of the Council of 5 July on the Fight against Fraud to the EU's financial interests by Means of Criminal Law, OJ EU L 198 of 28 July 2017, p. 29
PIF-Regulation	Council Regulation 2988/95/EC, Euratom of 18 December 1995 on the protection of the European Communities financial interests, OJ EC L 312/1 of 23 December 1995, p. 1
PJCC	Police and Judicial Co-operation in Criminal Matters
PNR	Passenger Name Records
pp.	pages
RBDi	*Revue Belge de Droit International*
Rev. Gral. Dcho. Europeo	*Revista General de Derecho Europeo*
RIDC	*Revue internationale de droit comparé*
RSC	*Revue de Science Criminelle et de Droit Pénal Comparé*
S.	Section
SIS (II)	Schengen Information System (II)
Sing. J.L.S.	*Singapore Journal of Legal Studies*
SJLS	*Silesian Journal of Legal Studies*
StPO	Strafprozessordnung (German Criminal Procedure Act)
Stud. Confl. Terror.	*Studies in Conflict & Terrorism*
TEC	Treaty Establishing the European Community
TEU	Treaty of the European Union
TFEU	Treaty on the Functioning of the European Union
TREVI	Terrorism, Radicalism, Extremism et Violence Internationale (a working group founded in 1975)

TUF	Testo unico delle disposizioni in materia di intermediazione finanziaria
UCLAF	Unité de coordination de la lutte anti-fraude (European Anti-Fraud Unit)
U. Pa. L. Rev.	*University of Pennsylvania Law Review*
UNTS	United Nations Treaty Series
Utrecht L. Rev.	*Utrecht Law Review*
Va. J. Int'l L.	*Virginia Journal of International Law*
VWLJ	*Virginia Environmental Law Journal*
wistra	*Zeitschrift für Wirtschafts- und Steuerstrafrecht*
Yale JIL	*The Yale Journal of International Law*
YEL	*Yearbook of European Law*
ZIS	*Zeitschrift für Internationale Strafrechtsdogmatik*
ZStW	*Zeitschrift für die gesamte Strafrechtswissenschaft*

Part I

Foundations of European Criminal Law

1 European Union and Council of Europe

Special Focus on Criminal Law

Krisztina Karsai and Liane Wörner

1.1 Introduction: European Criminal Law as an Umbrella Term

1.1.1 Dual Meaning

European criminal law (ECL) has acquired a dual meaning in professional and academic discourse: first, as a generic term for the description and classification of European legal integration in the context of criminal law.[1] It is, on the one hand, used to distinguish the realm of transnational and supranational law and standards with respect to penal law from the traditional national discipline of criminal law; on the other hand, it is meant to provide a separate identifiable discipline.[2] Second, ECL constitutes a branch of criminal law, with its own (criminal) policy, legal norms (more or less accepted), principles, and interpretative rules.[3] While there are some objections to this view, particularly vis-à-vis differences to classical national criminal law systems, there is consensus when speaking of a cross-sectional area of law.[4] At the same time, we may use the concept of ECL in a broader sense, including criminal law based on the European Convention on Human Rights (ECHR) as well as the crime control activities of the Council of Europe (CoE).[5]

Notwithstanding that ECL is incorporated into national criminal justice systems, the legal framework and the legal dynamics of influencing these national systems differ substantially. As to ECL as a broad concept, it may be argued – in line with Kettunen[6] – that respect of human dignity, as

[1] K. Ambos, *European Criminal Law*, Cambridge: Cambridge University Press, 2018, p. 14.

[2] A. Klip, *European Criminal Law*, 4th edn., Cambridge: Intersentia, 2021, p. 1; B. Hecker, *Europäisches Strafrecht*, 6th edn., Berlin: Springer, 2021, p. 7.

[3] Klip, European Criminal Law, p. 1. [4] Hecker, Europäisches Strafrecht, p. 8.

[5] Ambos, European Criminal Law, p. 14.

[6] M. Kettunen, *Legitimising European Criminal Law*, Berlin: Springer, 2020, p. 247 ('the ECHR regime requires that the contracting parties use criminal law measures to protect the basic Convention value of human dignity which is protected through the other Convention rights').

the very core of the European Court of Human Rights (ECtHR), is the general justification for criminal law.

1.1.2 The Academic Discourse and Its Spillover

As early as 1953, at the dawn of European integration, Hans-Heinrich Jescheck stated that 'European criminal law is no longer a question for the future, but a part of the living present.'[7] He was the first to use the term, referring to the exercise of the criminal law competence conferred upon supranational bodies by the European Coal and Steel Community (ECSC) and the draft European Defence Community. In the academic debate, the subject has been a permanent feature since the late 1960s and early 1970s of the twentieth century, with ECL receiving increased attention, primarily by formulating reasons for its non-existence.[8] Thus, for example, Bridge argued that there is no 'European criminal law', and indeed its construction as a supranational criminal law system would be a disproportionate answer to the relevant problems resulting from Community integration.[9]

The further discourse has been influenced by issues regarding the regulatory and doctrinal aspects of administrative criminal law as well as the relationship between EU and national criminal law. The procedural (due process) and proportionality issues arising from the European Commission's own sanctioning powers first came to the fore in the late 1980s. And by way of its Engel judgment,[10] the ECtHR set down the criteria for criminal charges, namely, the classification of the offence under national law, the nature of unlawful acts, and the nature and degree of severity of the penalty. As to the primacy and direct effect of EU law (then 'Community law'), the Court of Justice of the European Union's (CJEU) (then 'Court of Justice of the European Communities') case law had already established that national criminal law rules could entail unjustified restrictions on the four fundamental freedoms, and that their application in specific cases could therefore be contrary to Community law.[11]

[7] H.-H. Jescheck, 'Die Strafgewalt übernationaler Gemeinschaften', (1953) 65 *ZStW*, 498.

[8] Hecker, Europäisches Strafrecht, p. 20.

[9] J. W. Bridge, 'The European Communities and the Criminal Law', (1976) 1 *CLR*, 88 at 97.

[10] ECtHR, *Engel and Others v. The Netherlands*, Appl. Nos. 5100/71; 5101/71; 5102/71; 5354/72; 5370/72, 8 June 1976.

[11] CJEU, *Bickel and Franz*, No. C-274/96, Judgment, ECLI:EU:C:1998:563, 24 November 1998; *Rienks*, No. 5/83, Judgment, ECLI:EU:C:1983:382, 15 December 1983; *Cowan v. Trésor public*, No. C-186/87, ECLI:EU:C:1989:47, 2 February 1989.

The Greek Maize case[12] had clarified the Member States' (MS)-specific obligations under Community law when designing their internal criminal law systems (application of effective, proportionate, and dissuasive sanctions). At that time, there was no third pillar, that is no specific cooperation framework on criminal justice.[13]

Given that certain elements of EU integration had a considerable impact on the domestic criminal law systems of the MS, it became readily apparent that this process also influenced the everyday practice of criminal law and the criminal justice system in their entirety. The CJEU's judicial law making and, of course, the significant changes to the founding treaties have led to the question of legitimacy. With the amendments to the Amsterdam Treaty (and subsequent treaties), criminal law aspects of immigration and asylum have become part of Community law. Solid competence for implementing criminal law was embedded in the third pillar (backed up by appropriate instruments). The introduction of the principle of mutual recognition anticipated a further development in procedural law;[14] Schengen law established the transnational *ne bis in idem* principle,[15] and the CJEU was given jurisdiction to interpret and examine the validity of the newly introduced framework decisions (FDs) (if the respective MS has opted in, Art. 35 Treaty on European Union (TEU [old 1999][16]).

As of 1 December 2009, ECL became part of 'normal' EU policy, giving rise to a proper European criminal policy,[17] although such a policy had

[12] CJEU, *Commission of the European Communities v. Hellenic Republic*, No. 68/88, Judgment, ECLI:EU:C:1989:339, 21 September 1989.

[13] Klip, European Criminal Law, p. 223; Ambos, European Criminal Law, p. 14.

[14] Ambos, European Criminal Law, p. 415; D. Brodowski, 'European Criminal Justice: From Mutual Recognition to Coherence', in S. Carrera, D. Curtin, and A. Geddes (eds.), *20 Years Anniversary of the Tampere Programme*, San Domenico di Fiesole: European University Institute, 2020, p. 225. On mutual recognition, see also the chapter by Phillip Ronsfeld in this volume (Chapter 6).

[15] See Ambos, European Criminal Law, pp. 146 ff.; see also Martin Böse, 'Fundamental Rights Protection', Chapter 10 in this volume.

[16] See 'Information Note on References from National Courts for a Preliminary Ruling' of the ECJ, OJ 2005 C 143/1; for more details, see S. Lorenzmaier, 'The Legal Effect of Framework Decisions – A Case-Note on the Pupino Decision of the European Court of Justice', (2006) *ZIS*, 583, 587.

[17] Towards an EU criminal policy: ensuring the effective implementation of EU policies through criminal law. Communication from the Commission to the European Parliament, the Council, the European Economic and Social Committee and the Committee of the Regions. COM/2011/0573 final.

been identified in academic discourse before.[18] Other features include the fact that elements of the EU *ius puniendi* are now clearly visible[19] and that EU criminal law standard setting can lead to legislation with primary application and direct effect.[20] The Charter of Fundamental Rights of the European Union (CFREU), which contains, inter alia, fundamental rights provisions on criminal justice, has entered into force as a binding primary source of law.[21]

1.1.3 European Criminal Law Today

ECL is still not the traditional criminal law in the 'domestic' sense because its function is not to establish direct individual criminal responsibility. In fact, the EU does not (yet) aim to develop a proper criminal justice system.[22] However, given that the EU has, as a supranational organisation, autonomous values and interests that go, at least partly, beyond national interests, these interests are to be protected by the national criminal justice systems as long as no supranational EU criminal justice system exists.[23] Of course, there is some supranationality at the institutional level, most impressively and recently demonstrated by the European Public Prosecutor's Office (EPPO),[24] but this institutional supranationality remains fragmentary at best.[25] Further, it is to be noted that ECL entails the harmonisation of the domestic criminal justice systems,

[18] J. Vogel, 'Europäische Kriminalpolitik - europäische Strafrechtsdogmatik', (2002) 149 *GA*, 517.

[19] See B.3.; C.2.; Art. 82, 325 TFEU; in more depth by K. Nuotio, 'Supranational Criminal Law, Harmonisation and Approximation', Chapter 5 in this volume.

[20] D. Brodowski, 'Supranationale europäische Verwaltungssanktionen. Entwicklungslinien – Dimensionen des Strafrechts – Legitimität', in K. Tiedemann, U. Sieber, H. Satzger, C. Burchard, and D. Brodowski (eds.), *Die Verfassung moderner Strafrechtspflege. Erinnerung an Joachim Vogel*, Baden-Baden: Nomos, 2016, p. 141.

[21] Treaty of Lisbon, entered into force on 1 December 2009, 2007/C 306/01. In more depth by S. Allegrezza, 'European Public Prosecutor', Chapter 17 in this volume.

[22] Hecker, Europäisches Strafrecht, pp. 9, 17.

[23] Ambos, European Criminal Law, p. 19; L. Wörner, 'Kriminalitätsphänomen Terrorismus als unlösbare Aufgabe für das nationale materielle Strafrecht – Zur Relevanz europäischer bis internationaler Tatbestandsvorgaben', in K. Höffler (ed.), *Criminal Law Discourse of the Interconnected Society (CLaDIS)*, Baden-Baden: Nomos, 2020, p. 131 at 137.

[24] See S. Allegrezza, 'European Public Prosecutor', Chapter 17 in this volume.

[25] For an overview on the institutional framework, see Ambos, European Criminal Law, pp. 560ff. (Ch. 5).

especially of their criminal law and its interpretation and application in line with EU law.[26]

In sum, ECL may be divided threefold according to the subject matter and the objective pursued: (i) the protection of separate (mainly and recently financial) EU interests, (ii) the aim of effective joint crime control (in the MS), and (iii) the sanctioning of violations of EU law. In order to better understand the relationship and intersections between the EU law and CoE (inspired) law (D.), the routes (B.) and sources (C.) of ECL need to be discussed first.

1.2 Routes of European Criminal Law

1.2.1 Criminality-Related Challenges for the MS

The dynamic development of ECL and its sometimes revolutionary milestones can be traced back to two groups of factors that have affected the MS equally over the last decades.

The first is globalisation, which has had a significant impact on crime, its structure, and transnationalisation. Fast and cheap travel has made criminals mobile; the technological revolution and access to the Internet for all has not only given rise to new types of crime but also transformed 'traditional' crime through the use of new tools for committing crimes. Traditional forms of cooperation between States became ineffective, and often even inappropriate, and have created significant impunity gaps for new types of crime, for which a unified approach is now indispensable.

Another set of reasons is created by EU integration itself: supranational interests and values have emerged, the protection of which has become a vital issue for the EU as an international organisation, even independently of the MS. These include, in particular, financial interests, such as protecting the euro as a currency against counterfeiting or the protection of EU officials against corruption, as well as the legal acquis for economic integration and, in particular, the four freedoms, which has indirectly but necessarily led to the inclusion of criminal law in the integration process.[27] Thus, legal forms had necessarily to be found that aid in avoiding impunity gaps in the MS in relevant legal matters, help

[26] Hecker, Europäisches Strafrecht, p. 243.

[27] Klip, European Criminal Law, p. 25.

enforce the acquis and aims of EU legal integration, and ensure that the MS cooperate as effectively as possible in the fight against crime. With Sieber, 'paradoxical as it may sound, the only way to solve the problems caused by (incomplete) European integration is to go even further'.[28] However, the development of a supranational EU criminal justice system has not been an option either technically or politically. It is therefore critical that the EU deploys national criminal justice systems to conquer these challenges and aims.

In addition, a third factor has emerged that will continue to influence the present and future of ECL: the digital revolution. The development of new regulatory requirements in criminal justice and of a regulatory framework for cooperation between national authorities will have to reflect not only the above-mentioned general phenomena of admissible technology as such but also the social changes brought about by disruptive technologies: social media, big data, artificial intelligence, and machine learning. They give rise to new types of crime, require new types of crime control and new procedures, and thus new types of procedural rules – ones in which geographical considerations (territory, jurisdiction, and sovereignty) are less relevant.

1.2.2 The Rise and Fall of the Pillars

The Treaty of Lisbon, which entered into force on 1st December 2009,[29] has significantly and fundamentally changed the legal framework of the EU's justice and home affairs cooperation policy,[30] opening a new chapter in an already active area of integration. How did this come about?

In 1992, with the establishment of the European Union (Treaty of Maastricht), justice and home affairs cooperation derived as a 'matter of common interest' for the MS derived from the so-called third pillar, which provided a legal framework for intergovernmental cooperation. The TEU (in force from 1 November 1993 to 1 May 1999) did not entitle the EU to any legally relevant supranational room for manoeuvre but was significant in relation to the objectives of economic integration. It recognised other social interests and values to be protected, those that

[28] U. Sieber, 'Memorandum für ein Europäisches Modellstrafgesetzbuch', (1997) 52 *JZ*, 369 at 370.

[29] Treaty of Lisbon 2007/C 306/01.

[30] Ambos, European Criminal Law, p. 15.

traditionally fall within the scope of national criminal law. The Union considered the fight against them as its own from that time onwards. The institutionalisation of the third pillar beyond the level of political cooperation was based precisely on the realisation that the development of the Common Market and European economic integration could be jeopardised by terrorism, drug trafficking, international fraud, and other crimes of an international or transnational nature, and that the fight against these crimes should therefore be tackled at a higher level, if necessary, and not at a national level. The intergovernmental model of the third pillar was a compromise between the MS, as there were States that would have preferred more dynamic integration while others would have preferred slower progress in connection with any criminal justice at all.[31]

Article K.3 TEU (old 1993) established the legal framework for introducing European conventions[32] and allowed the Council to take joint action, as the Union's objectives can be better achieved through joint action than through the MS acting individually on account of the scale or effects of the action envisaged. The historical importance of the first version of the third pillar is indisputable, as it thematised joint action against crime at the EU level, and the legitimacy gained by its enshrinement in the Treaty also paved the way for further developments.

This balance is not altered by otherwise very cumbersome intergovernmental decision-making, lack of binding legal acts, and often unproductive legislation – the reasons that led to the failure of the first version of the third pillar and the reform. The landmark changes were brought about by the Treaty of Amsterdam (signed on 2 October 1997, in force from 1 May 1999 to 30 October 2009). These reforms gave both the European Commission and the CJEU autonomous powers (preliminary ruling) in the third pillar, that is the Union's supranational bodies could act 'in their own right' as far as delegation was concerned, thus losing the purely intergovernmental character of the third pillar. Among other FDs, legally binding legislation was introduced. The common migration and asylum policy was moved to the first pillar, and some – criminal justice-related – achievements of the Schengen acquis were incorporated into the legal structure of the third pillar. In the period following its entry into

[31] See also H. G. Nilsson, 'Some Memories of the Third Pillar', (2019) *eucrim*, 253–255 at 254.

[32] For example, Europol Convention, PIF directive on the protection of financial interests of the European Communities through criminal law, EU Convention on Corruption.

force, virtually nothing substantial happened for about two years, until the adoption of the first binding FD on the protection of the euro under criminal law. Then, following the first ruling by the CJEU acting under third pillar powers, criminal law-related legislation gained a significant boost, which continues to this day.

The Treaty of Nice (signed on 26 February 2001, in force since 1 February 2003) made an impact on the third pillar by making Eurojust the leading actor of judicial cooperation in criminal matters and further refining the rules of so-called enhanced cooperation.

The new paradigm of the reform introduced by the Treaty of Lisbon, finally, abolishes the pillars and reorganises the former third pillar issues into a separate, 'normal' EU policy. The 'area of freedom, security and justice' (AFSJ) is an EU policy of shared competencies. In order to adopt this institutional change that created a new supranational EU policy from its content, replacing previous intergovernmental cooperation, the MS have also set out specific compensatory mechanisms in the reform that could help ensure that the new paradigm is accepted and lived out in practice, such as, in general, no EU regulation on substantive criminal law shall be issued, the so-called emergency brake procedure, and the enhanced cooperation linked to it.

1.2.3 'Hunt' for European *ius puniendi*

The earliest reference to criminal law competence appeared in Article K.1 of TEU (old 1993), but this could by no means be considered as being part of *ius puniendi*. Instead, it was a significant stage in a longer development. The provision affirmed the competence of the newly formed EU to commence joint action in the field of criminal law, surpassed the former limitations of combatting crime at the national level, and paved the way for shared interests. This was followed by a broad academic debate on the justification of rules laid down by several directives or regulations aimed at applying necessary sanctions against entities (natural persons or legal bodies) infringing upon Community law on the level of the respective national (domestic) legal order. It included the question of whether the sanctions 'expected' by the Community should be of domestic criminal law nature or if MS should be given a margin of discretion in determining the sanctioning instrument, using *ius puniendi* when obliging the MS to sanction the infringement of EU law within its own criminal law framework.

Meanwhile, it became clear that the (Union Community) would need to take measures to safeguard its own interests, the protection of which could not be efficiently provided and achieved by the MS. However, the overall protection of criminal law throughout Europe and the European Union was not planned on the supranational level;[33] therefore, other means had to be introduced to fill the gaps. Protection of the financial interests of the (Union Community) by criminal law was established by a multilateral convention of the MS, which called for and set forth an obligation for the contracting parties (MS) to criminalise such conduct.[34] Not even the modifications introduced by the Treaty of Amsterdam established new *ius puniendi* competencies, although they afforded an abstract power to punish by way of FDs. These were aimed at approximating different MS laws in harmony with Article 34 paragraph 2 Nr b of TEU (old 1999) – as read together with Articles 29 and 31 TEU (old 1999). Third pillar legislation gained the power to decide on questions of criminal law as provided by the split or layered *ius puniendi* of the MS. The Council therefore has the competence to decide on the legislative use of FDs as protective measures or for combatting certain forms of criminality as well as on the further scope of FDs, namely, the use of national criminal laws to support the above-mentioned objective. The elements of *ius puniendi* were only transferred to the European level to a limited extent: the third pillar legislator was empowered only to approximate criminal laws in specific cases, and the decision on the severity of punishment and the choice between modalities of punishment were transferred to a limited extent, namely, only if the FDs set a minimum or maximum range for imprisonment. Yet, there was no power to create comprehensive sanction law frameworks or to define punishment and execute said punishment; all this remained in the hands of the MS.

It should be highlighted that the right to choose measures was a highly debated subject in connection with Article 42 TEU (old 1999), as per the '*passerelle*' clause. Central to the theoretical debate was whether the Community has such values or interests that their protection (or enforcement) requires the use of third pillar measures as well, that is, whether the transferred layers of *ius puniendi* should be

[33] L. Wörner, 'Kriminalitätsphänomen Terrorismus als unlösbare Aufgabe für das nationale materielle Strafrecht – Zur Relevanz europäischer bis internationaler Tatbestandsvorgaben', in K. Höffler (ed.), *Criminal Law Discourse of the Interconnected Society (CLaDIS)*, Baden-Baden: Nomos, 2020, p. 131 at 135.

[34] K. Karsai, *Alapelvi (r)evolúció az európai büntetőjogban*, Szeged: Iurisperitus Bt., 2015.

used in order to achieve purely Community objectives. The European legislator chose not to enforce this clause prematurely but instead applied a proper 'golden mean' to enhance protection for preferred Community interests. If a third pillar requirement surfaced, the legislator embarked on introducing parallel legislation, for example, in the event of unauthorised entry, transit, and residence, the Council issued a directive (2002)[35] distinguishing legal and illegal behaviour in terms of Community law (as administrative law). Simultaneously, an FD activated the criminal laws of the MS[36] in order to punish the most severe modalities of behaviour rendered illegal by the aforesaid Council directive. Theoretical debates on (ex) Article 42 TEU (old 1999) continued to remain on the agenda. The Commission then contributed added value to this 'maturing process' when, on 10 May 2006, it announced that the '*passerelle*' clause shall be applied in order to enable police and judicial cooperation in criminal matters, meaning that this area could be dealt with under the Treaty establishing the European Community (EC Treaty), with consequentially increased roles for the organs of the Community.[37] This was, of course, questioned from the viewpoint of national criminal law.

However, debates then suddenly froze. Following the Commission's aforementioned political communication, the CJEU took the first step in a new direction (Case C-176/03 Commission v. Council), which led to major legal consequences. Academic reactions were critical; authors referred to the birth of the Leviathan or the 'Brussels Octopus'.[38] As accurately summarised by the British Lords: until September 2005, it was commonly understood that the EC Treaty conferred no power to define criminal offences or prescribe criminal sanctions. The extent of the European Union's legislative competence concerning criminal law and procedure was generally limited to the 'Third Pillar'. That MS, or at least a majority of them, had seemingly been labouring under a

[35] Directive 2002/90/EC of 28 November 2002, OJ L 328, 5.12.2002, pp. 17–18.

[36] Council Framework Decision 2002/946/JHA of 28 November 2002 on the strengthening of the penal framework to prevent the facilitation of unauthorised entry, transit and residence, OJ L 328, 5 December 2002, pp. 1–3.

[37] Communication from the Commission to the European Council: a citizen's agenda: delivering results for Europe. Brussels, 10 May 2006, COM(2006) 211 final, 6.

[38] R. Hefendehl, 'Europäischer Umweltschutz: Demokratiespritze für Europa oder Brüsseler Putsch?', (2007) *ZIS*, 161 at 167.

misapprehension as to what they had agreed in the Treaties, and on what basis they had recently formulated the text of the Constitutional Treaty was revealed when, on 13 September 2005, the CJEU handed down its judgment in Case C-176/03[39] and clarified the distribution of powers in criminal matters between the first and third pillars based on converging legislative power between a directive and an FD in environmental policy through criminal law. The CJEU clearly stated whether competencies in criminal law could be attributed to the Community. The conclusion amounted to a valid – substantial – extension, introducing a similar split *ius puniendi* into first pillar legislation like the one already transferred to the third pillar. The extension (legislative procedure, sanctions in the case of non-implementation, deadlines, etc.) was quite different in its legal consequences than that in the third pillar, although supranational (limited) *ius puniendi* was thereby acknowledged by the Court in favour of the Community.[40] It is evident that the CJEU primarily envisaged clarifying the difference between the first and the third pillars and strengthening the sectoral regulation regime of Community law. However, the decision was used as legal justification to accelerate the establishment of criminal law competencies on a European level and opened new margins of interpretation for the competence of the Community, which were applied as part of the initiative of the Commission to replace FDs with new directives.[41] Resolving the opaque nature of the limited *ius puniendi* discovered in the text of the TEC by the CJEU, the Treaty on the Functioning of the European Union (TFEU) brings clarity by unifying the legal framework of EU law and building a common framework (legislative procedures, forms of legal acts, judicial remedies, etc.) for every policy.

[39] The Criminal Law Competence of the European Community. Report with Evidence. House of Lords, European Union Committee, 42nd Report of Session 2005–06, p. 7.

[40] See CJEU, *Commission of the European Communities v. Council of the European Union*, No. C-176/03, ECLI:EU:C:2005:542, 13 September 2005, paras. 41–42, 47–48, 51–53.

[41] The Parliament expressed almost the same opinion: implications of Case C-176/03. European Parliament resolution on the consequences of the judgment of the Court of 13 September 2005 (C-176/03 Commission *v.* Council) 2006/2007(INI). Two directives were enacted (already based on the TEC, old version): Directive 2005/35/EC of 7 September 2005 on ship-source pollution and on the introduction of penalties for infringements, OJ L 255, 30 September 2005, pp. 11–21; Directive 2008/99/EC of 19 November 2008 on the protection of the environment through criminal law, OJ L 328, 6 December 2008, pp. 28–37.

1.2.4 European Criminal Policy

Criminal policy is one of the tools for social control of crime,[42] viewed as an activity of the State that reacts to this social phenomenon. It formulates some favourable social aims and tries to achieve them through legal regulation while at the same time it is often used for general political support, for example, to gain votes, taking advantage of the sensitivity of the masses concerning punishability, sense of justice, and, of course, fear.[43] On 20 September 2011, the European Commission published a policy communication entitled 'Towards an EU criminal justice policy',[44] which for the first time set out a general strategy and principles for EU criminal law to ensure better implementation and to protect citizens' interests. This was an important milestone, as the Commission has a general power of legislative initiative. It is therefore in its interest to have a coherent policy vision for developing EU-wide criminal law standards. It remains questionable what the characteristics of such EU criminal policy are and whether these are comparable with the criminal policies of the MS.

Since creating the third pillar, criminal policy discourse has indeed been present in the EU arena. Notwithstanding legislative activities based on intergovernmental cooperation under the third pillar (i.e. FDs with substantive criminal law content), the MS' criminal justice systems and legislation continued to have a direct impact on crime definitions and criminal procedures. Therefore, national criminal law functioned as a perceivable 'buffer' that filtered and transformed EU criminal policy 'yields' before entering the domestic legal order.[45] As a consequence, EU criminal policy has developed its own characteristics, in which the aspects that politicise national criminal policy (symbolic functions) are less important, as no crime control on the part of the EU can take place directly, but only through the respective national law and law

[42] M. Ancel, *Social Defence: A Modern Approach to Criminal Law Problems*, London: Routledge, 1998; H. D. Barlow and S. H. Decker, *Criminology and Puplic Policy: Putting Theory to Work*, Philadelphia: Temple University Press, 2010.

[43] K. Karsai, 'European Criminal Policy', (2020) *FORVM Acta Juridica et Politica*, Hungary (2/17), 1.

[44] Towards an EU Criminal Policy: ensuring the effective implementation of EU policies through criminal law. Brussels, 20 September 2011 COM(2011) 573 final.

[45] K. Karsai, 'European Criminal Policy', (2020) *FORVM Acta Juridica et Politica*, Hungary (2/17), 3.

enforcement. The directions it takes are based on grounded scientific results, evidence-based research,[46] and actual criminal problems. The role of scientific ideas and criminal law schools in this field is quintessential. Many ideas that emerged later as legal norms were born in 'Petri dishes' of criminal law professors in Paris, London, Rome, Berlin, Luxemburg, and Brussels (etc.).[47]

Yet, abolishing the pillars and introducing clear competencies for criminal law-making will change the above-mentioned, both professional and naive nature of European criminal policy – for which several reasons exist. Legislative competencies have been devolved, and, as a rule, the ordinary legislative procedure is based on majority voting in favour of criminal law-related norms. The possibility of qualified majority voting implies political struggles ab ovo. The European Parliament will have the possibility to decide on completely new topics. The Council will have a new decision-making structure (even on topics already known). Öberg predicts that 'whilst the MS still formally may be the "captain of the ship"', members of Council will constitute 'the Council as an entity separate from national governments with a distinct [European] loyalty and which exercises some measure of genuine autonomous power. As the veto power in the field of criminal law is diluted – which is the ultimate power of the State to guard sovereignty – there appears thus to be a stronger direction of supranationalism in the area'.[48] Equally crucially, under current EU law, the role of national parliaments in decision-making has increased, and the orange and red card procedures can even allow for explicit national political interests to be reflected in decision-making. The emergency brake procedure of the AFSJ may also open up scope for political games, especially if the reference to the 'fundamental aspects' of its criminal justice system (Article 82 II, 83 III TFEU), which is seen as a standard component of national sovereignty (more recently national identity), is an obstacle to majority legislation. Not least, improvisation in criminal

[46] W. De Bondt, 'Evidence-Based EU Criminal Policy Making: In Search of Matching Data', (2014) 20 *Eur. J. Crim. Pol. Res.*, 23–49.

[47] Corjus Juris Europeae recommended introducing provisions for the purpose of protecting the financial interests of the European Union, under the direction of M. Delmas-Marty (1997); see European Criminal Policy Initiative, 'A Manifesto on European Criminal Policy', (2009) *ZIS*, 707–709.

[48] J. Öberg, 'Exit, Voice and Consensus – A Legal and Political Analysis of the Emergency Brake in EU Criminal Policy', (2021) 46 *Eur. L. Rev.*, 506 at 530.

law-making[49] occurs as a consequence of dramatic events (e.g. Dutroix, Charlie Hebdo, 57 dead Chinese in a container, the attacks on the WTC on 9/11) and makes politicians feel the need to show that they were acting, be it with a proposal from a delegation or sometimes the Commission, rapid negotiations, or heavy political pressure to produce expedited results.[50]

In order to be terminologically correct, the precise term European criminal policy on the AFSJ (in shared competence) covers the activities of the EU entitled by Articles 67–89 TFEU only and therefore only one of the elements of (establishing) European criminal policy, namely that of influencing national criminal law and national criminal justice.[51] Not less important, the other element of European criminal policy is derived from the goal of protecting the financial interests of the EU supranationally, if necessary, through criminal law (Article 325 TFEU). While European criminal policy also covers a triangle of aims, almost constantly criticised is the fact that the EU's criminal policy is geared towards extending the scope of criminalisation[52] and generally increasing the repressiveness and punishing power of national criminal justice in the EU.[53] After all, the TFEU issues a mandate concerning criminal offences, sanctions, and procedure, so the subject of the ruling can obviously and necessarily be nothing other than criminal offence-related matters. Consequently, minimum EU legislation will directly trigger criminalising legislation in those MS which have hitherto allowed acts to go unpunished. This provides a basis for a repressive EU criminal policy theory, while it is necessary to highlight the equally important process of a balanced rule of law. The effect of decriminalisation is triggered by European law itself through EU policies incorporated into areas of European law by primacy and its direct effect and by the prevailing legal guarantee of the four freedoms of the Common Market.[54]

[49] N. Corral-Maraver, 'Irrationality as a Challenge to European Criminal Policy', (2017) 7 *EuCLR*, 123 at 131.

[50] Nilsson, 'Some Memories of the Third Pillar', 253–255.

[51] K. Karsai, 'European Criminal Policy', (2020) *FORVM Acta Juridica et Politica*, Hungary (2/17), 3.

[52] For example, European Criminal Policy Initiative, 'Manifesto on European Criminal Policy', (2009) *ZIS*, 707.

[53] In detail N. Corral-Maraver, 'Irrationality as a Challenge to European Criminal Policy', (2017) 7 *EuCLR*, 123 or Hecker, Europäisches Strafrecht, p. 21.

[54] K. Karsai, 'European Criminal Policy', (2020) *FORVM Acta Juridica et Politica*, Hungary (2/17), 18.

1.3 Sources of European Criminal Law

The relevant doctrines of European law determine the sources of ECL: a distinction is made between primary and secondary sources of law and 'unwritten' law.[55] The sources of ECL can be classified in several ways: the rules concerning criminal responsibility and criminal justice, which are the result of EU legislation and have a regulatory content (joint actions, FDs, and directives), contain obligations for national legislation but – generally – do not have a direct effect on individuals. These rules can be further categorised based on their content to distinguish between substantive criminal law, procedural criminal law, law enforcement or judicial cooperation in criminal matters. Also, European rules could directly affect the individual's position concerning criminal responsibility or criminal procedural rules. Since harmonised national criminal law is closely linked to ECL (and can be part of its broader concept), the added value of ECL is the emergence of a legal framework for interpretation (so-called indirect effect of EU norms) that is different from, yet coherent with, that of the MS and derives from EU law.

1.3.1 Charter of Fundamental Rights of the European Union (CFREU)

As of 1 December 2009, the CFREU, now having legally binding character, became part of the primary sources of EU law. The catalogue of human rights presented therein affects criminal law legislation and practice in numerous points. Besides the CFREU, the (unwritten) general principles of law are additional sources of human rights: these and the CFREU constitute EU primary law.[56]

According to Article 6 TEU, 'the Union recognises the rights, freedoms and principles set out in the Charter of Fundamental Rights of the European Union [...], which shall have the same legal value as the Treaties'. An essential feature of the CFREU was not to create new fundamental rights nor to extend the scope of protection already achieved by EU law, but instead to mirror the status quo. Yet, its obligatory character opened up

[55] Summaries published regularly in the European Criminal Law Association Forum (eucrim), https://eucrim.eu (10/2021).

[56] In detail N. O'Meara (Chapter 2), 'Human Rights Protection through regional instruments', in this volume.

new horizons for enforcing fundamental rights within EU law. Moreover, the autonomous legislative and enforcement powers of EU bodies have made it necessary to develop a specific EU regime to protect human rights when exercising legislative or executive powers. As the AFSJ has become the legal basis for issuing norms within the scope of EU policy that can also have explicit criminal law content (legislative), EU human rights protection directly ensures the guaranteed legal position of individuals. Yet, procedures of the newly introduced EPPO will generate a new need for protection.

According to Article 51, the provisions of the CFREU address the institutions, bodies, offices, and agencies of the Union with due regard for the principle of subsidiarity and the MS only when they are implementing Union law. Therefore, they shall respect the rights, observe the principles, promote the application thereof by their respective powers, and respect the limits of the powers of the Union as conferred on it in the Treaties. As the CJEU explained in its Fransson decision,[57] the MS are addressees of the CFREU if they apply harmonised national norms (e.g. criminal law provisions). And as the CFREU does not accord the person concerned an individual and natural right of complaint, it is only applicable as an interpretative reference framework in national jurisprudence. National courts must then decide when to directly apply EU norms and when to implement them.

1.3.2 The Exercise of Competences and Legislative Processes in Criminal Law

In the third pillar legislation (Amsterdam version), the Commission and the MS have launched legislative processes in a 'race' to approximate national criminal laws. A striking feature during that period was the general acceptance of the principle of mutual recognition in legislative initiatives in the field of criminal justice, a revolutionary achievement in terms of its integration potential.[58] Legislative activity had reached a very significant level by 30 November 2009, with the Council having

[57] CJEU, *Åklagaren v. Hans Åkerberg Fransson*, No. C-617/10, Judgment, ECLI:EU:C:2013:105, 26 February 2013.

[58] C. Burchard, *Die Konstitutionalisierung der gegenseitigen Anerkennung. Die strafjustizielle Zusammenarbeit in Europa im Lichte des Unionsverfassungsrechts*, Frankfurt a. M.: Vittorio Klostermann, 2019, pp. 3, 394; E. Kloska, *Das Prinzip der gegenseitigen Anerkennung im Europäischen Strafrecht*, Baden-Baden: Nomos, 2016, p. 132.

adopted some 30 FDs. These can be grouped according to their central subject matter as follows: substantive criminal law,[59] procedural criminal law,[60] *ne bis in idem*,[61] and transnational cooperation between authorities.[62] Some FDs have since been amended by directives or regulations (so-called 'Lisbonisation'[63]), but many FDs still remain in force today.

According to the current legal understanding, the TFEU provides many legal bases for secondary EU acts with criminal law content. The classification matrix of legal bases is based on three criteria: (1) the extent to which the subject of the secondary norm may affect the criminal law and criminal justice systems of the MS,[64] (2) scrutinising the various legal sources because different secondary legal acts could have different legal consequences (in particular direct effect), and (3) analysing whether there is an emergency brake option as a compensatory mechanism for the specific situation of criminal law.

[59] See 2000/383/JHA FD of 29 May 2002; 2001/413/JHA FD of 28 May 2001; 2001/500/JHA FD of 26 June 2001; 2000/383/JHA FD of 6 December 2001; 2001/500/JHA FD of 26 June 2001; 2002/475/JHA FD of 13 June 2002; 2002/629/JHA FD of 19 July 2002; 2002/946/JHA FD of 28 November 2002; 2003/80/JHA FD of 27 January 2003; 2003/568/JHA FD of 22 July 2003; 2004/68/JHA FD of 22 December 2003; 2004/757/JHA FD of 25 October 2004; 2005/212/JHA FD of 24 February 2005; 2005/667/JHA FD of 12 July 2005; 2006/783/JHA FD of 6 October 2006; 2008/841/JHA FD of 24 October 2008; 2008/919/JHA FD of 28 November 2008; 2008/913/JHA FD of 28 November 2008.

[60] See 2001/220/JHA FD of 15 March 2001; 2002/584/JHA FD of 13 June 2002 (European Arrest Warrant); 2003/577/JHA FD of 22 July 2003 (freezing orders); 2005/214/JHA FD of 24 February 2005 (mutual recognition); 2008/909/JHA of 27 November 2008 (custodial sentences); 2008/947/JHA FD of 27 November 2008 (probation measures and alternative sanctions); 2008/977/JHA FD of 27 November 2008 (police and judicial cooperation in criminal matters); 2008/978/JHA FD of 18 December 2008 (European evidence warrant); 2009/299/JHA FD of 26 February 2009 (Amending FD 2002/584/JHA, 2005/214/JHA, 2006/783/JHA, 2008/909/JHA and 2008/947/JHA); 2009/829/JHA FD of 23 October 2009.

[61] See 2008/675/JHA FD of 24 July 2008; 2009/948/JHA FD of 30 November 2009.

[62] See 2002/465/JHA FD of 13 June 2002 (JIT); 2003/577/JHA FD of 22 July 2003 (freezing orders); 2006/783/JHA FD of 6 October 2006 (confiscation orders); 2006/960/JHA FD of 18 December 2006 (exchange of information); 2008/909/JHA FD of 27 November 2008 (custodial sentences); 2008/947/JHA FD of 27 November 2008 (probation measures); 2008/977/JHA FD of 27 November 2008 (personal data); 2008/978/JHA FD of 18 December 2008 (European evidence warrant); 2009/315/JHA FD of 26 February 2009 (criminal record); 2009/829/JHA FD of 23 October 2009 (supervision measures).

[63] P. Csonka and O. Landwehr, '10 Years after Lisbon – How "Lisbonised" is the Substantive Criminal Law in the EU?', (2019) *eucrim*, 261–267.

[64] This is because different EU law and national legal constraints apply if the content of the secondary norm is of substantive criminal law nature or if it contains procedural (organisational or institutional) rules.

Article 82(1) TFEU contains an explicit legislative competence, the subject matter of which is typically criminal procedure or cooperation in criminal matters; this can be done in any type of legal act and is not subject to the emergency brake procedure. Article 82(2) TFEU expands the power to adopt minimum rules, but restricted to the directive, and the emergency brake procedure remains an option during the legislative procedure.

Article 83(1) TFEU accords the right to set minimum rules, and, here too, the directive and the emergency brake procedure are used as restrictive mechanisms. However, it allows the establishment of minimum rules concerning the definition of criminal offences and sanctions in the areas of severe crime with a cross-border dimension. Article 83 (2) TFEU, which contains the 'annex competence', entitles the EU legislator to issue a directive if the approximation of criminal laws and regulations of the MS proves essential to ensuring the effective implementation of a Union policy in an area that has been subject to harmonisation measures. The emergency brake procedure is foreseen. Since the text does not limit the legal basis to directives, issuing any legal act (if the general requirements are met) is possible; the EU legislator may choose between directives and regulations.[65]

Article 86 TFEU entitles the EU to adopt regulations to combat crimes affecting the financial interests of the Union. Regulations shall determine the general rules applicable to the EPPO, the conditions governing the performance of its functions, the rules of procedure, as well as those governing the admissibility of evidence, and the rules applicable to judicial review. The legislation aims neither to establish a minimum ruling nor to approximate criminal law, but instead to lay down general rules of criminal procedure with direct effect and applicability.[66] Although the legislative procedure is specific, the emergency brake procedure is not applicable, or only by way of analogy.[67]

Article 325 (4) TFEU provides the legal basis for the legislative procedure to adopt the necessary measures to enact legislation concerning fraud and

65 A regulation on money laundering is currently under discussion.

66 Council Regulation (EU) 2017/1939 of 12 October 2017 implementing enhanced cooperation on the establishment of the European Public Prosecutor's Office ('the EPPO') OJ L 283, 31.10.2017, pp. 1–71.

67 D. Brodowski, 'Art. 22', in H. H. Herrnfeld, D. Brodowski, and C. Burchard (eds.), *European Public Prosecutor's Office – Regulation (EU) 2017/1939*, Baden-Baden: Nomos, 2021, p. 174.

any other illegal activities affecting the Union's financial interests. In this context, the term fraud must be understood in a broad sense, including certain fraud-related criminal offences. The argument can be made that this norm entitles the EU to enact provisions with criminal law content.

Finally, Article 79 TFEU, which describes the legal instruments of the common migration policy, includes a mandate under paragraph 2(d) requiring the adoption of measures to combat trafficking in human beings, particularly women and children. This norm entitles the EU to legislate generously by issuing directives or regulations for combatting trafficking through criminal law. And since it does not expressly contain any restrictions concerning available legal acts, it seems that the EU legislator is entitled to issue any of these. However, there is an ongoing debate in the legal doctrine whether Article 79 (2) TFEU [and Article 325 (4) TFEU] contain any entitlement for issuing legal acts with criminal law content. Contrarily, it is argued that the systematic interpretation of the TFEU does not allow for the provision of a genuine entitlement for issuing legal acts with criminal law content.[68] While Articles 82 and 83 entitle the EU in its shared competence to exercise its competencies in criminal matters (e.g. legislation), Article 79 remains silent. The possible assumption of an implied entitlement to issue legislation with criminal law content without specifically expressing it is hard to justify in the same policy field. Articles 82 and 83 include such entitlement and the limits for EU actions in the field of criminal law; the simple shift to Article 79 would make it possible to establish supranational criminal law without the balanced restrictions seen in Articles 82 and 83. Accordingly, the TFEU does not permit 'criminal law' legislation in the AFSJ solely on the basis of Article 79, but it does in combined application with Articles 82 or 83.[69] Additionally, there are no explicit restrictions in connection with Articles 82 and 83 (emergency brake and minimum legislation); this means that Article 79 paragraph 2 TFEU has more in common with Article 325 paragraph 4 than with the other entitlement norms.

With the advent of the (partial) *ius puniendi* in the EU, it also became necessary to extend the principle of legality at the European level. This is enshrined in Article 49 CFR, which sets the precise definitional limitations

[68] Hecker, Europäisches Strafrecht, p. 243.
[69] Ambos, European Criminal Law, pp. 319, 336.

of EU criminal legislation. In the Advocaaten Voor de Wereld[70] case, the CJEU ruled that the FD does not fall within the scope of the principle of legality (as a recognised EU legal principle) since the obligation to transpose the FD necessarily implies a legal transformation into national law. Then, compliance with the principle of legality from a fundamental and human rights perspective can be ensured by domestic legislation. However, the CJEU's jurisprudence on the principle of legality is changing, primarily because of the function of national law (including criminal law) to ensure the uniform application of EU law. Moreover, while in the Taricco case[71] the CJEU wanted to set a new course for the principle of legality at the EU level compared to the Berlusconi case,[72] it was forced to correct it (M.A.S. case[73]). In the case of a directive that contains substantive criminal law-related norms but needs to be incorporated into the domestic legal order [Article 83 (1)-(2) TFEU], the possibility of direct effect even creates a close link between the principle of legality and the directive's provisions. Since the possibility of direct effect may be opened up for the benefit of the individual (defendant) against the State, it has an extraordinary outcome in the context of criminal responsibility. Namely, this can only become relevant – by the very nature of the matter – if there are potentially compelling grounds for exclusion from criminal responsibility (e.g. if the directive explicitly regulates the impunity of an act).[74]

With the obligation to interpret the national norm in conformity with EU law, directives also acquire an indirect effect. The CJEU stated in its Kolpinghuis Nijmegen case[75] that national courts are required to interpret their national law in light of the wording and the purposes of the directive in order to achieve the result laid down in it. That obligation is limited by the general principles of law, which form part of Community law and the principles of legal certainty and non-retroactivity. Therefore, a directive cannot, in itself and independently of a national law adopted by a MS for its implementation, have the effect of determining or aggravating the

[70] CJEU, No. C-303/05, *Advocaten voor de Wereld VZW v. Leden van de Ministerraad*, ECLI:EU:C:2007:261, 3 May 2007.3

[71] C-105/14 *Ivo Taricco and others* [ECR] 2015 555.

[72] L. Wörner, 'Wirksam genug? – Normentheorie im Kontext funktionstüchtiger europäisierter Strafrechtspflege' in A. Schneider and M. Wagner (eds.), *Normentheorie und Strafrecht*, Baden-Baden: Nomos, 2018, p. 271 at 282.

[73] CJEU, *M.A.S. and M.B.*, No. C-42/17, Judgment, ECLI:EU:C:2017:936, 5 December 2017.

[74] See also the following subchapter.

[75] CJEU, *Kolpinghuis Nijmegen BV*, No. 80/86, Judgment, ECLI:EU:C:1987:431, 8 October 1987.

liability in criminal law of persons who act in contravention of the provisions of that directive. Yet, the emergence of a (partial) EU *ius puniendi* has the potential to relativise and weaken this limitation; it is not unlikely that the CJEU attempted such a weakening with the Taricco 'experiment'.

1.3.3 Minimum Harmonisation by Way of Secondary Law

When harmonising directives, the minimum regulatory method specified in the directive will still generate fundamental differences concerning specific questions, among the most important being punishability and impunity.[76] Some examples:

- the rules on limitation of actions of particular MS set the minimum time limits to a later period, while others set a different but earlier maximum time limit for punishability;
- different interpretations of the accessory character of participation may result in different judgments of the same aiding or abetting conduct;
- as a result of the fundamentally different dogmatic approaches related to the stages of perpetration, the same act could be considered a punishable attempt in one MS or preparation in another, depending on the acceptance of an objective or a subjective theory;
- the concrete conditions for sanctionability of legal persons can be fundamentally different (crimes by a natural person only; what causal relationships must be examined, etc.).

Such regulatory asymmetries are inevitable in this co-working system of European law and national criminal law, and only systematic research can provide an accurate prognosis in this regard. Mutual recognition cannot eliminate the risk of a 'relative gap of punishability'.[77] The activist jurisprudence of the CJEU cannot be an option because the critical issue here is a gap between punishability or – from the opposite point of view – acceptance of non-punishability.[78] And case law in criminal matters

[76] K. Karsai, 'External Effects of the European Public Prosecutor's Office Regime', (in Hungarian) (2019) 14 *Miskolci Jogi Szemle.*

[77] K. Ligeti, 'European Public Prosecutor's Office: How Should the Rules Applicable to its Procedure be Determined', (2011) 1 *EuCLR*, 123–148.

[78] L. Wörner, 'Kriminalitätsphänomen Terrorismus als unlösbare Aufgabe für das nationale materielle Strafrecht – Zur Relevanz europäischer bis internationaler Tatbestandsvorgaben' in K. Höffler (ed.), *Criminal Law Discourse of the Interconnected Society (CLaDIS)*, Baden-Baden: Nomos, 2020, p. 131 at 137.

cannot extend or establish criminal responsibility if the (written) law does not provide a solid basis. However, if we accept that the MS has granted EU partial *ius puniendi*, at least regarding the protection of financial interests, the CJEU will be entitled to act with more vigour.

As an important feature of the minimum harmonisation of directives and according to the well-accepted doctrine of European law and the practice of the CJEU, directives may have a direct effect in some instances in order to protect the rights of individuals (direct vertical effect). The preconditions are threefold: when the provisions of the directive are unconditional and sufficiently clear and precise; when the MS has not transposed the directive by the deadline (judgment of 4 December 1974, Van Duyn) or it did so, but incorrectly; and finally, only the individual can invoke the directive directly against the 'lazy' MS on the basis of the directive (judgment of 5 April 1979, Ratti). The question, therefore, is whether it is rationally conceivable for an individual to rely directly on a directive containing a legislative obligation on the part of the MS.

Meanwhile, the entitlement in Article 82 (2) TFEU provides the legal basis for minimum harmonisation in connection with procedural issues; Article 83 (2)-(3) TFEU gives two different legal bases for minimum ruling in connection with substantive criminal law (statutory elements of offences and sanctions). In the case of procedural harmonisation, the direct effects are immediately clear when viewed from a rational perspective, particularly for regulatory acts affecting the procedural position of the individual where the minimum protection under a directive is not provided in the MS concerned. Suppose the Pupino case was hypothetically brought before the CJEU in the present legal situation under directive rules: the CJEU would likely have ruled that the victim (his representative) could directly invoke the requirement for different interrogation circumstances. In the case of substantive criminal law, however, it is necessary to examine, before granting direct effect, the type of criminal law provision where minimum harmonisation exists. If it is about statutory definitions offered by the directive for implementation, the MS is entitled to decide to impose greater punishment or penalise other behaviour; in that case, the directive does not restrict it from acting accordingly. However, the MS is not entitled not to punish any of the minimum statutory offences. In the case of possible direct application, the question would arise of how the person affected by the direct application could enforce the directive's rules against the MS and in favour of himself.

The answer is that he cannot. If such minimum rules are absent from the domestic criminal code, the European limitation mentioned above restricts the consequences of relying on the directive, namely, EU law on its own cannot establish (or aggravate) criminal responsibility in the context of a national criminal procedure. The same is the case with minimum rules of sanctioning established by a directive under Articles 82 (2) or 83 (2)-(3) TFEU. Setting the minimum standards does not prohibit the imposition of other or more severe sanctions.

1.4 Status Quo: The Relationship and Intersections between EU Law and CoE Law

All EU countries are members of the CoE, but this has not always been the case. Historically important, all the Eastern European EU MS in particular first became part of the CoE (and especially the ECHR) after their regime change and only subsequently joined the EU through the EU accession process. Immediate accession to the ECHR resulted in the human rights compliance of their legal systems within a few years. The acquis of the CoE in the field of (criminal) justice also essentially filtered directly into the legal systems of those countries with a regime change (recommendations, training, monitoring).

While the dynamic development of EU-ECL over twenty-five years and its results today were not political or legally planned – primarily because of restrictive arguments of sovereignty – it was not surprising that in the late 1980s, precisely in order to delimit the CoE's achievements, the view was expressed that the EU (then the EEC) had no place in the international (regional) arena of crime control and cooperation in criminal matters. Only 'the Council of Europe [...] had both the substantive knowledge and the procedures to deal with this issue which, in addition, was intimately linked with the European Convention of Human Rights and the case-law of the Court'.[79] These views did not propagate and even lost their basis after the birth of the third pillar in its first version. The slow and persistently compromised development of cooperation in criminal matters among the EU MS under the auspices of the CoE have led to mechanisms where the two organisations reciprocally influence

[79] H. G. Nilsson, '25 Years of Criminal Justice in Europe', (2012) 2 *EuCLR*, 106 at 107.

(have reciprocally influenced) each other. When MS follow this path to find their own legal solutions, which is made possible by the different legal structure and legal order at the EU level (e.g. the European Arrest Warrant), CoE results can serve as sources of inspiration and reflection (e.g. the intergovernmental character of the third pillar in its first version). At the same time, legal solutions between EU MS following new concepts or principles can partly filter through to the sphere of influence of the CoE, giving a new horizontal impetus to the traditional cooperation framework (e.g. allowance of joint investigation teams).

As of today, there are three main fields of intersection between legal developments influenced by EU law and CoE law: (1) human rights protection and its implications in the legislation and jurisdiction of national systems, (2) the very important influence of CoE activities in initiating crime control and preparing international multilateral conventions for designing national criminal justice institutions, and (3) the international cooperation of States in criminal matters (extradition, legal assistance).

1.4.1 Crime Control and Monitoring Mechanisms

In 1958, the Committee of Ministers of the CoE tasked the European Committee on Crime Problems (CDPC) with overseeing and coordinating crime prevention and crime control activities. The CDPC identifies priorities for legal cooperation, makes proposals to the Committee of Ministers on activities regarding the entire criminal justice ecosystem, and implements these activities. Meanwhile, the CoE has adopted more than 100 resolutions or recommendations relevant to criminal law and initiated over 50 multilateral conventions[80] with criminal law-related regulatory content. Generally speaking, these conventions have in common that they identify a criminological phenomenon (organised crime, corruption, terrorism, cybercrime) and provide statutory definitions of offences belonging to this phenomenon that should be punishable Europe-wide and which the MS undertake to prosecute through signing the convention. Signing a convention a State also ensures closer judicial (and/or police) cooperation with other signatory MS regarding the offences in question (*aut dedere aut judicare*). Some criminal conventions additionally introduce

[80] www.coe.int/en/web/cdpc/conventions (10/2021).

convention-related monitoring mechanisms.[81] Such monitoring activities can support and persuade MS to improve their convention-related measures and thus better protect rights and values through refinement of criminal law legislation.

1.4.2 Judicial Cooperation between States

The international cooperation of States is a collaborative undertaking between sovereign national States that traditionally are not bound to satisfy a request.[82] However, the general willingness of States to assist in criminal procedures for other States has developed since the early twentieth century – following the decline of the sovereigns of the empires of the nineteenth century. In the second half of the twentieth century, especially within Europe, the desire for peace and stability and the evolvement of human rights had led to a broad array of multilateral (and bilateral) agreements between States.[83] The individual value of humans as recognised subjects of international cooperation (rather than as objects) was a cornerstone in this development. The expansion of human rights protection also affected the law on international cooperation of States, which can serve to restrict State interests under specific circumstances.

In European regional development, mutual legal assistance has meanwhile become an important pillar of jointly controlling (transnational) criminality. If States are prompt to assist each other in criminal

[81] Mechanisms (1) dealing with financial issues (Committee of Experts on the Evaluation of Measures to Combat Money Laundering and Terrorist Financing; GRECO, Group of States against Corruption), (2) protecting vulnerable groups, such as GRETA (Group of Experts on Action against Trafficking), GREVIO (Group of Experts on Action against Violence against Women and Domestic Violence), and Lanzarote Commission (Convention for the Protection of Children against Sexual Exploitation and Sexual Abuse), (3) monitoring cross-cutting fundamental rights protection, such as the CoE's European Committee for the Prevention of Torture and Inhuman or Degrading Treatment or Punishment (CPT) and the European Commission against Racism and Intolerance (ECRI).

[82] K. Karsai, 'Locus/Forum Regit Actum – a Dual Principle in Transnational Criminal Matters', (2019) 60 *Hung. J. Leg. Stud.*, 155 at 157; L. Wörner, 'Die Normen des IRG', in K. Ambos, S. König, and P. Rackow (eds.), *Rechtshilferecht in Strafsachen*, 2nd edn., Baden-Baden: Nomos, 2020, p. 1150.

[83] L. Wörner, 'Die Übermittlung von Informationen im Lichte des deutsch-polnischen Kooperationsvertrags und der EU-Rechtshilfevorgaben aus deutscher Sicht', in A. Ligocka, M. Malolepszy, and M. Soine (eds.), *Die grenzüberschreitende Informationsgewinnung und -verwertung am Beispiel der Zusammenarbeit der deutschen und polnischen Strafverfolgungsbehörden*, Berlin: Logos, 2018, p. 15.

investigations and trust each other, meaning that traditional legal and political struggles founded in any kind of mistrust are no longer relevant, the benefits for criminals of acting transnationally diminish. Mutual legal assistance is indispensable because evidence located abroad cannot be gathered by one State on the territory of another.[84] However, this might be the ultimate goal of integrating justice systems – this level of trust has not yet been achieved between any MS in the EU. European legal development (both CoE and European Union) paints a rather colourful picture concerning the existing institutions of legal assistance;[85] different and independent regimes operate in parallel, often acknowledging the same scopes of application. A general feature of the relevant legislation is a strong intersection between EU and CoE instruments, as the conventions concluded by the EU MS and the relevant secondary legislation reflect and reinforce previous CoE agreements. However, the MS also operate with innovative new instruments which reflect the determination to improve the effectiveness of criminal cooperation in criminal matters, and which is justified by the gradual process of European integration.

1.5 Conclusions

The picture drawn here of a developing ECL against the background of its routes and sources reveals several intersections between EU law and CoE law. This leads, in combination with the further development of European criminal policy, to two predictions: first, it is to be expected that, as a matter of policy, further harmonising directives will be enacted, and the Commission will increasingly use regulations as an instrument. Second, the EPPO will have a considerable integrating effect, both in terms of its involvement in national proceedings and ensuing changes to criminal procedures in the MS. Even if not all MS participate in the EPPO, those (as yet) not participating (Hungary, Poland, Sweden,[86] Denmark and Ireland) will not be able to divorce themselves entirely from it.[87] Yet, the answer to whether the EPPO

[84] L. Wörner, 'Die Europäische Ermittlungsanordnung (RL EEA)', in K. Ambos, S. König, and P. Rackow (eds.), *Rechtshilferecht in Strafsachen*, 2nd edn., Baden-Baden: Nomos, 2020, p. 1089.

[85] Ambos, *European Criminal Law*, p. 415.

[86] Pending www.pwclegal.be/en/news/the-european-public-prosecutor-s-office--eppo--has-officially-st.html (11/2021).

[87] For further details see S. Allegrezza, Chapter 17 'European Public Prosecutor', in this volume.

system should be generalised – obliging *all* MS to facilitate the EPPO's work and mechanisms – or relativisation of fundamental principles risked – is yet to be found. To find it, a deeper reflection on the meaning, effectiveness and operational reliability of EU criminal law is needed, hopefully resulting, ultimately, in the establishment of a legal theory of ECL.

Further Reading

D. Brodowski, 'European Criminal Justice: From Mutual Recognition to Coherence', in S. Carrera, D. Curtin and A. Geddes (eds.), *20 Years Anniversary of the Tampere Programme. Europeanisation Dynamics of the EU Area of Freedom, Security and Justice*, San Domenico di Fiesole: European University Institute, 2020, pp. 225–238.

C. Burchard, *Die Konstitutionalisierung der gegenseitigen Anerkennung. Die strafjustizielle Zusammenarbeit in Europa im Lichte des Unionsverfassungsrechts*, Frankfurt a.M.: Vittorio Klostermann, 2019.

W. De Bondt, 'Evidence-Based EU Criminal Policy Making: In Search of Matching Data', (2014) 20 *Eur J Crim Policy Res*, 23–49.

H. H. Jescheck, 'Die Strafgewalt übernationaler Gemeinschaften', (1953) 65 *ZStW*, 498.

M. Kettunen, *Legitimising European Criminal Law*, Berlin: Springer, 2020.

J. Vogel, 'Europäische Kriminalpolitik – europäische Strafrechtsdogmatik', (2002) 149 *GA*, 517–534.

2 The European Court System and Its Role in Shaping European Criminal Law

Liz Heffernan

2.1 Introduction

It is self-evident that in the 1950s the European Communities (ECs) established a *sui generis* legal order that departed from the traditional intergovernmental model of cooperation by creating independent institutions empowered to adopt rules legally binding on the Member States (MS) and to enforce them. In the Union's formative years, the Court of Justice of the European Union (CJEU) embodied that supranationalism when exercising its authority to definitively interpret EU law in its many forms and to review the actions of the political institutions and MS to ensure their conformity with Union precepts. The Court famously served as 'the motor of European integration', drawing on the doctrines of supremacy and direct effect (*effet utile*) to shape the European legal order and supervise the application of EU law in wide-ranging areas of economic and social activity.[1]

The ebb and flow of intergovernmentalism and supranationalism is a recurring motif in European Criminal Law.[2] It could not have been foreseen in the 1950s that European integration would eventually extend to crime, security, and policing and it is not surprising that the intergovernmental approach dominated this field until the entry into force of the Treaty of Lisbon in 2014. In the early years of European criminal law,

[1] T. Horsley, 'Reflections on the Role of the Court of Justice as the "Motor" of European Integration: Legal Limits to Judicial Lawmaking', (2013) 50 *CMLR*, 931–64; T. Tridimas, 'The Court of Justice and Judicial Activism', (1996) 26 *Eur. L. Rev.*, 199–210; H. Rasmussen, *On Law and Policy in the European Court of Justice: A Comparative Study in Judicial Policymaking*, Leiden: Brill/Nijhoff, 1986.

[2] K. Ambos, *European Criminal Law*, Cambridge: Cambridge University Press, 2018; S. Peers, *EU Justice and Home Affairs Law Volume II: EU Criminal Law, Policing and Civil Law*, 4th edn., Oxford: Oxford University Press, 2016; A. Klip, *European Criminal Law: An Integrative Approach*, 4th edn., Cambridge: Intersentia, 2021; S. Miettinen, *Criminal Law and Policy in the European Union*, London: Routledge, 2013; V. Mitsilegas, *EU Criminal Law after Lisbon: Rights, Trust and the Transformation of Justice in Europe*, Oxford: Hart Publishing, 2016.

the agenda was controlled by the MS acting unanimously with only limited scope for judicial review. While the traditional horizontal methods of doing business have waned post-Lisbon, and today there is greater transparency and accountability over EU action in the field, intergovernmentalism still applies to certain pre-Lisbon instruments and its broader history continues to cast a shadow over contemporary policy and practice.

The competence of the EU to formulate policies and adopt rules in relation to criminal matters has been a source of contention and the CJEU has been called upon to define the contours of European authority. Criminal law is an area where national sovereignty is pre-eminent; preventing crime and preserving security are primary responsibilities for the nation-state and normally embedded in national laws and constitutions. Nevertheless, the MS gradually recognised the need for co-operation in fighting transnational crimes such as terrorism, international fraud, and drug trafficking. Over time, the benefits of national authorities assisting each other, for example by sharing intelligence and extraditing suspects, became increasingly apparent. Fledgling international arrangements for police and judicial co-operation mushroomed over time into a complex body of rules, policies and practices, a development which was reflected in the transition of crime and security from the periphery to the heart of the EU Treaties.

Although not a transnational legal code in the strict sense, European criminal law is now a substantial, dynamic branch of EU law that supports 'an area of freedom, security and justice without internal frontiers'[3] (AFSJ). Nevertheless, it remains controversial for reasons beyond the historical factors noted above. Criminal law involves the balancing of distinct public interests and providing a framework that promotes pluralism, equality, justice, and solidarity is particularly challenging at a transnational level. Collective European endeavour requires reaching agreement on measures that apply within the markedly diverse national legal systems that span the civil law and common law traditions.[4] Not surprisingly, integration in crime, security, and policing has been complex and controversial, politically and legally.

[3] Article 3(2) TEU. The goal of free movement of EU citizens within this area operates 'in conjunction with appropriate measures with respect to external border controls, asylum, immigration and the prevention and combating of crime'. Ibid.

[4] A. Ryan, *Towards a System of European Criminal Justice: The Problem of Admissibility of Evidence*, London: Routledge, 2014; J. Jackson and S. Summers, *The Internationalisation of Criminal Evidence: Beyond the Common Law and Civil Law Traditions*, Cambridge: Cambridge University Press, 2012.

This chapter explores the role of the European court system in establishing the foundations of European criminal law and in addressing some of these difficult issues. Its focus is the CJEU and the contribution of its case law in two formative areas: the competence of the EU and the primacy of EU law; and the relationship between the principle of mutual recognition and the protection of fundamental rights. The chapter first sketches a brief overview of the European court system and the co-existence of the CJEU and the European Court of Human Rights (ECtHR).

2.2 The European Court System

The judicial branch of the European system comprises several different parts which exercise distinct but overlapping functions. Although we refer for present purposes to a 'European Court System', it is intuitive that there is no single homogenous judicial structure in Europe but rather an amalgamation of courts drawn from different legal orders. The European judicial process is shaped above all by the co-existence of two dynamic and powerful courts, the CJEU and the ECtHR, an international court established under the auspices of the Council of Europe (CoE) which hears applications alleging violations of the European Convention on Human Rights (ECHR). Another tier in the European system comprises the national courts located in the EU MS and in the States parties to the ECHR. Both EU law and the ECHR operate on the premise that laws that are internationally inspired should be applied and enforced locally in the first instance. The European court system thus ascribes a significant role to the national courts as fora for the implementation of European law and the percolation of issues to the CJEU and ECtHR.

The CJEU has been far less active in criminal matters comparable to other areas of EU law and this is a reflection of the more restricted jurisdiction that it was accorded historically. The ECs, as created in the 1950s, were focused squarely on economic integration and although they gradually embraced wide-ranging fields of competence, it was not until the Treaty on European Union (TEU) agreed at Maastricht in 1992 that arrangements for tackling serious cross-border crime were included in the Treaty's Third Pillar on Justice and Home Affairs (JHA). Prior to that time, criminal matters surfaced occasionally or incidentally, for example in relation to financial crimes or fraud against the Union or in context of immigration and border controls.

As a strand within the TEU's Third Pillar, the Union's criminal law competence was firmly intergovernmental: decision-making power resided in the Council acting unanimously, the instruments adopted were more akin to international agreements than legislation and, most pertinent to the present discussion, judicial oversight was severely restricted. In stark contrast to the mechanisms available under the First Pillar, which housed the law of the European Community (EC), infringement proceedings could not be brought under the Third Pillar and national courts could make references to the CJEU only where the MS in question had expressly signed up to a modified preliminary ruling procedure.[5]

The re-shaping of the constitutional architecture in the years following the Treaty of Maastricht involved the gradual re-location of European criminal law at the centre of Union activity. The process of adjustment, honed through the subsequent treaties of Amsterdam in 1997, Nice in 2001 and Lisbon in 2009, culminated in the inclusion of policing and criminal law within the First Pillar, essentially re-cast as the Treaty on the Functioning of the European Union (TFEU). This involved the embrace of supranational arrangements including the extended jurisdiction of the CJEU over EU criminal law. By lifting the prohibition on infringement actions and easing the restrictions on the preliminary ruling procedure,[6] the Lisbon Treaty enabled a more robust role for the Court in scrutinising the adoption of EU legislation and reviewing MS implementation.

While these changes were indeed momentous, the practical operation of EU criminal law is constrained by certain legal limitations which reflect the jealous guarding by the MS of their own domestic criminal laws, procedures, and traditions. First, the EU legislative process in relation to criminal matters is peppered with exceptions, caveats and provisos which allow the MS to curtail the adoption of measures.[7] Second, there remain some pre-Lisbon criminal law instruments that operate in the intergovernmental mould without the avenues for enforcement and

[5] Article 35 TEU as originally adopted.

[6] Articles 258–260 TFEU (proceedings against MS) and Arts. 263–266 (proceedings against institutions); Article 267 TFEU (preliminary ruling procedure).

[7] An example is the possibility under Arts. 82(3) and 83(3) TEU that a MS can operate an 'emergency brake' on the legislative process where it believes a draft directive would affect fundamental aspects of its criminal justice system. The ordinary legislative process is suspended and the matter may be referred to the European Council with a view to resolving the dispute or enabling some MS to proceed via 'enhanced cooperation'.

oversight available under mainstream Union law.[8] A third limitation is the tolerance within the Treaty of Lisbon of 'variable geometry', that is, differing levels of commitment to European integration among the MS. A notable example is the special positions negotiated by Denmark, Ireland and formerly the United Kingdom (UK) which have allowed them to participate selectively in criminal law measures.[9] Fourthly, cooperation in relation to criminal justice has generally followed the model of 'mutual recognition'[10] rather than 'harmonisation', thereby affording the MS greater flexibility in the manner in which they implement common standards and minimum rules, as will be explained in the following text. The emphasis on coordination and approximation preserves wide variation in national laws, procedures, and practices across the Union with attendant implications for the transparency and efficacy of EU law. Each of these limitations has had a spill-over effect on the role of the CJEU in developing European criminal law; the Court's jurisdiction may be broad in theory under the TFEU, but its influence is diminished by these inroads into its ability to exercise its authority in practice.

The ECtHR is grounded legally in the ECHR and has been operational since 1959. For the past sixty years, it has heard countless applications brought by individuals, and occasionally by States, alleging violations of the human rights protected in the Convention and its substantive protocols.[11] Included among the forty-six members of the CoE which have ratified the ECHR are the twenty-seven MS of the EU. The ECtHR's substantive competence is clearly far more limited than that of the CJEU because it extends exclusively to human rights – specifically to the lengthy catalogue of rights guaranteed in the ECHR which roughly

[8] Under complicated transitional rules, the old Third Pillar arrangements, including limitations on the CJEU's jurisdiction, still govern measures that were not repealed prior to the end of 2014 (cf. Article 10, Protocol 36 Lisbon Treaty).

[9] For example, under Protocol 21 Lisbon Treaty, Ireland opted out of any new criminal law initiatives but retained the right to opt in to any specific measure.

[10] Article 82 TFEU; Ambos, *European Criminal Law*, pp. 20–22.

[11] The ECtHR's authority to examine an issue is dependent on an application being brought by an individual, group or NGO alleging that a State party has violated their rights under the Convention. Article 34 ECHR. The Court also has jurisdiction to entertain complaints lodged by States parties against each other and, since 2018, to issue advisory opinions at the request of the CoE's Committee of Ministers. Article 33 ECHR and Articles 47–49 and Protocol No 16. Cf. P. van Dijk et al. (eds.), *Theory and Practice of the European Convention on Human Rights*, 5th edn., Cambridge: Intersentia, 2018; D. Harris et al., *Law of the European Convention on Human Rights*, 4th edn., Oxford: Oxford University Press, 2018.

corresponds to the civil and political rights contained in the EU Charter of Fundamental Rights (CFREU).[12]

Because the ECtHR is a creature of a multilateral treaty, the impact of its judgments is constrained by the vagaries of the international legal system. Where the Court finds that a State party has violated the Convention, its ruling is binding as a matter of international law and the State party is obliged give effect to it.[13] The execution of judgments and awards of compensation is monitored by the CoE's Committee of Ministers but neither that body nor the CoE's Parliamentary Assembly nor indeed the Court itself has the power to enforce the Court's judgments directly within national systems, for example by ensuring that national laws are changed or future violations prevented.[14] The legal effect of the ECHR within the domestic legal system is a matter that is determined by national law. There is a spectrum of practice in the legal orders of the States parties ranging from the monist stance that is dominant in the civil law tradition to common law adherence to the dualist position.[15] The limited penetrative effect of ECHR law within national legal systems contrasts starkly with the powerful reach of EU law, which in principle has the automatic impact of displacing conflicting domestic law provisions.

EU law and the ECHR are consistent for the most part in the nature and extent of their substantive coverage of civil and political rights. Historically

[12] The CFREU constitutes a primary source of Union law and it binds both the EU institutions and the MS when implementing EU law (Article 6(1) TEU and Article 5(1) CFREU). S. Peers et al. (eds.), *The EU Charter of Fundamental Rights: A Commentary* (Oxford: Hart Publishing, 2014). A more modern legal text than the ECHR, the CFREU is broader in substantive scope, notably because it also encompasses socio-economic rights. Cf. Ambos, *European Criminal Law*, p. 80 et seq. and p. 142 et seq. Central to European criminal law is the right of an accused person to a fair trial, a guarantee that is safeguarded by Article 6 ECHR and Articles 47 and 48 CFREU.

[13] Article 46 ECHR.

[14] The Assembly monitors human rights compliance by new MS and, exceptionally, this procedure can be applied to any MS. Its general powers include authority to recommend the suspension or even expulsion of a MS for serious violations of CoE standards. The Secretary General of the CoE also has a general supervisory power to request a MS to explain how its internal law complies with the Convention. Monitoring Committee, *The Monitoring Procedure of the Parliamentary Assembly*. AS/Mon/Inf (2013) 06rev3; Harris et al., *Law of the European Convention on Human Rights*, pp. 197–99; P. van Dijk et al. (eds.), *Theory and Practice of the European Convention on Human Rights*, 5th edn., Cambridge: Intersentia, 2018, pp. 296–306.

[15] In reality, the status of the ECHR within domestic legal systems is more complicated than these general labels would suggest. Ambos, *European Criminal Law*, pp. 74–76 (comparing the position in the UK, Russia and Germany).

the ECHR influenced the evolution by the CJEU of 'general principles' of EC law, and indeed Article 6(3) TEU now formally recognises the ECHR's fundamental rights as general principles of EU law. It is fair to say that the respective regimes of the EU and the ECHR run essentially in parallel and the relationship between the CJEU and the ECtHR in adjudicating potential rights violations is generally symbiotic. The CFREU expressly recognises that in so far as its rights correspond to ECHR guarantees, the meaning and scope of those rights shall mirror their counterparts under the Convention.[16] This 'requirement of homogeneity' has been acknowledged by Advocates General as requiring the interpretation of the rights of the defence under Article 47 CFREU in broadly equivalent terms to Article 6 ECHR[17] which implicitly entails following the Strasbourg case law. The CJEU has itself frequently relied on judgments of the ECtHR when developing rights relevant to the criminal process including the right to fair trial[18] and the right to informational privacy.[19]

Article 6(2) TEU asserts the EU's commitment to accede to the ECHR, a development which would ensure that the Union is bound by the Convention independently of the MS. Various steps were taken to lay the legal groundwork for accession culminating in the drafting of an accession agreement in 2013. However, in its *Opinion 2/13* the CJEU held that accession via the draft agreement would be incompatible with the TEU and 'liable to adversely affect the specific characteristics of EU law and its autonomy'.[20] Central among the CJEU's concerns was the institutional

[16] Article 52(3) CFREU. However, this provision shall not prevent Union law providing 'more extensive protection'. Ibid.

[17] CJEU, *Trade Agency Ltd*, No. C-619/10, Opinion of AG Kokott, ECLI:EU:C:2012:247, 26 April 2012, para.75 (civil proceedings); *Tupikas*, No. C-270/17, Opinion of AG Bobeck,ECLI:EU:C:2017:609 noting at para. 133 that 'there must be a minimum level of parallelism between the standards of protection provided for by the ECHR, on the one hand, and those existing in EU law, on the other hand'. But see *ZZ v. Secretary of State for the Home Department*, No. C-300/11, Opinion of AG Bot, ECLI:EU:C:2012:563, 12 September 2012, para. 111 (distinguishing expulsion proceedings from criminal proceedings).

[18] CJEU, *Orkem*, No. C-374/87, Judgment, ECLI:EU:C:1989:237, 13 June 1989, para.30; *Hoechst*, Joined Cases Nos. C-46/87 and 227/88, Judgment, ECLI:EU:C:1989:337, 21 September 1989, para. 18; *Rubach*, No. C-344/08, Judgment, ECLI:EU:C:2009:482, 16 July 2009, para. 31; *USB Europe SE and Others*, No. C-358/16, Judgment, ECLI:EU:2018:715, 13 September 2018, para. 59.

[19] See, for example, *Digital Rights Ireland*, Joined Cases Nos. C-293/12 and C-594/12, Judgment, ECLI:EU:C:2014:238, 8 April 2014.

[20] CJEU, *Opinion 2/13 (Accession of the EU to the ECHR)*, Opinion of the Court, ECLI:EU:C:2014:2454, 18 December 2014, para. 200. The Court had referred earlier in its Opinion to the EU's essential characteristics, its unique legal structure and the common

relationship between itself and the ECtHR and the prospect that it might be subject to the external control of the ECtHR on issues involving the interpretation of EU law.[21] The Court's rigid stance was a stumbling block to progressing the accession project and several years elapsed before negotiations were resumed in 2020. Accession is vital to ensuring that fundamental rights are applied and can be enforced throughout the Union against all sources of governmental authority whether national or European.[22]

2.3 EU Criminal Law: Competence and Primacy

'European criminal law' is an amalgamated term used to denote a miscellany of substantive offences, procedural rules, and institutional arrangements which supplement criminal governance at national level. The disparate nature of the law, coupled with dominance of national interests, makes it difficult to discern the nature and extent of Union authority. While it is customary to identify the inclusion of a criminal law competence in the TEU's Third Pillar as the catalyst for development, it is important not to overlook judicial engagement with criminal law issues prior to the Maastricht Treaty. During a formative era in the evolution of the European legal order, the CJEU delivered a series of seminal judgments that touched on the relationship between EC law and the criminal process. The general tenor of these judgments was to affirm the primacy of EC law and the corresponding obligation on national authorities to conform to its tenets even where this involved adapting national criminal law and process.

values on which it was founded. Ibid., paras. 167–70. The conditions surrounding accession are found in Article 6(2) TEU, Protocol No 8 TEU, and Article 218 TFEU.

[21] CJEU, *Opinion 2/13 (Accession of the EU to the ECHR)*, Opinion of the Court, ECLI:EU:C:2014:2454, 18 December 2014, paras. 181–86. The CJEU emphasised in particular that the EU's judicial system was designed to ensure consistency and uniformity in the interpretation of EU law. Ibid., para. 174. B. de Witte and Š. Imamović, 'Opinion 2/13 on Accession to the ECHR: Defending the EU Legal Order against a Foreign Human Rights Court', (2015) 40(5) *Eur. L. Rev.*, 683–705.

[22] Klip, *European Criminal Law*, p. 413. The delay in progressing negotiations is perhaps surprising given that the Union's commitment to accession is set down in Article 6(2) TEU but it is partly attributable to the complicated conditions outlined in CJEU, *Opinion 2/13 (Accession of the EU to the ECHR)*, Opinion of the Court, ECLI:EU:C:2014:2454, 18 December 2014. Lock, for example, has argued that accession involving the preservation of the doctrine of mutual trust would weaken rather than strengthen fundamental rights protection. T. Lock, 'The Future of EU Human Rights Law: Is Accession to the ECHR Still Desirable?', (2020) 7(2) *JICL*, 427–48.

A specific question that the CJEU was asked to consider during this period was whether the Community's competences in establishing the internal market and pursuing specific policies extended to the power to impose criminal sanctions for breaches of EC law (so called annex or ancillary competence). For legislatures vested with a general power to enact criminal laws, the imposition of criminal sanctions incidental to a non-criminal law objective is typically not controversial. However, given that the Community lacked any general criminal law competence, it was debatable whether the EC legislature could buttress the regulation of the internal market by requiring the MS to penalise infringements of Community law.[23]

The *Greek Maize* case[24] arose out of the exportation from Greece to Belgium of maize that had originated in Yugoslavia but had been declared by the Greek authorities to be of Greek origin. Because an agricultural levy had not been collected when the consignments had been imported into Greece, the enterprise involved a fraud on the Community budget in which the Greek authorities had been complicit. Giving judgment in infringement proceedings brought by the Commission against Greece, the Court recognised that the Community had the power to require the MS to punish infringements of EC law. The particular obligation on the MS to impose penalties derived from their broad duty to take all measures necessary to guarantee the application and effectiveness of Community law, later known as 'the principle of sincere cooperation'.[25]

The Court grounded the Community power to impose criminal sanctions in two principles, each of which has generated its own subsequent case law.[26] Where the nature and extent of the sanction for an infringement are not prescribed at European level, the MS have discretion to select an appropriate penalty. But this freedom is tempered by the principle that breaches of EC law must be treated in the same way as violations

[23] See F. Giuffrida, 'Effectiveness, Dissuasiveness, Proportionality of Sanctions and Assimilation Principle: The Long-Lasting Legacy of the Greek Maize Case', in V. Mitsilegas et al. (eds.), *The Court of Justice and European Criminal Law: Leading Cases in a Contextual Analysis*, Oxford: Hart, 2019, 108–21; M. Dougan, 'From Velvet Glove to Iron Fist: Criminal Sanctions for the Enforcement of Union Law', in M. Cremona (ed.), *Compliance and the Enforcement of EU Law*, Oxford: Oxford University Press, 2012, 74–131.

[24] CJEU, *Commission v. Greece*, No. 68/88, Judgment, ECLI:EU:C:1989:339, 21 September 1989.

[25] Article 5 EEC; Article 4(3) TEU.

[26] Klip, *European Criminal Law*, pp. 78–90.

of national law of 'a similar nature and importance'.[27] The implication is that national authorities may be obliged to use the criminal process to punish infringements of EC law if equivalent breaches of national law would be prosecuted criminally.[28] The second tenet that emerged from the *Greek Maize* case was that the substantive and procedural conditions under which penalties are imposed by national authorities for breaches of EC law must be such as to render the penalties 'effective, proportionate and dissuasive'.[29] In the absence of further elucidation by the Court, the meaning of these standards and the relationship between them remained uncertain. Nevertheless, the judgment appreciably influenced the subsequent development of criminal penalties as an effective means of enforcing European law.[30]

The advent of criminal law-making powers under the rubric of JHA later raised the possibility that the TEU's Third Pillar had become the sole basis on which the Union could legislate for criminal sanctions thereby displacing ancillary competence under the First Pillar's Community law provisions. Given the intergovernmental nature of the Third Pillar, this interpretation would have left decision-making about sanctions firmly in the control of the MS with only limited possibilities for judicial review. However, in the *Environmental Crimes* case,[31] the Court rejected any abridgement of the EC's authority to impose criminal sanctions incidental to essential Community objectives such as the protection of the environment.[32] This reasoning led the Court to annul a framework decision that the Council had adopted under the Third Pillar, on the basis that the measure encroached on the powers conferred on the Community by the EC Treaty.[33]

[27] CJEU, *Commission v. Greece*, No. 68/88, Judgment, ECLI:EU:C:1989:339, 21 September 1989, para. 24.

[28] Ibid., para. 26. CJEU, *Amsterdam Bulb*, No. 50/76, Judgment, ECLI:EU:C:1977:13, 2 February 1977; *Hansen*, No. C-326/88, Judgment, ECLI:EU:C:1990:291, 10 July 1990, para. 17.

[29] CJEU, *Commission v. Greece*, No. 68/88, Judgment, ECLI:EU:C:1989:339, 21 September 1989, para. 24.

[30] K. E. Sørensen, 'MS' Implementation of Penalties to Enforce EU Law: Balancing the Avoidance of Enforcement Deficits and the Protection of Individuals', (2015) 40(6) *Eur. L. Rev.*, 811–31.

[31] CJEU, *Commission v. Council*, No. 176/03, Judgment, ECLI:EU:C:2005:542,13 September 2005.

[32] Ibid., paras. 41 and 47–48. See also *Commission v. Council*, No. 440/05, Judgment, ECLI:EU:C:2007:625, 23 October 2007 (the 'ship-source pollution' case).

[33] Ibid., para. 53.

Plainly the Court's reasoning in the *Environmental Crimes* case had the effect of promoting 'the Community' as the maker of law and policy at the expense of the MS acting collectively. While consistent with the Court's tendency to support integration and supranationalism during this formative period, the judgment's liberal interpretation of Community competence was controversial. Two decades later, the Community power to enact criminal law incidental to the exercise of competence in a non-criminal policy area sits uneasily with the precept that the Union can act only where authority has been conferred by the MS (principle of conferral) and then only if the measure is necessary, appropriate and proportionate to the pursuit of a Community aim.[34]

The issue of incidental criminal sanctions was rendered largely moot by the Treaty of Lisbon in so far as criminal law powers now reside alongside internal market powers in the First Pillar, recast as the TFEU.[35] To the extent that criminal law matters are the subject of dedicated powers in Title V of the TFEU, the case for giving precedence to ancillary competences relating to other policy areas is logically less compelling.[36] Even so, there are risks to ringfencing criminal law competence exclusively within Title V. There may be instances where the inclusion of criminal sanctions within a measure related to a specific policy makes good legislative sense either because it is indeed essential to the achievement of a legitimate aim or its omission would undermine an overall legislative scheme. It might also be dangerous to foreclose entirely the possibility that an ancillary competence in a specific policy area might be used for a progressive end, such as safeguarding the fundamental rights of criminal suspects or the victims of crime. Realistically, the inclusion in Article 83(1) TFEU of a broad power for the Parliament and Council to adopt directives in areas of cross-border crime (including terrorism, organised crime, human trafficking, and computer crime)[37] should lead over time

[34] Article 5(2) TEU (principle of conferral); Articles 5(1), (3) and (4) TEU, Article 69 TFEU (principles of subsidiarity and proportionality); Ambos, *European Criminal Law*, p. 15; Klip, *European Criminal Law*, p. 37.

[35] But see n. 8 and n. 9.

[36] The opposite sides of this debate were illustrated in the process leading to the adoption Directive (EU) 2017/1371 of the European Parliament and the Council of 5 July 2017 on the fight against fraud to the Union's financial interests by means of criminal law [2017] OJ L 198/29. Although the Commission had initially proposed that the measure be adopted under the Union's broad power in Article 325(4) to take measures necessary to protect its finances, the legislature opted to invoke Article 83(2) as the legal basis.

[37] On that see Wade Ch. 8 in this volume.

to a gradual consolidation of legislative activity that will reduce the relevance of ancillary competence exponentially.

As for the efficacy of Community law, the principle of sincere cooperation, discussed in the *Greek Maize* case, was subsequently developed in the Treaties and secondary legislation. The obligation resting on the MS is substantial and wide-ranging and it may necessitate proactive as well as reactive responses to the interaction of EU law and national law. The Court has recognised, for example, that European law may require national authorities to displace conflicting provisions of national criminal law and procedure[38] or, conversely, to actively deploy the national criminal process in order to vindicate Community interests.[39] The contours of Union power and the implications of its exercise for the MS remain fluid questions in European criminal law that the CJEU will likely be tasked with resolving in future cases.

One of the ways in which the Court of Justice nurtured its role as the 'motor of European integration' was by developing the doctrine of direct effect as a means of protecting the interests of individuals in national court proceedings against MS. In *Van Gen den Loos,* the Court of Justice famously described the EC as 'a new legal order of international law', the subjects of which included 'not only MS but also their nationals'.[40] In the years that followed, the Court delivered landmark judgments on the relationship between national authorities and individuals and on the direct effect of treaty provisions and directives.[41] Specifically, the Court recognised that an individual can invoke a directive in a national court in circumstances where the MS has not implemented it within the prescribed period.[42] To allow the MS to rely on its own failure in order to defeat the individual's rights would

[38] CJEU, *Bordessa*, Joined Cases Nos. C-358/93 and C-416/93, Judgment, ECLI:EU:C:1995:54, 23 February 1995; *Taricco and Others*, No. C-105/14, Judgment, ECLI:EU:C:2015:555, 8 September 2015.

[39] CJEU, *Commission v. France*, No. C-265/95, Judgment, ECLI:EU:C:1997:595, 9 December 1997.

[40] CJEU, *Van Gend en Loos*, No. 26/62, Judgment, ECLI:EU:C:1963:1, 5 February 1963, at p.12.

[41] CJEU, *Costa,* No. 6/64, Judgment, ECLI:EU:C:1964:66, 15 July 1966; *Simmenthal,* No. 106/77, Judgment, ECLI:EU:C:1978:49, 9 March 1978; *Van Duyn,* No. 41/74, Judgment, ECLI:EU:C:1974:133, 4 December 1974.

[42] CJEU, *Becker,* No. 8/81, Judgment, ECLI:EU:C:1982:7, 19 January 1982. Direct effect may apply where the Member State has failed to implement the directive or where the directive has not been implemented correctly, provided the provisions in question are sufficiently clear and precise.

be inconsistent with the nature of directives as a source of law binding on the MS.[43] For this self-same reason, the direct effect of directives can be invoked only against national authorities; in European lexicon, directives can be used 'vertically' against MS, but not 'horizontally' to the detriment of individuals.[44] The Court also made plain that even in a case where the doctrine of direct effect is not applicable, the court must adopt a 'conforming' interpretation, that is, it must construe national law in a manner consistent with the directive to the extent that this is possible.[45]

The criminal law implications of these ground-breaking principles of Community law were subsequently teased out in a series of cases in the 1980s and 1990s. *Kolpinghuis Nijmegen*[46] involved the prosecution of a coffee shop for selling a beverage it called 'mineral water' that in fact comprised tap water mixed with carbon dioxide. The public prosecutor relied in part on a directive on the marketing of natural mineral waters that had not been implemented into national law at the material time. In a preliminary ruling, the Court of Justice recalled that because a directive is addressed to the MS, it cannot 'of itself' impose obligations on an individual; thus, the national authorities cannot plead a provision in the directive against the individual in a national court.[47] It dismissed the suggestion that the obligation on the national court to interpret national law and EC law consistently could facilitate the conviction of an individual by the backdoor:

> a directive cannot, of itself and independently of a national law adopted by a Member State for its implementation, have the effect of determining or aggravating the liability in criminal law of persons who act in contravention of the provisions of that directive.[48]

43 The MS is effectively estopped from relying on its failure. Case 148/78 *Ratti*, No. 148/78, ECLI:EU:C:1979:110, 5 April 1979.

44 CJEU, *Marshall*, No. 152/84, Judgment, ECLI:EU:C:1986:84, 26 February 1986.

45 CJEU, *Von Colson*, No. 14/83, Judgment, ECLI:EU:C:1984:37, 10 April 1984.

46 CJEU, *Kolpinghuis Nijmegen*, No. C-80/86, Judgment, ECLI:EU:C:1987:431, 8 October 1987. L. Martin, 'The General Principles of European (Criminal) Law as Limitation to the Enforcement of EU Law: The Kolpinghuis Nijmegen Rule', in V. Mitsilegas et al. (eds.), *The Court of Justice and European Criminal Law: Leading Cases in a Contextual Analysis*, Oxford: Hart, 2019, pp. 7–20.

47 CJEU, *Kolpinghuis Nijmegen*, No. C-80/86, Judgment, ECLI:EU:C:1987:431, 8 October 1987, paras. 9–10.

48 Ibid., at para. 13 (citing *Pretore di Salò v. X*, No. 14/86, Judgment, ECLI:EC:C:1987:275, 11 June 1987). For subsequent development see, for example, *Luciano Arcaro*, No. C-168-95, Judgment, ECLI:EU:C:1996:330, 17 September 1996; *X*, No. C-60/02, Judgment, ECLI:EU:C:2004:10, 7 January 2004.

One of the crucial aspects of *Kolpinghuis Nijmegen* was the Court's reliance on the general principles of legal certainty and non-retroactivity in its exegesis on the implications of directives for criminal prosecutions in the national courts. An unwritten source of primary law derived from principles common to the constitutional traditions of the MS and international human rights treaties to which they are parties, general principles have influenced reasoning and outcomes in other foundational cases.[49]

Berlusconi[50] was a later, high profile ruling in which the Court cemented its approach in *Kolpinghuis Nijmegen* by both extending its reasoning on direct effect and drawing from the wellspring of general principles. The case arose out of criminal proceedings instigated against Silvio Berlusconi, the former prime minister of Italy, and others for false corporate accounting. The prosecution was based on a national law that purported to implement EC company law directives but, after the proceedings had commenced, the Italian parliament passed a new law that, if applied to the case, would have had the effect of de-railing the prosecution. In a landmark judgment, the Court of Justice identified 'the retroactive application of the more lenient penalty that came into effect ex post facto' as a general principle of Community law which the national courts must respect when interpreting national legislation.[51] The Court took the view that, in the present case, leaving the manifestly more severe criminal penalty in place would be 'contrary to the limits which flow from the essential nature of any directive'.[52] *Berlusconi* thus reinforced the Court's commitment to protecting the individual in the context of a criminal prosecution by affording her/him the more favourable interpretation of the law.

Pupino[53] was another milestone in the relevant jurisprudence in which the Court further developed the doctrinal strands of direct effect and conforming interpretation. The instrument at the heart of the case was

[49] T. Tridimas, *General Principles of EU Law*, Oxford: Oxford University Press, 2007; Klip, *European Criminal Law*, pp. 159–65.

[50] CJEU, *Berlusconi and Others*, Joined Cases Nos. C-378/02 and C-391/02, Judgment, ECLI:EU:C:2005:270, 3 May 2005. F. Meyer, 'The Berlusconi Judgment: A Cornerstone of European Legality', in V. Mitsilegas et al. (eds.), *The Court of Justice and European Criminal Law: Leading Cases in a Contextual Analysis*, Oxford: Hart, 2019, pp. 38–54.

[51] CJEU, *Berlusconi and Others*, Joined Cases Nos. C-378/02 and C-391/02, Judgment, ECLI:EU:C:2005:270, 3 May 2005, paras. 68–69.

[52] Ibid., para. 77.

[53] CJEU, *Pupino*, No. C-105/03, Judgment, ECLI:EU:C:2005:386, 16 June 2005. M. Fletcher 'Extending "Indirect Effect" to the Third Pillar: The Significance of Pupino', (2005) 30 *Eur. L. Rev.*, 862–77.

not a First Pillar directive, however, but a framework decision (FD) on the Standing of Victims in Criminal Proceedings that had been adopted by the Council under the Third Pillar. The national proceedings involved the prosecution of a pre-school teacher for the alleged maltreatment of her pupils. The public prosecutor sought permission for eight children to give their evidence out-of-court in the preliminary enquiry phase. The case did not qualify for this special measure under the applicable national law even though the procedure was provided for under the FD. The national court sought a preliminary ruling from the CJEU on the compatibility of the national law with the FD having regard to the national court's obligation to interpret national law in conformity with EU law.

The decision in *Pupino* is renowned for the CJEU extending to FDs the principles regarding direct effect that govern directives. This necessitated drawing an analogy between the two types of instrument in terms of their binding character and the obligation that they impose on national courts to interpret national law in conformity with their terms.[54] Adopting a purposive approach to the defence of its preliminary rulings jurisdiction under TEU, Article 35, the Court opined:

> [T]hat jurisdiction would be deprived of most of its useful effect if individuals were not entitled to invoke framework decisions in order to obtain a conforming interpretation of national law before the courts of the Member States.[55]

Having acknowledged that the principle of conforming interpretation applied to FDs,[56] the CJEU ultimately ruled that the aims of this particular FD required giving national courts the authority to use special measures for vulnerable victims[57] while also noting that the procedures adopted must be compatible with the basic principles of the national system.[58] The principle of conforming interpretation is itself limited by other aspects of EU law including the general principles of law; applying the principles of legal certainty and non-retroactivity the Court affirmed

[54] CJEU, *Pupino*, No. C-105/03, Judgment, ECLI:EU:C:2005:386, 16 June 2005, paras. 33–34.

[55] Ibid., para. 38. The Court went on to expressly affirm that 'the principle of loyal cooperation' on the part of the MS applied in the area of police and judicial cooperation in criminal matters. Ibid., para. 42.

[56] Ibid., para. 43. [57] Ibid., para. 56.

[58] Ibid., para. 57. At the end of the day, whether a conforming interpretation was possible in the case was a matter for the national court to determine. Ibid., para. 48.

that a framework decision could not, of itself, establish a person's criminal liability. However, the Court was satisfied that the legal provisions at issue in Pupino's case did not concern criminal liability *per se* but rather criminal procedure and evidence.[59]

Pupino, and the other cases discussed in this section, highlight the complexity of the primacy of EU law and the challenges surrounding its implementation in national legal orders. These judgments were not delivered in a vacuum, but rather echoed foundational principles applied by the Court in core Community contexts. In the criminal law setting, however, promoting the efficacy of European law came at a controversial cost to the MS and it was inevitable that unresolved questions would generate subsequent case law. The judgments themselves did not expressly address the unique context of the criminal process including the sensitivities surrounding national sovereignty and the challenge of balancing societal interests and individual rights. Moreover, the disparate nature of European criminal cooperation, as it has developed in the years since, has added to the difficulty the CJEU faces in ensuring the uniform application of the law.[60]

2.4 Mutual Recognition and Fundamental Rights

The defining approach to the Europeanisation of criminal procedure is cooperation based on the principle of mutual recognition whereby decisions taken by judicial authorities in one MS are recognised and enforced in the other MS. Mutual recognition is premised on mutual trust: despite the substantial diversity in national systems and procedures, the MS trust each other to adhere to common values and minimum standards.[61] As a method of cooperation, it is more flexible than harmonisation because it leaves the MS considerable latitude as to how they implement EU law. For this reason, it has enabled the MS to collectively commit to various forms of legal assistance including the surrender of suspects, the

[59] Ibid., para. 46. [60] Klip, *European Criminal Law*, pp. 636–39.

[61] Miettinen, *Criminal Law and Policy in the European Union*, p. 5; Ambos, *European Criminal Law*, pp. 20–21; Klip, *European Criminal Law*, pp. 110–113 & 473–82; R. Sicurella, 'Fostering a European Criminal Law Culture: In Trust We Trust', (2018) 9(3) *NJECL*, 308–25.

transfer of evidence, and the execution of foreign judgments. By the same token, integration falls far short of standardisation since differences in the form and extent of national implementation are tolerated within a broad scheme of co-ordination and approximation.

The first and best known of the mutual recognition instruments is the Framework Decision on the European Arrest Warrant (FD EAW).[62] The EAW is a judicial decision issued in one MS which requires another MS to arrest an individual and transfer her/him to the issuing State to face prosecution or serve a sentence. The process is more expeditious than traditional extradition procedures because the arresting State must give immediate effect to the decision of the issuing State and has only limited grounds on which to refuse surrender. Mitsilegas has astutely characterised the process as 'a journey into the unknown' for the authorities executing the warrant because they take on faith the decision of the authorities issuing the warrant.[63] The FD EAW largely dispensed with certain classic bars to extradition: the tenet that a State is not obliged to surrender its own citizens (nationality principle), the requirement that the offence at issue must constitute an offence in both States (double criminality principle), and the practice of non-extradition in cases of political offences (the political offence exception). Even so, the length and technicality of the FD EAW reflect some of the complexity and compromise traditionally associated with the extradition of suspects and offenders. Not surprisingly, the EAW has been the subject of case law and contention at European and national levels.

In *Advocaten voor de Wereld*,[64] the CJEU upheld an early and robust challenge to the validity of the FD EAW. The Belgian *Arbitragehof* (Court of Arbitration) sought a preliminary ruling raising questions that went to the heart of the Union's competence to regulate extradition. The CJEU rejected the argument that the EAW should have been created through the adoption of a convention because framework decisions can be used only 'for the purpose of the approximation of the laws and regulations of the Member States'.[65] Advancing a broad reading of the powers vested in

62 FD 2002/584/JHA [2002] OJ L 190/1, 18.7.2002. Ambos, *European Criminal Law*, pp. 433–51.

63 V. Mitsilegas, 'The Constitutional Implications of Mutual Recognition in Criminal Matters in the EU', (2006) 43 *CMLR*, 82.

64 CJEU, *Advocaten voor de Wereld*, No. C-303/05, Judgment, ECLI:EU:C:2007:261, 3 May 2007.

65 Article 34(2)(b) TEU.

the Union to develop the AFSJ, the Court eschewed the suggestion that the legislature's authority to approximate laws via framework decisions was limited to substantive criminal law[66] or, indeed, that it was restricted in its method to a particular type of instrument.[67]

At issue in *Advocaten voor de Wereld* was the further matter of the compatibility of mutual recognition with the protection of fundamental rights. The FD EAW provides for the surrender of suspects in cases coming within a catalogue of thirty-two broadly defined categories of criminal behaviour which are not conditioned by the principle of double criminality.[68] This raises the possibility that a national court may be required to extradite an individual in respect of conduct that is not criminal in its own national legal system. This scenario exemplifies the pressure that the EAW brings to bear on the concept of mutual trust; categorising conduct as criminal or non-criminal engages national values to a greater extent than the internal market setting in which mutual recognition was initially nurtured. At the same time, because the FD EAW is 'a paradigmatic instrument'[69] the CJEU's decision to affirm the legislature's competence to adopt it had profound implications for the integration of criminal process through mutual recognition arrangements.

The CJEU summarily rejected the claim that by dispensing with the double criminality requirement, the FD EAW had infringed the general principles of legal certainty, equal treatment, and non-discrimination. The Court acknowledged the status of these standards as general principles and their relevance to judicial review of legislative action.[70] However, this ground was tersely dismissed, arguably without meaningful engagement. The Court sidestepped the argument that the offences for which surrender may be sought are inadequately defined in the FD EAW by concluding that the certainty of the offences should be decided

[66] CJEU, *Advocaten voor de Wereld,* No. C-303/05, Judgment, ECLI:EU:C:2007:261, 3 May 2007, para. 32 (interpreting Article 31(1)(a), (b) and (e) TEU).

[67] CJEU, *Advocaten voor de Wereld,* No. C-303/05, Judgment, ECLI:EU:C:2007:261, 3 May 2007, paras. 37–38 and 41.

[68] Article 2(2) EAW FD. Somewhat confusingly, Article 2(2) provides separately for the surrender of individuals in respect of serious offences where double criminality is a condition of transfer.

[69] Ambos, *European Criminal Law*, p. 417.

[70] CJEU, *Advocaten voor de Wereld,* No. C-303/05, Judgment, ECLI:EU:C:2007:261, 3 May 2007, paras. 45–46.

on the basis of the implementing national law.[71] The potential application of the principles of equal treatment and non-discrimination flowed from the fact that the FD EAW dispenses with the double criminality requirement in relation to the list of thirty-two offences but leaves open its possible retention in other cases. Any difference of treatment was objectively justified because the listed offences, by their nature and severity, warranted dispensing with the double criminality requirement.[72] Interestingly, this was not a conclusion reached independently by the Court but rather its endorsement of a decision that the Council had been entitled to take 'on the basis of the principle of mutual recognition and in the light of the high degree of trust and solidarity between the Member States'.[73]

The Court's deference to the legislature and its willingness to promote the efficacy of the FD EAW over the safeguarding of general principles is striking, particularly when compared with the emphasis in its earlier case law on protecting the individual (discussed in the previous section). Although *Advocaten voor de Wereld* has been cited on numerous occasions in subsequent judgments and opinions, the CJEU eventually arrived at a more progressive, rights-based assessment. The opinion of Advocate General (AG) Sharpston in *Radu*[74] paved the way in so far as it recognised that a national court might exceptionally refuse to surrender an individual on the ground of a grave risk to her/his fundamental right to a fair trial. The AG took the view that the express commitments to respect for fundamental rights in the Treaties and in the FD EAW implied that such rights might legitimately be taken into account by a national court when deciding not to execute a warrant.[75] The Court defied expectations, however, by declining to follow her lead; by reformulating the case as involving the narrower question of the consequences of national authorities

[71] Ibid., paras. 51–53. [72] Ibid., paras. 57–58. [73] Ibid., para. 57.

[74] CJEU, *Radu,* No. C-396/11, Opinion of AG Sharpston, ECLI:EU:C:2012:648, 18 October 2012. A. Tinsley, 'he Reference in Case C-396/11 Radu: When Does the Protection of Fundamental Rights Require the Non-Execution of a European Arrest Warrant?', (2012) 2(3) *EuCLR*, 338–52.

[75] CJEU, *Radu,* No. C-396/11, Opinion of AG Sharpston, ECLI:EU:C:2012:648, 18 October 2012, para. 71. She continued by quoting CJEU, *I.B.,* No. C-306/09, Opinion of AG Cruz Villalóns, ECLI:EU:C:2010:404, 6 July 2010: 'Although mutual recognition is an instrument for strengthening the area of security, freedom and justice, it is equally true that the protection of fundamental rights and freedoms is a precondition which gives legitimacy to the existence and development of this area'.

failing to afford the suspect an opportunity to be heard prior to issuing an EAW, the Court avoided the deeper doctrinal issues at play.[76]

The limits of mutual trust at the coalface of international cooperation and the potency of fundamental rights concerns were at the forefront of the Court's controversial decision in the subsequent case of *Melloni*.[77] The facts centred on the issuing by Italian authorities of an EAW for the surrender by Spain of an Italian national who had been tried and convicted *in absentia* in Italy. Trial *in absentia* is a practice on which the MS are divided and Spain is a country in which the right to be present at trial is protected by the Constitution. The FD EAW (as amended by a FD on judgments *in absentia*[78]) is equivocal on the point: it lists *trial in absentia* as a legitimate ground for refusal of surrender but this position is undercut by a wide exception,[79] which was relied on by the Italian authorities in Melloni's case. The Spanish Constitutional Court sought a preliminary ruling from the CJEU on the compatibility of surrender with fundamental rights in such circumstances. In a judgment emphasising the importance of the effective operation of the EAW, the Court upheld the restriction on the latitude of national authorities as consistent with the principle of mutual recognition. Noting that the entitlement of an accused to be present at trial is not absolute,[80] the Court concluded that the CFREU rights to fair trial and an effective remedy were not infringed by the EAW regime.[81] In a boon to the primacy of EU law and a corresponding blow to the protection of human rights, the CJEU affirmed that secondary EU law (specifically measures adopted under the Third Pillar) took precedence over national constitutional law even where the latter provided a higher level of rights protection.[82]

[76] In a relatively short judgment, the Court stated that the fact that a suspect has not been heard does not constitute a ground for refusing surrender under the FD EAW. Non-surrender was not mandated by the CFREU and would have the effect of undermining the efficacy of the EAW system. CJEU, *Radu*, No. C-396/11, Judgment, ECLI:EU:C:2013:39, 29 January 2013, paras. 38–40.

[77] CJEU, *Melloni*, No. C-399/11, Judgment, ECLI:EU:C:2013:107, 26 February 2013. L. Besselink, 'The Parameters of Constitutional Conflict After Melloni', (2014) 39(4) *Eur. L. Rev.*, 531–52.

[78] Council FD 2009/299/JHA of 26 February 2009 on the application of the principle of mutual recognition to decisions rendered in the absence of the person concerned at trial.

[79] FD EAW as amended, Article 4(1).

[80] CJEU, *Melloni*, No. C-399/11, Judgment, ECLI:EU:C:2013:107, 26 February 2013, para. 49.

[81] Ibid., para. 54. CFREU Articles 47–48.

[82] CJEU, *Melloni*, No. C-399/11, Judgment, ECLI:EU:C:2013:107, 26 February 2013, para. 58.

As in *Radu*, the backstop for the validity of Union law was the mutual trust invested by the MS; the Court took the view that allowing national authorities to refuse surrender on the facts presented in *Melloni* would subvert that trust, undermine the system of mutual recognition and consequently thwart the efficacy of the FD EAW.[83] As an exercise in judicial review of legislative action, the judgment in *Melloni* displays a remarkably light touch. The CJEU was unwilling to second-guess the balance between process and rights that the Council had struck in the FD EAW.[84] Judicial conservatism was not to last, however, and just a few years later, and in the wake of the entry into force of the Lisbon Treaty, the Court took a dramatically bolder and more progressive stance on the protection of fundamental rights within the EAW system.[85]

In *Aranyosi and Căldăraru,*[86] the CJEU acknowledged that there might be exceptional cases where national authorities could justifiably refuse to enforce an EAW due to human rights concerns. At issue in a request for a preliminary ruling from a German Appeals court was the possibility of resisting the surrender of individuals to Romania and Hungary in light of judgments of the ECtHR that conditions of detention in these countries violated the guarantee against inhuman and degrading treatment in Article 3 ECHR, which finds corresponding protection in Article 4 CFREU. The influence of the ECtHR is appreciable in this context: the landmark decision in *Soering v. UK*, delivered over thirty years ago, stands for the proposition that the act of a State transferring a person to a jurisdiction where there is a substantial risk that s/he will be ill-treated itself constitutes a violation of Article 3 ECHR.[87]

[83] Ibid., para. 63. The significance of mutual trust was emphasised in the CJEU's landmark opinion on EU accession to the ECHR. CJEU, *Opinion 2/13*, Opinion of the Court, ECLI:EU:C:2014:2454, 18 December 2014, paras. 191–92.

[84] For a more nuanced approach in the EAW context, see CJEU, *Jeremy F*, No. C-168/13 PPU, Judgment, ECLI:EU:C:2013:358, 30 May 2013.

[85] A pivotal step was the adoption by the CJEU of a more critical assessment of mutual recognition in the area of asylum. CJEU, *NS*, No. C-411/10, Judgment ECLI:EU:C:2011:865, 21 December 2011.

[86] CJEU, *Aranyosi and Căldăraru*, Joined Cases Nos. C-404/15 and C-695/15 PPU, Judgment, ECLI:EU:C:2016:198, 5 April 2016. G. Anagnostaras, 'Mutual Confidence is not Blind Trust! Fundamental Rights Protection and the Execution of the EAW: Aranyosi and Căldăraru', (2016) 53(6) *CMLR*, 1675–704.

[87] ECtHR, *Soering v. UK*, Appl. No. 14038/88, Judgment, 7 July 1989.

The judgment in *Aranyosi and Căldăraru* displaced the CJEU's earlier assumption that mutual recognition arrangements are inherently compliant with fundamental rights standards simply because the legislature has calibrated the appropriate level of protection within instruments such as the FD EAW. The CJEU thereby opened the door to judicial scrutiny of EAWs in executing MS while at the same time emphasising the highly exceptional nature of the practice. It recalled the importance of mutual recognition in the scheme of the FD EAW and, specifically, the existence of 'mutual confidence between the Member States that their legal systems are capable of providing equivalent and effective protection of the fundamental rights protected at EU level'.[88] But whereas mutual recognition is 'the cornerstone of judicial cooperation in criminal matters' and an essential bulwark for the AFSJ,[89] it is not an absolute principle and the FD EAW itself acknowledges that it should not have the effect of disturbing fundamental rights protection.[90]

A noteworthy aspect of *Aranyosi and Căldăraru* was the inclusion in the CJEU's judgment of practical guidance to national authorities on the test to be applied when concerns about breaches of the right to inhuman and degrading treatment are raised. When asked to surrender an individual, the national court must consider whether there exists 'a real risk' of inhuman or degrading treatment in the general conditions in which individuals are detained in the issuing MS; if satisfied that this general risk exists, the national court must go on to assess whether there are substantial grounds for believing the individual concerned will be exposed to that risk.[91] Both the generalised and specific risks of inhuman or degrading treatment must be established and the level of proof is relatively high.[92] Refusal to execute a warrant is also conditioned on a procedural step: the national court must request the authorities in the issuing State to provide as a matter of urgency 'all necessary supplementary information on the conditions in which it is envisaged that the

[88] CJEU, *Aranyosi and Căldăraru*, Joined Cases Nos. C-404/15 and C-695/15 PPU, Judgment, ECLI:EU:C:2016:198, 5 April 2016, para. 77.

[89] Ibid., paras. 78–79. [90] Ibid., paras. 82–83. [91] Ibid., paras. 88–92.

[92] The judgment refers, for example, to 'information that is objective, reliable, specific and properly updated on the detention conditions prevailing in the issuing Member State' which demonstrates deficiencies which may be 'systemic or generalised' or which may affect 'certain groups of people, or ... certain places of detention'. Ibid., para. 89.

individual concerned will be detained'.[93] If the fundamental rights concerns are not assuaged within a reasonable time, the national court in the executing MS must decide 'whether the surrender procedure should be brought to an end'.[94]

A factor that motivated the Court's more progressive, rights-based response in *Aranyosi and Căldăraru* was the absolute nature of freedom from inhuman and degrading treatment under Article 3 ECHR and Article 4 CFREU.[95] This implied that the authority of national courts to look behind EAWs might be more restricted where other more qualified rights are at stake. In the subsequent case of *LM*,[96] the CJEU ruled that the risk that an individual would be denied a fair trial, under Article 6 ECHR and Articles 47–48 CFREU, might justify refusing to execute an EAW. The backdrop to the case was the ongoing political controversy over the introduction by the far-right Polish government of reforms that seemingly compromise the independence of the judiciary. Prior to the Irish High Court seeking a preliminary ruling in the *LM* case, the European Commission had instigated the procedure in Article 7 TEU alleging a serious breach of Poland's commitment to the values set down in Article 2 TEU, on which the Union is founded. Thus, the questions referred in *LM* went beyond a potential breach of fundamental rights to the broader subject of a threat to the 'rule of law'. On the one hand, the CJEU made plain that the EAW regime could be set aside only on the basis of a unanimous decision of the Council under Article 7; on the other hand, and applying the principles distilled in *Aranyosi and Căldăraru*, it recognised the entitlement of a national court to resist executing a warrant if surrender would run the risk that the individual would not receive a fair trial. Even so, the extraordinary, politically contentious 'rule of law' aspect of the *LM* case arguably limits its value as a precedent from which generalisations might be drawn about the right to fair trial as a basis for refusal to surrender.[97]

[93] Ibid., para. 95. Execution of the warrant may be postponed at this point but cannot be abandoned altogether. Para. 98.

[94] Ibid., para. 104. [95] Ibid., paras. 85–87.

[96] CJEU, *LM*, No. C-216/18 PPU, Judgment, ECLI:EU:C:2018:586, 25 July 2018. N. Šubic, 'Executing a European Arrest Warrant in the Middle of a Rule of Law Crisis: Minister for Justice and Equality v LM (Celmer)', (2018) 21(1) *IJEL*, 98.

[97] P. Bárd and W. van Ballegooij, 'Judicial Independence as a Precondition for Mutual Trust? The CJEU in Minister for Justice and Equality v LM', (2018) 9(3) *NJECL*, 353–65.

2.5 Ongoing Development

The history of EU criminal law evinces a gradual growth in the depth and breadth of the EU's power and influence. The CJEU has played a significant hand in extending the EU's constitutional principles, initially to national implementation of Community law and later to the burgeoning Union competence in criminal matters. Traditionally the field was dominated by Treaty development and legislative action with the CJEU playing a limited role when compared to other areas of Union law. However, the entry into force of the Treaty of Lisbon marked a turning point for criminal law in general and judicial influence in particular. The relocation of Third Pillar competences within the First Pillar, the augmented jurisdiction of the CJEU, and the constitutionalisation of the CFREU, all combined to facilitate a heightened judicial role in the development of EU criminal law.

European criminal law is a broad and eclectic subject and while this chapter has focused on two particular formative episodes, the CJEU's case law has grown exponentially post-Lisbon in tandem with the flourishing of policy initiatives, legislative activity, and fundamental rights issues. The Court has delivered important decisions on wide-ranging issues including counter-terrorism measures,[98] data protection,[99] the right to interpretation and translation,[100] the presumption of innocence,[101] and the principle of *ne bis in idem.*[102]

[98] CJEU, *Ocalan,* No. C-229/05 P, Judgment, ECLI:EU:C:2007:32, 8 January 2007; *Commission and Others v. Kadi,* Joined cases Nos. C-584/10 P, C-593/10 P and C-595/10 P, ECLI:EU:C:2013:518, 18 July 2013.

[99] See, for example, CJEU, *Schrems,* No. C-362/14, ECLI:EU:C:2015:650, 6 October 2015; *Privacy International,* No. C-623/17, Judgment, ECLI:EU:C:2020:790, 6 October 2020; *La Quadrature du Net and Others,* Joined Cases Nos. C-511/18, C-512/18 and C-520/18, Judgment, ECLI:EU:C:2020:791, 6 October 2020; CJEU, *G.D.*, No. C-140/20, Judgment, ECLI:EU:C:2022:258, 5 April 2022.

[100] CJEU, *Mutsch,* No. C-137/84, Judgment, ECLI:EU:C:1985:335, 11 July 1985; CJEU, *Covaci,* No. C-216/14, ECLI:EU:C:2015:686, 15 October 2015; *Sleutjes,* No. C-278/16, ECLI:EU:C:2017:757, 12 October 2017.

[101] CJEU, *Rubach,* No. C-344/08, ECLI:EU:C:2009:482, 16 July 2009; *Milev, No.* 310/18 PPU, Judgment, ECLI:EU:C:2018:732, 19 September 2018; *RH,* No. C-8/19 PPU, Order ECLI:EU:C:2019:110, 12 February 2019.

[102] CJEU, *Gözütok and Brügge,* Joined Cases Nos. C-187/01 and C-385/01, Judgment, ECLI:EU:C:2003:87, 11 February 2003; *Gasparini,* No. C-467/04, ECLI:EU:C:2006:610, 28 September 2006; *Kretzinger,* No. C-288/05, Judgment, ECLI:EU:C:2007:441, 18 July 2007; *Bourquain,* No. C-297/07, Judgment, ECLI:EU:C:2008:708, 11 December 2008.

The cases discussed in this chapter reveal significant systemic challenges in the historical emergence and contemporary operation of European criminal law; while the CJEU has addressed these questions to some degree, it has not succeeded in putting them to rest. A recurrent theme is the deep-rooted tension in the relationship between the Union and the MS. The Court's early case law established guiding principles that set the parameters for the relationship without firmly settling the implications of EU action for national sovereignty in this delicate field. Mutual recognition has proved a mixed blessing as a vehicle for cooperation to the extent that it tolerates minimalist standards and incentivises national agendas. Against the background of the continued growth in mutual recognition instruments, it will fall to the CJEU to ensure that the EU legislature respects the authority of the MS and, at the same time, that the national authorities do not undermine the Union's objectives and values, including respect for fundamental rights.

The place that criminal justice occupies within the broad scheme of EU law is a related and long-running concern. Cases such as *Greek Maize* and *Environmental Crimes* reflect the Court's internal market orientation and its tacit assumption that constitutional principles honed in pursuit of economic regulation can and must be applied in the same way in non-economic fields. However, the organic growth of EU criminal law has revealed the need to adapt judicial thinking to better meet the specific demands of criminal justice. The erratic evolution of criminal law competence and the piecemeal augmentation in the Union's institutional power has created a somewhat chaotic system of legal rules and principles, many of them replete with technicality and qualification. Moving forward, as the volume of case law increases, the CJEU is likely to have opportunities to bring greater clarity, consistency, and predictability to cooperation in criminal matters.

As the dynamic development of EU criminal law continues, the CJEU will invariably be tasked with new controversies and additional dimensions in the relationships between the EU institutions and agencies, MS and individuals. A perennial challenge is how to ensure that EU criminal law and policy provides robust and effective protection for fundamental rights. This engages the general question of reconciling the societal interest in preserving public order and security with the imperative of safeguarding human rights and civil liberties. In liberal democracies, courts often provide a crucial 'due process' counterbalance to the 'crime control' tendencies of legislatures[103] but regrettably the CJEU has been slow to assume this mantle. The Court must strive to establish a better equilibrium between the interests of the national authorities and individuals, particularly through the evolution of its jurisprudence on general principles and fundamental rights. The more progressive trend in its recent case law is welcome and will hopefully lead to sustained, heightened judicial protection.

Further Reading

V. Mitsilegas et al. (eds.), *The Court of Justice and European Criminal Law: Leading Cases in a Contextual Analysis*, Oxford: Hart, 2019.

S. Peers, *EU Justice and Home Affairs Law Volume II: European Criminal Law, Policing and Civil Law*, 4th edn., Oxford: Oxford University Press, 2016.

[103] H. L. Packer, 'Two Models of the Criminal Process', (1964) 1 *U Pa L Rev*, 1.

Part II

Purposes and Principles

3 Human Rights Protection through the Lens of the EU Charter of Fundamental Rights and the ECHR

Noreen O'Meara

3.1 Introduction

The legal orders of the EU and Council of Europe (notably via the European Convention on Human Rights (ECHR)) have shaped the development of European Criminal Law over several decades. While both systems offer protection of fundamental rights, they are at different stages of evolution in human rights terms. On the EU's part, an emphasis on fundamental rights was initially gradual, both judicially and legislatively. The role and prominence of fundamental rights in EU legislation and case law became more marked from the 1970s, with a swathe of non-discrimination case law directly impacting national laws on, for example, equal pay and sex discrimination.[1] Over time, as EU competences grew and reached deeper into what are traditionally regarded as constitutionally sensitive policy areas (including security, asylum and immigration, criminal justice), the associated growth of EU fundamental rights law accelerated. Since the entry into force of the EU Charter of Fundamental Rights ('Charter' or 'CFREU') in 2009,[2] the Court of Justice has taken numerous opportunities to interpret and apply its provisions.

In their substance, many of the Charter's provisions echo those contained in the European Convention of Human Rights ('ECHR' or 'Convention'). The European Court of Human Rights ('ECtHR') is in its seventh decade delivering judgments across the broad spectrum of rights guaranteed by the Convention and its Protocols. Its reach includes 46 High Contracting Parties. Given its scope of jurisdiction,[3] it is unsurprising that the ECtHR has evolved into a highly impactful international human rights

[1] In the UK, rapid consolidation of equality and anti-discrimination legislation (Equal Pay Act 1970, Sex Discrimination Act 1975, Race Relations Act 1976) was partially informed by such developments at EU level.

[2] Charter of Fundamental Rights of the European Union (2007/C 303/01), 14 December 2007, C 303/1.

[3] See Articles 32–34, 46–47 ECHR.

court. This is due in no small part to the right of individual petition,[4] a right 'indissoluble' from the mission of the Court.[5] Thanks to the opportunity for individuals to submit complaints, albeit as a last-resort option, the Court receives tens of thousands of complaints annually.[6]

This chapter focuses on the roles and impacts of the EU Charter and the ECHR as the core regional instruments of rights protection of the EU and ECHR legal orders. While their fundamental rights missions are shared in key respects, both systems are at different stages of evolution and face their own challenges and crises. This chapter aims to consider both systems in their contexts, whilst exploring the structure and content of the Charter and Convention. As such, this chapter sets the scene for more detailed substantive analysis of the rights of individuals later in this collection.

3.2 EU Dimension: Fundamental Rights Protection and the Charter

3.2.1 Evolution of Fundamental Rights in EU Law

Fundamental rights considerations served as an important driver for establishing new institutions and pushing for greater reliance on multilateral co-operation in the post-World War II era. This goal of elevating fundamental rights protection and ensuring greater legal accountability of state governments at regional or international levels shaped the EU and Council of Europe.

Yet, the trajectory of the human rights tradition in EU law was somewhat unexpected. At least when compared with the protection envisaged in the resolutions of the *Comité d'études pour la constitution européenne* (CECE) in the early 1950s, and in the subsequent draft European

[4] Article 34 ECHR.

[5] P. Mahoney, 'Thinking a Small Unthinkable: Repatriating Reparation from the European Court of Human Rights to the National Legal Order' in L. Caflisch et al. (eds.), *Liber amicorum Luzius Wildhaber: Human Rights – Strasbourg Views*, Kehl et al.: Engel, 2007, p. 267. See also K. Dzehtsiarou and A. Greene, 'Restructuring the European Court of Human Rights: Preserving the Right of Individual Petition and Promoting Constitutionalism', (2013) *Public Law*, 710.

[6] In the year ending 31 December 2021, some 44,250 applications were allocated and 36,092 applications were disposed of judicially, a fall of 8% from 2020. By the end of 2021, there were 71,150 pending applications. ECtHR Analysis of Statistics 2021 (Council of Europe 2022), 4.

Political Community Treaty (1952–1953), at a time when ambitions for a European Defence Treaty and stronger forms of political integration were in play. As de Búrca has discussed, the drafters' vision for fundamental rights protection anticipated, in particular, (i) the EC having a strong monitoring, intervention, and review role on human rights protection in Member States (MS); (ii) a closely entwined constitutional relationship between the EC and ECHR; and (iii) a constitutional framework both outwardly and inwardly focused, aiming to protect against human rights abuses in both internal and external Community policies.[7] Contrasting that ambition with the post-Lisbon reality, de Búrca notes that the interventionist vision was scaled back to one which limits and restrains EU monitoring of rights in MS. Rather than emphasising both human rights protection in internal and external EU policies, the EU's efforts in promoting rights in external policies have tended to dominate.[8] As we know, while there is certainly evidence of engagement with ECtHR case law in CJEU judgments, efforts to concretize a 'closely entwined' relationship between the EU and ECHR in the form of EU accession to the ECHR have encountered major hurdles.[9] This formalisation of the EU–ECHR relationship remains under negotiation.[10]

Abandoning those proposals from the early 1950s, and the consequential absence in the Treaty of Rome (1957) of a role for the EC in human rights, coupled with market-focused policy agendas for European integration, led to a different fundamental rights landscape in EU law. One which often left fundamental rights concerns as marginal interests, if they were perceived as relevant at all. Rather, rights were framed as negative limitations to the policy agendas pursued in European integration,

[7] On the '1950's model' see G. de Búrca, 'The Evolution of EU Human Rights Law', in P. Craig and G. de Búrca (eds.), *The Evolution of EU Law*, 2nd edn., Oxford: Oxford University Press, 2011, pp. 465–475. See also, G. de Búrca, 'The Road not Taken: The European Union as a Global Human Rights Actor', (2011) 105(4) *AJIL*, 649.

[8] G. de Búrca, 'The Evolution of EU Human Rights Law', in P. Craig and G. de Búrca (eds.), *The Evolution of EU Law*, 2nd edn., Oxford: Oxford University Press, 2011, pp. 465–475.

[9] Opinion 2/94, Accession by the Community to the European Convention for the Protection of Human Rights and Fundamental Freedoms, 28 March 1996; ECLI:EU:C:1996:140. Opinion 2/13 of the Court of Justice of the European Union, 18 December 2014; ECLI:EU:C:2014:2454.

[10] Following Opinion 2/13, given the obstacles the CJEU identified preventing accession, political ambition for EU accession to the ECHR stalled. After informal meetings, negotiations only formally restarted in September 2020. Crit. on the opinion K. Ambos, *European Criminal Law*, Cambridge: Cambridge University Press, 2018, pp. 74 ff.

instead of an opportunity for the EU to make positive contributions in defining and protecting fundamental rights,[11] and identifying their centrality to policy goals as these broadened over time from the original market-focused objectives.

For decades, and in the absence of an overarching catalogue of fundamental rights, the human rights tradition thus matured in a piecemeal way, both legislatively and through the case law of the Court of Justice (ECJ). In its early evolution, the language of rights was used to shed light on the nature of EU law itself. Adjudicating in *Van Gend en Loos*, the ECJ found that 'Community law ... not only imposes obligations on individuals but is also intended to confer upon them rights which become part of their legal heritage'.[12] The Court famously identified the ways in which such EU-based rights arise, and its constitutionalizing jurisprudence – of which *Van Gend en Loos* is central – has been praised for its integrationist rigour against the background of political stasis.[13] Weiler does not place the Court of Justice on a pedestal in this regard, arguing that this constitutionalizing case law implicated the Court 'in the very issues of democratic and social legitimacy' more commonly viewed as exacerbated by the EU's political institutions.[14]

A trio of ECJ cases (*Stauder*,[15] *Internationale Handelsgesellschaft*,[16] *Nold*)[17] showed the Court's willingness to adjust its narrative on the constitutional role of human rights. This was enhanced by the powerful responses of the *Bundesverfassungsgericht*, notably in *Solange I*,[18] challenging the absolute vision of primacy in the face of apparent diluted rights protection at Community level. The Court of Justice's preparedness

[11] P. Eeckhout, 'Bold Constitutionalism and Beyond', in M. Poires Maduro and L. Azoulai (eds.), *The Past and Future of EU Law*, Oxford: Oxford University Press, 2010, p. 222.

[12] CJEU, *N.V. Algemene Transport- en Expeditie Onderneming van Gend en Loos*, No. 27/62, Judgment, ECLI:EU:C:1963:1, 5 February 1963, at 12.

[13] J. H. H. Weiler, 'Europe in Crisis – On "Political Messianism," "Legitimacy" and the "Rule of Law"', (2012) *Sing. J.L.S.*, 248, 263.

[14] J. H. H. Weiler, 'Deciphering the Political and Legal DNA of European Integration – An Exploratory Essay', in J. Dickson and P. Eleftheriadis (eds.), *Philosophical Foundations of European Union Law*, Oxford: Oxford University Press, 2012, p. 152.

[15] CJEU, *Erich Stauder v. City of Ulm-Sozialamt*, No. C-29/69, Judgment, ECLI:EU:C:1969:57, 12 November 1969.

[16] CJEU, *Internationale Handelsgesellschaft mbH v. Einfuhr- und Vorratsstelle für Getreide und Futtermittel*, No. C-11/70, Judgment, ECLI:EU:C:1970:114, 17 December 1970.

[17] CJEU, *J. Nold, Kohlen- und Baustoffgroßhandlung v. Commission of the European Communities*, No. C-4/73, Judgment, ECLI:EU:C:1974:51, 14 May 1974.

[18] BVerfG, Beschluss vom 29. Mai 1974 ('Solange I') – 2 BvL 52/71 -, BVerfGE 37, 271–305.

to view fundamental rights as general principles of Community (now Union) law signalled alignment with a substantive approach to the rule of law, setting fundamental rights as a condition for the legality of acts of the Union.[19] The increased expansiveness of the ECJ in addressing human rights, and the willingness of often lower courts and tribunals making preliminary references, led to sectoral progress on aspects of equality. Notwithstanding that, the Court has regularly faced accusations of being insufficiently expansive or humane in its approaches to individual rights.

The history of the EU may be one of 'political and legal action and reaction',[20] though the ECJ at times fails to do either – whether by avoiding persuasive calls for revolution made by Advocates General or by accepting such invitations with opaque reasoning that can create uncertainty.[21] Although infringement actions under Articles 258–260 TFEU can serve as a practical and impactful method of holding MS to account for alleged infringements of fundamental rights and the rule of law, it is an inherently selective enforcement tool. At a broader political level, the EU's reticent approach to the activation of the Article 7 TEU mechanism[22] in the face of rule of law crises in Poland and Hungary is indicative of a failure to exploit the Union's human rights potential.

EU Criminal law has emerged and developed in parallel with the rise in prominence of fundamental rights protection in EU law and policy over the past two decades. In the years leading up to the adoption of the Lisbon Treaty, the EU's priorities for criminal justice matters were shaped by a series of multiannual political agendas: the Tampere Programme (1999), the more security-oriented Hague Programme (2004) and the Stockholm Programme (2009), which purported to place the citizen at

[19] For a notable form of this type of fundamental rights review in EU law, see CJEU, *Kadi and Al Barakaat International Foundation v. Council and Commission*, Joined Cases Nos. C-402/05 P and C-415/05 P, Judgment, EU:C:2008:461 ('*Kadi I*'), 3 September 2008.

[20] C. Murphy and D. Acosta Arcarazo, 'Rethinking Europe's Freedom, Security and Justice', in C. Murphy and D. Acosta Arcarazo (eds.), *EU Security and Justice Law*, Oxford: Hart, 2014, p. 8.

[21] On the nature of the 'revolution' of Ruiz Zambrano, see H. van Eijken, 'Connecting the Dots Backwards, What Did Ruiz Zambrano Mean for EU Citizenship and Fundamental Rights in EU Law?', (2021) 23(1) *Eur. J. Migr. Law*, 48.

[22] Article 7 TEU can be activated (following an investigation process) in the event of an alleged clear risk of a breach of the values on which the EU is based (Article 2 TEU). Introduced in the Treaty of Amsterdam, this 'rule of law mechanism' was activated for the first time against Poland in 2017, and against Hungary in 2018. On the role of Article 7 TEU, see T. Konstadinides, *The Rule of Law in the European Union*, Oxford: Hart, 2017, pp. 161–165.

its heart.[23] The Stockholm Programme's continued focus on security, but with a greater emphasis on rights-oriented measures, set the scene for a series of Directives extending procedural rights for defendants. The passage of legislation on the right of access to a lawyer, the right to interpretation and translation, and the right to information in criminal proceedings[24] realised the early ambitions of the Stockholm Programme, while a second wave of legislation focused on the presumption of innocence and the right to be present at trial, procedural safeguards for children in criminal proceedings, and legal aid.[25] Entering into force in 2009, the Lisbon Treaty aimed to have a galvanising effect on criminal law and policy in the Area of Freedom, Security and Justice (AFSJ).[26] It sought to do this through a shift away from an intergovernmental to a supranational approach for the adoption of legislation in justice and home affairs, enhancing the EU's legislative power in areas of crime and security, and ending the pillar structure which had largely shielded these areas from the ECJ's jurisdiction. Lisbon also marked the long-awaited entry into force of the Charter. This paved the way for the ECJ to rely on the Charter as a legally binding source in the context of these fast-evolving and constitutionally sensitive policy areas.

[23] N. O'Meara, 'Lisbon via Stockholm, Strasbourg and Opinion 2/13: Prospects for Citizen-Centred Protection of Fundamental Rights?', in N. Ferreira and D. Kostakopoulou (eds.), *The Human Face of the European Union – Are EU Law and Policy Humane Enough?*, Cambridge: Cambridge University Press, 2016, p. 74. See generally K. Ambos, *European Criminal Law*, Cambridge: Cambridge University Press, 2018, pp. 136 ff.

[24] Directive 2010/64/EU of the European Parliament and of the Council of 20 October 2010 on the right to interpretation and translation in criminal proceedings, L 280/1, 26.10.2010; Directive 2013/48/EU of the European Parliament and of the Council of 22 October 2013 on the right of access to a lawyer in criminal proceedings and in European arrest warrant proceedings, and on the right to have a third party informed upon deprivation of liberty and to communicate with third persons and with consular authorities while deprived of liberty, OJ L 294, 6.11.2013; Directive 2012/13/EU of the European Parliament and of the Council of 22 May 2012 on the right to information in criminal proceedings, OJ L 142, 1.6.2012.

[25] Directive 2016/343 of the European Parliament and of the Council of 9 March 2016 on the Strengthening of Certain Aspects of the Presumption of Innocence and of the Right to be Present at the Trial in Criminal Proceedings OJ L 6, 11.03.2016; Directive 2016/800 of the European Parliament and of the Council of 11 May 2016 on procedural safeguards for children who are suspects or accused persons in criminal proceedings, OJ L 132, 21.05.2016; Directive 2016/1919 of the European Parliament and of the Council of 26 October 2016 on legal aid for suspects and accused persons in criminal proceedings and for requested persons in European Arrest Warrant proceedings, OJ L 297, 4.11.2016.

[26] Developed on the basis of the Tampere (1999), Hague (2004), and Stockholm Programme (2009). Note Article 3(2) TEU.

3.2.2 The Charter of Fundamental Rights: Substance and Scope of Protection

For many years before action was taken to formally draft the Charter, calls had been made – politically and in academic literature – for the adoption of a comprehensive Charter of rights at EU level.[27] Fundamental rights protection increased incrementally from the Single European Act onwards, along with a momentum for developing greater EU competences in fields where rights are more obviously central. These developments, and the steering role of Germany's Council Presidency in 1999, helped create the context for establishing a Convention to draft the Charter. Following an intensive and swift process,[28] the Charter was proclaimed by the European Parliament, Council and Commission in 2000.[29] Due to the failure of the proposed Constitutional Treaty in 2005, there followed an unexpectedly long phase when the Charter had the status of non-binding, soft law. This phase provided scope to further adjust aspects of the Charter in readiness for its entry into force, notably its horizontal provisions (Articles 51–54 Charter).[30] On the Lisbon Treaty's entry into force on 1 December 2009, the Charter gained binding status as primary law of the Union as a Charter of rights for the EU's 450 million citizens.[31]

3.2.3 Protection of Rights: The Charter's Substantive Provisions

With its goal of rendering fundamental rights more visible,[32] the Charter is structured in a way that presented different categories of rights as one thematic whole, building on the 'invisible, universal values of human dignity, freedom, equality and solidarity' on which the Union is based.[33] This eliminates any distinction in status between civil, political, social,

[27] See, for example, P. Alston and J. H. H. Weiler, 'An "Ever Closer Union" in Need of a Human Rights Policy' (1998) 9 *EJIL*, 658.

[28] The Praesidium of the Charter Convention steered the drafting the Charter of Fundamental Rights between December 1999 and October 2000.

[29] Charter of Fundamental Rights of the European Union OJ C 364/01, 7.12.2000. On the background to the Charter's drafting and travaux préparatoires, see N. Coghlan and M. Steiert (eds.), *The Charter of Fundamental Rights of the European Union: the 'travaux préparatoires' and selected documents*, Florence: European University Institute, 2020.

[30] Ibid., 26.

[31] Article 6(1) TEU granted the Charter of Fundamental Rights primary law status.

[32] Charter Preamble: fourth recital. [33] Charter Preamble: second recital.

and economic rights; a tendency which can be evident in national constitutions. However, given the distinctions on justiciability of rights and principles, this should be considered in the light of Article 52(5) CFREU.

Dignity – Articles 1–5 Charter (Title I): The opening cluster of rights protected by the Charter of Fundamental Rights falls under the essential theme of human dignity – the basis of all rights. Article 1 CFREU's provision on the inviolability of human dignity echoes the preamble to the Universal Declaration of Human Rights 1948.[34] This category encompasses the right to life (Article 2 CFREU, which corresponds to Article 2 ECHR and Article 2 of Protocol No. 6 ECHR); the right to integrity of the person (Article 3 CFREU);[35] the prohibition on torture and inhuman or degrading treatment or punishment (Article 4 CFREU, corresponding to Article 3 ECHR with identical wording); and a prohibition covering slavery, servitude, forced and compulsory labour and trafficking in human beings (Article 5 CFREU, corresponding to Article 4 ECHR). While trafficking is not explicitly prohibited by Article 4 ECHR, the case law of the ECtHR brought trafficking within the ambit of that provision by reference to the positive obligations of States Parties.[36]

Freedoms – Articles 6–19 Charter (Title II): The provisions under the heading of 'Freedom' protect a series of essential civil and political rights. These include the right to liberty and security (Article 6 CFREU, corresponding with Article 5 ECHR), which has relevance for the adoption of criminal justice measures on the basis of Articles 82, 83, and 85 TFEU. The right to respect for private and family life is protected under Article 7 CFREU (corresponding to Article 8 ECHR, using the term 'communications' in place of the Convention wording 'correspondence'). Personal data is protected under Article 8 CFREU, the right to marry and found a family under Article 9 CFREU (a wider construction than the corresponding right under Article 12 ECHR), and the freedom of thought, conscience, and religion is protected under Article 10 CFREU (corresponding to Article 9 ECHR). The Charter protection of freedom of expression (Article 11 CFREU, corresponding to Article 10 ECHR) contains a specific provision on freedom and pluralism of the media. Of the remaining provisions relevant to

[34] Preamble, UDHR 1948: first recital.

[35] The principles of Article 3 of the Charter are already included in the Convention on Human Rights and Biomedicine, adopted by the Council of Europe (ETS 164 and additional protocol ETS 168).

[36] ECtHR, *Rantsev v. Cyprus and Russia*, Appl. No. 25965/04, Judgment, 7 October 2010, para. 282.

criminal justice, Article 19 CFREU guarantees protection in the event of removal, expulsion, or extradition. This provision covers both Article 4(1) of Protocol No. 4 ECHR and relevant case law on rights of individuals facing deportation or extradition to third countries under Article 3 ECHR.[37]

Equality – Articles 20–26 Charter (Title III): Under the 'equality' heading, the Charter of Fundamental Rights primarily protects classic forms of discrimination: with an overarching equality provision (Article 20 CFREU) and a more detailed non-discrimination provision (Article 21 CFREU) which protects against discrimination on the grounds of sex, race, colour, ethnic or social origin, among others.[38] It should apply in conformity with Article 14 ECHR insofar as it corresponds with it. Article 21(2) CFREU corresponds with Article 18(1) TFEU. Additional rights protected under the equality heading include the rights of the child, of the elderly, and the integration of persons with disabilities.[39]

Solidarity – Articles 27–38 Charter (Title IV): The protection of classic social rights and principles falls under the 'solidarity' heading of the Charter. These include various workers' rights and the protection of children (e.g., right of collective bargaining and action, Article 27 CFREU, prohibition of child labour, Article 32 CFREU), principles on access to benefits (e.g., Article 34 CFREU) and the right of access to healthcare (Article 35 CFREU), along with principles on environmental and consumer protection (Articles 37 and 38 CFREU, respectively).

Citizens' Rights – Articles 39–46 Charter (Title V): The emphasis of the 'citizens' rights' are on rights available to citizens of the EU (e.g., voting rights protected under Articles 39–40 CFREU, and the citizens' rights guaranteed under Articles 43–46 CFREU). Certain administrative rights are also available to non-EU citizens who are living in the EU, and to other legal persons, such as companies registered in the EU (e.g., the right of access to documents, Article 42 CFREU).

Justice – Articles 47–50 Charter (Title VI): Fundamental rights protected under the 'justice' heading focus on procedural rights and principles of greatest salience to the development of European criminal law. These rights underpin access to justice, starting with the right to an effective remedy and to a fair trial (Article 47 CFREU). The wording of

[37] ECtHR, *Ahmed v. Austria*, Reports of Judgments and Decisions 1996-VI, 17 December 1996; *Soering v. the United Kingdom*, Series A No. 161, Judgment, 7 July 1989.

[38] Article 21(1) CFR. [39] Articles 24, 25, and 26 CFR, respectively.

Article 47 CFREU is inspired by both Article 13 ECHR and Article 6(1) ECHR, albeit with a more expansive effect in Union law (e.g., the guarantee of an effective remedy before a court, with a fair hearing covering both civil rights and obligations and criminal charges).[40] The right to the presumption of innocence and the right of defence (Article 48 CFREU) mirror the substantive protection contained in Article 6(2) and 6(3) ECHR, and have generated contrasting litigation before the Court of Justice.[41]

The principles of legality and proportionality of criminal sanctions are protected under Article 49 CFREU; comprising a rule of non-retroactivity of laws and sanctions in criminal matters which takes as its inspiration Article 7 ECHR. In *Taricco I* (a case concerning limitation periods in national law for certain criminal offences and their effect on the Union's financial interests) the Court of Justice's ruling provoked responses in the Italian appellate and constitutional courts, and tensions with the principle of legality as provided for in the Italian Constitution.[42]

Finally, Article 50 CFREU protects the right not to be tried or punished twice in criminal proceedings for the same offence (the 'double jeopardy' or '*ne bis in idem*' principle). This right has a basis in Article 4 of Protocol No. 7 ECHR, though under the Charter it applies both within and between the MS. The parameters of this provision were given a wide interpretation in *Åkerberg Fransson*, whilst giving national court the opportunity to apply a potentially more generous national rule of *ne bis in idem*.[43] The distinctions between Article 50 CFREU and Article 54 of the Convention Implementing the Schengen Agreement (CISA) and the relationship between them proved to be contentious questions. Though inspired by the jurisprudence of the ECtHR, CJEU case law has not always been consistent.[44]

[40] In the light of the EU's basis on the rule of law; CJEU, *'Les Verts' v. European Parliament*, No. 294/83, Judgment, ECLI:EU:C:1986:166, 23 April 1986.

[41] For example, CJEU, *Kadi and Al Barakaat International Foundation v. Council and Commission*, Joined Cases Nos. C-402/05 P and C-415/05 P, Judgment, EU:C:2008:461 ('*Kadi I*'), 3 September 2008; *Criminal proceedings against Nikolay Kolev and others*, No. C-612/15, Judgment, ECLI:EU:C:2018:392, 5 June 2018.

[42] CJEU, *Taricco I*, No. C-105/14, Judgment, ECLI:EU:C:2015:555, 8 September 2015; *M.A.S. and M.B. ('Taricco II')*, No. C-42/17, Judgment, ECLI:EU:C:2017:936, 5 December 2017.

[43] CJEU, *Åklagaren v. Hans Åkerberg Fransson*, No. C-617/10, Judgment, ECLI:EU:C:2013:105, 26 February 2013. See B. Schima, 'EU Fundamental Rights and Member State Action After Lisbon: Putting the ECJ's Case Law in Its Context', (2015) 38 *Fordham ILJ*, 1098, 1112.

[44] Notably, Article 50 CFR lacks the final enforcement element contained in Art. 54 CISA, and both provisions differ in their scope of application – Article 50 CFR applying to all

3.2.4 Scope of Protection: The Charter's Horizontal Provisions

3.2.4.1 Field of Application (Article 51 CFREU)

The field of application of the Charter is defined by Article 51 CFREU, albeit with vague wording which required clarifications by the ECJ. Article 51(1) CFREU provides that the Charter applies to the institutions, bodies, offices, and agencies of the Union, but is only applicable to MS when they are implementing EU law.[45] The Charter was not intended to extend the field of application of Union law, or to extend the competences or tasks of the Union beyond those provided for in the Treaties.[46] The framing of Article 51(1) CFREU, in particular, reinforces the trend of MS' minimalist approach to subjecting themselves to EU scrutiny of their compliance with fundamental rights. While the ECJ ruled that the Charter binds EU institutions whether or not they are acting within the scope of EU law,[47] questions linked to the Charter's scope of application *vis-á-vis* MS proved more contentious.[48] The difficulty of defining exactly when MS are or are not 'implementing' EU law, for the purposes of the Charter, became a potent debate.[49] In *Dereci*, the Court provided welcome clarity that to 'implement' for the purposes of Article 51(1) CFREU encompasses a MS acting within the scope of EU law.[50] The Court's case law on this point proved to take an expansive stance to

EU Member States and Article 54 CISA applying to Schengen states. For a detailed exposition of Article 54 CISA and double jeopardy, see further K. Ambos, *European Criminal Law*, Cambridge: Cambridge University Press, 2018, p. 147.

45 Article 51(1) CFR. On the drafting history of Article 51 CFR, see G. de Búrca, 'The Drafting of the EU Charter of Fundamental Rights', (2001) 26 *Eur. L. Rev*, 214; see also K. Ambos, *European Criminal Law*, Cambridge: Cambridge University Press, 2018, pp. 142 ff.

46 Article 51(2) CFR.

47 CJEU, *Ledra Advertising*, Joined Cases Nos. C-8/15 and 10/15 P, Judgment, ECLI:EU:C:2016:701, 20 September 2016.

48 On the scope of application, see for example X. Groussot, L. Pech, and G. T. Petursson, 'The Scope of Application of EU Fundamental Rights on Member States' Action: In Search of Certainty in EU Adjudication', Eric Stein Working Paper No. 1/2011; B. Pirker, 'Mapping the Scope of Application of EU Fundamental Rights: A Typology', (2018) 3(1) *European Papers*, 133.

49 See, for example, early post-Charter *Åklagaren v. Hans Åkerberg Fransson*, No. C-617/10, Opinion of AG Cruz Villalon, ECLI:EU:C:2012:340, 12 June 2012 and *Gerado Ruiz Zambrano*, No. C-34/09, Opinion of AG Sharpston, ECLI:EU:C:2010:560, 30 September 2010. On the scope of 'implementation' note for example *NS v. Secretary of State for the Home Department*, Joined Cases Nos. C-411/10 and C-493/10, Judgment, ECLI:EU:C:2011:865, 21 December 2011.

50 See *Dereci*, No. C-256/11, Judgment, ECLI:EU:C:2011:734, 15 November 2011, para. 72.

the application of the Charter to MS.[51] When delimiting the boundaries of Article 51(1) CFREU, it could be far from clear whether the Charter should apply to MS action. In *Siragusa*, the Court set guidance on how closely connected EU law and national law must be for the Charter to apply.[52] Questions also arose as to whether the Charter altered the scope of EU fundamental rights as confirmed in existing ECJ case law – an issue for MS in situations when, for example, they are bound to implement and enforce EU law, or when derogating from EU law.[53] The post-Charter era also brought the prospect of fresh jurisprudence emerging on aspects of rights where there was no overlap between the Charter and ECHR, though as AG Sharpston noted, that would have been likely to happen in the ordinary context of EU law.[54]

3.2.4.2 Horizontal Application of the Charter

The Charter's silence on whether it can have horizontal application – invoked against an individual – has not prevented the ECJ from finding that it can, in certain circumstances. The potential for horizontal direct effect of Charter rights emerged in the non-discrimination context (*Mangold*,[55] *Kücükdeveci*),[56] the Court later implicitly confirming its applicability beyond non-discrimination (*AMS*).[57] This possibility can arise in the context of a directive (which cannot itself be invoked horizontally) where that directive provides for the content of rights contained in the Charter.

[51] Note an expansive reading in the context of harmonising national rules in an area (VAT) closely connected with the internal market (CJEU, *Åklagaren v. Hans Åkerberg Fransson*, No. C-617/10, Judgment, ECLI:EU:C:2013:105, 26 February 2013), and a more minimalist approach in the context of co-ordinating national rules (*McB*, No. C-400/10 PPU, Judgment, ECLI:EU:C:2010:582, 5 October 2010).

[52] CJEU, *Siragusa*, No. C-206/13, Judgment, ECLI:EU:C:2014:126, 6 March 2014, para. 24.

[53] On the latter, note CJEU, *Schmidberger*, No. C-112/00, Judgment, ECLI:EU:C:2003:333, 12 June 2003; *Elliniki Radiophonia Tiléorassi AE and Others v. Dimotiki Etairia Pliroforissis (ERT)*, No. C-260/89, Judgment, ECLI:EU:C:1991:254, 18 June 1991.

[54] See, for example, *Gerado Ruiz Zambrano*, No. C-34/09, Opinion of AG Sharpston, ECLI:EU:C:2010:560, 30 September 2010, para. 147.

[55] CJEU, *Werner Mangold v. Rüdiger Helm*, No. C-144/04, Judgment, ECLI:EU:C:2005:709, 22 November 2005.

[56] CJEU, *Seda Kücükdeveci v. Swedex GmbH & Co.*, No. C-555/07, ECLI:EU:C:2010:21, 19 January 2010.

[57] CJEU, *Association de mediation sociale v. Union locale des syndicats GCT*, No. C-176/12, Judgment, ECLI:EU:C:2014:2, 15 January 2015. See, K. Lenaerts, 'Making the EU Charter of Fundamental Rights a Reality for All: 10th Anniversary of the Charter Becoming Legally Binding', Keynote Speech (12 November 2019), 16.

3.2.4.3 Scope of Rights and Principles (Article 52 CFREU)

The scope of rights and principles, as provided in Article 52 CFREU, proved to be one of the most taxing issues in post-Charter caselaw before the Court of Justice. Article 52(1) CFREU is a general derogation clause, providing that any limitation on the exercise of rights and freedoms recognised by the Charter must: (i) be provided by law, (ii) respect the essence of those rights; (iii) comply with the principle of proportionality; and (iv) be necessary to meet the objectives of general interest recognised by the Union or the need to protect the rights and freedoms of others. The wording of Article 52(1) CFREU was inspired by the approach of the Court of Justice in *Wachauf* and *Kjell Karlsson.*[58] Article 52(2) CFREU confirms that Treaty-based rights shall be exercised 'under the conditions and within the limits defined by those Treaties'.

Turning to paragraphs addressing consistency of interpretation, Article 52(3) CFREU confirms that insofar as Charter rights correspond to rights protected by the ECHR, 'the meaning and scope of those rights shall be the same'. This provision allows scope for Union law to provide more extensive protection. Article 52(4) CFREU requires Charter rights which result from the 'constitutional traditions common to the Member States' to be 'interpreted in harmony with those traditions'. Over a decade after the entry into force of the Charter, the rights/principles distinction in Article 52(5) CFREU remains a much-debated aspect of the Charter.[59] Lock suggests that this distinction is not related to the classification of specific rights (as civil, political, social, or economic), but is rooted in political choices made by the drafters. The classification 'right' or 'principle' is important in determining justiciability; as provided in Article 52(5) CFREU, principles are judicially cognisable 'only in the interpretation of such acts and in the ruling on their legality'.

3.2.4.4 Harmonious Interpretation (Article 53 CFREU), Abuse of Rights (Article 54 CFREU)

An emphasis on harmonious interpretation is also reflected in Article 53 CFREU, which provides that the protection offered by the Charter shall

[58] CJEU, *Kjell Karlssson and others,* No. C-292/97, ECLI:EU:C:2000:202, 13 April 2000, para. 45; *Wachauf,* No. 5/88, Judgment, ECLI:EU:C:1989:321, 13 July 1989, para. 18.

[59] See, J. Krommendijk, 'Principled Silence or Mere Silence on Principles? The Role of the EU Charter's Principles in the Case Law of the Court of Justice', (2015) 11(2) *Eur. Const. L. Rev.*, 321; T. Lock, 'Rights and Principles in the EU Charter of Fundamental Rights', (2019) 56(5) *CMLR,* 1201.

not fall below the level of protection in international law, in international agreements to which the Union or all MS are party to (such as the ECHR), and MS' constitutions. This aspect was contested in *Melloni*, where in the context of the execution of a European Arrest Warrant *in absentia*, the Court of Justice interpreted Article 53 CFREU to confirm that a higher level of protection under the Spanish Constitution could not override the level of protection offered by the Charter.[60] In relation to overlaps between the Charter and ECHR in this regard, there are various corresponding fundamental rights in the criminal realm, including the prohibition against inhuman and degrading treatment, the right to liberty in extradition procedures, and the principle that penalties must be defined by law.[61] Finally, Article 54 CFREU is an abuse of rights provision, similar to the drafting of Article 17 ECHR, which rules out any right to engage in any activity aimed at the destruction of any of the rights and freedoms contained in the Charter.

As is evident from this overview, following its entry into force, the Charter had an immediate impact on the ECJ's adjudication. The 'primary importance' of the Charter was recognized in a statement by the Presidents of the ECJ and ECtHR.[62] As such, the Charter is viewed as the 'reference text and the starting point' for the assessment of fundamental rights by the ECJ,[63] and has been used in a wealth of cases across the spectrum of rights protected under the Charter.

3.3 The Council of Europe Dimension: Fundamental Rights Protection and the ECHR

3.3.1 ECHR Mission and Evolution

As an 'ideological response to war', the protection of rights at international level emerged during World War II as an element for shaping a

[60] CJEU, *Melloni v. Ministerio Fiscal*, No. C-399/11, Judgment, ECLI: EU:C:2013:107, 26 February 2013. Note also (in the context of *ne bis in idem*) *Menci*, No. C-524/15, Judgment, ECLI:EU:C:2018:197, 5 June 2018. See further G. de Búrca, 'After the Charter of Fundamental Rights: The Court of Justice as a Human Rights Adjudicator?' (2013) 20 *Maastricht J. Eur. Comp. L.*, 168.

[61] K. Lenaerts, 'The ECHR and the CJEU: Creating Synergies in the Field of Fundamental Rights Protection' (speech, 26 January 2018), 5.

[62] Joint Communication from Presidents Costa and Skouris, 27 January 2011, available at: www.echr.coe.int/Documents/UE_Communication_Costa_Skouris_ENG.pdf (accessed: 30 June 2021).

[63] Ibid., para. 1.

more secure new world order.[64] While security concerns were a primary factor for the development of the UN at that time, an emphasis on seeking multilateral cooperation on human rights led to a range of proclamations on their importance and status. In the Preamble to the UN Charter (1945), states reaffirmed 'faith in fundamental human rights, in the dignity and worth of the human person, in the equal rights of men and women and of nations large and small'.[65] The barbarity inflicted on victims of World War II was explicitly referenced in the Universal Declaration of Human Rights (1948), juxtaposed with a recognition of 'inherent dignity and of the equal and inalienable rights of all' as being the 'foundation of freedom, justice and peace in the world'.[66] As states negotiated options, it would not take long for such declarations to be concretised through the creation of new international bodies aiming to safeguard rights, and values of democracy and the rule of law, with scope for the creation of international courts where individuals could seek justice against their state governments.

Despite not being enamoured by the prospect of international supervision,[67] and scepticism about federalist movements in Europe, the UK played a leading role in these efforts. In doing so, the UK had some influence at the UN level, and a real impact at European level. Churchill's 'Zurich' speech in 1946, coupled with the momentum of the Hague Congress in 1948, soon led to the adoption of the treaty constituting the Statute of the Council of Europe in 1949.[68] The swift drafting and adoption of the ECHR in 1950 on this wave of momentum was a moment of genuine ambition illustrating the capacity of states to push ahead despite objections linked to sovereignty and the problems the Convention could pose for colonial powers. While acceptance of the ECtHR, and the right of individual petition to it, was optional for states, the Convention set in train the prospect of building a jurisprudence of the Court which could, in

[64] On the efforts of the British and American governments at this time, see A. W. Brian Simpson, *Human Rights and the End of Empire: Britain and the Genesis of the European Convention*, Oxford University Press, 2004, Chapter 4.

[65] Preamble to the UN Charter (1945).

[66] Preamble to the Universal Declaration of Human Rights: first and second recitals.

[67] A reticence linked to the winding down of colonialism; A. W. Brian Simpson, *Human Rights and the End of Empire: Britain and the Genesis of the European Convention*, Oxford University Press, 2004, Chapter 5.

[68] Initially signed by ten states on 5 May 1949: Belgium, Denmark, France, Ireland, Italy, Luxembourg, The Netherlands, Norway, Sweden and the United Kingdom. Greece, Turkey, Germany, Iceland ratified over the course of 1949–1950.

time, profoundly influence rights protection at national level. The Council of Europe and the ECtHR may have been inspired by a fear of totalitarianism among states, but they helped foster a vision of multilateralism in which safeguarding rights was a central, non-negotiable expectation.[69]

The UK was the first country to ratify the Convention,[70] which has now gained 46 High Contracting Parties. The EU remains committed to pursuing the objective set in the Lisbon Treaty to accede to the ECHR, with a new phase of negotiations ongoing. The Convention itself could be viewed as a 'mission statement' of democratic values on one hand,[71] albeit one which was drafted with the potential of being a true European bill of rights. As Bates notes, the original mission of the Court was to serve as an 'alarm bell' for democracy in Europe.[72] Yet, it proved to be more prepared than states for the implications of its role in interpreting the rights in the Convention – which were, for the most part, generally worded and non-absolute rights. Some transformational judgments have had the spill-over effect of enhancing rights protection at national level, both in caselaw and in the adoption of new national legislation.[73] In states where legislative challenges typically involved challenges on constitutional grounds, the possibility of invoking Convention-based arguments broadened the options for human-rights based arguments in judicial review applications.[74]

3.3.2 The European Convention on Fundamental Rights: Substance and Scope of Protection

The ECHR is primarily focused on the protection of essential civil and political rights. A few limited exceptions to this were adopted shortly

[69] See further, E. Bates, *The Evolution of the European Convention on Human Rights: From Its Inception to the Creation of a Permanent Court of Human Rights*; Oxford University Press, 2010, 64–65. In detail on the constitutional framework and the rights relevant for criminal justice K. Ambos, *European Criminal Law*, Cambridge: Cambrdige University Press, 2018, pp. 80 ff.

[70] The UK ratified the ECHR on 8 March 1951.

[71] L. Hoffmann, 'The Universality of Human Rights' (2009) 125 *L. Q. Rev.*, 416, 418 and 423.

[72] L. Bates, *The Evolution of the European Convention on Human Rights: From Its Inception to the Creation of a Permanent Court of Human Rights*, Oxford University Press, 2010, p. 54.

[73] On the added value of the ECtHR to the UK specifically, see M. Amos, 'The Value of the European Court of Human Rights to the United Kingdom' (2017) 28(3) *EJIL*, 763.

[74] In the Irish criminal justice context, see U. Ní Raifeartaigh, 'The European Convention on Human Rights and the Criminal Justice System' (2007) 2 *JSIJ*, 18.

after the Convention itself, due to difficulties reaching consensus when the main provisions were drafted: namely, the protection of property (Article 1 of Protocol 1 ECHR) and the right to education (Article 2 of Protocol 1 ECHR). This part highlights the rights and freedoms protected in Section I of the Convention. Further substantive rights were protected in subsequent Protocols – specifically Protocols 1 (protection of property, the right to education, the right to free elections); 4 (extending various rights of liberty and security), 6 (abolition of the death penalty), 7 (*ne bis in idem*, and other criminal procedural safeguards), 12 (prohibition of discrimination), and 13 ECHR (abolishing the death penalty in all circumstances). The remaining Protocols primarily focused on the administration of justice and procedural reforms at the ECtHR, notably Protocols 11, 14, 15, and 16 ECHR. As the Court developed its quasi-constitutional role – through setting minimum standards in human rights protection, through its principles of interpretation, and the increasing impacts of its jurisprudence at national level[75] – the scale of applications to the Court has proven to be a challenge which its procedural reforms have only ever partially succeeded in tackling.

3.3.3 Protection of Rights: The Convention's Substantive Provisions

Article 1 ECHR requires states to secure the rights defined in Section I of the Convention to 'everyone within their jurisdiction'. Section I comprises a set of classic fundamental rights and freedoms, which are selectively outlined as follows.

The right to life is protected under Article 2 ECHR, which provides that everyone's right to life shall be protected by law, with no intentional deprivation of life permitted save in the execution of a death penalty lawfully imposed following conviction for a crime (Article 2(1) ECHR). This element must be viewed in the light of both protocols to the Convention which later outlawed the death penalty (Protocol 6 ECHR) in all circumstances (Protocol 13 ECHR). Article 2(2) ECHR identifies situations where the deprivation of life may not infringe Article 2 ECHR where 'the use of

[75] S. Greer, J. Gerards and R. Slowe, *Human Rights in the Council of Europe and European Union – Achievements, Trends and Challenges*, Cambridge: Cambridge University Press, 2018, p. 21.

force is no more than absolutely necessary'. The ECtHR has articulated an increasingly expansive approach to positive obligations under Article 2 ECHR (*Öneryıldız v. Turkey*; *Stoyanovi v. Bulgaria*).[76] The substantive dimension of this provision includes case law on intentional killing by the state (*McCann v. UK*),[77] deaths in custody (*Trubnikov v. Russia*),[78] while the procedural dimensions of Article 2 ECHR were explored most deeply in the context of the high death-toll incurred in the Beslan school siege (*Tagayeva and others v. Russia*).[79] Extensive case law on the abortion and reproductive rights (*Vo v. France*; *Tysiac v. Poland*; *A, B, C v. Ireland*),[80] the 'right to die' (*Pretty v. UK*)[81] and withdrawal of life-sustaining treatment (*Lambert v. France*)[82] has placed state regulation of start- and end of life decisions under close scrutiny by the Court.

In its case law on the prohibition of torture (Article 3 ECHR), the Court reinforces the absoluteness of the prohibition. As noted in *Gäfgen v. Germany*, a case that provoked intense debate in Germany and beyond, the 'philosophical basis underpinning the absolute nature of the right under Article 3 does not allow for any exceptions or justifying factors or balancing of interests'.[83] Is the level of protection offered under Article 3 ECHR so absolute in reality? The fidelity of the Court to the 'absoluteness' of Article 3 ECHR has been questioned,[84] with many voices

76 ECtHR, *Öneryıldız v. Turkey*, Appl. No. 48939/99, Judgment, 30 November 2004; *Stoyanovi v. Bulgaria*, Appl. No. 42980/04, Judgment, 9 November 2010.

77 ECtHR, *McCann and Others v. the United Kingdom*, Appl. No. 18984/91, Judgment, 27 September 1995.

78 ECtHR, *Trubnikov v. Russia*, Appl. No. 49790/99, Judgment, 5 July 2005.

79 ECtHR, *Tagayeva and Others v. Russia*, Appl. Nos. 26562/07 and 6 others, Judgment, 13 April 2017.

80 ECtHR, *Vo v. France*, Appl. No. 53924/00, Judgment, 8 July 2004; *Tysiąc v. Poland*, Appl. No. 5410/03, Judgment, 20 March 2007; *A, B and C v. Ireland* [GC], Appl. No. 25579/05, Judgment, 16 December 2010.

81 ECtHR, *Pretty v. the United Kingdom*, Appl. No. 2346/02, Judgment, 29 April 2002.

82 ECtHR, *Lambert and Others v. France* [GC], Appl. No. 46043/14, Judgment, 5 June 2015.

83 ECtHR, *Gäfgen v. Germany* [GC], Appl. No. 22978/05, Judgment, 1 June 2010, para. 107; *Derman v. Turkey*, Appl. No. 21789/02, Judgment, 31 May 2011, para. 27. On *Gäfgen*, see further K. Ambos, 'May a State Torture Suspects to Save the Life of Innocents?', (2008) 6 *JICJ*, 261.

84 See, for example, M. Nowak, 'Challenges to the Absolute Nature of the Prohibition of Torture and Ill-treatment' (2005) 23(4) *Neth. Q. Hum. Rts.*, 674; H. Battjes, 'In Search of a Fair Balance: The Absolute Character of the Prohibition of Refoulement under Article 3 ECHR re-assessed' (2009), 22 *LJIL*, 587; N. Mavronicola, 'What is an "Absolute Right"? Deciphering Absoluteness in the Context of Article 3 of the European Convention on Human Rights' (2012) 12(4) *HRLR*, 724.

proposing alternative approaches to framing it. Mavronicola has argued for a narrower construction of Article 3 ECHR to target violations which harm human dignity and agency,[85] whereas Smet has proposed a stronger focus on aggravating factors of ill-treatment which should be necessary for a violation to be found.[86] The interpretation of Article 3 ECHR is further complicated by the three aspects covered: torture, inhuman, and degrading treatment. Notwithstanding Greer's assessment that according all three elements of Article 3 ECHR absolute protection is indefensible, the case law does not follow that trajectory.[87] The unclear boundary between 'inhuman' and merely 'degrading' treatment and punishment, however, and the minimum level of severity required to engage an Article 3 ECHR violation – a threshold that varies between cases – can trigger accusations of a dilution of the absolute nature of Article 3 ECHR rights.[88] Though dilution of rights is something states can be fully prepared to argue for before the ECtHR.[89]

In prohibiting slavery and forced labour, Article 4 ECHR has, until recently, generated limited case law. Early cases often focused on aspects of alleged forced labour, and the exceptions open to states under Article 4(3) ECHR – for example, service during public emergencies threatening the community (Article 4(3)(c) ECHR) or normal civic obligations (Article 4(3)(d) ECHR). However, the recent rise in Article 4 ECHR cases has focused more on the absolute right contained in Article 4(1) ECHR, which protects individuals from slavery or servitude, and on Article 4(2) ECHR, which protects individuals from forced or compulsory labour. Milestone

[85] N. Mavronicola, 'Güler and Öngel v. Turkey: Article 3 of the European Convention on Human Rights and Strasbourg's discourse on the justified use of force' (2013) 76 *MLR*, 375.

[86] S. Smet, 'The "Absolute" Prohibition of Torture and Inhuman or Degrading Treatment in Article 3 ECHR – Truly a Question of Scope Only?', in E. Brems and J. Gerards (eds.), *Shaping Rights in the ECHR – The Role of the European Court of Human Rights in Determining the Scope of Human Rights*, Cambridge: Cambridge University Press, 2013, p. 273 at p. 284.

[87] Note Greer's criticism in (for example) S. Greer, 'Is the Prohibition against Torture, Cruel, Inhuman and Degrading Treatment Really "Absolute" in International Human Rights Law?' (2015) 15 *HRLR*, 101.

[88] In reaction to, for example, ECtHR, *Bouyid v. Belgium* [GC], Appl. No. 23380/09, Judgment, 28 September 2015.

[89] The UK government's unsuccessful arguments to that effect in ECtHR, *Saadi v. Italy* [GC], Appl. No. 37201/06, Judgment, 28 February 2008 illustrate this in relation to Article 3 ECHR.

cases have highlighted the suffering of often young, vulnerable victims and the slowness of states to take action to protect individuals from domestic servitude (*Siliadin v. France*; *C.N. and V v. France*; *C.N. v. UK*),[90] trafficking (*Rantsev v. Cyprus and Russia*)[91] and exploitation for prostitution (*S.M. v. Croatia*).[92] Legislative steps such as the UK's Modern Slavery Act 2015 have shown that strengthening the legal framework still presents huge challenges identifying victims and enforcing obligations against businesses.

Article 5 ECHR provides the right to liberty and security, with the aim of protecting individuals against arbitrary detention and the abuse of state power. As the ECtHR ruled in *Kurt v. Turkey*, this provision protects both 'physical liberty of individuals as well as their personal security in a context which, in the absence of safeguards, could result in a subversion of the rule of law and place detainees beyond the reach of the most rudimentary forms of legal protection'.[93] Whilst Article 5(1) ECHR provides an overarching right to liberty and security to everyone, Article 5(2) ECHR stipulates six categories in which detention may be justified if carried out in accordance with a procedure prescribed by law. As such, Article 5 ECHR has been invoked by applicants in diverse contexts, from stop-and-search (*Gillan and Quinton v. UK*)[94] and 'kettling' as a form of crowd-control (*Austin v. UK*)[95] to newer applications including involuntary placement in psychological care (*Stanev v. Bulgaria*)[96] and detention of sea migrants (*Khlaifia and others v. Italy*).[97]

Closely related is the right to a fair trial as protected under Article 6 ECHR. This multifaceted right has often come under pressure and scrutiny over the decades and came under particular strain given the impact of COVID-19 on the administration of justice. Article 6(1)

[90] ECtHR, *Siliadin v. France*, Appl. No. 73316/01, Judgment, 26 July 2005; *C.N. and V. v. France*, Appl. No. 67724/09, Judgment 11 October 2012; *C.N. v. the United Kingdom*, Appl. No. 4239/08, Judgment, 13 November 2012.

[91] ECtHR, *Rantsev v. Cyprus and Russia*, Appl. No. 25965/04, Judgment, 7 October 2010.

[92] EctHR, *S.M. v. Croatia* [GC], Appl. No. 60561/14, Judgment, 25 June 2020.

[93] ECtHR, *Kurt v. Turkey*, Appl. No. 15/1997/799/1002, Judgment, 25 May 1998, paras. 122–124.

[94] ECtHR, *Gillan and Quinton v. the United Kingdom*, Appl. No. 4158/05, 12 January 2010.

[95] ECtHR, *Austin and Others v. the United Kingdom* [GC], Appl. Nos. 39692/09 and 2 others, 15 March 2012.

[96] ECtHR, *Stanev v. Bulgaria* [GC], Appl. No. 36760/06, Judgment, ... 17 January 2012.

[97] ECtHR, *Khlaifia and Others v. Italy* [GC], Appl. No. 16483/12, Judgment, 15 December 2016.

ECHR provides an overarching protection of the right to a fair trial for the determination of 'civil rights and obligations' or criminal charges. To engage Article 6 ECHR a dispute must be of a genuine and serious nature, with a decisive outcome,[98] and the multiple aspects of protection are more tightly applied to criminal proceedings. Article 6 ECHR is detailed and prescriptive in articulating the safeguards offered,[99] perhaps unsurprisingly the most intensively invoked provision of the Convention. Yet, the ECtHR still finds scope for novelty – in *Ćwik v. Poland* recently examining the admission of evidence in criminal proceedings which was forcibly obtained through ill-treatment, in the absence of the actions or approval of state authorities.[100] In *V.C.L and A.N. v. United Kingdom*, the ECtHR had its first opportunity to consider Article 4 ECHR in relation to the right to a fair trial under Article 6(1) ECHR.[101] The applications concerned Vietnamese children trafficked to work on a cannabis farm, convicted despite credible suspicion as to their trafficked status, who later lost their appeals against conviction. In a ruling that should make states more mindful of the level of protection they must provide to potential victims of trafficking, the ECtHR found violations of both provisions.

Shifting from primarily procedural to substantive protection in criminal proceedings, Article 7 ECHR protects the guarantee of no punishment without law, offering individuals protection against arbitrary prosecution, conviction, and punishment. Article 7(1) ECHR is absolute, the principle contained (*nullem crimen, nulla poena sine lege* – no punishment without law) an uncontroversial and essential element of the rule of law. Both the ECtHR and the ECJ have sought to rely on Article 7(1) ECHR / Article 49 Charter jurisprudence when interpreting these respective provisions.[102] The ECtHR has addressed Article 7 ECHR in challenging contexts such as marital rape (*SW v. UK*; *CR v. UK*), and more recently (and less

[98] ECtHR, *Sporrong and Lönnroth v. Sweden*, Appl. No. 7151/75; 7152/75, Judgment, 23 September 1982, para. 81.

[99] P. Mahoney, 'Right to a Fair Trial in Criminal Matters under Article 6 ECHR', (2004) 4(2) *JSIS*, 107.

[100] ECtHR, *Ćwik v. Poland*, Appl. No. 31454/10, Judgment, 5 November 2020; ECtHR Annual Report 2020 (Council of Europe – European Court of Human Rights 2021).

[101] ECtHR, *V.C.L. and A.N. v. the United Kingdom*, Appl. Nos. 77587/12 and 74603/12, Judgment, 16 February 2021.

[102] For example, alignment of these provisions in ECtHR, *Scoppola v. Italy (no. 2)* [GC], Appl. No. 10249/03, Judgment, 17 September 2009.

controversially) in the second advisory opinion delivered under Protocol 16 ECHR, on the request of the Armenian Constitutional Court.[103]

On reaching Articles 8–11 ECHR, the structure of rights changes to a two-part formula. The first paragraph articulates the right protected, and the second paragraph specifies the circumstances in which state interference may be lawful on the basis that it is justified as necessary in a democratic society to achieve a legitimate aim. The right to respect for private and family life (Article 8 ECHR), freedom of thought, conscience, and religion (Article 9 ECHR), freedom of expression (Article 10 ECHR) and freedom of assembly and association (Article 11 ECHR) are the classic examples of this two-part construction.

These rights are being tested in new ways, gaining a reach which would never have been anticipated by the drafters of the Convention. In respect of the right to respect for private and family life (Article 8 ECHR), this provision has gained a reputation in some quarters over being heavily relied on by applicants – for example, bringing private and family life arguments to the fore in cases where applicants are resisting extradition or deportation. ECtHR case law continues to break new ground in the context of legal recognition of same-sex unions (*Fedotova v. Russia*), an aspect of private life in which the ECtHR has taken a very gradual and cautious approach to setting positive obligations for states.[104] Technological advances are creating new frontiers for Article 8 ECHR in the online realm in areas of data protection, surveillance, and security (*López Ribalda*; *Big Brother Watch*).[105] The freedom of thought, conscience, and religion

[103] ECtHR, *S.W. v. the United Kingdom*, Appl. No. 20166/92, Judgment, 22 November 1995; *C.R. v. the United Kingdom*, Appl. No. 20190/92, Judgment, 22 November 1995; Advisory opinion concerning the use of the 'blanket reference' or 'legislation by reference' technique in the definition of an offence and the standards of comparison between the criminal law in force at the time of the commission of the offence and the amended criminal law [GC], request no. P16-2019-001, Armenian Constitutional Court, 29 May 2020. See generally K. Ambos, *European Criminal Law*, Cambridge: Cambridge University Press, 2018, pp. 127 ff.

[104] ECtHR, *Fedotova and Others v. Russia*, Appl. Nos. 40792/10 and 2 others, Judgment, 13 July 2021. On the background to this strand of caselaw, note ECtHR, *Schalk and Kopf v. Austria*, Appl. No. 30141/04, 24 June 2010; *Vallianatos and Others v. Greece* [GC], Appl. Nos. 29381/09 and 32684/09, Judgment, 7 November 2013; *Oliari and Others v. Italy*, Appl. Nos. 18766/11 and 36030/11, Judgment, 21 July 2015.

[105] Recent case examples include ECtHR, *López Ribalda and Others v. Spain* [GC], Appl. Nos. 1874/13 and 8567/13, Judgment, 17 October 2019; *Big Brother Watch and Others v. the United Kingdom* [GC], Appl. Nos. 58170/13 and 2 others, Judgment, 25 May 2021; *Centrum för rättvisa v. Sweden* [GC], Appl. No. 35252/08, Judgment, 25 May 2021.

(Article 9 ECHR) has been consistently viewed by the ECtHR as essential to democracy since the first case (*Kokkinakis v. Greece*).[106] Yet, Article 9 ECHR has proven to be the source of highly contentious cases particularly on state restrictions on the manifestation of one's religious belief.[107] It should be noted that freedom of conscience (Article 9(1) ECHR) is an absolute right, though embedded in a provision with an extensive justification clause – which provides scope for states to lawfully interfere with freedom to manifest one's religion or beliefs.[108] In relation to freedom of expression (Article 10 ECHR), the ECtHR also recognised free speech as 'one of the essential foundations' of a democratic society (*Handyside v. UK*).[109] From Holocaust denial (*Lehideux*)[110] and its instrumentalization (*PETA Deutschland*)[111] to political speech (e.g., *Lingens v. Austria; Baldassi v. France*),[112] artistic expression (*Vereinigung Bildener Künstler v. Austria*),[113] and more recently to hate speech (*Lilliendahl v. Iceland*),[114] jurisprudence under Article 10 ECHR (occasionally in conjunction with Article 17 ECHR) always provides a new boundary to push.

Thematically, the freedom of assembly and association (protected under Article 11 ECHR) covers the right to peaceful protest and membership or alignment with organisations (such as trade unions, political parties, and religious organisations). The unprecedented restrictions on movement and gatherings across many European countries during the COVID-19 pandemic have had implications for this right, not least (in the UK) for

[106] ECtHR, *Kokkinakis v. Greece*, Appl. No. 14307/88, Judgment, 25 May 1993.

[107] For two of many examples, note ECtHR, *Dahlab v. Switzerland*, Appl. No. 42393/98, Judgment, 15 February 2001; *S.A.S. v. France* [GC], Appl. No. 43835/11, Judgment, 1 July 2014 (extracts).

[108] J. Gerards, *General Principles of the European Convention on Human Rights*, Cambridge: Cambridge University Press, 2019, p. 20.

[109] ECtHR, *Handyside v. the United Kingdom*, Appl. No. 5493/72, Judgment, 7 December 1976.

[110] *Lehideux and Isorni v. France*, Appl. No. 24662/94, 23 September 1998.

[111] ECtHR, *PETA Deutschland v. Germany*, Appl. No. 43481/09, 8 November 2012.

[112] ECtHR, *Lingens v. Austria*, Appl. No. 9815/82, Judgment, 8 July 1986; *Baldassi and Others v. France*, Appl. Nos. 15271/16 and 6 others, Judgment, 11 June 2020; on this case see K. Ambos, 'Freedom of Expression and Political Controversy: The ECtHR's BDS Judgment', *Just Security*, 30 June 2020, www.justsecurity.org/71083/freedom-of-expression-and-political-controversy-the-ecthrs-bds-judgment/, (last accessed 20 February 2022).

[113] ECtHR, *Vereinigung Bildender Künstler v. Austria*, Appl. No. 68354/01, Judgment, 25 January 2007.

[114] ECtHR, *Carl Jóhann Lilliendahl v. Iceland*, Appl. No. 29297/18, Decision of inadmissibility, 12 May 2020.

protests on issues such as 'Black Lives Matter', 'Reclaim These Streets' and against the COVID-19 restrictions themselves.[115] The right to marry and found a family (Article 12 ECHR) was drafted in a manner which explicitly protects the right to marriage between a man and a woman. The ECtHR's first opportunity to consider the right to same-sex marriage (*Schalk and Kopf v. Austria*)[116] was – in the absence of European consensus on this right – deferential to national law. Some gradual progress has been made in protecting non-heterosexual unions (*Oliari and others v. Italy; Fedotova v. Russia*),[117] though with more scope for progress invoking Articles 8 and 14 ECHR. The right to an effective remedy under Article 13 ECHR requires 'an effective remedy before a national authority' for victims of violations of the Convention. Neither Article 1 ECHR nor Article 13 ECHR feature in the Human Rights Act 1998 (HRA) in the UK, on the basis that the incorporation of Convention provisions in the HRA itself satisfies their requirements. It should be noted that the general prohibition of discrimination contained in Article 14 ECHR can only be invoked in conjunction with another substantive provision of the Convention.

The final set of substantive rights contained in Section I of the Convention provides scope for additional restrictions in specific circumstances. The derogation in time of emergency (Article 15 ECHR) allows states to derogate from most Convention rights 'in time of war or other public emergency threatening the life of the nation' provided that measures taken do not violate other obligations under international law (Article 15(1) ECHR).[118] Caveats to this derogation provision are found in Article 15(2) ECHR, which prevents derogation from Article 2 ECHR (except in respect of deaths resulting from lawful acts of war) or from

[115] On the UK Government's response on this area, note: Joint Committee on Human Rights, Thirteenth Report: The Government Response to COVID-19: freedom of assembly and the right to protest HC 1328, accessible at: https://publications.parliament.uk/pa/jt5801/jtselect/jtrights/1328/132805.htm (accessed: 30 June 2021).

[116] ECtHR, *Schalk and Kopf v. Austria*, Appl. No. 30141/04, Judgment, 24 June 2010.

[117] ECtHR, *Oliari and Others v. Italy*, Appl. Nos. 18766/11 and 36030/11, Judgment, 21 July 2015; *Fedotova and Others v. Russia*, Appl. Nos. 40792/10 and 2 others, Judgment, 13 July 2021.

[118] On recent debate on the decision to invoke Article 15 ECHR in the COVID-19 context, compare A. Greene, 'Derogating from the European Convention on Human Rights in Response to the Coronavirus Pandemic: If not Now, When?' (2020) *EHRLR*, 262; K. Dzehtsiarou, 'Article 15 Derogations: Are they Really Necessary during the COVID-19 Pandemic?' (2020) *EHRLR*, 359.

Articles 3, 4(1), and 7 ECHR. Restrictions on political activity of aliens (Article 16 ECHR) – a dated provision with scant caselaw – adds a gloss to the interpretation of Articles 10, 11 and 14 ECHR, providing that they shall not be regarded as preventing states from imposing restrictions on the political activity of foreign nationals.

The prohibition on abuse of rights (Article 17 ECHR) confirms that the Convention cannot be interpreted as implying a right for any State, group, or person 'any right to engage in any activity aimed at the destruction of any of the rights and freedoms' of the Convention, or from limiting them to a greater extent than the Convention provides for. Notably, Article 17 ECHR has been engaged by the ECtHR in relation to holocaust denial cases under Article 10 ECHR. Finally, the limitation on use of restrictions of rights (Article 18 ECHR) provides that the restrictions, rights, and freedoms under the Convention shall not be applied for any other purpose, other than those prescribed by the Convention.

The reach of the Convention and its case law is unprecedented in international human rights law, even if that case law and the legitimacy of the ECtHR itself are often subject to challenge. Political backlashes against the Convention system and a lack of political and legal mechanisms to ultimately enforce compliance with ECtHR may undermine confidence in the system. However, as it matures in its eighth decade, its influence on the development of standards of rights protection at national levels – and in the jurisprudence of the Court of Justice – is likely to continue.

3.4 Conclusion

This chapter has explored the substantive rights protection offered under the EU Charter of Fundamental Rights and the ECHR, in the light of the context in which both legal orders evolved. Despite their many differences, it is evident that both the EU and ECHR legal orders have shared missions in the fundamental rights sphere and shared expectations for rights-based criminal justice which conforms to the rule of law. While the mandates of the EU and Council of Europe are broad, commitments to fundamental rights and the rule of law are deeply embedded in both systems. When reflecting on the development of emerging European Criminal law, the most important shared impact in both EU law and the law of the ECHR is arguably the galvanising effects of both the ECJ and

ECtHR. Conversely, the most striking distinction is the sharp difference between both systems regarding how individuals can engage with the ECJ and ECtHR as victims of rights violations. Their rights-based case law has the power to influence changes to both EU and national law, and at least in the case of the ECtHR, provides direct opportunities for victims to hold their state to account.

With the reach of EU competences growing to encompass areas such as criminal justice and asylum law, the ECJ's 'intense commitment' to fundamental rights[119] is being tested in new fields and in challenging contexts. There is now a much closer fusion between the ECJ's own rhetoric on the essential role of fundamental rights in EU law and the expanding legislative reach in policy areas where rights are increasingly salient. The EU can sometimes appear slow to react politically in the face of existential pressures – whether linked to populism or migration, security, or financial instability. Yet in the post-Charter era, fundamental rights and the rule of law are reinforced as core to the identity of both the European Union and determinative to the constitutional identities of its MS.[120]

The accommodation of the ECHR by states has not been without incident. Allegations questioning the Court's lack of legitimacy have persistently targeted the Strasbourg court.[121] Explicit backlashes against the Court's perceived overreach are increasingly common in political discourse – not least in the UK, where resistance to the Convention system was illustrated in occasional ambivalence at executing judgments, and calls to withdraw from the ECHR as an even more appealing alternative to Brexit.[122] At a broader level, the rates of execution of judgments are questionable in various countries.[123] Efforts to manage the ECtHR's

[119] T. Tridimas, 'Fundamental Rights, General Principles of EU Law, and the Charter', (2013–2014) 16 *CYELS*, 361, 363.

[120] L. Besselink, 'The Protection of Fundamental Rights Post-Lisbon', General Report FIDE 2012, 5–6.

[121] For example, K. Dzehtsiarou, *European Consensus and the Legitimacy of the European Court of Human Rights*, Cambridge: Cambridge University Press, 2015; B. M. Oomen, 'A Serious Case of Strasbourg-Bashing? An Evaluation of the Debates on the Legitimacy of the European Court of Human Rights in the Netherlands', (2016) 20 *IJHR*, 407.

[122] 'Home Secretary's speech on the UK, EU and our place in the world', delivered by Theresa May, 25 April 2016, accessible at: www.gov.uk/government/speeches/home-secretarys-speech-on-the-uk-eu-and-our-place-in-the-world (accessed: 30 June 2021).

[123] See Supervision of the Execution of Judgments and Decisions of the European Court of Human Rights 2020, 14th Annual Report of the Committee of Ministers (Council of Europe 2021).

volume of applications continue, with victims of violations often facing lengthy proceedings. Achieving reforms at the ECtHR can be slow process,[124] but the fact that the ECtHR remains a popular destination for applicants still owes far more to the actions of states than to the Court's failure to provide optimum processes for the administration of justice. In the eighth decade of the Convention, there remains much to achieve for the individuals it aims to protect.

Further Reading

P. Alston and J. H. H. Weiler, 'An "Ever Closer Union" in Need of a Human Rights Policy' (1998) 9 *EJIL*, 658.

E. Bates, *The Evolution of the European Convention on Human Rights: From Its Inception to the Creation of a Permanent Court of Human Rights*, Oxford: Oxford University Press, 2010.

G. de Búrca, 'The Road not Taken: The European Union as a Global Human Rights Actor' (2011) 105(4) *AJIL*, 649.

K. Dzethsiarou, T. Lock, T. Konstadinides, and N. O'Meara (eds.), *Human Rights Law in Europe: The Influence, Overlaps and Contradictions of the EU and ECHR*, London: Routledge 2014.

S. Greer, J. Gerards, and R. Slowe, *Human Rights in the Council of Europe and European Union – Achievements, Trends and Challenges*, Cambridge: Cambridge University Press, 2018.

T. Lock, 'Rights and Principles in the EU Charter of Fundamental Rights', (2019) 56(5) *CMLR*, 1201.

N. Mavronicola, *Torture, Inhumanity and Degradation under Article 3 of the ECHR – Absolute Rights and Absolute Wrongs*, Oxford: Hart 2021.

V. Mitsilegas, *EU Criminal Law after Lisbon: Trust, Rights and the Transformation of Justice in Europe*, Oxford: Hart 2016.

[124] Protocol 15 ECHR opened for signature in 2013 entered into force on 1 August 2021. The reduction of the time limit to apply to the ECtHR from six months to four months (under Protocol 15, Article 4 ECHR) was applied from 1 February 2022.

4 Primacy, Duty of Loyalty and Interpretation

Emanuela Fronza

4.1 Introduction

Approaching the European criminal justice system – characterised by the relations between European law and national criminal law – we find ourselves in an intricate and multi-layered system of norms that changes form and morphology depending on the perspective. At the heart of this system, we encounter various intersections between European law and national norms. To systematise this field means giving an order to the structure of these relations.

The basic *enjeu* is the articulation of norms, which ultimately dictates the articulation of powers and competences. European criminal law, in particular, does not replace the existing law, but supplements it. In fact, the notion of European Criminal Law (ECL) does not refer to a complete and independent legal system, like the national ones. It not only comprises European norms which substitute national norms. On the contrary, ECL is, by definition, composed of both national and European norms. In fact, the history of European criminal law remains one of problematic interferences, where the problem lies in the difficulty of combining the two systems. It is then a matter of coupling the logics of legitimation of the EU with those proper to national criminal law. Prevalence of ECL, in fact, does not entail challenging national law: it is the ability of ECL to penetrate the domestic system, a characteristic that distinguishes ECL from international treaty law – also prevalent but lacking this ability to penetrate.[1] However, this penetration has its own peculiarities as we move to a criminal law context, where the principle of legality of crimes and punishments applies. From here stems the paradox of this juridical universe: in the realm of domestic criminal law both EU and subordinate national

[1] A. von Bogdandy, "Pluralism, Direct Effect, and the Ultimate Say: On the Relationship between International and Domestic Constitutional Law," (2008) 6 *ICON*, 397.

provisions (co-)exist. Traditionally, even if not prevailing, domestic provisions are empowered with competence in the criminal sector.

Another peculiarity of the European system is its structure. The European criminal justice system is a complex space, composed of multiple levels and thus functioning on several systems. It became even more sophisticated after the Lisbon Treaty, which marked a turning point. ECL is, in fact, characterised by the interference between EU and domestic norms that may regulate the same fact in the context of the same judgment. As a consequence, difficulties arise in reconciling conflicting norms by way of judicial interpretation or otherwise. European criminal law relies on national judges as allies. In this, it differs from international law, which does necessitate such an active role of the judicial branch. In examining the relationship between EU law and national laws, it should indeed be borne in mind that the main player of the European criminal justice system is the judge, especially the national judge. The keystone of the system is represented by the fact that every national judge, and in particular every ordinary judge, becomes the European judge, albeit remaining a national judge. Yet s/he is not alone: the criminal judge converses with domestic Constitutional Courts and the European Court of Justice (ECJ), all of which have very different perspectives and approaches to judicial decision-making. As the main actor in this legal universe, the judge must implement the indications coming from the ECJ and the Constitutional Courts. The ultimate problem, again, lies in the difficulty of harmonizing the systems.

All this complexity is embedded in the principles and mechanisms of penetration that are analysed here. These principles and mechanisms are interconnected and complement each other. They are fundamental for the system, but at the same time different visions of primacy, loyal cooperation and interpretation are introduced, depending on how they are understood and applied in domestic systems. These principles bear continuous interconnections. Primacy implies conforming interpretation, but the latter is also a way of completing what primacy alone cannot accomplish.[2] In this sense, the limits of primacy must be overcome by interpretation and loyal cooperation. To exemplify the connection between these

[2] As for the interconnections among EU law's interpretation and the domestic margin of appreciation, M. Delmas Marty and M. L. Izorche, "Marge nationale d'appréciation et internationalisation du droit. Réflexions sur la validité formelle d'un droit commun pluraliste," (2000) 4 *RIDC*, 765.

principles, this chapter, after explaining them, analyses selected case law, which further demonstrates the specific impact of EU law on the domestic criminal law systems.

4.2 The Two Levels of the Interconnection between EU Law and National Laws

ECL is, by definition, 'multi-layered'.[3] It is composed of both national and European rules: two systems that interact with each other in a perspective of 'interference'. This process happens on two levels. On the one hand, it entails the influence of EU law on national criminal policymaking through the attribution of competencies to the Union and the correspondent duty for national States to implement EU law in criminal matters.[4] On the other, EU law penetrates Member States' (MS) walls through the duty imposed on national judges to interpret national criminal law in conformity or in accordance with EU law.

With regard to the first aspect of interference, it is important to underline that the Lisbon Treaty represented a 'breakthrough' for ECL: it established the competence of the EU to adopt criminal law rules in certain sectors of transnational criminal law (Art. 83 (1) TFEU). The coordination between EU criminal law and domestic criminal law is carried out through two doctrinal categories: competence and the hierarchy of sources as an authoritative criterion for resolving possible conflicts. The 'revolution' brought about by the Treaty of Lisbon is embodied in the introduction of Article 83 TFEU which establishes two types of indirect criminal competence of the EU. This is the competence of the European Parliament and the Council to deliberate 'minimum standards', aiming at harmonising the legal systems of the MS. The competence of the EU is established in nine areas ('spheres of crime'), listed in para. 1 of Article 83: terrorism, trafficking in human beings and sexual exploitation of women and children, illicit drug trafficking, illicit arms trafficking, money laundering, corruption, counterfeiting of means of payment, computer crime and organised crime. In the second paragraph of this same provision a further harmonization competence regarding

[3] N. Walker, 'The European Union's Unresolved Constitution', in M. Rosenfeld and A. Sajo (eds.), *The Oxford Handbook of Comparative Constitutional Law*, Oxford: Oxford University Press, 2012, 1185 ff.

[4] K. Ambos, *European Criminal Law*, Cambridge: Cambridge University Press, 2018, p. 336.

minimum rules on the definition of offences and penalties is established in order to ensure the effective implementation of certain Union policies. Thus, Art. 83(2) TFEU establishes an annex competence for criminal law 'approximation' to enforce harmonization in certain policy areas.[5]

In addition, it is important to note that the principle of primacy applies also to directives that have not yet been implemented: what is allowed in terms of conduct at the European law level cannot form the object of criminalisation under national law.[6] This might strike as odd, if we consider that, in principle, directives are not directly applicable, and leave to MS the national implementing measure that transposes into domestic law their objectives. This is especially true for directives that contain criminal obligations. These types of directives cannot have a direct domestic effect without the implementation of local operative legislation.[7] In this context, criminal law traditionally becomes the qualifying area of disruption of the primacy of EU law. 'If we had to summarize in one sentence the innovations introduced as a result of the entry into force of the Treaty of Lisbon, we could say that, with the new rules on criminal matters, the European Union becomes definitively competent to judge the necessity of punishment, but not to exercise punitive power'.[8] These words describe the contradiction that characterises ECL. ECL thus constitutes a 'paradoxical legal universe' due to the different logics of legitimation that underlie the EU, on the one hand, and national criminal law, on the other.[9]

However, a possibility to interfere directly in the domestic criminal law system for the EU arises. In fact, the Treaty of Lisbon seems to be equipping the EU with legislation that is directly aimed at protecting its financial interests. According to Art. 86 TFEU in order to combat crimes affecting the financial interests of the Union, the Council – by a unanimous decision after obtaining the consent of the European Parliament – may establish a European Public Prosecutor's Office (EPPO) from Eurojust.

[5] A. Bernardi, 'La competenza penale accessoria dell'Unione Europea: problemi e prospettive' (2012) 1 *DPC*, 43–78, archiviodpc.dirittopenaleuomo.org.

[6] K. Ambos, *European Criminal Law*, pp. 336 ff.

[7] CJEU, *Kolpinghuis Nijmegen*, No. 80/86, Judgment, ECLI:EU:C:1987:431, 8 October 1987, para. 14; *Berlusconi et al.*, Joined Cases Nos. C-387/02, C-391/02 and C-403/02, Judgment, ECLI:EU:C:2005:270, 3 May 2005, para. 74; *Pupino*, No. C-105/03, Judgment, ECLI:EU:C:2005:386, 16 June 2005, para. 45.

[8] C. Sotis, 'Il Trattato di Lisbona e le competenze penali dell'Unione Europea', (2010) 3 *Cassazione Penale*, 326.

[9] Ibid., 327.

The EPPO shall be responsible for investigating, prosecuting and bringing to judgment the perpetrators of, and accomplices in, offences against the Union's financial interests, as determined by the regulation provided for in paragraph 1. The EPPO shall exercise the function of prosecuting these crimes in the courts of the MS. Hence, the EPPO is conceived as endowed with the power to directly act in criminal proceedings before national courts. A confirmation of this possibility to interfere directly in the criminal law system for the EU, albeit limited to the protection of financial interests, seems also to follow from Art. 325 TFEU. According to its para. 1,

The Union and the Member States shall counter fraud and any other illegal activities affecting the financial interests of the Union through measures to be taken in accordance with this Article, which shall act as a deterrent and be such as to afford effective protection in the Member States, and in all the Union's institutions, bodies, offices and agencies.

Article 325(3) TFEU establishes that The Member States shall coordinate their action aimed at protecting the financial interests of the Union against fraud and adopt the necessary measures in the fields of the prevention of and fight against fraud affecting the financial interests of the Union with a view to affording effective and equivalent protection in the Member States and in all the Union's institutions, bodies, offices and agencies.

The ECJ confirmed the direct effect of Art. 325 TFEU to 'counter illegal activities affecting the financial interests of the European Union through dissuasive and effective measures' and 'to take the same measures to counter fraud affecting those interests as they take to counter fraud affecting their own financial interests'; the Court also affirmed that national provisions unable to give full effect to Art. 325 TFEU are to be disapplied.[10] Thus, the influence, both direct and indirect, of EU law in the criminal justice area has progressively increased in recent years: the axiom of a lack of competence of the EU in criminal matters can now be said to have been definitely overcome.

Regarding the second aspect of the aforementioned 'interference' process, this is represented by the penetration of EU law through judicial decisions. The judge is, as previously stated, a key actor in European criminal law. This power/duty derives from the principles of primacy and

[10] CJEU, *Taricco and Others*, No. C-105/14, Judgment, ECLI:EU:C:2015:555, 8 September 2015, paras. 49–52, particularly para. 51. See also Ambos, European Criminal Law, pp. 18 f.

of sincere cooperation but also carries with it limits that are typical of criminal law such as the principle of legality and the respect for fundamental rights established by national norms.

In sum, it can be affirmed that we are in presence of a sort of paradoxical legal system, made of originally incompetent, yet dominant, European law combined with competent, yet subordinate, national law.[11] This complex universe is governed by several principles, namely the principle of primacy and the duty of loyalty, which will be the focus of the next two paragraphs.

4.3 Primacy

The ECJ, called on to determine the scope and validity of EU law, upheld the primacy of Community (now European) law, starting with the historic *Costa v. Enel* judgment of July 15, 1964.[12] Subsequently, on the basis of the conclusions of *Van Gend en Loos*,[13] the Court definitively affirmed the prevalence of Community law over national law with the *Simmenthal* judgment:[14]

> In accordance with the principle of the precedence of Community law, the relationship between provisions of the Treaty and directly applicable measures of the institutions on the one hand and the national law of the Member States on the other is such that those provisions and measures not only by their entry into force render automatically inapplicable any conflicting provision of current national law but – in so far as they are an integral part of, and take precedence in, the legal order applicable in the territory of each of the Member States – also preclude the valid adoption of new national legislative measures to the extent to which they would be incompatible with Community provisions.

The relevance of this principle – placed at the very heart of the structure of the European system – also had an impact on the sphere of criminal law. Until a few years ago, in fact, the system of the European Union's competence in criminal matters was based on one simple assumption: the

11 C. Sotis, *Il diritto senza codice. Uno studio sul sistema penale europeo vigente*, Milano: Giuffrè, 2007, pp. 88 f.

12 CJEU, *Costa v. ENEL*, No. 6/64, Judgment, ECLI:EU:C:1964:66, 15 July 1964.

13 CJEU, *Van Gend & Loos v. Netherlands Inland Revenue Administration*, No. 26/62, Judgment, ECLI:EU:C:1963:1, 5 February 1963.

14 CJEU, *Simmenthal*, No. 106/77, Judgment, ECLI:EU:C:1978:49, 9 March 1978.

EU did not possess the authority to enact criminal norms. This position has changed over time, especially after the implementation of the principle of primacy, as developed in the case law of the ECJ.[15] Hence, even criminal law (and consequently all the principles that form the identity of the respective domestic systems – *in primis* the principle of legality) had to cope with the primacy of EU law. There can as a result be no domestic criminal law sanction which is incompatible with EU law, that is domestic criminal law is 'neutralised' by EU law.[16]

Thus, the effects of the primacy principle are for the most part twofold: the obligation to interpret domestic legislation in accordance with EU law (primary and secondary)[17] and the non-application of national criminal norms which contravene or undermine EU law. Primacy operates with reference to criminal law rules that are more severe than what are required by EU law and vice versa, granting full effectiveness to EU law within the domestic criminal sphere. Moreover, primacy, as said, affects every branch of the law (from criminal to constitutional law); it is now capable of neutralizing a domestic criminal law sanction.[18]

The interference between criminal law and European law determines, therefore, a plurality of effects that can be defined as mediated or indirect and can generally be summarised in three aspects: integration of domestic law; interpretation and non-application. Primacy must, in fact, be construed with a view to its ability to penetrate. If we think of the interaction between ECL and national law as busy crossroad, then the judge becomes a sort of traffic control officer, who has the role to manage the legal traffic.

The above-mentioned difficulty of matching domestic criminal law and European law clearly comes to light in the case law of the ECJ, in particular in the cases of *Melloni, Taricco,* and *El Dridi, Åkerberg Fransson* and *Garlsson* to be discussed in the following text.[19]

15 V. Mitsilegas, *EU Criminal Law after Lisbon. Rights, Trust and the Transformation of Justice in Europe*, Oxford: Hart Publishing, 2016; J. A. E. Vervaele, *European Criminal Justice in the Post Lisbon Area of Freedom, Security and Justice*, Naples: Editoriale Scientifica, 2014.

16 K. Ambos, European Criminal Law, p. 341.

17 For a first statement of this obligation see CJEU, *Von Colson & Kamann v. Land Nordrhein-Westfalen*, No. 14/83, Judgment, ECLI:EU:C:1984:153, 10 April 1984.

18 However, considering the boundaries imposed by the principles of subsidiarity and proportionality, see K. Ambos, European Criminal Law, p. 17.

19 CJEU, *Melloni v. Ministerio*, No. C-399/11, Judgment, ECLI:EU:C:2013:107, 26 February 2013; *Taricco and Others*, No. C-105/14, Judgment, ECLI:EU:C:2015:555, 8 September 2015; *El Dridi*, No. C-61/11, Judgment, ECLI:EU:C:2011:268, 28 April 2011.

4.4 The Duty of Loyalty

The principle of primacy is not only directed to national judges but also (and primarily) towards MS, which are bound to respect and enforce the rules and laws of the EU so as to secure full effectiveness to the rights provided for by the Treaties.[20] In this sense, the ECJ has gradually transformed primacy from a general principle of constitutional law to a specific obligation on States (and thus on their judges) to effectively enforce EU law in domestic courts.[21]

Hence, domestic criminal law is also affected by the duty of loyalty enshrined in Article 4 (3) TEU: 'pursuant to the principle of sincere cooperation, the Union and the Member States shall, in full mutual respect, assist each other in carrying out tasks which flow from the Treaties'. This principle imposes an obligation on MS to actively ensure compliance with the EU legal framework, to facilitate the achievement of Union tasks and to abstain from any contravening measures. Furthermore, it encompasses the responsibility of States to protect the Union's legal interests (protection of financial interests as well as other interests which concern the existence and functioning of the Union).[22] In the words of the ECJ,

> this principle not only requires the Member States to take all the measures necessary to guarantee the application and effectiveness of Community law, if necessary by instituting criminal proceedings,[23] but also imposes on Member States and the Community institutions mutual duties of sincere cooperation.[24]

From the principle of sincere cooperation derives another postulate: States, in applying the content of a directive in their national legal

[20] V. Mitsilegas, 'The Normative Foundations of European Criminal Law', in R. Schütze (ed.), *Globalization and Governance*, Cambridge: Cambridge University Press, 2018; C. Briére and A. Weyembergh, *The Needed Balances in EU Criminal Law. Past, Present and Future*, Oxford: Hart Publishing, 2018; A. Klip, *European Criminal Law. An Integrative Approach*, 4th edn., Cambridge: Intersentia, 2021, pp. 25 ff.

[21] M. Klamert, *The Principle of Loyalty in EU Law*, Oxford: Oxford University Press, 2013.

[22] K. Ambos, European Criminal Law, p. 18.

[23] See CJEU, *Commission of the European Communities v. Hellenic Republic*, No. 68/88, Judgment, ECLI:EU:C:1989:339, 21 September 1989, paras. 23, 2965.

[24] CJEU, *J. J. Zwartveld and Others*, No. C-2/88, Order of the Court, ECLI:EU:C:1990:440, 6 December 1990, para. 8; see also *Grand Duchy of Luxembourg v. European Parliament*, No. 230/81, Judgment, ECLI:EU:C:1983:32, 10 February 1983, paras. 37, 255.

system, must not simply transpose it through their legislative organs but are also obliged to effectively apply it through their judicial bodies, using their discretional assessment so as to respect the rationale of the supranational act.[25] As a matter of fact, the ECJ

> [...] observed that where Community legislation does not specifically provide any penalty for an infringement or refers for that purpose to national laws, regulations and administrative provisions, Article 5 of the Treaty requires the Member States to take all measures necessary to guarantee the application and effectiveness of Community law. For that purpose, whilst the choice of penalties remains within their discretion, they must ensure in particular that infringements of Community law are penalized under conditions, both procedural and substantive, which are analogous to those applicable to infringements of national law of a similar nature and importance and which, in any event, make the penalty effective, proportionate and dissuasive.[26]

This entails a minimum level of criminal law protection under Union Law.[27] On the other hand, MS must intervene in producing legislation that provides effective protection to EU law and interest.[28] It is important to note that violations of such norms are to be punished under conditions that are equal to those applicable in case of infringement of national laws of a similar nature (principle of equal treatment amounting to the assimilation of Union and national law of MS).[29] In this context, it has been noted that Art. 325 (2) TFEU serves as *the concretisation and consolidation of assimilation by means of criminal law*.[30] Notwithstanding its precise placement in Art. 4 (3) TEU, the duty of loyalty became a general principle of Union law that certainly applies beyond the specific wording of Art. 4.[31] The MS, therefore, have the duty to apply the principle of loyal cooperation, intended as a positive obligation to act and as a negative duty to refrain from acting against EU interests. This principle,

[25] M. Caianiello and V. Manes, *Introduzione al diritto penale europeo*, Turin: Giappichelli, 2020, p. 6.

[26] CJEU, *Commission of the European Communities v. Hellenic Republic*, No. 68/88, Judgment, ECLI:EU:C:1989:339, 21 September 1989, para. 24.

[27] K. Ambos, European Criminal Law, pp. 338 ff.

[28] Ibid. [29] Ibid.

[30] V. Mitsilegas, 'From Overcriminalisation to Decriminalisation: The Many Faces of Effectiveness in European Criminal Law', (2014) 5 *NJECL*, 419.

[31] M. Klamert, The Principle of Loyalty in EU Law, p. 11.

however, also creates tensions in the field of criminal law, especially with regard to judicial activity. In this context the question arises as to how a conflict between EU law and the founding constitutional principles of a specific country should be handled from the perspective of sincere cooperation.[32]

4.5 Mechanisms of Penetration of EU Law

EU law penetrates the national legal systems of the MS through the actions of the judges, which can either carry out a conforming interpretation of national norms according to EU law or disapply a domestic rule contravening EU law.

4.5.1 The Power of Disapplying National Criminal Law Contravening EU Law

National judges have the power and the duty to disapply domestic criminal law when it is in contrast with an EU rule that has direct effects or is directly applicable. This can be seen as the tool that resolves antinomies without giving rise to abrogation or other forms of cancellation of domestic norms incompatible with EU law. This power represents the most relevant and disruptive manifestation of the 'internal' criminal effects of EU law. In other words, through disapplication EU non-criminal law acquires the strength to directly affect the criminal regimes of the MS. This has been the subject of the well-known *Taricco* affair.[33] As to the power (and the duty) of the national judge to disapply internal rules incompatible with directly applicable EU provisions, we can refer to an illustrative case concerning a preliminary ruling referred by the Tribunal of Larino (*case C-338/04*) in the joint cases *C-338/04*, *C-359/04* and *C-360/04*. Here the ECJ, after affirming that, in principle, criminal legislation is reserved to the competence of MS, points out that European law limits this competence, since it

[32] K. Ambos, European Criminal Law, pp. 338 ff.

[33] F. Giunta, 'Europa e Diritto penale, tra line di sviluppo e nodi problematici', (2020) *Criminalia*, 9.

must not entail a restriction of the fundamental freedoms guaranteed by EU law.[34] The Court concluded that European provisions must be interpreted as precluding national legislation sanctioning those who engaged in collecting bets without the required license not issued by the MS, in breach of European law.[35]

4.5.2 Interpretation

A further consequence of primacy is that MS must construe and interpret their national (criminal) law in a way that achieves compliance with EU law.[36] Otherwise the respective national law would have to be superseded by EU law.[37] Thus, once again, national courts play a central role in the application and interpretation of EU law. As mentioned above, when called upon to settle a dispute between private parties in which the national legislation in question is contrary to EU law, national courts must ensure that individuals are afforded the judicial protection resulting from the provisions of EU law and guarantee its full effectiveness.[38] It should be noted that the principle of interpretation not only concerns substantive rules but also those of a procedural nature.[39] Generally speaking, however, interpretation cannot and should not expand punishment.[40] Therefore, the decision-making process of the domestic judge in resolving conflicts and inconsistencies between national and European law unfolds in two ways: interpretation in accordance with EU law or disapplication of national laws contravening EU law. The option to disapply a national provision, however, *arises only if no conforming interpretation of this provision is possible.*[41]

[34] See CJEU, *Calfa*, No. C-348/96, Judgment, ECLI:EU:C:1999:6, 19 January 1999, para. 17.

[35] See CJEU, *Placanica et al.*, Joined Cases Nos. C-338/04, C-359/04, C-360/04, Judgment, ECLI:EU:C:2007:133, 6 March 2007, para. 64.

[36] H. Satzger, *International and European Criminal Law*, Oxford: Hart Publishing, 2018; V. Mitsilegas, *EU Criminal Law*, Oxford: Hart Publishing, 2009, pp. 107 ff.

[37] K. Ambos, European Criminal Law, p. 343.

[38] See CJEU, *Dansk Industri (DI), acting on behalf of Ajos A/S v. Estate of Karsten Eigil Rasmussen*, No. C-441/14, Judgment, ECLI:EU:C:2016:278, 19 April 2016.

[39] K. Ambos, European Criminal Law, p. 344. [40] Ibid., p. 345.

[41] CJEU, *Maribel Dominguez v. Centre informatique du Centre Ouest Atlantique and Préfet de la région Centre*, No. C-282/10, Judgment, ECLI:EU:C:2012:33, 24 January 2012, para. 23. On the limits of EU primacy towards interpretation, see recently *Poplawski*, No. C-573/17, Judgment, ECLI:EU:C:2019:530, 24 June 2019, para. 109.

4.6 Relevant Case Law

4.6.1 *Stefano Melloni v. Ministerio Fiscal*: (Higher) National Standards and Cooperation in Criminal Matters

The case *Stefano Melloni v. Ministerio Fiscal* concerns the relationship between the standards of protection adopted by EU law on fundamental rights in cases of cross-border cooperation in criminal matters and those of the MS, which may impose a higher level of protection in comparison. In fact, this case encompasses many of the contradictions mentioned above. The ECJ was called upon to examine the compatibility of Article 4 *bis* of framework decision (FD) 2002/584/JHA, as amended by Framework Decision 2009/299/JHA (that is the FD on the European Arrest Warrant, EAW), with Articles 47 and 48 (2) of the EU Charter of Fundamental Rights. The referring court asked for a clarification of Article 53 of the Charter, that is, whether it is possible to derogate from the principle of primacy of EU law when national constitutional provisions ensure a higher standard of protection.[42]

Mr. Melloni was convicted by the Court of Ferrara in an *in absentia* proceeding. The Attorney General of the Bologna Court of Appeal issued a EAW against Mr. Melloni, who was then arrested in Spain. The competent Spanish judge authorised the execution of the warrant, but Melloni lodged a *recurso de amparo* before the *Tribunal Constitucional*, alleging an indirect violation of the mandatory requirements of the right to a fair trial enshrined in Article 24(2) of the Spanish Constitution. The Spanish court referred three questions to the ECJ: firstly, it asked for an interpretation of Article 4*bis* of FD 2009/299/JHA in order to establish whether it requires the executing judicial authority to make the execution of a EAW subordinate to the condition that the conviction pronounced *in absentia* may be reviewed in the issuing MS; secondly, to assess the compatibility of Article 4*bis* of the FD with Articles 47 and 48(2) of the Charter; lastly, whether Spain could rely on Article 53 of the Charter to safeguard, also in the context of the application of the FD, the highest level of protection guaranteed by the national Constitution. Article 53, labelled '*level of protection*', reads as follows:

[42] S. Peers, T. Hervey, J. Kenner and A. Ward (eds.), *The EU Charter of Fundamental Rights*, Oxford: Hart Publishing, 2021.

Nothing in this Charter shall be interpreted as restricting or adversely affecting human rights and fundamental freedoms as recognised, in their respective fields of application, by Union law and international law and by international agreements to which the Union, the Community or all the Member States are party, including the European Convention for the Protection of Human Rights and Fundamental Freedoms, and by the Member States' constitutions.

At first sight, this provision recalls Article 53 of the European Convention on Human Rights, which establishes the subsidiary nature of the level of protection guaranteed by the Convention with respect to the possibly higher level of protection guaranteed by national law or other law applicable in the Contracting States. However, if this were the case, one would have to conclude that Article 53 of the Charter would make an exception to the principle of primacy of Union law given that a higher level of constitutional protection should always be maintained. Yet, the ECJ has peremptorily ruled out this interpretation of Article 53 on the grounds that it 'would undermine the principle of the primacy of EU law'.[43] The Court recalled that 'it is settled case-law that, by virtue of the principle of primacy of EU law, which is an essential feature of the EU legal order [...] rules of national law, even of a constitutional order, cannot be allowed to undermine the effectiveness of EU law on the territory of that State'.[44]

The ECJ, therefore, rejected the argument that a MS, to avoid a lowering of its constitutional protection, could invoke Article 53 of the Charter to make the surrender of a person sentenced *in absentia* conditional upon the possibility of a review of the sentence in the MS having issued the EAW. The Court concluded that Spain could not reject Mr. Melloni's extradition on this ground since this would undermine the primacy and effectiveness of Union law.

4.6.2 The El Dridi Case: The Objective of Ensuring the Effectiveness of European Union law

This proceeding concerned an Algerian citizen, Hassen El Dridi, who had illegally entered Italy without a residence permit and had been sentenced in the first instance, on April 28, 2011, to one year of imprisonment for

43 CJEU, *Melloni v. Ministerio*, No. C-399/11, Judgment, ECLI:EU:C:2013:107, 26 February 2013, para. 50.

44 Ibid., para. 59; see also CJEU, *Winner Wetten GmbH v. Bürgermeisterin der Stadt Bergheim*, No. C-409/06, Judgment, ECLI:EU:C:2010:503, 8 September 2010, para. 61.

not complying with the order to leave the Italian territory issued on the basis of an expulsion decree. The Court of Appeal of Trento asked the ECJ to assess whether the Italian sentence was compatible with Articles 15 and 16 of Directive 2008/115/EC, which regulate conditions, methods and limits of detention of foreigners in special temporary centres during the administrative procedure of return.

Primacy of European law can lead either to a *widening* or a *narrowing* of the scope of national criminal law. In fact, in case the national criminal legal system already has a relevant criminal offense, the application of EU law might paralyze its application. In other words, EU law can overcome national rules that lead to a deprivation of liberty, with an ensuing enhancement of liberty. Nonetheless, such direct effectiveness depends on the clarity and precision of the EU rule, as clearly emerged in the case of *El Dridi*. In this case, the Return Directive (2008/115/EC) proved sufficiently precise as to paralyze Italian domestic law, that is, which provided for the imprisonment of third-country nationals who illegally remained on the territory of the State, failing to comply with the order to leave the country. According to the Court, national legislation must be interpreted in a way that does not frustrate the *effet utile* of EU rules and thus the achievement of the objective underlying the Directive.

Concerning the impact of Union law on the law of MS, the Luxembourg judges enunciated the following principle: 'States may not apply rules, even criminal law rules, which are liable to jeopardise the achievement of the objectives pursued by a directive and, therefore, deprive it of its'.[45] It follows that if the *effect utile* of domestic legislation is rendered vain by domestic legislation, the Italian judge will have to disapply it.

In particular, the directive aims to reconcile the effectiveness of return procedures and the protection of the fundamental rights of aliens. To this end, the Court specified that 'even the use of the latter measure, which is the most serious constraining measure allowed under the directive under a forced removal procedure, is strictly regulated, pursuant to Articles 15 and 16 of that directive, inter alia in order to ensure observance of the fundamental rights of the third-country nationals concerned'.[46] The Court therefore pointed out that the establishment of a mandatory maximum duration of detention 'serves the purpose of limiting the deprivation

[45] CJEU, *El Dridi*, No. C-61/11, Judgment, ECLI:EU:C:2011:268, 28 April 2011, para. 55.
[46] Ibid., para. 46.

of third-country nationals' liberty in a situation of forced removal'.[47] The Court also noted that Article 8 (4) of the Directive allows the State to take all coercive measures necessary to enforce the return decision through the removal of the alien, including those of a criminal nature, 'aimed inter alia at dissuading those nationals from remaining illegally on those States' territory'.[48] Detention, however, is to be distinguished from imprisonment and arrest as punishments.

Consequently, the Member States may not, in order to remedy the failure of coercive measures adopted in order to carry out forced removal pursuant to Article 8(4) of that directive, provide for a custodial sentence, such as that provided for by Article 14(5b) of Legislative Decree No 286/1998, on the sole ground that a third-country national continues to stay illegally on the territory of a Member State after an order to leave the national territory was notified to him and the period granted in that order has expired; rather, they must pursue their efforts to enforce the return decision, which continues to produce its effects.[49]

In fact, in addition to jeopardising the protection of the fundamental rights of individuals, a prison sentence results in delaying the execution of the return decision, thus jeopardising the achievement of the objective pursued by the directive, namely, the establishment of an effective policy for the removal and repatriation of illegally staying third-country nationals.[50]

The national court, called upon, within the exercise of its jurisdiction, to apply and give full effect to European Union law provisions, will have to refuse to apply any provision of the Legislative Decree No 286/1998 resulting in contrast with the result of Directive 2008/115, including Article 14(5b) of that legislative decree.[51]

That was in accordance with the established case law of the Court originating with the *Simmenthal* case.

The *El Dridi* case had an impact on Article 14, paragraph 5-ter of Legislative Decree no. 286/98, leading, in fact, to the abolition of the mentioned crime. As a result of this case, the Italian legislator replaced the penalty for the offence of irregular entry and stay with a fine, except for the case of irregular re-entry, which is still punished with imprisonment.

[47] Ibid., para. 43. [48] Ibid., para. 52.
[49] Ibid., para. 58. [50] Ibid., para. 59. [51] Ibid., para. 61.

4.6.3 The *Taricco* Case: Obligation to Disapply Provisions of National Law Liable to have an Adverse Effect on the Fulfilment of Member States' Obligations under EU Law

In the *Case C-105/14 Ivo Taricco and Others, of the 8 of September 2015,* the ECJ imposed upon MS (*in casu* Italy) the duty to effectively sanction fraud against the EU budget in violation of national procedural rules. The Taricco saga illustrates several critical issues, such as those related to the separation of powers and rule of law. It shows how the principle of sincere cooperation has significantly limited the power of national judicial authorities and their interpretative discretion, calling for an interpretation of national law consistent with European law.[52] It also demonstrates how the duty of loyal cooperation has been pushed to the point of infiltrating the autonomy that was traditionally reserved to States in the field of criminal law. Fostering the boundaries of European primacy, Taricco challenges the direct effects implied by the EU law when the 'counter-limit doctrine'[53] is involved. In particular, in the criminal arena, the 'dialogue' between the domestic Constitutional Court and the ECJ strengthens the core of national identity, allowing the supranational provisions to take a step back whenever fundamental rights risk being jeopardised.

Following a preliminary appeal by the Court of Cuneo,[54] on September 8, 2015, the ECJ established the so-called *Taricco rule*:[55] this is the obligation of a national court to disapply domestic provisions on the statute of limitations when such rules prevent the imposition of effective and dissuasive sanctions in a case of fraud against the financial interests of EU, because the statute of limitations' period becomes shorter than that established by national law for similar cases

[52] R. Schütze, 'Direct Effect and Indirect Effects of Union Law', in R. Schütze and T. Tridimas (eds.), *Oxford Principles of European Union Law Vol. I*, Oxford: Oxford University Press, 2017, pp. 265 ff.

[53] The Italian Constitutional Court has identified the fundamental principles enshrined by the Constitution as an absolute limit to the primacy principle so that, in case of contrast, the national provision shall prevail (i.e. the 'counter-limits doctrine'): see M. Caianiello and V. Manes, *Introduzione al diritto penale europeo*, Turin: Giappichelli, 2020, p. 28.

[54] The request for a preliminary ruling under Article 267 TFEU from the Tribunale di Cuneo (Italy) has been made by decision of 17 January 2014.

[55] CJEU, *Taricco and Others*, No. C-105/14, Judgment, ECLI:EU:C:2015:555, 8 September 2015.

of fraud to the detriment of the financial interests of another MS.[56] On this basis, the court found an infringement of EU primary law by the national provisions as follows:

> A national rule in relation to limitation periods for criminal offences such as that laid down by the last subparagraph of Article 160 of the Penal Code, as amended by Law No 251 of 5 December 2005, read in conjunction with Article 161 of that Code – which provided, at the material time in the main proceedings, that the interruption of criminal proceedings concerning serious fraud in relation to value added tax had the effect of extending the limitation period by only a quarter of its initial duration – is liable to have an adverse effect on fulfilment of the Member States' obligations under Article 325(1) and (2) TFEU if that national rule prevents the imposition of effective and dissuasive penalties in a significant number of cases of serious fraud affecting the financial interests of the European Union, or provides for longer limitation periods in respect of cases of fraud affecting the financial interests of the Member State concerned than in respect of those affecting the financial interests of the European Union, which it is for the national court to verify. The national court must give full effect to Article 325(1) and (2) TFEU, if need be by disapplying the provisions of national law the effect of which would be to prevent the Member State concerned from fulfilling its obligations under Article 325(1) and (2) TFEU.[57]

In the Court's view, the 'Taricco Rule' does not violate the principle of legality as enshrined in Article 49 (3) of the Charter, interpreted according to Article 7 of the ECHR, because statutes of limitations are procedural in nature and therefore not covered by the principle of legality.[58] However, the Italian courts considered the Court's position to be in conflict with Articles 3, 11, 24, 25 second paragraph and 27 third paragraph, 101 second paragraph of the Italian Constitution, hence proceeding with a constitutional assessment of the law that ratified the Lisbon Treaty. It was especially noted that the application of Article 325 TFEU (establishing a shared responsibility of MS and the Union to protect its financial

[56] Press Office of the Italian Constitutional Court, *Frodi UE e prescrizione: la 'regola Taricco' è incostituzionale per contrasto con il principio di determinatezza in materia penale* (2018). Disposable at: www.cortecostituzionale.it/documenti/comunicatistampa/CC_CS_20180531112725.pdf.

[57] CJEU, *Taricco and Others*, No. C-105/14, Judgment, ECLI:EU:C:2015:555, 8 September 2015, para. 66.

[58] ECtHR, *Coëme and Others v. Belgium*, Appl. Nos. 32492/96, 32547/96, 32548/96, 33209/96 and 33210/96, Judgment, 22 June 2000, paras. 145–149.

interests) entailed the disapplication of the Italian Penal Code's provisions on the statute of limitations. Thus, from the national judicial perspective, the Taricco rule violates Article 25, para. 2, Italian Constitution, on three points: (i) the primacy of statutory law in criminal matters (*riserva di legge*): in civil law systems, only a politically accountable and democratically legitimised body – the Parliament – can create criminal law norms; (ii) requirement of certainty (s.c. *determinatezza/precisione*): judges are bound by positive law, they cannot make legislative judgments, such as the ones required by the Taricco rule (based on vague notions such as 'serious fraud' or 'significant number of cases' – judges enjoying too much room for discretion would 'legislate from the bench', with arbitrary and unpredictable results); (iii) prohibition of retroactivity: harsher punishment than the one the person could reasonably foresee at the time of the commission of the offense.

The Constitutional Court was asked by national judges to activate the s.c. *controlimiti doctrine*, that is, to apply the supreme principles of the Italian constitutional order that cannot be infringed even by the primacy of EU law (*conditional primacy*). This was followed by a further preliminary referral to the ECJ by the Constitutional Court. The ECJ then ruled that the national judge has the power to apply the domestic legislation in exceptional circumstances, namely if its non-application gave rise to a conflict with the principle of legality. The Court stated in the M.A.S. judgement:

> article 325(1) and (2) TFEU must be interpreted as requiring the national court, in criminal proceedings for infringements relating to value added tax, to disapply national provisions on limitation, forming part of national substantive law, which prevent the application of effective and deterrent criminal penalties in a significant number of cases of serious fraud affecting the financial interests of the European Union, or which lay down shorter limitation periods for cases of serious fraud affecting those interests than for those affecting the financial interests of the MS concerned, unless that disapplication entails a breach of the principle that offences and penalties must be defined by law because of the lack of precision of the applicable law or because of the retroactive application of legislation imposing conditions of criminal liability stricter than those in force at the time the infringement was committed.[59]

[59] CJEU, *Criminal proceedings against M.A.S. and M.B.*, No. C-42/17, Judgment, ECLI:EU:C:2017:936, 5 December 2017.

This decision was followed by a final ruling of the Constitutional Court (sentence n. 115 of 2018) which affirmed the absolute inapplicability of the 'Taricco rule'.[60] The Constitutional Court concluded that 'the inapplicability of the "Taricco rule," as recognized by the M.A.S. judgment, arised not only from the Constitution of the Republic [of Italy], but in Union law itself' and that the questions of constitutionality raised on the basis that the law was, instead, applicable, were unfounded. The Court affirmed:

> It remains well-established that it is only for the Court of Justice to interpret Union law in a uniform manner, and specify whether it has direct effect, it is also undoubted that, as recognized in the M.A.S. judgment, an interpretation that does not conform to the principle of certainty in criminal matters does not have any place in our legal system.[61]

4.6.4 The Åkerberg Fransson Decision: Applying National Law contravening EU Fundamental Rights

The Åkerberg Fransson decision[62] is considered a landmark judgment on the scope of application of the EU Charter in criminal matters and the interpretation of the *ne bis in idem* principle. The case regarded Åkerberg Fransson, a fisherman who had allegedly provided false information regarding his income tax and VAT, which resulted in a loss of wealth for the Swedish government. In 2007 Fransson had received administrative fines for the violations committed from 2004 to 2005. In 2009 he was indicted for serious tax offences, based on the same false information that had resulted in the administrative fines. Fransson argued that the criminal charges violated the *ne bis in idem* principle as provided in Article 50 Charter. Therefore, he asked for a dismissal of the charges on the ground that he had already been punished for the same acts in other proceedings. As the sanctions were established by Swedish national law,

[60] Italian Constitutional Court, Judgment No. 115, 10 April 2018, official translation available at www.cortecostituzionale.it/documenti /download/doc/recent_judgments/S_2018_115_EN.pdf.

[61] Ibid., para. 12. On the issue, see V. Manes, 'Taricco Endgame', in V. Mitsilegas, A. di Martino and L. Mancano (eds.), *The Court of Justice and European Criminal Law: Legal Cases in a Contextual Analysis*, Oxford: Hart Publishing, 2019, p. 188.

[62] CJEU, *Åklagaren v. Hans Åkerberg Fransson*, No. C-617/10, Judgment, ECLI:EU:C:2013:105, 26 February 2013.

the issue was whether the principles of the Charter were applicable to national rules for administrative and criminal sanctions regarding the violation of VAT legislation adopted in the implementation of Union law (Directive 2006/112/EC).

The Grand Chamber of the ECJ decided, in general, that MS need to comply with the rights set forth in the Charter whenever national legislation falls within the scope of Union Law.[63] In other words, the Charter is a constituent part of primary EU law and, as such, it is subject to the principles that regulate its relationship with national norms. More specifically, the Court ruled, first, that '[t]he *ne bis in idem* does not preclude a Member State from imposing successively, for the same acts of non-compliance to the VAT regulation, a tax penalty and a criminal penalty as long as the first penalty is not criminal in nature (a matter which is subject to national courts' scrutiny)'.[64] This has been criticised as the starting point of a 'problematic set of cases that water down the *ne bis in idem* guarantee under the Charter and set the Court of Justice on a course which may result in a conflict with the European Court of Human Rights (ECtHR)'.[65] Secondly, the Court affirmed that in cases where there is a conflict between provisions of domestic law and rights guaranteed by the Charter, the national court that has to apply EU law has the duty to give 'full effect to those provisions, if necessary refusing of its own motion to apply any conflicting provision of national legislation, even if adopted subsequently' and that the national court can do so without requesting or awaiting 'the prior setting aside of such a provision by legislative or other constitutional means'.[66] Hence, if the national judge ascertains that the first sanction issued was criminal in nature, the *ne bis in idem* principle as provided by Article 50 of the Charter applies. This means that the national judge has the duty/power to dismiss the case without having to wait for new legislation to be enacted.

[63] T. Lock, 'Fishing for Better Rights Protection: The Court of Justice on the Application of the Charter in the Member States and the Reach of ne bis in idem', in V. Mitsilegas, A. di Martino and L. Mancano (eds.), *The Court of Justice and European Criminal Law: Legal Cases in a Contextual Analysis*, Oxford: Hart Publishing, 2019, p. 245.

[64] CJEU, *Åklagaren v. Hans Åkerberg Fransson*, No. C-617/10, Judgment, ECLI:EU:C:2013:105, 26 February 2013.

[65] T. Lock, 'Fishing for Better Rights Protection: The Court of Justice on the Application of the Charter in the Member States and the Reach of ne bis in idem', in V. Mitsilegas, A. di Martino and L. Mancano (eds.), *The Court of Justice and European Criminal Law: Legal Cases in a Contextual Analysis*, Oxford: Hart Publishing, 2019, p. 245.

[66] CJEU, *Åklagaren v. Hans Åkerberg Fransson*, No. C-617/10, Judgment, ECLI:EU:C:2013:105, 26 February 2013, para. 45.

4.6.5 Garlsson Real Estate and Others v. Consob: National Legislation Providing for both an Administrative and a Criminal Penalty for the Same Acts

In the Garlsson Real Estate and Others v. Consob (the Italian national Stock Exchange Commission, *Commissione Nazionale per le Società e la Borsa*) decision of 2018 the ECJ addressed once again the issue of the scope and limits of application of the *ne bis in idem* principle. In 2007, the Italian Consob imposed an administrative fine on Mr. Ricucci, Magiste International and Garlsson Real Estate for anomalous price movements which had resulted in market manipulation. In 2008 Mr. Ricucci was also condemned in a criminal trial to three years of imprisonment for the same conducts, which were deemed extinguished through judicial pardon.

Under Article 14(1) and Article 5 of Directive 2003/6, MS are obliged to impose effective, proportionate and dissuasive administrative measures or sanctions against the persons responsible for market manipulation. The administrative sanctions have to be imposed without prejudice to the right of States to impose criminal penalties. Such dispositions were transposed into Article 187b(3)(c) of the Italian *Testo unico delle disposizioni in materia di intermediazione finanziaria* ('TUF').

Therefore, the referring court asked the ECJ two questions: firstly, whether Article 50 of the Charter must be interpreted as precluding the possibility of bringing administrative proceedings under national legislation against a person for market manipulation, even if the same person was already convicted in a criminal forum; secondly, whether the *ne bis in idem* principle grants a directly applicable right in the context of such disputes.

As was stated in Fransson, the principle of *ne bis in idem* prohibits the duplication of proceedings (and penalties that are criminal in nature) for the same acts against the same person. The Court affirmed that to assess whether the sanctions imposed by the TUF are criminal in nature, three criteria must be followed: the legal classification of the offence under national law, the intrinsic nature of the offence and the degree of severity of the penalty that the person concerned is liable to incur. This is to be determined by the referring court, so that the ECJ can provide clarification in its preliminary ruling. The Court affirmed that the fiscal breach embodied a criminal sanction and as such triggered the operation of Article 50, and in turn the operation of Article 52 (1) of the Charter.[67] With regards to the second question, following the reasoning made in Fransson, the ECJ reaffirmed that the Charter is an act of EU primary law and its application does not require further action from the EU or national authorities. It follows that the *ne bis in idem* principle grants individuals a directly applicable right, which can be raised in the context of a national dispute. Therefore, when national judges are faced with assessing the compatibility of national norms with the rights enshrined in the Charter they have a duty to give full effect to the provision of the Charter. This could result in a non-application of the potentially conflicting national norm, even when adopted after the Charter, without having to wait for the legislator to solve such a contradiction.[68]

4.7 Conclusions

The cases examined show the difficulties of interlocking two very different logics, such as the one behind EU law and the one behind criminal law. They also show both that criminal law has some very specific characteristics when interfering with EU law and that EU law encounters specific limits when encountering criminal law. In this regard and considering the most recent European jurisprudence however, it should be noted that the ECJ's approach is increasingly careful so as to safeguard fundamental rights and guarantees. On the one hand, this shows that, as previously mentioned, the three principles have destabilised the criminal sphere and in particular the principle of legality. On the other hand, these principles allowed the very principle of legality to renew and consolidate in its parameters.[69]

[67] 'Any limitation on the exercise of the rights and freedoms recognised by this Charter must be provided for by law and respect the essence of those rights and freedoms. Subject to the principle of proportionality, limitations may be made only if they are necessary and genuinely meet objectives of general interest recognised by the Union or the need to protect the rights and freedoms of others'.

[68] CJEU, *Garlsson Real Estate and Others,* No. C-537/16, Judgment, ECLI:EU:C:2018:193, 20 March 2018, paras. 64–68.

[69] On the issue, see the CJEU case law on EAW protecting the fundamental rights granted at the national level, even undermining the Union law's primacy: *Aranyosi* and *Căldăraru,* Joined Cases Nos. C-404/15 and C-659/15, Judgment, ECLI:EU:C:2016:198, 5 April 2016; *Celmer,* No. C-216/18, Judgment, ECLI:EU:C:2018:586, 25 July 2018. A similar path has recently been followed on the ground of right to remain silent and to avoid self-incrimination: *Consob,* No. C-481/19, Judgment, ECLI:EU:C:2021:84, 2 February 2021.

The system necessarily readjusts itself to reflect the evolution of this complex process. However, in doing so, it must follow a path of integration and dialogue. The approach is indeed one of 'unity within diversity' (*see Constitutional Court Taricco*).[70]

The key lies in, despite obvious limits, the dialogue between the courts, primarily deriving from the value of what is at stake: people's freedom.

Further Reading

K. Ambos, 'Comments on the Model Penal Code and European Criminal Law', in A. Klip (ed.), *Substantive Criminal Law of the European Union*, Antwerp: Maklu, 2011, pp. 227–232.

A. Klip, 'European Integration and Harmonisation and Criminal Law', in D. M. Curtin, J. M. Smits, A. Klip and J. A. McCahery (eds.), *European Integration and Law*, Antwerp: Intersentia, 2006, pp. 109–150.

K. Ligeti, 'Criminal Liability of Heads of Business', (2015) 4 *eucrim*, 145–150.

V. Mitsilegas, 'The Uneasy Relationship between the UK and the European Criminal Law: From Opt-Outs to Brexit', (2016) 63 *CLR*, 517–536.

J. Vogel, 'Why Is the Harmonisation of Penal Law Necessary? A Comment', in A. Klip and H. van der Wilt (eds.), *Harmonisation and Harmonising Measures in Criminal Law*, Amsterdam: Koninklijke, 2002, pp. 55–64.

[70] See V. Manes, 'Taricco Endgame', in V. Mitsilegas, A. di Martino and L. Mancano (eds.), *The Court of Justice and European Criminal Law: Legal Cases in a Contextual Analysis*, Oxford: Hart Publishing, 2019, pp. 188 ff.

5 Supranational Criminal Law, Harmonisation and Approximation

Kimmo Nuotio

5.1 Introduction

European Union (EU) criminal law as we know it is a product of intensive legal development on both legislative and judicial levels, accompanied by significant changes in the Treaty framework. In this article we will discuss the emergence and nature of harmonisation efforts with an emphasis especially on substantive criminal law. Our claim is that whereas during the Amsterdam era harmonisation of substantive criminal law was mainly regarded a competence issue, since entering of the Lisbon Treaty and together with strengthening of the role of the fundamental rights and human rights in the law of the EU the debates concerning European criminal law take place mainly on the level of adjudication. Harmonisation relates not only to the cornerstone principle of mutual recognition, but has a link as well to the debates on increased supranationalism as expressed by the 'Taricco saga' and the establishment of the European Public Prosecutor's Office (EPPO).[1]

In this article we will look at certain features of European criminal law, namely the ways in which harmonisation and approximation of the national criminal law systems should be understood as well as the features of supranational criminal law in this setting. We will look at these phenomena less from a technical legal theory point of view but rather from a broader perspective, including some remarks on the development of the principles as well as on how far European criminal law has developed within the current treaty framework. The development of European criminal law is part of the larger development of the European law, but it has its specificities as well.

If we look back at the history and development of European criminal law, in the early days it was not that self-evident which model of common approach would be followed and given a priority. The more renowned site of European interstate cooperation in the field of criminal

[1] Concerning EPPO, see also the article by S. Allegrezza, Chapter 17 in this volume.

policy, the Council of Europe (CoE), had promoted collaboration between the State parties and even beyond by means of international conventions addressing a variety of issues reaching out from conventions on extradition, mutual assistance in criminal matters to conventions on substantive criminal law matters. The CoE is thus using the typical tools of public international law and it has done so in a highly successful manner as it is exercising an impact regionally in Europe and it can even be considered a point of reference to many other regions in the world. The CoE has built its approach on a value basis which colours its activities.

In legal terms the European law on human rights was the key product. Even though the human rights law is often being enforced by soft means, in Europe the idea was to take rights seriously and to give a court, the European Court of Human Rights (ECtHR), the powers to look at how the State parties are performing. It was even given the right to deal directly with complaints from individual citizens. The Court, however, exercises external control as it only has the mandate to judge on whether the State in case has fulfilled its obligations stemming from the European Convention of Human Rights (ECHR). There may also be expert committees following up the performance as required by the various crime prevention conventions.

The CoE was and still is working in matters of substantive criminal law solely on the basis of international conventions which meant that the supranational elements were minimal and absent. Conventions in the field of substantive criminal do have a harmonizing effect on the legal orders of the State parties, but the State parties can pretty freely choose whether they are part of the particular conventions. The substantive issues dealt with were mostly not specifically ones of cross-border criminality. It was also possible to make reservations to the obligations arising from the conventions. Over the years the CoE has created specific European models and paved the way for a further European integration in the setting of the EU law. In some areas, such as law on terrorist offences, the CoE runs parallel to EU criminal law.

The story of the European Union (EU) follows a different path. Already in the 1960s the European Court of Justice (CJEU) held that the European law should be seen as a genuine legal order.[2] The Court has ever since worked to interpret and develop the norms and principles of European Community law, and later, when its mandate was expanded, European

[2] CJEU, *Van Gend en Loos*, No. 26–62, Judgment, ECLI:EU:C:1963:1, 5 February 1963.

law. Since the European law has the character of a genuine legal order, the legal effects of that order have the ability of being internal to the Member State's (MS) legal orders. In the 1990s, the EU, founded by the Maastricht Treaty, already knew Justice and Home Affairs cooperation, but all this had to happen and be coordinated by using conventional international law tools. Europol was founded, and in 1995 the Convention for the protection of the financial interests of the European union (PIF) was adopted.

The development of cooperation in Justice and Home Affairs was in several ways taking shape differently from what was the approach of the CoE. Interests of the Union itself started getting a weight, the general legal setting of the Union was very different, and also the threats posed by cross-border criminality were real. There was a clear awareness that the criminal law cooperation would need to be strengthened as also the Schengen arrangement, which was still not directly part of the EU framework, had progressed and the internal border controls were relaxed in that area. In the 1990s the consciousness grew that clearly something more was needed. Only few treaties had been negotiated and it took years to have them ratified and step into force.

5.2 The Origins of Supranationalism

Let me first state that when we deal with transnational legal phenomena, we are not always very precise in our use of the concepts. Often the word 'transnational' works well enough, if we wish to highlight that we speak of internationally legally regulated cross-border issues. Here I would distinguish 'supranational' from 'transnational' by referring to the feature that supranationality indicates a conferral of legal powers to institutions beyond the State in a qualitatively different manner.

Neil Boister has recently suggested that we should conceptualize as transnational criminal law the part of law which addresses serious cross-border criminality which often is organized and profit-driven since it seeks illegal economic benefit.[3] For Boister, the international Treaty on Organized Crime, the Palermo Convention from 2000 with its protocols, is the prototype of transnational criminal law.

[3] N. Boister, *An Introduction to Transnational Criminal Law*, 2nd edn., Oxford: Oxford University Press, 2018.

Much of what we have seen happening in the EU fits with the catchword transnational criminal law. The phenomenon of cross-border criminality has necessitated the interstate cooperation as a complementary measure, and the abolition of internal border checks has further reinforced that need.

The European Economic Community (and later the European Union) has created an internal legal order and is operating through established institutions. The normalization of criminal law cooperation in the EU has strengthened the distinct supranational features of it, and the recent establishment of EPPO is a clear sign that the legal integration has progressed far beyond being merely transnational. The history of supranationalism begins with the history of general EU law. In the context of community law, supranationalism is an important and debated issue, and without a doubt several community law principles are an expression of supranationalism.[4]

Even though the European Communities (EC) did not have the competence to issue criminal legislation, it was clear that EC law was relevant and could have legal implications on how the national criminal justice should be working. In the famous Greek Maize judgement the CJEU confirmed that an MS had the duty to protect the financial interests of the EC by means of criminal justice in a similar way it protected its own financial interests. This reasoning has played a crucial role with a view to the MS's shared responsibility in protecting the financial issues of the Union: '...whilst the choice of penalties remains within their discretion, they must ensure in particular that infringements of Community law are penalized under conditions, both procedural and substantive, which are analogous to those applicable to infringements of national law of a similar nature and importance and which, in any event, make the penalty effective, proportionate and dissuasive'.[5]

In the academic discussions ambitious proposals were being tabled. Most famous of them was the so-called *Corpus Iuris* proposal.[6] The idea of that proposal was to introduce a Penal Code for the territory of the

[4] See, for example, J. Weiler, 'The Community System: The Dual Character of Supranationalism', in F. G. Jacobs (ed.), *Yearbook of European Law 1981*, Oxford: Oxford University Press, 1982, pp. 267–306.

[5] CJEU, *Commission of the European Communities v. Hellenic Republic*, No. 68/88, Judgment, ECLI:EU:C:1989:339, 21 September 1989, para. 24.

[6] On the different models proposed, see for example C. Gómez-Jara Díez, 'Models for a System of European Criminal Law: Unification v. Harmonisation', (2010) 1 *NJECL*, 385–402.

European Union.[7] The Code would have entailed an embryo, a core of a truly European Penal Code. The substantive criminal law provisions were divided into two groups: offences committed by anyone and offences committed by officials.

The Corpus Iuris also included clearly supranational features. A European Public Prosecutor for these offences would have been provided, and a particular Judge of Freedom would have been appointed to secure the effectivity of the new system as well as to safeguard the legal guarantees of the accused and prosecuted persons. Further, it included a proposal for a European Arrest Warrant that a Judge of Freedom would have issued.

The academic discussion proceeded its way. The imagination of the professors was not limited by political realities or even realities related to the legal bases that the EU treaties provided. There is nothing wrong with that as such. But it was clear from the beginning that there would be no fast avenue which could lead to the adoption of the model in the short term.

5.3 Mutual Recognition and Minimum Harmonisation of Substantive Criminal Law

What happened in real life was rather a move away from supranationalism. In the Tampere EU Summit of 1999 the mutual recognition principle was set as the cornerstone principle for criminal law collaboration within the European Union. Harmonisation of substantive criminal law should be limited to the minimum, and it would be subordinated to the mutual recognition rationale which it would serve.

In fact, during the Amsterdam era, when framework decisions (FDs) were used as the harmonizing instruments, it all followed this logic of minimum harmonisation. If we look at the institutional development, the founding of Eurojust in 2000 as the body of collaboration with regard to prosecution of European cross-border cases was the main step taken. Eurojust was, however, not a supranational actor, but rather a kind of coordination unit through which national prosecutors could collaborate.[8]

[7] See the so-called Florence proposal from 2000. https://ec.europa.eu/anti-fraud/sites/antifraud/files/docs/body/corpus_juris_en.pdf.

[8] K. Ambos, *European Criminal Law*, Cambridge: Cambridge University Press, 2018, pp. 569 ff.

Together with the advancing of European integration it became increasingly evident that a new type of coordination was needed. If in the early days two States needed to cooperate in order to enforce the laws, now the criminality itself at issue was becoming of a cross-border type.

European Arrest Warrant (EAW) become reality rather quickly, since in the aftermath of 11 September (2001) the EU wanted to show a capability for fast action, and it issued two FDs simultaneously, one on terrorist offences,[9] the other on EAW.[10] The system of enforcing the EAWs was, however, built into the existing criminal justice structures, following the cornerstone principle of mutual recognition.

One could easily suggest that legal instruments such the EAW do not aim at any harmonisation since they are based on the principle of mutual recognition. This is, however, not the entire truth. The purpose of these instruments is to harmonize the rules of international criminal procedure through the backdoor, so to say, which make the mutual recognition principle work.[11] In this sense, the actual running of the EAW system was a promotor of increased approximation of substantive criminal law.

The specific history of how criminal law cooperation has entered the scene of EU law is still today relevant for understanding the character of the entire exercise. Criminal justice cooperation was something qualitatively different from creating a common market, which was the origin of an EU legal order. But, as we saw earlier, the general EU law also started exercising an influence on this field. Criminal law is a domain which has been traditionally almost exclusively been connected with state sovereignty. Only sovereign states may exercise criminal justice and this exercise is then also an expression of sovereignty. The Europeanisation of criminal justice – that was the term earlier in use – and the birth of European criminal law has therefore required specific adjustments.

EU criminal law grows out of this landscape. It deals for instance with crimes threatening the EU budget. But even more so, it deals with cross-border criminality, which often is being carried out in organized forms, as organized crime and with an economic motive. In substantive terms,

9 Council Framework Decision of 13 June 2002 on combating terrorism, OJ L 164, 22.6.2002, 3–7.

10 2002/584/JHA: Council Framework Decision of 13 June 2002 on the European arrest warrant and the surrender procedures between Member States, OJ L 190, 18.7.2002, 1–20.

11 P. Asp, *The Procedural Criminal Law Cooperation of the EU*, Stockholm: Stockholms universitet, Juridiska fakultetens skriftserie, 2016, p. 22.

the crimes that are of interest to the EU are the ones having an impact on European interests and values.

The first decade of the new millennium saw an active use of FDs which enabled approximation of the national laws in the MS for specific areas of criminality. This was the heyday of actual harmonisation of substantive criminal law.

In the architecture of the Amsterdam Treaty, the cooperation in criminal matters was still being dealt with separately and it followed its own legislative procedure. The aim was 'to provide citizens with a high level of safety within an area of freedom, security and justice by developing common action among the Member States'. The text of the Treaty did not yet define strictly the areas in which common action would be taken, but rather listed examples. At this point the MS were still controlling the development in this field since the Council had to decide unanimously on the measures to be taken. The Union Treaty provided in its Article 31 (e) that the common action in criminal matters shall include 'progressively adopting measures establishing minimum rules relating to the constituent elements of criminal acts and to penalties in the fields of organised crime, terrorism and illicit drug trafficking'.

There was a rush to create a European-wide approach to certain identified forms of cross-border criminality, and the minimum harmonisation was the means to get there. A full unification was completely rejected. During the Amsterdam era it was still a bit unclear what the powers of the European Communities were and what the EU could do. A famous dispute between the Council and the Commission concerned the fact whether a proposed FD on Protection of the Environment by means of criminal law infringed the powers of the European Communities. And since it did, the FD was annulled.[12] Another similar dispute concerned the fact whether the FD concerning the ship source pollution infringed the powers of the European Communities. Also in this case the FD was annulled.[13] The CJEU determined, however, that there was a difference between the powers of the European Communities and those of the EU: The 'determination of the type and level of the criminal penalties to be applied does not fall within the Community's sphere of competence'.[14]

[12] See CJEU, *Commission v. Council*, No. C-176/03, Judgment, ECLI:EU:C:2005:542, 13 September 2005.

[13] CJEU, *Commission v. Council*, No. C-440/05, Judgment, ECLI:EU:C:2007:625, 23 October 2007.

[14] Ibid., paras. 70, 71.

It is interesting to look at a book published in 2005 in which the situation as regards harmonisation of criminal law was being addressed.[15] In this book, Walter Perron described the very deficient European system in which the significant differences between the various European legal orders were seen as obstacles that would one way or another have to be overcome in order to realise a true area of freedom, security and justice with citizens trusting European institutions.[16] In that picture the rapid regulatory action coming through the European legislature, the Council, was not regarded as a way to reach that goal, since the problems reached deeper. The comparative knowledge of the differences between the legal orders was far too limited and it had become obvious that criminal law is profoundly embedded in national legal cultures. The case with criminal procedure was not that different, albeit in that area the human rights law had a shaping impact on the national systems. Perron was hoping that the European Parliament would be given a larger role and that hectic lawmaking would be avoided. He also pointed out that the EUCJ could play a bigger role in the field the way, as in fact it had in other fields. He even saw that a European Prosecutor – if ever established – would have a special impact on the harmonisation process. Perron was thus somewhat sceptical, but he still considered that in the long run, things could improve: '..., there is hope that with the harmonisation of statutes the application of the law will also move towards a more common European standard. With the coming together of the different societies we also have an approximation of sense of justice, which might lead one day to genuine European criminal law'.[17]

Petter Asp, in turn, discusses (in 2005) the link between mutual recognition and harmonisation. In the first place it seems that priority was given to the principle of mutual recognition simply as an alternative to harmonisation, as a way to avoid in-depth harmonisation in this sensitive field. The priority of the mutual recognition principle introduces a kind of enforcement perspective in which recognition of foreign decisions and judgements are seen as tools for enforcement, as enforcement

[15] E. J. Husabø and A. Strandbakken (eds.), *Harmonisation of Criminal Law in Europe*, Antwerpen: Intersentia, 2005.

[16] W. Perron, 'Perspectives of the Harmonisation of Criminal Law and Criminal Procedure in the European Union', in E. J. Husabø and A. Strandbakken (eds.), *Harmonisation of Criminal Law in Europe*, Antwerpen: Intersentia, 2005, pp. 5–22.

[17] Ibid., pp. 21–22.

orders. Such a view implies that also harmonisation, when combined with the mutual recognition principle, operates in the same instrumental setting. Recognition without harmonisation of substantive criminal law brings in the issue of trust, since it involves 'a journey to the unknown'.[18] If the mutual recognition instruments, such as the EAW, are not backed up by substantive harmonisation, albeit minimum harmonisation, it may be difficult to maintain the necessary trust since real life will teach us about differences of approach. Asp claims that it is easier to introduce and apply the principle of mutual recognition if there is at least a minimum level of harmonisation. He expects to see a dialectical development where the development in the two areas, mutual recognition and harmonisation, will mutually affect each other.[19]

In April 2004, the European Commission presented its Green Paper on the approximation, mutual recognition and enforcement of criminal sanctions in the EU. This took place on the eve of enlargement, namely, on the last day before ten new MS joined the EU. The awareness was rising that significant differences between the systems of punishment were causing problems in relation to creating/establishing a European area of justice and that harmonisation measures could help not only in securing the acceptance of mutual recognition of judgments, but more generally and symbolically send out a symbolic message. The approximation of penalties would 'give the general public a shared sense of justice' which is again one of the conditions for establishing the area of freedom, security and justice. Approximation of the definition of the offence and of the level of the penalty incurred for it, 'provides effective and equivalent protection for citizens throughout the Union against a phenomenon that strikes against the principles and values shared by the Member States'.[20]

This part of the Commission Green Paper did not have much consequences. The Green Paper summarised the findings of a research project which published its results also in book format. The key finding of the

[18] V. Mitsilegas, *EU Criminal Law*, Oxford: Hart, 2009, 119.

[19] P. Asp, 'Mutual Recognition and the Development of Criminal Law Cooperation within the EU', in E. J. Husabø and A. Strandbakken (eds.), *Harmonisation of Criminal Law in Europe*, Antwerpen: Intersentia, 2005, pp. 23–40.

[20] COM (2004) 334 final, 30 April 2004, at p. 9–10. See the discussion in K. Nuotio, 'Harmonisation of Criminal Sanctions in the European Union – Criminal Law Science Fiction', in E. J. Husabø and A. Strandbakken (eds.), *Harmonisation of Criminal Law in Europe*, Antwerpen: Intersentia, 2005, pp. 79–101.

exercise was that there are indeed deep variations between the systems of punishment of the selected MS, even though the systems of the ten new MS were not covered.[21]

The academics saw the landscape rather accurately. Nothing more than a minimum harmonisation could be expected and the mutual recognition principle had the lead. But this created a deadlock since the overriding enforcement paradigm maintained the model in which truly European interests could not really be expressed in this emerging system of European criminal justice, and also the deficient constitutional law setup and the deficient protection of the rights of the accused rendered any short-term real development unlikely. Anyway, the seeds were there and much more could be built on the premises, especially in the long-term perspective.

André Klip has pointed out that European criminal law should be seen in the larger setting of European law. The CJEU adopts a long-term perspective on legal issues and it has proven it can strike different balances and work out a European law approach to various issues. The CJEU has the ability to exercise its authority in a way that inevitably increases the role of Union law in this area at the cost of national law.[22]

5.4 The Lisbon Treaty as the Game-Changer

Together with the Lisbon Treaty, which entered into force in 2009, the normative framework of the European criminal law was once again reformed. The legislative work would now finally follow ordinary legislative procedures and directives would be used as instruments. The principle of mutual recognition of judgements and decisions is still the lead principle. Only when necessary to facilitate it shall directives for approximation of MS' legislation be adopted. Such directives may only contain minimum rules, and the differences between legal traditions shall be taken into account when adopting them. Approximation in terms of minimum harmonisation is subordinated to the practical needs in terms of the mutual recognition principle.

[21] M. Delmas-Marty, G. Guidicelli Delage and E. Lambert Abdelgawad (eds.), *L'harmonisation des sanctions pénales en Europe. Avec le soutien de la Commission Européenne et de la Mission de recherche Droit et Justice*, Société de législation comparée, 2003.

[22] A. Klip, *European Criminal Law*, Cambridge: Intersentia, 2021, Chapter 10.

The Lisbon Treaty normalized much of the position of criminal law within the EU law. Institutional development meant that standard legislative procedure would be applied even in this field. Powers of the CJEU were broadened. Procedural law could be addressed by means of harmonizing measures, with a special mention of admissibility of evidence, rights of the accused and rights of the victim.[23]

In what sense could then the legal traditions of the MS to be taken into account? Arguably, minimum rules should not be used to demolish central features in European legal traditions. This provision shows that the 'Masters of the Treaty' have still wanted to emphasize that the key features of criminal justice are linked with deeper values embedded in the national laws which make them fundamental. Another similar indication is the so-called emergency brake system. If MS see that a proposed directive would affect fundamental aspects of its criminal justice system,[24] it may refer the matter to the European Council; thus to a political discussion on a high level. A single reluctant MS can, however, not prevent others from proceeding.

The emergency break arrangement was created in order to calm down MS when the ordinary legislative procedure was adopted: a single MS can no longer stop the proceedings. Even though in principle the existence of such a mechanism is significant, in practice it has remained a dead letter. The difference to the previous legislative practice with unanimous voting in the Council is not that huge since even then the threshold of individual MS to stop a proposal during the negotiations was quite high. The mechanism of enhanced cooperation as such has been known already for long, and it has been used from time to time.

TFEU Article 83 provides the central rules on establishing minimum rules in this area. Minimum rules can be established concerning 'the definition of criminal offences and sanctions in the areas of particularly serious crime with a cross-border dimension resulting from the nature or impact of such offences or from a special need to combat them on a common basis'. The areas of crime have been expressly listed as follows: terrorism, trafficking in human beings and sexual exploitation of women and children, illicit drug trafficking, illicit arms trafficking, money laundering, corruption, counterfeiting of means of payment, computer crime

[23] See Art. 83(2) TFEU. [24] Art. 83(3) TFEU.

and organised crime. The Council may adopt a decision identifying even other areas of crime on the basis of developments in crime, but for such a decision unanimity is required. However, so far no new areas of crime have been added to the list.

TFEU Article 83(2) provides for the so-called annex competence in areas which already have been subject to previous harmonisation measures. If the approximation of criminal laws and regulations of the MS proves essential to ensure the effective implementation of a Union policy, directives may establish minimum rules with regard to the definition of criminal offences and sanctions in the area concerned. The TFEU provides for a clearer and more mature legal framework for approximation of the criminal law and norms of criminal procedure than the previous Amsterdam Treaty.[25]

The protection of the financial interests of EU against fraud never stopped being a central area of interest in the development of the normative setting of the European criminal even though the supranational elements were not particularly stressed. The EU had OLAF as a supranational enforcement institution, originally in the first pillar. The treaties were addressing it as well. The Lisbon Treaty entailed a revival of a certain supranational approach as the Article 86 TFEU set the scene for the establishment of EPPO arising out of Eurojust. The EPPO shall, among others, exercise the functions of the prosecutor in the competent courts of the MS to ensure a better protection of the Union's financial interests.

Article 325 TFEU restated the obligations of the MS to counter fraud affecting the financial interests of the Union through measures to be taken according to this article. Article 325 created a small world in itself since its position in the Treaty made it somewhat independent of the more cautiously written Article 83 with its emergency brake and other reservations.

After more than a decade, the thoughts originally drafted by the academics in the Corpus Iuris exercise became relevant again. The significance of EPPO is further underlined by the fact that its mandate could be further extended to cover other forms of serious crime with a cross-border element. The real new driver from now on would be the establishment of the EPPO, even though the reasons behind why it was needed as well as the expectations of what it could deliver were varying.[26]

[25] Art. 83(2) TFEU.

[26] See, for example, the discussion in Asp, The Procedural Criminal Law Cooperation of the EU, Chapter 7.

In 2017 the EPPO and the cooperation of the MS with it have been finally regulated.[27] The road to the 2017 Regulation was not smooth since there was no unanimity and thus the route of enhanced cooperation had to be taken.[28] After some delays, the EPPO finally started its operation on 1 June 2021.

The development of European criminal law has been a gradual process in which both the Masters' of the Treaty, the MS, and the CJEU have contributed. Strengthening of the protection of fundamental rights in establishing the criminal law cooperation in the EU has been one such clear feature. It is interesting that much of the harmonisation of the substantive criminal law through the means of FDs took place already before, or rather, parallel to the increase of the importance and the gaining of formal legal validity of the Charter of Fundamental Rights of the European Union (CFREU).

The more recent human rights focus has created new constellations to the logic of the way mutual recognition principle should be understood. We are familiar with this effect in light of certain EAW cases, Melloni (C-399/11), for instance. The judgments of the CJEU in Aranyosi and Căldăraru (C-404/15 and C-659/15) opened up the avenue that the strict logic of mutual trust as a kind of blind trust would require additional tests. The case LM, C-216/18, took the matter to another level, that is, rule of law and judicial independence. The CJEU has been forced to create a room for discretion, albeit a narrow corridor, for circumstances in which the surrender should be refused.

As regards the particular area of protection of the financial interests of the Union, the Taricco saga deserves a special mention. It highlights the novel landscape of EU criminal law in which the strive for effectivity in order to protect the financial interests of the EU may threaten the constitutional values of the MS, in this case the principle of legality and the law on statutory limitations. The much-discussed Taricco I case raised this issue and suggested that the domestic court would have to solve the tension by not compromising the effective protection of the EU financial

[27] Council Regulation (EU) 2017/1939 of 12 October 2017 implementing enhanced cooperation on the establishment of the European Public Prosecutor's Office ('the EPPO').

[28] The Regulation has been amended by the Commission delegated regulation (EU) 2020/2153 of 7 October 2020 as regards the categories of operational personal data and the categories of data subjects whose operational personal data may be processed in the index of case files by the EPPO.

interests and by ensuring that EU law is given full effect, even if this entails the displacement of national legislation. The Italian court which referred the case to CJEU was worried that the amendments of the Italian law concerning the complex system of limitation periods were rendering them so short that in fact a sort of impunity resulted since in a majority of cases the limitation would operate as a bar to effective prosecution.

The CJEU sent a strong message to the MS, stressing, inter alia, that the rules on statutory limitation could have an adverse effect on fulfilment of the MS' obligations under Articles 325(1) and (2) TFEU if such rules prevent the imposition of effective and dissuasive penalties in a significant number of cases of serious fraud affecting the financial interests of the EU: 'The national court must give full effect to Article 325(1) and (2) TFEU, if need be by disapplying the provisions of national law the effect of which would be to prevent the Member State concerned from fulfilling its obligations under Article 325(1) and (2) TFEU.'[29] The CJEU doubted of whether the Italian legislature had ensured the effective criminalisation of the acts in question, and it instructed the domestic court accordingly.

At any rate, this did not close the issue since another referral for a preliminary ruling followed, now by the Constitutional Court of Italy. The so-called Taricco II judgement of the EUCJ did not technically concern the same criminal proceedings, but rather related to the principle and the outcomes of the Taricco I judgment.[30] In the latter setting two Italian courts had already taken the stance that they would disapply the relevant limitation period as indicated by Taricco I. The Constitutional Court, however, expressed its doubts on whether such an interpretation would interfere with the legality principle, that is, that offences and penalties must be defined by law in a precise manner and cannot be applied retroactively.

The Constitutional Court explained that in the Italian legal system the rules on limitation in criminal matters are substantive in character and fall within the scope of the legality principle as understood in Article 25 of the Italian Constitution. Those rules must therefore be established by provisions that are precise and are in force at the time when the offence in question was committed. The Constitutional Court considered that it is

[29] CJEU, *Taricco et al.*, No. C-105/14, Judgment, ECLI:EU:C:2015:555, 8 September 2015.

[30] CJEU, *M.A.S., M.B. ('Taricco II')*, No. C-42/17, Judgment, ECLI:EU:C:2017:936, 5 December 2017.

for the national courts to decide whether the Taricco rule complies with the requirement of 'determination' indispensable for criminal law.

The CJEU reminded that Article 325 TFEU builds on the idea of shared competence and thus, even though the MS have discretion in how they formulate their rules on statutory limitation, they however need to ensure that criminal proceedings may be successfully completed within the given time limits. The CJEU concluded that the national courts should respect and give due concern to the principle of legality and non-retroactive criminal legislation. Thus, the role of these criminal law principles as constitutional principles needs to be taken into account even at the cost that the respective MS would be in breach of its obligations under Article 325. It would then be the duty of the legislature to amend the domestic legislation accordingly.[31]

We can thus see the affirmation of the legality principle, but at the same time the MS' obligation to effectively protect the Union budget by means of their criminal law. The CJEU differentiated between the legislative and the adjudicative level. It also managed to restrict the consequences of its latter more fundamental rights friendly view which threatened to soften the more absolutist pro-EU approach taken in Taricco I.

The Taricco saga shows once again the CJEU's ability to defend the core principles of the general EU law, such as its primacy, as well as of EU criminal law more specifically without risking a too direct conflict with the constitutional values of the MS. There is only a narrow corridor in which this can be successfully done, but the CJEU has demonstrated its ability to navigate in this zone.[32] This also shows that criminal law cases invite constitutional courts and the CJEU to engage in a dialogue on how to approach such tensions.[33]

Taricco I raised the challenge, and there were a variety of interpretations of what was happening. Was the CJEU mainly seeking to strengthen the constitutional dimension of EU criminal law by stressing the primacy of EU law? Silvia Allegrezza has put this judgement in the context of the negotiations of the PIF directive. According to

[31] CJEU, *M.A.S., M.B. ('Taricco II')*, No. C-42/17, Judgment, ECLI:EU:C:2017:936, 5 December 2017.

[32] V. Manes, 'Some Lessons from the Taricco Saga', (2018) 9(1) *NJECL*, 12–17. The role of the constitutional principles has later been further underlined in CJEU, *Dzivev et al.*, No. C-310/16, Judgment, ECLI:EU:C:2019:30, 17 January 2019.

[33] M. Bonelli, 'The Taricco Saga and the Consolidation of Judicial Dialogue in the European Union', (2018) 25(3) *Maastricht J. Eur. Comp. L.*, 357–373.

that view the CJEU wanted to highlight that EU criminal law obligations can be extended to VAT frauds and that this is a pre-existing obligation stemming directly from the treaties.[34] There is a further edge on this lesson as well, namely, that the national discretion has to do with the fact that the limitation periods were not harmonised at the European level. Once that happens, the possibilities of the national legislature and courts to determine scope of the legality principle will be put an end.[35] This has been taken up by the PIF directive from 2017[36] which finally replaced the PIF convention, stating in its article 12(1): 'Member States shall take the necessary measures to provide for a limitation period that enables the investigation, prosecution, trial and judicial decision of criminal offences ... for a sufficient period of time after the commission of those criminal offences, in order for those criminal offences to be tackled effectively.'

5.5 From a Narrow Dialectic towards a Broader Justice Framework

As concerns our topic of the shifting role of harmonisation in EU criminal law and policy, here we find that the entire setting has clearly become much more complex than before. The legal issues regarding the limits of legislative competence have been replaced by much more complicated settings.[37] The problematic national legal norms on the limitation periods as regards tax frauds were risking the effectivity of the fight against fraud threatening the EU budget. At the same time this situation created a conflict with domestic constitutional principles which apparently call for the application of statute of limitations. The EU response to this was to harmonise these rules in the context of the protection of the EU's financial interests and thus to make effective and successful criminal proceedings possible. Thus, while in the traditional context harmonisation was needed

[34] S. Allegrezza, 'On Legality in Criminal Matters between Primacy of EU Law and National Constitutional Traditions. A Study of the Taricco Saga', in V. Mitsilegas, A. di Martino and L. Mancano (eds.), *The Court of Justice and European Criminal Law*, Oxford: Hart 2019,165, 165 ff.

[35] Ibid, V.

[36] Directive (EU) 2017/1371 of the European Parliament and of the Council of 5 July 2017 on the fight against fraud to the Union's financial interests by means of criminal law, OJ L 198/29, 28.7.2017.

[37] This was observed already in Mitsilegas, EU Criminal Law, p. 110.

to increase trust and make mutual recognition instruments work, now harmonisation may be needed to solve the possible arising tensions with constitutional criminal law principles.

The logic of the development is rather interesting. We should think back and remember that in the very beginning the mutual recognition principle was chosen as the cornerstone principle in order to get around the need to (fully) harmonise substantive criminal law in the first place. But when adopting instruments based on the mutual recognition principle, such as the EAW, there are obvious benefits to combine at least some harmonising measures with it. The larger EU law setting has affected this dialectic in several ways. The principle of primacy of EU law has given the CJEU a tool to strengthen the European perspective. In the context of the discussion on defence rights issues relevant in transnational procedural justice going beyond one single legal order have been addressed. Fundamental rights which could have acted as a limiting force have become drivers of mutual recognition.

If we refer back to the early days and the views that scholars had almost twenty years ago, we will see that the European criminal law has matured significantly. The fast minimum harmonisation during the Amsterdam area in a variety of fields was causing too simplified expectations of what criminal justice can deliver. It was built on a rather simplistic belief in securing effective control. In the shadows of this development other things took place as well. The Lisbon treaty framework was already more balanced, and the CFREU complemented that renewed setting significantly. The CJEU has elaborated on the existing normative materials and sought to integrate EU criminal law in the general EU law, at the same time recognising the sensitivities related to this area, as has been realized also by the Treaty makers. The tensions between general EU law and EU criminal law have not disappeared, but the process of 'learning through experience' continues.[38]

Protection of the financial interests of the Union has shown to be an important driver as well. It represents truly European interests, and the approach adopted already in the 1980s has carried all the way through to these days. With the EPPO now fully operational, we will be witnessing

[38] E. Herlin-Karnell, *The Constitutional Dimension of European Criminal Law*, Oxford: Hart, 2012, 237. For a useful discussion, see M. Kettunen, *Legitimizing European Criminal Law: Justification and Restrictions*, Cham: Springer, 2020. See also K. Nuotio, 'European Criminal Law', in M. Dubber and T. Hörnle (eds.), *Oxford Handbook of Criminal Law*, Oxford: Oxford University Press, 2014, pp. 1115–1138.

one more step in this development. As indicated earlier, the powers of EPPO might later be even further extended to cover serious forms of cross-border criminality.

European criminal law is an evolving concept, and we can see that the emphasis has shifted several times depending on which principle has taken the lead. The dialectic between mutual recognition and harmonisation which dominated the scene in the early years has been developed into a much richer landscape of principles and dimensions. Together with a certain constitutionalisation of the normative frameworks and the norms themselves the legal realm of European criminal law has matured and been complemented. The European dimension has been strengthened as the automatism originally presupposed by the mutual recognition paradigm has been transformed into a mutual recognition based on trust, albeit only in a very limited sense of the word. Rights of the individual have been elevated from the national legal orders to that of the Union itself, and procedural rights as well as rights of the victim have been addressed in the context of a criminal procedure with cross-border elements.

European criminal law has been born out of the need to provide citizens with high level of safety when the forces of European integration have increased the opportunities of crime in Europe, in particular cross-border crime. The policymakers have responded by suggesting measures to be adopted, and over a period of almost thirty years a rich body of law has emerged. In the early days the tone was often that effectivity was the main goal and criminal law was seen as the law which is having an impact in the society almost by definition. As the MS were not ready to adopt a European Penal Code, the remaining option was to build something fitting the already-existing body of EU law. At the same time, European criminal law would also become an area which called for further development of the Union itself. It is precisely this area in which the Lisbon Treaty really made a difference.

At the early stage the idea, or the concept, we might say, of European criminal law was clearly much more utilitarian. It was a tool for advancing freedom, security and justice. It was to be measured against its performance. The concept was not that different from transnational criminal law á la Boister.[39] Over the years the transnational character has changed

[39] N. Boister, *An Introduction to Transnational Criminal Law*, 2nd edn., Oxford: Oxford University Press, 2018.

and European criminal law represents a genuine European legal approach much more than before. Criminal law cooperation falls within a shared competence between the MS and the European institutions.

Together with the maturing of European criminal law also new nuances are born. New understanding of the role of mutual recognition feeds into the minimum harmonisation as trust no longer can be blind and harmonisation is a way of ensuring that there are grounds for trust. A more holistic view is also being born as harmonisation of substantive criminal law does not happen in isolation, but is supported by other harmonizing measures ensuring rights of the victims or procedural safeguards of the suspects and accused.

Thus, the part of European criminal law which has grown out of the fear of increased cross-border criminality has been somewhat tamed as the institutional and constitutional development has elevated the rights of the individual on the level of European law. Simultaneously also the tension caused by an enforcement type of logic of transnational law stressing the effectivity and the traditional domestic criminal law logic stressing justice has been relaxed and alleviated. On the one hand, justice concerns have been included in the European normativity. On the other hand, the traditional problems with the minimum harmonisation of criminal law and the mutual recognition principle have not disappeared.

Differences between the details as well as principles of the national legal orders continue to exist. We should also be mindful that the general doctrines of penal liability have only indirectly been the object of harmonizing measures. Obviously, the case law of the ECJ will continue addressing issues of this kind.[40]

One particular area in which the enforcement paradigm links with a very strong symbolical dimension is the FD on racism and xenophobia.[41] It is actually a legal instrument which goes beyond the competence that was provided for in the Amsterdam Treaty. It deals also with qualitatively different type of criminality compared to typical profit-driven organized crime, for instance, since racism and hate speech affect the foundations of society in a qualitatively different manner and have links to questions

[40] Cf., for example, R. Sicurella, 'Fostering a European Criminal Law Culture: In Trust We Trust', (2018) 9(3) *NJECL*, 308–325.

[41] Council Framework Decision 2008/913/JHA of 28 November 2008 on combating certain forms and expressions of racism and xenophobia by means of criminal law. OJ L 328, 6.12.2008, 55–58.

of limits to law, politics and democracy, freedom of speech, and discrimination, even though usually such offences lack a cross-border element. The symbolic character also means that this body of law has an expressive dimension.[42]

These issues continue to be central for the EU since they have very close links to the values on which the Union has been founded.[43] A Union which would fail to address these issues would risk losing its identity. The European response speaks to these European values. The response in itself also has a direct link to justice and equality and brings issues of justice to the European negotiating table. The sensitivities linked with the constitutional traditions of protecting the right to free speech render such a harmonizing effort complicated. This fact has even been identified as the Article 7 of the FD on racism, and xenophobia states that it 'shall not have the effect of modifying the obligation to respect fundamental rights and fundamental legal principles…'. As the constitutional law traditions may vary in this respect, these adjustments may further weaken the minimum harmonizing effect of this FD.[44]

We might also be tempted to say that combatting racism and xenophobia on a common basis matter for concerns of a European sense of justice. Even if views on the limits of freedom of speech vary, the concern for these phenomena is shared. But what do we understand by 'sense of justice'? Is it a mere irrational expression of sentiment, or are there deeper empirically justified foundations? According to Paul H. Robinson communities only develop shared understandings of the core features of criminal law regulations. A (shared) sense of justice does not give answers as to the underlying values in detail. A community may share a sense of justice in the sense of recognizing the relative blameworthiness of different offences.[45]

42 J. Iontcheva Turner, 'The Expressive Dimension of EU Criminal Law', (2012) 60 *AJCL*, 555. I have dealt with this observation in K. Nuotio, 'A Legitimacy-based Approach to European Criminal Law: Maybe We Are Getting There, After All', (2020) 11(1) *NJECL*, 20–39. see also E. Herlin-Karnell, 'Effectiveness and Constitutional Limits in European Criminal Law', (2014) 5(3) *NJECL*, 267–273.

43 Communication from the Commission to the European Parliament, the Council, the European Economic and Social Committee and the Committee of the Regions: EU anti-racism action plan 2020–2025, A Union of equality: EU anti-racism action plan 2020–2025. Brussels, 18.9.2020 COM(2020) 565 final.

44 See, for example, Mitsilegas, EU Criminal Law, pp. 98–101.

45 P. H. Robinson, *Intuitions of Justice and the Utility of Desert*, Oxford: Oxford University Press, 2013.

We could link this finding to the question of possible harmonisation of criminal penalties, an issue briefly discussed earlier. Robinson's finding may partly explain why the approach of approximation of criminal penalties by setting rigid requirements concerning the penalty scales for specific crimes ('minimum maximum penalty range') has not been very successful as a means of harmonizing the national rules on levels of criminal sanctions.

A new approach, focusing instead on the relative comparability of the severity of the offence in different national legal orders, seems to be more fitting and promising. We would accordingly wish to make sure that in the national legal order the respective punishments enjoy a similar relative position. A category approach has been proposed meaning that the European rule only would refer to the relevant blameworthiness in terms of gravity, without indicating the precise minimum or maximum penalties in the MS' legal orders. Such an approach would go with the idea that European criminal law touches on the symbolic level of the criminal law and promotes the emergence of a European way of looking at certain crimes. Prima facie, it would help to avoid some of the obvious flaws of the previous 'minimum maximum range' model.[46] Such an approach would build more on the values enshrined in the national legal orders than the current model which uses rather blunt instruments to approximate penal sanctions. Especially in the long run, an approach built on relative comparability of categories of offences would enable European law to build more directly on the coherence of the national legal orders. Today, approximation presents itself as an intervention securing only harmonisation as to a minimum level of seriousness.

The last significant driver of current development is the EPPO and the protection of the financial interest of the Union by means of criminal law. Compared to the symbolical and expressive use of criminal law to fight racism and intolerance, letting the foundational values of the Union surface in this way, the protection of the Union's financial interests combines a similar symbolical and expressive function with a highly concrete need to provide effective prosecution in such cases, even at the cost of national sovereignty. This unique setting expresses in a way a distrust in the operation of national authorities, but the interests at stake have been

[46] H. Satzger, 'The Harmonisation of Criminal Sanctions in the European Union', (2019) 2 *EurCLR*, 115.

so significant that the *Herren der Verträge*, masters of the treaty, opened the door to such an arrangement. In some sense the EPPO as a phenomenon proves that even highly unlikely developments may happen when only the drivers are right. The EU has been prone to react by means of an institutional development on the European level, but establishing the EPPO is a big step in this direction.

The overall development after Lisbon has changed the various balances that European criminal law is all about. The strengthening of fundamental and human rights has shifted the focus to the level of individuals, the actual beneficiaries of European criminal law. European criminal law is no longer as State-oriented as it used to be.[47] The focus has as well shifted somewhat from the level of legislature to the level of the judiciary. It is the duty of the courts to give effective protection to citizens, either as accused or victims of crime. The driving forces and interests behind the emergence of European criminal law have, however, not disappeared. Together with the various processes of transformation the discussions about limits of approximation of substantive criminal law take these days place in a different context. As a large body of law with a harmonizing effect has already been adopted even before the entry into force of the Lisbon Treaty, the weight of such discussions may be somewhat smaller than what was the case twenty years ago, when the story really began.

Further reading

E. Herlin-Karnell, *The Constitutional Dimension of European Criminal Law*, Oxford: Hart, 2012.

M. Kettunen, *Legitimizing European Criminal Law. Justification and Restrictions*, Cham: Springer, 2020.

[47] Mitsilegas, EU Criminal Law after Lisbon, p. 271.

Mutual Recognition and Mutual Trust 6

Philipp Ronsfeld

6.1 Introduction

In 1985, English hooligans caused a mass panic during an English-Italian football match in the Belgian Heysel stadium. In the end, 39 people died and more than 450 people were injured. The following prosecution of the perpetrators is an important example for both success and challenges of international mutual legal assistance in criminal matters. The review of the Belgian extradition request for twenty-six English suspects took more than a year because of doubts about the procedural fairness of the Belgian criminal proceedings.[1]

Member States (MS) of the European Union (EU) must increasingly rely on mutual legal assistance in order to deal with cases that have occurred in several MS. The procedures have become even more transnational since 1985. Free movement of people and goods, the major achievements of the Schengen agreement and the European internal market, favour at the same time the rise of transnational crime. In order to keep up with the Europeanisation of crime, the MS have to adapt their criminal proceedings constantly. The EU is currently solving this issue by applying the principle of mutual recognition, which means that each MS executes foreign decisions by other MS like his own. Indirectly, each MS thus trusts that the decision has been taken correctly and in compliance with EU law. However, numerous obstacles can arise in the concrete application.

This essay examines the challenges of implementing the principle of mutual recognition – even when there is a lack of trust between MS.[2]

[1] *New York Times*, Steve Lohr Sept. 3, 1987, Section B, Page 13, Britain to Extradite 26 Fans for Riot Trial; http://news.bbc.co.uk/onthisday/hi/dates/stories/september/9/newsid_2503000/2503885.stm.

[2] P. Ronsfeld, *Rechtshilfe, Anerkennung und Vertrauen. Die Europäische Ermittlungsanordnung*, Berlin: Duncker & Humblot, 2015.

6.2 Principle of Mutual Recognition

6.2.1 Classification

The Heysel stadium case is one of the first examples of large-scale successful cooperation between European criminal authorities in the context of international mutual legal assistance. On an international level mutual legal assistance often applies without a treaty. In Europe, however, a number of bilateral and multilateral agreements have codified the application of mutual legal.

Of particular relevance for Europe are the agreements of the Council of Europe, the EU and the Schengen Group. The MS of the EU cooperate on the basis of the principle of mutual recognition of judicial decisions. In 1997, through the Treaty of Amsterdam, the MS committed themselves to creating an area of freedom, security and justice. An essential element of this area is the principle of mutual recognition. The first and most effective legal instrument was the Framework Decision on the European Arrest Warrant (FD EAW).[3] A decisive impulse for further regulations came from the targets set in the Lisbon Treaty of 2009 and the Stockholm Programme of the European Council of 2010.[4] According to Article 67(3) of the Treaty on the Functioning of the European Union (TFEU), the EU

> shall endeavour to ensure a high level of security [...] through the mutual recognition of judgments in criminal matters and, if necessary, through the approximation of criminal laws.

The principle of mutual recognition is specified in Article 82(1) TFEU:

> 1. Judicial cooperation in criminal matters in the Union shall be based on the principle of mutual recognition of judgments and judicial decisions and shall include the approximation of the laws and regulations of the Member States in the areas referred to in paragraph 2 and in Article 83.
>
> The European Parliament and the Council, acting in accordance with the ordinary legislative procedure, shall adopt measures to:

[3] Ibid., pp. 70–1; Council Framework Decision of 13 June 2002 on the European arrest warrant and the surrender procedures between Member States (2002/584/JHA), OJ L 190/01, 18.7.2002; see Chapter 11 by P. Caeiro and M. Costa in this volume.

[4] European Council, *The Stockholm Programme – An Open and Secure Europe Serving and Protecting Citizens*, OJ C 115/01, 4.5.2010.

(a) lay down rules and procedures for ensuring recognition throughout the Union of all forms of judgments and judicial decisions; [...]

In addition to the FD EAW, there is, inter alia, secondary law on the following judicial decisions: freezing and confiscation orders, probation orders, pre-trial orders, decisions on financial penalties, decisions on criminal proceedings in the absence of the person concerned, decisions on the protection of victims, decisions on the execution of sentences and decisions on supervision measures as an alternative to pre-trial detention.

A well-known application of the principle of mutual recognition from the recent past is the prosecution of offences in connection with the riots during the G20 summit in Hamburg on 7 and 8 July 2017. Both peaceful and violent protestors travelled from all over Europe to northern Germany. About 31,000 police officers were deployed to protect the summit and the city. More than 2,000 cases were filed, covering various offences, such as damage to property, severe bodily harm, breach of the peace, aggravated breach of the peace, arson and resistance against police officers. At the request of German authorities, nine properties were searched in France, Spain, Italy and Switzerland. German authorities issued an EAW against a French suspect and several European Investigation Orders (EIO)[5] in France and Italy. The requests for mutual legal assistance were directed via Eurojust to the respective competent authorities in Italy, France and Spain.[6] Unlike in the Heysel stadium case, at no point was the rule of law of the requesting State questioned.

6.2.2 From Request to Order

In the EU, a distinction is made between traditional and new judicial cooperation in criminal matters, to which the principle of mutual recognition is applied. According to the Commission, traditional mutual assistance law is based on a 'request' principle. The requested State may refuse to respond to the request submitted to it. By contrast, the EU puts mutual legal assistance on a new footing with the principle of mutual recognition as 'the

[5] On the EIO, see Chapter 12 by L. Bachmaier Winter in this volume.

[6] Kleine Anfrage die LINKE, Bürgerschaft der Freien und Hansestadt Hamburg, Drucksache 21/13507; www.welt.de/regionales/hamburg/article168060024/Soko-Schwarzer-Block-ermittelt-in-mehr-als-2000-Faellen.htm (accessed 5 March 2022).

cornerstone of judicial co-operation'.[7] The aim here is not only the territorial but also the extraterritorial effectiveness of judicial decision within the EU. According to the Commission, 'a decision taken by a judge [...] – in so far as it has extranational implications – would automatically be accepted in all other Member States, and have the same or at least similar effects there'.[8] The pure form of the principle of mutual recognition gives a judicial decision extraterritorial effect. By contrast, traditional mutual legal assistance requires an act of transformation ('exequatur') for the execution of a request.[9]

According to the Commission,

> '[i]deally [under the new principle of mutual recognition], there should be no need at all for such a procedure: mutual recognition would work directly and automatically, without any additional procedural step. In practice, this seems impossible in most cases' [...]
>
> '[r]ecognising a decision means first and foremost to do what is ordered in the decision, to enforce it.'[10]

According to the Council,

> 'mutual recognition comes in various shapes and must be sought at all stages of criminal proceedings, before, during or after conviction, but it is applied differently depending on the nature of the decision or the penalty imposed. In each of these areas the extent of the mutual recognition exercise is very much dependent on a number of parameters which determine its effectiveness. [...]'.

This includes, inter alia, according to the Council, 'the definition of minimum common standards' and the scope of the 'double criminality requirement' and of the 'validation procedure'.[11] Since the EU's concept of mutual recognition is based on these preconditions, it introduces this concept in a weakened form until these preconditions are met. The respective

[7] European Council, *The Tampere Programme – Towards a Union of freedom, security and justice*, No. SN 200/99, 15./16.10.1999, para. 33.

[8] Commission, Communication, *Mutual Recognition of Final Decisions in Criminal Matters*, COM(2000)495 final, p. 2; K. Ligeti, *Strafrecht und strafrechtliche Zusammenarbeit in der Europäischen Union*, Berlin: Duncker & Humblot, 2005, pp. 181–2.

[9] Ronsfeld, *Rechtshilfe, Anerkennung und Vertrauen. Die Europäische Ermittlungsanordnung*, pp. 80–1.

[10] Commission, Communication, *Mutual Recognition of Final Decisions in Criminal Matters*, COM(2000)495 final, pp. 8, 17.

[11] Council, *Programme of Measures to Implement the Principle of Mutual Recognition of Decisions in Criminal Matters*, OJ C 12/10, 15.1.2012, pp. 11–2.

secondary law offers MS a broad framework for implementation. The MS have the choice between a direct effect or a conversion of a decision into their national law. German law, for example, mainly follows the latter alternative.[12]

6.2.3 Forum Shopping

Critics are concerned that law enforcement agencies could abuse the principle: Coercive measures such as interception of communications could be carried out in the MS with the least restrictions ('forum shopping'). They fear that this would lead to a levelling of those rights to the lowest common denominator ('race to the bottom').[13] In principle, two critical scenarios must be considered:

1. Both MS are entitled to order a measure, but the law of the requested State facilitates the implementation of that measure.
2. Only the law of the requested State permits the ordering of a measure. A request to do so would thus circumvent the requesting State's own national law.

The first scenario is to be seen positively in terms of European integration. It facilitates the transnational process and cooperation within the area of freedom, security and justice. The second scenario concerns the illegal abuse of a request for mutual legal assistance. Therefore, only for this scenario the term *forum shopping* should be used.[14] In order to prevent such *forum shopping* between the MS, the Directive regarding

[12] Ronsfeld, *Rechtshilfe, Anerkennung und Vertrauen. Die Europäische Ermittlungsanordnung*, p. 87.

[13] S. Allegrezza, 'Critical Remarks on the Green Paper on Obtaining Evidence in Criminal Matters from One Member State to another and Securing Its Admissibility', (2010) 5 *ZIS*, 569, 575: The consequence of this would be to lower down European and national standards of procedural safeguards and thus to reduce the protection of human rights; C. W. Heydenreich, 'Die Europäische Ermittlungsanordnung. Der endgültige Abschied von der Fiktion einer Waffengleichheit', (2012) *StV*, 439, 441; M. Möstl, 'Preconditions and Limits of Mutual Recognition', (2010) 47 *CMLR*, 405, 421; F. Zimmermann, S. Glaser, and A. Motz, 'Mutual Recognition and Its Implications for the Gathering of Evidence in Criminal proceedings: A Critical Analysis of the Initiative for a European Investigation Order', (2011) 1 *EuCLR*, 56, 73; K. Ambos, *European Criminal Law*, Cambridge: Cambridge University Press, 2018, p. 136.

[14] Ronsfeld, *Rechtshilfe, Anerkennung und Vertrauen. Die Europäische Ermittlungsanordnung*, pp. 118 ff.

the EIO contains some precautions. For example, the issuing of an EIO requires that the desired measure is permissible in the two States involved and the issuing authority must also explicitly confirm this in the standard form.

Yet, the concrete practice of the investigating authorities poses major challenges for the judiciary. Transnational cooperation generates a high degree of complexity. This becomes particularly clear when dealing with encrypted mobile phone data. In Europe, members of organised crime have been communicating by using an end-to-end encrypted smartphone application (EncroChat) since 2016. Due to the high level of encryption, the criminals felt safe to talk freely about their plans and accomplices and refrained from using code words or other methods of obfuscation. French authorities eventually managed to decrypt the data traffic. In the framework of police cooperation, France informed other concerned MS. At a mutually agreed time, numerous objects were searched by the competent authorities in the respective MS. Numerous investigations and criminal proceedings followed and more than 1,000 suspects got arrested. As a result, EncroChat, with its about 60,000 users, ceased its activities.[15] On 2 June 2020, the General Public Prosecutor's Office in Frankfurt am Main sent an EIO to the competent French prosecution authorities in order to be able to use the available investigation results in its own criminal proceedings. This investigation order was recognised by the competent investigating judge in Lille on 13 June 2020, and the transmission of the requested data was set in motion. This transnational cooperation touches on the issue of *forum shopping*. Many related decisions in Germany dealt with the use of results from EIOs, as German and French criminal procedure law are structured differently, and this type of *forum shopping* could be illegal. However, the decisions clarify that, pursuant to the trust to be assumed in the context of mutual recognition, French criminal proceedings would not be examined more closely without concrete indications. There were no indications for an illegal fishing expedition, and therefore, the *ordre public* had not been violated.[16] Mostly, the respective decisions assume

[15] www.europol.europa.eu/media-press/newsroom/news/dismantling-of-encrypted-network-sends-shockwaves-through-organised-crime-groups-across-europe (accessed 5 March 2022).

[16] For a different view, see K. Ambos et al., 'Die Europäische Ermittlungsanordnung aus Verteidigersicht', (2021) 41 *StV*, 126.

that computer network surveillance in German procedural law is comparable to the coercive measures in French law, so that there was no illegal *forum shopping.*[17] Although these decisions confirm the measures in this transnational cooperation, they also show the real danger of negligent *forum shopping.* Even an unintentional breach of Article 6(1)(b) of the EIO Directive can have serious consequences for the persons concerned. As a consequence, an adaptation of national law through secondary law is necessary.

Moreover, transnational proceedings can also offer a defendant – albeit limited – room for manoeuvre. If necessary, the defendant can work towards proceedings against him being conducted in a favourable participating MS. This tactical use of exclusion of double jeopardy (*ne bis in idem*) could prevent prosecution in another MS. Since the defendant prefers a specific jurisdiction, this approach is also called *ne bis in idem*-shopping.[18] Reasons for *ne bis in idem*-shopping can be more favourable legal circumstances such as a lower expectation of punishment or procedural simplifications in the criminal proceedings of the preferred MS. For instance, in Greece, illicit traffic in narcotics results in a higher level of penalties than in other MS. However, in addition to the maximum penalty, the enforcement practice applied in the MS must also be taken into account. MS with high penalties often refrain from enforcing the penalty in full, while MS with low penalties regularly enforce the penalty in full. Apart from this the accused may also avoid to be prosecuted in certain places for personal reasons such as his/her social status. The sinking of the cargo ship Lucona in the Indian Ocean in 1977, in which six crew members died, provides a shining example here. Arrest warrants for murder were issued in Austria against the German Hans-Peter Daimler and his accomplice, the Austrian Udo Proksch. Daimler fled to Germany and took up residence in the North. He surrendered to the public prosecutor's office in Kiel, which brought charges against him. According to his own statements, he hoped for a fairer trial in Germany than in Austria. In Germany, Daimler enjoyed

[17] OLG Hamburg, order of 29.01.2021, 1 Ws 2 /21, para. 57 f., 88, 89; OLG Schleswig, order of 29.04.2021, 2 Ws 47/21; OLG Celle, order of 12.08.2021, 2 Ws 250/21; KG Berlin, order of 30.08.2021, 2 Ws 79/21.

[18] CJEU, *Gasparini and Others,* No. C-467/04, Opinion of Advocate General Sharpston, ECLI:EU:C:2006:406, 15 June 2006, para. 104; Ronsfeld, *Rechtshilfe, Anerkennung und Vertrauen. Die Europäische Ermittlungsanordnung,* p. 117.

protection under the European Convention on Extradition (ECE), Article 6(1)(a), in conjunction with Article 16(2) German Basic Constitutional Law. Furthermore, he hoped that a sentence by a German court would prevent his extradition to Austria on the basis of Article 9 ECE (exclusion of double jeopardy). Eventually, the Kiel Regional Court sentenced Daimler to fourteen years' imprisonment for, among other things, aiding and abetting murder. Previously, Proksch had been sentenced to life imprisonment in Austria for the same offence.[19]

6.2.4 Abolition of the Double Criminality Requirement

According to the principle of double criminality, mutual assistance is only granted if the conduct contained in the request of the requesting State would also constitute a criminal offence in the requested/executing State. The partial abolition of this principle is fundamental to the principle of mutual recognition. In the framework of traditional mutual legal assistance, the principle of double criminality allows for broad discretion and it is up to the sovereign decision of the requested State to either insist on or to waive this requirement.[20] Furthermore, the principle of double criminality grants personal rights. As a rule, citizens expect that they won't be prosecuted in their State of residence for an offence that does not exist in its legal system. Therefore, the principle of double criminality in the EU can only be abolished at the exchange of new procedural safeguards, such as a European *ordre public*.[21] At present, the EU envisages the abolition of the principle only under certain conditions.

[19] K.-U. Drews, S. Hiebner, and H. Wisser, 'Muss der Bundesgerichtshof über die Zuständigkeit im Fall Daimler entscheiden?', *Kieler Nachrichten*, 5.4.1989, p. 3; '"Lucona" – Ein Fall für Kiel?', *Holsteinischen Courier* of 3.4.1989, p. 8; 'Der Daimler, das arme Schwein', *Der Spiegel*, 1992 Issue 29, pp. 76–78; report of *Hamburger Morgenpost* of 28.6.2001. For an English (albeit incomplete) summary, see https://en.wikipedia.org/wiki/Lucona (accessed 3 March 2022).

[20] P. Rackow and C. Birr, 'Recent Developments in Legal Assistance in Criminal Matters', (2010) 2 *GoeJIL*, 1087, 1091.

[21] Very critical L. Bachmaier Winter, 'European Investigation Order for Obtaining Evidence in the Criminal Proceedings. Study of the Proposal for a European Directive', (2010) 5 *ZIS*, 580, 585: 'In sum, in my opinion, only if the evidence can be collected without resorting to the restriction of fundamental rights, the dual criminality requirement could be disregarded'; L. Bachmaier Winter, 'The Role of the Proportionality Principle in Cross-Border Investigations Involving Fundamental Rights', in Stefano Ruggeri (ed.), *Transnational inquiries*, Heidelberg, New York, Dordrecht, London: Springer, 2013, pp. 85, 102.

These include the deliberate entry into a foreign jurisdiction, the seriousness of the offence and its typical cross-border dimension. The last two criteria should be cumulative.[22]

6.3 Mutual Trust and Mutual Recognition

6.3.1 Mutual Trust as a Prerequisite

In many of its documents, the EU identifies trust as a fundamental prerequisite for cooperation. This applies in particular to mutual recognition in criminal matters:

> Implementation of the principle of mutual recognition of decisions in criminal matters presupposes that Member States have trust in each others' criminal justice systems. That trust is grounded, in particular, on their shared commitment to the principles of freedom, democracy and respect for human rights, fundamental freedoms and the rule of law.[23]

Accordingly, the object of reference of mutual trust is the rule of law of the respective criminal justice systems of the MS. At the same time, the EU assumes that a 'high level of confidence between Member States' already exists.[24]

Critics doubt that trust is a suitable basis for intergovernmental cooperation.[25] They even doubt that trust in the rule of law exists within the EU

[22] Ronsfeld, *Rechtshilfe, Anerkennung und Vertrauen. Die Europäische Ermittlungsanordnung*, p. 87 and, in detail, C. Penkuhn, *Der ordre-public-Vorbehalt als Auslieferungshindernis im europäischen Auslieferungsverkehr*, Berlin: Duncker & Humblot, 2020.

[23] Council, *Programme of Measures to Implement the Principle of Mutual Recognition of Decisions in Criminal Matters*, OJ C 12/10, 15.1.2012, p. 11.

[24] Council Framework Decision of 13 June 2002 on the European arrest warrant and the surrender procedures between Member States (2002/584/JHA), OJ L 190/01, 18.7.2002, Recital 10; CJEU, *Melloni*, No. C-399/11, Judgment, 26 February 2013, para. 37; Council Framework Decision 2008/909/JHA of 27 November 2008 on the application of the principle of mutual recognition to judgments in criminal matters imposing custodial sentences or measures involving deprivation of liberty for the purpose of their enforcement in the European Union, OJ L 327/27, 5.12.2008, Recital 5; Council Framework Decision 2008/978/JHA of 18 December 2008 on the European evidence warrant for the purpose of obtaining objects, documents and data for use in proceedings in criminal matters, OJ L 350/72, 30.12.2008, Recital 8.

[25] Möstl, 'Preconditions and Limits of Mutual Recognition', 405, 419; P. Rackow, 'Das Anerkennungsprinzip auf dem Prüfstein der Beweisrechtshilfe', in K. Ambos (ed.), *Europäisches Strafrecht post-Lissabon*, Göttingen: Universitätsverlag Göttingen, 2011,

at all. The dull repetition of a phrase does not make it true. For example, Ambos argues that the assumption of trust 'contains hardly any substance [...] increasingly becoming, as the Union expands further and further, a mere Brussels or Luxembourg phantasmagoria'.[26] It is further argued that in actual fact, not all MS have a criminal procedure (practice) in line with rule of law principles. Trust can not merely be assumed. Furthermore, it is said to be unclear, what minimum level of the rule of law is sufficient as a basis for trust.[27] They argue trust presupposes a direct relationship, which can only be built by individual persons, in this case the citizens of the EU, and furthermore, the significance of trust as a whole in the principle of mutual recognition has not been clarified scientifically.[28]

6.3.2 Trust in International Legal Relations

In many legal systems, there exist 'bases of trust' (*Vertrauenstatbestand)* from which legitimate expectations can be derived). One important example in this respect is the Full Faith and Credit Clause in Article IV, Section 1, of the US Constitution. But, at any rate, the concept of trust itself is rather defined in interdisciplinary discourses. Sociology and political philosophy provide essential insights: Hobbes developed basic theories on trust as the basis of human coexistence in general and of legal relations in particular.[29] The following propositions are essentially based on Luhmann's and Sztompka's concepts of trust from the perspective of systems theory.[30]

p. 117, 128; Ambos, *European Criminal Law*, p. 435; Zimmermann, Glaser, and Motz, 'Mutual Recognition and Its Implications for the Gathering of Evidence in Criminal proceedings', 56, 61; C. Heard and D. Mansell, 'The European Investigation Order. Changing the Face of Evidence-Gathering in EU Crossborder Cases', (2011) 2 *NJECL*, 353, 354.

26 Ambos, *European Criminal Law*, p. 435.

27 Frank Meyer, 'Die Aussagefreiheit und das Prinzip der gegenseitigen Anerkennung', (2007) 154 *GA*, 15, 25.

28 V. Mitsilegas, 'The Constitutional Implications of Mutual Recognition in Criminal Matters in the EU', (2006) 43 *CMLR*, 1277, 1306; V. Mitsilegas, *EU Criminal Law*, Oxford, Portland, OR: Hart Publishing, 2016, p. 151. The following observations are essentially based on Luhmann's and Sztompka's concepts of 'trust'. For further reading, Ronsfeld, *Rechtshilfe, Anerkennung und Vertrauen. Die Europäische Ermittlungsanordnung*, p. 199.

29 T. Hobbes, *De Cive*, Angel in Ivie-Lane, 1651, Chapter 2; T. Hobbes, *Leviathan or the Matter, Forme and Power of a Commonwealth Ecclesiasticall and Civil*, St. Paul's Churchyard: Green Dragon, 1651, Chapter XIV.

30 N. Luhmann, *Vertrauen. Ein Mechanismus der Reduktion sozialer Komplexität*, 4th edn., Stuttgart: Lucius & Lucius, 2000; P. Sztompka, *Trust. A Sociological Theory*, Cambridge, New York: Cambridge University Press, 1999.

A subject and an object can be connected through trust as a social relationship. They thus form a common system. Such systems arise above all where the individual cannot assert himself alone but is dependent on cooperation with others. The more complex the situation, the greater the effort for the individual to make a conscious decision about his/her behaviour. Trust however can reduce complexity. For the modern age, the granting of trust has become characteristic, as globalisation and Europeanisation have led to a very complex social environment. This also applies to international relations, and transnational law enforcement in particular, since States want to reduce complexity just as much as individuals do. Mutual recognition is a way of implementing this relationship of trust.

According to the EU 'authorities and services in the different Member States and decision-makers' apply both as the object and subject of mutual trust.[31] Similarly, all other actors in the criminal process, such as lawyers and defendants, are considered as subjects of trust.[32] In international relations, the reliability of the partner is, in line with reciprocity (*do ut des*), sufficient. In mutual recognition, however, demands must be higher, since civil rights are affected. The reference point of trust is not the institutions themselves but the rule of law, the integrity of the competent authorities and the quality of the services they provide.[33] This ensures a reliable, non-arbitrary and fair criminal procedure. If these conditions exist, it can be assumed that the foreign decisions are equivalent or similar to domestic decisions.[34]

[31] European Council, *The Stockholm Programme*, para. 1.2.1; Resolution of the Council of 30.11.2009 on a Roadmap for strengthening procedural rights of suspected or accused persons in criminal proceedings, OJ C 295/01, 4.12.2009, Recital 8.

[32] Directive 2013/48/EU of the European Parliament and of the Council of 22 October 2013 on the right of access to a lawyer in criminal proceedings and in European arrest warrant proceedings and on the right to have a third party informed upon deprivation of liberty and to communicate with third persons and with consular authorities while deprived of liberty, OJ L 294/01, 6.11.2013, Recital 6.

[33] European Council, *The Hague Programme: Strengthening Freedom, Security and Justice in the European Union*, OJ C 53/01, 3.3.2005, para. 3.2; Directive 2013/48/EU of the European Parliament and of the Council of 22 October 2013 on the right of access to a lawyer in criminal proceedings and in European arrest warrant proceedings, and on the right to have a third party informed upon deprivation of liberty and to communicate with third persons and with consular authorities while deprived of liberty, OJ L 294/01, 6.11.2013, Recital 6.

[34] Ronsfeld, *Rechtshilfe, Anerkennung und Vertrauen. Die Europäische Ermittlungsanordnung*, pp. 218 ff.

6.3.3 Building Trust

Trust relies on free will. No one can be forced to trust another person. 'Blind trust' is thus a contradiction in terms. Trustworthiness must be voluntarily attributed to the object of trust.[35]

One can distinguish between two types of trustworthiness: self-acquired or derived. Self-acquired trustworthiness leads the subject of trust to believe that the object of trust is sincere and capable, while derived trustworthiness is based on external influences.[36] The decisive factor is always the good impression of the object of trust. One's own perception (visibility of the object) and familiarity (closeness of the object) are often decisive for trusting or distrusting an object of trust.[37] External factors – not based in the object of trust itself – include all forms of 'accountability', 'pre-commitment' and any 'trust-inducing situations'. In complex systems, 'closeness' and 'visibility' can also be established through appropriate regulations and organisation.[38] However, this can change the way trust is established. While the trust in social relationship is usually based on individual behaviour, in a complex system the basis for trust is rather the functioning of organisation and institutions. These systems are characterised by a higher degree of abstraction. The reference object of trust is no longer the behaviour of an individual, but the functioning of the system based on the behaviour of all participants.[39] In some systems, personal trust emerges alongside this abstract trust. It depends on the type of organisation. Direct contact of members of the system with decision-makers is not a prerequisite, but probably the rule. Through this, the system itself can gain trustworthiness; the system is given a symbolic face.[40]

These observations can also be transferred to mutual legal assistance within the EU. Established mutual legal assistance relations between individual MS are not sufficient for systemic trust in the EU. In an area of

[35] Sztompka, *Trust. A Sociological Theory*, p. 107, according to Sztompka, 'the functionality or dysfunctionality of trust is relative to its epistemological foundations: trustworthiness of the target.'

[36] Ibid., pp. 70 ff.

[37] Luhmann, *Vertrauen. Ein Mechanismus der Reduktion sozialer Komplexität*, pp. 22–23, 40.

[38] Sztompka, *Trust. A Sociological Theory*, pp. 94–5.

[39] Luhmann, *Vertrauen. Ein Mechanismus der Reduktion sozialer Komplexität*, p. 124.

[40] A. Giddens, *The Consequences of Modernity*, Stanford: Stanford University Press, 1990, p. 88; Sztompka, *Trust. A Sociological Theory*, pp. 135–6.

freedom, security and justice, all MS must trust each other. In order for such systemic trust to emerge, the EU and its members must conceptually ensure that their national criminal justice systems generally receive and retain trustworthiness. According to the European Council '[e]nsuring trust and finding new ways to increase reliance on, and mutual understanding between, the different legal systems in the Member States will thus be one of the main challenges for the future'.[41]

Confidence-building measures are a key element for achieving this goal. The most important measures support the formation of understanding of foreign law and its application, provide transparency of justice and strengthen the integrity and professional competence of the judiciary.[42] Above all, a common reference system, which is monitored and maintained by an independent body, conveys trustworthiness. Common minimum rules concerning criminal procedure, to which all MS are committed, could at least create trust in the legality and fairness in the legislation of other MS. In addition to the possible partial application of foreign law (*forum regit actum*), common minimum rules also offer an opportunity to overcome structural differences between the legal systems of the MS. However, existing system differences can still lead to legal gaps or double burdens, especially for the person concerned.

The European Convention for the Protection of Human Rights and Fundamental Freedoms (ECHR) is such an existing reference system. According to Article 6(3) TEU, the ECHR and the case law of the European Court of Human Rights (ECtHR) 'constitute general principles of the Union's law'. Across Europe, the ECHR and the case law of the ECtHR have already introduced sufficient and proven minimum standards for criminal proceedings. The adoption, codifying and amendment of its fundamental rights and procedural safeguards in the Charter of Fundamental Rights of the EU (Charter) and the secondary law contribute to legal certainty.[43]

As rightly stated in the Directive on the right of access to a lawyer:

> Strengthening mutual trust requires detailed rules on the protection of the procedural rights and guarantees arising from the Charter, the ECHR and the ICCPR.

[41] European Council, *The Stockholm Programme*, para. 1.2.1.

[42] Ibid., para. 3.2; European Council, *The Hague Programme*, para. 3.2.

[43] Ronsfeld, *Rechtshilfe, Anerkennung und Vertrauen. Die Europäische Ermittlungsanordnung*, pp. 227 ff.; on the instruments based on the Stockholm Programme, see Ambos, *European Criminal Law*, p. 137.

> It also requires, [...] further development within the Union of the minimum standards set out in the Charter and in the ECHR. [...] Common minimum rules should lead to increased confidence in the criminal justice systems of all Member States, which, in turn, should lead to more efficient judicial cooperation in a climate of mutual trust and to the promotion of a fundamental rights culture in the Union. Such common minimum rules should also remove obstacles to the free movement of citizens throughout the territory of the Member States.[44]

Article 53 of the Charter prevents harmonising standards below the level of protection of the ECHR (race to the bottom).

However, abandoning the principle of double criminality leads to ambiguities about the scope of foreign criminal law. The right answer to this would be a comprehensive harmonisation of criminal offences. This would generate trust and legal certainty since in each MS there are functional equivalents to the national criminal offences in the areas of crime concerned. This harmonisation of substantive law is driven by several international conventions and secondary law instruments.[45] Supranational criminal procedural law has an even stronger effect than harmonisation and can lead to mutual trust in the long term.[46]

6.4 Mutual Trust and Control

6.4.1 Scrutiny and Mutual Recognition

Mutual recognition has a long reach but is not unlimited. According to Bachmaier Winter, the principle of mutual recognition is not 'equivalent to a blind and automatic recognition and execution of the measure requested, but as a rule, the grounds for refusal are restricted to a minimum'.[47]

[44] Directive 2013/48/EU of the European Parliament and of the Council of 22 October 2013 on the right of access to a lawyer in criminal proceedings and in European arrest warrant proceedings, and on the right to have a third party informed upon deprivation of liberty and to communicate with third persons and with consular authorities while deprived of liberty, OJ L 294/01, 6.11.2013, Recitals 6, 8.

[45] Ambos, *European Criminal Law*, pp. 317 ff.

[46] On the minimum requirements of the rule of law for international criminal procedural law, see, for example, K. Ambos, *Treatise on International Criminal Law*, Vol. III, Oxford: Oxford University Press, 2016, pp. 57 ff.

[47] L. Bachmaier Winter, 'European Investigation Order for Obtaining Evidence in the Criminal Proceedings. Study of the Proposal for a European Directive', 580, 582; likewise Ambos, *European Criminal Law*, p. 437.

In a case of international mutual legal assistance, not based on a treaty, the executing authority has wide discretion. However, the recognition of a judicial decision can no longer be refused on political grounds. Still, legal objections are admitted as grounds for postponement and refusal.[48] At any rate, the emphasis is shifting from a unilateral, final decision to a consensual approach. In this way, a common practice between friendly states is codified. An efficient mutual legal assistance system is to be created by

- interpreting incoming requests in a friendly manner
- informing about legal reservations and
- consulting with a view to dispute resolution.

In the context of mutual recognition, this also applies to all cases of refusal, postponement, modification or delay of enforcement. In order to deal with legal and factual problems at an early stage, the authorities of the issuing state may participate in the enforcement procedure in an assisting capacity. For example, after the aforementioned G20 riots, twelve German police officers assisted the measures abroad. An obstacle to mutual assistance or enforcement usually exists if there is an obvious lack of connection between the evidence present and the suspicion of the respective offence or if such a suspicion has not even been convincingly presented. The Commission therefore recommends including certain necessary steps for mutual recognition like translation, validation check on criminal matter, scope, competence and procedural safeguards but warns that an overly rigorous vetting process hinders the creation of an area of freedom, security and justice:

Indeed, with every additional point that one foresees to be checked before a decision is recognised in the executing Member State, the validation procedure becomes more complicated and lengthier, thereby detracting from mutual recognition's main advantages, speed and simplicity. Too heavy a validation procedure

[48] According to Rackow is this a 'neuralgischer Punkt', Rackow, 'Das Anerkennungsprinzip auf dem Prüfstein der Beweisrechtshilfe', 117, 131; Rackow and Birr, 'Recent Developments in Legal Assistance in Criminal Matters', 1087, 1093: 'The assisting State is in principle obliged to carry out the order, possibly even in the manner in which the ordering State wants it done. In practice, however, the contrast occasionally may not be as evident since mutual-recognition as the case may be – depending on the content and scope of the grounds to refuse the execution of a mutual-recognition-instrument – may converge towards traditional mutual assistance.'

would have the effect of only allowing a mutual recognition regime that in practice would work very much as the traditional 'request' regime.[49]

6.4.2 Lack of Trust

Violations of fundamental rights by implementing and applying secondary law are prohibited by primary law, cf. Article 6(3) TEU (*ordre public*). This applies in particular to secondary law of mutual recognition of judicial decisions. Such violations refute the assumption of mutual trust. While primary law prohibits any violation, secondary law is rarely clear. Fundamental rights are often only mentioned in the recitals, but rarely in the enacting terms. Recently, secondary law has however provided for clear guidance in the Regulation on the mutual recognition of freezing orders and confiscation orders (EU) 2018/1805 in its Recital 34 according to which:

> [...] in exceptional situations, where there are substantial grounds to believe, on the basis of specific and objective evidence, that the execution of a freezing order or confiscation order would, in the particular circumstances of the case, entail a manifest breach of a relevant fundamental right as set out in the Charter, the executing authority should be able to decide not to recognise and execute the order concerned. [...].[50]

This is then concretely implemented in Article 8(1)(f) of Regulation (EU) 2018/1805.[51] Such a clause should be provided for by any secondary law based on mutual recognition. Indeed, assistance to foreign proceedings involving prosecution contrary to the rule of law, capital punishment and disproportionately high sentences cannot be admitted. Also, outgoing requests must not indirectly initiate such proceedings in the requested State. Credible assurances from non-governmental organisations about a real risk of a violation of the Charter are sufficient to assume such a violation. This assumption can then only be countered by a legally binding assurance of the requesting State that it will abide by international standards in its

[49] Commission, Communication, *Mutual Recognition of Final Decisions in Criminal Matters*, COM(2000)495 final, p. 19; Council, *Programme of Measures to Implement the Principle of Mutual Recognition of Decisions in Criminal Matters*, OJ C 12/10, 15.1.2001, pp. 11 ff., p. 19.

[50] A corresponding guideline can also be found in Recital 19 of the Directive regarding the EIO.

[51] The EIO Directive also contains a parallel provision with Art. 11(1)(f).

procedures. If the requested State considers these assurances to be unreliable, the execution of the requested measure must be denied. The following case on the refusal to surrender a person on the basis of an EAW is a paradigmatic example of the recourse to the *ordre public*. The Court of Justice of the European Union (CJEU) ruled in the case of Aranyosi and Căldăraru[52] that

> where there is objective, reliable, specific and properly updated evidence with respect to detention conditions in the issuing Member State that demonstrates that there are deficiencies, which may be systemic or generalised [...], the executing judicial authority must determine, specifically and precisely, whether there are substantial grounds to believe that the individual concerned by a European arrest warrant [...] will be exposed, because of the conditions for his detention in the issuing Member State, to a real risk of inhuman or degrading treatment, within the meaning of Article 4 of the Charter, in the event of his surrender to that Member State.

The risk of systemic deficiencies plainly undermines the assumption of a general mutual trust. The requested State must consider in each individual case whether such a deficiency can be remedied by additional measures taken by the requesting State so that the danger of a serious rights' violation is eliminated.[53] In the long term, such systemic deficiencies must, of course be adressed, by the respective MS and the EU, so that trust in the rule of law in Europe is not fundamentally shaken. In addition to that, a refusal of enforcement on the basis of a purely national *ordre public* is ruled out. This has been confirmed by the CJEU in Melloni:

> Consequently, allowing a Member State to avail itself of Article 53 of the Charter to make the surrender of a person convicted in absentia conditional upon the conviction being open to review in the issuing Member State, a possibility not provided for under Framework Decision 2009/299, in order to avoid an adverse effect on the right to a fair trial and the rights of the defence guaranteed by the constitution of the executing Member State, by casting doubt on the uniformity of the standard of protection of fundamental rights as defined in that framework decision, would undermine the principles of mutual trust and recognition which that decision purports to uphold and would, therefore, compromise the efficacy of that framework decision.[54]

[52] CJEU, *Aranyosi und Căldăraru*, Joined Cases Nos. C-404/15 and C-659/15 PPU, Judgment, 5 April 2016, paras. 84 ff.

[53] OLG Bremen, order of 3.9.2021, 1 Ausl.A 45/20.

[54] CJEU, *Melloni*, No. C-399/11, Judgment, 26 February 2013, para. 63; *Melloni*, No. C-399/11, Opinion of Advocate General Bot, ECLI:EU:C:2012:600, 2 October 2012, para. 102–3.

As a consequence, national law only takes precedence in precisely defined cases.[55]

6.4.3 Control in Case of Systemic Deficiencies

Trust is not established all at once but is the result of a gradual process (accumulation). Likewise, once granted trust decays with the gradual loss of trustworthiness. The shaking of abstract or concrete trust can disrupt trust in the entire system.[56] Abstract trust is destroyed in particular by organisational and institutional deficiencies, whereas individual misconduct can destroy concrete trust. If such individual breaches of trust exceed, in their accumulation, a critical threshold overall, the loss of abstract trust ensues too.

European law enforcement as an abstract system is always at risk of losing trust. It is also exposed to the danger of a breakdown in general trust. At present, the massive system dependence on trust can be observed due to various disturbances. The development of European cooperation (including judicial cooperation) is currently showing signs of a gradual slowdown, which seems to be due to a fundamental crisis of trust.

All MS are within the scope of primary law, but systemic deficiencies are reported in a different kind of manner. States acceding to the EU must fulfil certain accession requirements (Copenhagen criteria) including 'stability of institutions guaranteeing democracy, the rule of law, human rights and respect for and protection of minorities'.[57] The Commission observes and monitors these criteria for new MS during the accession process and during the transition period afterwards. In 2007, after identifying shortcomings for some new MS in the fields of judicial reform, corruption and organised crime, the Commission set up the Cooperation and Verification Mechanism (CVM) as a transitional measure to assist the respective States to remedy these shortcomings.[58] In 2012,

55 Cf. Art. 2 (d)(2) Directive 2014/41/EU of the European Parliament and of the Council of 3 April 2014 regarding the European Investigation Order in criminal matters, OJ L 130/01, 1.5.2014.

56 Luhmann, *Vertrauen. Ein Mechanismus der Reduktion sozialer Komplexität*, pp. 96 ff.

57 https://ec.europa.eu/neighbourhood-enlargement/enlargement-policy/glossary/accession-criteria_en (accessed 5 March 2022).

58 https://ec.europa.eu/info/policies/justice-and-fundamental-rights/upholding-rule-law/rule-law/assistance-bulgaria-and-romania-under-cvm/cooperation-

a respective close monitoring process and transitional measures by the Commission were regulated in the Croatian accession act in conjunction with the Croatian accession treaties.[59] This ongoing process depends on fulfilling the recommendations set out by the Commission. The detailed reported analysis of the Commission shows systemic deficiencies in each MS which leads to criticism and a lack of trust in the respective MS. As stated above, only the new MS, but not the old ones, are monitored by the Commission with regard to the Copenhagen criteria. However, these States have voluntarily placed themselves under increased observation and scrutiny by the Commission through their accession agreements. Compared to other MS, rule of law deficits are therefore particularly well documented. The European Parliament's Committee on Civil Liberties, Justice and Home Affairs called this in 2013 the 'Copenhagen dilemma': '[W]hereby the EU remains very strict with regard to compliance with the common values and standards on the part of candidate countries but lacks effective monitoring and sanctioning tools once they have joined the EU.' The Committee recommended to the EU institutions 'setting up a new mechanism to enforce Article 2 TEU effectively' and requested 'that Member States be regularly assessed on their continued compliance with the fundamental values of the Union and the requirements of democracy and the rule of law, avoiding any double standards'.[60]

In recent years, the EU has been confronted with crisis events in old MS, which revealed systemic threats to the rule of law.[61] Since 2020, the Commission has reported on the rule of law situation in the EU. According to these reports and EU press releases, the rule of law situation in Poland and Hungary is concerning: in Poland, the EU criticises

and-verification-mechanism-bulgaria-and-romania_en (accessed 5 March 2022); Commission, *Report on Progress in Romania under the Cooperation and Verification Mechanism*, COM(2021) 370 final, p. 1.

59 Treaty between the MS of the European Union and the Republic of Croatia concerning the accession of the Republic of Croatia to the European Union, OJ L 112/10, 1.5.2012; Act concerning the conditions of accession of the Republic of Croatia and the adjustments to the Treaty on European Union, the Treaty on the Functioning of the European Union and the Treaty establishing the European Atomic Energy Community, OJ L 112/2, 1.5.2012.

60 European Parliament's Committee on Civil Liberties, Justice and Home Affairs, Report on the situation of fundamental rights: standards and practices in Hungary (pursuant to the European Parliament resolution of 16 February 2012), Rapporteur: Rui Tavares, 24.6.2013, A7-0229/2013, p. 35.

61 https://ec.europa.eu/info/policies/justice-and-fundamental-rights/upholding-rule-law/rule-law/rule-law-framework_en (accessed 5 March 2022).

significant shortcomings in the independence of the judiciary, freedom of the media and freedom from discrimination against minorities due to 'LGBT ideology-free zones'. In Hungary, media freedom and the anti-corruption framework are also being weakened. The weakening of independent institutions and the growing pressure on civil society undermine the separation of powers. There is a lack of commitment to implement the EU's recommendations on the rule of law on the ground.[62] On 27 October 2021, Poland was ordered by the CJEU to pay the Commission a daily penalty payment in an amount of 1,000,000 euro 'as it has not suspended the application of the provisions of national legislation relating, in particular, to the areas of jurisdiction of the Disciplinary Chamber of the Supreme Court'. Polish President Andrzej Duda announced to dismantle this Disciplinary Chamber.[63] According to the CJEU, '[c]ompliance with the interim measures ordered on 14 July 2021 is necessary in order to avoid serious and irreparable harm to the legal order of the European Union and to the values on which that Union is founded, in particular that of the rule of law'.[64] Such situations of conflicts undermine trust in the rule of law in the respective MS.

For these reasons, the respective principle of mutual trust should be incorporated in primary law to strengthen it, just like the principle of mutual recognition. A simple suspension procedure could be standardised in primary or secondary law through a reform of Article 7 TEU.[65] This is all the truer since Article 7 TEU, with its high formal requirements, entails a lengthy and complex procedure. Even in well-documented cases, such as Poland and Hungary, Article 7 TEU does not provide an effective tool for control. It should be possible to prevent deficiencies in the rule of law

[62] Commission, Communication, *2020 Rule of Law Report. The Rule of Law Situation in the European Union*, COM (2020) 580 final; Commission, Commission staff working document, *2020 Rule of Law Report Country Chapter on the Rule of Law Situation in Hungary*, SWD (2020) 316 final; Commission, Commission staff working document, *2020 Rule of Law Report Country Chapter on the Rule of Law Situation in Poland*, SWD (2020) 320 final.

[63] www.reuters.com/world/europe/polish-president-submits-bill-move-end-rule-law-row-with-eu-2022-02-03/ (accessed 5 March 2022).

[64] CJEU, *Commission v. Poland*, No. C-204/21 R, Press Release No 192/21, Order of the Vice-President of the Court, 27 October 2021.

[65] M. Ruffert, 'Art. 7 EUV', in C. Calliess and M. Ruffert (eds.), *EUV/AEUV. Das Verfassungsrecht der Europäischen Union mit Europäischer Grundrechtecharta. Kommentar*, 4th edn., München: C. H. Beck, 2011, para. 32; P. Wilkitzki, 'Regionalisierung des internationalen Strafrechts', (1993) 105 *ZStW*, 821, 845.

even below the threshold of Article 7 TEU by way of a preliminary non-compliance procedure. The CVM and the control procedure in the Croatian accession agreements by the Commission have proven to be practicable and effective. For example, in September 2013, after several warnings, the Commission 'launched' a corresponding 'procedure on Croatia' and thus 'activated the justice and home affairs safeguard clause in Croatia's Accession Treaty'.[66] The reason for this was a Croatian law which, in contradiction to the provisions of the FD EAW, provided for time limits for the application of an EAW and, at least from the EU's perspective, deliberately made the apprehension of suspected war criminals more difficult.[67] The following case was particularly interesting in this context: The former secret service employee and politician Josip Perković was wanted in connection with a murder in Bavaria in the 1980s. Germany therefore issued an arrest warrant in 2004. As of 2013, Croatia, now an EU MS, was obliged to implement the FD EAW in Croatia. However, the time limits in the said law were not in compliance with secondary law and released Croatia from the obligation to extradite Perković. The sanctions procedure threatened Croatia to further suspend its accession to the Schengen area and hold off a payment of 80 million euro from the EU regional fund. Croatia finally gave in and withdrew and announced that it would repeal the said law. After a Croatian court had rejected the final appeal against extradition, President Ivo Josipović conceded: 'We have to respect the independent judiciary, and that's it.'[68] As a result, the proceedings against Croatia were discontinued, and Croatia put its promise into practice. In 2016, Perković was surrendered to Germany and convicted of murder.

However, the supervisory procedure of the accession treaties is unsuitable for eliminating structural and long-term deficiencies. For it only applies for

[66] Cf. Art. 39 Act concerning the conditions of accession of the Republic of Croatia and the adjustments to the Treaty on European Union, the Treaty on the Functioning of the European Union and the Treaty establishing the European Atomic Energy Community, OJ L 112/2, 1.5.2012, in conjunction with Art. 1(3) Treaty between the Member States of the European Union and the Republic of Croatia concerning the accession of the Republic of Croatia to the European Union, OJ L 112/10, 1.5.2012.

[67] Memo of the Commission on 18.9.2013, MEMO/13/793, p. 2, according to the Commission 'the limitation of the European Arrest Warrant is a clear and serious violation of EU law. It thwarts the legitimate expectations of other Member States to be able to request the surrender of alleged and convicted criminals from Croatia as of the countries' accession to the EU, under a rapid and efficient European Arrest Warrant system'.

[68] www.bbc.com/news/world-europe-25882256.

a limited period of time to new MS on a transitional basis. The difficult procedure to change primary law makes a swift reform of Article 7 TEU rather unlikely. It is more probable to come to an adjustment of secondary law[69] by including in the relevant legal instruments a suspension procedure. Insofar, the most reasonable approach would be to complement the case-by-case examination, as provided for in the freezing order, by a general suspension clause. Only the Commission should be allowed to suspend recognition in a general form to ensure legal unity. This required measure could be modelled on Article 39 Act of Accession of Croatia. Similarly, a rule of law clause should be integrated as a condition in secondary law on subsidies and funds. The example of Croatia has shown that this is an effective instrument.[70]

In such a scenario, the Commission would be the competent supervisory body since it already performs such a task vis-à-vis new MS and regularly evaluates the legal instruments on the principle of mutual recognition. It could be supported by the Fundamental Rights Agency. If the Commission does not act swiftly, an appeal to the CJEU, not least for the sake of the separation of power, should be made possible.

The suspension of the principle of mutual recognition merely means that the requested MS's obligation to execute a request from the respective MS no longer applies. Mutual legal assistance in the traditional sense will still be possible if an assurance is given that a rule of law-based procedure will be followed in the respective case at hand. This approach is in line with the CJEU's ruling in Aranyosi and Căldăraru. Case-by-case regulation to uphold human rights is necessary, but it always assumes non-intentional, remediable non-compliance with primary and secondary law. Serious negligence and intent that lead to systemic and structural violations in general can only be countered at a government and institutional level. At any rate, one must not overlook that a suspension

[69] Ronsfeld, *Rechtshilfe, Anerkennung und Vertrauen. Die Europäische Ermittlungsanordnung*, pp. 276 ff.

[70] First tendencies in this direction can be found in Recital 25 of the Regulation (EU) 2020/2221 amending Regulation (EU) No 1303/2013 as regards additional resources and implementing arrangements to provide assistance for fostering crisis repair in the context of the COVID-19 pandemic and its social consequences and for preparing a green, digital and resilient recovery of the economy (REACT-EU), OJ L 437/30, 28.12.2020; www.politico.eu/article/poland-lgbtq-steep-price/ in 2021 five Polish towns abolished their so called 'LGBT-free zones' because the Commission stopped regional funding as a result of Charter violations.

also entails a partial disenfranchisement of the respective MS and will therefore certainly not be uncontroversial if implemented in secondary law. The States addressed may feel as being stigmatised as generally unreliable and not up to the general rule of law standards.

6.5 Conclusion

Transnational criminality requires enforcement cooperation. All States can use traditional mutual legal assistance for this purpose. However, the EU has created legal instruments based on the principle of mutual recognition, for a simpler and more secure cooperation. International relations always depend on the perceived trustworthiness of the partner State. The term 'trust' is therefore frequently recalled in preambles, but its jurisprudential conceptualisation is still pending. Trust is in any case closely linked to respect for fundamental rights.

At all stages of a new member's accession, the EU works towards transparency, integrity and the rule of law, using confidence-building measures. In each MS, the ECHR and the Charter apply. Nevertheless, the observance of fundamental rights must be constantly monitored. This task is currently mainly carried out by NGOs and the Venice Commission of the Council of Europe. Yet, the EU is increasingly taking the initiative in this area, such as with the Commission's 2020 Rule of Law Report.[71] Lack of trust – not only in law enforcement – leads to Euroscepticism, and even to Europe fatigue (Brexit). The EU must therefore address the shortcomings identified in the said report and regain lost trust.

For mutual recognition based on mutual trust, the rule of law of all MS must be constantly reviewed and adapted. Human rights violations such as inhumane detention conditions can also be remedied with financial support and consulting. The EU Rule of Law Mechanism, which entered into force in 2021, can make an important contribution in this regard if it is properly applied. At the same time, European institutions must be strengthened and the exchange and cooperation between law enforcement agencies must be intensified.

[71] Commission, Communication, *2020 Rule of Law Report. The Rule of Law Situation in the European Union*, COM(2020) 580 final.

Further Reading

P. Ronsfeld, *Rechtshilfe, Anerkennung und Vertrauen. Die Europäische Ermittlungsanordnung*, Berlin: Duncker & Humblot, 2015.

P. Sztompka, *Trust. A Sociological Theory*, Cambridge, New York: Cambridge University Press, 1999.

N. Luhmann, *Vertrauen. Ein Mechanismus der Reduktion sozialer Komplexität*, 4th edn., Stuttgart: Lucius & Lucius, 2000.

Part III

European Substantive Criminal Law

Protection of the Financial Interests of the EU (Art. 325 TFEU) 7

Stefanie Bock

7.1 Introduction: The Importance of Protecting the European Union's Financial Interests

The protection of the EU's financial interests has always been the driving force behind the development of European Criminal Law.[1] The regulatory instruments and techniques originally developed in this field have often served as legislative blueprints, and they have frequently been transferred to other areas of criminal law.[2] It might be argued that the protection

[1] Cf., for example, V. Covolo, *L'émergence d'un droit pénal en réseau. Analyse critique du système européen de lutte antifraude*, Baden-Baden: Nomos, 2015, p. 83; B. Hecker, *Europäisches Strafrecht*, 6th edn., Berlin: Springer, 2021, § 13 mn. 4; C. Gómez-Jara Díez, *European Federal Criminal Law – The Federal Dimension of EU Criminal Law* Cambridge: Intersentia, 2015, p. 76; S. Bock, 'Der Schutz der finanziellen Interessen der Union. Überlegungen zur Betrugsbekämpfungsrichtlinie 2017/1371', in K. Ambos and S. Bock (eds.), *Aktuelle und grundsätzliche Fragen des Wirtschaftsstrafrechts/Questions actuelle et fondamentales du droit pénal des affaires*, Berlin: Duncker & Humblot, 2019, pp. 155–180 at p. 156.

[2] For example, the principle of assimilation was originally developed by the Court of Justice of the European Union (CJEU) to guarantee an effective protection of the EU's financial interests (see note 29 and accompanying text). In the meantime, however, it has come to be applied to all supranational legal interests that concern the EU's existence and functioning. See K. Ambos, *European Criminal Law*, Cambridge: Cambridge University Press, 2018, p. 339. European definitions of active and passive corruption were set up for the first time in the Protocol drawn up on the basis of Art. K.3 of the Treaty on European Union to the Convention on the protection of the European Communities' financial interests, OJ C 313, 23.10.1996, p. 1. These definitions were later included, with only minor modifications, in the Convention drawn up on the basis of Art. K.3 para. 2 lit. (c) of the Treaty on the European Union on the fight against corruption involving officials of the European Communities or officials of Member States of the European Union, OJ C 192, 15.6.1997, p. 1. The Council's standard model provision on the liability of legal persons (Council, *Council Conclusions on Guidelines for Future Criminal Law in EU legislation*, 9 October 2009, Doc. 14162/09, pp. 9–10) is based on Art. 3 und 4 Second Protocol, drawn up on the basis of Art. K.3 of the treaty on European Union, to the Convention on the protection of the European Communities' financial interests, OJ C 221, 19.7.1997, p. 11.

of financial interests – the so-called 'PIF-sector'[3] – has assumed such a pioneering role because it provides a fundamental condition for the existence and effective functioning of the EU.[4] This is particularly true of the EU's financial and subsidies policies, which are closely intertwined with its political priorities.[5] For example, direct payments to farmers[6] clearly aim 'to ensure a fair standard of living for the agricultural community'.[7] Moreover, however, they are linked with a complex system of obligations[8] and cross-compliances requirements.[9] In effect, they serve as a tool for the EU's environmental and climate policy. With its structural investments, the EU aims to promote a broadly harmonious development, strengthen its economic, social and territorial cohesion, and reduce disparities between the levels of development of the various regions (cf. Art. 174 TFEU). In much the same way, the gamut of EU customs duties[10] not only provide a measure for generating income; they

[3] The broad legal field that relates to the 'protection of financial interest' is commonly referred to by its French acronym 'PIF' (*protection des intérêts financiers*).

[4] Cf. also B. Weißer, 'Strafgesetzgebung durch die Europäische Union: Nicht nur ein Recht, sondern auch eine Pflicht?', (2014) 161 *GA*, 433–452 at 434.

[5] S. Magiera, 'Art. 325 AEUV', in E. Grabitz, M. Hilf and M. Nettesheim (eds.), *Das Recht der Europäischen Union*, München: C.H. Beck, 74th supply, September 2021, mn. 11; Bock, 'Der Schutz der finanziellen Interessen der Union. Überlegungen zur Betrugsbekämpfungsrichtlinie 2017/1371', p. 157; cf. also H. Spitzer and U. Stiegel, 'Art. 325 AEUV', in H. von der Groeben, J. Schwarze and A. Hartje (eds.), *Europäisches Unionsrecht. Vertrag über die Europäische Union, Vertrag über die Arbeitsweise der Europäischen Union, Charta der Grundrechte der Europäischen Union*, 7th edn., Baden-Baden: Nomos, 2015, mn. 10.

[6] Cf. in particular Arts. 21 f. Regulation 1307/2013/EU of the European Parliament and of the Council of 17 December 2013 establishing rules for direct payments to farmers under support schemes within the framework of the common agricultural policy and repealing Council Regulation (EC) No 637/2008 and Council Regulation (EC) No 73/2009, OJ L 347, 10.12.2013, p. 608.

[7] Art. 39 (1) (b) TFEU.

[8] Cf., for example, Art. 44 Regulation 1307/2013 on crop diversification or Art. 46 Regulation 1307/2013 on ecological focus areas.

[9] Beneficiaries of direct payments have to obey the rules on cross-compliance which relate to areas of (a) environment, climate change and good agricultural condition of land, (b) public, animal and plant health and (c) animal welfare, cf. Art. 93 read with Annex II of the Regulation (EU) No 1306/2013 of the European Parliament and of the Council of 17 December 2013 on the financing, management and monitoring of the common agricultural policy and repealing Council Regulations (EEC) No. 352/78, (EC) No. 165/94, (EC) No. 2799/98, (EC) No. 814/2000, (EC) No. 1290/2005 and (EC) No. 485/2008, OJ L 347, 20.12.2013, p. 549.

[10] In order to realise the common market and guarantee the free movement of goods, the EU comprises a customs union, Art. 28 TFEU. Between individual EU Members,

also function as a critical means by which the Union influences trade and pursues its economic interests.[11]

Clearly, then – and as these examples show – any loss of revenue or misallocation of funds damages the EU's financial interests. More than this, however, such setbacks threaten to jeopardise the implementation of EU policies.[12] The EU thus has a vital interest in effectively protecting its budget and in promoting the development of criminal law in this area.

However, these efforts may run into spirited opposition from the individual Member States (MS). Indeed, the financial interests of the EU and those of its MS are in many ways interconnected. Protective measures adopted at the European level often affect national budgets and financial policies. Traditionally, such policy areas have typically been perceived as '[p]articularly sensitive for the ability of a constitutional state to democratically shape itself'.[13] Discussions on the adoption of protective financial measures thus inevitably touch upon even more fundamental questions concerning the division of sovereign spheres within the EU. They also impact delicate questions around the preservation of the national (cultural and legal) autonomy of EU MS.[14] This basic conflict becomes particularly appreciable if the EU elects to fight fraudulent

customs duties and charges having equivalent effect shall be prohibited, Art. 30 TFEU; customs are only collected at the external frontier of the EU. Revenues from the common customs tariff (cf. Art. 31 TFEU) and other duties established in respect of trade with third countries are collected by the Member States but then transferred to the budget of the EU.

[11] See, in more detail, H.-M. Wolffgang, '§ 33. Zollrecht', in R. Schulze, M. Zuleeg and S. Kadelbach (eds.), *Europarecht. Handbuch für die deutsche Rechtspraxis*, 3rd edn., Baden-Baden: Nomos, 2015, pp. 2025–2058 at mn. 4–8; see also Bock, 'Der Schutz der finanziellen Interessen der Union. Überlegungen zur Betrugsbekämpfungsrichtlinie 2017/1371', p. 158.

[12] European Commission, *On the Protection of the Financial Interests of the European Union by Criminal Law and by Administrative Investigations – An Integrated Policy to Safeguard Taxpayers' Money*, 26 May 2011, COM(2011) 293 final, p. 3.

[13] German Constitutional Court, Judgement of 30 June 2009, *BVerfGE* 123, pp. 267–437 at 359 – English translation available at www.bundesverfassungsgericht.de/SharedDocs/Entscheidungen/EN/2009/06/es20090630_2bve000208en.html;jsessionid=78683F879FE461D7EC3384186A5CEF5A.1_cid392 (last accessed 13 November 2022).

[14] Cf. on the lengthy discussion on the adoption of the Directive 2017/1371/EU of the European Parliament and of the Council of 5 July on the Fight against Fraud to the EU's financial interests by Means of Criminal Law, OJ L 198, 28.7.2017, p. 29 – PIF-Directive) Bock, 'Der Schutz der finanziellen Interessen der Union. Überlegungen zur Betrugsbekämpfungsrichtlinie 2017/1371', p. 155.

conduct by drawing on criminal law. This is another especially sensitive area when it comes to the sovereign identity of national states.[15] Against this background, it might be argued that the 'protection of financial interests' not only comprises the driving force behind the development of European Criminal Law; it could be taken as an indicator of the status of the entire process of European integration.

7.2 Art. 325 TFEU – The Primary Law Basis of the PIF Regime

The importance of the PIF Regime is clearly indicated by its settled status in primary law. Its main elements are outlined in Art. 325 of the Treaty of the Functioning of the European Union (TFEU). This fundamental provision

- obliges the EU and the MS to counter fraud and any other illegal activities affecting the financial interests of the EU through deterrent measures which afford effective protection (para. 1);
- obliges the MS to apply the same measures to counter fraud which affects the EU's financial interests as they take to counter fraud which affects their own, independent financial interests (para. 2);
- obliges the MS to coordinate their actions with respect to protecting the financial interests of the EU, in conjunction with the Commission (para. 3);
- empowers the European Parliament and the Council to adopt the necessary measures in the fields of the prevention of and fight against fraud which affects the financial interests of the EU (para. 4); and
- obliges the Commission to report to the European Parliament and to the Council on a yearly basis on the measures taken to prevent and combat fraud and any other illegal activities affecting the financial interests of the EU (para. 5).

[15] German Constitutional Court, Judgement of 30 June 2009, *BVerfGE*, 123 pp. 267–437 at 359 – English translation available at www.bundesverfassungsgericht.de/SharedDocs/Entscheidungen/EN/2009/06/es20090630_2bve000208en.html;jsessionid=78683F879FE461D7EC3384186A5CEF5A.1_cid392 (last accessed 13 November 2022).

7.3 Scope of Application – Definition of Terms

7.3.1 The Financial Interests of the European Union

Art. 325 TFEU obliges the EU and the MS to fight fraud and any other financial activities directed against the financial interests of the EU. However, at no point does it expressly define these interests. How, then, do we interpret this Article? First, it is necessary to consider that Art. 325 TFEU is part of the TFEU's Title on 'Financial Provisions'. The protection of the EU's financial interests is thus closely linked to the EU's budget.[16] Certainly, Art. 2 (1) (a) of the PIF-Directive[17] defines the 'Union's financial interests' as 'all revenues, expenditures and assets covered by, acquired through, or due to: (i) the EU budget; (ii) the budgets of the EU institutions, bodies, offices and agencies established pursuant to the Treaties or budgets directly or indirectly managed and monitored by them.' Clearly, then, the core purpose of Art. 325 TFEU lies in the protection of the EU's public money, wherever this money is collected or spent.[18]

That said, this Article is not concerned with the protection of the EU's overall monetary system, or with the price stability of the euro area. In fact, these factors exert no more than an indirect effect on the EU's financial resources. The same applies to the protection of the EU's currency, the Euro, against counterfeiting,[19] and to the protection of the integrity of the common market.[20]

[16] Bock, 'Der Schutz der finanziellen Interessen der Union. Überlegungen zur Betrugsbekämpfungsrichtlinie 2017/1371', p. 159.

[17] Directive 2017/1371/EU of the European Parliament and of the Council of 5 July 2017 on the Fight against Fraud to the Union's Financial Interests by Means of Criminal Law, OJ L 198/29, 28.7.2017, p. 29.

[18] European Commission, *Commission Staff Working Paper: Impact Assessment (Part I) Accompanying the Document, Proposal for a Directive of the European Parliament and of the Council on the Protection of the Financial Interests of the European Union by Criminal Law,* 11 July 2012, SWD(2012) 195 final, p. 27.

[19] For a different view, see J. Vogel, 'Die Strafgesetzgebungskompetenzen der Europäischen Union nach Art. 83, 86 und 325 AEUV', in K. Ambos (ed.), *Europäisches Strafrecht post-Lissabon*, Göttingen: Göttingen University Press, 2011, pp. 41–49 at p. 48.

[20] A different view is apparently taken by C. Gómez-Jara, 'European Federal Criminal Law: What Can Europe Learn from the US System of Federal Criminal Law to Solve Its Sovereign Debt Crisis?', (2013) 3 *EuCLR*, 170–193. On pp. 184–186, the author seems to frame the market abuse directive (Directive 2014/57/EU of the European Parliament and of the Council of 16 April 2014 on criminal sanctions for market abuse, OJ L 173/179, 12 June 2014, p. 179) as a measure to protect the EU's financial interests.

Against this background, it seems clear that the protection of the EU's financial interests must be strictly distinguished from the EU's monetary or economic policies. Anything else would overstretch Art. 325 TFEU, and it would risk interfering with other (special) treaty provisions. These include, for example, Art. 127 TFEU, which defines the tasks of the European System of Central Banks in the areas of price stability and monetary and exchange rate policy.[21]

7.3.2 Fraud and Other Illegal Activities Affecting the Financial Interests of the EU

Art. 325 TFEU differentiates between two types of harmful conduct: fraud, and other illegal activities affecting the EU's financial interests. Certainly, drawing a clear distinction between these two categories is no easy task. However, it carries myriad and significance implications. The power of the EU to adopt protective measures in terms of Art. 325 (4) TFEU applies only to fraud – but *not* to other illegal activities.[22]

Broadly speaking, fraud entails some kind of deliberate deception or willful misrepresentation.[23] This could take the form of using or presenting false, incorrect or incomplete statements or documents (cf. Art. 3 (2) (a) (i) PIF-Directive). Fraud can also be committed by omission – that is, misleading a person by failing to disclose relevant information in violation of a specific obligation to do so (cf. Art. 3 (2) (a) (ii) PIF-Directive). This includes the misapplication of EU funds or assets for purposes other than those for which they were originally granted (cf. Art. 3 (2) (a) (iii) PIF-Directive). The beneficiary is required to inform the financing body of any non-compliance with or violation of the overall obligations and conditions inherent to the allocation of money. In addition, this deceptive behaviour

[21] Bock, 'Der Schutz der finanziellen Interessen der Union. Überlegungen zur Betrugsbekämpfungsrichtlinie 2017/1371', pp. 160–161.

[22] H. Satzger, 'Art. 325 AEUV', in R. Streinz (ed.), *EUV/AEUV*, 3rd edn., München: C.H. Beck, 2018, mn. 8, 28; P. Asp, '(More Than) Two Decades Later – Does the Principle of Assimilation Still Have a Role to Play within European Criminal Law?', in G. Freund *et al.* (eds.), *Grundlagen und Dogmatik des gesamten Strafrechtssystems – Festschrift für Wolfang Frisch zum 70. Geburtstag*, Berlin: Duncker & Humblot, 2013, pp. 1389–1401 at p. 1393; for a different view, see Magiera, 'Art. 325 AEUV', mn. 15.

[23] See K. Tiedemann, 'Strafrecht im Europäischen Verfassungsvertrag', in H. Müller-Dietz *et al.* (eds.), *Festschrift für Heike Jung* (Baden-Baden: Nomos, 2007) pp. 987–1003 at p. 997; see also Satzger, 'Art. 325 AEUV', mn. 28.

must result in property damage or an economic loss for the EU. This might comprise a wrongful retention of funds, or an illegal diminution of EU resources (cf. Art. 3 (2) (a) PIF-Directive). The term 'other illegal activities' covers all conduct other than fraud[24] which at least endangers[25] EU property. Concrete examples include the (non-fraudulent) appropriation of property belonging to the EU.

7.3.3 Member States' Duty to Protect: The Principles of Assimilation and Minimum Protection

According to Art. 325 (1) TFEU, the EU and its MS share responsibility for the effective protection of the Union's financial interests.[26] The MS are presented as 'protector guarantors',[27] charged with a protective duty towards the EU. This requires them to act on their own initiative in order to actively combat fraud and other illegal activities which threaten the interests of the EU.[28]

The details of this arrangement are set out in Art. 325 (1), (2) AEUV. These passages codify the fundamental principles established in 1989 by the European Court of Justice (ECJ), the predecessor to the Court of Justice of the European Union (CJEU), in its ground-breaking 'Greek Maize' judgement.[29] This judgement concluded a legal case around two consignments of maize exported to Belgium and officially declared to be Greek – despite the fact that both came from Yugoslavia. The relevant authorities treated the maize as if it had originated within the European

[24] Spitzer and Stiegel, 'Art. 325 AEUV', mn. 23.

[25] Fraud requires the actual occurrence of financial harm. However, other illegal activities need only affect the EU's financial interests. This formulation is broad enough to cover crimes of (concrete) endangerment. See Satzger, 'Art. 325 AEUV', mn. 9; Vogel, 'Die Strafgesetzgebungskompetenzen der Europäischen Union nach Art. 83, 86 und 325 AEUV', pp. 48–49.

[26] Cf. CJEU, *Criminal Proceedings against M.A.S. and M.B.*, No. C-42/17, Judgment, ECLI:EU:C:2017:936, 5 December 2017, para. 43.

[27] Generally, on the terminology and the foundation of duties to act, see K. Ambos, 'Omissions', in K. Ambos *et al.* (eds.), *Core Concepts in Criminal Law and Criminal Justice. Volume 1* Cambridge: Cambridge University Press, 2020) pp. 17–53 (at pp. 27–38).

[28] Hecker, *Europäisches Strafrecht*, § 7 mn. 26. Member States' obligation to act proactively, even when they are not given express instruction to take concrete measures, is covered more thoroughly in Ambos, *European Criminal Law*, p. 339.

[29] ECJ, *Commission of the European Communities v. Hellenic Republic*, No. 68/88, Judgment, ECLI:EU:C:1989:339, 21 September 1989.

Community. Consequently, they did not collect the agricultural tariff levied against maize imported from a third country. Despite several requests from the European Commission, Greek authorities refused to take criminal or disciplinary actions against the Greek officials allegedly involved in the incident.

The ECJ took the view that Greece had violated its duty of loyalty and the principle of sincere cooperation. Art. 5 EEC Treaty (now: Art. 4 (3) TEU) required all MS to take appropriate measures in order to ensure fulfilment of the obligations arising from European treaties or resulting from the acts of the Community's institutions (that is, of today's EU). According to the ECJ, this provision

> [...] requires the Member States to take all measures necessary to guarantee the application and effectiveness of Community law.
>
> For that purpose, whilst the choice of penalties remains within their discretion, they must ensure in particular that infringements of Community law are penalized under conditions, both procedural and substantive, which are analogous to those applicable to infringements of national law of a similar nature and importance and which, in any event, make the penalty effective, proportionate and dissuasive.
>
> Moreover, the national authorities must proceed, with respect to infringements of Community law, with the same diligence as that which they bring to bear in implementing corresponding national laws.[30]

This judgment is based on the assumption that the MS have a protective duty towards the EU, but that they can, in principle, freely decide how to fulfill this duty. In particular, they have some latitude with respect to how they sanction violations of EU interests. However, their discretion is limited by two fundamental principles. These principles are highly relevant for the protection of the EU's financial interests and for the Europeanisation of national criminal law in general. They are (i) the principle of assimilation and (ii) the principle of minimum protection.[31]

The principle of assimilation is vividly reflected in Art. 325 (2) TFEU. It requires the relevant MS to protect the EU interests in the same way that it would protect its own national interests.[32] Let us suppose, for example,

[30] Ibid., paras. 23–25. [31] Ambos, *European Criminal Law*, pp. 339–340.

[32] Asp, '(More Than) Two Decades Later – Does the Principle of Assimilation Still Have a Role to Play within European Criminal Law?', p. 1389.

that a particular MS defines the evasion of national taxes as a criminal offence that might result in imprisonment of up to five years (see, e.g., S. 370 (1) of the German Fiscal Code). Under such circumstances, this MS must apply the same penalty with respect to import or export duties – a functional equivalent[33] of taxes[34] – collected for the benefit of the EU (see, e.g., S. 370 (6) of the German Fiscal Code).[35]

Clearly, then, the principle of assimilation is a special, non-discriminative rule. It requires that violations of national interests, on the one hand, and of corresponding EU interests, on the other, be dealt with equally in law and practice.[36] However, this also means that the scope of protection of European interests depends on the relevant national legal system. Ultimately, if a MS does not protect its own interests to a reasonable degree, then the principle of assimilation carries few consequences. In the end, this principle only guarantees an *analogous* level of protection.[37]

In order to circumvent these legal loopholes, the EU's financial protection regime complements the principle of assimilation with the principle of *minimum protection.* In its 'Greek Maize' judgement, the ECJ established a 'minimum trias'.[38] This stipulated that any sanctions for violations of European interests must be effective, proportionate and dissuasive. The equivalent paragraph in EU primary law is now Art. 325 (1) TFEU; it calls for 'deterrent and effective measures'. In fact, however, this new wording does not change the substance of the principle of minimum protection as it was first articulated in the 'Greek Maize' judgement.[39] Then as now, it is expected that MS sanctions be

[33] Cf. S. Gröblinghoff, *Die Verpflichtung des deutschen Strafgesetzgebers zum Schutz der Interessen der Europäischen Gemeinschaften*, Heidelberg: C.F. Müller, 1996, p. 24; H. Satzger, *Die Europäisierung des Strafrechts*, Köln: Carl Heymanns Verlag, 2001, p. 263; Asp, '(More Than) Two Decades Later – Does the Principle of Assimilation Still Have a Role to Play within European Criminal Law?', p. 1393.

[34] Spitzer and Stiegel, 'Art. 325 AEUV', mn. 45.

[35] See also A. Klip, *European Criminal Law – An Integrative Approach*, 4th edn., Cambridge: Intersentia, 2021, p. 80 and CJEU, *Nikolay Kolev and Others*, No. C-612/15, Judgment, ECLI:EU:C:2018:392, 5 June 2018, para. 54.

[36] Hecker, *Europäisches Strafrecht*, § 7 mn. 26–27; Klip, *European Criminal Law – An Integrative Approach*, p. 80; H. Satzger, *International and European Criminal Law*, 2nd edn., München et al.: C. H. Beck, Hart Publishing, Nomos, 2018, § 7 mn. 27.

[37] Cf. Klip, *European Criminal Law – An Integrative Approach*, p. 80; Satzger, *International and European Criminal Law*, § 7 mn. 27; Spitzer and Stiegel, 'Art. 325 AEUV', mn. 46.

[38] Ambos, *European Criminal Law*, p. 340.

[39] Cf. also Spitzer and Stiegel, 'Art. 325 AEUV', mn. 27.

sufficiently stringent to (i) discourage the perpetrator from re-offending (theory of special prevention), (ii) deter the general public from violating the EU's financial interests (theory of negative general prevention), and (iii) restore confidence in the (European) legal order (theory of positive general prevention).[40] Moreover, the sanction must correspond to the severity of the violation.[41]

Significantly, these minimum requirements apply independently from the level of protection already offered by national law. This means that, if a MS does not already meet the standard of Art. 325 (2) TFEU, then it is obliged to introduce additional (and, if necessary, criminal)[42] sanctions in order to enhance the protection of the EU's financial interests.[43]

It is against this background that we can understand the verdict arrived at by the CJEU in its *Taricco* judgement.[44] In this case, the Court targeted specific national provisions related to the interruption of limitation periods which had the effect that, 'in a considerable number of cases, the commission of serious fraud will escape criminal punishment, since the offences will usually be time-barred before the criminal penalty laid down by law can be imposed by a final judicial decision.' Consequently, in the view of the CJEU, these provisions 'could not be regarded as effective and dissuasive' in accordance with the meaning of Art. 325 (2) TFEU.[45] As EU law takes precedence over national law,[46] the CJEU concluded that national criminal courts are obliged to disapply any

[40] Gröblinghoff, *Die Verpflichtung des deutschen Strafgesetzgebers zum Schutz der Interessen der Europäischen Gemeinschaften*, pp. 25–26; Spitzer and Stiegel, 'Art. 325 AEUV', mn. 30; Satzger, *International and European Criminal Law*, § 7 mn. 27; see for more detail Klip, *European Criminal Law – An Integrative Approach*, pp. 81–88.

[41] Satzger, *International and European Criminal Law*, § 7 mn 27; see also Spitzer and Stiegel, 'Art. 325 AEUV', mn. 39.

[42] CJEU, *Criminal Proceedings against Ivo Taricco and Others*, No. C-105/14, Judgment, ECLI:EU:C:2015:555, 8 September 2015, para. 39; CJEU, *Criminal Proceedings against M.A.S. and M.B.*, No. C-42/17, Judgment, ECLI:EU:C:2017:936, 5 December 2017, para. 34.

[43] Satzger, *International and European Criminal Law*, § 7 mn. 27; Ambos, *European Criminal Law*, p. 340; Hecker, *Europäisches Strafrecht*, § 7 mn. 27.

[44] On the 'Taricco saga' in more detail, see Fronza in this volume.

[45] CJEU, *Criminal Proceedings against Ivo Taricco and Others*, No. C-105/14, Judgment, ECLI:EU:C:2015:555, 8 September 2015, para. 47.

[46] On the principle of the primacy of EU law and its meaning for national criminal law, see Ambos, *European Criminal Law*, pp. 340–343; Satzger, *International and European Criminal Law*, § 7 mn. 78.

national provisions on limitation which conflict with the principle of minimum protection.[47] Ultimately, then, Art. 325 (2) TFEU effectively neutralises national provisions that are incompatible with the duty of the MS to provide for a dissuasive and effective protection of the EU's financial interests.[48]

Critics argue that the CJEU's *Taricco* judgement paves the way for an undue degree of European interference in national criminal proceedings, without paying sufficient attention to fundamental legal guarantees such as the the *nullum crimen sine lege* principle.[49] Such objections are undeniably weighty. However, it is also important to note that the CJEU has limited the neutralising effect of Art. 325 (2) TFEU. It has done so by pointing out that the disapplication of national provisions must be compatible with the fundamental rights of the accused, in particular the principles of legality and proportionality as enshrined in Art. 49 of the EU Charter of Fundamental Rights. In the view of the CJEU, however, this does not prohibit a retroactive extension of limitation periods.[50]

Indeed, in a later case, the CJEU once again had to deal with the effects of (too) short statutes of limitations. The CJEU clarified that the task of the national legislator is, above all, to ensure that national law fulfils

[47] CJEU, *Criminal Proceedings against Ivo Taricco and Others,* No. C-105/14, Judgment, ECLI:EU:C:2015:555, 8 September 2015, para. 52; cf. also CJEU, *Criminal Proceedings against Petar Dzivev and Others,* No. C-310/16, Judgment, 17 January 2019, para. 32.

[48] Cf. CJEU, *Criminal Proceedings against Ivo Taricco and Others,* No. C-105/14, Judgment, ECLI:EU:C:2015:555, 8 September 2015, para. 59. On the neutralising effect on EU law, see Satzger, *International and European Criminal Law,* § 7 mn. 78 f.

[49] Cf. E. Billis, 'The European Court of Justice: A Quasi-Constitutional Court in Criminal Matters: The Taricco Judgment and Its Shortcomings', (2016) 7 *NJECL,* 20–38; G. Hochmayer, 'Unionstreue trotz Verjährung. Anmerkung zum Urteil des Europäischen Gerichtshofs (Große Kammer) vom 8. September 2015 (C-105/14 – Taricco) = HRRS 2015 Nr. 1007', (2016) 17 *HRRS,* 239–243.

[50] CJEU, *Criminal Proceedings against Ivo Taricco and Others,* No. C-105/14, Judgment, ECLI:EU:C:2015:555, 8 September 2015, paras. 53–58. With reference to the relevant case law of the European Court of Human Rights (ECtHR), see only ECtHR, *Scoppola v. Italy (No. 2),* Appl. No. 10249/03, 17 September 2009 para. 110. In this judgment, the EctHR confirmed that the rules on retrospectives (Art. 7 of the European Convention of Human Rights, ECHR) apply only to provisions defining offences and the penalties for them, but not to procedural laws like rules on limitation. This was confirmed in CJEU, *Criminal Proceedings against M.A.S. and M.B.,* No. C-42/17, Judgment, ECLI:EU:C:2017:936, 5 December 2017, para. 42, 46; CJEU, *Nikolay Kolev and Others,* No. C-612/15, Judgment, ECLI:EU:C:2018:392, 5 June 2018, paras. 68–69; CJEU, *Criminal Proceedings against Petar Dzivev and Others,* No. C-310/16, Judgment, 17 January 2019, paras. 33 f.

the minimum standard of Art. 325 (2) TFEU.[51] At the same time, the CJEU granted the national courts a margin of interpretation to determine whether or not the disapplication of national laws conflicting with Union law is compatible with human rights standards and fundamental principles of criminal law. Ultimately, national courts are not obliged to give full effect to Art. 325 (2) TFEU if the neutralisation of the national norm at issue (be it procedural or substantive)[52] leads to a 'situation of uncertainty [...], which would be in breach of the principle that the applicable law must be precise'.[53]

7.3.4 The Power of the EU to Adopt the Necessary Measures to Prevent and Fight Fraud

Art. 325 (1), (2) TFEU thus impose a range of duties on EU MS in the area of financial protection. In addition, Art. 325 (4) TFEU empowers and requires the European Parliament and the Council to adopt all necessary measures in the fields of the prevention of and fight against fraud directed at the EU.[54] Notably, the specific phrasing of Art. 325 (4) TFEU is broad indeed. This Article does not limit the EU to the enactment of specific measures (at least, not at first sight, as discussed in more detail *infra*). Instead, the Article grants broad discretion to the EU in the development of a comprehensive and effective protection regime. All measures based on Art. 325 (4) TFEU are adopted in accordance with the conventional legislative procedure. This is based on a qualified majority decision from the Council (see Art. 294 TFEU).

[51] CJEU, *Criminal Proceedings against M.A.S. and M.B.*, No. C-42/17, Judgment, ECLI:EU:C:2017:936, 5 December 2017, para. 41; cf. also CJEU, *Nikolay Kolev and Others*, No. C-612/15, Judgment, ECLI:EU:C:2018:392, 5 June 2018, para. 65; CJEU, *Criminal Proceedings against Petar Dzivev and Others*, No. C-310/16, Judgment, 17 January 2019, para. 31.

[52] Cf. also CJEU, *Criminal Proceedings against Petar Dzivev and Others*, No. C-310/16, Judgment, 17 January 2019, para. 39.

[53] CJEU, *Criminal proceedings against M.A.S. and M.B.*, No. C-42/17, Judgment, ECLI:EU:C:2017:936, 5 December 2017, paras. 59, 61. For a comparison between the Taricco and M.A.S. cases, see G. Dannecker, 'Der unionsrechtliche Grundrechtsschutz im Wirtschaftsstrafrecht', in K. Ambos and S. Bock (eds.), *Aktuelle und grundsätzliche Fragen des Wirtschaftsstrafrechts/Questions actuelle et fondamentales du droit pénal des affaires*, Berlin: Duncker & Humblot, 2019, pp. 115–154, at pp. 142 f. and F. Meyer, 'Anmerkung zu EuGH, Urteil v. 5.12.2017 – C-42/17 M.A.S. und M.B.', (2018) 73 *JZ*, 304–308.

[54] On the differentiation between fraud and other illegal activities, see *supra* notes 23 f. and accompanying text.

7.4 The Institutionalisation of the Fight Against Fraud: OLAF

With its broad scope, Art. 325 (4) TFEU provides a legal basis for creating new or shaping existing institutions[55] mandated with the prevention of and fight against EU-fraud.[56] The most prominent example of such an institution is the European Anti-Fraud Office (OLAF).[57] It is tasked with carrying out independent investigations of an administrative nature[58] into fraud, corruption and other misconduct involving EU funds.[59]

7.4.1 Administrative Measures

Another tier of an effective, holistic anti-fraud concept is the establishment of a homogenous system of administrative checks, measures and penalties. Such a regime was introduced in 1995 by the PIF-Regulation.[60] Today, this would have to be based on Art. 325 (4) TFEU. These legal provisions underpin a tripartite protection regime: prevention, restitution, and sanction.

First, EU MS are obliged to take appropriate and proportionate measures 'to ensure the regularity and reality of transactions involving the Communities' financial interests' (Art. 8 PIF-Regulation). Second, any irregularity[61] affecting EU budgets shall involve withdrawal of the

[55] Cf. the reference to Art. 325 AEUV in Regulation 2020/2223/EU, Euratom of the European Parliament and of the Council of 23 December 2020 amending Regulation (EU, Euratom) No 883/2013, as regards cooperation with the European Public Prosecutor's Office and the effectiveness of the European Anti-Fraud Office investigations, OJ L 437/49, 28.12.2020, p. 49.

[56] This, of course, assumes that there is no more specific provision taking precedent over the general Art. 325 (4) TFEU (see, e.g., Art. 86 TFEU, which concerns the creation of a European Public Prosecutor Office, – on the EPPO, see Allegrezza in this volume and M. A. Zöller and S. Bock, '§ 22. Europäische Staatsanwaltschaft', in M. Böse (ed.), *Europäisches Strafrecht* (Baden-Baden: Nomos, 2nd ed., 2021) pp. 1073–1103, for more detail).

[57] See also M. A. Zöller and S. Bock, '§ 23. OLAF', in M. Böse (ed.), *Europäisches Strafrecht* (Nomos, 2nd ed., 2021) pp. 1139–1160.

[58] Ambos, *European Criminal Law*, p. 561.

[59] For more detail, see O. Cahn in this volume.

[60] Council Regulation 2988/95/EC, Euratom of 18 December 1995 on the protection of the European Communities financial interests, OJ L 312/1, 23.12.1995, p. 1.

[61] Irregularity is defined here as any 'infringement of a provision of Community law resulting from an act or omission by an economic operator, which has, or would have,

wrongly obtained advantage, in particular by an obligation to pay or repay the amounts due or wrongly received (Art. 4 (1) PIF-Regulation). The same applies to abuses of European Law which aim to obtain an advantage contrary to the objectives of these laws (Art. 4 (3) PIF-Regulation). Third, irregularities that were caused intentionally or negligently may be sanctioned with administrative[62] penalties. These can include payment of an administrative fine, the temporary withdrawal of the approval or recognition necessary for participation in an EU aid scheme, or the loss of a security or deposit (Art. 5 PIF-Regulation).

7.4.2 Criminal Measures

Art. 325 (4) TFEU is broadly worded, however. This gives rise to a number of questions. For example, does this Article also authorise the EU to adopt fraud-related criminal law measures and to harmonise national criminal laws? Does it provide the grounds for the establishment of supranational criminal offences that are immediately applicable?[63]

On first glance, one might wonder if such additional measures are even necessary. As a rule, EU MS protect their financial interests in a satisfactory way. Moreover, they tend to prosecute fraud – or, at least, serious cases of it – as a criminal offence. As noted, the principle of assimilation requires that MS extend the same degree of safeguarding to EU financial interests as to their own, while the minimum trias serves as a gap-filling tool. Together, these principles seemingly provide for a fairly comprehensive protection of the EU's financial interests.[64]

the effect of prejudicing the general budget of the Communities or budgets managed by them, either by reducing or losing revenue accruing from own resources collected directly on behalf of the Communities, or by an unjustified item of expenditure' (Art. 1 (2) PIF-Regulation).

62 On the administrative character of the PIF penalties, see ECJ, *Maizena Gesellschaft mbH and others v. Bundesanstalt für landwirtschaftliche Marktordnung (BALM)*, No. 137/85, Judgment, ECLI:EU:C:1987:493, 18 November 1987, para. 13; ECJ, *Germany v. Commission of the European Communities*, No. C-240/90, Judgment, ECLI:EU:C:1992:408, 27 October 1992, para. 25; ECJ, *Käserei Champignon Hofmeister GmbH & Co. KG v. Hauptzollamt Hamburg-Jonas*, No. C-210/00, Judgment, ECLI:EU:C:2002:440, 11 July 2002, paras. 36, 42.

63 On the notion of supranational criminal law, see Ambos, *European Criminal Law*, p. 14.

64 Asp, '(More Than) Two Decades Later – Does the Principle of Assimilation Still Have a Role to Play within European Criminal Law?', p. 1394.

However, the principle of assimilation refers to the relevant national law of the individual MS. These laws are taken – and applied – as they are found. This entails a basic acceptance of the differences between the national legal regimes. It does not lead to the development of unified rules, and it cannot contribute to an *equivalent* protection of the EU's financial interests in all MS and across the EU, as envisioned in Art. 325 (4) TFEU.[65]

In the area of combating fraud, this is cause for concern, for two key reasons. First – and as the European Commission has pointed out – divergencies in national laws and practices may hamper international co-operation in cross-border cases. This could well have a detrimental effect on the effectiveness of the EU's fraud protection regime.[66] Inconsistent criminal sanctions and penalties can reduce the deterrent effect of the respective criminal provisions. This danger is particularly acute if some MS allow certain fraudulent conduct to go unpunished, or if they elect to impose unduly lenient penalties on the perpetrators.[67] According to the Commission, legal loopholes or enforcement deficits such as these can lead to a kind of 'forum shopping'. Under such circumstances, perpetrators (especially those involved in organised crime) might consciously take advantage of legal inconsistencies by moving 'to

65 Bock, 'Der Schutz der finanziellen Interessen der Union. Überlegungen zur Betrugsbekämpfungsrichtlinie 2017/1371', p. 163; in a similar vein, W. C. Pabsch, *Der strafrechtliche Schutz der überstaatlichen Hoheitsgewalt*, Bonn: Ludwig Röhrscheid Verlag, 1965, p. 176; Covolo, *L'émergence d'un droit pénal en réseau. Analyse critique du système européen de lutte antifraude*, p. 163.

66 European Commission, *Proposal for a Directive of the European Parliament and of the Council on the Fight against Fraud to the Union's Financial Interests by Means of Criminal Law*, 11 July 2012, COM(2012) 363 final, pp. 3–4. For more detail, see European Commission, *Commission Staff Working Paper: Impact Assessment (*Part I*) Accompanying the Document, Proposal for a Directive of the European Parliament and of the Council on the Protection of the Financial Interests of the European Union by Criminal Law*, 11 July 2012, SWD(2012) 195 final, pp. 14 f.; J. Sunderland et al., *Study on the Legal Framework for the Protection EU Financial Interests by Criminal Law*, 4 Mai 2012, pp. 72 f.

67 European Commission, *Protection of the Financial Interests*, p. 7; European Commission, *Commission Staff Working Paper: Impact Assessment (Part I) Accompanying the Document, Proposal for a Directive of the European Parliament and of the Council on the Protection of the Financial Interests of the European Union by Criminal Law*, 11 July 2012, SWD(2012) 195 final, pp. 22–23; see also J. Sunderland *et al.*, *Study on the Legal Framework for the Protection EU Financial Interests by Criminal Law*, 4 Mai 2012, p. 82; Covolo, *L'émergence d'un droit pénal en réseau. Analyse critique du système européen de lutte antifraude*, p. 154.

more lenient jurisdictions within the Union to exercise their intentional illegal activities'.[68]

The second cause for concern is the prospect that differences in the legal frameworks of individual MS may result in an unequal treatment of comparable cases. For example, a situation might arise whereby different MS impose different sanctions on cases of fraudulent conduct which are similar in terms of their gravity and character. Such discrepancies might well lead to feelings of injustice or resentment. They might even impinge upon the credibility of and public trust in the European criminal justice system.[69] Violations of the financial interests of the EU are, 'by nature, and from the start, placed at the EU level'. They thus transcend the national jurisdiction of the individual MS. But the principles of equality before the law and non-discrimination require that such infringements are treated on a common basis and according to comparable standards – regardless of where the relevant act is committed or prosecuted.[70] Consequently, in order to achieve an equivalent protection of the EU's financial interests across the Union, it is not enough to merely assimilate the (divergent) national laws of individual MS. In order to fulfil the mandate of Art. 325 (4) TFEU, the EU must actively Europeanise and standardise its anti-fraud measures.

The PIF-Regulation[71] applies automatically in and across all MS. It does not need to be transposed into national law. This is clearly a step in the direction of standardisation, because it provides a common basis for sanctioning irregularities affecting the EU's budget. That said, this

[68] European Commission, *Proposal for a Directive of the European Parliament and of the Council on the Fight against Fraud to the Union's Financial Interests by Means of Criminal Law*, 11 July 2012, COM(2012) 363 final, p. 4; see also European Commission, *Protection of the Financial Interests*, p. 12; J. Sunderland et al., Study on the *Legal Framework for the Protection EU Financial Interests by Criminal Law*, 4 Mai 2012, p. 73.

[69] Cf. D. D. Spinellis, 'Das Corpus Juris zum Schutz der finanziellen Interessen der Europäischen Union', (1999) 82 *KritV*, 141–161 at 144; I. E. Fromm, *Der strafrechtliche Schutz der Finanzinteressen der EG – Die Frage der Einführung einer supranationalen Strafrechtskompetenz durch Artikel 280 IV EGV*, Berlin, Heidelberg: Springer, 2004, p. 52.

[70] Pabsch, *Der strafrechtliche Schutz der überstaatlichen Hoheitsgewalt*, p. 28; Bock, 'Der Schutz der finanziellen Interessen der Union. Überlegungen zur Betrugsbekämpfungsrichtlinie 2017/1371', p. 164; see also European Commission, *Proposal for a Directive of the European Parliament and of the Council on the Fight against Fraud to the Union's Financial Interests by Means of Criminal Law*, 11 July 2012, COM(2012) 363 final, pp. 7–8.

[71] *Supra* note 60 and accompanying text.

regulation is limited to administrative sanctions. Of particular note here is that the PIF-Regulation does not allow for the imposition of prison sentences – not even in the form of default imprisonment in case a fine cannot be recovered.[72] The Commission assumes that criminal provisions are more effective than administrative ones. This partly owes to

(i) a widely shared sense in society that there are strong detrimental effects on reputation, in particular for the typically socially previously well placed offenders in the field of financial crime, to be tried or convicted for a criminal offence ('stigmatising effect'), (ii) the harsh sanctions potentially resulting from such conduct ('higher disruption risk') and (iii) the stricter investigative procedure, allowing in particular to better trace illegal transactions ('higher detection risk').[73]

Moreover, as the Commission argued in 2012, some 25% to 33% of total misallocations of EU-funds could be prevented or recovered through the enactment of criminal law measures.[74] Admittedly, this statement might betray the Commission's overestimation of the preventive effect of criminal law. Ultimately, this effect is hard to predict, and indeed, the concrete calculations presented by the Commission to prove the effectiveness of criminal proceedings are rather difficult to comprehend. Nevertheless, the particular harshness of criminal sanctions (i.e., the risk of imprisonment), coupled with the specific social and ethical judgement of unworthiness associated with a criminal conviction, surely makes for a potent cocktail. Given this, the European legislator is arguably justified in attributing a higher deterrent effect to criminal sanctions – at least in light of its legislative freedom and prerogative of assessment.[75] It thus seems plausible to conclude that the effective protection of the EU's

[72] Cf. also Satzger, *Die Europäisierung des Strafrechts*, pp. 76–77, 79, 84.

[73] European Commission, *Commission Staff Working Paper: Impact Assessment (Part I) Accompanying the Document, Proposal for a Directive of the European Parliament and of the Council on the Protection of the Financial Interests of the European Union by Criminal Law*, 11 July 2012, SWD(2012) 195 final, p. 36.

[74] Ibid., p. 10.

[75] Cf. also Fromm, *Der strafrechtliche Schutz der Finanzinteressen der EG – Die Frage der Einführung einer supranationalen Strafrechtskompetenz durch Artikel 280 IV EGV*, p. 35; M. Kaiafa-Gbandi, 'The Commission's Proposal for a Directive on the Fight against Fraud to the Union's Financial Interests by Means of Criminal Law (COM (2012) 363 final) – An Assessment Based on the Manifesto for a European Criminal Policy', (2012) 2 *EuCLR*, 319–337 at 324.

financial interests in terms of Art. 325 (4) TFEU requires that criminal sanctions be imposed on – at the very least – serious forms of fraud.[76]

7.4.3 Art. 325 (4) TFEU as a Legal Basis for Criminal Harmonisation?

Clearly, then, the EU has long held a legitimate interest in standardising the national criminal laws of its MS with respect to EU fraud. Against this background, in 2012 the Commission presented a first proposal for a new PIF-Directive that was based on Art. 325 (4) TFEU. The Commission's explanatory memorandum suggested that this provision 'includes the power to enact criminal law provisions in the context of the protection of the Union's financial interests against all angles of illegal attack'.[77] However, both the Council[78] and the Parliament[79] took the contrary view that a harmonisation of national criminal law could only occur in accordance with Art. 83 TFEU. They wanted to base the new directive on the annex competence outlined in Art. 83 (2) TFEU. At this point, thrashing out the precise legal basis for the EU's new anti-fraud regime quickly became one of the most controversial aspects of the legislative process. This controversy owed largely to the significant consequences of this point for the scope and extent of the EU's regulatory powers.

[76] See the example given in Hecker, *Europäisches Strafrecht*, § 7 mn. 49; in the same vein, CJEU, *Criminal Proceedings against Ivo Taricco and Others*, No. C-105/14, Judgment, ECLI:EU:C:2015:555, 8 September 2015, para. 39 ('criminal penalties may nevertheless be essential to combat certain serious cases of VAT evasion in an effective and dissuasive manner'). Crit. S. Braum, 'Das "Corpus Juris" – Legitimität, Erforderlichkeit und Machbarkeit', (2000) 55 *JZ*, 493–500.

[77] European Commission, *Proposal for a Directive of the European Parliament and of the Council on the Fight against Fraud to the Union's Financial Interests by Means of Criminal Law*, 11 July 2012, COM(2012) 363 final, p. 7.

[78] See, for example, Council, *Protecting the Union's Financial Interests by Means of Criminal Law*, 3 June 2013, 10232/13, p. 2; Council, *Proposal for a Directive of the European Parliament and of the Council on the Fight Against Fraud to the Union's Financial Interests by Means of Criminal Law – General Approach*, 6 June 2013, 10729/13, p. 2.

[79] See European Parliament legislative resolution of 16 April 2014 on the proposal for a directive of the European Parliament and of the Council on the fight against fraud to the Union's financial interests by means of criminal law (COM(2012)0363 – C7-0192/2012 – 2012/0193(COD)) (Ordinary legislative procedure: first reading), OJ C 443, 22.12.2017, pp. 982–993 at p. 982.

The annex competence of Art. 83 (2) TFEU allows for an approximation of the criminal laws of the individual MS in areas that have been subject to harmonisation measures. To a very great extent, the law concerning the financial interests of the EU, its budget, revenues and expenditures, was already determined by EU law. We might think here of the customs law,[80] the VAT-Directive[81] or the public procurement law.[82] Clearly, then, the fight against fraud is – as a matter of principle – suitable for an ancillary harmonisation of criminal law.[83]

And yet, Art. 83 (2) TFEU only affords empowers the EU to 'establish minimum rules with regard to the definition of criminal offences and sanctions'. Consequently, the EU is merely in a position to introduce common minimum standards regarding the extent to which certain conduct should be made punishable. However, the MS retained significant latitude to go beyond these requirements and to criminalise other acts.[84] Clearly, the prospect that such a minimum harmonisation would eliminate legal differences between the MS was doubtful, to say the least.

By contrast, Art. 325 (4) TFEU is more ambitious. It calls for the establishment of a uniform protection system. This implies that the EU may strive for a full harmonisation of national laws – though always within the limits of the principles of proportionality, subsidiarity, and minimally invasive treatment of criminal law.[85] In much the same way, the harmonising effect of measures based on Art. 83 (2) TFEU is further limited by the fact that Denmark[86] and Ireland[87] do not participate

[80] Cf. in particular Regulation 952/2013/EU of the European Parliament and of the Council of 9 October 2013 Laying Down the Union Customs Code, OJ L 269, 10.10.2013, p. 1.

[81] Council Directive 2006/112/EC of 28 November 2006 on the Common System of Value Added Tax, OJ L 347, 11.11.2006, p. 30.

[82] See, for example, Regulation 1307/2013/EU.

[83] European Commission, *Towards an EU Criminal Policy: Ensuring the Effective Implementation of EU Policies Through Criminal Law,* 20 September 2011, COM(2011) 573 final, p. 10.

[84] Ambos, *European Criminal Law*, p. 320; Satzger, *International and European Criminal Law*, § 7 mn 42; P. Asp, *The Substantive Criminal Law Competence of the EU*, Stockholm: Stiftelsen Skrifter, 2012) p. 121.

[85] R. Sicurella, 'Some Reflections on the Need for a General Theory of the Competence of the European Union in Criminal Law', in A. Klip (ed.), *Substantive Criminal Law in European Union*, Antwerp et al.: Maklu Publishers, 2011, pp. 233–249 at p. 237; Bock, 'Der Schutz der finanziellen Interessen der Union. Überlegungen zur Betrugsbekämpfungsrichtlinie 2017/1371', p. 171 with further references.

[86] Art. 1 Protocol No 22 on the Position of Denmark, OJ C 83, 30.03.2010, p. 299.

[87] Art. 1 Protocol No 21 on the Position of the United Kingdom and Ireland in Respect of the Area of Freedom, Security and Justice, OJ C 83, 30.03.2010, p. 295.

in measures enacted by the EU in the area of freedom, security and justice. Consequently, these two MS are not bound by Art. 83 directives. However, Art. 325 TFEU provides for no such opt-out clauses in anti-fraud measures.[88] Finally, and similarly, EU MS have the right to veto any draft Art. 83 directive if they can convincingly argue that it would affect fundamental aspects of their criminal justice system (Art. 83 (3) TFEU). By contrast, Art. 325 TFEU contains no such provision for an 'emergency brake'.[89]

Against this background, the Council and some scholarly commentators have argued that Art. 83 TFEU should be considered *lex specialis* to Art. 325 (4) TFEU. They maintain that the former already serves to define the EU's powers in the realm of criminal law. They insist that the restrictions contained in the annex competence must not be undermined by recourse to Art. 325 (4) TFEU.[90] They marshal some strong arguments in support of their claim – but their case is not entirely convincing.

Certainly, Art. 325 (4) TFEU does not explicitly refer to criminal law measures. However, the term 'combat' (see the official headline of Title II Chapter 6 of the TFEU: 'Combating Fraud') is used in other provisions

[88] Council, *Opinion of the Legal Service – Proposal for a Directive of the European Parliament and of the Council on the Fight against Fraud to the Union's Financial Interests by Means of Criminal Law (12683/12 DROIPEN 107 JAI 535 GAF 15 FIN 547 CADREFIN 349 CODEC 1924) – Legal Basis*, 22 October 2012, 15309/12, mn. 22.

[89] Some authors argue that Art. 83 (3) TFEU should also be applied by way of analogy to anti-fraud measures in terms of Art. 325 (4) TFEU. See, for example, Ambos, *European Criminal Law*, p. 323; Hecker, *Europäisches Strafrecht*, § 8 mn. 25. However, this argument is unconvincing, for two key reasons. First, Art. 83 (3) TFEU is a derogation rule (it allows for derogation from the ordinary legislative procedure). As such, it must be applied restrictively. Second, Art. 83 TFEU and Art. 325 TFEU deal with different situations. The annex competence is used to enhance the efficiency of an EU policy that lies in the common interests of the MS. By contrast, Art. 325 TFEU aims at the effective protection of an original EU interest that exists beyond the sphere of the MS. It therefore seems logical that national interests play a less crucial role in the fight against EU fraud than in the enforcement of general EU policies. See Bock, 'Der Schutz der finanziellen Interessen der Union. Überlegungen zur Betrugsbekämpfungsrichtlinie 2017/1371', pp. 171–172 and, in the same vein, Magiera, 'Art. 325 AEUV', mn. 77; Vogel, 'Die Strafgesetzgebungskompetenzen der Europäischen Union nach Art. 83, 86 und 325 AEUV', p. 49.

[90] Council, *Legal Basis*, mn. 12 f.; M. Böse, 'Die Entscheidung des Bundesverfassungsgerichts zum Vertrag von Lissabon und ihre Bedeutung für die Europäisierung des Strafrechts', (2010) 5 *ZIS*, 76–91 at 87–88; M. Huomo-Kettunen, 'EU Criminal Policy at a Crossroads between Effectiveness and Traditional Restraints for the Use of Criminal Law', (2014) 5 *NJECL*, 301–326.

of the TFEU in a criminal law context. Art. 83 (1) TFEU allows for the approximation of national criminal laws if this is necessary to 'combat' crimes with a cross-border dimension. Moreover, Art. 86 TFEU foresees the establishment of a European Public Prosecutor's Office 'to combat crimes affecting the financial interests of the Union.'[91] Significantly, the principles of assimilation and the minimum trias as enshrined in Art. 325 (1), (2) TFEU stem from the Greek Maize Judgement.[92] These principles were thus developed in a criminal law context. It would be inconsistent to, on the one hand, apply the first two paragraphs of Art. 325 TFEU to criminal measures but, on the other, to limit the scope of para. 4 to preventive and administrative sanctions.[93] The legislative record offers additional proof of this. Unlike its predecessor,[94] Art. 325 (4) TFEU does not exclude measures which 'concern the application of national criminal law'.[95] This phrase was commonly understood as preventing the EU from adopting criminal law measures.[96]

91 Bock, 'Der Schutz der finanziellen Interessen der Union. Überlegungen zur Betrugsbekämpfungsrichtlinie 2017/1371', pp. 172–173; cf. also Asp, *Criminal Law*, p. 143; Sicurella, 'Some Reflections on the Need for a General Theory of the Competence of the European Union in Criminal Law', p. 237 ('the term fight [...] clearly refers to measures of a repressive nature').

92 See *supra* note 29 and accompanying text.

93 Hecker, *Europäisches Strafrecht*, § 4 mn. 69; Bock, 'Der Schutz der finanziellen Interessen der Union. Überlegungen zur Betrugsbekämpfungsrichtlinie 2017/1371', p. 173; cf. also European Commission, *Proposal for a Directive of the European Parliament and of the Council on the Fight against Fraud to the Union's Financial Interests by Means of Criminal Law*, 11 July 2012, COM(2012) 363 final, p. 8; Fromm, *Der strafrechtliche Schutz der Finanzinteressen der EG – Die Frage der Einführung einer supranationalen Strafrechtskompetenz durch Artikel 280 IV EGV*, p. 27.

94 The old Art. 280 (4) EEC Treaty read as follows: 'The Council, acting in accordance with the procedure referred to in Article 251, after consulting the Court of Auditors, shall adopt the necessary measures in the fields of the prevention of and fight against fraud affecting the financial interests of the Community with a view to affording effective and equivalent protection in the Member States. *These measures shall not concern the application of national criminal law or the national administration of justice.*'

95 See, for example, European Commission, *Commission Staff Working Paper: Impact Assessment (Part I) Accompanying the Document, Proposal for a Directive of the European Parliament and of the Council on the Protection of the Financial Interests of the European Union by Criminal Law*, 11 July 2012, SWD(2012) 195 final, pp. 26–27; Hecker, *Europäisches Strafrecht*, § 4 mn. 68; Ambos, *European Criminal Law*, pp. 18–19; Satzger, *International and European Criminal Law*, § 6 mn. 24, § 7 mn. 50.

96 See European Commission, *Commission Staff Working Paper: Impact Assessment (Part I) Accompanying the Document, Proposal for a Directive of the European Parliament and of the Council on the Protection of the Financial Interests of the European Union*

However, the change in wording indicates that the MS wanted to expand the EU's powers in the fight against fraud.[97] Such a broad, inclusive interpretation of Art. 325 (4) TFEU does not create inconsistencies with Art. 83 TFEU. Indeed, the EU's general harmonisation competencies are limited in several respects (in particular, and as noted, minimum harmonisation and the emergency break). However, these competencies were intended to provide a tool for enforcing the common interests of the MS on the European level that implies that the MS can expect the EU to consider and respect their national sovereign interests when using these powers. By contrast, Art. 325 TFEU aims at the protection of a basic EU interest that exists beyond the sphere of the individual MS. It thus seems logical that national interests (such as the preservation of fundamental aspects of national legal orders) should play a less crucial role in the fight against EU fraud than in the enforcement of general EU policies.[98]

In sum, it seems more apposite to conceptualise Art. 325 TFEU as a *special enabling clause* that takes precedence over the general Art. 83 TFEU. The former article exclusively regulates the powers and competencies of the EU in the protection of its financial interests – regardless of the type and nature of the measure it wants to adopt. Despite this, however, in 2017, the European Parliament and Council finally decided to base the PIF-Directive on the annex competence (Art. 83 (2) TFEU).

7.4.4 Excursus: The PIF-Directive

Regardless of its legal basis, the aim and content of the PIF-Directive clearly delineate it as a measure to protect the EU's financial interests.[99] The Directive obliges MS to criminalise the following acts: fraud that affects

by Criminal Law, 11 July 2012, SWD(2012) 195 final, p. 5; see for more detail Fromm, *Der strafrechtliche Schutz der Finanzinteressen der EG – Die Frage der Einführung einer supranationalen Strafrechtskompetenz durch Artikel 280 IV EGV*, pp. 107 f.

[97] Ambos, *European Criminal Law*, p. 19; Bock, 'Der Schutz der finanziellen Interessen der Union. Überlegungen zur Betrugsbekämpfungsrichtlinie 2017/1371', p. 175 with further references.

[98] cf. also Sicurella, 'Some Reflections on the Need for a General Theory of the Competence of the European Union in Criminal Law', p. 237; J. Sturies, 'Ermächtigt der Vertrag von Lissabon wirklich zum Erlass supranationaler Wirtschaftsstrafgesetze?', (2012) 13 *HRRS*, 273–288 at p. 280; and Bock, 'Der Schutz der finanziellen Interessen der Union. Überlegungen zur Betrugsbekämpfungsrichtlinie 2017/1371', p. 174 with further references.

[99] cf. also in recital (1) of the PIF-Directive.

EU financial interests (Art. 3 PIF-Directive); money laundering involving property derived from criminal acts affecting the EU's financial interests (Art. 4 (1) PIF-Directive); acts of active and passive corruption which damage or endanger the EU's financial interests (Art. 4 (2) PIF-Directive); and misappropriation of EU funds by public officials (Art. 4 (3) PIF-Directive). The MS are also required to ensure that inciting, aiding and abetting, and attempting these offences are punishable (Article 5 PIF-Directive).

At first glance, this seems a fairly comprehensive package of legal regulations. And yet it has several shortcomings. One of these concerns fraudulent revenues arising from the value added tax (VAT) of the individual MS. Each year, EU members are obliged to transfer a percentage of their estimated national VAT income to the EU's coffers.[100] However, fraud in this area only falls within the remit of the PIF-Directive if it amounts to a 'serious offence against the common VAT system', one that requires that the relevant act is connected with the territory of two or more MS of the EU and involves total damages of at least EUR 10 000 000 (Art. 2 (2) PIF-Directive).[101] A second shortcoming is that the Directive does not provide autonomous definitions of complex concepts such as instigation or attempt. Instead, it leaves the concretisation of such concepts to the relevant national laws and legal bodies. Inevitably, then, the exact scope of the criminal provisions differs from MS to MS.

To be sure, the PIF-Directive serves to enhance and concretise common minimum standards in the fight against EU fraud. Ultimately, however, these two examples show that the Directive does not lead to a truly uniform protection of the EU's financial interest across all MS.

7.5 A Look to the Future: Art. 325 (4) TFEU as a Legal Basis for Supranational Criminal Law Legislation?

It seems reasonable to argue that Art. 325 (4) TFEU does indeed allow for the adoption of criminal law legislation and that it does not limit the EU to certain types of measures (e.g., to directives – as Art. 83 TFEU does).

[100] See Council Regulation 1553/89/EEC, Euratom of 29 May 1989 on the definitive uniform arrangements for the collection of own resources accruing from value added tax, OJ L 155, 7.6.1989, p. 9.

[101] On the background to this limitation, see Bock, 'Der Schutz der finanziellen Interessen der Union. Überlegungen zur Betrugsbekämpfungsrichtlinie 2017/1371', pp. 176–178.

It thus seems logical to conclude that this provision also grants the EU the right to introduce directly applicable criminal provisions to fight EU fraud by way of regulation.[102] Nonetheless, a weighty question remains: can such a supranational criminal law *stricto sensu* ever be adequately reconciled with the principles of proportionality and subsidiarity and, if so, under what conditions? Whatever our answer to this question, such a regulation arguably offers the only means by which the EU can conceivably introduce fully equivalent (criminal) protection standards throughout the EU. Nevertheless, it seems unlikely that the near future will see the emergence of a 'European Criminal Code on the fight against fraud to the EU's financial interests'. This scepticism is based not least on the reluctant stance of the Council and the Parliament, as shown in their conspicuously restrictive interpretations of Art. 325 (4) TFEU.

Further Reading

P. Asp, '(More Than) Two Decades Later – Does the Principle of Assimilation Still Have a Role to Play within European Criminal Law?', in G. Freund *et al.* (eds.), *Grundlagen und Dogmatik des gesamten Strafrechtssystems – Festschrift für Wolfang Frisch zum 70. Geburtstag*, Berlin: Duncker & Humblot, 2013, pp. 1389–1401.

S. Bock, 'Der Schutz der finanziellen Interessen der Union. Überlegungen zur Betrugsbekämpfungsrichtlinie 2017/1371', in K. Ambos and S. Bock (eds.), *Aktuelle und grundsätzliche Fragen des Wirtschaftsstrafrechts / Questions actuelle et fondamentales du droit pénal des affaires*, Berlin: Duncker & Humblot, 2019, pp. 155–180.

V. Covolo, *L'émergence d'un droit pénal en réseau. Analyse critique du système européen de lutte antifraude*, Baden-Baden: Nomos, 2015.

I. E. Fromm, *Der strafrechtliche Schutz der Finanzinteressen der EG – Die Frage der Einführung einer supranationalen Strafrechtskompetenz durch Artikel 280 IV EGV*, Berlin, Heidelberg: Springer, 2004.

S. Gröblinghoff, *Die Verpflichtung des deutschen Strafgesetzgebers zum Schutz der Interessen der Europäischen Gemeinschaften*, Heidelberg: C.F. Müller, 1996.

[102] See, for example, Ambos, *European Criminal Law*, pp. 15 f; Satzger, *International and European Criminal Law*, § 6 mn. 25; see for more detail Weißer, 'Strafgesetzgebung durch die Europäische Union: Nicht nur ein Recht, sondern auch eine Pflicht?', 433 f.; crit., for example, J. Sturies, 'Ermächtigt der Vertrag von Lissabon wirklich zum Erlass supranationaler Wirtschaftsstrafgesetze?', (2012) 13 *HRRS*, pp. 237 f.

M. Kaiafa-Gbandi, 'The Commission's Proposal for a Directive on the Fight against Fraud to the Union's Financial Interests by Means of Criminal Law (COM (2012) 363 final) – An Assessment Based on the Manifesto for a European Criminal Policy', (2012) 2 *EuCLR*, 319–337.

W. C. Pabsch, *Der strafrechtliche Schutz der überstaatlichen Hoheitsgewalt*, Bonn: Ludwig Röhrscheid Verlag, 1965.

J. Sunderland et al., Study on the Legal Framework for the Protection EU Financial Interests by Criminal Law, 4 *Mai* 2012.

B. Weißer, 'Strafgesetzgebung durch die Europäische Union: Nicht nur ein Recht, sondern auch eine Pflicht?', (2014) 161 *GA*, 433–452.

8 Cross-Border Crimes

Marianne L. Wade*

8.1 Introduction

Substantive EU criminal law features a number of developmental strands. Some appear more innovative, matching the novel nature of the EU itself. Thus, a major strand relates to the protection of the Union's financial interests, another usually less prominent[1] relates to criminal justice mechanisms engaged in core areas of EU policy.[2] The one international lawyers will be less surprised by is the inclusion of a number of cross-border crimes, the substance of which might well be described as a mutation of more conventional transnational criminal law.

This strand of EU work was provided for by the Treaty of Lisbon, more specifically the Treaty of the Functioning of the European Union (hereinafter TFEU) reading in its Article 83 as follows:

> 1. The European Parliament and the Council may, by means of directives adopted in accordance with the ordinary legislative procedure, establish minimum rules concerning the definition of criminal offences and sanctions in the areas of particularly serious crime with a *cross-border dimension* resulting from the nature or impact of such offences or from a special need to combat them on a common basis [*emphasis added*].

The criminal phenomena focused upon ring familiar to anyone even vaguely acquainted with transnational criminal law, a classic area of multi-lateral treaty activity. The qualified inclusion of this list of crimes within the penumbra of legitimate EU action (to define minimum rules concerning the 'definition of criminal offences and sanctions')

* Reader in Criminal Justice, Birmingham Law School. Thanks are due to Aishling Seymour Pellew for research assistance.

1 With cases CJEU, *Commission v. Council*, No. C-176/03, Judgment, ECLI:EU:C:2005:542, 13 September 2005 and *Commission v. Council*, No. C440/05, Judgment, ECLI:EU:C:2007:625, 23 October 2007 – and ensuing Commission policy papers – forming notable exceptions.

2 The later are regulated in Art. 83(2) TFEU, OJC 326, 26.10.2012.

as subject to them being 'particularly serious crimes' characterised by 'a cross-border dimension resulting from the nature or impact of such offences or from a special need to combat them on a common basis' is a very clear expression of the limited extent to which the Member States (MS) are willing to cede initiative to the Commission. So whilst EU activity is legislated for, the normal path to EU legislation does not appear to be favoured.

To underline this further, the MS saw fit to include (in Article 83 (1) TFEU) an exhaustive list of the crimes for which this kind of EU action is appropriate.

These areas of crime are the following: terrorism, trafficking in human beings and sexual exploitation of women and children, illicit drug trafficking, illicit arms trafficking, money laundering, corruption, counterfeiting of means of payment, computer crime and organised crime.

The suffix: 'on the basis of developments in crime, the Council may adopt a decision identifying other areas of crime that meet the criteria specified in this paragraph. It shall act unanimously after obtaining the consent of the European Parliament' combined with the fact that the list of crimes may be supplemented only via the extraordinary legislative procedure (requiring Council unanimity and only European Parliament consent) apparently emphasises that this area of EU activity is fundamentally reserved for the systems of the MS. Because the Council – populated as it is solely by representatives of MS governments – retains legislative control and can expand the field of EU activity only when all MS agree to it so doing, this remains an area of EU work with parameters (envisaged as) set by the MS. Only where they unanimously agree that EU action is warranted – for the purposes outlined – will a basis for this be created. This Treaty provision thus clearly reflects a core feature of classic transnational criminal law, reflecting the view that criminal justice is traditionally a matter for close control by sovereign States. Supranational activity is legislated for as an exception, provided for only when the Council – acting as a multi-lateral collective of all MS – deems it appropriate.[3]

[3] For critical discussion of the lack of effective legal limitation, see K. Ambos, *European Criminal Law*, Cambridge: Cambridge University Press, 2018, p. 320, and see below for a factual assessment.

The umbrella legislative provision for EU activity relating to cross-border crime is furthermore clearly characterised by the fundamental tension that runs throughout EU criminal justice. Article 83(3) TFEU on the one hand delivers an emergency break procedure to MS for whom activity goes too far (because a development is viewed as 'affect[ing] fundamental aspects of its criminal justice system') but equally goes on to ensure those who do not wish to be slowed down can proceed via enhanced cooperation. Article 83 TFEU therefore legislates for a very specific context within which MS can advance common interests to combat cross-border crime, at different speeds.

So whilst it is clear that cross-border crime is of relevance to the EU, one might be surprised at first sight of the apparently limited extent to which the Union is fundamentally tasked with playing a real, substantive role in relation to them. Its competence has not, for example, developed as a corollary to EU characteristics such as freedom of movement, but in accordance with the criminal justice needs recognised by the Council. Provisions in the TFEU lay out a role very clearly subsidiary to MS criminal justice systems. The EU role exists purely to facilitate MS cooperation[4] in relation to a select number of crimes. Defining which crimes fall into this group remains within the hands of the MS acting akin to intergovernmental organisations (i.e., not on the basis of qualified majority voting) rather than normal EU processes as embodied by the ordinary legislative procedure. One might argue (endlessly) over whether this body of EU law stems from MS instincts to use the EU as a convenient forum or is a logical and principled corollary to a unique community opening up traditional notions of borders to revolutionise trade. Ensuring the illegitimate economy does not benefit from EU freedoms seems entirely appropriate given its broader activity. It is undeniable, however, that the criminal offence areas now known as *Eurocrimes* because they feature in Article 83 TFEU are decisively similar to those dealt with by other frameworks producing cooperative, transnational criminal law.[5]

Cognisant of that, it is worth remembering the unique character of the EU marked as it is by the integration of the Schengen Accord. It is an enormous area marked by freedom of movement with traditional national

4 Thus Art. 83 activity is limited to 'establish[ing] minimum rules concerning the definition of criminal offences and sanctions.'

5 See N. Boister, *An Introduction to Transnational Criminal Law*, 2nd edn., Oxford: Oxford University Press, 2018.

borders – which, crucially, fundamentally remain the borders of criminal justice systems – and the security systems normally associated with them, rarely visible.[6] This set-up might lead one to consider cross-border crime of a different nature to logically be addressed by any common legislative framework. If the MS are concerned that those with illegitimate ends can take advantage of freedom of movement, surely EU action might be directed at that? The rules of hot pursuit and others developed under the Schengen framework[7] indicate that open borders are not an issue only for loftier crimes and corresponding action. Criminal bands stealing cars and conventional boiler-room schemes can be rendered more difficult to pursue where freedom of movement is deployed to foil law enforcement. This is, however, seemingly not regarded as adequate reason to overcome traditional understandings of sovereignty. So whilst mechanisms based upon mutual recognition such as the European Arrest Warrant (hereinafter EAW) are certainly available for use in relation to such crimes, these are decisively not featured in the list of offences for which more managerial EU legislative action is permitted. Cross-border crime is important, but it is the more traditional transnational 'usual suspects' which are deemed *Eurocrimes*, not all cross-border crime is focused upon.[8]

8.2 Activity under Article 83 TFEU

EU activity relating to the *Eurocrimes* provided for by Article 83 TFEU is detailed in the following relating to each area set out in the provision.

[6] Border enforcement has not, of course, disappeared but is characterised as 'smart'; for more detail, see European Commission, https://ec.europa.eu/home-affairs/what-we-do/policies/borders-and-visas/smart-borders_en (last accessed 5 July 2021).

[7] See, in particular, Arts. 40 and 41 of the Convention Implementing the Schengen Agreement (CISA); also M. Daman, 'Cross-Border Hot Pursuit in the EU', (2008) 16 *ECCL*, 171–207. See also Chapter 13 by K. Ambos and P. Rackow of this volume.

[8] Thus, for example, German press reports of mass car crimes perpetrated by Polish gangs (e.g. Anon (auto-de) Kripo jagt Autodiebe an der polnischen Grenze, 7.8.2013) have not galvanised EU-level action nor have frauds perpetrated against German pensioners from the Canary Islands – as reported by German Prosecutor Roth, L. (21 March 2013) *Prosecutors Coordinating Investigations across the EU*. Panel Discussion at the Institute for Judicial Administration: The Challenges of Transnational Investigations Conference, the University of Birmingham. Although such crimes are substantively covered by organised crime legislation, the point is that they do not provide the kind of policy impetus other crimes, such as terrorism and trafficking human beings (THB), do.

8.2.1 Terrorism

Terrorism is the criminal phenomenon with the longest history of treatment within the EU context with most academic commentary identifying the informal TREVI group meetings of the 1970s as the MS first impulse to utilise this governance context for matters of criminal justice concern. It is doubtlessly an area of prime importance,[9] often driving EU criminal justice related development.[10] The EU can clearly be described as a counter-terrorism actor; its prominence is often driven by individual MS whose EU Council Presidencies provide them opportunity to focus attention on this as a priority issue.[11]

The core piece of EU legislation is the Directive (EU) 2017/541 of 15 March 2017 on combating terrorism.[12] As should be expected after a reading of Article 83 TFEU, the Directive centrally established minimum rules for offence definitions and sanctions relating to terrorism.[13] Those familiar with transnational criminal law will know that defining terrorism is the ultimate bugbear of criminal justice cooperation.[14] Preamble 8 of the Directive thus sets out that only those offences listed within it are considered terrorist offences. This exhaustive list is featured in Article 3:

- attacks upon a person's life which may cause death;
- seizure of aircraft, ships or other means of public or goods transport;
- release of dangerous substances, or causing fires, floods or explosions, the effect of which is to endanger human life; and
- threatening to commit any of the acts listed in (a) to (i).

[9] See, for example C. C. Murphy, 'Transnational Counter-Terrorism Law: Law, Power and Legitimacy in the "Wars on Terror"', (2015) 6(1) *Transnational Legal Theory*.

[10] For more detail as the EAW, see W. van Ballegooij, 'European Implementation Assessment 2004–2020 on the EAW', (2020) *eucrim*, 149–154.

[11] Thus, the UK Presidency in 2004 was a key driver behind initial legislation – see Secretary of State for Foreign and Commonwealth Affairs, *Prospects for the European Union in 2006 and retrospective of the UK's Presidency of the EU, 1 July to 31 December 2005*, Cm 6735, London: The Stationary Office, 2006, p. 4. See also the confidence the UK had in its Brexit negotiations that the value it brings via counter-terrorism cooperation would be a key negotiating point – C. Morris, 'Brexit: Will the UK and EU cooperate on Security?', *BBC News*, 20 October 2020, available at www.bbc.co.uk/news/54613967 (last accessed 15 June 2021).

[12] And replacing Council Framework Decision 2002/475/JHA and amending Council Decision 2005/671/JHA.

[13] Directive EU 2017/541 of 15 March 2017 on combating terrorism, OJ L 88, 31.3.2017, Art. 1.

[14] See, for example A. Greene, 'Defining Terrorism: One Size Fits All?', (2017) 66 *ICLQ*, 411–440.

Whilst offences relating to a terrorist group are to be found in Article 4:

- directing a terrorist group and
- participating in the activities of a terrorist group – with knowledge of the fact that it is a terrorist group.[15]

The Directive also remains true to the more controversial aspects of EU counter-terrorism law which see it prescribe offences criminalising activity traditionally excluded from the remit of MS' criminal law[16] such as public provocation to commit a terrorist offence (regulated in Article 5), recruitment for terrorism (Article 6), providing training for terrorism (Article 7), receiving training for terrorism (Article 8), travelling for the purpose of terrorism (Article 9) and organising or otherwise facilitating travelling for the purpose of terrorism (Article 10). These offences cover behaviour traditionally viewed as insufficiently proximate to harm to warrant criminalisation,[17] and so this Directive sees the EU as a key actor driving the expansive nature of counter-terrorism law in the criminal justice arena.[18]

Whilst these last Articles also provide regulation for the key concerns featured in international discussions of terrorism in recent years (terrorist training camps and foreign fighters), the Directive also addresses another area of major concern by providing for the criminalisation of terrorist financing (in Article 11).[19]

[15] The offences detailed in Art. 4 are required to be punishable by custodial sentences with a maximum sentence of no less than fifteen years (Art. 4(a)) and no less than eight years (Art. 4(b)), respectively (see Art. 15).

[16] On this, see D. Korosec, 'Anti-Terrorism Related Law Reforms and Human Rights in Slovenia', in M. L. Wade and A. Maljević (eds.), *A War on Terror? The European Stance on a New Threat, Changing Laws and Human Rights Implications*, New York: Springer, 2009, pp. 245–259 and D. Derenčinović, 'The Evolution of the Antiterror Legal and Institutional Framework in Croatia', in M. L. Wade and A. Maljević (eds.), *A War on Terror? The European Stance on a New Threat, Changing Laws and Human Rights Implications*, New York: Springer, 2009, pp. 305–320.

[17] See K. S. Stubbs and F. Galli, 'Inchoate Offences: The Sanctioning of an Act Prior to and Irrespective of Harm', in F. Galli and A. Weyembergh (eds.), *EU Counter-Terrorism offences*, Brussels: Editions de l'Universite de Bruxelles, 2012, pp. 291–303.

[18] See M. L. Wade, 'The European Union as a Counter-Terrorism Actor: Right Path, Wrong Direction?', (2014) 62 *Crime, Law and Social Change*, 355–383.

[19] Note that other activity under Art. 83 is emphasised as a key component of this with the following cited as the relevant legislation to counter terrorist financing by the Counter-Terrorism Agenda for the EU, p. 2: Directive (EU) 2018/1673 of 23 October 2018 on combating money laundering by criminal law, OJ L 284, 12.11.2018. And Directive (EU)

8.2.2 Trafficking in Human Beings and Sexual Exploitation of Women and Children

Another very high-profile area of activity grounded in Article 83 TFEU relates to THB. The flagship legislation is Directive 2011/36/EU of the European Parliament and of the Council of 5 April 2011 on preventing and combating trafficking in human beings and protecting its victims.[20] Parallel to terrorism, the legislative history in this area demonstrates EU commitment to it as post-Lisbon legislation was quickly introduced to replace that produced in the previous inter-governmental era under the so-called Third Pillar.

Again the Directive ensures compact provision of the sort one would expect from legislation facilitating cooperation between states in this area. Its stated aim is to provide a basis for 'close cross-border cooperation, including the sharing of information and the sharing of best practices' whilst viewing 'continued open dialogue between the police, judicial and financial authorities of the Member States, [as] essential'.[21] As this reveals, provision is in fact made for more comprehensive action than one might expect from an entity laying down minimal rules and sentences – even if the EU may ultimately, to a degree, be driven by its MS in this context. This perhaps best reflects the role the EU plays in relation to combatting the cross-border criminal phenomena agreed to fall within its remit. The reality of its role goes well beyond what negotiators were willing to stipulate in Treaty provision – if one looks at the concrete secondary legislation to ultimately assess what action is taken by the EU and what left to the MS. This particular legislation for example goes on to state that 'This Directive adopts an integrated, holistic, and human rights approach to the fight against trafficking in human beings.'[22] It should be clarified that this fight is spurned not only by Article 83 TFEU but is also directly related to the prohibition of slavery found in Article 5 of the Charter of Fundamental Rights of the European Union.[23] One core consideration to bear in mind is that no matter what the MS' intention may have been when they introduced work relating to cross-border crime

2018/843 of 30 May 2018 amending Directive (EU) 2015/849 on the prevention of the use of the financial system for the purposes of money laundering or terrorist financing, and amending Directives 2009/138/EC and 2013/36/EU, OJ L 156/43, 19.6.2018.

[20] OJ L 101/1, 15.4.2011. [21] Ibid., Preamble 5. [22] Ibid., Preamble 7.

[23] (2000/C 364/01) OJ C 364/1, 18.12.2000.

to the auspices of the European Communities, the EU is now a supranational body that also converses in terms of fundamental values. And some cross-border criminal activity stands in opposition also to those.

Substantively, Article 2 of the Directive replicates the UN[24] definition of THB laying down an obligation upon MS to criminalise:

> The recruitment, transportation, transfer, harbouring or reception of persons, including the exchange or transfer of control over those persons, by means of the threat or use of force or other forms of coercion, of abduction, of fraud, of deception, of the abuse of power or of a position of vulnerability or of the giving or receiving of payments or benefits to achieve the consent of a person having control over another person, for the purpose of exploitation.

In subparagraph 1, it goes on to define vulnerability and exploitation in greater detail as well as to state that victim consent is irrelevant.[25]

Article 4 requires that MS ensure that any crime defined in Article 2 is subject to a maximum term of imprisonment of at least five years. So, once again, in reality the EU is exercising considerable powers, laying down sanctions to be imposed on individual citizens. MS are further required to entitle authorities 'not to prosecute or impose penalties on victims of trafficking in human beings for their involvement in criminal activities ... as a direct consequence of being subjected to any acts referred to in Article 2'.[26]

Preamble 5 furthermore highlights the expectation that MS avail themselves of the breadth of tools the Union offers to combat this cross-border criminal phenomenon reading: 'The coordination of investigations and prosecutions of cases of trafficking in human beings should be facilitated by enhanced cooperation with Europol and Eurojust, the setting-up of joint investigation teams' and other measures. It is thus abundantly clear that the EU wants to achieve far more than classic transnational criminal law agreements would in this arena. In the EU, legislative agreement on definitions is the beginning of and reference point for criminal justice work, not the aim itself. This supra-national body is not just the creator

[24] Found in Art. 2 of the Protocol to Prevent, Suppress and Punish Trafficking in Persons, Especially Women and Children, supplementing the United Nations Convention against Transnational Organized Crime *[hereinafter UNTOC]*, 15 November 2000, in force 25 December 2003, Vol.2237 p. 319; Doc.A/55/383.

[25] Again, mirroring the provisions of the UNTOC Protocol.

[26] See Art. 8.

of suppression conventions. MS are expected to use the toolbox the EU provides to effectively counter the criminal phenomenon viewed as a common problem.

The particular nature of EU work in this setting is well reflected by discussion of the follow-up work undertaken to ensure the effectiveness of this legislation.[27] The EU Strategy on Combatting Trafficking in Human Beings[28] sets out that legislation is a key tool but highlights that several years of monitoring and dialogue with MS are necessary to ensure successful transposition alone. The Strategy further highlights that the provision of funding for studies, creation of systems for the exchange of best practices and a variety of measures to ensure consistency of approaches across the MS, as well as measures at the policy and operational level are necessary to secure the kind of comprehensive approach the EU foresees as necessary to counter this heinous criminal phenomenon.

The specificities of EU criminal justice can also be perceived in measures flanking flagship legislation of a specific criminal justice nature. Earlier legislation concerned with THB (undertaken within the Third Pillar) was also accompanied by legislation and action in relevant areas of core EU policy. Thus, Council Directive 2004/81/EC on the residence permit issued to third-country nationals who are victims of trafficking in human beings[29] forms an important basis for the work of MS dealing with individual THB victims. Specifically, minimal provision is outlined corresponding to the EU's role in ensuring MS have a common immigration policy.[30] The broader EU context thus means that criminalising legislation is only a starting point in tackling cross-border crime. Detailed provision can be made for further action in related policy areas to complement work undertaken (by the Commission particularly) in ensuring political intent to act translates into concrete action across the Union.

Whilst the sexual exploitation of women and children is viewed by Article 83 TFEU as a matter tied to THB, specific legislative activity has also been undertaken to tackle this criminal phenomenon as viewed through a

[27] See Commission Communication: On the EU Strategy on Combating Trafficking in Human Beings 2021–2025, COM/2021/171, 14 April 2021, p. 3.

[28] European Commission Communication on the EU Strategy on Combatting Trafficking in Human Beings 2021–2025, Brussels, 14.4.2021 COM(2021) 171 final, p. 3.

[29] 29 April 2004, OJ L 261/19, 6.8.2004. The UK, Ireland and Denmark were (and are) not bound by this Directive – see Preambles 21 and 22.

[30] See Preamble 1.

broader lens. Centrally, the 2011 Directive on combating the sexual abuse and sexual exploitation of children and child pornography[31] is overtly identified as 'fully complementary' with the Directive on preventing and combating trafficking in human beings as there is an identified overlap.[32] The sexual abuse and exploitation Directive lays down requirements for offences of sexual abuse with the prison sentences foreseen ranging from at least one year (for causing a child to witness sexual activities without having to participate) to at least ten years (if the child has not reached the age of sexual consent) or at least five years for coercing, forcing or threatening a child into sexual activities with a third party, in Article 3. Article 4 tackles sexual exploitation offences requiring criminalisation and punishments ranging from at least two years for attending a pornographic performance involving the participation of a child to at least ten years for coercing or forcing a child into child prostitution or threatening a child for such purposes. Article 5 details obligations relating to offences concerning child pornography. These range from at least one year for acquisition or possession of child pornography to at least three years for the production of child pornography. Article 6 sets out minimal provision relating to the soliciting of children for sexual purposes, and Article 7 lays down requirements that MS foresee and punish accessorial liability.

8.2.3 Illicit Drug Trafficking

Activity relating to other 'classic' transnational criminal phenomenon witnesses the EU as (more recently) less concerned with flagship legislation[33] and more focused upon the pursuit of commonly agreed policy advances. In relation to drug trafficking, this is marked by an understanding of the criminal phenomena as forming only a part of a much broader problem. Given the diversity of views on illicit narcotics across the EU, as well as the

[31] Directive 2011/93/EU, OJ L 335, 17.12.2011 with Corrigendum, OJ L 018, 21.1.2012, p. 7 (2011/93).

[32] Preamble 7.

[33] Work of this nature was – to a fairly limited extent – undertaken under the Third Pillar however with the Council Framework Decision 2004/757/JHA of 25 October 2004 laying down minimum provisions on the constituent elements of criminal acts and penalties in the field of illicit drug trafficking OJ L 335, 11.11.2004. This piece of legislation required comprehensive criminalisation relating to drug trafficking as well as relating to accessorial liability. It required regulation and suggested punishments for legal persons involved as well as minimum sanctions more broadly.

plethora of UN instruments already in place to counter drug trafficking, it is perhaps not surprising that a less criminal justice focused approach is taken.

EU drugs policy more broadly is centred around Drugs Strategies. The most recent of these was approved by the Council in December 2020 and is the EU Drugs Strategy 2021–2025 of 18 December 2020. This clearly sets any treatment of the cross-border crime of drug trafficking in a much broader framework stating:

'The Strategy aims to protect and improve the well-being of society and of the individual, to protect and promote public health, to offer a high level of security and well-being for the general public and to increase health literacy. The Strategy takes an evidence-based, integrated, balanced and multidisciplinary approach to the drugs phenomenon at national, EU and international level. It also incorporates a gender equality and health equity perspective.'[34]

The criminal phenomenon of drug trafficking is characterised as something to be addressed in the course of a drugs supply reduction agenda:

> In the field of drug supply reduction, the objective of the Strategy is to respond, through an evidence-based approach, to the challenging development of European drug markets, which is characterised by a high availability of various types of drugs, ever larger seizures, increasing use of violence and huge profits. The Strategy therefore aims to contribute to the disruption of traditional and online illicit drug markets, the dismantling of organised crime groups that are involved in drug production and trafficking, efficient use of the criminal justice system, effective intelligence-led law enforcement, a reduction in the levels of violence associated with the illicit drug markets, and increased intelligence sharing that will ensure a common approach on the part of all responsible stakeholders.[35]

In relation to this, a number of action points are identified as the priority for the next four years. These strategic priorities are to: (1) disrupt and dismantle high-risk drug-related organised crime groups operating in, originating in or targeting the EU MS; address links with other security threats and improve crime prevention, (2) increase the detection of illicit wholesale trafficking of drugs and drug precursors at EU points of entry and exit, (3) tackle the exploitation of logistical and digital channels for medium- and small-volume illicit drug distribution and increase seizures

[34] Council of the European Union, EU Drugs Strategy 2021–2025, 14178/20, 18 December 2020, p. 2.

[35] Ibid., p. 5.

of illicit substances smuggled through these channels in close cooperation with the private sector, and (4) dismantle illicit drug production and counter illicit cultivation, prevent the diversion and trafficking of drug precursors for illicit drug production and address environmental damage.[36]

In this regard, it seems clear that the EU is focused upon adding value to the MS criminal justice and broader societal combatting of problems related to narcotics. This follows previous work in this area[37] but if also perhaps indicative of attitudes within the EU. Whilst there is an earnest desire to combat the criminal phenomena associated with narcotics, the 'War on Drugs' is not one with which the EU identifies.

8.2.4 Organised Crime

Counter THB and drug trafficking efforts are ones targeted at criminal activity frequently associated with organised crime.[38] So the discussion that follows should be viewed in close nexus with that above. It is key to recognise also, of course, that the EU does not – nor does it perceive itself as – operate[ing] in a vacuum. Just as the definition of THB makes reference to and indeed adopts United Nations legislation (and counter-terrorism indeed mirrors it; for good and for bad),[39] so the approach to organised crime more broadly should be viewed with UN activity as a

[36] Ibid, at pp. 6–11.

[37] See Council Recommendation on improving investigation methods in the fight against organised crime linked to organised drug trafficking: simultaneous investigations into drug trafficking by criminal organisations and their finances/assets, OJ C 114, 25.4.2002; Council Framework Decision 2008/841/JHA on the fight against organised crime, OJ L 300, 24.10.2008; Council of the European Union, European pact to combat international drug trafficking – disrupting cocaine and heroin routes, 3 June 2010; Commission Communication: Evaluation of the implementation of the EU Drugs Strategy 2013–2020 and of the EU Action Plan on Drugs 2013–2016: a continuous need for an EU Action Plan on Drugs 2017–2020, COM/2017/0195 final, 15 May 2017; Directive (EU) 2016/681 on the use of passenger name record (PNR) data for the prevention, detection, investigation and prosecution of terrorist offences and serious crime, OJ L 119, 4.5.2016, pp. 132–149; with relevant offences listed in Annex 2 as referred to by Art. *3(9)*; 2017 Drugs Directive (Directive (EU) 2017/2103) amending Framework Decision 2004/757/JHA, OJ L 305, 21.11.2017.

[38] For definitions, see Klaus von Lampe, Definitions of Organized Crime, www.organized-crime.de/organizedcrimedefinitions.htm (last accessed 5 July 2021).

[39] See, for example, CJEU [GC], *Yassin Abdullah Kadi and Al Barakaat International Foundation v. Council of the European Union and Commission of the European Communities,* Joined cases Nos. C-402/05 P and C-415/05 P, Judgment, ECLI:EU:C:2008:461, 3 September 2008.

vital background.[40] Undeniably, the UNTOC dominates efforts to counter organised crime. However, specific EU efforts focus regional work and provide for a more detailed, tailored approach.

The 2015 European Agenda on Security[41] underlines this point. Whilst International Organised Crime is identified as the second of three priorities identified following (1) terrorism and radicalisation and (2) cybercrime, this is immediately explained to mean 'countries neighbouring the EU will be more closely involved in operational activities. Greater efforts will be made to tackle crime financing and confiscate assets, and to counter people-smuggling and human trafficking.'

On 14 April 2021, the Commission presented a new five-year strategy to tackle organised crime[42] described as 'focusing on boosting law enforcement and judicial co-operation, tackling organised crime structures and high priority crimes, removing criminal profits and ensuring a modern response to technological developments'. Again we see the EU very much as a capacity building arena focused upon enhancing capacities and facilitating smooth and efficient law enforcement cooperation across borders.[43] The efforts described are targeted ones to ensure data and intelligence exchange regimes (developed under the Prüm Framework[44]) are integrated into EU policy and built upon. Core areas of focus are further to consolidate all cooperative arrangements previously developed into one comprehensive framework as well as to undertake, for example negotiations for a cooperative agreement with Interpol. The EU is thus the forum for significantly enhancing cooperation of MS authorities but also the one that adds value; negotiating as it does with the mandate of twenty-seven sovereign nations.

[40] For example, the 2006/617/EC Council Decision on the conclusion, on behalf of the European Community, of the Protocol Against the Smuggling of Migrants by Land, Sea and Air, supplementing the UN Convention against Transnational Organised Crime concerning the provisions of the Protocol, in so far as the provisions of the Protocol fall within the scope of Part III, Title IV of the Treaty establishing the European Community of 24 July 2006, OJ L 262, 22.9.2006, is overtly presented as such.

[41] COM/2015/185 final of 28 April 2015.

[42] See https://ec.europa.eu/commission/presscorner/detail/en/ip_21_1662 (last accessed 5 July 2021).

[43] See the Commission Staff Working Document, EMPACT, the flagship EU instrument for cooperation to fight organised and serious international crime, SWD/2021/74 final, which accompanies the Commission Communication: On the EU Strategy to tackle Organised Crime 2021–2025 COM/2021/170 final.

[44] Prüm Decisions (2008/615/JHA and 2008/616/JHA).

Legislation is a less important feature in this overarching area, but the key piece stems from the pre-Lisbon era: the Council Framework Decision on the fight against organised crime.[45] This lays down the definition of a criminal organisation and structured association in the same terms as the UNTOC[46] except that two people suffice to form a 'criminal organisation'.[47] Provision is also made for minimum maximum sentence length, accessorial liability and that of legal persons in parallel with, for example THB legislation.

Organised crime is clearly a matter of concern for the MS and as such has become an important aspect of EU criminal justice work, logically also recognised in Article 83 TFEU. This can be seen for as long as criminal justice activity has been integrated into the EU framework. The 'European Union action plan on common action for the Russian Federation on combating organised crime of 13 April 2000'[48] and 'the prevention and control of organised crime: a European Union strategy for the beginning of the new millennium' of 3 May 2000,[49] for instance, provide early examples.

As one would expect from the rhetoric of policy documents, recovery of the proceeds of crime and deterrence (because the profitability of such crimes is reduced) forms a heart of legislative activity with several instruments making detailed provisions produced in the past decade.[50] It is also an area for which the European Parliament has established a special committee[51] and regularly produces suggestions for policy initiatives.[52]

[45] (2008/841/JHA) 24 October 2008, OJ L 300/42, 11.11.2008.

[46] See Annex 1, Art. 2.

[47] Art. 1(1).

[48] OJ C 106, 13.4.2000.

[49] OJ C 124, 3.5.2000.

[50] See the Commission Communication: Proceeds of organised crime: ensuring the 'crime does not pay' of 20 November 2011, COM/2008/0766 final; the Directive 2014/42/EU on the freezing and confiscation of instrumentalities and proceeds of crime in the European Union of 3 April 2014, OJ L 127, 29.4.2014; Regulation (EU) 2018/1805 on the mutual recognition of freezing orders and confiscation orders of 14 November 2018, OJ L 303, 28.11.2018; Directive (EU) 2019/1153 laying down rules facilitating the use of financial and other information for the prevention, detection, investigation or prosecution of certain criminal offences. Repealed Council Decision 2000/642/JHA of 20 June 2019 OJ L 186, 11.7.2019.

[51] See European Parliament Decision on setting up a special committee on organised crime, corruption and money laundering, its powers, numerical composition and term of office of 14 March 2012, OJ C 251E, 31.8.2013.

[52] See, for example – European Parliament Resolution on organised crime in the European Union of 25 October 2011, OJ C 131E, 8.5.2013; European Parliament Resolution on organised crime, corruption and money laundering: recommendations on action and initiatives to be taken (interim report) of 11 June 2013, OJ C 65, 19.2.2016 and below.

8.2.5 Money Laundering

Given the priorities identified in the Strategy against Organised Crime, money laundering logically constitutes an area of particular focus for the EU. In recent years, two major pieces of legislation have been passed: Directive (EU) 2015/849 on the prevention of the use of the financial system for the purposes of money laundering or terrorist financing[53] and the 2018 Criminal Anti-Money Laundering Directive.[54] Article 2 of the former sets out definitions of offences clearly demonstrating this as building on work done in legislation relating to i.a. organised crime, THB and terrorism in order to provide for effective countering tools more broadly. Article 3 provides details of offences to be criminalised, Article 5 requires them to be punishable by a maximum term of at least four years imprisonment and the Directive requires liability of legal persons and provides suggestion for the punishment of these[55] in a manner now familiar to readers of EU legislation. Preamble 4 clarifies that this Directive builds directly upon and importantly enhances provision previously made in the Council Framework Decision of the 26 June 2001 on money laundering, the identification, tracing, freezing, seizing and confiscation of instrumentalities and the proceeds of crime.[56] So this area of work provides another example of the longevity and importance of anti-cross-border crime efforts undertaken in the pre-Lisbon Third Pillar now featured in fully fledged EU activity against such offences.

It is vital to recognise this as an area of intense EU activity with a broad, practical reach. It is flanked by a number of mechanisms that transform this policy area into one of very considerable dynamism. A further three Directives have been issued to update, refine and sharpen the provisions of the 2015 Directive.[57]

53 See note 19, which amended Regulation (EU) No 848/2012 and repealed Directive 2005/60/EC.

54 See note 19. Directive on Combating Money Laundering by Criminal Law, PE/30/2018/REV/1, 23 October 2018. OJ L 284, 12.11.2018.

55 In Arts. 7 and 8.

56 OJ L 182, 5.7.2001. Incisive examples are further provided by the Commission's supranational risk assessment mechanism – based on a mandate created in the 4th Money Laundering Directive, its 3rd Country Risk list – as foreseen by Art. 9 of the 2015 Directive and further legislation like Regulation (EU) 2021/369 establishing the technical specifications and procedures required for the system of interconnection of central registers referred to in Directive (EU) 2015/849, OJ L 141, 5.5.2015.

57 The Fourth Money Laundering Directive, 26 June 2017; The Fifth Money Laundering Directive, 10 January 2020; The Sixth Money Laundering Directive, 3 June 2021. The

8.2.6 Further Areas of Activity

The further criminal offences listed in Article 83 TFEU are matters of lesser profile politically but nevertheless the subject of considerable EU effort. Current legislation described here often replaced Framework Decisions of the pre-Lisbon era.

Illicit arms trafficking is a matter of direct concern highlighted by the European Agenda on Security of 28 April 2015 followed by a flurry of legislative activity,[58] also very clearly demonstrating how EU work fills the gaps and provides for aspects of preventive and repressive policy MS would struggle to on their own. Legislating predating this also highlights Union work as dovetailing with broader global efforts in a manner seen in relation to other phenomena.[59]

Corruption also forms a significant area of work in this regard. It should also be noted that it is one of particular interest also to other strands of EU criminal justice work and development as anti-corruption constitutes a major aspect of OLAF's work (see Chapter 7 by Bock and Chapter 14 by Cahn).[60] Developments surrounding the European Public Prosecutor's

relevance of which becomes immediately apparent upon searching the Internet which is brimming with companies offering advice to commercial compliance divisions on the effects of these updates.

58 And accompanying consideration, see Council Conclusions on the adoption of an EU strategy against illicit firearms, small arms and light weapons and their ammunition, 13581/18, 19 November 2018; Commission Communication: The European Agenda on Security, COM(2015) 185 final, 28 April 2015: EU action plan against illicit trafficking in and use of firearms and explosives, COM(2015) 624 final, 2 December 2015; Council Decision 2018/1788. In support of SEESAC for the implementation of the Regional Roadmap on combating illicit arms trafficking in the Western Balkans, OJ L 293, 20.11.2017; Council Decision 2019/2111. In support of SEESAC disarmament and arms control activities in South-East Europe reducing the threat of illicit small arms and light weapons and their ammunition, OJ L 318/147, 9.12.2019, as well as Commission Communication: 2020–2025 EU action plan on firearms trafficking, COM(2020) 608 final, 24 July 2020.

59 Regulation No. 258/2012- implementing Art. 10 of the UNs' Protocol against the illicit manufacturing of and trafficking in firearms, their parts and components and ammunition, supplementing the UN Convention against Transnational Organised Crime (UN Firearms Protocol), and establishing export authorisation, and import and transit measures for firearms, their parts and components and ammunition, OJ L 94, 30.3.2012; Commission Communication: Firearms and the internal security of the EU: protecting citizens and disrupting illegal trafficking, COM/2013/0716 final, 21 October 2013. See also the Draft European Action Plan to combat illegal trafficking in the so-called 'heavy' firearms that could be used or are used in criminal activities. 16427/1/10, 29 November 2010.

60 See Regulation (EU) 2021/785 establishing the Union Anti-Fraud Programme, OJ L 172, 29.4.2021.

Office have focused attention on financial crime and also saw renewed legislative vigour in this area.[61] This builds on legislation stemming from the Commission scandal of the 1990s and work flowing from that.[62]

The inclusion of the *counterfeiting of means of payment* as a cross-border crime of priority for the Union is of no surprise given that it is a governance level with its own currency.[63] Given that the Union alone has the reach to deal with some related criminal activity (consider e.g., matters of jurisdiction if Euros are being counterfeited in a non-EU member country), this constitutes a major area of work both for institutions such as Europol (see Chapter 15 by Ligeti/Giuffrida) and of legislative activity.

Centrally the 2014 Directive on the protection of the euro against counterfeiting (Directive 2014/62/EU) regulates details for a number of offences in Article 3, such as fraudulent making or altering of currency and import, export, transport, receiving or obtaining of counterfeit currency with a view to uttering the same and with knowledge that it is counterfeit. Article 5 provides the lowest threshold of maximum penalties as is standard in EU legislation of this kind.[64]

The particular position of the EU in relation to offences of this nature is also reflected in Article 11, which requires that the MS to submit data to the Commission on the number of offences and the number of people prosecuted and convicted at least every two years.

As highlighted by the current Security Strategy, *computer crime* is a major priority when framed as cybercrime. The 2013 Cybercrime

[61] Commission Communication: Fighting corruption in the EU, COM(2011) 308 final, 6 June 2011; Report from the Commission to the Council on the modalities of the European Union participate in the Council of Europe Group of States against Corruption (GRECO), COM(2011) 307 final, 6 June 2011; European Commission, EU Anti-Corruption Report, COM(2014) 38 final, 3 February 2014.

[62] Convention on the fight against corruption involving officials of the European Communities or officials of Member States of the European Union, OJ C 195/1, 26.5.1997; Commission Communication: On a comprehensive EU policy against corruption, COM(2003) 317 final, 28 May 2003; Council Framework Decision 2003/568/JHA on combating corruption in the private sector, OJ L 192/54, 22.7.2003.

[63] The official currency of nineteen out of twenty-seven member states – see https://europa.eu/european-union/about-eu/euro/which-countries-use-euro_en (last accessed 5 July 2021).

[64] Offences in Art. 3(1) are punishable by a maximum term of at least eight years whilst those defined in Art. 3(b) and (c) are punishable by a maximum term of at least five-year imprisonment.

Directive[65] on attacks against information systems highlights this as an area of increasing concern, especially in terms of attacks linked to organised crime.[66] This legislation requires the criminalisation of behaviour qualified as illegal access to information systems,[67] illegal system interference (seriously hindering or interrupting the functioning of an information system through a number of different methods),[68] illegal data interference[69] and illegal interception.[70]

This measure is now augmented by more recent legislation reflecting current concerns: Directive (EU) 2016/1148 concerning measures for a high common level of security of network and information systems across the Union[71]; Regulation (EU) 2019/881 of the European Parliament and of the Council on ENISA and on information and communications technology cybersecurity certification[72] as well as Council Decision 2021/796 amending Decision 2019/797 concerning restrictive measures against cyber-attacks threatening the Union or its MS.[73] EU activity has previously complemented work undertaken under the auspices of the Council of Europe,[74] but the efforts of the last years and the priority lent to this criminal phenomenon in the new Security Agenda clearly demonstrate the need for agile regulation that the EU is recognised as well placed to provide.

As should now have become clear, the EU has emerged – from perhaps being viewed as a convenient forum for the MS in which they could further efforts to ensure their needs for cooperation across borders were met in relation to prioritised cross-border crimes – as a governance level with considerable expertise, featuring institutions which take initiative in relation to such offences.

[65] Directive 2013/40/EU, OJ L 218, 12.8.2013.

[66] Preamble 3. [67] Art. 3. [68] In Art. 4.

[69] Deleting, damaging, deteriorating, altering or suppressing computer data, or rendering such data inaccessible in Art. 5.

[70] The interception of non-public transmissions of computer data in Art. 6.

[71] COM/2017/0476 final, 6 July 2016.

[72] And repealing Regulation (EU) No 526/2013 (Cybersecurity Act), OJ L 151, 17.4.2019.

[73] OJ L 1741, 17.5.2021.

[74] See P. W. Brunst, 'Terrorism and the Internet: New Threats Posed by Cyberterrorism and Terrorist Use of the Internet', in M. L. Wade and A. Maljević (eds.), *A War on Terror? The European Stance on a New Threat, Changing Laws and Human Rights Implications*, New York: Springer, 2009, pp. 51–78.

8.3 The Specific Meaning of Substantive Law in the EU Context: Flanking Institutions

The final statement above is particularly clear with evidence that a more holistic view, recognising the EU as a criminal justice actor in relation to these cross-border crimes, is now common. Although the legislation explored above may not appear so radically different to texts anyone familiar with transnational criminal law created in other contexts might expect, it is important to recognise that these are flanked in a number of deeply meaningful ways within the EU context.

As EU law, they are subject to evaluation proceedings to check compliance, ultimately enforced via corresponding court proceedings initiated by the Commission if MS fail to comply.[75] EU legislation is not mere lip service to a criminal justice effort. Within a few years of production, at the latest, this is internationally agreed substantive criminal legislation that has real world effects. Cross-border crime legislated for in the ways described above, constitute a very serious expression of intent, often driven by powerful MS. The Commission also takes its role as Guardian of the Treaties (and all that flows from them) seriously.

Thus, for example, Article 13 of the 2018 Money Laundering Directive requires MS to transpose this piece of legislation by 3rd December 2020. The Commission is in turn obliged by Article 14 to submit a report to the Parliament and Council by 3rd December 2022 reporting on the compliance of MS in this regard. Precisely one year later, the Commission is required to report to the same on the value added by the Directive as well as its impact on Fundamental Rights.

Furthermore, various, more organically developed, contexts mean the EU as a governance landscape is populated with a variety of organs to ensure effective cooperation against serious cross-border crime.[76] The ability to legislate is but one tool in the EU's hands, and it is utilised in dialogue with a plethora of others. A core feature is that these tools also influence each other. As a criminal justice actor, the EU has grown

[75] See Art. 258 TFEU. See, for example, action being taken against Poland and Hungary, at the time of writing, demonstrating these MS as being regarded as in breach of the EU's founding values by discriminating against LGBTIQ citizens, available at https://ec.europa.eu/commission/presscorner/detail/en/ip_21_3668.

[76] For an overview of the relevant criminal justice institutions, see Ambos, *European Criminal Law*, pp. 560–616.

not simply because it could legislate substantive law. Just as national politicians found the EU a useful umbrella under which to discuss their concerns, anti-fraud professionals, senior police chiefs, etc. also found an EU table at which they could sit. The Council of Police Chiefs evolved into structures now housed within Europol (see Chapter 15 by Ligeti/ Giuffrida), and DG Home, OLAF (see Chapter 14 by Cahn) provides a powerful focal point for international anti-fraud efforts; Eurojust's (see Chapter 16 by Jiménez-Villarejo Fernández/Hernández) development is unimaginable without the efforts of prosecutors informally reaching out to one another, then developing the European Judicial Network which in turn found support from EU structures. The EU's criminal justice efforts may have begun as legislative. However, because the EU also provided an institutional go to (employees within the Commission and Council tasked initially with supporting such legislative tasks), the demands upon it and its remit countering cross-border crime have expanded from this.

Article 83 TFEU reflects the role of the EU in relation to cross-border crime the MS could agree (in the early years of this century), publicly, that the EU should play. The analytical work files within Europol, specialist working groups within Eurojust[77] and indeed organs situated within the Council, which developed to ensure the effectiveness of substantive EU criminal law, have rendered this governance level an intelligence hub. They mean Threat Assessments written by[78] and opinions within these agencies drive policy agendas and further action.[79] The EU's resolve to stand united against terrorism and THB was and is also, very effectively, expressed also in the presence of institutions such as SitCen (which evolved into EU INTCEN)[80] and the Counter-Terrorism[81] and Anti

77 And indeed, its very existence meaning those requesting measures have somewhere to go to chase lagging responses for mutual assistance up.

78 See www.europol.europa.eu/activities-services/main-reports (last accessed 5 July 2021).

79 Note that even in the midst of Brexit negotiations, when the UK prime minister required a threat assessment to report to the public in the immediate aftermath of the Manchester Arena bombing, her stated authoritative source was the Director of Europol – BBC News, 'Manchester attack: Theresa May Terror Threat Speech in Full' (23 May 2017) at www.bbc.co.uk/news/uk-40023457 (last accessed 5 July 2021).

80 See UK House of Lords, 'Select Committee on European Union Seventh Report. Appendix 5. Joint Situation Centre (JSC)' (11 February 2003), archived on 16 June 2012 and EEAS Factsheet 05/02/2015 EU INTCEN.

81 www.consilium.europa.eu/en/policies/fight-against-terrorism/counter-terrorism-coordinator/ (last accessed 5 July2021).

THB[82] Coordinators within the Council. Only time will tell what will develop from these informal, intergovernmental organs in the future. The creation of the Fundamental Rights Agency should also be viewed as a development related to the Union's criminal justice powers. Some of the crimes analysed above may also receive greater attention and evolve should they emerge in practice as ancillary offences relevant to the work of the EPPO.[83]

As key, and indeed impressive, as EU substantive criminal law may be, it cannot be emphasised enough that to understand the law in the books is not to understand the true nature of EU work and influence in relation to cross-border crimes. This chapter must be read in connection with those detailing institutional development within the EU for a reader to hope to understand the very particular importance, also of substantive EU criminal law.[84] This area of law is rendered far more effective because it is part of a criminal justice system. It provides the basis for procedural instruments of mutual recognition, such as the EAW, and ensures that powerful agencies – such as Europol and Eurojust – can intervene to support national criminal justice systems in unprecedented manners.

8.4 Future Development

A final note should attend to the fact that, as a governance level, the EU has a range of tools at its disposal which influence it strongly, also in relation to cross-border crime. As is noted above, for instance, the European Parliament has made organised crime a focus of considerable work and policy consideration.[85] There are further ways in which its activities also directly relate to cross-border crime that have a less

[82] https://ec.europa.eu/anti-trafficking/eu-anti-trafficking-coordinator_en (last accessed 25 October 2021).

[83] J. E. Guerra, 'The Material Competence of the EPPO and the Concept of Inextricably Linked Offences', (2021) *eucrim*, 49–50.

[84] See, for example, F. Meyer, *Verbundstrafverfolgung in der EU*, in: F. Herzog et al. *Rechtsstaatlicher Strafprozess und Bürgerrechte: Gedächtnisschrift für Edda Weßlau*, Berlin: Duncker & Humblot, 2016, pp. 193–215; id., *Strafrechtsgenese in internationalen Organisationen*, Baden-Baden: Nomos, 2012, pp. 295–484.

[85] Producing for example: European Parliament recommendation to the Council on developing a strategic concept on tackling organised crime, OJ C 102E, 24 April 2008, pp. 464–468.

obvious nexus to criminal justice responses and have more to do with the protection parliamentarians view EU citizens as deserving. Because the European Parliament is now an actor within the ordinary legislative procedure, this also influences substantive EU criminal law.

For instance when Slovakia's political elite appeared to deserve the attention of a murder investigation due to dubious connections to organised crime, MEPs stepped in to demand adequate protection and criminal justice responses for citizens and victims.[86] This was doubtlessly a particular case, but it also forms part of MEP's activities to protect journalists more broadly.[87] These are clearly issues relevant to cross-border crime and will feed into, also substantive, understanding of the problem. They are also activities resonating strongly with a broader idea of a genuinely European Area of Freedom, Security and Justice, marked by certain expectations of social values as well as criminal justice provision. This in turn will be captured by substantive criminal law. So it cannot be more apparent that the EU context means recognition of a criminal phenomenon as a cross-border crime of relevance (to that governance level) will often lead to resonance in other policy areas; with effects that go well beyond facilitation of cooperation between MS authorities.

Noting Article 83's reservation of expansion considerations for the exceptional legislative procedure (so only requiring the consent of the Parliament after unanimity is reached in the Council), it appears important to track the *factual* working impulses of EU institutions in this area. These reveal a view of Article 83 as far more than an instrument of cooperation between the MS. No matter what it may look like on paper, the reality of EU law is very much as one feature of a powerful, supra-national governance level. Against the background of concerted effort to combat racism in the name of European values,[88] the Commission is pursuing an initiative to recognise hate crime and speech as 'other crimes' within Article 83(1)

[86] See J. Rankin, 'Bring in EU Police over Journalist's Murder, MEPs Urge Slovakia', *The Guardian*, 13 March 2018, www.theguardian.com/world/2018/mar/13/slovakia-should-hand-over-journalist-murder-inquiry-say-meps (last accessed 5 July 2021).

[87] See, for example, European Parliament Resolution 2018/2965(RSP) of 28 March 2019 on the situation of the rule of law and the fight against corruption in the EU, specifically in Malta and Slovakia, Preamble A.

[88] See the Commission Communication, A Union of equality: EU anti-racism action plan 2020–2025, COM/2020/565 final, 18 September 2020.

TFEU[89] and the European Parliament has passed a Resolution including a request to the Council that gender-based violence be included.[90] Article 83 TFEU may only foresee the Council as having the right to take initiative in relation to expanding its remit, the lived reality of the EU bears witness to other institutions also having influence. Introducing the concept of cross-border crime to the EU context has consequences irrespective of any apparent intentions of those drafting Treaties.

As has been noted above, identification as a cross-border crime falling within the ambit of the EU resonates into a variety of realities and actions. Where a *Eurocrime* is committed, this is also, for instance, being viewed as a breach of important values, meaning that qualification as such has profound effects for citizens convicted of these offences.[91]

The particular nature of EU criminal justice stems from the reach of its substantive criminal law both via its (monitored) transposition into MS law but also its practical operationalisation via the institutional framework – formal and informal – which surrounds it. Even if the MS initially intended to utilise the EU as an additional forum in which to create cooperative frameworks, this makes it uniquely potent. Politically powerful voices find – sometimes very swift – resonance within the EU context.[92] And it is not without consequence that informal policing networks have grown into a European Agency as definitions of crimes of relevance have been developed. The EU legislative process has provided a definition of terrorism, but the Europol TE-SAT drives a common understanding of associated criminal phenomena, emerging threats and paths forward. The discussion of and approach to cross-border crimes focused upon by the EU, is subject to evolution; potentially very fast indeed.

If one compares the various strands of EU criminal law and justice one might well note the tortuous process associated with the creation

89 See Directorate-General for Justice and Consumers, Roadmap, available at https://op.europa.eu/en/publication-detail/-/publication/0d868aaf-75df-11eb-9ac9-01aa75ed71a1/language-en (last accessed 5 July 2021).

90 Art. 3, and European Parliament Resolution of 25 February 2014 with recommendations to the Commission on combating Violence against Women, 2013/2004(INL).

91 For critical discussions of recent CJEU jurisprudence, for example see L. Mancano, 'Criminal Conduct and Lack of Integration into the Society under EU Citizenship: This Marriage Is Not to Be Performed', (2015) 6(1) *NJECL*, 53–77 and V. Mitsilegas, *EU Criminal Law after Lisbon*, Oxford: Hart, 2016, pp. 231–2.

92 See, for example the history of the EAW – Chapter 11 by P. Caeiro and M. J. Costa in this volume; W. van Ballegooij, 'European Implementation Assessment 2004–2020 on the EAW', (2020) *eucrim*, pp. 149–154.

of a European Public Prosecutors Office (EPPO) for the protection of the EU's financial interests (Ch. 17 Allegrezza).[93] Given how difficult Council negotiations surrounding that Office proved, one might be surprised to learn that the Commission put forward a proposal for a counter-terrorism EPPO in 2018.[94] At the time of writing, that is a legislative proposal sitting in the drawer. Students of EU criminal law and justice may well like to note that the same was true of the EAW until September 2001. Cross-border crimes lent priority in the EU context drive revolution.

Further Reading

C. Brière, 'Transnational Responses to Trafficking in Human Beings in Europe: Models for More Inclusive Governance Mechanisms', in R. Pereira, A. Engel and S. Miettinen (eds.), *The Governance of Criminal Justice in the European Union*, Cheltenham: Edward Elgar, 2020.

J. E. Guerra, 'The Material Competence of the EPPO and the Concept of Inextricably Linked Offences' (2021) *eucrim*, 49–50.

E. Herlin-Karnell, G. Conway, and A. Ganesh, *European Union Law in Context* London: Bloomsbury, 2021, Chapter 5.

J. Jones and J. Winterdyk, 'Human Trafficking: Challenges and Opportunities for the 21st Century. Outcomes and Proposals', (2018) 8(1) *Oñati Socio-Legal Series*, 165–173.

C. Kaunert and S. Léonard, 'The Collective Securitisation of Terrorism in the European Union', (2019) 42 *West European Politics*, 261–277.

C. C. Murphy, 'Transnational Counter-Terrorism Law: Law, Power and Legitimacy in the "Wars on Terror"', (2015) 6(1) *Transnational Legal Theory*, 31–54.

[93] For an earlier account, see Ambos, *European Criminal Law*, pp. 574–80.

[94] Commission Communication: A Europe that protects: an initiative to extend the competences of the European Public Prosecutor's Office to cross-border terrorist crimes, COM/2018/641 final, 12 September 2018.

9 Further Areas

Jan Stajnko, Petra Weingerl and Miha Šepec

9.1 Introduction

This chapter examines the Union's competence to require Member States (MS) to harmonize substantive criminal law in certain areas, particularly its competence to require MS to set out criminal law offences and penalties in 'further areas', besides the cross-border crimes discussed in Chapter 8. The Union's competence to harmonize substantive criminal law is addressed by the first two paragraphs of Article 83 TFEU.

Article 83(1) TFEU provides for the creation of 'minimum rules concerning the definition of criminal offences and sanctions in the area of particularly serious crime with a cross-border dimension', while Article 83(2) TFEU introduces an ancillary or annex competence to regulate criminal offences and sanctions for the purpose of the effective implementation of EU policies. We focus on Article 83(2) TFEU and divide the chapter into four parts. The first part traces the development of the EU's competence in the further areas of substantive criminal law prior and after the Treaty of Lisbon's entry into force. The second part provides an overview of further harmonized areas, while the third part looks at possible future areas of harmonization. The fourth part concludes the chapter by discussing bits and pieces of a general part of substantive criminal law found in the existing harmonization measures at the EU level.

9.2 The Union's Competence to Regulate Further Areas of European Substantive Criminal Law

9.2.1 Before the Treaty of Lisbon: From No Formal Role to Implied Powers

Before the entry into force of the Treaty of Lisbon, the competence of the (then) European Community to require MS to impose criminal sanctions was a controversial topic.[1] Initially, the European Community had no formal role in relation to justice and home affairs policy.[2] Efforts to harmonize substantive criminal law at EU level began to develop after the entry into force of the Treaty on European Union (TEU), the Maastricht Treaty, in 1993.

The CJEU played an important role in bringing criminal law closer to the EU's authority. It repeatedly stressed that, '[a]s a general rule, neither criminal law nor the rules of criminal procedure fall within the Community's competence'.[3] However, it contributed to the strengthening of EU competence in criminal law in at least two important ways.

First, the CJEU developed general principles that required MS to enforce Community rules by criminal law at least to some extent to ensure their effectiveness.[4] Second, the CJEU confirmed that the Community indeed had some criminal law competence. While the CJEU reiterated the 'general rule' that 'neither criminal law nor the rules of criminal procedure fall within the Community's competence', this rule was a presumption that could be overturned.[5] The CJEU held that the rule 'does not prevent the Community legislature, when the application of effective, proportionate and dissuasive criminal penalties by the competent national authorities is an essential measure for combating serious environmental offences, from taking measures which relate to the criminal law of the MS which it considers necessary in order to ensure that the rules which it lays down on

[1] See S. Peers, *EU Justice and Home Affairs Law: Volume II: EU Criminal Law, Policing, and Civil Law*, 4th edn, Oxford: Oxford University Press, 2016, p. 174.

[2] See, for example Art. 135 EC Treaty (Customs cooperation) and Art. 280 EC Treaty (Fraud against the EU Budget). See Peers, *EU Justice and Home Affairs Law*, p. 9.

[3] See, for example CJEU, *Commission v. Council*, No. C-176/03, Judgment, ECLI:EU:C:2005:542, 13 September 2005, para. 47, referring to *Lemmens*, No. C-226/97, Judgment, ECLI:EU:C:1998:296, 16 June 1998, para. 19.

[4] See, for example Peers, *EU Justice and Home Affairs Law*. For the landmark cases on the effective enforcement, see, for example the *Greek Maize* case (CJEU, *Commission v. Greece*, No. 68/88, Judgment, ECLI:EU:C:1989:339, 21 September 1989); CJEU, *Imm, Zwartveld and others*, No. C-2/88, Judgment, ECLI:EU:C:1990:440, 6 December 1990; and the ship source pollution case (CJEU, *Commission v. Council*, ECLIEU:C:2007:625, 23 October 2007). For an interesting discussion on the *Greek Maize* case in relation to the requirements of the principles of equivalence, effectiveness and proportionality, see, for example M. Dougan, 'From the Velvet Glove to the Iron Fist: Criminal Sanctions for the Enforcement of Union Law', in M. Cremona (ed.), *Compliance and the Enforcement of EU Law*, Oxford: Oxford University Press, 2012, p. 74.

[5] See Peers, *EU Justice and Home Affairs Law*, p. 174.

environmental protection are fully effective.'[6] Thus, the CJEU developed an ancillary or annex competence in in areas of environmental crime and ship-source pollution based on the doctrine of 'implied powers' or *effet utile.*[7] According to the doctrine of 'implied powers' the Community enjoys the powers to achieve a given objective or task attributed to it. Thus, for example, the Union's environmental protection objective would be deprived of its *effet utile* if the Union legislature did not have the power to adopt the criminal law measures necessary to ensure that the rules regarding environmental protection are fully effective.[8]

9.2.2 Treaty of Lisbon: Codification of the Ancillary or Annex Competence

The Treaty of Lisbon expressly recognised the competence of the Union to ensure a high level of security through the approximation of criminal laws. Article 83(2) TFEU expressly codifies the aforementioned ancillary or annex competence developed by the case law of the CJEU. This provision authorises the European Parliament and the Council, acting on a proposal from the Commission, to establish 'minimum rules with regard to the definition of criminal offences and sanctions,' where the approximation of criminal laws and regulations of the MS is essential to ensure the effective implementation of a Union policy in an area that has been subjected to harmonisation measures. This provision expressly recognized the autonomous function of approximation of the penal laws of the MS,[9] thereby making unnecessary any recourse to aforementioned unwritten 'implied powers'.[10] In the AFSJ, it is particularly important to strike a balance between the ius puniendi of the MS and transnational harmonization at the EU level. For this reason, this provision is subject to a number of safeguards discussed below.

6 See, for example CJEU, *Commission v. Council*, No. C-176/03, Judgment, ECLI:EU:C:2005:542, 13 September 2005, para. 47, para. 48.

7 For their usage as synonyms and a thorough explanation, see E. Herlin-Karnell, *The Constitutional Dimension of European Criminal Law*, Oxford: Hart Publishing, 2012, pp. 69–70.

8 Cf. R. Pereira, *Environmental Criminal Liability and Enforcement in European and International Law*, Leiden: Brill Nijhoff, 2015, p. 191, at notes 104–106 and references therein.

9 Ibid., p. 153.

10 See, for example P. Asp, *The Substantive Criminal Law Competence of the EU*, Stockholm: Skrifter utgivna av juridiska fakulteten vid Stockholms universitet, 2012, p. 136.

While Article 83(2) TFEU does not establish an exhaustive list of specific crimes, i.e., there is no absolute limitation *ratione materiae*, there are still two conditions for its applicability. First, the criminal law measures have to be 'essential' for the implementation of an EU policy, 'essential' being a highly ambiguous term.[11] Second, the use of Article 83(2) TFEU is qualified with making the prior adoption of harmonisation measures a precondition for the adoption of criminal law measures at the EU level. As highlighted by Peers, it could not be said that there is a 'Union policy' that needs implementing effectively in the absence of harmonization in specific areas of law.[12] EU institutions need to make policy choices in terms of the use or non-use of criminal law (instead of other measures, such as administrative sanctions) as tools to enforce legislation and to decide which EU policies require the use of criminal law as an additional enforcement tool.[13] Thus, Article 83(2) TFEU links the EU competence to harmonise criminal law to a need for the effective implementation of a Union policy. Therefore, it is expected that effectiveness will continue to play a significant role in future initiatives to harmonise criminal law in the EU.[14] To this end, in 2011, the Commission issued specific guidance on this point outlining the principles that should guide EU criminal law legislation and the policy areas.[15]

As regards the substantial questions, the first issue is the relationship between Article 83(1) and (2). Besides the potentially different decision-making procedure in each of them, different substantive criteria would apply to the adoption of measures under the two paragraphs. Article 83(2) TFEU subjects the harmonisation of criminal law mainly to a test of 'effectiveness', while Article 83(1) requires EU criminal law to address

[11] V. Mitsilegas, *EU Criminal Law*, Oxford: Hart Publishing, 2009, p. 108.

[12] Peers, *EU Justice and Home Affairs Law*, p. 121.

[13] P. Csonka and O. Landwehr, '10 Years after Lisbon – How "Lisbonised" Is the Substantive Criminal Law in the EU?', (2019) *eucrim*, 261–267.

[14] Pereira, *Environmental Criminal Liability and Enforcement in European and International Law*, p. 215; for the discussion on the role of effectiveness in the development of EU criminal law, see, for example E. Herlin-Karnell, 'The Constitutional Dimension of European Criminal Law'; E. Herlin-Karnell, 'Effectiveness and Constitutional Limits in European Criminal Law' (2014) 5 *NJECL*, 267.

[15] Communication from the Commission to the European Parliament, the Council, the European Economic and Social Committee and the Committee of the Regions, 'Towards an EU Criminal Policy: Ensuring the effective implementation of EU policies through criminal law', COM(2011) 573 final.

'particularly serious crime'. As to their relationship, Peers argues that each paragraph should logically be considered to be a *lex specialis* as regards the other paragraph. Therefore, the scope of para. 1 cannot be extended by the Council to cover offences within the scope of para. 2, and para. 2 cannot be interpreted to cover items expressly listed in para. 1.[16] Article 83(2) can be used to adopt measures asserting jurisdiction in relation to specific offences, and not only to define offences but also to prescribe sanctions in respect of those offences. However, the other policing and criminal law provisions of the Treaties have to be used to adopt measures concerning conflicts of jurisdiction, procedure and investigations.

Another substantive issue is the scope of Article 83(2) TFEU as compared to the Treaty's other policing and criminal law provisions. The question is whether it is still possible to adopt 'EU criminal law' on the basis, for example, of the EU's environmental law competence (Article 192 TFEU), rather than Article 83(2) TFEU? Or does Article 83(2) TFEU prevail over the other provisions?[17] The answer to this question is important as regards the applicability of Protocols 21 and 22 to the Treaty of Lisbon and the emergency break provided for by Article 83(3) TFEU. Concerning Protocols 21 and 22, Ireland and Denmark have the possibility to opt out from the EU initiatives in criminal law only.[18] What is more, the emergency break may be triggered by any MS with regard to measures based on Article 83(1) or (2) TFEU[19] and if the planned EU measures were to affect 'fundamental aspects' of the respective MS's criminal justice system. But who should define such 'fundamental aspects'? Should it be left to the MS as suggested by the German Federal Constitutional Court?[20]

The answer to the question whether Article 83(2) TFEU prevails over the other provisions is that both Article 83(1) and (2) are *leges speciales* regarding the adoption of criminal law measures concerning specific listed crimes (Article 83(1)) and ensuring effective harmonization (Article

[16] Peers, *EU Justice and Home Affairs Law*, pp. 168–169.

[17] See, for example S. Miettinen, 'Implied Ancillary Criminal Law Competence after Lisbon', (2013) 3 *EuCLR*, 194; Peers, *EU Justice and Home Affairs Law*, p. 169; Asp, *The Substantive Criminal Law Competence of the EU*, p. 141.

[18] Peers claims that the Danish and Irish opt-outs from Title V of TFEU arguably do not apply to paragraph 2, whereas they undoubtedly apply to paragraph 1. Peers, *EU Justice and Home Affairs Law*, p. 168.

[19] Ibid.

[20] BVerfGE 123, 267 [decision on the Lisbon Treaty]. See W. Schroeder, 'Limits to European Harmonisation of Criminal Law', (2020) *eucrim*, 147–148.

83(2)).[21] Thus, it seems that the correct legal basis for the future harmonisation of (environmental) criminal law is Article 83 TFEU.[22] As with all other open questions regarding the interpretation of EU law, it is for the CJEU to have a final say on this matter.

Another issue is the possibility of the use of the flexibility clause enshrined in Article 352 TFEU for the purposes of the harmonization of criminal law. This Article can only be invoked by the Council acting unanimously as a secondary option when 'the Treaties have not provided the necessary powers'. One can ask whether there can be situations where the use of criminal law is not essential, i.e., it is not possible to make use of Article 83(2) TFEU, but where the respective measures can be based on Article 352 TFEU.[23]

It is important to note that Article 83(2) TFEU refers specifically to approximation of criminal laws, and the adoption of minimum standards with regard to the definition of criminal offences and sanctions, which implies a limited degree of integration.[24] So far, only two directives have been based on Article 83(2): the Market Abuse Directive 2014/57[25] and the Directive 2017/1371 on the fight against fraud to the Union's financial interests by means of criminal law (the PIF Directive).[26] The overview of further harmonized areas, based on the pre-Lisbon implied powers or Article 83(2) TFEU, are outlined in the remainder of this contribution. The breakdown of further harmonized areas follows legal interests of the EU which have been protected in the respective harmonization instrument.[27]

[21] Peers, *EU Justice and Home Affairs Law*, p. 179.

[22] Ibid., p. 160; M. Kettunen, *Legitimizing European Criminal Law: Justification and Restrictions*, Cham: Springer, 2020, pp. 226–229. For a different view, favouring the possibility of 325(4) as a legal basis for the adoption of supranational criminal law legislation, see, for example K. Ambos, *European Criminal Law*, Cambridge: Cambridge University Press, 2018, pp. 18–19; H. Satzger, *International and European Criminal Law*, 2nd edn., München: C. H. Beck, Hart, Nomos, 2018, pp. 66–67.

[23] Asp, *The Substantive Criminal Law Competence of the EU*, p. 137; Kettunen, *Legitimizing European Criminal Law: Justification and Restrictions*, p. 219.

[24] Mitsilegas, *EU Criminal Law*, p. 108.

[25] Directive 2014/57/EU of the European Parliament and of the Council of 16 April 2014 on criminal sanctions for market abuse (market abuse directive), OJ L 173/179, 12.7.2014.

[26] Directive (EU) 2017/1371 of the European Parliament and of the Council of 5 July 2017 on the fight against fraud to the Union's financial interests by means of criminal law, OJ L 198, 28.7.2017, pp. 29–41.

[27] For a similar breakdown of the special part of the European substantive criminal law with regard to the protected 'legal value', see A. Klip, *European Criminal Law: An Integrative Approach*, 3rd edn., Cambridge: Intersentia, 2016, pp. 231–238. Compare with

While the Europeanisation of national substantive criminal law is also brought about by Council of Europe conventions,[28] the following overview is limited to EU harmonization.

9.3 Overview of Further Harmonized Areas

9.3.1 Environmental Protection

The first legal interest protected by EU criminal legislation which does not fall within the scope of Article 83(1) TFEU is the environment.[29] Harmonization of environmental criminal law at EU level has a long and debated history, previous to the Lisbon Treaty and the introduction of the TFEU. Initially, the role that criminal law played in most of the environmental legislation was relatively modest.[30] It was up to MS to choose how to react to breaches of environmental legislation of European origin.[31] This, however, changed in 2003 with the adoption of Framework Decision 2003/80 on the protection of environment,[32] wherein the Council stressed that environmental offences increasingly extend beyond the borders of MS in which they are committed. Complementary, the Framework Decision 2005/667 against ship-source pollution[33] was adopted by the Council in 2005. It aimed at combating environmental crime through

S. Coutts, 'Supranational Public Wrongs: The limitations and Possibilities of European Criminal Law and a European Community', (2017) 54 *CMLR*, 787–792, who identifies a number of 'European public goods', the violation of which constitutes a 'public wrong' as understood by Duff.

[28] For an exhaustive list of relevant conventions, see Ambos, *European Criminal Law*, pp. 317–318.

[29] Ibid., p. 788.

[30] M. Faure, 'The Revolution of Environmental Criminal Law in Europe', (2017) 35 *VELJ*, 321. Criminal law aiming at the protection of the environment usually came as an appendix to legislation having largely an administrative character. Ibid., 325.

[31] G. M. Vagliasindi, 'The EU Environmental Crime Directive', in A. Farmer, M. Faure and G. M. Vagliasindi (eds.), *Environmental Crime in Europe*, Oxford: Hart Publishing, 2017, p. 32.

[32] Council Framework Decision 2003/80/JHA of 27 January 2003 on the protection of the environment through criminal law, OJ L 29/55, 5.2.2003. This Framework Decision also took into account the Council of Europe Convention on the protection of the environment through criminal law from 1998.

[33] Council Framework Decision 2005/667/JHA of 12 July 2005 to strengthen the criminal-law framework for the enforcement of the law against ship-source pollution, OJ L 255/164, 30.9.2005.

discouraging the parties involved in the transport of hazardous cargoes by sea from engaging in substandard practices.

However, the adopted framework decisions aimed at the protection of environment were at the centre of a broader institutional conflict regarding the competence of adopting criminal law measures, as discussed above. The Commission introduced a Proposal for the Directive on the Protection of the Environment through Criminal Law already in 2001.[34] Disagreeing, the Council argued that adopting such measures went beyond the powers attributed to the (then) Community by the Treaty establishing the European Community. Hence, it instead adopted the framework decisions as instruments within the framework of the third pillar.[35]

The Commission, however, argued that the competence to take criminal law measures related to the protection of the environment belonged within the first pillar. It therefore brought with the support of the European Parliament actions for annulments against both framework decisions. As aforementioned, the CJEU stressed in environmental crimes case[36] that as a general rule, neither criminal law nor the rules of criminal procedure fall within the first pillar (para. 47). However, it went on to explain that this does not mean that even limited first pillar harmonisation of criminal law through Directives must always be ruled out (paras. 48 and 52). In cases where criminal law measures are necessary in order to ensure the full effectiveness of the protection of environment, they fall within the first pillar. In other words, the legal basis upon which the Council adopted the framework decision was not correct. The CJEU therefore annulled the Framework Decision 2003/80 on the protection of environment. A similar line of argumentation was adopted by the CJEU in ship-source pollution case,[37] where it annulled the Framework Decision 2005/667 against ship-source pollution (para. 66).

34 Proposal for a Directive of the European Parliament and of the Council on the Protection of the Environment through Criminal Law, Submitted by the Commission on 15 March 2001), COM(2001) 139 final – 2001/0076(COD), OJ C 180 E/238, 26.6.2001.

35 The Police and Judicial Co-operation in Criminal Matters (PJCC) Pillar, established by the Maastricht Treaty and abolished by the Lisbon Treaty. For an overview of pre-Lisbon EU competences in criminal matters and adopted instruments, see S. Miettinen, 'The Evolution of Competence Distribution between the European Union and the Member States in the Criminal Field', in C. Brière and A. Weyembergh (eds.), *The Needed Balances in EU Criminal Law*, Oxford: Hart Publishing, 2018, pp. 40–57.

36 CJEU, *Commission v. Council*, No. C-176/03, Judgment, ECLI:EU:C:2005:542, 13 September 2005.

37 CJEU, *Commission v. Council*, No. C-440/05, Judgment, ECLI:EU:C:2007:625, 23 October 2007.

These judgments of the CJEU are important for the understanding of the (pre-Lisbon) implicit (also implied) substantive criminal law competence and the equilibrium between the Communities (EC and EU) and the MS.[38] Division of competences for adopting criminal legislation in general and for further areas in particular is, however, discussed in other parts of this monograph and of this chapter.[39] For the purposes of this overview of European environmental criminal law development, it is more important to stress that new first pillar instruments replaced the framework decisions annulled by the CJEU: Directive 2008/99 on the protection of the environment[40] and Directive 2009/123 on ship-source pollution.[41]

Directive 2008/99 on the protection of the environment lays out definitions of nine criminal offences that need to be transposed into national legislation. They cover a wide area of environmental crime,[42] ranging from waste transport and management crimes to the destruction and trading in specimens of protected wild fauna or flora species (Article 3).

All these offences need to be committed *unlawfully*, meaning in infringement of environmental legislation listed in the Annexes to Directive 2008/99. This condition, together with partly unclear wording of the Directive[43] ('is likely to cause [...] substantial damage'), leaves a wide margin of possible interpretations regarding the question if environmental crimes should be understood as either abstract or concrete endangerment crimes[44] and the administrative dependence of the environmental

[38] Kettunen, *Legitimizing European Criminal Law*, pp. 131–135.

[39] See, for example, Chapter 9.

[40] Directive 2008/99/EC of the European Parliament and of the Council of 19 November 2008 on the protection of the environment through criminal law, OJ L 328/2, 6.12.2008.

[41] Directive 2009/123/EC of the European Parliament and of the Council of 21 October 2009 amending Directive 2005/35/EC on ship-source pollution and on the introduction of penalties for infringements, OJ L 280/52, 27.10.2009.

[42] For a useful categorization of offences in European environmental crime legislation, see Pereira, *Environmental Criminal Liability and Enforcement in European and International Law*, pp. 242–267.

[43] Some scholars are pinpointing at the problematic usage of 'quantitative non-numeric concepts' which allow for a lot of discretion in the selection of the actual criminalized conduct. A. Farmer, M. Faure and G. M. Vagliasindi, 'Environmental Crime in Europe: State of Affairs and Future Perspectives', in A. Farmer, M. Faure and G. M. Vagliasindi (eds.), *Environmental Crime in Europe*, Oxford: Hart Publishing, 2017, pp. 320–321.

[44] On the difference between concrete and abstract endangerment crimes in the context of environmental crime, see Faure, 'The Revolution of Environmental Criminal Law in Europe', 346–348. Compare G. Heine and C. Ringelmann, '*Towards an European Environmental Criminal Law – Problems and Recommendations*', Budapest: Studia Iuridica Auctoritate Universitatis Pecs Publicata, 2005, pp. 51–53.

criminal law.[45] However, it should be noted that such vague definitions might be used on purpose as to allow MS discretion on how to reach the objectives established in the Directive.[46]

The drafting approach and structure of Directive 2009/123 on ship-source pollution differs from the Directive 2008/99 on the protection of the environment. The former functions as an amendment of the existing Directive 2005/35 on ship-source pollution,[47] introducing criminal offences to the existing first pillar legal framework. Hence, the amended Directive 2005/35 now defines the criminal offence of illicit ship-source discharges of polluting substances, imposing an obligation on MS to transpose the offence (Arts. 4, 5 and 5a).

Interestingly, the definition explicitly excludes minor cases of pollution, except when 'repeated minor cases do not individually but in conjunction result in deterioration in the quality of water' (Article 5a(3)). Such potentially unlimited clustering of individual (minor or administrative) offences into a single overarching (criminal) offence can pose problems in terms of its compatibility with fundamental principles and other established mechanisms of national criminal law, such as the *ne bis in idem* principle or the temporal limitation rules. Hence, such definitions of criminal offences inevitably lead to problems during the legal transposition and practical application alike and should therefore be avoided in future harmonization attempts.

9.3.2 Market Abuse and Protection of the Financial Sector

Another legal interest that was identified early on and protected by European criminal law is the financial sector of the EU.[48] Most criminal

[45] Farmer, Faure and Vagliasindi, 'Environmental Crime in Europe: State of Affairs and Future Perspectives', p. 323.

[46] G. M. Vagliasindi, 'The EU Environmental Crime Directive', in A. Farmer, M. Faure and G. M. Vagliasindi (eds.), *Environmental Crime in Europe*, Oxford: Hart Publishing, 2017, pp. 47–48. Compare I. M. Ragaišytė, 'Challenges in Harmonising and Implementing the Environmental Crime Directive', (2021) 118 *Teisė*, 140–141.

[47] Directive 2005/35/EC of the European Parliament and of the Council of 7 September 2005 on ship-source pollution and on the introduction of penalties for infringements, OJ L 255/11, 30.9.2005.

[48] A. Klip, *European Criminal Law*, pp. 233–234; Coutts, 'Supranational Public Wrongs', p. 789; M. Kettunen, *Legitimizing European Criminal Law: Justification and Restrictions*, Cham: Springer, 2020, p. 141.

offences dealing with the protection of the financial sector, such as counterfeiting of Euro,[49] money laundering[50] and offences related to payment instruments,[51] would nowadays fall within the scope of Article 83(1) TFEU and are, therefore, not discussed in this chapter. However, the EU institutions already enacted further legislation which very clearly extends beyond the so-called euro-crimes defined in Article 83(1) TFEU, namely legislation protecting the financial sector from market abuse, which includes insider dealing and market manipulation.

The necessity for coordinated supranational rules on combating transfrontier insider dealing was identified by the EU already before the adoption of the Maastricht Treaty.[52] This resulted in the adoption of the Directive 89/594 on insider dealing,[53] which forced MS to harmonize rules regarding the prohibition (but not necessarily criminalization) of insider dealing. With the Market Abuse Directive 2003/6,[54] the harmonization extended to prohibition of market manipulation. Proper harmonization of substantive criminal[55] law finally took place with the adoption of Market Abuse Directive 2014/57,[56] which took effect in conjunction

[49] Directive 2014/62/EU of the European Parliament and of the Council of 15 May 2014 on the protection of the euro and other currencies against counterfeiting by criminal law, and replacing Council Framework Decision 2000/383/JHA, OJ L 151/1, 21.5.2014.

[50] The fourth Anti-Money Laundering Directive, Directive (EU) 2015/849 of the European Parliament and of the Council of 20 May 2015 on the prevention of the use of the financial system for the purposes of money laundering or terrorist financing, amending Regulation (EU) No 648/2012 of the European Parliament and of the Council, and repealing Directive 2005/60/EC of the European Parliament and of the Council and Commission Directive 2006/70/EC, OJ L 141/73, 5.6.2015. Regarding the striking choice to use Art. 114 TFEU as the sole legal basis for the fourth Anti-Money Laundering Directive, see V. Mitsilegas and N. Vavoula, 'The Evolving EU Anti-Money Laundering Regime: Challenges for Fundamental Rights and the Rule of Law', (2016) 23 *Maastricht J. Eur. Comp. L.*, 268–269.

[51] Directive (EU) 2019/713 of the European Parliament and of the Council of 17 April 2019 on combating fraud and counterfeiting of non-cash means of payment and replacing Council Framework Decision 2001/413/JHAPE/89/2018/REV/3, OJ L 123/18, 10.5.2019.

[52] For an overview of harmonization of EU insider trading law, see M. G. Faure, and C. Leger, 'The Directive on Criminal Sanctions for Market Abuse: A Move towards Harmonizing Insider Trading Criminal Law at the EU Level', (2014) 9 *BRJCFCL*, 395–397.

[53] Council Directive 89/592/EEC of 13 November 1989 coordinating regulations on insider dealing, OJ L 334/31, 18.11.1989.

[54] Directive 2003/6/EC of the European Parliament and of the Council of 28 January 2003 on insider dealing and market manipulation (market abuse), OJ L 096/16, 12.4.2003.

[55] M. Cerizza, 'The New Market Abuse Directive', (2014) *eucrim*, 86.

[56] Directive 2014/57/EU of the European Parliament and of the Council of 16 April 2014 on criminal sanctions for market abuse (market abuse directive), OJ L 173/179, 12.6.2014.

with the Market Abuse Regulation 596/2014.[57] This harmonisation of sanctioning regimes represented the first exercise of the competence introduced by Article 83(2) TFEU.[58]

The Market Abuse Directive 2014/57 (also dubbed by some as the 'Directive on Bankers')[59] needs to be assessed with a view to the financial crisis of 2008 and its consequences for financial markets.[60] The Commission argued in 2010 that the confidence of investors in financial markets needs to be restored by taking firm action against those actors who abuse the system.[61] These considerations were of vital importance for the adoption of the Market Abuse Directive 2014/57, aimed at ensuring compliance with the rules on market abuse by harmonizing criminal sanctions and thereby increasing the deterrent effect on potential offenders.[62]

Three criminal offences are defined by the Market Abuse Directive in order to protect the integrity of the financial market. Firstly, MS are obliged to criminalize insider dealing – the use of insider information for acquiring or disposing of financial instruments to which that information relates (Article 3). The aim of this criminal offence is to ensure a level playing field for all entities participating in the financial market by preventing the insiders ('persons in the know') from abusing their unfair advantage. A member of the managerial board may for example be acquainted very early on with the decision that a major acquisition of another company will be made. As it is likely that such an acquisition will increase the price of company's shares, it would be unfair if he would use this information to acquire a significant number of such shares, beating the 'ordinary' investor.[63]

[57] Regulation (EU) No 596/2014 of the European Parliament and of the Council of 16 April 2014 on market abuse (market abuse regulation) and repealing Directive 2003/6/EC of the European Parliament and of the Council and Commission Directives 2003/124/EC, 2003/125/EC and 2004/72/EC, OJ L 173/1, 12.6.2014.

[58] M. Miglietti, 'The First Exercise of Article 83(2) TFEU under Review: An Assessment of the Essential Need of Introducing Criminal Sanctions', (2014) 5 *NJECL*, 12–16.

[59] Peers, *EU Justice and Home Affairs Law*, p. 167.

[60] Miglietti, 'The First Exercise of Article 83(2) TFEU under Review: An Assessment of the Essential Need of Introducing Criminal Sanctions', 14; E. Herlin-Karnell,' White-Collar Crime and European Financial Crises: Getting Tough on EU Market Abuse', (2012) 37 *Eur. L. Rev.*, 487.

[61] Regulating Financial Services for Sustainable Growth, 2. 6. 2010, COM(2010) 301 final, pp. 6–7.

[62] Recitals 6 and 7 of the Directive.

[63] M. Janovec, 'How Not to Abuse the Market', in P. Mrkývka, J. Gliniecka, E. Tomášková, E. Juchniewicz, T. Sowiński and M. Radvan (eds.), *The Financial Law towards Challenges of the XXI Century: Conference Proceedings*, Brno: Masaryk University, 2020, pp. 603–606.

The second criminal offence (Article 4) relates to unlawful disclosure of inside information to third persons, except in cases where this is required or permitted by law (for example reporting to a regulatory body in order to fulfil a legal obligation),[64] while the third criminal offence (Article 5) relates to various forms of market manipulation. The latter encompasses manipulative conduct such as spreading false or misleading signals, price securing and the employment of fictitious devices or other forms of deception or contrivance. Similar to Arts. 3 and 4, prohibition and criminalization of market manipulation also aims at ensuring 'full and proper market transparency, which is a prerequisite for trading for all economic actors in integrated financial markets'.[65] All the above-described cases of market abuse should constitute criminal offences, at least in serious cases.[66]

9.3.3 Migration and Fair Competition between Employers

Although not as thoroughly protected against various forms of abuses as the financial market, the labour market is another recognizable legal interest protected by European criminal law. While not explicitly mentioned, the urge to protect the labour market is apparent from the Directive 2009/52 on employer sanctions.[67] In the impact assessment report on the proposed directive, the Commission for example listed 'distortion of the labour market by downward pressure on wages and conditions'[68] amongst negative impacts of employment of illegal migrants for nationals (workers), while distortion of competition between employers is listed amongst negative impacts for companies who do not employ illegal immigrants.

Directive 2009/52 on employer sanctions explicitly prohibits the employment of illegally staying third-country nationals in order to fight illegal immigration (Articles 1 and 3). What is more, it stipulates

64 P. Hauck, 'Europe's Commitment to Countering Insider Dealing and Market Manipulation on the Basis of Art 83 Para 2 TFEU: A Critical Evaluation', (2015) 10 *ZIS*, 344.

65 Recital 15 of the Market Abuse Directive 2003/6.

66 This criterion was described as highly ambiguous and open for interpretation, although some additional clarification is provided by recital 11 of the Directive. Compare Hauck, 'Europe's commitment to countering insider dealing and market manipulation on the basis of Art 83 para 2 TFEU' 341.

67 Directive 2009/52/EC of the European Parliament and of the Council of 18 June 2009 providing for minimum standards on sanctions and measures against employers of illegally staying third-country nationals, OJ L 168/133, 30.6.2009.

68 Impact assessment, 16.5.2007, SEC(2007) 603, pp. 8–9.

that a violation of this prohibition constitutes a criminal offence when committed intentionally and under five distinct circumstances, which range from persistently repeated infringement of the prohibition to illegal employment of a minor illegal immigrant (Article 9).[69]

Further areas of immigration criminal law[70] which do not fall within the scope of Article 83(1) TFEU have also been subject to harmonization. Framework Decision 2002/946 on unauthorised entry[71] called upon MS to adopt criminal sanctions for the facilitation of unauthorized entry, transit and residence, i.e., human smuggling. While human trafficking involves an element of (usually longer term) victim exploitation, human smugglers merely move people and provide a bridge between various countries for migrants.[72] Criminalization of human smuggling therefore far exceeds criminalization of human trafficking, which falls within the scope of Article 83(1) TFEU.

Framework Decision 2002/946 reflects an expansive approach to the criminalisation of human smuggling since it 'dispenses with the condition of obtaining a financial or other material benefit for the smuggling offence to be established'.[73] There is, however, a discretionary provision allowing MS to limit the scope of criminalisation by not imposing (criminal) sanctions in cases where the aim is to provide humanitarian assistance to the migrant.[74]

[69] For a critical assessment of these additional criteria, see S. Peers, 'Legislative Update: EC Immigration and Asylum Law Attracting and Deterring Labour Migration: The Blue Card and Employer Sanctions Directives', (2009) 11 *Eur J Mig Law*, 419–420.

[70] In the light of increasing entanglement of criminal and immigration law, some scholars are pointing out that the so called crimmigration trends are on the rise in the EU and globally. N. K. Šalamon, B. Frett and E. S. Ketchum, 'Global Crimmigration Trends', in N. K. Šalamon (ed.), *Causes and Consequences of Migrant Criminalization*, Cham: Springer, 2020, p. 22.

[71] Council framework Decision of 28 November 2002 on the strengthening of the penal framework to prevent the facilitation of unauthorised entry, transit and residence (2002/946/JHA), OJ L 328/1, 5.12.2002. On the same date, the Council Directive 2002/90/EC of 28 November 2002 defining the facilitation of unauthorised entry, transit and residence, OJ L 328/17, 5.12.2002, was also adopted.

[72] E.R. Kleemans and M. Smit, 'Human Smuggling, Human Trafficking and Exploitation in the Sex Industry', in L. Paoli (ed.), *The Oxford Handbook of Organized Crime*, Oxford: Oxford University Press, 2014, pp. 381–382.

[73] V. Mitsilegas, '*The Criminalisation of Migration in Europe: Challenges for Human Rights and the Rule of Law*', Cham: Springer, 2015, p. 52.

[74] Art. 1(2) of the Council Directive 2002/90/EC defining the facilitation of unauthorised entry, transit and residence, OJ L 328/17, 5.12.2002. On the importance of this clause

9.3.4 Human Dignity, Discrimination and Hate Speech

A number of harmonized criminal offences that (amongst other legal interests) protect the human dignity were already mentioned (for example human trafficking, sexual abuse of children and employment of illegal immigrants). A further area of harmonized substantive criminal law protecting human dignity[75] which does not (yet) fall within the scope of 83(1) TFEU[76] relates to European non-discrimination legislation.

While the existing[77] as well as the proposed[78] Directives prohibit various forms of discrimination, they do not oblige MS to use criminal law to address acts of discrimination. Instead, the only instrument that introduces an EU-wide criminal ban of certain forms of discrimination is the Framework Decision 2008/913 on Racism and Xenophobia,[79] replacing the Joint Action 96/443 on Racism and Xenophobia.[80]

Although not explicitly stated in the Framework Decision itself, there is a general consensus that it focuses on criminalizing (at least certain forms) of illegal hate speech.[81] This is achieved by defining two groups of offences that need to be criminalized by MS. The first group relates to

for organisations and individuals who provide advice or assistance to migrants, see Mitsilegas, 'The Criminalisation of Migration in Europe', p. 53.

[75] Klip, *European Criminal Law*, p. 235.

[76] Compare *below*, ref. 110; Peers, *EU Justice and Home Affairs Law*, p. 181; Ambos, *European Criminal Law*, p. 361.

[77] Council Directive 2000/43/EC of 29 June 2000 implementing the principle of equal treatment between persons irrespective of racial or ethnic origin, OJ L 180/22, 19.7.2000; Council Directive 2000/78/EC of 27 November 2000 establishing a general framework for equal treatment in employment and occupation, OJ L 303/16, 2.12.2000; Directive 2006/54/EC of the European Parliament and of the Council of 5 July 2006 on the implementation of the principle of equal opportunities and equal treatment of men and women in matters of employment and occupation (recast), OJ L 204/23, 26.7.2006; Council Directive 2004/113/EC of 13 December 2004 implementing the principle of equal treatment between men and women in the access to and supply of goods and services, OJ L 373/37, 21.12.2004.

[78] Proposal for a Directive against discrimination based on age, disability, sexual orientation and religion or belief beyond the workplace of 2 July 2008, COM(2008) 426 final.

[79] Council Framework Decision 2008/913/JHA of 28 November 2008 on combating certain forms and expressions of racism and xenophobia by means of criminal law, OJ L 328/55, 6.12.2008.

[80] Joint Action of 15 July 1996 adopted by the Council on the basis of Article K.3 of the Treaty on European Union, concerning action to combat racism and xenophobia (96/443/JHA), OJ L 185/5, 24.7.1996.

[81] N. Alkiviadou, 'Regulating Hate Speech in the EU', in S. Assimakopoulos, F. H. Baider and S. Millar (eds.), *Online Hate Speech in the European Union: A Discourse-Analytic Perspective*, Cham: Springer, 2017, pp. 6–7.

crimes of publicly inciting to violence or hatred directed against a group of persons or a member of such a group defined by reference to race, colour, religion, descent or national or ethnic origin. The second group instead focuses on crimes of publicly condoning, denying or grossly trivialising crimes such as the Holocaust, but also other core international crimes such as genocide, crimes against humanity and war crimes (Article 1(1)).[82]

The harmonization framework is softened by allowing MS 'to punish only conduct which is either carried out in a manner likely to disturb public order or which is threatening, abusive or insulting' (Article 1(2)). This provision is important because it allows for far-reaching restrictions on the hate speech crimes, effectively limiting their reach to cases of concrete endangerment or even harming of further legally protected interests (public order or the affected person's honour and reputation).[83]

The Framework Decision furthermore touches upon other crimes that are performed with racist and xenophobic motivation, giving MS a choice to either consider such motivation as an aggravating circumstance or leave it to national courts to consider it while determining the severity of sanctions in concrete cases (Article 4).

9.3.5 Offences against or by Public Officials

The integrity of public administration is a legal interest,[84] which is perhaps most notably protected by the Convention against corruption involving public officials.[85] There is, however, a further body of legislation which does not fall within the scope of Article 83(1) TFEU and nonetheless impacts the protection of the integrity of public administration through criminal law. We are referring to various provisions on offences against or by officials during operations in another MS.

[82] P. Lobba, 'Punishing Denialism beyond Holocaust Denial: EU Framework Decision 2008/913/JHA and Other Expansive Trends', (2014) 5 *NJECL*, 64–65.

[83] N. Alkiviadou, 'Regulating Hatred: Of Devils and Demons?', (2018) 18 *Int. J. Discrim. Law*, 228.

[84] Klip, *European Criminal Law*pp. 236–237.

[85] Convention drawn up on the basis of Article K.3 (2) © of the Treaty on European Union on the fight against corruption involving officials of the European Communities or officials of Member States of the European Union, OJ C 195/2, 25.6.1997.

Already the Convention on mutual assistance in criminal matters[86] stated in Article 15 that during operations related to controlled deliveries, joint investigation teams and covert investigations, 'officials from a Member State other than the Member State of operation shall be regarded as officials of the Member State of operation with respect of offences committed against them or by them.' Similar clauses were later introduced to the Framework Decision 2002/465 on joint investigation teams (Article 2), Decision 2008/615 on the stepping up of cross-border cooperation, particularly in combating terrorism and cross-border crime (Article 22), Europol Decision 2009/371 (Article 6) and Directive 2014/41 on the European Investigation Order (Article 17).

The far-reaching implications of such provisions should not be underestimated since national criminal law often treats crimes committed by or against a public official as aggravating offences (for example unlawful visual recording by an official). What is more, MS also typically protect the integrity of public administration by introducing a number of offences against official duties (for example abuse of office and acceptance of bribes). Hence, national criminal law needs to be harmonized in order to allow for an extension of such offences to officials of other MS while they are performing operations and other activities performed under the outlined legislation.

9.3.6 Perjury and Fair Administration of Justice

A further legal interest protected by European criminal law is fair administration of justice.[87] One would indeed be hard pressed to argue for the competence of the EU to harmonize criminal substantive law protecting national judicial authorities and administration of justice in national judicial proceedings. However, preventing various forms of obstruction of justice such as perjury in proceedings before the CJEU is of vital importance for the EU and proper functioning of its institutions. It is therefore not surprising that the Statute of the Court of Justice of the European Union (CJEUSt) in Article 30 stipulates that MS should 'treat

[86] Convention established by the Council in accordance with Article 34 of the Treaty on European Union, on Mutual Assistance in Criminal Matters between the Member States of the European Union, OJ C 197/3, 12.7.2000.

[87] Klip, *European Criminal Law*, pp. 237–238.

any violation of an oath by a witness or expert in the same manner as if the offence had been committed before one of its courts with jurisdiction in civil proceedings'.

The implications of this clause for the national criminal legal systems and its nature are somewhat controversial. In line with the prevailing opinion, it constitutes a self-executing, directly applicable (supranational) European law.[88] It was, however, pointed out – and rightly so – that the necessary prerequisites for the direct effectiveness of Article 30 CJEUSt are not fulfilled. Without a corresponding provision in a national criminal legal system, this clause does not constitute a criminal offence. It furthermore leaves a wide margin of discretion to MS when it comes to its implementation, for example regarding the exact scope of the perjury offence and legal consequences of such an offence.[89] This means that Article 30 CJEUSt does not constitute directly applicable (supranational) criminal law. At any rate, it is clear that this clause at least constitutes an obligation for MS to reform their national legal systems. What is more, the existing national provisions on perjury should be subject to interpretation in conformity with Article 30 CJEUSt if possible.[90]

9.4 Future Areas of Harmonization

Taking into account limitations posed by (inter alia) principles of conferral, subsidiarity and proportionality,[91] the competence for harmonization of criminal law given by Article 83(2) TFEU can potentially expand in parallel with the evolution of any area of EU action not covered by Article 83(1).[92] While an extended approximation of criminal law could prove controversial in practice and therefore lack a necessary political consensus, there are some key areas of criminal law that can be identified as more prone to future harmonization.

[88] Ambos, *European Criminal Law*, p. 329.

[89] Satzger, *International and European Criminal Law*, pp. 62–64.

[90] Ambos, *European Criminal Law*, p. 330.

[91] For more on the principles of conferral, subsidiarity and proportionality and their relation to the ultima ratio principle, see, for example Ambos, *European Criminal Law*, pp. 15–17; M. Kettunen, *Legitimizing European Criminal Law: Justification and Restrictions*, Cham: Springer, 2020, pp. 169–173.

[92] Miglietti, 'The First Exercise of Article 83(2) TFEU under Review: An Assessment of the Essential Need of Introducing Criminal Sanctions', 8.

Firstly, some areas that are already subject to partial harmonization of criminal law ought to be mentioned. These are for example areas where the harmonization of definitions of offences is lacking a common grid of sanctions[93] (for example environmental law[94] and employment of illegal immigrants[95]) or where the protection is simply lacking because of too narrow definitions (for example inciting of violence against individuals based on their sexual orientation, age or disabilities not covered by the hate speech framework decision[96]).

Secondly, we might see the extension of European criminal law to areas already subject to explicit prohibitions and penalties, but not to harmonization of criminal law. These might include legislation on intellectual property,[97] road transport (for example rules restricting lorry-drivers' driving hours), data protection legislation or customs rules. The Commission already explicitly indicated that in all of these areas, 'the potential role of criminal law as a necessary tool to ensure effective enforcement could be explored further'.[98]

Alas, areas not (yet) subject to harmonization of prohibitions or penalties (or even any harmonization at all) could also be subject to future harmonization of criminal law aspects. The Commission, for example suggested

93 This category mainly refers to First Pillar pre-Lisbon harmonization of substantive criminal law which was limited by the CJEU to defining criminal offences, while the harmonization of sanctions was to be established under the Third Pillar. Mitsilegas, *EU Criminal Law after Lisbon: Rights, Trust and the Transformation of Justice in Europe*, Oxford: Hart Publishing, 2016, p. 56.

94 'The Commission will consider the need to strengthening compliance monitoring and enforcement [of environmental crimes], for instance by [...] further approximating criminal sanctions throughout the EU.' The European Agenda on Security, COM(2015) 185 final, 28 April 2015, p. 18. The approximation of sanctions was later proposed as a possible action in Evaluation of Directive 2008/99/EC of the European Parliament and of the Council of 19 November 2008 on the protection of the environment through criminal law (Environmental Crime Directive), 28. 10. 2020, SWD(2020) 259 final, p. 80. On possible future amendments to EU environmental crime legislation in general, see Pereira, *Environmental Criminal Liability and Enforcement in European and International Law*, pp. 200–202.

95 'The Commission will assess how to strengthen the effectiveness of the Employers Sanctions Directive and evaluate the need for further action.' New Pact on Migration and Asylum of 23 September 2020, COM(2020) 609 final, p. 16.

96 'In 2021, the Commission will present an initiative to extend the list of "EU crimes" under Article 83 (1) of the Treaty on the Functioning of the European Union (TFEU) to cover hate crime and hate speech, including when targeted at LGBTIQ people.' Union of Equality: LGBTIQ Equality Strategy 2020–2025, 12 November 2020, COM(2020) 698 final, p. 14.

97 Proposal for a European Parliament and Council Directive on criminal measures aimed at ensuring the enforcement of intellectual property rights, 12 July 2005, COM(2005)276 final.

98 Towards an EU Criminal Policy: ensuring the effective implementation of EU policies through criminal law (Communication), 20 September 2011, COM(2011) 573 final, p. 10.

in 2019 that it might be appropriate to establish minimum rules concerning the definition of criminal offences and sanctions in the area of election manipulation.[99] Another example could be potential harmonization of criminal offences and sanctions in the area of public health, especially in the wake of the COVID-19 crisis and its implications. Moreover, suggestions have been made for the criminal prohibition of spreading disinformation and fake news, which can be linked to the enduring rule of law crisis in the EU.[100]

9.5 General Part of Substantive Criminal Law

Even though a Pan-European criminal code was never adopted, this does not mean that there is a complete lack of interest for harmonization or even unification of general principles of substantive criminal law on the European level. Already in 1971, the Council of Europe discussed the possibility of a European Model Penal Code. The idea was dismissed at the time, however brought back in 1993 on the agenda of the Committee on Legal Affairs and Human Rights of the Council of Europe. Even if adopted, such model penal code would ideally not aim at mandatory harmonization, but rather at non-binding, 'soft' approximation of the General Part.[101] The flexibility of the non-binding model would however mean that its harmonizing and unifying effect would be much weaker than that of a binding convention or EU directive.[102]

However, it is unlikely that political consensus for a binding directive could be achieved in the foreseeable future. What is more, the EU does not have the mandate to harmonise or codify criminal law comprehensively.[103] The harmonization competence of the EU in Article 83

[99] Presidency document 9726/19, The future of EU substantive criminal law – Policy debate, 28 May 2019, p. 9.

[100] J. Bayer (ed.), *Disinformation and Propaganda – Impact on the Functioning of the Rule of Law in the EU and Its Member States*, European Parliament, LIBE Committee, Policy Department for Citizens' Rights and Constitutional Affairs, 2019, p. 139. Authors of the study suggest that 'any envisaged criminal rule should build heavily upon the method rather than the content – the manipulative techniques, the automated dissemination methods, the misuse of personal data and the violation of political party financing'.

[101] U. Sieber, 'Memorandum on a European Model Penal Code', (1999), 1, *Eur J Law Reform*, 470.

[102] Ibid., 465.

[103] Csonka and Landwehr, '10 Years after Lisbon – How "Lisbonised" Is the Substantive Criminal Law in the EU?', 262.

TFEU is limited to 'rules concerning the definition of criminal offences and sanctions'. EU therefore lacks the competence to harmonise generally applicable national principles and concepts. For example, it lacks the competence to adopt legislation that would focus on the definition of attempt in general, also covering non-harmonized areas such as attempted murder, theft, rape and so on.

It is, however, inevitable for the EU to deal with some General Part related issues even when focusing on harmonization of specific areas of the Special Part.[104] As rightly pointed out by Ambos: 'General and Special Part are interrelated; the former cannot be understood without recourse to the latter and, more importantly in our context, the scope of criminalization in the Special Part depends on the rules of the General Part'.[105] It is therefore not surprising that some General Part related concepts can be found in existing harmonization instruments. These include, inter alia, intent, negligence, participation and attempt.[106] Hence, harmonization instruments each produce their own General Part provisions with regard to specific harmonized area of the Special Part.[107] What is more, it has been argued that read together, these harmonization instruments can be considered to provide a shared embryonic set of rules on key General Part concepts.[108] Some shared concepts, for example on liability of legal persons, were even codified in non-binding Council Conclusions on model provisions, guiding the Council's criminal law deliberations[109] from 2009. It is however true that the EU has not been very consistent, systematic or precise when introducing these general concepts and, as a consequence, the emerging General Part of European criminal law is still fragmented and full of grey areas.[110]

It is therefore not ideal that the CJEU does not seem to be too keen on facilitating the emergence of shared criminal law concepts. Even the principle of guilt as the most basic principle in continental criminal law

[104] Klip, *European Criminal Law*, p. 184.

[105] K. Ambos, 'Is the Development of a Common Substantive Criminal Law for Europe Possible? Some Preliminary Reflections' (2005) 12 *Maastricht J. Eur. Comp. L.*, 175.

[106] Klip, *European Criminal Law*, pp. 208–227. [107] Ibid., p. 196.

[108] S. Miettinen, *Criminal Law and Policy in the European Union*, London: Routledge, 2013, p. 134.

[109] Council document 16542/2/09, Draft Council Conclusions on model provisions, guiding the Council's criminal law deliberations, 27 November 2009.

[110] Klip, *European Criminal Law*, p. 196.

doctrine was never unified or harmonized. Similar to the European Court of Human Rights, the CJEU understands guilt in a procedural sense to be inferred from the presumption of innocence. And while the CJEU qualifies the principle of *nulla poena sine culpa* as a principle typical of criminal law, so far it has only done so in cases unrelated to criminal law. In multiple cases,[111] in which national law had created strict (objective) criminal liability – omitting a subjective element of guilt – the CJEU found this to be compatible with Union law.[112]

Further Reading

K. Ambos, 'Is the Development of a Common Substantive Criminal Law for Europe Possible? Some Preliminary Reflections.' (2005) 12 *Maastricht J. Eur. Comp. L.*, 173–191.

P. Csonka, and O. Landwehr, '10 Years after Lisbon. How "lisbonised" Is the Substantive Criminal Law in the EU?', (2019) *eucrim*, 261–267.

M. Kettunen, *Legitimizing European Criminal Law: Justification and Restrictions*, Cham: Springer, 2020.

V. Mitsilegas, *EU Criminal Law after Lisbon: Rights, Trust and the Transformation of Justice in Europe*, Oxford: Hart Publishing, 2016.

V. Mitsilegas, M. Bergström, and T. Konstadinides (eds.), *Research Handbook on EU Criminal Law*, Cheltenham: Edward Elgar, 2016.

J. Öberg, *Limits to EU Powers: A Case Study of EU Regulatory Criminal Law*, Oxford: Hart Publishing, 2019.

S. Peers, *EU Justice and Home Affairs Law: Volume II: EU Criminal Law, Policing, and Civil Law*, 4th edn, Oxford: Oxford University Press, 2016.

N. Peršak, 'EU Criminal Law and Its Legitimation: In Search for a Substantive Principle of Criminalisation.' (2018) 26 *ECCL*, 20–39.

I. Topa, 'Where Do We Stand with Harmonization of Substantive Criminal Law in EU? Remarks on the Changes Introduced by the Lisbon Treaty.' (2012) *SJLS*, 89–99.

I. Wieczorek, *The Legitimacy of EU Criminal Law*, Oxford: Hart Publishing, 2020.

[111] CJEU, *Anklagemyndigheden v. Hansen & Soen I/S*, No. C-326/88, Judgment, ECLI:EU:C:1990:291, 10 July 1990; *Käserei Champignon Hofmeister GmbH & Co. KG v. Hauptzollamt Hamburg-Jonas*, No. C-210/00, Judgment, ECLI:EU:C:2002:440, 11 July 2002.

[112] P. H. van Kempen and J. Bemelmans, 'EU Protection of the Substantive Criminal Law Principles of Guilt and ne bis in idem under the Charter of Fundamental Rights: Underdevelopment and Overdevelopment in an Incomplete Criminal Justice Framework', (2018) 9 *NJECL*, 256.

Part IV

European Criminal Procedure

10 Fundamental Rights Protection

Martin Böse

10.1 Introduction

The Council of Europe and the European Union have established common European standards for the protection of fundamental rights and the rights of the defendant in criminal proceedings in particular. The guarantees enshrined in the European Convention of Human Rights (ECHR) and the Union's Charter of Fundamental Rights (CFREU) have become essential parts of the national criminal justice systems of the Member States (MS). In the Area of Freedom, Security and Justice (Article 67 of the Treaty on the Functioning of the European Union – TFEU), the rights of the defendant have also gained a transnational dimension in the framework of cross-border cooperation in criminal matters. This new dimension of procedural rights is closely linked to the principle of mutual recognition (Article 67(3), 82(1) TFEU): on the one hand, the transnational dimension of a procedural right can be regarded as an emanation of the principle of mutual recognition (the *ne bis in idem* principle, Article 54 Convention Implementing the Schengen Agreement – CISA); on the other hand, common standards for the effective protection of defence rights (e.g., the presumption of innocence and the right to be present at trial) constitute essential preconditions for mutual trust in the MS' criminal justice systems and may facilitate the mutual recognition of judgments in criminal matters (Article 82(2) TFEU). Taking up the aforementioned connection to the principle of mutual recognition, this chapter will elaborate on the *ne bis in idem* principle and the right to a fair trial with a particular focus on the transnational dimension of these guarantees and their impact on cross-border cooperation in criminal matters within the Union.

10.2 The *ne bis in idem* Principle (Article 54 CISA, Article 50 CFREU)

The *ne bis in idem* principle protects the accused from double punishment, or more precisely: from double prosecution. According to the traditional understanding, this protection is limited to the criminal justice system in which the final decision (conviction or acquittal) was rendered (i.e., the sentencing state). Article 54 CISA takes the *ne bis in idem* principle a step further, stating that a person whose trial has been finally disposed of in one Contracting Party may not be prosecuted in another Contracting Party for the same acts. Barring proceedings in a state other than the sentencing state, Article 54 CISA has provided the *ne bis in idem* principle with a transnational effect.

Article 54 CISA was not invented by EU MS but has originated from previous international treaties.[1] The transnational dimension of the *ne bis in idem* principle was firstly recognized in Article 9 of the European Convention on Extradition (1957).[2] According to that provision, extradition shall not be granted if a court of the requested state has passed final judgment upon the person in respect of the offence for which extradition is requested (Article 9 clause 1). If the competent authorities have terminated proceedings in respect of the same offence by a decision other than a judgment, the requested state 'may' refuse extradition (Article 9 clause 2). So, the mandatory extradition obstacle requires a 'final judgment', that is, a decision having the authority of *res iudicata* in the requested state whereas a decision merely terminating criminal proceedings because there are no grounds for prosecution (e.g., an *ordonnance de non-lieu*) is only considered an optional ground for refusal.[3] Furthermore, even if a 'final judgment' was rendered in the requested state, the protection of the convicted or acquitted person is limited to extradition proceedings: Article 9 of the European Convention on Extradition does not bar criminal proceedings in

[1] W. Schomburg, 'Internationales "ne bis in idem" nach Art 54 SDÜ', (1997) 17 *StV* 383; John Vervaele 'Ne bis in idem: Towards a Transnational Constitutional Principle in the EU?', (2013) 9 (4) *Utrecht L. Rev.* 211, 213 ff.

[2] European Convention on Extradition of 13 December 1957 (ETS No. 24).

[3] Explanatory Report to the European Convention on Extradition 8, 9.

another state when the sentenced person has been arrested in that state and there is no need for an extradition request.[4]

The apparent *lacuna* in the protection from double prosecution has been addressed by subsequent treaties containing self-standing provisions on the *ne bis in idem* principle. In 1970, the European Convention on the International Validity of Criminal Judgments[5] provided this principle with a transnational effect by stating that 'a person in respect of whom a European criminal judgment has been rendered may for the same act neither be prosecuted nor sentenced nor subjected to enforcement of a sanction in another Contracting State' (Article 53(1) of the Convention). Since the Convention was ratified by a few states only,[6] the MS of the European Communities drafted a new treaty, namely the Convention on Double Jeopardy (1987).[7] The wording of Article 1 of the Convention served as a blueprint for the transnational dimension of the *ne bis in idem* principle as finally adopted by Article 54 CISA (1990).[8] The Schengen acquis was integrated into the legal framework of the Union by the Treaty of Amsterdam (1997) and Article 54 CISA became part of the EU legislation.[9] As the ban on double prosecution forms part of

[4] J. Vervaele 'Ne bis in idem: Towards a Transnational Constitutional Principle', (2013) 9 (4) *Utrecht L. Rev.*, 217.

[5] European Convention on the International Validity of Criminal Judgments of 28 May 1970 (ETS No. 70).

[6] In 1985, only six states had ratified the Convention (Austria, Cyprus, Denmark, Norway, Sweden and Turkey); in the meantime, the Convention has been ratified and entered into force in twenty-three states.

[7] Convention between the Member States of the European Communities on Double Jeopardy of 25 May 1987 (Übereinkommen zwischen den Mitgliedstaaten der Europäischen Gemeinschaften über das Verbot der doppelten Strafverfolgung), German Federal Law Gazette (Bundesgesetzblatt) 1998 II 2227.

[8] Explanatory memorandum of the German government to the Convention on Double Jeopardy, Bundestagsdrucksache No. 13/8195 (10 July 1997), p. 9.

[9] Protocol integrating the Schengen acquis into the framework of the European Union OJ C 340, 10.11.1997, p. 93; Council Decision 1999/435/EC of 20 May 1999 concerning the definition of the Schengen acquis for the purpose of determining, in conformity with the relevant provisions of the Treaty establishing the European Community and the Treaty on European Union, the legal basis for each of the provisions or decisions which constitute the acquis OJ L 176, 10.7.1999, p. 1; Council Decision 1999/436/EC of 20 May 1999 determining, in conformity with the relevant provisions of the Treaty establishing the European Community and the Treaty on European Union, the legal basis for each of the provisions or decisions that constitute the Schengen acquis OJ L 176, 10.7.1999, pp. 17, 21.

the international human rights standard (Article 14(7) ICCPR,[10] Article 4 Protocol No. 7 to the ECHR[11]), the *ne bis in idem* principle is also enshrined in the Charter of Fundamental Rights (Article 50) that expressly acknowledges its transnational effect ('within the Union').

The rationale of the *ne bis in idem* principle and its transnational dimension are twofold: As a fundamental right, Article 50 CFREU shall protect the individual from double punishment and ensure the principle of legal certainty: When the court has taken a final decision on the case, the convicted (or acquitted) person can be sure that he will not be subject to criminal prosecution again (for the same conduct).[12] On the other hand, Article 54 CISA has an objective coordinating function as it resolves (potential) conflicts of jurisdiction and thereby contribute to an effective transnational law enforcement.[13] This objective function reflects the origins of Article 54 CISA in international treaties on cooperation in criminal matters. Accordingly, the Convention's chapter on the *ne bis in idem* principle is embedded between the chapters on mutual legal assistance (Article 48 to 53 CISA) and extradition (Articles 59 to 66 CISA).

10.2.1 Scope and Limits of the *ne bis in idem* Principle and its Transnational Effect

According to Article 54 CISA, the transnational effect of the *ne bis in idem* principle (a ban on further prosecution) is subject to four requirements: (i) criminal proceedings in the sentencing state must have resulted in a final decision (*res iudicata)*, (ii) the proceedings in the sentencing state and the prosecuting state must relate to the same facts (*idem*), (iii) the penalty imposed by the sentencing state has been enforced is actually in

[10] International Covenant on Civil and Political Rights of 16 December 1966 (UNTS Vol. 999, I-14668).

[11] Protocol No. 7 to the Convention for the Protection of Human Rights and Fundamental Freedoms of 1 November 1988 (ETS No. 117).

[12] J. Lelieur 'Transnationalising ne bis in idem: How the Rule of ne bis in idem Reveals the Principle of Personal Legal Certainty' (2013) 9 (4) *Utrecht L. Rev.*, 198, 210.

[13] M. Böse 'Der Grundsatz "ne bis in idem" in der Europäischen Union (Art. 54 SDÜ)', (2003) 150 *GA*, 744, 751–752; see also for the link to the principle of mutual recognition: CJEU, *Gözütök and Brügge*, Joined Cases Nos. C-187/01 and C-385/01, Opinion of Advocate General Ruiz-Jarabo Colomer, ECLI:EU:C:2002:516, 19 September 2002, paras. 124 ff.

the process of being enforced or can no longer be enforced under the laws of the sentencing state (enforcement element) and (iv) non-applicability of exceptions (Article 55 CISA).

(i) In its first case on Article 54 CISA, the Court of Justice (CJEU) had to rule on the notion of *res iudicata*. In contrast to the traditional understanding in international treaty law, the Court held that the term 'finally disposed of' did not require a court decision but applied to any decision of the public prosecutor's office whereby criminal proceedings were discontinued once the accused had paid a certain amount of money and further prosecution was barred (*Einstellung unter Auflagen,*[14] *transactie*[15]).[16] In essence, the reasoning of the Court was based on the effect of the relevant decisions under national law: Once the accused has paid the amount of money determined by the prosecutor, he enjoys protection from further prosecution.[17] The Court argued that restricting the scope of application to court decisions (judgments) would result in an interpretation of the *ne bis in idem* principle that would benefit perpetrators of serious crimes only, but not defendants having committed minor offences who were prosecuted in the framework of simplified procedures.[18] The integration of the Schengen acquis was aimed at enhancing European integration and developing the Union as an area of freedom, security and justice in which the citizens of the Union enjoy the right to free movement (Article 21 TFE), and the exercise of this right to free movement would be significantly hampered if persons having fulfilled the obligations for a discontinuation of proceedings were still facing the risk of being prosecuted in another MS.[19]

In subsequent judgments, the Court re-affirmed the broad interpretation of Article 54 CISA and made its application mainly dependent upon whether or not the decision adopted in the sentencing MS was to be considered final. Whereas the final acquittal for lack of evidence (*van*

[14] German Code of Criminal Procedure (Strafprozessordnung), section 153a.

[15] Dutch Criminal Code (wetboek van strafrecht), Art. 74.

[16] CJEU, *Gözütok and Brügge*, Joined Cases Nos. C-187/01 and C-385/01, Judgment, ECLI:EU:C:2003:87, 11 February 2003, para. 48.

[17] German Code of Criminal Procedure (Strafprozessordnung), section 153a(1)5; Dutch Criminal Code (wetboek van strafrecht), Art. 74(1)2.

[18] CJEU, *Gözütok and Brügge*, Joined Cases Nos. C-187/01 and C-385/01, Judgment, ECLI:EU:C:2003:87, 11 February 2003, para. 40.

[19] CJEU, *Gözütok and Brügge*, Joined Cases Nos. C-187/01 and C-385/01, Judgment, ECLI:EU:C:2003:87, 11 February 2003, paras. 35–38.

Straaten)[20] or for prosecution being time-barred (*Gasparini*)[21] fell within the scope of application of Article 54 CISA, the transnational *ne bis in idem* effect was not triggered by a decision that did not have the effect of *res iudicata* under domestic law and, thus, did not bar a new investigation related to the same facts (*Turanský*).[22] In the light of this case law, it was hardly surprising that the Court ruled in *criminal proceedings against M* that a court decision to discontinue criminal proceedings (*ordonnance de non-lieu*[23]) fell within the scope of application of Article 54 CISA, too, because the *ordonnance de non-lieu* precluded new criminal proceedings on the basis of the same facts and evidence in the sentencing MS.[24] In addition, the Court argued that Article 54 CISA had to be interpreted in the light of Article 50 CFREU and Article 4 of Protocol No 7 to the ECHR.[25] Thereby, the Court expressly recognized the transnational dimension of the *ne bis in idem* principle as a fundamental right in order to justify its broad interpretation of Article 54 CISA.

By contrast, the most recent judgment (*Kossowski*) followed a more restrictive approach according to which a final decision had to meet two conditions, namely the effect of *res iudicata* in the domestic criminal justice system and, secondly, a determination as to the merits of the case.[26] The second requirement was not considered to be met if the authorities of the sentencing state were apparently not able to verify the evidence and, thus, to examine the merits of the case.[27] In contrast to its former judgments where the principle of mutual recognition had been given particular weight, the Court held that mutual trust could prosper only if the second MS was able to satisfy itself that the final decision taken in the first MS met the criteria set out in Article 54 CISA.[28] In the eyes of

20 CJEU, *van Straaten*, No. C-150/05, Judgment, ECLI:EU:C:2006:614, 28 September 2006, paras. 60–61.

21 CJEU, *Gasparini*, No. C-467/04, Judgment, ECLI:EU:C:2006:610, 28 September 2006, paras. 25, 33.

22 CJEU, *Turanský*, No. C-491/07, EU:C:2008:768, 22 December 2008, paras. 36, 40, 45.

23 Belgian Code of Criminal Procedure (Code d'Instruction Criminelle), Art. 128.

24 CJEU, *Criminal proceedings against M*, No. C-398/12, EU:C:2014:1057, 5 June 2014, paras. 33, 41.

25 Ibid., paras. 35, 37.

26 CJEU, *Kossowski*, No. C-486/14, Judgment, ECLI:EU:C:2016:483, 29 June 2016, para. 42; see also *Miraglia*, No. C- 469/03, Judgment, ECLI:EU:C:2005:156, 10 March 2005, paras. 30, 35.

27 CJEU, *Kossowski*, No. C-486/14, Judgment, ECLI:EU:C:2016:483, 29 June 2016, para. 48.

28 Ibid., paras. 52–53.

the Court, Article 54 CISA had to be interpreted in the light of the need to promote the combating of crime within the area of freedom, security and justice.[29] In *Kossowski,* the concerns about the application of Article 54 CISA were originating from a dysfunctional coordination of criminal proceedings because the 'final' decision had not been taken in the MS where the crime had been committed (Germany) and were to bar further prosecution by that state whereas in its preceding case law (*criminal proceedings against M*), the final decision had been adopted in the MS where the criminal conduct had occurred. In this regard, Article 55(1)(a) CISA provides for an exception from the *ne bis in idem* principle that is based upon the legitimate interest of a MS in exercising jurisdiction over crimes committed within its own territory because the assessment by the court of another MS is based upon extraterritorial jurisdiction and, thus, might be not be completely exhaustive. Recourse to this provision would take the MS' (and the Union's) interest in effective criminal law enforcement into consideration but would still maintain the character of the *ne bis in idem* principle as a fundamental right (Article 50 CFREU) and not leave the defendant in a limbo of uncertainty whether or not the decision in the sentencing state is based upon a determination of the merits of the case, that is a 'proper' evaluation of the evidence.[30]

(ii) The second requirement under Article 54 CISA is that the criminal proceedings in the sentencing state and the prosecuting state relate to 'the same acts' (*idem*). In its case law, the Court of Justice construed the *idem* as identity of the material acts, irrespective of the legal classification and the protected legal interest (*van Esbroeck*).[31] The Court based its interpretation on the wording of Article 54 CISA ('acts') that differed from the corresponding term in Article 4 of Protocol No. 7 to the ECHR ('offence') but also referred to the principle of mutual trust in the sentencing state's criminal justice system and the rationale of the *ne bis in*

[29] Ibid., para. 47.

[30] See for a critical appraisal of the Court's approach: M. Böse, 'The Transnational Dimension of the ne bis in idem principle and the Notion of res iudicata in the European Union' in M. Böse, M. Bohlander, A. Klip, and O. Lagodny (eds.) *Justice Without Borders Essays in Honour of Wolfgang Schomburg*, Leiden, Boston: Brill 2018, p. 49, 59 ff.; for the contrary view (in favour of a merits test), see K. Ambos, 'C-486/14 – Kossowski – Judgment (Grand Chamber) C-486/14 Piotr Kossowski, 29 June 2016' in V. Mitsilegas, A. di Martino and L. Mancano (eds.), *The Court of Justice and European Criminal Law*, Oxford: Hart 2019, p. 227, at 232.

[31] CJEU, *van Esbroeck*, No. C-436/04, ECLI:EU:C:2006:165, 9 March 2006, para. 42.

idem principle to protect the Union's citizen from further prosecution on account of his or her having exercised the right to free movement (Article 21 TFEU).[32] Accordingly, the identity of the conduct (*idem*) is determined by the material acts, that is a set of facts that are inextricably linked together.[33] This broad and human-rights-oriented approach was consistently upheld in subsequent case law.[34]

(iii) Thirdly, the transnational effect of the *ne bis in idem* principle is subject to proper enforcement: If criminal proceedings in the sentencing state have resulted in a guilty verdict and a penalty has been imposed upon the convicted person, Article 54 CISA requires that the penalty has been fully enforced is actually in the process of being enforced (e.g., where the convicted person serves a prison sentence or is under probation[35]) or can no longer be enforced under the laws of the sentencing state (e.g., because enforcement is time-barred or the convicted person has been pardoned[36]). The enforcement condition shall avoid a situation in which the convicted person can no longer be prosecuted for the same acts in another MS despite the fact that the respective decision has not been enforced. Thus, ultimately, impunity shall be avoided and thus made sure that the public interest in criminal law enforcement will be satisfied.[37] Even though Article 50 CFREU does not provide for this further requirement, the CJEU considered it to be compatible with Article 50 CFREU because Article 52(1) CFREU allows for limitations of the *ne bis in idem* principle that are provided for by law and comply with the principle of proportionality.[38] According to the Court, the enforcement condition is necessary to prevent impunity given that the cooperation instruments on cross-border enforcement of penalties are subject to various conditions and grounds for refusal and require a decision of the sentencing

32 Ibid., paras. 28, 30, 33. 33 Ibid., paras. 36, 42.

34 CJEU, *Gasparini*, No. C-467/04, Judgment, ECLI:EU:C:2006:610, 28 September 2006, para. 54; *van Straaten*, No. C-150/05, Judgment, ECLI:EU:C:2006:614, 28 September 2006, para. 48; *Kretzinger*, No. C-288/05, Judgment, ECLI:EU:C:2007:441, 18 July 2007, paras. 29, 37; *Kraaijenbrink*, No. C-367/05, Judgment, ECLI:EU:C:2007:444, 18 July 2007, para. 36; *Mantello*, No. C-261/09, ECLI:EU:C:2010:683, 16 November 2010, para. 39.

35 CJEU, *Kretzinger*, No. C-288/05, Judgment, ECLI:EU:C:2007:441, 18 July 2007, para. 42.

36 See in this regard, CJEU, *Bourquain*, No. C-297/07, Judgment, ECLI:EU:C:2008:708, 11 December 2008, para. 45.

37 CJEU, *Kretzinger*, No. C-288/05, Judgment, ECLI:EU:C:2007:441, 18 July 2007, para. 51; *Spasic*, No. C-129/14, Judgment, ECLI:EU:C:2014:586, 27 May 2014, para. 58.

38 CJEU, *Spasic*, No. C-129/14, Judgment, ECLI:EU:C:2014:586, 27 May 2014, paras. 54–74.

state to initiate transnational enforcement proceedings.[39] However, the implementation of the mutual recognition principle has established an effective framework of the transnational enforcement of sentences, and it seems doubtful whether *lacunae* in the enforcement regime (in particular where a lack of enforcement results from the unwillingness of the sentencing state to use the corresponding cooperation instruments) provide sufficient reason for initiating new criminal proceedings against the convicted person instead of eliminating the obstacles to the execution of the judgment of the sentencing state in the first place.[40]

(iv) Finally, Article 55 CISA allows the MS to establish exceptions from the *ne bis in idem* principle and to exercise their *ius puniendi* even though the offender has been subject to criminal prosecution in another MS. These exceptions are limited to three situations, namely crimes committed within the territory of the MS claiming jurisdiction (Article 55(1)(a) CISA), crimes against essential interests of that state (Article 55(1)(b) CISA), and crimes committed by officials of that state in violation of their duties (Article 55(1)(c) CISA). Several MS have issued such declarations (Austria, Denmark, Finland, Germany, Greece and Sweden).[41] They mostly refer to the whole list of exceptions, only two are limited to Article 55(1) (a) and (b) CISA (Germany and Sweden). The exceptions (and the corresponding reservations) under Article 55 CISA are based upon the MS' concern that their public interest to maintain the rule of law and to protect core state interests is not satisfied by a final decision rendered in another MS because it is based upon extraterritorial jurisdiction and, thus, limited to certain aspects of the criminal conduct (Article 55(1)(a) CISA) or the law of the sentencing state does not protect interest

[39] CJEU, *Spasic*, No. C-129/14, Judgment, ECLI:EU:C:2014:586, 27 May 2014, para. 69.

[40] For a critical assessment of the Court's reasoning, see M. Böse, 'Einschränkungen des transnationalen ne bis in idem – notwendiges Korrektiv oder Anachronismus?', in G. Hochmayr (ed.), *'Ne bis in idem' in Europa*, Baden-Baden: Nomos 2015, 171, 173 ff; F. Meyer, 'Transnationaler ne-bis-in-idem-Schutz nach der GRC – zum Fortbestand des Vollstreckungselements aus Sicht des EuGH', (2014) 15 *HRRS*, 269, 270 ff.

[41] Commission Staff Working Document, Annex to the Green Paper on Conflicts of Jurisdiction and the Principle of ne bis in idem in Criminal Proceedings of 23 December 2005, SEC (2005) 1767, p. 47. The reservations of the French and the Italian government have not been deposited within the time-limit under Art. 55 CISA, see in this regard, M. Böse, 'Chapter 3: Fundamental Rights of the EU Charter', in M. Böse, F. Meyer, and A. Schneider (eds.), *Conflicts of Jurisdiction in Criminal Matters in the European Union. Volume II: Rights, Principles and Model Rules*, Baden-Baden: Nomos 2014, p. 132.

of a foreign state (Article 55(1)(b) and (c) CISA). Like the enforcement condition (Article 54 CISA), the exceptions under Article 55 CISA may be considered as limitations to the *ne bis in idem* principle enshrined in Article 50 CFREU, provided that they comply with the requirements set out in Article 52(1) CFREU.[42] The procedural background in *Kossowski* has revealed that there may be good reasons for recourse to the exceptions and giving territorial jurisdiction priority over extraterritorial jurisdiction of the sentencing state (Article 55(1)(a) CISA).[43] However, the harmonization of the MS' criminal law (e.g., in the area of terrorism and corruption) have raised doubts on whether recourse to the exceptions under Article 55(1)(b) and (c) CISA is still necessary and proportionate.[44]

10.2.2 The *ne bis in idem* Principle in Transnational Proceedings

As a fundamental right, Article 50 CFREU (and Article 54 CISA) impose binding obligations upon MS that do not only apply to domestic criminal proceedings but also to cross-border cooperation in criminal matters. The EU legislator has expressly acknowledged these obligations in the Framework Decision on the European arrest warrant (FD EAW)[45] and provided that an EAW must not be executed if the requested person has been finally judged by an MS in respect of the same acts provided that the sentence has been served or is currently being served or may no longer be executed under the law of the sentencing MS (Article 3(2) FD EAW). This mandatory ground for refusal corresponds, in scope and limits, to Article 54 CISA and prohibits the executing MS from surrendering a person whose prosecution in the issuing MS is in breach with the *ne bis in idem* principle (Article 50 CFREU, Article 54 CISA).[46] Thus, Article 3(2) FD EAW can be considered as an expression of the obligation of the

[42] Explanations to the CFREU prepared under the authority of the Presidium of the Convention, OJ C 303, 14.12.2007, pp. 17, 31.

[43] For the contrary view, see *Kossowski*, No. C-486/14, Opinion of Advocate General Yves Bot, ECLI:EU:C:2015:812, 15 December 2015, paras. 48–68.

[44] For a detailed analysis, see M. Böse, 'Chapter 3: Fundamental Rights of the EU Charter' in M. Böse, F. Meyer, and A. Schneider (eds.), *Conflicts of Jurisdiction. Volume II*, Baden-Baden: Nomos 2014, pp. 131 ff, 139 ff.

[45] Framework Decision of 13 June 2002 on the European arrest warrant and the surrender procedures between Member States, OJ L 190, 18.7.2002, p. 1.

[46] CJEU, *Mantello*, No. C-261/09, Opinion of Advocate General Yves Bot, ECLI:EU:C:2010:501, 7 September 2010, paras. 86 ff.

executing MS to respect fundamental rights (Article 1(3) FD EAW), that, in turn, limits the principle of mutual recognition and the obligation of the executing MS to surrender the requested person.[47]

However, the principle of mutual recognition might gain particular importance where the final decision has been adopted in the MS that has been issued the EAW and whose competent authority has expressed the view that the *ne bis in idem* principle does not bar further criminal prosecution in the issuing MS – and the decision to issue an EAW to that end. In this particular setting, it is not the transnational, but the intranational effect of the *ne bis in idem* principle that is at stake. However, neither the wording nor the objective and purpose of Article 3(2) FD EAW support an interpretation that limits the scope of this ground for refusal to cases in which the acts referred to in the EAW formed the subject-matter of a final judgment in a sentencing state other than the issuing MS. On the contrary, the *ne bis in idem* principle equally applies to the effect of a final decision (*res iudicata*) in any MS where this decision has been adopted (i.e., the intranational effect).[48] Accordingly, the CJEU followed a comprehensive interpretation of the refusal ground in Article 3(2) FD EAW that covers final decisions rendered in the issuing MS as well (*Mantello*).[49] However, the effect of *res iudicata* in the national criminal justice system is governed by the law of the sentencing (and issuing) state (see *supra* with regard to the first requirement of Article 54 CISA). The Court's case law on the *ne bis in idem* principle illustrates that Article 54 CISA applies to final decisions that do not have full, but only limited authority of *res iudicata* and allow for a re-opening of proceedings if certain conditions are met (e.g., if new facts or evidence are revealed).[50] According to the division of tasks and responsibilities between the sentencing (and issuing) MS on the one hand and the executing MS on the other, it is first and foremost upon the courts of the former state to decide upon whether or not the authority of *res iudicata* bars criminal proceedings related to

[47] ibid., para. 88; see in general CJEU, *Aranyosi and Căldăraru*, Joined Cases Nos. C-404/15 and C-659/15 PPU, Judgment, ECLI:EU:C:2016:198, 5 April 2016, paras. 83 ff.

[48] CJEU, *Mantello*, No. C-261/09, Opinion of Advocate General Yves Bot, ECLI:EU:C:2010:501, 7 September 2010, paras. 84 ff.

[49] CJEU, *Mantello*, No. C-261/09, Judgment, ECLI:EU:C:2010:683, 16 November 2010, paras. 32 ff.

[50] CJEU, *Gözütok and Brügge*, Joined Cases Nos. C-187/01 and C-385/01, Judgment, ECLI:EU:C:2003:87, 11 February 2003, para. 48; *Criminal proceedings against M*, No. C-398/12, Judgment, EU:C:2014:1057, 5 June 2014, para. 40.

the acts referred to in the EAW.[51] Thus, if the competent authorities of the issuing MS expressly state that the earlier judgment delivered under its legal system does not have the (full) authority of *res iudicata* and therefore does not preclude further criminal prosecution of the respective conduct, the executing authority has no reason to apply the ground of mandatory non-execution under Article 3(2) FD EAW.[52] This interpretation does not render the *ne bis in idem* principle wholly irrelevant in surrender proceedings. The issuing MS is still, notwithstanding its margin of appreciation, obliged to respect the essence of the *ne bis in idem* principle and the legitimate expectations of the acquitted or convicted person not to be tried again (Article 50, 52(1) CFREU). If the issuing state does not live up to this obligation and initiates criminal proceedings violating the *ne bis in idem* principle, the executing MS may (and, in fact, must) refuse to surrender the requested person.

10.3 The Right to a Fair Trial and *in absentia* Proceedings (Article 47, 48 CFREU)

The right to fair trial (Article 47(2) CFREU, Article 6(1) ECHR) is an essential element of any criminal justice system committed to the rule of law and respect for human rights. This right entails several specific rights such as the presumption of innocence (Article 48(1) CFREU, Article 6(2) ECHR) and the rights of the defence (Article 48(2) CFREU), Article 6(3) ECHR). Beyond their intrinsic value for the national criminal justice systems in the Union, the MS' commitment to these fundamental procedural guarantees is the basis for mutual trust in the legitimacy of each other's criminal justice system and the smooth functioning of cross-border cooperation based upon the principle of mutual recognition. In order to strengthen and foster mutual trust between the MS and to facilitate mutual recognition of judgments and cooperation in criminal matters, the EU legislator may establish minimum rules on the rights of individuals in criminal procedure (Article 82(2)(b) TFEU) that further develop the standards set out in the ECHR and the CFREU. To that end, the Council

[51] CJEU, *Mantello*, No. C-261/09, Judgment, ECLI:EU:C:2010:683, 16 November 2010, paras. 47, 49 f.

[52] Ibid., para. 51.

adopted a roadmap for strengthening procedural rights of the individual in criminal proceedings[53] that resulted in the following legislative measures on the rights of the defendant.

10.3.1 The Directives on Procedural Rights of the Defendant

As the first measure implementing the roadmap, Parliament and Council adopted Directive 2010/64/EU on the right to interpretation and translation in criminal proceedings[54] that specified content and scope of the right under Article 6(3)(e) ECHR, e.g., with regard to the availability of interpretation for communication with defence counsel (Article 2(2) Directive 2010/64/EU) and mandatory translation of essential documents such as arrest warrants, indictments and judgments (Article 3(1), (2) Directive 2010/64/EU) and penal orders in particular.[55] Directive 2010/64/EU, however, does not establish a right to lodge a remedy against a penal order in a language other than that of the proceedings even if the defendant does not have a command of that language.[56]

The second measure (Directive 2012/13/EU[57]) established a common minimum standard on the right to information in criminal proceedings. This standard covers the right to be informed of the nature and the cause of the accusation (Article 6(3)(a) ECHR) and, as far as the defendant is in custody, the reasons for arrest and detention (Article 6 Directive 2012/13/EU) as well as the right of arrested persons to access to the file (Article 7 Directive 2012/13/EU). Furthermore, the Directive entails an obligation of the MS to inform the defendant of his/her rights in criminal proceedings such as the right of access to a lawyer, any entitlement to free legal advice and the conditions for obtaining such advice, the right to be informed of the accusation, the right to interpretation and translation and the right to remain silent (Article 3 Directive 2012/13/EU). Arrested

[53] Council of the European Union Resolution of the Council of 30 November 2009 on a Roadmap for strengthening procedural rights of suspected or accused persons in criminal proceedings, OJ C 295, 4.12.2009, p. 3.

[54] Directive 2010/64/EU of 20 October 2010 on the right to interpretation and translation in criminal proceedings, OJ L 280, 26.10.2010, p. 1.

[55] CJEU, *Sleutjes*, No. C-278/16, Judgment, ECLI:EU:C:2017:757, 12 October 2017, paras. 31, 34.

[56] CJEU, *Covaci*, No. C-216/14, Judgment, ECLI:EU:C:2015:686, 15 October 2015, para. 51.

[57] Directive 2012/13/EU of 22 May 2012 on the right to information in criminal proceedings, OJ L 142, 1.6.2012, p. 1.

persons shall be provided with a 'letter of rights' that contains – in addition to the aforementioned information – the right to access the file, the right to have consular authorities and one person informed, the right of access to urgent medical assistance, the maximum number of hours or days suspects or accused persons may be deprived of liberty before being brought before a judicial authority, and the legal remedies against his/her detention (Article 4 Directive 2012/13/EU).

The procedural rights to which the letter of rights in Directive 2012/13/EU referred were further developed by Directive 2013/48/EU.[58] According to the Directive, defendants shall have access to a lawyer (Article 6(3)(c) ECHR) without undue delay, in particular before they are questioned by law enforcement or judicial authorities, after arrest or where they have been summoned to appear before a court in criminal proceedings (Article 3(2) Directive 2013/48/EU). MS shall ensure that the defendant has the right to meet and communicate with defence counsel prior to questioning and to be assisted effectively by his lawyer when the defendant is questioned or certain investigative measures (identity parades, confrontations, reconstruction of the crime-scene) are carried out (Article 3(3) Directive 2013/48/EU). Police and judicial authorities shall respect the confidentiality of any communication between defendant and defence counsel (Article 4 Directive 2013/48/EU). Furthermore, the Directive establishes common standards on the right of the arrested person to have a third party informed upon deprivation of liberty (Article 5 Directive 2013/48/EU) and the right of the detained person to communicate with third persons (Article 6 Directive 2013/48/EU) and with consular authorities (Article 7 Directive 2013/48/EU) while deprived of liberty.

The minimum rules on the right of access to criminal lawyer were supplemented by Directive 2016/1919/EU that provided for a common standard on legal aid for defendants in criminal proceedings.[59] Furthermore, the EU legislator established minimum rules on procedural safeguards for children who are suspects or accused persons in criminal proceedings in

[58] Directive 2013/48/EU of 22 October 2013 on the right of access to a lawyer in criminal proceedings and in European arrest warrant proceedings, and on the right to have a third party informed upon deprivation of liberty and to communicate with third persons and with consular authorities while deprived of liberty, OJ L 294, 6.11.2013, p. 1.

[59] Directive (EU) 2016/1919 of 26 October 2016 on legal aid for suspects and accused persons in criminal proceedings and for requested persons in European arrest warrant proceedings, OJ L 297, 4.11.2016, p. 1.

order to preserve their potential for development and reintegration into society and to address the vulnerability of juvenile defendants (Directive 2016/800/EU).[60]

Finally, Directive 2016/343/EU refined core elements of the right to a fair trial, namely the presumption of innocence (Article 48(1) CFREU, Article 6(2) ECHR) and the right to be present at the trial (Articles 47(2), 48(2) CFREU, Article 6(1), (3)(c) ECHR). As far as the presumption of innocence is concerned, the Directive follows a broad understanding of this guarantee that includes a prohibition of presentations or public statements referring to the defendant as being guilty (Articles 4, 5 Directive 2016/343/EU) and the privilege against self-incrimination (Article 7 Directive 2016/343/2016). The following part will further elaborate on the second main chapter of Directive 2016/343/EU on the right to be present at the trial which is of particular relevance in a transnational setting, that is surrender proceedings on the basis of an EAW.

10.3.2 The Right to be Present at the Trial

The right to be present at the trial forms integral part of the right to a fair trial (Article 47(2) CFREU, Article 6(1) ECHR) and can be derived from the defence rights enshrined in Article 6(3) ECHR, such as the right of the accused person to defend himself in person (Article 6(3)(c) ECHR) and to examine witnesses (Article 6(3)(d) ECHR) because the defendant cannot exercise these rights without being present.[61]

As the Convention establishes rights rather than obligations, it is up to the defendant to appear at the hearing or to waive the exercise of this right. However, according to the case law of the European Court of Human Rights, such a waiver must be established in an unequivocal manner and be attended by minimum safeguards commensurate to the importance of the right to take part in the hearing.[62] These safeguards shall ensure that the waiver constitutes a knowing and informed relinquishment of the right to be present at the trial.[63] If these conditions are not met, the trial must not

[60] Directive (EU) 2016/800 of 11 May 2016 on procedural safeguards for children who are suspects or accused persons in criminal proceedings, OJ L 132, 21.5.2016, p. 1.

[61] ECtHR, *Colozza* v. *Italy,* Appl. No. 9024/80, 12 February 1985, para. 27.

[62] EctHR, *Poitrimol* v. *France,* Appl. No. 14032/88, 23 November 1993, para. 31; EctHR, *Sejdovic* v. *Italy,* Appl. No. 56582/00, 10 November 2004, para. 86.

[63] EctHR, *Makarenko* v. *Russia,* Appl. No. 5962/03, 12 November 2009, para. 135.

be held in the accused's absence. A conviction *in absentia*, however, does not violate the right to a fair trial if the convicted person can subsequently obtain a fresh judicial determination of the merits of the charge pursuant to a hearing.[64] Once again, it is up to the accused to decide whether to apply for review or to waive the exercise of this right. Thus, the accused person can waive both the right to be present at the trial and the right to a new trial.

However, the assumption that the absent defendant has waived his right to defend himself in person might be fallacious. This is why the Strasbourg Court requires a waiver that has been established in an unequivocal manner. This condition is not met if the accused person is detained in another state and, for that reason, unable to attend the trial; in this case, the sole fact that the defendant does not appear in court cannot be interpreted as his/her intention to waive the right to be present at the trial and to defend him-/herself in person;[65] rather, in such a situation, the absence of the accused person cannot be considered to be based upon his free will, but upon coercion (detention). The accused's detention is the most obvious, but not the only situation where the assumption of a voluntary waiver is subject to serious doubts. Likewise, it must be doubted whether an accused person who faces immediate arrest and a risk of several years of imprisonment can be expected to take a voluntary decision on whether to exercise or waive his/her right to be present at the hearing.

The Strasbourg Court did not take up these concerns, but even went a step further and held that a trial may be conducted in the absence of a defendant who seeks to escape from justice.[66] A defendant who has been notified of the charges should reasonably have foreseen the consequences of his conduct and, thus can be tried *in absentia*.[67] In other words, the accused forfeits his right to participate in the hearing. Whereas the waiver is based upon the voluntary decision of the accused whether to exercise his rights or not, the idea of a forfeiture is predicated on the assumption that the accused is not only entitled, but obliged to appear at the trial. If the defendant does not comply with this obligation, he is deprived of his right to defend himself in person at a later stage of proceedings. This concept touches upon core

64 EctHR, *Poitrimol* v. *France*, Appl. No. 14032/88, 23 November 1993, para. 31.

65 EctHR, *F.C.B.* v. *Italy*, Appl. No. 12151/86, 28 August 1998, para. 33; EctHR, *Hokkeling* v. *the Netherlands*, Appl. NO. 30749/12, 14 February 2017, para. 60.

66 EctHR, *Medenica* v. *Switzerland*, Appl. No. 20491/92, 14 June 2001, paras. 55 ff; EctHR, *Sejdovic* v. *Italy*, Appl. No. 56581/00, 10 November 2004, paras. 97, 102.

67 EctHR, *Atanasova* v. *Bulgaria*, Appl. No. 72001/01, 2 October 2008, para. 52; EctHR, *Demebukov* v. *Bulgaria*, Appl. No. 68020/01, 28 February 2008, paras. 57–58.

elements of the defendant's right to a fair trial. An obligation to appear in court is tantamount to a duty of the defendant to give himself up to prison and thereby strikingly contradicts to the privilege against self-incrimination and the principle that the defendant must not be forced to actively contribute to his own conviction.[68] The right to a fair trial must not be used as a sort of whip to make the accused appear in court.[69]

By Directive 2016/343/EU, the EU legislator has taken care of these concerns and established a common standard that is well above the minimum level of protection guaranteed by Article 6 ECHR and the case law of the Strasbourg Court. This standard maintains the right of the accused person to be present at the trial (Article 8(1) Directive 2016/343/EU) but strictly limits the conditions for trials *in absentia*: a trial must not be held in the absence of the accused person unless he has been informed of the trial and the consequences of non-appearance and waived his right either by non-appearance (Article 8(2)(a) Directive 2016/343/EU)[70] or by a decision to mandate a lawyer to represent him at the trial (Article 8(2)(b) Directive 2016/343/EU). If these conditions were not met, the person convicted in his absence has the right to a new trial, or to another legal remedy, which allows a fresh determination of the merits of the case, including examination of new evidence, and which may lead to the judgment being reversed (Article 9 Directive 2016/343/EU).

This common minimum standard is binding upon the MS. As a consequence, trials *in absentia* can no longer be based upon the reasoning that a person who seeks to escape from justice forfeits his right to be present at the trial. If a person has not been summoned or provided with official information about the date and the place of the trial and the consequences of non-appearance and the judgment has been rendered *in absentia*, the convicted person has the right to a new trial. This rule even applies if the whereabouts of the accused person are unknown. Admittedly, Directive 2016/343/EU allows for a decision to be taken and even enforced, but when the accused and convicted person has been apprehended, he still enjoys the right to a new trial (Article 8(4) Directive 2016/343/EU).

68 EctHR, *Funke* v. *France*, Appl. No. 10828/84, 25 February 1993, para. 44; EctHR, *J.B.* v. *Switzerland*, Appl. No. 31827/96, 6 April 2000, paras. 63–71; EctHR, *Jalloh v. Germany*, Appl. No. 54810/00, 11 July 2006, para. 122.

69 For a more detailed discussion, see M. Böse, 'Harmonizing Procedual Rights Indirectly. The Framework Decision on Trials in Absentia', (2011) 37 *N.C. J. Int'l L.*, 489, 500 ff.

70 See in this regard, CJEU, *TX and UW*, No. C-688/18, Judgment, ECLI:EU:C:2020:94, 13 February 2020, paras. 28 ff.

10.3.3 The Transnational Dimension of Fair Trial Rights (EAW Proceedings)

The aforementioned directives aim at establishing minimum standards on procedural rights in criminal proceedings in the MS, irrespective of whether or not these proceedings have a cross-border dimension. Nevertheless, essential elements of this standard also apply in a transnational setting: in proceedings on the execution of an EAW, the arrested person has a right to translation and interpretation (Article 1(1) Directive 2010/64/EU), to information about his/her rights (Article 5 Directive 2012/13/EU) and the right of access to a lawyer in surrender proceedings (Article 10 Directive 2013/48/EU; see also Article 5 Directive 2016/1919/EU). However, the scope of these rights is still limited and does not extend to the right to be informed of the nature and the cause of the accusation (Article 6 Directive 2012/13/EU) and the right of arrested persons to access to the file (Article 7 Directive 2012/13/EU).[71]

Similarly, the minimum standards on the presumption of innocence and the right to be present at the trial do not apply to surrender proceedings because the decision to execute an EAW is neither a verdict of guilt (or innocence) nor based upon a criminal trial. Nevertheless, judgments rendered *in absentia* raise serious human rights concerns, and these concerns have resulted in obstacles to international cooperation in criminal matters. In particular, extradition for the purpose of carrying out a sentence resulting from *in absentia* proceedings may be refused because these proceedings did not satisfy the minimum rights of defence.[72] Likewise, the FD EAW, mentioned above, provided for a refusal ground on trials *in absentia* (Article 5(1) FD EAW)[73] that has been replaced by Framework Decision 2009/299/JHA on trials *in absentia* (Article 4a FD EAW).[74]

71 CJEU, *IR*, No. C-649/19, Judgment, ECLI:EU:C:2021:75, 28 January 2021, para. 62.

72 See, for example Art. 3 of the second additional protocol to the European Convention on extradition of 17 March 1978 (ETS No. 98).

73 Framework Decision 2002/584/JHA of 13 June 2002 on the European arrest warrant and the surrender procedures between Member States, OJ L 190, 18.7.2002, p. 1.

74 Framework Decision 2009/299/JHA of 26 February 2009 amending Framework Decisions 2002/584/JHA, 2005/214/JHA, 2006/783/JHA, 2008/909/JHA and 2008/947/JHA, thereby enhancing the procedural rights of persons and fostering the application of the principle of mutual recognition to decisions rendered in the absence of the person concerned at the trial, OJ L 81, 27.3.2009, p. 24.

Unlike Directive 2016/343/EU, Framework Decision 2009/299/JHA was not designed to harmonise national legislation on trials *in absentia* and to establish a common minimum standard but to redefine the grounds for non-recognition of an EAW and other cooperation instruments (Recitals (4), (6) and (14) Framework Decision 2009/299/JHA). In close orientation to the case law of the European Court of Human Rights, the Framework Decision was based on the principle that judgments rendered *in absentia* could be recognized if the accused had unequivocally waived his right to be present at the trial (Recitals (1), (8) FD 2009/299/JHA). A waiver of the right to a hearing cannot be derived merely from the deliberate absence of the accused who received official information of the scheduled date and place of the trial and the consequences of his failure to appear in court (Article 4a(1)(a) FD EAW) but requires in addition a mandate to a defence counsel (Article 4a(1)(b) FD EAW). In this case, the accused must be aware of the scheduled trial when giving the mandate. In addition, the waiver requires that the defence counsel effectively appears at trial to defend the accused. The latter requirement is meant to ensure that the accused can effectively exercise his defence rights, albeit in an indirect manner.

If, however, the aforementioned conditions for a waiver are not met and the accused has been convicted *in absentia* the executing MS may subject surrender to the condition that the convicted person is afforded with the right to a retrial, or an appeal, in which he has the right to participate and which allows to re-examine the case on its merits, including fresh evidence. To that end, the convicted person must be served with the judgment and expressly be informed about the right to retrial or appeal and the time frame applicable to the request for a retrial or an appeal (Article 4a(1)(d) and (2) FD EAW). Again, the right to a new trial can be subject to a waiver, either by the explicit statement of the accused person not to challenge the judgment rendered *in absentia* or by not lodging a request for retrial or appeal within the applicable time-frame (Article 4bis(1)(c) FD EAW).

In sum, Framework Decision 2009/299/JHA does not only re-formulates the case law of the Strasbourg Court but also precisely determines the conditions for a waiver of the right to be present at the trial and thereby corresponds to the minimum requirements established by Directive 2016/343/EU. Nevertheless, Article 4a FD EAW merely defines an optional ground for non-execution of an EAW and, thus, does not establish a minimum, but a maximum standard on the conditions for surrender on the basis of an EAW: the executing state must not insist upon a higher standard to be applied; in particular, the execution of an EAW must not be refused for grounds derived from constitutional law (*Melloni*). As Article 4a FD EAW contains a specific and exhaustive provision on the non-execution of EAWs that are based upon judgments *in absentia*, the executing state may not rely on the national constitution in order to make surrender conditional upon a review of the judgment rendered *in absentia*.[75]

Moreover, instead of establishing a common minimum standard, Article 4a FD EAW leaves it up to the executing state to apply a lower threshold. Even though Framework Decision 2009/299/JHA does not follow the reasoning of the European Court of Human Rights that an accused who seeks to evade justice forfeits his right to participate in the hearing, the MS are still free to follow this approach and to accept and execute an EAW for the purpose of enforcing a judgment that has been rendered *in absentia*. Accordingly, the German law implementing Framework Decision 2009/299/JHA expressly allows for the execution of an EAW in such cases.[76] The mandatory standards established by Directive 2016/343/EU have raised the question whether such national provisions are still in conformity with EU law or whether the refusal ground (Article 4a FD EAW) must be interpreted in the light of Directive 2016/343/EU so that the execution of an EAW must (instead of 'may') be refused if it is based upon a judgment *in absentia* that does not meet the common minimum standard under Directive 2016/343/EU.[77]

In a most recent decision, the Court of Justice answered this question in the negative and held that the standard established by Directive 2016/343/EU could not be invoked as a ground for refusal in surrender proceedings because these proceedings were specifically regulated by the Framework Decision on the EAW and the exhaustive list of refusal grounds, in particular with regard to the execution of judgments rendered

[75] CJEU, *Melloni*, No. C-399/11, Judgment, ECLI:EU:C:2013:107, 26 February 2013, paras. 63–64.

[76] Act on International Cooperation in Criminal Matters (Gesetz über die Internationale Rechtshilfe in Strafsachen), section 83(2) No. 2; see for the legislative process, M. Böse, 'Neue Standards für Abwesenheitsverfahren in "Fluchtfällen"? Zu den Auswirkungen der Richtlinie 2016/343/EU auf die Auslieferung und Vollstreckungshilfe in der Europäischen Union' (2017) 37 *StV*, 754, 756, 758.

[77] For a more detailed discussion, see M. Böse 'Neue Standards für Abwesenheitsverfahren in "Fluchtfällen"?' (2017) 37 *StV* 754, 759–760.

in absentia (Article 4a FD EAW).[78] In fact, the Court's reasoning followed the Advocate General who strictly distinguished between the rules and standards in domestic criminal proceedings (Directive 2016/343/EU) and the framework of surrender proceedings and grounds for refusal in particular (Article 4a FD EAW); with regard to the latter, it were not a matter for the executing state to assess whether criminal proceedings in the issuing state were compatible with EU standards.[79] Such review would run counter the very idea of mutual recognition and mutual trust and, thus, should be limited to exceptional cases where a breach of fundamental rights (Article 47, 48 CFREU) were at stake.[80]

This reasoning, however, ignores the functional link between the principle of mutual recognition and common minimum standards on the rights of the defendant in criminal proceedings that shall be established 'to the extent necessary to facilitate mutual recognition of judgments' (Article 82(2) TFEU). If these standards are to strengthen mutual trust between MS, it is crucial that they are properly implemented into the MS' criminal justice systems. Moreover, if EU legislation provides for a higher level of protection than international human rights standards (the ECHR and the corresponding case law), this common minimum standard gives shape to the European *ordre public* and, thereby, necessarily has repercussions on the level of protection in transnational proceedings: the commitment to the strengthening of fundamental rights and the right to a fair trial in particular (recital (9) Directive 2016/343/EU) implies an obligation of MS to insist on these common standards to be respected by other MS in cross-border cooperation rather than to confine themselves to maintaining international human rights standards. This holds especially true with regard to the execution of judgments *in absentia* where a corresponding ground for refusal already exists (Article 4a FD EAW). Thus, reference to the standard established by Directive 2016/343/EU will not have the effect of extending the list of grounds for refusal nor their scope of application, but merely transform an optional ground for refusal into a mandatory one: According to Article 4a FD EAW, the executing authority 'may' refuse the execution of an EAW that is based upon a judgment *in absentia* if the minimum standards are not met. It is generally accepted

[78] CJEU, *TR*, No. C-416/20 PPU, ECLI:EU:C:2020:1042, 17 December 2020, paras. 45 ff.

[79] CJEU, *TR*, No. C-416/20, Opinion of Advocate General Evgeni Tanchev, ECLI:EU:C:2020:1020, 10 December 2020, paras. 60–61.

[80] Ibid., paras. 61, 64–65.

that the executing state's obligation to respect fundamental rights, turns 'may' into 'must' if the execution of the judgment would be in breach with the right to a fair trial (Articles 47(2), 48 CFREU).[81] As the EU legislator has further developed the right to be present at trial and established a common standard, it is hardly conceivable that it is still within the executing MS' discretion to execute a judgment *in absentia* without taking this standard into consideration.[82] By contrast, maintaining such discretion to surrender persons convicted *in absentia* even if it is obvious that the trial in the issuing state did not meet the standards established by Directive 2016/343/EU would seriously undermine the credibility of the efforts to establish a common minimum standard for the rights of the defendant.

10.4 Conclusion

Fundamental rights such as the *ne bis in idem* principle (Article 50 CFREU) and the right to a fair trial (Articles 47(2), 48 CFREU) are essential elements of the Area of Freedom, Security and Justice. The rights and guarantees established by Article 54 CISA and the Directives on the rights of the defendant in criminal proceedings do not only have an impact upon the national criminal justice systems of the MS but also affect transnational criminal law enforcement in the Union because MS will have to comply with the new minimum standard when executing mutual recognition instruments. *Prima facie*, this seems to contradict the idea of mutual trust and the principle of mutual recognition. According to the division of tasks and responsibilities between the issuing and the executing MS, it is a matter for the issuing state to implement these standards and to ensure that criminal proceedings against the person to be surrendered are conducted in conformity with the right to a fair trial and the corresponding procedural guarantees. If, however, the issuing state does not live up to its obligations, there is a residual competence (and responsibility) of the executing state to protect the defendant's right to a fair trial. The road map and the development of minimum standards for procedural safeguards have always been driven by the intention to establish a common basis for cooperation in criminal matters (such as

[81] Ibid., para. 64. [82] For the contrary view, see ibid., para. 68.

the ECHR and the CFREU). If these standards should be more than empty phrases and mere lip service, non-compliance must have consequences for transnational criminal law enforcement. Thus, an MS insisting on compliance with EU standards on procedural rights cannot be regarded as hampering the smooth functioning of cooperation in criminal matters but contributes to the enforcement of this common standard as a key element of the Area of Freedom, Security and Justice.

Further Reading

K. Ambos, 'C-486/14 – Kossowski – Judgment (Grand Chamber) C-486/14 Piotr Kossowski, 29 June 2016', in V. Mitsilegas, A. di Martino, and L. Mancano (eds.), *The Court of Justice and European Criminal Law*, Oxford: Hart 2019, p. 227.

M. Böse, 'Harmonizing Procedual Rights Indirectly. The Framework Decision on Trials in Absentia', (2011) 37 *N.C. J. Int'l L.*, 489.

M. Böse, 'The Transnational Dimension of the ne bis in idem principle and the Notion of res iudicata in the European Union', in M. Böse, M. Bohlander, A. Klip, and O. Lagodny (eds.), *Justice without Borders Essays in Honour of Wolfgang Schomburg*, Leiden, Boston: Brill 2018, p. 49.

J. Lelieur, 'Transnationalising ne bis in idem: How the Rule of ne bis in idem Reveals the Principle of Personal Legal Certainty', (2013) 9 (4) *Utrecht L. Rev.*, 198.

S. Quattrocolo and S. Ruggeri (eds.), *Personal Participation in Criminal Proceedings*, Cham, Springer:2019.

J. Vervaele, 'Ne bis in idem: Towards a Transnational Constitutional Principle in the EU?', (2013) 9 (4) *Utrecht L. Rev.*, 211.

W. Schomburg, 'Internationales "ne bis in idem" nach Art 54 SDÜ', (1997) 17 *StV*, 383.

11 Extradition and Surrender

From a Bilateral Political Arrangement to a Triangular Legal Procedure

Pedro Caeiro and Miguel João Costa

11.1 The Classic Framework of Extradition

Extradition (*lato sensu*) is the *transfer of an individual from one State to another to prosecute/try him/her or enforce a penal sanction to which he/she has been convicted.* It is a coercible procedure, as the consent of the individual is not necessary, and it takes place at the request of the State that holds the penal claim (the 'requesting State').

Taken broadly, extradition also encompasses the transfer of individuals by the States to international tribunals. However, this modality is generally referred to as 'surrender', which encapsulates a model of vertical cooperation where the requested State is expected to comply with the request, in contrast with the traditional paradigm of horizontal interstate relations, where the requested State has ample powers of refusal.[1] This helps to explain why 'surrender' came to be used also in certain interstate relations where high levels of cooperation are intended to be achieved[2] – notably in the EU, with the EAW, and in the Nordic States.[3]

The earliest legal instrument providing for the reciprocal transfer of persons is the thirteenth-century BCE Treaty between Hittite King Hattusili III and Pharaoh Ramesses II of Egypt,[4] which is also the earliest

[1] See A. Cassese, *The Human Dimension of International Law: Selected Papers*, in P. Gaeta and S. Zappalà (eds.), Oxford et al.: Oxford University Press, 2008, p. 520.

[2] See P. Caeiro, 'O procedimento de entrega previsto no Estatuto de Roma e a sua incorporação no Direito Português', in V. Moreira et al., *O Tribunal Penal Internacional e a Ordem Jurídica Portuguesa*, Coimbra: Coimbra Editora, 2004, pp. 74–79.

[3] While the Nordic Arrest Warrant is in force only since 2012, Denmark, Finland, Iceland, Norway and Sweden already had in place for many decades special extradition arrangements where several of the traditional grounds for refusal did not apply, and such arrangements served as an inspiration for the EAW: see G. Mathisen, 'Nordic Cooperation and the European Arrest Warrant: Intra-Nordic Extradition, the Nordic Arrest Warrant and Beyond', (2010) 79 *Nordic J. Int'l L.*, pp. 1–16.

[4] See §§ 17–18, in S. Langdon and A.H. Gardiner, 'The Treaty of Alliance between Ḫattušili, King of the Hittites, and the Pharaoh Ramesses II of Egypt', (1920) 3 *JEA*, pp. 179–181.

known diplomatic document.[5] The Bible contains relevant references,[6] and this practice is reported to have been used in ancient Greece and Rome,[7] in ancient China,[8] as well as throughout the Middle Ages[9] and in the Early Modern Period.[10] However, extradition as we understand it today has its origins in the late eighteenth-century Europe,[11] largely due to the impulse and the prolific treaty-making activity of France.[12] Belgium too played a key role with the enactment of a pioneer national statute on extradition in 1833,[13] characterised by a high level of detail in the regulation of this subject matter.[14] Whereas ancient practices were fundamentally concerned with political offenders and other particular problems – such as the desertion of troops and sailors, modern extradition was in principle excluded for political acts and it expanded to common criminality.[15] The late modern era was the period when not only the

[5] See *v.g.* P. Bernard, *Traité Théorique et Pratique de l'Extradition*, Paris: Arthur Rosseau Éditeur, 1883, pp. 30–32; C.L. Blakesley, 'The Practice of Extradition from Antiquity to Modern France and the United States: A Brief History', (1981) 4 *B.C. Int'l & Comp. L. Rev.*, pp. 41–42.

[6] See *Judges* 15 and 20; and H. Grotius, *On the Law of War and Peace*, Batoche Books, 2001, p. 217.

[7] See F. de Cardaillac, *De l'Extradition: Droit International*, Tarbes: Émile Croharé, 1878, pp. 5–7; C. Phillipson, *The International Law and Custom of Ancient Greece and Rome: Volume I*, London: McMillan and Co., 1911, pp. 349–374.

[8] See M.C. Bassiouni, *International Extradition: United States Law and Practice*, 6th edn., Oxford et al.: Oxford University Press, 2014, p. 2.

[9] See A. Quintano Ripollés, *Tratado de Derecho Penal Internacional e Internacional Penal: Tomo II*, Madrid: Instituto Francisco de Vitoria, 1955, p. 157.

[10] See Bassiouni, *International Extradition: United States Law and Practice*, p. 6; W. Magnuson, 'The Domestic Politics of International Extradition', (2012) 52 *Va. J. Int'l L.*, p. 848.

[11] According to A. Billot, *Traité de l'Extradition: suivi d'un recueil de documents étrangers et des conventions d'extradition conclues par la France et actuellement en vigueur*, Paris: E. Plon et Cie, 1874, p. 34, the term *extradition* was first used in an official document by France in the Decree of 19 February 1791.

[12] Before the nineteenth century, France had already concluded extradition treaties with all neighbouring States to the exception of England, see I.A. Shearer, *Extradition in International Law*, Manchester: Manchester University Press, 1971, p. 17.

[13] Law no. 1195 (*Loi sur les extraditions*), of 1.10.1833, available in *Pasinomie: Collection complète des lois, décrets, arrêtés, et règlements généraux qui peuvent être invoqués en Belgique, Troisième Série, Tome Troisième, Règne de Léopold 1er – Année 1833*, Librairie de Jurisprudence de H. Tarlier, 1834, p. 239.

[14] See F. von Martitz, *Internationale Rechtshilfe in Strafsachen. Beiträge zur Theorie des Positiven Völkerrechts der Gegenwart*, Leipzig: H. Haesel, 1897, p. 747.

[15] Although there is not a causal relationship between the two: see M.J. Costa, *Extradition Law: Reviewing Grounds for Refusal from the Classic Paradigm to Mutual Recognition and Beyond*, Leiden et al.: Brill, 2019, pp. 327–330.

political exception emerged but also several other rules were established which remain central in international cooperation to this day, such as the nationality exception and the principle that extradition should only be granted for acts that the requested State itself deems to be of a criminal character (double criminality).

A second significant transformation would occur in the aftermath of WWII, with the advent of human rights and the acknowledgement of the individual as a subject of international law. Although the late modern period already revealed some consideration for individual interests (as reflected for instance in the death penalty exception),[16] their protection was secondary to State policy and did not translate into proper *rights.*[17] It was only later that individuals were granted standing in extradition proceedings entitling them to an active defence, and that rules were enacted to the specific end of protecting them from abusive State action (as reflected for instance in the *non-refoulement* rule). As a consequence, certain safeguards initially set in place in the interest of the requested State could no longer be waived freely by this State (as reflected for instance in the speciality rule).[18] In a word, extradition shifted from a bilateral arrangement where only the two involved States were relevant, to a triangular procedure with the individual as a vertex.[19]

[16] See, *v.g.*, Art. 3 of the 1873 Extradition Treaty between the Helvetic Confederation and Portugal.

[17] See B. Swart, 'Human Rights and the Abolition of Traditional Principles', in A. Eser and O. Lagodny (eds.), *Principles and Procedures for a New Transnational Criminal Law*, Freiburg: Max Planck Institut, 1992, p. 508.

[18] See J. Dugard and C. van den Wyngaert, 'Reconciling Extradition with Human Rights', (1998) 92 *AJIL*, p. 188; and see, *v.g.*, Art. 14(1) and (3) of the 1957 CoE Convention. The speciality rule is paramount, for in the absence of a rule preventing a State from prosecuting a person for acts other than those for which it obtained extradition, the very extradition proceedings carried out by the requested State would be to a large extent superfluous. In this sense, speciality may even be understood as a 'precondition' of extradition law: Costa, *Extradition Law: Reviewing Grounds for Refusal from the Classic Paradigm to Mutual Recognition and Beyond*, pp. 432–433. Nevertheless, this rule would later become again more flexible, see Art. 10 of the 1996 EU Convention on Extradition and Art. 27 of the FD EAW, as well as the judgments of the Court of Justice of the European Union (CJEU), *Leymann and Pustovarov*, No. C-388/08 PPU, Judgment, ECLI:EU:C:2008:669, 1. December 2008, and *Generalbundesanwalt beim Bundesgerichtshof*, No. C-195/20 PPU, ECLI:EU:C:2020:828, 14. October 2020.

[19] See A. Eser, 'Basic Issues Concerning Transnational Cooperation in Criminal Cases: A Problem in Outline', in E.M. Wise (ed.), *Criminal Science in a Global Society: Essays in Honor of Gerhard O. W. Mueller*, Littleton: Fred B. Rothman & Co., 1994, pp. 6, 14–15.

This triangular scheme, where the person is regarded as the holder of fundamental rights vis-à-vis the two States, and the wide discretion of the requested State while deciding on the request, form the conceptual framework on which present-day extradition continues to rely. Nevertheless, the variants of extradition brought under the concept of 'surrender' have shaken to a significant extent both of those premises. Based on shared cultural traditions, legal standards and political institutions, certain clusters of States have narrowed considerably the grounds for refusing extradition insofar as concerns both the rights of the sought person and the interests of the requested State. There is some parallel between this evolution and that of national criminal procedural legislation. The paradigm arisen from the Enlightenment (and reinvigorated in post-WWII liberal democracies) cared essentially for protecting individuals against arbitrariness. However, as democratic institutions and the rule of law became more mature, on the one hand, and as new challenges emerged such as terrorism and highly organised crime, on the other hand, even liberal States allowed themselves to develop starker approaches to criminal procedure, with correspondent limitations to individual rights. A similar enhancement of their repressive capacity took place at the transnational level, in reaction to those challenges and against the background of a globalising world.

Even institutions such as the ECtHR, whose primary task is safeguarding human rights, have never overlooked the importance of good extradition relations, in that these also contribute to the well-being of communities and the individuals that form them[20] – especially in such highly symbolic cases as those involving terrorism.[21] But while this crime-tackling dimension of extradition has always been acknowledged, it has recently been taken to a new level by the ECtHR – precisely, and yet again, in a case concerning terrorism.[22] This ruling marks the first occasion in which the ECtHR (or any other such institution) found that a decision

[20] This is clear from the very outset: cf. ECtHR, *Soering v. UK*, Appl. No. 14038/88, Judgment, 7 July 1989, para. 86.

[21] As illustrated by ECtHR, *Trabelsi v. UK*, Appl. No. 140/10, Judgment, 7 October 2014, para. 117.

[22] ECtHR, *Romeo Castaño v. Belgium*, Appl. No. 8351/17, Judgment, 9 July 2019. The applicants were the five children of Colonel Ramón Romeo and claimed that their right to an effective investigation into the murder of their father had been breached as a result of the Belgian courts' decisions – based on Art. 3 ECHR – to refuse the execution of multiple EAWs issued by Spain for N.J.E., suspected murderer of the Colonel, shot in 1981 by a commando unit claiming to belong to ETA.

not to extradite[23] had breached human rights.[24] It has been criticised by some for approving of a certain crime control approach; others recalled that the ECtHR had already recognised the existence of positive duties in this context, including a duty to *request* extradition in certain cases.[25] Regardless of its possible flaws and virtues, what is noteworthy is that this ruling appears as a symptom of a wider trend whereby even human rights can assist the sword function of extradition.[26] This reflects on the progressive adjustment of several of the most classic grounds for refusal, including the double criminality rule, the political offence exception and the nationality exception.

11.2 The History of the EAW

It is unsurprising that the trend described above would find fertile ground in the EU. The idea of having a swift mechanism for the surrender of fugitives in the EU, which would replace the slow and often ineffective extradition procedure, has been put forward for the first time by French President Giscard d'Estaing.[27] As he addressed the European Council in its Brussels meeting of 5–6 December 1977, d'Estaing stated that building a EU (as an 'organised area') implied the need to go beyond the establishment of a common market, towards an ampler concept that would match the European people's awareness of their unity of fate ('*unité de destin*'). In a moment in time where terrorist attacks and kidnappings were a major cause for concern across Europe, there was political momentum to foster the creation of a single judicial area ('*espace judiciaire unique*'),

23 More precisely, a decision not to execute an EAW.

24 In the case at hand, the right to life enshrined in Art. 2 ECHR. The Court underscored that a real risk of torture or ill-treatment could carry the refusal of extradition, but held that, given the existence of third-party rights (*sc.*, the rights of the applicants under Art. 2, in its procedural limb), the conclusion that such a risk exists must rely on a 'sufficient factual basis' (paras. 85–92).

25 An analysis of the ruling can be found in S. Top and P. de Hert, 'Castaño Avoids a Clash between the ECtHR and the CJEU, but Erodes Soering. Thinking Human Rights Transnationally', (2021) 12 *NJECL*, 52–68.

26 On the dichotomy 'sword/shield', more generally, see F. Tulkens, 'The Paradoxical Relationship between Criminal Law and Human Rights', (2011) 9 *JICJ*, 577–595; more recently, K. Ambos, 'Ius puniendi and Constitution. A Comparative (Canadian German) Perspective', (2020) 14 *ICL Journal*, 271–272.

27 J. Charpentier 'Vers un espace judiciaire européen', (1978) 24 *Annuaire français de droit international*, 927–941.

which included, as its first element, the establishment of a convention providing for 'automatic extradition' for perpetrators of the most serious offences, assorted with appropriate guarantees.[28]

The French proposal was never adopted as such, but its constituent parts[29] would eventually be revisited, two decades later, in the development of judicial cooperation within the 'third pillar' of the EU put in place by the Treaty of Maastricht (1993). The endeavour to establish a simplified legal framework for the extradition between Member States (MS) was furthered with the adoption of the EU Conventions of 1995 and 1996.[30] But at the end of the twentieth century, three events crucially fuelled the move for swifter and more effective judicial cooperation in the EU, which would eventually crystallise in the establishment of the EAW.

The first, of a normative nature, was the entry into force of the Treaty of Amsterdam, which included a provision that referred explicitly to the 'facilitation of extradition between MS' as part of the common action on judicial cooperation in criminal matters (Article 31(1)(b)).

The second, of a political nature, was the European Council of Tampere, whose Conclusions urged MSs to 'speedily ratify the 1995 and 1996 EU Conventions on extradition' and recovered the project of replacing the formal extradition procedure regarding fugitives who had been finally sentenced with 'a simple transfer of such persons, in compliance with Article 6 TEU'. For the remaining cases, 'consideration should also be

[28] *Proposition de M. Valéry Giscard d'Estaing concernant l'espace judiciaire européen (Bruxelles, 5 décembre 1977)*, which can be found at www.cvce.eu/en/obj/proposition_de_valery_giscard_d_estaing_sur_la_mise_en_place_d_un_espace_judiciaire_europeen_bruxelles_5_decembre_1977-fr-c7f7171f-f73a-4ab4-829e-faa221acaeca.html (last accessed 18 June 2021). See also P. Berthelet, 'Police et justice dans l'Union Européenne – Document de travail', Ed. Parlement Européen, Série *Libertés publiques*, LIBE112FR, 11-2000 FR, p. 5.

[29] Along with the convention on extradition, the proposal also included the improvement of mutual legal assistance in criminal matters, the establishment of a procedure for the transfer of criminal proceedings, the recognition of foreign judgments in criminal matters and the establishment of a procedure for the transfer of prisoners: in more detail, see C. Gueydan, 'Cooperation between Member States of the European Community in the Fight against Terrorism', in R. Higgins and M. Flory (eds.), *Terrorism and International Law*, London et al.: Routledge, 1997, pp. 101–104; and A. Weyembergh, *L'harmonisation des législations: condition de l'espace pénal européen et révélateur de ses tensions*, Brussels: Ed. Université Libre de Bruxelles, 2004, pp. 13–15.

[30] Respectively, Council Act of 10 March 1995, adopted on the basis of Article K.3 of the TEU, drawing up the Convention on simplified extradition procedure between the Member States of the European Union, OJ C 78, 30.03.1995, and Council Act of 27 September 1996, adopted on the basis of Article K.3 of the TEU, drawing up the Convention relating to extradition between the Member States of the European Union, OJ C 313, 23.06.1996.

given to fast track extradition procedures, without prejudice to the principle of fair trial'.[31] Such improvements should take place in the context of the principle of mutual recognition of judicial decisions, which was thereby erected as 'the cornerstone of judicial co-operation in both civil and criminal matters within the Union'.[32]

The third important event, of an empirical nature, was the terrorist attack of 11.09.2001 in the USA. In its immediate aftermath, the European Commission (which was already working on the file) submitted a first 'Proposal for a Council framework Decision on the EAW and the surrender procedures between the Member States', dated 19.09.2001.[33]

The Framework Decision was eventually adopted by the Council, with significant changes, in June 2002.[34] It was amended by Framework Decision 2009/299/JHA, concerning trials *in absentia,*[35] and complemented by several directives on procedural rights, especially Directive 2010/64/EU, on the right to interpretation and translation, and Directive 2013/48/EU, on the right of access to a lawyer.

11.3 The EAW and Mutual Recognition: A New Paradigm of Cooperation in Criminal Matters?

The purpose of improving extradition between MSs, both in terms of effectiveness and expeditiousness, has translated into the two main revolutionary features of the EAW. At the substantive level, European law sets out a limited number of admissible grounds for 'non-execution' of a warrant and does not allow for MSs to expand them. At the procedural level, proceedings take place exclusively between judicial authorities, thereby preventing any intervention by the executive based on political convenience. Those innovative features limit the discretion of the 'executing' (no longer requested) State in deciding over the 'warrants' (no longer the requests) for the 'surrender' (instead of extradition) of the sought

[31] *Tampere European Council 15 and 16 October 1999. Presidency Conclusions*, Conclusion 35.
[32] Ibid., Conclusion 33.
[33] COM/2001/0522 final – CNS 2001/0215, OJ C 332E, 27.11.2001.
[34] 2002/584/JHA, Council Framework Decision of 13 June 2002 on the European arrest warrant and the surrender procedures between Member States, OJ L 190, 18.7.2002 (hereinafter, FD EAW).
[35] OJ L 81, 27.3.2009.

person issued by the 'issuing' (instead of requesting) State. Furthermore, problems that may emerge in the execution of an EAW regarding the interpretation of the applicable law are solved, on a routine basis, by a third entity (the CJEU).

The regime of the EAW is built on the principle of mutual recognition that governs the common market, which is based on an assumption of mutual trust among MSs of the Union.[36] According to that principle, MSs recognise the decisions uttered by the authorities of other MSs as if they were their own.[37] This would lead to a quasi-automatic execution of EAWs, with a minimum of formality and few questions asked by the executing authorities.[38]

There is no doubt that the EAW has fostered and improved the surrender of suspects within the EU, both in terms of expediency and effectiveness of the warrants.[39] From this perspective, it certainly deserves to be deemed a 'success story'. Moreover, the exclusion of any interference by the executive power in the cooperation procedure is a major step towards a single judicial area in criminal matters (even if combined with legal pluralism). As a matter of fact, the easy application and swiftness of the new mechanism have led to a dramatic increase in the issuance of warrants across Europe, which in turn has eventually raised concerns from the perspective of the proportionality principle.[40]

[36] As a matter of fact, such assumption is not confirmed by reality, where distrust often arises: see A. Klip, 'European Integration and Harmonisation and Criminal Law', in D. Curtin, J. Smits, A. Klip, and J. McCahery (eds.), *European Integration and Law*, Antwerp et al.: Intersentia, 2006, p. 137 ('[t]his confidence is so great that it must be ordained at regular intervals that there shall be mutual confidence'); K. Ambos, *European Criminal Law,* Cambridge: Cambridge University Press, 2018, p. 436 (mutual trust 'is increasingly becoming, as the Union expands further and further, a mere Brussels or Luxembourg phantasmagoria').

[37] On mutual recognition, see C. Janssens, *The Principle of Mutual Recognition in EU Law*, Oxford: Oxford University Press, 2013, and W. van Ballegooij, *The Nature of Mutual Recognition in European Law*, Cambridge et al.: Intersentia, 2015.

[38] V. Mitsilegas, *EU Criminal Law after Lisbon*, Oxford: Hart, 2016, pp. 127–129.

[39] The procedure lasts on average 16–17 days after the arrest in cases where the requested person consents to his/her surrender (which accounts for more than half of the total), and around 45 days in cases where there is no consent (*Report from the Commission to the European Parliament and the Council on the implementation of Council Framework Decision of 13 June 2002 on the European arrest warrant and the surrender procedures between Member States*, COM(2020) 270 final, 2.07.2020, p. 1).

[40] See European Parliament resolution of 27.02.2014, OJ C 285, 29.8.2017, p. 135, and *Report from the Commission to the European Parliament and the Council on the*

However, one may question the extent to which the EAW and mutual recognition mean an actual change of paradigm in judicial cooperation.

The word 'mutual' rightly points to a procedure between *two* MSs. This is quite different from issuing an arrest warrant with a pan-European scope, to be executed by the authorities of any MS where the sought person is found and leading to the latter's immediate and automatic surrender. Even when the location of the individual is unknown and the EAW is entered as an alert for arrest in the Schengen Information System,[41] his/her eventual surrender, once apprehended, follows a bilateral formal procedure between the issuing and the executing States similar to classic extradition.

Moreover, when the 'execution' of the European warrant takes place, the *surrender* of the individual is not really an act of execution of *that* warrant, issued by a foreign authority. On the contrary, it enforces a decision with constitutive effects taken by the authorities of the executing MS, just like in traditional extradition proceedings. It may be instructive to compare, in this respect, the European *warrants* with *final decisions* in criminal matters: whereas the ultimate effect of the former (surrender) depends on decisions taken by another jurisdiction, the latter generate a *ne bis in idem* effect on their own, across the whole EU, even where there is a foreign decision *declaring* (recognising) that the requirements on which *ne bis* depends are fulfilled.

In the third place, the common legal framework underlying the EAW is not a single and univocal body of law, because the FD EAW has left some leeway for the MSs to make choices in its implementation, in particular in what concerns the so-called 'optional grounds for non-execution'.[42] As a consequence, the law applicable in this respect – where the decision on the warrant is ultimately taken – follows a pattern of *variable geometry*,[43]

implementation of Council Framework Decision of 13 June 2002 on the European arrest warrant and the surrender procedures between Member States, COM(2020) 270 final, 2.07.2020, p. 9.

41 See Arts. 26 to 31 of Council Decision 2007/533/JHA of 12 June 2007 on the establishment, operation and use of the second-generation Schengen Information System (SIS II) (OJ L 205, 7.8.2007, p. 63).

42 See A. Klip, *European Criminal Law. An Integrative Approach*, 4th edn., Cambridge et al.: Intersentia, 2021, pp. 501–505, and Ambos, *European Criminal Law*, p. 446; see also below, under 'Mandatory and optional grounds for non-execution of an EAW'.

43 For a comprehensive overview of the differences in national implementation, see *Report from the Commission to the European Parliament and the Council on the implementation of*

which explains why the same EAW can have a different fate depending on the MS to which it is addressed. This legal framework is still quite deferent to executing States, especially when compared with other models of cooperation where they enjoy virtually no discretion regarding the enforcement of warrants.[44]

Finally, the whole concept of 'recognition' supposes that the Other, being different, is seen not in her otherness, but in her resemblance to oneself, as a condition for acknowledging her status as a peer. There is, of course, huge common ground between States who enter a political union such as the EU, namely in what concerns the values they share and the duties binding upon them vis-à-vis the protection of human rights (enshrined in the CFREU and the ECHR). However, the level of compliance with those duties varies in space and time, even within the area of freedom, security and justice. As recent developments have made apparent, the lack of practical enforcement or even sheer violation of such obligations by MSs can lead to distrust and put recognition in jeopardy.[45]

In sum, it is clear that the EAW has made judicial cooperation in the EU much simpler, swifter and more effective, but it falls short of the 'automatic extradition' envisaged by Giscard d'Estaing, which would translate into judicial cooperation in criminal matters the paradigm of recognition in force in the internal market.

Additionally, one should also bear in mind that, in its current version, classic extradition is not left to considerations of pure convenience either: instead, it is usually based on legally binding obligations, even if they leave a wider margin of discretion for the States to decide on the requests.

Council Framework Decision of 13 June 2002 on the European arrest warrant and the surrender procedures between Member States, COM(2020) 270 final, 2.07.2020, p. 15, passim.

[44] See, for example Arts. 86 and 89(1) of the Rome Statute of the International Criminal Court.

[45] See, for example CJEU, *Aranyosi and Căldăraru*, Joined Cases Nos. C-404/15 and C-659/15 PPU, Judgment, ECLI:EU:C:2016:198, 5 April 2016, and the rule of law-related infringement actions against Poland (for example No. C-192/18, 05.11.2019 and No. C-619/18, 24.06.2019). The difference between the CJEU's bold jurisprudence in infringement cases and the weaker stance taken in preliminary rulings is hardly justifiable (P. Bárd and W. van Ballegooij, 'The effect of CJEU case-law concerning the rule of law and mutual trust on national systems', in V. Mitsilegas, A. di Martino, and L. Mancano (eds.), *The Court of Justice and European Criminal Law. Leading Cases in a Contextual Analysis*, Oxford: Hart, 2019, p. 460), even if it may aim at safeguarding mutual trust (L. Pech, P. Wachowiec, and D. Mazur, 'Poland's Rule of Law Breakdown: A Five-Year Assessment of EU's (In)Action', (2021) 13 *HJRL*, p. 36).

Hence, characterising surrender under the EAW as a radical change of paradigm vis-à-vis extradition might be an overstatement.

11.4 The Role of the Executive in Extradition Proceedings: From Exclusive to Excluded

Even after the focus of extradition steered from political onto common criminality, extradition requests continued to be regarded as an issue to be dealt with by political and diplomatic entities. However, the rise of the individual and his/her rights in the context of extradition had a profound impact on the nature and institutional configuration of the proceedings, which shifted from a purely administrative to a hybrid model where the intervention of the political branch was supplemented by a judicial phase. The former remained in place to uphold the interests of the requested State; the latter aimed at an effective safeguard of individual rights.[46]

By contrast, one of the most important features of the EAW is the full judicialisation of the procedure: the warrants must be issued and executed by 'judicial authorities' (Article 6(1) FD EAW), with no interference of the executive power. To this extent, the surrender of suspects and convicts within the EU is now governed exclusively by the law.

The first consequence that comes to mind is that the political interests of the executing State cannot serve as grounds for refusing judicial cooperation and preventing criminal justice from being served. Additionally, there is a strong link between full judicialisation, mutual trust and the exclusion of the political offence exception from the list of grounds for refusal.[47] Reserving the competence for *issuing* an EAW to judicial

[46] See J. Lemontey, *Du Rôle de l'Autorité Judiciaire dans la Procédure d'Extradition Passive*, Paris: R. Pichon et R. Durant-Auzias, 1966, pp. 5–30. This hybrid model remains in place in all the EU MS in their extradition relations with third States (albeit with differences, namely regarding the order in which the executive and the judicial branches intervene): see Ambos, *European Criminal Law*, pp. 419–421. The 1957 CoE Convention established that extradition proceedings should in principle be governed by the law of the requested State (Art. 22), but it did not safeguard the customary sovereignty and *ordre public* clause, such that political refusals of extradition under this Convention became rather anomalous. Similar considerations apply to the 1996 EU Convention on Extradition and the 1995 EU Convention on Simplified Extradition Procedure (Art. 15).

[47] The political offence exception was already excluded by the 1996 EU Convention: see below, under 'The political offence exception'.

authorities should reinforce trust in that respect since judicial bodies are deemed to be subject only to the law and are expected not to avail themselves of judicial cooperation to prosecute or punish someone for political reasons. The CJEU has taken judicialisation very seriously and drafted an autonomous concept of 'judicial authority'[48] in several judgments,[49] the most notorious being those that excluded the German and Dutch public prosecutors from, respectively, the concepts of 'issuing'[50] and 'executing judicial authority'.[51] The rationale was the same: both entities can receive specific instructions from the government over a concrete case.[52]

Finally, the importance of judicialisation is also visible in the recent case law of the Court regarding the provision of guarantees against ill-treatment of prisoners subject to an EAW. In cases where the detention conditions in the issuing State present systemic or generalised deficiencies, posing a serious risk of inhuman or degrading treatment, the executing State shall not proceed with surrender until it can discard

[48] See V. Mitsilegas, 'Autonomous Concepts, Diversity Management and Mutual Trust in Europe's Area of Criminal Justice', (2020) 57(1) *CMLR*, 45–78.

[49] The discussion over the notion of 'judicial authority' in the context of the EAW started with the judgments CJEU, *Poltorak*, No. C-452/16 PPU, ECLI:EU:C:2016:858; *Kovalkovas*, No. C-477/16, ECLI:EU:C:2016:861; and *Özcelik*, No. C-453/16, ECLI:EU:C:2016:860, all of 10 November 2016, where the Court found that a body of the executive, such as the Ministry of Justice or a police body, cannot be designated as an issuing judicial authority.

[50] CJEU, *OG and Pi*, Joined cases Nos. C-508/18 and C-82/19 PPU, Judgment, ECLI:EU:C:2019:456, 27 May 2019, 27 May 2019. Some months later, the Court refined the concept in *JR and YC*, Joined cases Nos. C-556/19 PPU and C-626/19 PPU, Judgment, ECLI:EU:C:2019:1077; *XF*, No. C-625/19 PPU, Judgment, ECLI:EU:C:2019:1078; *ZB*, No. C-627/19 PPU, Judgment, ECLI:EU:C:2019:1079, all of 12 December 2019; and *AZ*, No. C-510/19, Judgment, ECLI:EU:C:2020:953, 24 November 2020. For a comprehensive critique of the case law of the Court in this regard (including the cases mentioned in the previous footnote), see T. Wahl, 'CJEU: German Public Prosecution Office Is Not a "Judicial Authority" in the EAW Context', (2019) *eucrim*, pp. 31–34; id., 'CJEU Clarifies Its Case Law on Concept of "Judicial Authority" Entitled to Issue EAWs', (2019) *eucrim*, 242–245; and K. Ambos, 'The German Public Prosecutor as (no) Judicial Authority within the Meaning of the European Arrest Warrant: A Case Note on the CJEU's Judgment in OG (C-508/18) and PI (C 82/19 PPU)', (2019) 10 *NJECL*, 339–407.

[51] CJEU, *AZ*, No. C-510/19, Judgment, ECLI:EU:C:2020:953, 24 November 2020.

[52] The Court found that the German public prosecutor office is not independent enough from the executive because they are exposed, in the abstract, 'to the risk of being subject, directly or indirectly, to directions or instructions in a specific case from the executive, such as a Minister for Justice, in connection with the adoption of a decision to issue a European arrest warrant'. In turn, Dutch prosecutors do not qualify as executing judicial authorities because 'they may receive in exercising his or her decision-making power an instruction in a specific case from the executive'.

the existence of such a risk.[53] In that context, the issuing State can 'give assurances concerning the actual and precise conditions in which the person concerned will be detained';[54] when those guarantees have been 'given, or at least endorsed, by the issuing judicial authority, (...) the executing judicial authority (...) must rely on that assurance (...)'. Paradoxically, assurances provided by the executive or a minister, who bear the competence to bind the State at the international level, 'must be evaluated by carrying out an overall assessment of all the information available to the executing judicial authority' – in other words, they are only to be taken into consideration as a piece of relevant information.[55]

11.5 Mandatory and Optional Grounds for Non-Execution of an EAW

The FD EAW provides for an exhaustive list of grounds for non-execution of an EAW and MSs may not refuse to surrender an individual based solely on their national law (or even on their constitution[56]). Some of the traditional grounds for refusal are simply irrelevant (*e.g.*, nationality) or have their scope significantly reduced (*e.g.*, double criminality).[57] Additionally, the FD EAW has established a distinction between mandatory and optional grounds for refusal: when the former are present, MSs are bound not to surrender the individual, whereas the transposition of the latter into domestic law is left to their discretion.

53 CJEU, *Aranyosi and Căldăraru,* Joined Cases Nos. C-404/15 and C-659/15 PPU, Judgment, ECLI:EU:C:2016:198, 5 April 2016, paras. 98, 103–104.

54 CJEU, *ML,* No. C-220/18 PPU, Judgment, ECLI:EU:C:2018:589, 25 July 2018, para.110; in a similar vein, *Dorobantu,* No. C-128/18, Judgment, ECLI:EU:C:2019:857, 15 October 2019, paras. 67–69.

55 This understanding seems to be at odds with the case law of the ECtHR on the subject, but the provision of assurances regarding the EAW may well qualify as a successful candidate to the application of the *Bosphorus* doctrine: see P. Caeiro, '«Scenes from a Marriage»: Trust, Distrust and (re)assurances in the Execution of a European Arrest Warrant', in S. Carrera, D. Curtin, and A. Geddes (eds.), *20 Year Anniversary of the Tampere Programme. Europeanisation Dynamics of the EU Area of Freedom, Security and Justice*, European University Institute, 2020, pp. 239–250.

56 CJEU, *Melloni,* No. C-399/11, Judgment, ECLI:EU:C:2013:107, 26. February 2013.

57 This approach had already been tested in the 1996 EU Convention, with the binding suppression or narrowing down of the scope of some grounds for refusal.

Mandatory grounds (Article 3 FD EAW) embody a common view of the situations where judicial cooperation must be excluded – a true EU extradition policy – whereas optional grounds serve for accommodating the concerns and particular views of the several MS. However, the decision on the application of optional grounds for refusal does not have to be left to judicial discretion.[58] Once national legislators decide to adopt them, they should be implemented either as binding or discretionary for the courts according to whether, by their nature, they should apply in general (*e.g.*, lack of double criminality) or rather be subject to a concrete assessment (*e.g.*, prospects of better rehabilitation in the executing MS). The judgment of the CJEU in *Popławski*[59] in fact confirms this view. The Court held that the executing judge must have some discretion over the application of the optional ground for non-execution contained in Article 4(6) FD EAW. Thus, it relied precisely on the 'objective' (the teleology) of that particular obstacle – and not on its formal quality of *optional* as opposed to mandatory.[60] Only a concrete assessment can ascertain

[58] The conflation of the two dimensions is present also in official documents; see *Report from the Commission to the European Parliament and the Council on the implementation of Council Framework Decision of 13 June 2002 on the European arrest warrant and the surrender procedures between Member States*, COM(2020) 270 final, 2.07.2020, p. 15, p. 17, p. 18, passim (while addressing how the MSs have transposed optional grounds for non-execution).

[59] CJEU, *Popławski*, No. C-579/15, Judgment, ECLI:EU:C:2017:503, 29 June 2017. The case concerned the application of Art. 4(6) FD EAW, which provides that '[t]he executing judicial authority may refuse to execute the European arrest warrant (...) if the European arrest warrant has been issued for the purposes of execution of a custodial sentence or detention order, where the requested person is staying in, or is a national or a resident of the executing Member State and that State undertakes to execute the sentence or detention order in accordance with its domestic law'. The Court found that '[i]t is clear from the actual wording of Art. 4(6) of Framework Decision 2002/584 that, where a Member State chose to transpose that provision into domestic law, the executing judicial authority must, nevertheless, have a margin of discretion as to whether or not it is appropriate to refuse to execute the EAW. In that regard, that authority must take into consideration the objective of the ground for optional non-execution set out in that provision, which, according to the Court's settled case law, means enabling the executing judicial authority to give particular weight to the possibility of increasing the requested person's chances of reintegrating into society when the sentence imposed on him expires (...)' (para. 21).

[60] The CJEU seems to have put more weight on the literal element of the provision in its judgment *Criminal Proceedings against X*, No. C-665/20 PPU, ECLI:EU:C:2021:339, 29 April 2021, esp. paras. 42–44, by ruling that the executing judicial authority must have a certain discretion as to whether or not it is appropriate to refuse to execute an EAW under Art. 4(5) FD EAW (*ne bis in idem* based on judgments in third States). While it is clear that this is also a ground for refusal that must be assessed *in concreto*, by the

whether the non-execution of the warrant will increase the chances of rehabilitation of the requested person. But this does not apply to the operation of every 'optional' ground: for instance, it is hard to figure out how the refusal of an EAW on the basis of lack of double criminality (within the limits set in Article 4(1) FD EAW) could be left to judicial discretion, since it contends with the general policy regarding judicial cooperation, and the decision (not) to cooperate in those circumstances does not depend on the particular features of the case.[61]

A large part of the legal doctrine of extradition relates to the interpretation and application of grounds for refusal. The following considerations address some of those obstacles, especially from the perspective of the EAW.

11.5.1 Mandatory Grounds for Non-Execution

An *amnesty* in the executing MS – as long as it has jurisdiction over the offence – is a traditional impediment[62] that has been maintained by the FD EAW. Its rationale is clear-cut: if a State renounces the prosecution of certain offences, it is also prevented from cooperating with other States in prosecuting and punishing the respective perpetrators.

The second mandatory obstacle is the transnational *ne bis in idem.* In line with Article 54 CISA – providing for a transnational *ne bis* within the EU[63], Article 3(2) FD EAW states that a warrant cannot be executed when the sought person has been judged by a MS for the same acts, 'provided that, where there has been sentence, the sentence has been served or is currently being served or may no longer be executed under the law of the sentencing Member State'. This 'execution clause' is not explicitly required by Article 50 CFREU, the *ne bis in idem* provision of the Charter. Such apparent disparity could lead to a bizarre situation: if the requested person had not served the sentence to which he/she had been convicted,

executing judge, on the basis of several (unwritten) criteria, it is submitted that the judgment mixes the need for a judicial *ascertainment* of the conditions for refusal (which also applies to mandatory grounds!) with judicial '*discretion*' (see esp. paras. 44 and 47–48).

61 P. Caeiro and S. Fidalgo, 'The Portuguese Experience of Mutual Recognition in Criminal Matters: Five Years of European Arrest Warrant', in G. Vernimmen-Van Tiggelen, L. Surano and A. Weyembergh (eds.), *The Future of Mutual Recognition in Criminal Matters in the European Union*, Brussels: Ed. ULB, 2009, pp. 452–456.

62 See *v.g.* Art. 3 (e) of the UN Model Treaty on Extradition.

63 See the seminal judgment by the CJEU, *Gözütok and Brügge*, Joined Cases Nos. C-187/01 and C-385/01, Judgment, ECLI:EU:C:2003:87ECR I-1345, 11 February 2003.

e.g., in Spain, Germany would be bound, as the custodial State, to enforce the warrant issued for the same acts by Italy, which however would not be entitled to prosecute/try the individual (Article 50 CFREU). Arguably, Italy would not even have (adjudicative) jurisdiction over the case after the Spanish sentence became final,[64] preventing it from issuing or maintaining a warrant from then on. Nevertheless, the CJEU has ruled, in *Spasic*,[65] that the execution clause contained in Article 54 CISA is not incompatible with Article 50 CFREU but rather a permissible restriction of the fundamental right contained therein. In a way, the Court has read the 'constitution' (the CFREU) in conformity with an instrument of secondary law passed in an intergovernmental setting (the CISA); this has rightly prompted harsh criticism in the literature.[66] In any case, the restriction of the scope of Article 50 CFREU means that the odd situation illustrated with the example above cannot ensue, since Italy *would have* jurisdiction to prosecute and try the requested person. The complexity of the issue increases because *ne bis* is indeed one of the fields where the mingling between EU law and the ECHR (more precisely, Article 4 of Protocol VII) – including the case law of the Luxembourg and Strasbourg Courts – is more frequent and intense, in an ongoing process of cross-fertilization.[67]

The third mandatory obstacle is the circumstance that the requested person 'may not, owing to his *age*, be held criminally responsible for the acts on which the arrest warrant is based under the law of the executing State' (Article 3(3) FD EAW, emphasis added). The broadness of the expression intends to accommodate the differences between the several

[64] Transnational *ne bis in idem* is a limit to adjudicative jurisdiction: see P. Caeiro, *Fundamento, Conteúdo e Limites da Jurisdição Penal do Estado – O Caso Português*, Coimbra: Wolters Kluwer and Coimbra Ed., 2010, pp. 332, 339.

[65] CJEU, *Spasic*, No. C-129/14, Judgment, ECLI:EU:C:2014:586, 27 May 2014. For a comprehensive assessment of *ne bis in idem*, in its manifold dimensions, within the EU (before *Spasic*), see I. Armada and A. Weyembergh, 'The Principle of ne bis in idem in Europe's Area of Freedom, Security and Justice', in V. Mitsilegas, M. Bergström, and T. Konstadinides (eds.), *Research Handbook on EU Criminal Law*, Cheltenham: Edward Elgar Publishing, 2009, pp. 189–209; J. Vervaele, 'Ne bis in idem: Towards a Transnational Constitutional Principle in the EU?', (2013) 9 *Utrecht L. Rev.*, 211–229.

[66] See F. Meyer, 'Transnationaler ne-bis-in-idem-Schutz nach der GRC – Zum Fortbestand des Vollstreckungselements aus Sicht des EuGH – zugleich Besprechung zu EuGH', (2014) 15 *Höchstrichterliche Rechtsprechung zum Strafrecht*, p. 269–278; J. Vervaele, 'Schengen and Charter-Related ne bis in idem Protection in the Area of Freedom, Security and Justice: M and Zoran Spasic', (2015) 52 *CMLR*, 1339–1359.

[67] See, for example G. Lasagni and S. Mirandola, 'The European *ne bis in idem* at the Crossroads of Administrative and Criminal Law', (2019) *eucrim*, 126–135.

laws, not only in respect of the age threshold itself but also of the moment when the bar operates (when the act is perpetrated or when the individual is charged)[68]. The assessment of this ground should be quite straightforward, as there is no need for the executing judge to 'consider any additional conditions, relating to an assessment based on the circumstances of the individual, to which the prosecution and conviction of a minor for such acts are specifically subject under the law of that Member State'.[69]

11.5.2 Protection of Human Rights by the Requested/ Executing State

The positive obligation impending on the requested State to protect fundamental rights in extradition procedures was affirmed by the ECtHR in *Soering*, a landmark ruling issued in 1989 regarding a German citizen whose extradition was requested to the UK by the USA, where he might be subjected to capital punishment.[70] The Convention does not explicitly apply to extradition, and the requesting State was not a party to it. Notwithstanding, in an unprecedented decision, the ECtHR held that extradition in those circumstances would breach human rights. The Court found that there was an actual risk that Jens Soering would plunge into the state of severe emotional distress known as the 'death row phenomenon', which would trigger the prohibition of ill-treatment enshrined in Article 3 of the Convention.[71] *Soering* was followed by numerous rulings – by the ECtHR and other international judicial bodies[72] – disallowing extradition on grounds of prospective ill-treatment in the requesting

[68] See *Commission Notice – Handbook on How to Issue a European Arrest Warrant* (2017/C 335/01), JO C 335, 6.10.2017, p. 30.

[69] CJEU, *Piotrowski*, No. C-367/16, Judgment, ECLI:EU:C:2018:27, 23 January 2018, para. 62.

[70] ECtHR, *Soering v. UK*, Appl. No. No. 14038/88, Judgment, 7 July 1989. Soering was eventually extradited in 1990, under a guarantee that the death penalty would not be carried out. Soering has always claimed his innocence, and his case has been supported by innocence projects – see Costa, *Extradition Law: Reviewing Grounds for Refusal from the Classic Paradigm to Mutual Recognition and Beyond*, p. 533. At the end of 2019, after more than three decades of imprisonment, he was released (though not pardoned) and deported to Germany: see www.newyorker.com/culture/culture-desk/a-new-chapter-in-a-double-murder-case (last accessed 18 June 2021).

[71] See W.A. Schabas, 'Soering's Legacy: The Human Rights Committee and the Judicial Committee of the Privy Council Take a Walk Down Death Row', (1994) 43 *ICLQ*, 913–915.

[72] In the field of extradition, the ECtHR has been the reference for other international human rights bodies such as the UN Human Rights Committee (see *v.g.* HRC, *Ng v. Canada*, Communication No. 469/1991, U.N. Doc. CCPR/C/49/D/469/1991 (1994), 7.

State. Other provisions have occasionally been engaged in extradition cases (notably Article 2, on the right to life, and Article 6, on fair trial), but never, thus far, in a fully self-standing manner.

In turn, the CJEU ruled, for more than ten years, that warrants could not be refused on grounds other than those provided for by the FD EAW, which does not specifically contemplate the protection of human rights of the sought person against the issuing State.[73] The common commitments enshrined in the ECHR and the CFREU would establish a safety net sufficient for the smooth operation of the EAW under the sign of mutual ('blind') trust. However, in *Aranyosi and Căldăraru*, the Court eventually acknowledged – with a formulation full of detailed caveats – that a MS is not bound to execute an EAW when it cannot discount an actual risk of inhuman or degrading treatment of the requested person in the issuing MS due to systemic or generalised deficiencies in the existing detention conditions.[74] In the face of an absolute right, the executing State may not ponder it with other considerations (such as the nature of the offence at stake[75] or countering impunity), and therefore it is legitimate to consider it as a (fourth) mandatory ground for refusal. Arguably, this brings the EAW in line with the obligations derived not only from the CFREU but also from the ECHR: notwithstanding the *Bosphorus* doctrine,[76] the

January 1994, the equivalent to *Soering* in the UNHRC's case law) and even for courts of countries that are not parties to the ECHR, such as Canada (see Supreme Court of Canada, *Kindler v. Canada (Minister of Justice)*, [1991] 2 SCR 779, 26 September 1991). Human rights case law on extradition is often mentioned as a paradigmatic example of the judicial creativity of international courts, see D.J. Bederman, *The Spirit of International Law*, Athens et al.: University of Georgia Press, 2002, pp. 64, 236.

73 See, for example CJEU, *Radu*, No. C-396/11, Judgment, ECLI:EU:C:2013:39, 29 January 2013. On the way(s) MSs tried to solve the conflict of obligations arising from this jurisprudence, see I. Wieczorek, 'The Implication of Radu at a National Level: National Courts' Diversified Response to Conflicting Obligations', in V. Mitsilegas, A. di Martino, and L. Mancano (eds.), *The Court of Justice and European Criminal Law. Leading Cases in a Contextual Analysis*, Oxford: Hart, 2019, pp. 380–392.

74 Above (fn. 45).

75 A.P. van der Mei, 'The European Arrest Warrant system: Recent Developments in the Case-Law of the Court of Justice', (2017) 24 *Maastricht J. Eur. Comp. L.*, 900.

76 In ECtHR, *Bosphorus Hava Yolları Turizm ve Ticaret Anonim Şirketi v. Ireland*, Appl. No. 45036/98, Judgment, ECLI:CE:ECHR:2005:0630JUD004503698, 30 June 2005, the ECtHR found that there is a presumption according to which 'a State has not departed from the requirements of the Convention when it does no more than implement legal obligations flowing from its membership of [an international] organisation', as long as the relevant organisation protects human rights 'in a manner which can be considered at least equivalent to that for which the Convention provides' (para. 155–156).

ECtHR might as well wish to look at the issue at some point – as it did in *Romeo Castaño*[77] and in *Bivolaru and Moldovan*.[78]

The judgment in *Aranyosi and Căldăraru* constitutes a revolution in the field of the EAW, although the Court had already ruled in a similar direction in an asylum case in 2011.[79] The explanation for the co-existence of the two diverging approaches for almost five years may be that refraining from returning an asylum seeker does not have the same implications as refusing to surrender a suspect/convict. The former affects only technical rules of the asylum system, whereas the latter impacts negatively on the effectiveness of cooperation and, ultimately, on the penal claim of another MS. As noted above, the Court has accepted the possibility of setting aside the risk of ill-treatment via the provision of guarantees by the issuing State. However, the full implications of such jurisprudence (namely in what concerns its consequences for the rights of the requested person) are still unclear and need to be unfolded in future decisions.[80]

More recently, the Court has extended the scope of the protection of fundamental rights by the executing authority to the right to a fair trial[81] and has reaffirmed the need to assess the risk of violation in two steps:[82] first, an evaluation of the deficiencies the issuing system may present in the abstract; second, the establishment of an actual and concrete risk for the rights of that particular individual.

11.5.3 Double Criminality

The double criminality rule, according to which a State will only extradite a person for acts that are also offences in its legal system, is the successor of the catalogue model, where States would not extradite for acts other than

77 Above (fn. 22).

78 ECtHR, *Bivolaru and Moldovan* v. *France*, Appl. Nos. 40324/16 and 12623/17, 25 March 2021.

79 CJEU, *N.S. and M.E. and Others*, Joined Cases Nos. C-411/10 and C-493/10, Judgment, ECLI:EU:C:2011:865, 21 December 2011. On this, see V. Mitsilegas, *EU Criminal Law*, 2nd edn., Oxford et al.: Hart, 2022, p. 207.

80 Caeiro, '«Scenes from a Marriage»: trust, distrust and (re)assurances in the execution of a European Arrest Warrant', in S. Carrera, D. Curtin, and A. Geddes (eds.), *20 Year Anniversary of the Tampere Programme. Europeanisation Dynamics of the EU Area of Freedom, Security and Justice*, pp. 243–245.

81 CJEU, *LM*, No. C-216/18 PPU, Judgment, ECLI:EU:C:2018:586, 25 July 2018.

82 CJEU, *L and P*, Joined Cases Nos. C-354/20 PPU and C-412/20 PPU, Judgment, ECLI:EU:C:2020:1033, 17 December 2020.

those enumerated in the applicable legal instrument (usually a treaty).[83] The list was prone to becoming outdated, and it sometimes failed to cover criminal conduct for which States would likely have been willing to cooperate. Double criminality solved those problems entirely (by reference to the ever-updated criminal law of the requested State), whilst leaving fundamentally intact the concept implicit in the enumerative system: it conveys a common view of the relevant States over the criminal nature of the acts and thus justifies cooperation against crime. In a sense, double criminality has *normalised* extradition: *any* act that qualifies as an offence from that double perspective can trigger extradition and the refusal to extradite becomes the exception.[84] It was already on double criminality that Article 2(1) of the 1957 CoE Convention relied on for defining extraditable acts, and the same approach was followed in Article 2(1) of the 1996 EU Convention.

The EAW, however, brought a momentous change in this respect: Article 2 FD EAW has abolished the control of double criminality in respect of 32 'areas of criminality' which are not necessarily harmonised under EU law or even under EU jurisdiction (Article 83 TFEU). Whenever the acts at hand constitute an offence that, according to the law of the issuing State, falls under one of those areas and is punishable by the same law with imprisonment for at least three years, the executing MS cannot refuse surrender on the basis that its law does not criminalise such act. Regarding offences not included in the catalogue (irrespective of the gravity of the applicable sanctions), it is open for the MSs to keep this ground for refusal. The Court has rightly ruled that dispensing with double criminality as a requisite for surrender does not violate the legality principle,[85] which does not govern such issues as arrest and surrender.[86] The (less dense) right to legal certainty vis-à-vis the latter is covered by the domestic laws that

[83] But not all States have completely relinquished the list-of-offences system: see Bassiouni, *International Extradition: United States Law and Practice*, pp. 500, 508–513.

[84] This shift can be considered the first great reform of the concept of 'extraditable acts' in the modern era, the second great reform being the shift from an *in abstracto* approach (which required semantic identity of offences) to the *in concreto* approach (which deems sufficient that the acts integrate any offence in both States): see Costa, *Extradition Law: Reviewing Grounds for Refusal from the Classic Paradigm to Mutual Recognition and Beyond*, p. 453.

[85] CJEU, *Advocaten voor de Wereld*, No. C-303/05, Judgment, ECLI:EU:C:2007:261. 3 May 2007.

[86] See also P. Asp, A. von Hirsch and D. Frände, 'Double Criminality and Transnational Investigative Measures in EU Criminal Proceedings: Some Issues of Principle', (2006) 11 *ZIS*, 514.

transpose the FD EAW, as they provide a fair warning that, in designated cases, those procedures do not depend on double criminality.[87]

The common area of freedom, security and justice means that the relevance of penal claims from the other MSs does not necessarily require an agreement on the criminal nature of the particular act that triggers the procedure. Such accord 'takes place in more abstract terms, whereby Member States simply recognise the worthiness of each other's criminal policy and provide mutual assistance for its execution'.[88] This concurs to shaping mutual recognition as 'an amplifier, a driver for the pan-European reach of the criminal policy of every single Member State'.[89]

11.5.4 The Nationality Exception

Another ground for refusal with deep roots in the European extradition history is the nationality exception, founded on the distrust of foreign justice and the fear of unfair treatment and bias against foreigners. Ancient Greece and Rome would not normally deliver their citizens to foreign polities.[90] The same happened also in the early modern period, for instance between France and the Netherlands, based on Dutch ordinances enacted in 1736, reportedly with support on the old Bulle Brabantine of 1355.[91]

87 In more detail, P. Caeiro, 'The Contribution of Advocaten voor de Wereld for the Protection of Human Rights in the Context of Supra-State Law and for the Doctrine of Double Criminality', in V. Mitsilegas, A. di Martino, and L. Mancano (eds.), *The Court of Justice and European Criminal Law. Leading Cases in a Contextual Analysis*, Oxford: Hart, 2019, pp. 357–360.

88 Ibid., p. 358.

89 P. Caeiro, S. Fidalgo and J. Prata Rodrigues, 'The Evolving Notion of Mutual Recognition in the CJEU's Case-Law on Detention', (2018) 25 *Maastricht J. Eur. Comp. L.*, p. 702.

90 See I.A. Shearer, 'Non-Extradition of Nationals – A Review and Proposal', (1966) 2 *Adelaide L. Rev.*, 274.

91 The Bulle ensured Dutch inhabitants the right not to be 'withdrawn from the application of the local courts', and 'France reciprocated': Harvard Research in International Law: Extradition, (1935) 29 *AJIL*, 123. Religious rivalries between Catholics and Protestants in the eighteenth century are certainly consistent with this reluctance to extraditing own nationals to each other – which is supported by the fact that, *v.g.*, France and Spain, both predominantly Catholic, concluded a treaty in 1765 where extradition of nationals was explicitly admitted – but, on the other hand, the Bulle Brabantine was issued long before the Reformation, which means that it 'probably reflected a more general feeling that the citizens of one State or region would be always at a grave disadvantage in securing justice from the courts of another': Shearer, 'Non-Extradition of Nationals – A Review and Proposal', (1966) 2 *Adelaide L. Rev.*, 274.

However, not all European countries refrain from extraditing their nationals. In the UK, for instance, the view prevails that the nationality exception rests upon 'sentimental considerations' and is underpinned by 'no valid reason'.[92] Since the nationality exception does not correspond to any fundamental individual right or principle of justice, it is only natural that the 1957 CoE Convention conceived of it as a mere right of the Contracting Parties, and attached an *aut dedere aut judicare* obligation to its exercise.[93] The 1996 EU Convention took one step further towards the abolition of this obstacle among the MSs of the EU,[94] and the FD EAW eventually suppressed it, which is consistent with the overall wariness of the European project concerning different treatment on that basis.

However, Article 4(6) FD EAW allows for the non-execution of a warrant issued for the execution of a custodial sentence when the requested person is a national, a resident, or is staying in the executing MS,[95] as long as the latter enforces the sentence itself. In the same vein, Article 5(3) allows for the executing MS to subject surrender to the condition that the requested national or resident, if convicted to a custodial sentence in the issuing MS, be returned to the former to serve his/her sentence there. These obstacles to surrender are based on the endeavour of 'increasing the requested person's chances of reintegrating into society when the sentence imposed on him expires'[96] (and arguably also during its enforcement) and bear no relation with the protection of national citizens against discrimination from foreign powers.[97]

92 J.B. Moore, *A Treatise on Extradition and Interstate Rendition*, Boston: The Boston Book Company, 1891, p. 157; S. Baker, D. Perry, and A. Doobay, *A Review of the United Kingdom's Extradition Arrangements*, 2011, in www.homeoffice.gov.uk, p. 222.

93 See Art. 6(1)(a) and (2). 94 See Art. 7.

95 The expressions 'resident' and 'staying in' are autonomous concepts of EU law: CJEU, *Kozlowski*, No. C-66/08, Judgment, ECLI:EU:C:2008:437, 17 July 2008, paras. 43 and 54.

96 CJEU, *Popławski*, No. C-579/15, Judgment, ECLI:EU:C:2017:503, 29 June 2017, para. 21.

97 The German legislator seems to have adopted a different understanding of nationality as an obstacle to surrender. Section 80 of the current law on international judicial cooperation (IRG), which regulates the EAW, discriminates foreigners (including foreign residents) from German citizens in respect of 'purely domestic offences' on the sheer basis of nationality. The surrender of the latter is prohibited, whereas the surrender of the former *can* be allowed, even for acts that are not criminalised under German law: in more detail, see Ambos, *European Criminal Law*, pp. 444–446, with further references.

11.5.5 The Political Offence Exception

The political offence exception is compulsory in any account of extradition. The very concept of 'political offence' is a creation of modern extradition law,[98] rather than a transnational projection of a domestic law concept. It emerged from the liberal revolutions and the desire of the new European republics to provide shelter to fellow revolutionaries from other countries, and it was instantly imprinted into the French Constitution of 1793. The traditional arguments in support of this rule are that it is legitimate to defy oppressive regimes and that it protects individuals from trials that are likely to be biased, all the while preventing States from meddling in the affairs of other States.[99] Arguably, the fair trial dimension was rendered somewhat redundant by the appearance of human rights-related grounds for refusal, such as the *non-refoulement* principle, already mentioned before. As for the non-interference argument, it has always been rather fragile, because refusing to assist a State which is explicitly requesting assistance can also easily be seen to express support for the cause of the opponents.

This exception soon entered a process of contraction. Both in actual practice and through the enactment of norms excluding certain classes of acts from its scope, starting with the famous *attentat* clause (developed again at the impulse of France and Belgium, in the aftermath of an attempt on the life of Napoleon III by French citizens residing in Belgium) and gradually expanding to other acts including core international crimes and terrorism.[100] This evolution is faithfully mirrored in the 1957 CoE Convention: initially, it only 'depoliticised' the 'taking or attempted taking of the life of a Head of State or a member of his family',[101] but the 1975 Additional Protocol excluded several other classes of acts, such as the crimes against humanity enshrined in the 1948 UN Convention on the Prevention and Punishment of the Crime of Genocide, certain violations of the 1949 Geneva Conventions, and 'any comparable violations' of the laws and customs of war.[102] To no surprise, the 1996 EU Convention took a sizeable step towards the eradication of this obstacle among the MS of the EU by plainly excluding its applicability – although MSs were allowed to

[98] See C. van den Wyngaert, *The Political Offence Exception to Extradition: The Delicate Problem of Balancing the Rights of the Individual and the International Public Order*, Deventer et al.: Kluwer, 1980, pp. 4–5.

[99] Ibid., pp. 2–4, and passim. [100] Ibid., pp. 10–18. [101] See Art. 3 (3). [102] See Art. 1.

declare that they would continue to apply the exception to offences other than terrorism or conspiracy to commit terrorism.[103] At the background of this shift was a political resolve to mitigate the chances of Belgium granting asylum to individuals charged in Spain for terrorist acts[104] – precisely the setting of the mentioned *Romeo Castaño* case at the ECtHR and of the current Catalan leaders crisis, still unresolved at the time of writing.[105]

In theory, this exception seems hardly tenable among States that enter a political *union*. Abolishing this obstacle was the legal correlate of the political transformation achieved with the EU: States formerly jealous of their sovereignty, which easily waged war against each other, became partners in a larger collective venture, bound by democracy and the rule of law. Political offences against another MS are not just another dispute for power in a foreign land: they have become value-laden and of collective concern. Attacking the political structures of one MS should be perceived – so the argument goes – as an attack against the whole and the principles by which it abides.

In a way, this had been implied all along by the French Constitution of 1793. The new French Republic did not promise a safe haven to *all* political offenders: it pledged asylum only to those who had been banished 'for the cause of liberty'.[106] Nevertheless, history shows abundantly how thin and volatile the divide is between the fight for freedom and criminal behaviour, and placing a case in one field or the other is a power that rests ultimately with each State. This still applies, to some extent, within the EU, which has not achieved a 'single political area' regarding the protection of fundamental rights against abuse from fellow MSs; rather, the EU is a paradigmatic example of the inextricable 'entanglement'[107]

[103] See Art. 5.

[104] See E. Bribosia and A. Weyembergh, 'Extradition et Asile: Vers un Espace Judiciaire Européen?', (1997) 30 *RBDI*, 71–72.

[105] For the latest developments, see S. Top, 'The Waiver of Immunity of Catalan MEPs: Reintroducing Politics in EU Extradition Law', 11.3.2021, *EJIL:Talk!*, www.ejiltalk.org/the-waiver-of-immunity-of-catalan-meps-reintroducing-politics-in-eu-extradition-law/ (last accessed 13 February 2022).

[106] Art. 120: '*[Le Peuple français] donne asile aux étrangers bannis de leur patrie pour la cause de la liberté. – Il le refuse aux tyrans*'.

[107] S. Top, 'The Waiver of Immunity of Catalan MEPs: Reintroducing Politics in EU Extradition Law', 11.3.2021, *EJIL:Talk!*; see also Costa, *Extradition Law: Reviewing Grounds for Refusal from the Classic Paradigm to Mutual Recognition and Beyond*, pp. 384–397.

between extradition and politics. Instructively, not less than nine MSs have declared, while ratifying the 1996 EU Convention, that they would continue to apply the political offence exception in the terms permitted by Article 5. Additionally, Sole Article, lit. (d), of Protocol (No 24) to the TFEU, on asylum for nationals of MS of the EU,[108] allows for a unilateral decision of a MS granting political asylum to a national of another MS. In turn, the FD EAW does not provide explicitly for the political offence exception, but acknowledges, in its recital 12, that an EAW can be issued for persecuting a person for, among other things, her political opinions – and clarifies that nothing in that legal instrument may be interpreted as prohibiting MSs to deny surrender in those cases.

Be it as it may, and notwithstanding that they might overlap, it is crucial to make a distinction between the political offence exception – which relates to the nature of the act – and the risk of political persecution – which is tied to the purpose of the EAW. The former is no obstacle to surrender, whereas the latter constitutes unwarranted discrimination (Article 21 CFREU), which might also put in jeopardy several fundamental rights (equality, freedom of thought, fair trial, etc.). As such, there is no reason to exempt this particular kind of discrimination from the judicial control of the respect for fundamental rights by the issuing State. This is a *legal* issue proper and does not amount to reinstating political decisions based on *ordre public*, political convenience or national interest, which are actually beyond the courts' remit and could only be taken by the executive.

Hence, as long as the EAW implies the *responsibility* of the executing MS for the (constitutive) decision to surrender, namely in what concerns the protection of individual rights, it does not seem possible – nor indeed appropriate – to amputate the courts from such competence. Otherwise, the 'depoliticisation' of extradition/surrender in that sense would paradoxically run counter the historic process that associates judicialisation with more effective enforcement of individual rights.

11.6 Extradition from Member States to Third States

The normative action of the EU over judicial cooperation is not limited to the relations between the MS, but it rather extends, in different ways,

[108] OJ C 115, 09.05.2008, pp. 305–306.

to the relations with third States. Parallel to replacing classic extradition with the more expeditious EAW mechanism at the internal level, the EU concluded, under its competence for external action,[109] extradition agreements with third States to which it is linked by particular historical and strategic ties, namely with the USA (in force since 1 February 2010) and Iceland and Norway (in force since 1 November 2019).[110] The purpose of intensifying cooperation is especially visible in the latter agreement, where the Parties have chosen the term 'surrender' instead of 'extradition', and which is inspired in the EAW model,[111] although only to a lesser extent does it abolish traditional grounds for refusal.

Recently, an issue has emerged where primary EU law and classic international cooperation intersect and conflict; a peculiar area where essential rules of EU law impose limits on MS' traditionally unconstrained prerogative to extradite individuals to third States. With its ground-breaking ruling in *Petruhhin,*[112] the CJEU gave further impulse to the development of EU nationality,[113] by asserting that MSs must refuse extradition of citizens of other MSs if they would refuse extradition of their citizens in identical circumstances, provided that this refusal does not cause a situation of impunity – one such situation being possible to avoid through the issuing of an EAW by the MS of which the requested person is a national.

Ironically, this ruling gave an EU dimension to the nationality exception found in several MSs by making use of the same device that had suppressed it in the relations among the MSs: the EAW. This has contributed to deepening the divide between internal and external cooperation, enhancing the specificity of the area of freedom, security and justice. Moreover, *Petruhhin* is to be credited for confirming that the CFREU – notably Article

[109] Arts. 205–222 TFEU.

[110] See Ambos, *European Criminal Law*, p. 417.

[111] See A. Klip, *European Criminal Law. An Integrative Approach*, 4th edn., Cambridge et al.: Intersentia, 2021, p. 477.

[112] CJEU, *Petruhhin,* No. C-182/15, Judgment, ECLI:EU:C:2016:630, 6 September 2016. Analyses of this ruling may be found *v.g.* in A. Klip, 'Europeans First!: Petruhhin, an Unexpected Revolution in Extradition Law', (2017) 25 *ECCL*, 195–204; M. Böse, 'Mutual Recognition, Extradition to Third Countries and Union Citizenship: Petruhhin', (2017) 54 *CMLR*, 1781–1797; M.J. Costa, 'The Emerging EU Extradition Law: Petruhhin and Beyond', (2017) 8 *NJECL*, 192–215.

[113] The judgment has also sparked reflection on the concept of 'EU territory' itself: see N.N. Shuibhne, 'The "Territory of the Union" in EU Citizenship Law: Charting a Route from Parallel to Integrated Narratives', (2019) 38 *YEL*, 267–319, esp. 294–306.

19 (2), on torture, ill-treatment and the death penalty – applies not only among MSs but also in extradition proceedings to third States.

The CJEU has subsequently issued several rulings that gave continuation and depth, in different directions, to the principle originally devised in *Petruhhin.*[114] More recently, however, the Court strongly suggested that the MS of which the sought person is a national has no duty to issue an EAW, and it explicitly held that the requested MS has no duty, either, to exert its criminal jurisdiction in order *to avoid* extraditing the EU citizen to a third State.[115] Arguably, this approach gravely curtails the potential of *Petruhhin* and is inconsistent with its rationale: *Petruhhin* relied on the articulation of equal treatment and freedom of movement, whereas the Court is now suggesting that MS have a prerogative – but not an actual duty – to enforce these fundamental commandments of EU law.

11.7 Concluding Remarks

The EAW has brought a significant change to international cooperation in criminal matters. It established new levels of cooperation that are unprecedented among such a wide and diverse set of States and laid down the basis for a true European area of criminal justice. It also inspired other regional initiatives such as the Mercosul/Mercosur Arrest Warrant.

Nevertheless, it was perhaps not as paradigm-shifting as it is generally perceived to have been. In part, because classic extradition had already evolved into more effectiveness-friendly models. But also because the decision to surrender pursuant to an EAW is still an autonomous decision of the executing MS, which may apply (EU) rules different from those in force in the issuing State.

[114] CJEU, *Schotthöfer and Steiner,* No. C-473/15, Order ECLI:EU:C:2017:633, 6 September 2017; *Pisciotti,* No. C-191/16, Judgment, ECLI:EU:C:2018:222, 10 April 2018; *Raugevicius,* No. C-247/17, Judgment, ECLI:EU:C:2018:898, 13 November 2018; and *Ruska Federacija,* No. C-897/19 PPU, Judgment, ECLI:EU:C:2020:262, 2 April 2020.

[115] CJEU, *Generalstaatsanwalt Berlin (Extradition vers l'Ukraine),* No. C-398/19, Judgment, ECLI:EU:C:2020:1032, 17 December 2020. An assessment of the main legal and practical challenges arisen form the case law initiated in *Petruhhin* is carried out in the 'Joint report of Eurojust and the European Judicial Network on the extradition of EU citizens to third countries', November 2020, available at www.eurojust.europa.eu/sites/default/files/2020-12/2020-11_Eurojust-EJN-report-on-extradition-of-EU-citizens.pdf (last accessed 25 June 2021).

This tendency for convergence between traditional extradition and surrender should neither be expected nor envisaged to lead to the complete identity of conditions. Certain approaches are only conceivable and desirable in highly specific political contexts such as the EU.

At any rate, the EAW has managed to overcome many important challenges in this field, namely the combination between national sovereignty, legal pluralism (including different national transpositions of the same European instrument), different material resources at the national level, common binding standards, positive obligations vis-à-vis the protection of human rights and mutual recognition. In sum, it can be said that the EAW has led mutual recognition as close as possible – in a union of sovereign States after all – to a point beyond which recognition is replaced by the plain enforcement of warrants issued by foreign authorities (extraterritorial adjudicative jurisdiction).

The case law of the CJEU deserves much of the credit for this 'success story', despite some more ancient, less fortunate decisions that have arguably 'fetishized' mutual trust and the need for effective cooperation while downplaying concerns with the protection of fundamental rights. In the times to come, it is likely that the assumption of mutual trust, based on the presumption of homogenous compliance with the rule of law and fundamental rights across the EU, will continue to be bluntly confronted with the reality. Should that be the case, the CJEU will play a key role in the preservation of the whole mechanism of judicial cooperation – in working condition.

Further Reading

N. Boister, 'Global Simplification of Extradition: Interviews with Selected Extradition Experts in New Zealand, Canada, The US and EU', (2017) 29 *CLF*, 327–375.

C. Brière and A. Weyembergh (eds.), *The Needed Balances in EU Criminal Law: Past, Present and Future*, Oxford: Hart, 2018.

M. Fichera, *The Implementation of the European Arrest Warrant in the European Union*, Cambridge et al.: Intersentia, 2011.

J. Jansson, *Terrorism, Criminal Law and Politics: The Decline of the Political Offence Exception to Extradition*, London et al.: Routledge, 2019.

V. Mitsilegas, 'The Limits of Mutual Trust in Europe's Area of Freedom, Security and Justice: From Automatic Inter-State Cooperation to the Slow Emergence of the Individual', (2012) 31 *YEL*, 319–372.

J. Ouwerkerk, *Quid Pro Quo? A Comparative Law Perspective on the Mutual Recognition of Judicial Decisions in Criminal Matters*, Cambridge et al.: Intersentia, 2011.

C.H. Pyle, *Extradition, Politics, and Human Rights*, Philadelphia: Temple University Press, 2001.

J.R. Spencer, 'Extradition, the European Arrest Warrant and Human Rights', (2013) 72 *CLJ*, 250.

A. Suominen, *The Principle of Mutual Recognition in Cooperation in Criminal Matters*, Cambridge et al.: Intersentia, 2011.

A. Willems, *The Principle of Mutual Trust in EU Criminal Law*, Oxford: Hart, 2021.

E. Xanthopoulou, *Fundamental Rights and Mutual Trust in the Area of Freedom, Security and Justice: A Role for Proportionality?*, Oxford: Hart, 2020.

Further Mutual Legal Assistance 12

The European Investigation Order

Lorena Bachmaier Winter

12.1 Introduction

Judicial cooperation in criminal matters is necessary whenever evidence to be obtained in a criminal procedure is located abroad. Such cooperation will be needed for carrying out investigative measures, for example to interview witnesses residing abroad, to carry out an entry and search of a home, to search and seizure documents, to intercept communications, to get samples of DNA, or to get bank information and confiscate assets.

The need for cross-border judicial cooperation has grown steadily in the last decades since many criminal proceedings present transnational elements these days. This is a consequence of the increasing mobility of persons and capital, the increase of complex forms of transnational organized crime, and the rapid digitalization of contemporary societies. Traditionally, judicial cooperation in criminal matters has been articulated through instruments of mutual legal assistance (MLA), governed by bilateral or multilateral international conventions. Within the EU,[1] it was considered that these traditional MLA instruments, with the involvement of executive authorities and broad grounds for refusal, did not respond adequately to the present needs in fighting effectively transnational crime. Therefore, the EU has implemented the principle of mutual recognition in the cooperation in criminal matters.[2]

Based on the principle of mutual recognition, various European instruments for judicial cooperation in criminal proceedings have been adopted.

[1] On the principles of European transnational criminal proceedings, see for example T. Krüssmann, *Transnationales Strafprozessrecht*, Baden-Baden: Nomos, 2009; S. Gless, *Beweisgrundsätze einer grenzüberschreitenden Strafverfolgung*, Baden-Baden: Nomos, 2007.

[2] See on this principle in more detail L. Wörner and K. Karsai in this book. Critically however, P. Rackow, 'Überlegungen zu dem Gesetz zur Änderung des IRG vom 5.1.2017', (2017) 2 *KriPoz*, 79–87 (considering that reforming the MLA Conventions might have been sufficient to improve judicial cooperation).

Among them, the EAW[3] has played a prominent role, because of not only its extensive use in practice but also for bringing to the forefront the need to improve the protection of fundamental rights of suspects or accused in the EU area of freedom, security, and justice (AFSJ). I will not provide a specific analysis of the EAW framework here, for this is done in Chapter 11 of this book.

Although there are other significant instruments for cooperation in criminal matters – for instance, in the field of confiscation orders,[4] victim protection[5] or enforcement of criminal judgments[6] – this chapter will analyse the main instrument for gathering cross-border evidence: the European investigation order (EIO).

On 3 April 2014, the Directive 2014/41/EU regarding the European Investigation Order in criminal matters (DirEIO)[7] was approved, and it entered into force on 22 May 2017. The EIO is a 'judicial' decision ordering/requesting the gathering of evidence,[8] which already exists or is to be obtained through investigative measures (Article 1 DirEIO) in another Member State (MS). The EIO can also include the request to secure or freeze evidence.[9] It will be applied to any 'criminal'

[3] Council Framework Decision 2002/584/JHA, of 13 June 2002 on the European arrest warrant and the surrender procedures between Member States, OJ L 190, 18.7.2002; Council Framework Decision 2009/299/JHA of 26 February 2009 amending Framework Decisions 2002/584/JHA, 2005/214/JHA, 2006/783/JHA, 2008/909/JHA and 2008/947/JHA, thereby enhancing the procedural rights of persons and fostering the application of the principle of mutual recognition to decisions rendered in the absence of the person concerned at the trial,OJ L 81, 27.3.2009.

[4] Cf. Regulation (EU) 2018/1805 of the European Parliament and of the Council of 14 November 2018 on the mutual recognition of freezing orders and confiscation orders, OJ L 303, 28.11.2018.

[5] Cf. Directive 2011/99/EU of the European Parliament and of the Council of 13 December 2011 on the European protection order, OJ L 338, 21.12.2011.

[6] Cf. Council Framework Decision 2008/909/JHA of 27 November 2008 on the application of the principle of mutual recognition to judgments in criminal matters imposing custodial sentences or measures involving deprivation of liberty for the purpose of their enforcement in the European Union, OJ L 327, 5.12.2008.

[7] Directive 2014/41/EU of the European Parliament and of the Council of 3 April 2014 regarding the European Investigation Order in criminal matters, OJ L 130, 1.5.2014.

[8] The terms order and request will be used here as equivalent, although the term 'order' is linked to the principle of mutual recognition and the term 'request' is the usual one in instruments of MLA.

[9] Before it was regulated in the Council Framework Decision 2003/577/JHA of 22 July 2003, on the execution in the European Union of orders freezing property or evidence, OJ L 196, 2.8.2003.

investigative measure with a European cross-border dimension, except the establishment and functioning of the joint investigation teams (JITs),[10] and surveillance measures. Its purpose is to facilitate and speed up the gathering and transfer of evidence, overcoming the undesirable fragmentation of the legal instruments aimed at collecting and transferring evidence between MS.[11]

The aim of this chapter is to provide a general overview of the EIO, without entering into details and its application in the MS. For the same reason, bibliographical references will be kept to a minimum.[12] The chapter begins with a brief introduction about EIO's historical precedents and its founding principles. I will then analyse the essential content of the Directive, its impact on the fundamental rights of suspects or accused, and its interaction with other instruments. Finally, I will address the problems detected in practice, as well as the questions that remain to be solved in order to make the EIO an effective mechanism to prosecute efficiently cross-border crime, while keeping the highest standard of procedural safeguards for the suspects and defendants.

12.2 Towards the Principle of Mutual Recognition in the Gathering of Evidence: Historical Background

As explained in other chapters, creating a single European area of freedom, security and justice entails that judicial cross-border cooperation is based upon the principle of mutual recognition. Article 67(3) TFEU provides that the Union shall endeavour to guarantee a high level of security through police and judicial cooperation, 'as well as through the mutual

[10] Cf. Council Framework Decision of 13 June 2002 on joint investigation teams, OJ L 162, 20.6.2002.

[11] See Recital 7 of the Explanatory Memorandum. See also L. Bachmaier Winter, 'The Role of the Proportionality Principle in the Cross-Border Investigations Involving Fundamental Rights' in S. Ruggeri (ed.), *Transnational Inquiries and the Protection of Fundamental Rights in Criminal Proceedings*, Heidelberg, New York: Springer, 2013, pp. 85–108.

[12] There is a vast academic literature on transnational evidence in the EU and, in particular, on the EIO. See, for example K. Ambos, *European Criminal Law*, Cambridge: Cambridge University Press, 2018, pp. 456–461, and the vast list of references included there. See also L. Bachmaier Winter, 'Transnational Evidence: Towards the Transposition of the Directive 2014/41 Regarding the European Investigation Order in Criminal Matters', (2015) *eucrim*, 47–59.

recognition of judgments in criminal matters and, if necessary, through the approximation of criminal laws'.[13]

Article 82(1) TFEU provides that 'judicial cooperation in criminal matters in the Union shall be based on the principle of mutual recognition of judgments and judicial decisions'. Articles 82(2) and 83(1) TFEU declare the EU (Parliament and Council) competent to establish minimum rules, respectively, on matters related to criminal procedure and to substantive criminal law. Mutual recognition and approximation of laws are, therefore, the axis of the policy on judicial cooperation on criminal matters, also regarding the gathering of cross-border evidence.

Nevertheless, the EIO is not, strictly speaking, an instrument of mutual recognition. As stated in the Explanatory Memorandum (E.M.) of the DirEIO, although this instrument is based on the principle of mutual recognition, it still keeps some of the flexibility of the MLA instruments.[14] While it is true that the executing State cannot control the adequacy, necessity and proportionality of the measure requested, and it has to trust the assessment made by the issuing State, the recognition will not apply automatically but is subject to certain requirements, conditions and checks.

The list of grounds of refusal – or non-recognition – included in Articles 9 to 11 of the DirEIO shows the flexibility of the principle of mutual recognition, resembling in many aspects the MLA system. The Directive has decided to avoid imposing the obligation to execute measures on the executing State that would infringe its own constitutional principles. Executing States can also refuse to carry out investigative measures that would not be allowed in comparable domestic proceedings. Thus, the DirEIO seeks to provide coherence and prevent the executing State from applying different standards to purely national criminal investigations and to investigations requested by another MS pursuant to an EIO.[15]

[13] The next paragraph mentions again the principle of mutual recognition and Art. 70 TFEU states that the principle of mutual recognition is the objective to be achieved within the EU.

[14] Recital 6 of the Explanatory Memorandum.

[15] See Winter, 'The Role of the Proportionality Principle in the Cross-Border Investigations Involving Fundamental Rights', pp. 105 ff. At the end, the scope of application of the principle of mutual recognition of the EIO has been limited when compared to the model adopted in the EAW FD of 2002.

Despite the Directive's flexible understanding of the principle mutual recognition, the journey that led to the adoption of the EIO has been long and difficult.[16] Previously, mutual assistance in matters of evidence had been governed by the European Convention on Mutual Assistance in Criminal Matters (EuCMACM) of 20 April 1959,[17] complemented by the Protocols of 17 March 1978[18] and 8 November 2001.[19] Further rules were developed by the Convention Implementing the Schengen Agreement of 14 June 1985 (CISA),[20] which provided for a simplified procedure for the transmission of requests, allowing in general the direct communication between judicial authorities of the requesting and executing States. On 29 May 2000, the European Convention on Mutual Assistance in Criminal Matters (EUMAC) was adopted. This Convention is based upon the same principles as the 1959 Convention but represents a significant step forward in the development of the judicial cooperation in criminal matters.[21]

While the MLA instruments were being updated and further developed the EU continued working towards the establishment of the principle of mutual recognition. The conclusions of the European Council of Tampere of 1999 determined that the principle of mutual recognition should apply to and facilitate the gathering of evidence in the European judicial area.[22]

[16] See on EIO and mutual recognition from the perspective of the (German) travaux, K. Ambos and P. Rackow, 'Grundsatz gegenseitiger Anerkennung und Europäische Ermittlungsanordnung', (2021) 76 *JZ*, 329–337.

[17] CoE, Treaty Series, Nr. 30; entry into force 17.7.1962.

[18] CoE, Treaty Series, Nr. 99; entry into force in 12.4.1983.

[19] CoE, Treaty Series, Nr. 182; entry into force 1.2.2004.

[20] Convention Implementing the Schengen Agreement of 14 June 1985 between the Governments of the States of the Benelux Economic Union, the Federal Republic of Germany and the French Republic on the gradual abolition of checks at their common borders, OJ L 239, 22.9.2000. Cf. specifically Arts. 48 to 53. Under the provisions of the CISA, the grounds to refuse the execution of a mutual assistance request were reduced and the requirement of double incrimination was also restricted (Art. 51).

[21] OJ C 197, 12.7.2000. It took more than five years until a sufficient number of States had signed the Convention in order to enter into force the 23 August 2005. It is complemented by the Additional Protocol of 16 October 2001, OJ C 326, 21.11. 2001; entry into force 5.10.2005.

[22] Point 36 of the Conclusions of the European Council of Tampere of 15 and 16 October 1999: 'The principle of mutual recognition should also apply to pre-trial orders, in particular to those which would enable competent authorities quickly to secure evidence and to seize assets which are easily movable; evidence lawfully gathered by one Member State's authorities should be admissible before the courts of other Member States, taking into account the standards that apply there.'

On this basis the Commission and the Council started working with the aim of extending the principle of mutual recognition to the gathering of cross-border evidence.

In 2001, the 'Programme of measures to implement the principle of mutual recognition of decisions in criminal matters' identified already the gathering and securing of evidence as one of the highest priorities.[23] Three years later, the Hague Programme[24] mentioned specifically the gathering and admissibility of evidence among the measures to implement the principle of mutual recognition in criminal matters.[25]

The 2009 'Green Paper on obtaining evidence in criminal matters from one MS to another and securing its admissibility'[26] soon led to the presentation of the first proposal of an EIO on April 2010.[27] In the meantime, the Framework Decision (FD) on the European Evidence Warrant (EEW) was passed,[28] but its limited scope made clear from the outset that it would have little practical impact. After several years of efforts, the DirEIO was approved. The EIO will substitute the rules on

[23] OJ C 12, 15.1.2001, in particular, see 2.1.1.

[24] 'Strengthening freedom, security and justice in the European Union', OJ C 53, 3.3.2005, approved in the European Council of 4 and 5 November 2004, known also as Tampere II. This document defines the objectives for the next five years for the establishing of the EU AFSJ.

[25] See point 3.3.1 of The Hague Programme.

[26] Done in Brussels 11.11.2009, COM (2009) 624 final, available at http://eur-lex.europa.eu/LexUriServ/LexUriServ.do?uri=COM:2009:0624:FIN:EN:PDF. On this Green Paper, see K. Ambos, 'Transnationale Beweiserlangung: 10 Thesen zum Grünbuch der EU-Kommission "Erlangung verwertbarer Beweise in Strafsachen aus einem anderen Mitgliedstaat"', (2010) *ZIS*, 557–567; and in the same issue, see S. Allegrezza, 'Critical Remarks on the Green Paper on Obtaining Evidence in Criminal Matters from One Member State to Another and Securing Its Admissibility', (2010) *ZIS*, 569–579.

[27] Brussels, 29.4.2010 (COPEN 115). On the proposal for a DirEIO, see, among others L. Bachmaier Winter, 'European Investigation Order for Obtaining Evidence in the Criminal Proceedings: Study of the Proposal for a European Directive', (2010) *ZIS*, 580–589 and also 'The Role of the Proportionality Principle in the Cross-Border Investigations Involving Fundamental Rights', in S. Ruggeri (ed.), *Transnational Inquiries and the Protection of Fundamental Rights in Criminal Proceedings*, Heidelberg, New York: Springer, 2013 pp. 85–107.

[28] Council Framework Decision 2008/9787/JHA of 18 December 2008 on the European evidence warrant for the purpose of obtaining objects, documents and data for use in proceedings in criminal matters, OJ L 350, 30.12.2008. On this instrument, see L. Bachmaier Winter, 'El exhorto europeo de obtención de pruebas en el proceso penal. Estudio y perspectivas de la propuesta de Decisión Marco', in T. Armenta, F. Gascón, L. Bachmaier (eds.), *El derecho procesal penal en la Unión Europea. Tendencias actuales y perspectivas de futuro*, Madrid: Colex 2006, pp. 131–178;

transnational evidence contained in the EEW and in the ECMACM,[29] among others.[30]

Now that the long road travelled until the approval of this new legal instrument for the cross-border gathering of evidence in criminal proceedings is over, it is time to focus on its content and practical implementation.

12.3 The European Investigation Order

12.3.1 Scope of Application

The question of which measures can be requested through the EIO has a relatively easy answer. The DirEIO is applicable to all types of investigative measures directed to the gathering of evidence in criminal proceedings, except, as mentioned above, the JITs and the evidence they may collect.[31] However, in practice, it is not always clear whether certain measures fall under police or judicial cooperation. This is the case, for example, of cross-border surveillance and covert investigations, with certain States considering them as investigative measures and others as police preventive measures. In principle, the EIO is aimed at gathering evidence in criminal proceedings, and (preventive) surveillance measures would as a rule fall outside its material scope.

When regulating the requirements and the grounds for refusal, the DirEIO makes a distinction between 'coercive' and 'non-coercive' measures.[32] Although at the EU level, there is not a common understanding of the concept of 'coercive measure', this notion is usually identified with those measures restricting fundamental rights and that are therefore subject to a judicial authorisation.

[29] Council Act of 29 May 2000 establishing in accordance with Article 34 of the Treaty on European Union the Convention on Mutual Assistance in Criminal Matters between the Member States of the European Union (2000/C 197/01).

[30] The international conventions, framework decisions and directives that are substituted and/or amended by the present Directive are listed in Art. 34 DirEIO.

[31] The establishment of a JIT is not based on the principle of mutual recognition but on a case-by-case agreement of the MS involved; it is meant mainly for carrying out comprehensive investigations in complex criminal cases rather than for requesting the execution of single investigative measures.

[32] See Recital 16, where it is explained that, for example non-coercive measures are those that do not interfere with the right to privacy or the right to property.

It is more difficult to determine in which types of procedures the EIO can be used. The Directive specifies that the EIO can be issued to gather evidence in 'criminal proceedings' but also in administrative sanctioning proceedings 'where the decision may give rise to proceedings before a court having jurisdiction, in particular, in criminal matters.' (Article 4 DirEIO). The aim of Article 4 DEIO is clearly to include in the scope of application of the EIO those administrative proceedings that can be reviewed 'in particular' before a criminal court. However, the boundaries of what must be considered as 'criminal proceedings' within the scope of the EIO are still somewhat vague. The CJEU had the opportunity to define this concept in the judgment on the *Marián Baláz* case,[33] which involved a fine imposed by an administrative authority (an Austrian *Verwaltungsstrafbehörde*) for a road traffic offence; the fine amounted to EUR 220, but this could converted into imprisonment if the payment is not done within a certain time.[34] The CJEU decided that the concept of a 'court having jurisdiction in particular in criminal matters' is an autonomous concept of EU law and must be interpreted as covering any court or tribunal that applies a procedure that satisfies the essential features of criminal proceedings.[35]

Further in this context, the term 'criminal proceedings' should also include those stages that, according to the national law of the issuing State, are within the criminal jurisdiction, such as the enforcement stage, including the breach of parole conditions. The EIO could therefore also be issued, for example, for identifying and freezing assets with the aim of establishing the factual basis of a non-conviction-based confiscation measure.[36]

It has also been debated whether an EIO can be issued within OLAF investigation proceedings.[37] The answer is not easy because so far OLAF has no sanctioning powers but carries out a preliminary investigation

[33] CJEU, *Marián Baláž*, No. C-60/12, ECLI:EU:C:2013:733, 14 November 2013.

[34] The Austrian administrative authorities asked a Court in the Czech Republic to recognize the certificate with the fine, as Baláž had been informed of his right to challenge the decision before a court having jurisdiction 'in particular' in criminal matters, which filed the preliminary question to the CJEU.

[35] CJEU, *Marián Baláž*, No. C-60/12, ECLI:EU:C:2013:733, 14 November 2013, para. 42.

[36] Regulation (EU) 2018/1805 of the European Parliament and of the Council of 14 November 2018 on the mutual recognition of freezing orders and confiscation orders, OJ L 303, 28.11.2018.

[37] On OLAF and its proceedings see Chapter 14 by O. Cahn in this volume.

in case of allegations of fraud, corruption and any other illegal activity affecting the financial interests of the EU. Although the implications of expanding the use of the EIO also by certain administrative authorities are counterbalanced with an increase in the procedural safeguards for the persons investigated, it should not be dismissed lightly that OLAF could be regarded as 'issuing authority' of the EIO, subject of course to validation by either a national authority involved in the investigation or by the European Public Prosecutor Office (EPPO), if the investigation falls within its competence.[38]

The Directive expressly mentions that the EIO can also be issued within proceedings for establishing the criminal or administrative liability of legal persons (Article 4 (d) DirEIO). Finally, regarding the request of tax data, although there are specific instruments for the exchange of data between tax administrations,[39] the authority investigating a tax criminal offence could resort to the EIO to gather the relevant evidence (Article 3 DirEIO).

With regard to the gathering of e-evidence, the EIO rules will be complemented by the future Regulation on electronic evidence.[40]

Finally, the territorial scope of application for the moment does neither include Ireland nor Denmark.[41]

12.3.2 Competent Authorities

12.3.2.1 The Issuing Authority

According to Article 2 DirEIO, 'issuing authority' shall be a court, judge, public prosecutor, or any other investigating authority that has powers to order the collection of evidence under the national legislation. In the

[38] See L. Bachmaier Winter, *Code of Best Practices for Investigation Order in criminal proceedings. Proposal for 100 Best Practices*, March 2019, p. 32, available at https://eurocoord.eu/wp-content/uploads/2019/06/D4.4-Final-version-of-the-Code-of-Best-Practices_rev.pdf.

[39] Directive 2011/16/EU of 15 February 2011 on administrative cooperation in the field of taxation and repealing Directive 77/799/EEC.

[40] Proposal for a Regulation of the European Parliament and the Council on European Production and Preservation Orders for electronic evidence in criminal matters, COM (2018) 225 final.

[41] See Recitals 43–45 of the E.M. of the Directive. See also the information on the European Judicial Network (EJN) webpage (www.ejn-crimjust.europa.eu/ejn/libcategories.aspx?Id=120).

latter case, however, the EIO shall be validated by a judicial authority, which might also 'be regarded as an issuing authority for the purposes of transmission of the EIO' (Article 2 (c) (ii) DirEIO).

The concept of 'issuing authority' in the DirEIO takes into account the fact that criminal investigations in most EU MS are directed or supervised by the public prosecution, which are consequently accorded investigative powers. Nevertheless, a preliminary question was referred to the CJEU,[42] asking whether the public prosecutor could be considered as 'judicial authority' for the purpose of issuing an EIO, taking into account that some public prosecution authorities are not completely independent being subject to instructions from the executive branch. The Court, sitting as the Grand Chamber, ruled that the concepts of 'judicial authority' and 'issuing authority', within the meaning of the EIO Directive, 'include the public prosecutor's office of a Member State, even though they are in a relationship of legal subordination to the executive and might be directly or indirectly subject to individual instructions regarding the issuing of an EIO'.[43]

In this judgment, the Court makes clear that the requisites for issuing the EAW, in particular the independence of the issuing judicial authority, as expressed by the ECJ in its judgment of 27 May 2019,[44] are not strictly applicable for issuing the EIO. In case the issuing authority is not a judge, the DirEIO provides for an additional safeguard: the judicial validation of the EIO when a judicial warrant is required either in the issuing or in the executing State. This solution is not only coherent with the diverse legal systems of the EU MS and the different conceptions of coercive measures,

42 See CJEU, *Staatsanwaltschaft Wien v. A. and Others,* No. C-584/19, Judgment, ECLI:EU:C:2020:1002, 8 December 2020.

43 Ibid., para. 75.

44 CJEU, *OG and PI,* Joined Cases Nos. C-508/18 and C-82/19 PPU, Judgment, ECLI:EU:C:2019:456, 27 May 2019, on the request for a preliminary ruling filed by the Supreme Court of Ireland, concerning the interpretation of Art. 6 (1) FD EAW. The executing Court asked whether the German public prosecutors (prosecution offices of Lübeck and Zwickau) could be defined as 'judicial authority' for the aims of issuing an EAW. The ECJ held that this concept 'must be interpreted as not including public prosecutors' offices of a Member State which are exposed to the risk of being subject, directly or indirectly, to directions or instructions in a specific case from the executive, such as a Minister for Justice, in connection with the adoption of a decision to issue a European arrest warrant' (para. 90). On this decision, see K. Ambos, 'German Public Prosecutor as (No) Judicial Authority within the Meaning of the European Arrest Warrant: A Case Note on the CJEU's Judgment in OG (C-508/18) and PI (C 82/19 PPU)', (2019) 10 (4) *NJECL*, 399–407.

but also ensures a higher standard of procedural safeguards. If the executing State receives the EIO without court validation, and the rules of the executing State require such a validation, the executing State shall proceed to its validation, but not refuse the execution of the EIO (Article 2(d) DirEIO). For example, if the measure requested is a DNA identification or metadata of electronic communications, and in the forum State this can be ordered by the public prosecutor, but in the requested State, such measure is subject to judicial authorisation, the executing State shall not deny such request because of this reason but seek for a judicial validation before getting the DNA samples. In doing so, it will not infringe its own laws and at the same time ensure an efficient cooperation.

With a view to strengthen the prosecution of cross-border criminality, the DirEIO seeks to limit the grounds for refusal to a minimum, while ensuring at the same time that the constitutional principles in both issuing and executing State are respected.[45] Requiring a judicial validation either in the issuing or in the executing State to my mind, seems to strike a right balance between efficiency and respect for the diversity of the different legal systems involved in the judicial cooperation, although the defence rights could be better protected.

Most of the States have designated the judge/judicial authority and/or the public prosecutor as issuing authorities, because those are the authorities competent to order the gathering of evidence in domestic criminal investigations. However, some MS have designated administrative and law enforcement institutions as issuing authorities. This is the case, for example, of Poland, where a police officer can issue the EIO, although it needs to be validated by the public prosecutor.[46]

As to the role of the defendant in the issuing of the EIO, Article 1(3) DirEIO provides that it 'may the requested by the suspect or accused person, or by a lawyer on his behalf', in conformity with the defence rights applicable under the national rules of the criminal procedure.

[45] Indeed, during the negotiations, one of the most criticised points was precisely that it was not required for the issuing authority to be a court, which could lead to problems for the implementation of the principle of mutual recognition, especially when coercive measures were requested. See Bachmaier Winter, 'European Investigation Order for Obtaining Evidence in the Criminal Proceedings: Study of the Proposal for a European Directive', 587.

[46] See Art. 589, para. 2, in relation with Arts. 307, 311, paras. 2 and 312 of the Criminal Procedure Code of Poland. As long as the validation by a judicial authority does not end being a mere formality, this provision should not raise concerns.

Thus, the moment, conditions and formal requirements for ensuring that the defendant has also the chance to request the issuing of the EIO remain in the hands of each MS. But this approach does not seem to be sufficient to guarantee effectively the right recognized under Article 6(3)(d) ECHR and the principle of equality in an adversarial criminal procedure, as the mere filing of a request by the defendant involves the disclosure of the defensive strategy to the accusing party.

12.3.2.2 The Executing Authority

The executing authority is the one 'having competence to recognise an EIO and ensure its execution in accordance with this Directive and the procedures applicable in a similar domestic case'. The DirEIO requires that EIO is transmitted between judicial authorities. Each State shall designate the authority that is competent to execute the EIO (Article 7 DirEIO). In most EU MS, the same authority receiving the EIO is also competent to recognize and execute it. Usually, it will be the public prosecutor, who will receive, register, recognise and also execute the EIO, unless the requested measure has to be executed by a judge. However, in certain countries the authority might change depending on the procedural stage in which the EIO is received.[47]

In case of complex EIOs that request several measures, some of which can be executed by the public prosecutor and some others need to be transferred to a judge, the execution might be divided between the two authorities. However, some countries have opted for allocating the execution of all the measures – be they coercive or not – in the hands of a judge.

Practical difficulties might also arise when the various measures requested are to be executed in different judicial districts, and therefore, different authorities have territorial competence. For example, in a case where different victims are located within several (local) jurisdictions in the same country or in different countries, identifying the executing authority might be challenging. In such cases, while the execution will need to be divided, it would be useful that the coordination remains under one single authority, to prevent that the EIO is scattered among diverse authorities and also to speed up the process of transmission of the evidence gathered. In any event, conflicts of competence among the executing authorities that would entail delays in the execution should

[47] See Bachmaier Winter, *Code of Best Practices for Investigation Order in criminal proceedings. Proposal for 100 Best Practices*, pp. 53–54.

be avoided. In these types of cases where different MS are involved, the assistance of Eurojust has proved to be very useful.[48]

12.3.3 Requirements: Proportionality and Necessity

Pursuant to Article 6(1) DirEIO, the EIO shall only be issued when it is 'necessary and proportionate for the purpose of the proceedings' and the requested measure could have been issued 'under the same conditions in a similar domestic case'.[49] In the EIO form, the issuing authority shall describe which are the criminal offences being investigated, the applicable criminal law and the type of measure requested. The proportionality and necessity of the EIO will be assessed exclusively by the issuing authority and the requested authority is not pursuant to the principle of mutual recognition, entitled to check such assessment or refuse the execution for this reason.[50] However, the executing authority shall have some margin to check the proportionality of the EIO, precisely when the requested measure is not in conformity with the constitutional principles of the executing State or the measures requested are economically too costly.[51] There is also possibility to replace the measure requested by another one which is less intrusive but would provide the same results (Article 10(3) DirEIO). This reflects a certain flexibility on the blind operation of the principle of mutual recognition, but it does not mean that the executing authority can review the assessment made by the issuing authority.

[48] See *Report on Eurojust's casework in the field of the European Investigation Order*, November 2020, p. 30, available at www.eurojust.europa.eu/report-eurojusts-casework-field-european-investigation-order-0.

[49] Regarding the interpretation of Article 6 DirEIO, a preliminary request has been filed by the Landesgericht Berlin as of 19 October 2022. The questions asked deal mainly with the rules on the issuing authority and the use as evidence in Germany of information gathered in France under surveillance laws (Encrochat case).

[50] Winter, 'The Role of the Proportionality Principle in the Cross-Border Investigations Involving Fundamental Rights', in S. Ruggeri (ed.), *Transnational Inquiries and the Protection of Fundamental Rights in Criminal Proceedings*, pp. 101 ff.

[51] Art. 6 DirEIO, which reads:

'3. Where the executing authority has reason to believe that the conditions referred to in paragraph 1 have not been met, it may consult the issuing authority on the importance of executing the EIO. After that consultation the issuing authority may decide to withdraw the EIO.'

The meaning of this provision is unclear. Literally it allows the executing authority to 'consult' the issuing one, when there are doubts as to the compliance of the conditions of proportionality and necessity.

Any proportionality assessment shall take into account the following factors: the seriousness of the offence; the necessity of the evidence for the investigation and adjudication of the offence; the existence of other less intrusive investigative measures which would achieve the same aim; the consequences of the adoption of the measures for the persons affected; and finally – and generally – whether the measure is proportionate with a view to its aims.[52] Nevertheless, the Directive does not exclude the possibility of issuing the EIO for the investigation of minor criminal offences (Article 4 DirEIO). Such an approach might be positive from the point of view of facilitating the cooperation in transnational evidence gathering but may entail an excessive use of the instrument and thus lead to an excessive burden for executing authorities. It is also questionable in terms of proportionality. Ultimately, it may have a negative impact on the willingness to cooperate, that is execute the EIO.

If there are doubts as to the proportionality of an EIO Article 6(3) DirEIO provides, as already mentioned, for a consultation procedure, and 'after that consultation the issuing authority may decide to withdraw the EIO'. When the economic costs appear to be exceptionally high the executing authority shall consult on the relevance of the evidence (i) to the proceedings, (ii) to the criminal policy and (iii) to the overall costs. The general social interest has to be considered when the problem of exceptionally high costs of an investigative measure arises.

Although Article 6(3) DirEIO looks like one of those rules that are included in a legal instrument just to pave the way towards its adoption and overcome the opposition of certain MS, it clearly gives rise to several questions of some significance. This is due to the fact that, on the one hand, Article 6(3) does not state that the consultations will be limited to the costs of the execution of the EIO; and on the other hand, because through these 'consultations' as to costs there may be a risk that the cooperation will be hindered, or even that the cooperation will be provided only if the costs are not 'exceptional' in the eyes of the executing authorities, or if those costs are assumed by the requesting State.

[52] Winter, 'The Role of the Proportionality Principle in the Cross-Border Investigations Involving Fundamental Rights', pp. 100–101; S. Allegrezza, 'Collecting Criminal Evidence across the European Union: The European Investigation Order between Flexibility and Proportionality', in S. Ruggeri (ed.), *Transnational Evidence and Multicultural Inquiries in Europe*, Heidelberg, New York: Springer 2014, pp. 51–67, p. 59 ff.

It is to be expected that the practice will have to clarify what is to be understood as 'exceptional costs', because not only the legal differences but also the economic differences between EU MS are considerable and thus the cost issue may have a negative impact on a smooth cooperation. Common understanding on what are proportional requests and proportional or reasonable costs in the execution of EIOs should be reached with the aim to create an environment that facilitates transnational cooperation.

12.3.4 Recognition and Execution of the EIO

During the process of drafting the DirEIO, it was discussed at length how the grounds for refusal should be regulated with a view to strengthen the principle of mutual recognition instead of creating (further) distrust among the MS.[53] In a nutshell, the adopted instrument does not move towards an automatic recognition of an EIO for it allows for certain grounds of refusal although these are strictly limited.

12.3.4.1 The Grounds for Substitution and Refusal of the Requested Measure

The Directive has tried to limit the grounds for refusal, providing for the possibility of substituting the requested measure if this would be beneficial for the cooperation (Article 10 DEIO).

12.3.4.1.1 Recourse to a Different Type of Investigative Measure Article 10 DirEIO regulates the cases where the executing authority, prior to consultation with the issuing authority, can or shall apply a different measure than the one requested.[54] When the measure does not exist in the executing State or is not applicable in the case described in the EIO, if there is no other alternative measure, the issuing

[53] Cf. Bachmaier Winter, 'European Investigation Order for Obtaining Evidence in the Criminal Proceedings: Study of the Proposal for a European Directive', 584–585.

[54] The situations are mainly three:
(i) The investigative measure indicated in the EIO does not exist under the law of the executing State (Art. 10(1) (a) DirEIO); or
(ii) The investigative measure indicated in the EIO would not be available in a similar domestic case (Art. 10(1) (b) DirEIO); or
(iii) The measure exists and could be applied, but the same result could be achieved by a less intrusive measure (Art. 10(3) DirEIO).

authority shall be informed about the impossibility to comply with the EIO. This can only happen regarding coercive measures because it is assumed that non-coercive measures shall exist in any MS and thus be enforceable. For example, if in the executing State, the remote search of computers is not regulated, there might be the possibility to access to the data of the computer by way of a physical search instead of dismissing the respective EIO out of hand. This substitution would promote cooperation even if the requested measure does not exist in the relevant State.

Finally, if the executing State does not provide for an equivalent measure as the one requested, the EIO shall be refused. This is not considered a 'refusal' of the request, but an 'impossibility to provide the assistance requested' based on legal reasons (Article 10(5) DirEIO). Here the principle of mutual recognition is relaxed and comes closer to the traditional MLA system in order to protect the coherence of the legal system of the executing State: the obligation to execute an investigative measure that is not provided in the law of the executing State would not only be inconsistent with its constitutional principles but also contrary to the ECtHR's case law on the quality of regulations providing for and the foreseeability of any restrictions of human rights within a criminal investigation to be in accordance with the Covention.[55]

12.3.4.1.2 Grounds for Refusal of Recognition or Execution

The structure and content of the grounds for refusal of an EIO follow basically the same pattern as the one found in the MLA conventions of 1959 and of 2000, albeit excluding the *ordre public* clause and the double incrimination requirement (except for the list of thirty-two offences (Article 11 (1)(g) DirEIO)), it includes a general ground for refusal when the measure requested would be against the fundamental rights recognised in the EU Charter.[56]

The general grounds for refusal are listed under Article 11 DirEIO. They are to be completed by other grounds that make the EIO execution

[55] See, for example ECtHR, *Copland v. United Kingdom*, Appl. No. 62617/00, 3 April 2007; *Dumitru Popescu v. Romania*, Appl. No. 71525/01, 26 April 2007; *Liberty and Others v. United Kingdom*, Appl. No. 58243/00, 1 February 2008. See Winter, 'The Role of the Proportionality Principle in the Cross-Border Investigations Involving Fundamental Rights', p. 98.

[56] Art. 11 (1) (f) DirEIO: 'there are substantial grounds to believe that the execution of the investigative measure indicated in the EIO would be incompatible with the executing State's obligations in accordance with Article 6 TEU and the Charter.'

impossible (as, for example Article 24(2) DirEIO, when the defendant does not consent to appear through video link).

The refusal ground that 'there are substantial grounds to believe that the execution of the investigative measure indicated in the EIO would be incompatible with the executing State's obligations in accordance with Article 6 TEU and the Charter' (Article 11(1)(f) DirEIO) is consistent with Article 1(4) DirEIO, which makes clear that the Directive does not modify the obligation to respect the fundamental rights enshrined in Article 6 TEU. This ground is quite broad as it is based on 'substantial grounds to believe' that the execution of the EIO may cause such infringement.[57] In fact, this ground comes close to a European *ordre public* clause,[58] and, as long as it is used correctly, represents a specific safeguard for the protection of the fundamental rights.

Before taking a decision on the refusal, the executing authority shall contact the issuing authority to try to overcome the doubts relating to possible grounds of refusal (Article 11(4) DirEIO). Thus, smooth communication should be the guiding principle in the AFSJ.

In any event, the grounds for refusal should be interpreted in a very flexible way. It must be recalled that these grounds should, as a rule, have been regulated as optional and not mandatory. Therefore, the MS whose legal framework has 'transformed' the grounds for refusal into mandatory ones, should not primarily use them to avoid cooperation, but rather apply them in a flexible way.

12.3.4.2 The Execution of the EIO

12.3.4.2.1 The Applicable Law The rules applied in the gathering of evidence in a foreign (requested) State may determine the admissibility of this evidence in the requesting State. The procedural rules of some MS require that the evidence has been obtained in accordance with their own national rules (*lex fori*), while other systems recognize its validity if the rules of the executing State (*lex loci*) have been respected. There are still other countries where foreign evidence is admitted without checking how it was obtained. This is the so-called *principle of non inquiry*, when the

[57] This provision refers to the rights recognised in the European Charter – as interpreted by the CJEU – which will not always be identical to the fundamental rights recognised in the national Constitutions of the MS.

[58] In the same sense, M. Böse, 'Ermittlungsanordnung – Beweistransfer nach neuen Regeln?', (2014) *ZIS* 154.

issuing authority does not check whether the formalities or norms that governed the evidence-gathering process have been fully complied with in the executing state.[59] The diversity of solutions existing in each of the MS, on the one hand, prevents or impairs the free circulation of criminal evidence; on the other hand, it may have an impact on the defendant's rights of defence.

To prevent possible obstacles to the admissibility of evidence obtained abroad, the issuing State should indicate the formalities to be followed when executing the EIO. Such accommodation of the investigative measure to the *lex fori* was already foreseen in the 2000 European MLA Convention (Article 4 DirEIO), and it is provided also in Article 9 DirEIO: indications of the issuing State shall be followed if they are not contrary to the principles of the executing State. This is a pragmatic approach to ensure the correct execution of the EIO, as well as the admissibility of evidence obtained abroad, although it may be questioned if it suffices to provide an adequate level of protection of the defendant's rights.

The transnational dimension of a process must indeed foster cooperation but not at the cost of distorting fundamental procedural principles and overly restricting defence rights.[60] This is the reason why many scholars have argued, for a long for time, that it is necessary to establish specific rules applicable to transnational criminal processes in Europe,[61] not least to ensure defence rights. This is a pending issue in the construction of a AFSJ where security should not become the prevailing leitmotiv.

Article 14(7) DirEIO at least introduces a general rule aimed at advancing in the protection of the defence rights also in transnational proceedings:

> 'Without prejudice to national procedural rules Member States shall ensure that in criminal proceedings in the issuing State the rights of the defence and the fairness of the proceedings are respected when assessing evidence obtained through the EIO.'

[59] A. van Hoek and M. Luchtman, 'Transnational Cooperation in Criminal Matters and the Safeguarding of Human Rights', (2005) 1 (2) *Utrecht L. Rev*, 1–39, 15.

[60] van Hoek and Luchtman, 'Transnational Cooperation in Criminal Matters and the Safeguarding of Human Rights', 16: 'the current inter-state practice thus creates a gap in legal protection that does not exist in purely national cases'.

[61] See, T. Krüssman, *Transnationales Strafprozessrecht*, Baden-Baden: Nomos, 2009, pp. 134 ff; S. Gless and J. Vervaele, 'Law Should Govern: Aspiring General Principles for Transnational Criminal Justice', (2013) 9(4) *Utrecht L. Rev.*, 1–10. In the same issue, see S. Gless, 'Transnational Cooperation in Criminal Matters and the Guarantee of a Fair Trial: Approaches to a General Principle', (2013) 9(4) *Utrecht L. Rev.*, 90 ff.

Even though this rule does not explicitly abolish the principle of *non-inquiry*, it clarifies that the courts must scrutinize the way evidence was obtained in another State and check that the defendant's fundamental guarantees have been respected.

There are still numerous questions that remain open regarding the admissibility of evidence. For example, what should be done in the case where the evidence was obtained legally but only for the purpose of administrative proceedings in violation of the right to self-incrimination? If according to the rules of the executing State, such evidence could only be used in administrative proceedings, but it is transferred in execution of an EIO, could this evidence be used in a criminal procedure, or should it be inadmissible because it was obtained against a fundamental right?

12.3.4.2.2 Other Issues Arising during the Execution of the EIO There are several other issues that are not addressed by the DirEIO, but they may raise difficult questions in practice. First, it is unclear whether the executing authority shall check if the requesting authority identified in the EIO form as judicial authority in fact complies with the requirements to be considered as such. This problem has been identified when certain countries consider, for example, customs authorities or police authorities as 'judicial authority' in their national law. As a rule, the executing authority should not be checking compliance with Article 2 DirEIO as a requisite for the execution, and only where there are manifest reasons that the issuing authority might not be a 'judicial authority', open consultations to find a solution, or proceed to validation.

Another question is whether the information transferred by way of an EIO can be used as *notitia criminis* in the executing State to trigger a domestic investigation. As a rule, the executing authorities should not use this way to challenge the jurisdiction of the issuing State with regard to the alleged crime but resort to the channels established in the FD 2009/498/JHA[62] on conflicts of jurisdiction.

Another question relates to possible casual findings of evidence during the execution of an EIO. It is not easy to determine how the executing authority shall proceed in such a case, for example if it finds evidence

[62] Council Framework Decision 2009/948/JHA of 30 November 2009 on prevention and settlement of conflicts of exercise of jurisdiction in criminal proceedings. See, for example P. Caeiro, 'Jurisdiction in Criminal Matters in the EU: Negative and Positive Conflicts, and beyond', (2010) 93(4) *KritV*, 366–379.

regarding the commission of another crime. It would be reasonable with a view to prevent conflicts of jurisdiction that the issuing authority should be consulted if the newly discovered offence has some connection with the EIO offence.

It is interesting to have a look at the practice on the use of the evidence obtained by the executing authorities regarding the interrogation of witnesses. It is unclear if the speciality principle should apply so that such evidence could only be used in the proceedings where the EIO was issued. The usual practice is to request permission of the executing State to change the destiny of the evidence obtained in the executing State. In another case, it was the executing MS which wanted to make subsequent use of the witness statements obtained as evidence while executing an EIO for another MS. In this case, it was considered that if the executing authority wished to use such evidence, it should issue a new EIO directed to the (original) issuing State, in order to officially obtain the outcome of the witness interrogation and be able to use as evidence the witness' statements they themselves had previously sent to the issuing authority in execution of an EIO.[63]

12.3.5 Rights of the Defendant and Third Parties

There is a clear risk of imbalance between the powers of the prosecution and the defendant in the process of gathering evidence abroad, which could undermine the principle of equality of arms.[64] This uneven position of the respective parties is not new and not generated by the EIO, but they may be exacerbated in the application of the EIO, notwithstanding Article 1(3) DirEIO providing access to cross-border evidence to the defendant.[65]

Another discussion is whether the defence can intervene in the execution of the EIO in the requested State and the possibility to challenge the

[63] These examples are found in the *Report on Eurojust's casework in the field of the European Investigation Order*, November 2020, pp. 31–32.

[64] Bachmaier Winter, 'European Investigation Order for Obtaining Evidence in the Criminal Proceedings: Study of the Proposal for a European Directive', 587; K. Ambos, P. Rackow and S. Schork, 'Die Europäische Ermittlungsanordnung aus Verteidigersicht', (2021) 2 *StV*, 126–133.

[65] Critically also for not providing for the participation of the defence lawyer in the execution of an EIO, S. Ruggeri, 'Introduction to the Proposal of a European Investigation Order: Due Process Concerns and Open Issues', in S. Ruggeri (ed.), *Transnational Evidence and Multicultural Inquiries in Europe* Heidelberg, New York: Springer 2014, pp. 3–25, p. 17.

issuing and/or execution of an EIO. The E.M. of the DirEIO recalls that it shall be applied in light of the Directives providing for fundamental defence rights,[66] but it is questionable whether such a reference is enough to ensure an effective protection of such rights.

In fact, the grounds for issuing an EIO can only be challenged before the courts of the requesting State 'without prejudice to the guarantees of fundamental rights in the executing State' (Article 14(2) DirEIO). The executing authority has to ensure that fundamental rights are duly respected (Article 1(4) DirEIO) and should have the possibility to refuse the execution of the EIO when there are serious reasons to think that it would cause a violation of those rights (Article 11(1) (f) DirEIO).

In accordance with Article 14(1) DirEIO, MS also have to ensure that all measures adopted in execution of an EIO can be challenged through the same channels as available in domestic proceedings ('equivalent to those available in a similar domestic case'), that is under the same conditions as if a national authority had decided the measure. However, when and under which conditions the defence must be informed about the execution of an EIO is not set out in the Directive but left at the discretion of the national legislature which must take the confidentiality of the measure into account (Article 14(3) DirEIO). Thus, this rule does not add anything substantial to the general right to a remedy except for the generic requirement that domestic rules must allow the 'effective exercise' of those remedies when they become applicable. In the form for the issuing an EIO, it is not even mandatory to describe which are the remedies against the EIO in the issuing state, but only to specify if any of the available remedies has been sought. According to the ECJ, the form shall inform whether such remedies have been used, but not in general whether legal remedies exist, and which they are.[67] Such a formalistic approach avoided addressing the core problem, namely the absence of any possibility to challenge the EIO on search and seizure in the issuing

[66] See Recital 15 E.M.

[67] See CJEU, *Ivan Gavanozov*, No. C-324/17, Judgment, ECLI:EU:C:2019:892, 24 October 2019. In this case, no legal remedy was available under Member State law (Bulgaria) against the order for search and seizure requested to be carried out in the executing state (Czech Republic). The ECJ then very formally stated that the form only required to express the 'if a legal remedy has been sought against an EIO' (para. 29), with the aim of informing the executing authority if a remedy has been sought in the issuing state, but not to inform the parties on the possible available remedies.

State. This situation led to a second preliminary question filed by the same court in Bulgaria, asking precisely whether it is contrary to the EU Charter of Fundamental Rights the issuing of an EIO for a search and seizure when there is no possibility to challenge such measure in the issuing State, because no remedy is provided for it under national law.[68] In this occasion finally the ECJ decided that such situation is against Article 47 of the European Charter of Fundamental Rights.[69]

Finally, the Directive does not contain any provision regarding the protection of the rights of third parties that may be affected when executing an EIO, save the rules on witness' and experts' testimonies through videoconference, telephone or other audio-visual means (Articles 24 and 25 DirEIO). In so far as third parties' fundamental rights can be encroached upon by the adoption of certain investigative measures –as, for example interception of communications (Articles 30 and 31 DirEIO) or controlled deliveries (Article 28 DirEIO) – the domestic laws should provide for the information of these third persons and instruct them how to protect their rights.

12.4 Conclusions

When compared to the EAW, in the case of the EIO, MS seem to have been more reluctant to accept blindly the application of the principle of mutual recognition, especially taking into account the fundamental rights affected and their own constitutional principles and traditions. This may explain the broader grounds for refusal in the DirEIO and their implementation as mandatory and not just optional in several MS.[70] All in all, the EIO constitutes an important step forward in the consolidation of the common AFSJ. In practice, it has contributed significantly to foster and simplify the judicial cooperation in criminal matters in the EU,

68 See ECJ Judgment C-852/19, *Ivan Gavanozov (II)*, of 11 November 2021 (ECLI:EU:C:2021:902)

69 This ECJ Judgment also addresses a question regarding the interrogation of witnesses by way of videconference, which is solved in a similar way as the question regarding to the measure of search and seizure, making in both cases the issuing of an EIO subject to the condition that there is a legal remedy to challenge its lawfulness and necessity in the issuing State.

70 See L. Bachmaier Winter, 'Prueba transnacional en Europa: la Directiva 2014/41 relativa a la orden europea de investigación', (2015) *Rev. Gral. Dcho. Europeo*, 1–35, 34.

although there is still a long way to go until cross-border evidence will be available as if gathered within one's own jurisdiction.

While the proceedings and formalities for issuing an EIO, transferring it to the executing authority and getting it executed within a reasonable time have improved greatly, there is still much more to be done to secure transnational evidence and ensuring its admissibility across the Union. For that reason, the European Commission is working on the e-evidence Digital Exchange System (e-EDES), part of the broader Digital Criminal Justice project,[71] which includes the establishment of a single electronic platform to exchange the most frequently applied judicial cooperation instruments with a view to a reliable transfer of electronic evidence and ensuring its authenticity and integrity and thus admissibility. While all these instruments shall facilitate an efficient transnational crime prosecution, this must go hand in hand with the strengthening of the protection of fundamental rights of the suspects and accused persons.

Further Reading

L. Bachmaier Winter, 'Transnational Criminal Proceedings, Witness Evidence and Confrontation: Lessons from the ECtHR's Case Law', (2013) 9(4) *Utrecht L. Rev.*, 126–148.

K. Ligeti, *Strafrecht und strafrechtliche Zusammenarbeit in der Europäischen Union*, Berlin: Duncker & Humblot 2005.

S. Ruggeri (ed.), *Transnational Inquiries and the Protection of Fundamental rights in Criminal Proceedings*, Heidelberg, New York: Springer 2013.

B. Schünemann (ed.), *Ein Gesamtkonzept für die europäische Strafrechtspflege*, Köln: Carl Heymanns Verl. 2006.

G. Vermeulen et al., *EU Cross-Border Gathering and Use of Evidence in Criminal Matters. Towards Mutual Recognition of Investigative Measures and Free Movement of Evidence?*, IRCP-series Volume 37 (2010), available at www.ejtn.eu/PageFiles/6335/evidence%20study.pdf.

[71] See the Communication from the Commission 'Digitalisation of justice in the European Union. A toolbox of opportunities', Brussels, 2.12.2020, COM(2020) 710 final, available at https://eur-lex.europa.eu/legal-content/EN/ALL/?uri=COM:2020:710:FIN.

13 Police Cooperation

Kai Ambos and Peter Rackow

13.1 The Development of Police Cooperation in Europe

13.1.1 Before the Second World War

Early forms of cross-border police cooperation in Europe can be traced back even before the Napoleonic era,[1] while in the nineteenth century, an intensification of pragmatic police cross-border cooperation could be observed in the face of phenomena such as, in particular, the emergence of anarchist movements in various European States;[2] by contrast, judicial cooperation focused on the area of extradition.[3] It is remarkable that these early forms of cooperation were strongly influenced by personal contacts between law enforcement officials.[4]

Around 1900, the International Union of Penal Law, or Union Internationale de Droit Pénal (I.U.P.L./U.I.D.P), founded by *Adolphe Prins* (Brussels), *Franz von Liszt* (Halle) and *Gerardus Antonius van Hamel* (Amsterdam), provided impetus for more formal international police cooperation between States.[5] This was seen as a reaction to an emerging 'international criminality',[6] which was attributed to factors such as increasing cross-border mobility and travel.[7] The Premier Congrès de

[1] Cf. C. Fijnaut, *A Peaceful Revolution*, Cambridge: Intersentia, 2019, pp. 10 ff.; id., 'Revolution or Evolution through the Treaty of Lisbon', in H. Aden (ed.), *Police Cooperation in the European Union under the Treaty of Lisbon*, Baden-Baden: Nomos, 2015, p. 26.

[2] Fijnaut, *A Peaceful Revolution*, pp. 13 ff.

[3] Ibid., pp. 18–21.

[4] C. Fijnaut, in H. Aden (ed.), *Police Cooperation in the European Union under the Treaty of Lisbon*, Baden-Baden: Nomos, 2015, p. 26.

[5] Fijnaut, *A Peaceful Revolution*, p. 21.

[6] G.A. Hopff, 'Das internationale Verbrechertum und seine Bekämpfung', (1997) 13 *Mitteilungen der Internationalen Kriminalistischen Vereinigung/Bulletin de l'Union Internationale de Droit Pénal*, 206.

[7] H. Lindenau, 'Das internationale Verbrechertum und seine Bekämpfung', (1997) 13 *Mitteilungen der Internationalen Kriminalistischen Vereinigung/Bulletin de l'Union Internationale de Droit Pénal*, 194.

Police Internationale in Monaco in 1914, promoted by *Prince Albert of Monaco*,[8] called, in particular, for the establishment of an International Bureau of Identification ('Bureau International d'Identification').[9]

After the end of the First World War, initiatives by individuals from the police sector, in particular by the Dutch police officer *van Houten* and the head of the Austrian State police *Schober*, led to the founding of the International Criminal Police Commission (ICPC) at the Congress of Vienna in 1923,[10] which tasked itself with 'organising extensive mutual administrative assistance by all security agencies within the framework of the existing laws of the individual States and taking all necessary measures to successfully shape the fight against ordinary criminals'.[11] At the Congress of Vienna, further far-reaching ideas were discussed, some of which can be read as anticipating much more recent parallel discussions, such as the question of whether an international 'mobile brigade' should be created, or whether it would be preferable not to create a central agency but instead to promote direct communication between all police authorities.[12]

After initial scepticism about formalising international police cooperation, by the beginning of the Second World War, the most important European (and a number of non-European States) had recognised and joined the ICPC.[13] However, a darker part of the picture is that, at the latest with the 'Anschluss of Austria' in the 1930s, a process of 'Nazification of the Commission' began,[14] culminating in the assumption of the presidency

[8] See, J. Sheptycky, 'Brand Interpol', in S. Hufnagel and C. McCartney (eds.), *Trust in International Police and Justice Cooperation*, Oxford, Portland, OR: Hart Publishing, 2017, p. 103.

[9] Fijnaut, *A Peaceful Revolution*, p. 26.

[10] H. J. Hoeveler, 'Die Entwicklung der internationalen Polizeikriminalistik', in H.J. Hoeveler (ed.), *Internationale Bekämpfung des Verbrechens*, Hamburg: Verlag Deutsche Polizei GmbH, 1966, pp. 30 ff.; Fijnaut, *A Peaceful Revolution*, pp. 27 ff.; id., in H. Aden (ed.), *Police Cooperation in the European Union under the Treaty of Lisbon*, Baden-Baden: Nomos, 2015, p. 29.

[11] Fijnaut, *A Peaceful Revolution*, p. 33; for details, cf. Hoeveler, in Hoeveler, *Internationale Bekämpfung des Verbrechens*, Verlag Deutsche Polizei GmbH, 1966, p. 36.

[12] Fijnaut, *A Peaceful Revolution*, p. 36.

[13] See in detail Hoeveler, in Hoeveler, *Internationale Bekämpfung des Verbrechens*, Hamburg: Verlag Deutsche Polizei GmbH, 1966, p. 37.

[14] Fijnaut, *A Peaceful Revolution*, p. 52, pp. 52 ff.; furthermore, see Hoeveler, 'Die Entwicklung der internationalen Polizeikriminalistik', pp. 38–40; furthermore, see J. Sheptycky, 'Brand Interpol', in S. Hufnagel and C. McCartney (eds.), *Trust in International Police and Justice Cooperation*, Oxford, Portland, OR: Hart Publishing, 2017, p. 105 ('ICPC network was most certainly used in the fulfilment of Nazi aims, but it was not wholly subjugated to them').

of the ICPC by the infamous Reinhard *Heydrich* (1940),[15] since 1939 head of Nazi-Germany's *Reichssicherheitshauptamt* (Reich Security Main Office), and the relocation of the ICPC-General Secretariat to Berlin, which 'meant that the commission had come to be regarded as an SS body'.[16]

13.1.2 From Interpol to TREVI

After the end of the Second World War, a Belgian police officer tried to revive the ICPC,[17] but its past as a nazified organisation eventually led to its re-establishment in 1956 (with significant help from France[18]) under a different name, namely International Criminal Police Organization (ICPO, Interpol).[19] As a further consequence of the Nazi past, Interpol now pretended to stay away from politics focusing on what it called 'ordinary law crimes'.[20] This depoliticisation was (arguably) one reason for the US-American FBI (under J. Edgar *Hoover*) to temporarily suspend cooperation with Interpol.[21]

In the aftermath of the Second World War, it did not take long for the States of Europe to come together under the umbrella of the Council of Europe (CoE) (1949) and later (1957) the European Economic Community (EEC). While judicial cooperation in criminal matters in Europe was, as

15 Cf. C. Fijnaut, in H. Aden (ed.), *Police Cooperation in the European Union under the Treaty of Lisbon*, Baden-Baden: Nomos, 2015, p. 30; H.J. Hoeveler, in H.J. Hoeveler (ed.), *Internationale Bekämpfung des Verbrechens*, Hamburg: Verlag Deutsche Polizei GmbH, 1966, pp. 39–40.

16 Fijnaut, *A Peaceful Revolution*, p. 64; id., 'Revolution or Evolution through the Treaty of Lisbon', in H. Aden (ed.), Police Cooperation in the European Union under the Treaty of Lisbon, p. 30 ('merger between the IKPK and the *Zentrale des Terrors*'); M. Anderson, *Policing the World*, Oxford: Clarendon, 1989, p. 41 ('catastrophic episode').

17 Cf. Hoeveler, 'Die Entwicklung der internationalen Polizeikriminalistik', pp. 42–3.

18 Anderson, *Policing the World*, p. 42.

19 J. Sheptycky, 'Brand Interpol', in S. Hufnagel and C. McCartney (eds.), *Trust in International Police and Justice Cooperation*, Oxford, Portland, OR: Hart Publishing, 2017, p. 106.

20 According to Art. 2(b) of its original 1956 constitution Interpol aims 'to contribute effectively to the prevention and suppression of ordinary law crimes'; on this term, see Sheptycky, 'Brand Interpol', p. 107: 'The concept of "ordinary law crimes" is important, but its meaning is complicated. In French the term is *criminalité de droit commun*, but the term is not common parlance in either language'.

21 On this, see Sheptycky, 'Brand Interpol', pp. 107–108 referring, inter alia, to the case of the hijacking of three Czechoslovak planes to West Germany in 1950. According to Sheptycky, J. Edgar *Hoover* wanted to classify this as a political act and invoked this case – despite the issuing of red notices – as one of the main reasons for cutting the FBI's ties with Interpol. Also, see Anderson, *Policing the World*, pp. 45–50 on '[t]he intrusion of political issues'.

a result of this development, increasingly governed by multilateral CoE conventions,[22] police cooperation remained first outside this legal framework. Only during the negotiations of the European Convention on Mutual Assistance in Criminal Matters (EuCMACM) of 1959, consideration was given to include a regulation providing for 'information concerning a criminal matter to be exchanged directly between "police authorities acting in an auxiliary capacity to the judicial authorities"'.[23] Yet, '[t]he majority of the experts were in favour of making no such provision. They thought it best not to force the existing practice of the police into a rigid mould, besides which, the Statute of the International Criminal Police Organisation (Interpol) already regulated mutual assistance between police authorities.'[24] Even with the existence of the EEC police cooperation initially remained of an intergovernmental nature, based on international treaties[25] or characterised by pragmatic informal networks, such as the Dutch-Belgian-German Police Working Group, founded in 1969.[26] Yet, with the increasing cross-border political or terrorist violence of the 1970s, there was a need to go beyond the existing framework, which, after all, too much reminded of the initiatives during the above mentioned nineteenth-century anarchism.[27] For example, the German Red Army Faction crossed borders, especially operating in and from Belgium and the Netherlands.

Interestingly a major factor for this European development was the fact, already mentioned above,[28] that Interpol took an apolitical approach, apparently excluding political offences committed by left-wing and also right-wing groups from its mandate,[29] at least until its General Assembly

[22] Of particular interest are the European Convention on Mutual Assistance in Criminal Matters (EuCMACM) of 20 April 1959 (ETS 30) and its Additional Protocols (AP I EuCMACM of 17 March 1978 and AP II EucMACM of 8 November 2011, ETS 99 and 182).

[23] Explanatory Report – ETS 30 – Mutual Assistance in Criminal Matters (Convention), p. 3, available at https://rm.coe.int/16800c92bd (accessed 4 March 2022).

[24] Ibid; for more details on this, see also Fijnaut, *A Peaceful Revolution*, pp. 99–100.

[25] H. Aden, 'Europäische Rechtsgrundlagen und Institutionen des Polizeihandelns', in M. Bäcker et al. (eds.), *Handbuch des Polizeirechts*, 6th edn., Munich: C.H. Beck, 2018, p. 1627.

[26] It established, inter alia, direct radio or fax links and appointed contact officers in the Meuse-Rhine Region. See T. Spapens, 'Building Trust and More', in S. Hufnagel and C. McCartney (eds.), *Trust in International Police and Justice Cooperation*, Oxford, Portland, OR: Hart Publishing, 2017, p. 149 with further examples of cooperation initiatives in border regions.

[27] See main text to fn. 21. On this similarity, see Anderson, *Policing the World*, p. 28.

[28] See main text to fn. 2.

[29] Fijnaut, *A Peaceful Revolution*, pp. 130–131.

of 1984.[30] At any rate, at the European level the TREVI Group (Terrorism, Radicalism, Extremism et Violence Internationale) was set up on the initiative of the United Kingdom.[31] TREVI differs from Interpol in several ways. While Interpol (as well as its predecessor ICPC) was not created by an agreement between States but resulted from an informal meeting of police officers as an intergovernmental organisation,[32] TREVI was founded in Rome in 1975 by the interior ministers of the EEC Member States (MS)[33] thus was, as an explicit State decision under the umbrella of the CoE, from the outset more firmly integrated into the respective States' security.[34] Nevertheless, tensions became quickly apparent with regard to the question of whether TREVI – although linked to State structures – should rather represent a forum for practical, case-related quick solutions to crime problems or whether it should be understood as an instrument of European integration in the field of internal security. While France and the United Kingdom preferred the former view, Germany always perceived TREVI as a further element of European integration.[35]

13.1.3 Developing Police Cooperation within the European Union Legal Framework

With the founding of the European Union (EU) through the Treaty of Maastricht in 1993, provisions on police cooperation found, for the first time, their way into the primary law, namely into the former Third Pillar,

[30] At that point, Interpol modified its restrictive Interpretation of Art. 3 Statut de l'O.I.P.C.-INTERPOL and has become more active with regard to terrorist crimes (see Anderson, *Policing the World*, pp. 28 and 144–145). It is obvious that this expansion of Interpol has its downside since it may be instrumentalised by certain States within the framework of their politically motivated investigations (see Aden, 'Europäische Rechtsgrundlagen und Institutionen des Polizeihandelns', p. 1663).

[31] E. Oberloskamp, *Codename TREVI*, Oldenbourg: De Gruyter, 2017, pp. 81 ff.; Fijnaut, *A Peaceful Revolution*, pp. 131–32;

[32] Anderson, *Policing the World*, p. 57.

[33] A. Weyemberg, 'History of the Cooperation', in R. E. Kostoris (ed.), *Handbook of European Criminal Procedure*, Cham: Springer, 2018, p. 175 ('initial structure from which police cooperation within the European Union originated').

[34] Fijnaut, *A Peaceful Revolution*, p. 132; id., 'Revolution or evolution through the Treaty of Lisbon', in H. Aden (ed.), Police Cooperation in the European Union under the Treaty of Lisbon, p. 33.

[35] See E. Oberloskamp, *Codename TREVI*, Oldenbourg: De Gruyter, 2017, pp. 192 ff. In France, the political left's reservations about West Germany's methods in its fight against left-wing terrorism in the 1970s probably contributed to this (p. 193).

characterised by intergovernmental cooperation.[36] Probably the most visible achievements of the Third Pillar are the Convention establishing Europol[37] and (in the field of mutual legal assistance) the European Convention on Mutual Assistance in Criminal Matters (EUMAC) of 2000.[38] However, police cooperation has largely developed outside the European (EEC/EU) Integration process, as can be seen from the fact that one of its most important instruments, the 1990 Convention Implementing the 1985 Schengen Agreement (CISA),[39] has been adopted as a multilateral treaty outside the EU framework.[40] One of the main reasons for this seems to be that there are important forms of police cooperation in everyday practice which – unlike extradition as the classic feature of judicial cooperation – by their very nature only concern neighbouring States. For example, a hot pursuit regulation between Germany and Spain, lacking common borders, is simply not necessary. Given the different situation in the Schengen area, the five[41] founding MS regulated important elements of police cooperation outside the framework of the EEC or the EU, although later to be transferred to the Third Pillar by the Amsterdam Treaty of 1999[42] and, as a result of Protocol 19 to the Lisbon Treaty, now applicable in the 27 EU States and four non-EU States.[43] Clearly, the practical needs of cross-border cooperation (beyond the exchange of information) always seemed to be more regional or specific[44] than the forms of judicial cooperation in criminal matters.

[36] D. Kugelmann, 'Europäische Polizeiliche Kooperation', in M. Böse (ed.), *Europäisches Strafrecht – Enzyklopädie Europarecht*, 2nd edn., Baden-Baden: Nomos, 2021, p. 892. For a detailed account of the development of the primary law framework of police cooperation in the EU, see Weyemberg, 'History of the Cooperation', pp. 178 ff.

[37] On Europol, see Chapter 15 by K. Ligeti and F. Giuffridaof this volume.

[38] OJ C 197, 12.7.2000, p. 1. [39] OJ L 239, 22.9.2000, p. 10.

[40] D.A. Heid, 'Before and after the Treaty of Lisbon', in H. Aden (ed.), *Police Cooperation in the European Union under the Treaty of Lisbon*, Baden-Baden: Nomos, 2015, p. 67 ('core part of EU law'). Interestingly, proposals of Nebegedeagpol (see above main text at fn. 26) eventually made their way into Art. 39 and 46 CISA, see T. Spapens, 'Building Trust and More', pp. 155–6.

[41] France, Germany and the Benelux States.

[42] See Protocol integrating the Schengen acquis into the framework of the European Union, OJ C 340, 10.11.1997, p. 93. For more details, see Heid, 'Before and after the Treaty of Lisbon', pp. 72–5.

[43] See Lisbon Treaty, Protocol (No. 19) on the Schengen Acquis Integrated into the Framework of the EU, OJ C 326, 26.10.2012, p. 290. For more details on this, see K. Ambos, *European Criminal Law*, Cambridge: Cambridge University Press, 2018, p. 412.

[44] See, for example below with regard to the European Investigation Order main text to fn. 58.

The so-called (bilateral) police treaties further confirm that the concrete needs for police cooperation differ considerably even within the EU. Thus, Germany, for example, has, given its relatively long land borders in the middle of the EU, concluded police agreements with all neighbouring States.[45] These treaties, which allow direct cooperation between police authorities differ significantly in content and scope and continue to supplement CISA (which remains in force) pursuant to Art. 39(5) CISA.[46] A case similar to the Schengen law (CISA) is the Prüm Treaty of 2005 as a current core element of European police cooperation,[47] which, like Schengen, is based on an agreement adopted outside the EU legal framework,[48] only later transferred to the legal framework of EU law.[49] The Prüm approach, demonstrating again the specificity of police cooperation compared to judicial cooperation in criminal matters in Europe, combines (in a rather heterogeneous-pragmatic way) very different repressive and preventive forms of police activity, ranging from joint patrols to information exchange (to be dealt with in more detail below[50]). Yet, compared to CISA, forms of information exchange are more prominent here, with the addition that the Prüm Treaty implemented the principle of availability for the first time.[51] Given that this kind of cooperation did not meet consensus yet in the beginning of the twentieth century within the EU, the Prüm EU Member States felt compelled to take the lead.[52]

Yet, only a year after Prüm, the EU adopted a legislative instrument on information exchange.[53] The particular importance of this so-called

[45] See Kugelmann, 'Europäische Polizeiliche Kooperation', p. 929. Yet, also see Anderson, *Policing the World*, p. 21 interestingly suspecting (older) police agreements to be seemingly 'designed to limit rather than extend police contacts'.

[46] Kugelmann, 'Europäische Polizeiliche Kooperation', pp. 929–30.

[47] In this vein, Kugelmann, 'Europäische Polizeiliche Kooperation', p. 920.

[48] Founding members are Germany, France, Luxembourg, the Netherlands, Austria and Spain. See Gaetano De Amicis, 'Horizontal Cooperation', in R. E Kostoris (ed.), *Handbook of European Criminal Procedure*, Cham: Springer, 2018, p. 257.

[49] See Council Decision 2008/616/JHA of 23 June 2008 on the implementation of Decision 2008/615/JHA on the stepping up of cross-border cooperation, particularly in combating terrorism and cross-border crime, OJ L 210, 6.8.2008, p. 12.

[50] See main text at fn. 110. [51] See main text at fn. 111 ff.

[52] Kugelmann, 'Europäische Polizeiliche Kooperation', p. 919.

[53] Framework Decision 2006/960/JHA on simplifying the exchange of information and intelligence between law enforcement authorities of the Member States of the European Union of 18 December 2006, OJ L 386, 29.12.2006, p. 89.

'Swedish Framework Decision'[54] (SFD) stems from the fact that it envisages, based on the principle of availability, the direct exchange of information between police authorities (without the intermediation of central offices).[55] While the subsequent Lisbon Treaty finally abandoned the pillar structure, the regulation of police cooperation at the level of primary law remained sketchy.[56] The 2014 Directive on the European Investigation Order (EIO Directive),[57] explicitly based on the principle of mutual recognition, primarily deals with judicial cooperation, but also contains provisions specifically tailored to the police sector. This applies in particular to Art. 29 EIO Directive on undercover investigations. Art. 29(3)(b) and (4) EIO Directive make cross-border personal investigations subject to the conclusion of corresponding 'arrangements for the covert investigations' at the level of the police (Art. 29(4) EIO Directive). In effect, this means that it is still completely in the hands of the police whether such cooperation takes place at all.[58] Indeed, subjecting undercover personal investigations to the principle of mutual recognition is hardly a realistic scenario. And, thus, Art. 29 EIO Directive shows once more the limits of this principle.[59]

13.2 The State of Affairs in 2022

On the basis of the above considerations, it is fair to say that police cooperation within the EU rests on somewhat fragmented normative foundations. In practice, it is largely based on the CISA, the Prüm Treaty, the SFD and – to a considerable extent – on bilateral police agreements. Against this background, it seems more appropriate to discuss the current

[54] It was based on a 'Swedish Initiative', see, for example W. Bogensberger, 'Police Cooperation', in Manuel Kellerbauer et al. (eds.), *The EU Treaties and the Charter of Fundamental Rights*, Oxford: Oxford University Press, 2019, p. 927.

[55] Kugelmann, 'Europäische Polizeiliche Kooperation', pp. 923–4.

[56] See S. Gleß. 'Police and Judicial Cooperation between the European Union Member States', in C. Fijnaut and Jannemieke Ouwerkek (eds.), *The Future of Police and Judicial Cooperation in the EU*, Brill: Leiden, 2010, p. 26 ('the treaties of the European Union do not define police and/or judicial cooperation as such'), 40 ('the Lisbon Treaty sketches its vision of police cooperation only very roughly in Arts 87-89') and very critical at p. 41 ('Reorganisation of police cooperation is thus not possible under the Lisbon Treaty').

[57] Directive 2014/41/EU of 3 April 2014, OJ C 18, 1.5.2014, p. 1.

[58] Cf. P. Rackow, 'Überlegungen zu dem Gesetz zur Änderung des IRG vom 5.1.2017', (2017) 2 *KripoZ*, 84–5.

[59] On the principle of mutual recognition, Chapter 6 by P. Ronsfeld of this volume.

state of affairs not so much focusing on the legal foundations, but on the possible forms of cooperative police activity.

Given the practice of undercover cross-border investigations (as well as the type of investigations carried out by Joint Investigation Teams (JITs)), it seems to be clear that it would be too narrow to limit the concept of 'police cooperation involving all the MS' competent authorities' within the meaning of Art. 87(1) TFEU to such forms of activity that only involve police authorities and/or do not require judicial authorisation.[60] In the following, our considerations shall be limited to forms of direct, case-related cooperation.[61] Thus, for example, mere cooperation in the area of education and training (especially within the framework of the Collège Européen de Police, CEPOL)[62] will not be considered. At any rate, given the variety of different forms of 'direct cooperation' and the limited extension of this contribution, a restriction to the most important or problematic forms of cooperation is necessary.[63]

13.3 Forms of Activity

13.3.1 Direct Cross-Border Police Activity

Direct police operations across the EU include, inter alia, on the one hand, open hot pursuit and cross-border covert surveillance and, on the other, such forms of police criminal investigations that, by definition, are designed to take place abroad.[64]

60 For example, under German law, covert investigations require the consent of the public prosecutor (§ 110b (1) StPO) and JITs are often led by (investigating) judges or public prosecutors (see below, main text at fn. 76). Cf. also W. Bogensberger, 'Police Cooperation', in Manuel Kellerbauer et al. (eds.), *The EU Treaties and the Charter of Fundamental Rights*, Oxford: Oxford University Press, 2019, p. 923 ('notion ... is very broad').

61 See G. Meško, 'Police Cooperation in the European Union, Supported by Strengthening the EU Internal Security's External Dimension', (2017) 25 *ECCL*, 113 ('exchange of information and data, and operational measures').

62 See www.cepol.europa.eu/ (accessed 4 March 2022).

63 Thus, the exchange of liaison officers cannot be treated in the following (for more details on this, see Amicis, 'Horizontal Cooperation', p. 254). On the 'Police Cooperation Centers', that is liaison offices of neighbouring States, which are particularly important for Germany due to its central geographical location and in which multlingual officials (without executive powers) coordinate or support investigations on both sides of the border, see Kugelmann, 'Europäische Polizeiliche Kooperation', p. 931.

64 Cf. M. Fahrner, *Handbuch Internationale Ermittlungen*, München: C.H. Beck, 2020, pp. 62–63.

13.3.1.1 Cross-Border Surveillance

Cross-border surveillance is of particular relevance across the EU given the high number of States with common borders in a relatively small geographical area.[65] Cross-border surveillance could be regulated by secondary legislation pursuant to Art. 89 TFEU[66] but is still carried out on the basis of Art. 40 CISA or, if applicable, a more far-reaching bilateral treaty (Art. 39(5) CISA). The 2017 EIO Directive is not applicable.[67] Under Art. 40(1) CISA, cross-border surveillance requires, as a rule, the consent of the territorial State and is limited to extraditable offences. However, Art. 40(2) CISA allows for the continuation of the surveillance for certain offences listed in Art. 40(7) CISA without the prior consent of the territorial State.[68] Police officers who cross a State border in the course of such a surveillance may carry their service weapons with them, but only use them in self-defence (Art. 40(3)(d) CISA). They are neither allowed to enter private homes and places nor to make arrests (Art. 40(3)(e–f) CISA). However, some bilateral police treaties go beyond Art. 40 CISA allowing for cross-border surveillance for the purpose of ensuring the execution of custodial sentences imposed for extraditable offences.[69]

13.3.1.2 Cross-Border Hot Pursuit

Cross-border hot pursuit is regulated in Art. 41 CISA in a manner similar to cross-border surveillance under Art. 40 CISA. However, in a case of hot pursuit, it will often not be possible to obtain the prior consent of the territorial (target or destination) State. Art. 41(1) CISA therefore allows the border to be crossed if, due to the 'particular urgency of the situation', it is not possible to inform the competent authorities of the target State or they are not able to continue the pursuit.[70] The pursuing officer

[65] See K. Ambos, *European Criminal Law*, Cambridge: Cambridge University Press, 2018, p. 412.

[66] Cf. Aden, 'Europäische Rechtsgrundlagen und Institutionen des Polizeihandelns', p. 1697.

[67] Cf. recital 9 ('This Directive should not apply to cross-border surveillance as referred to in the Convention implementing the Schengen Agreement').

[68] Cf. M. Kubiciel, 'Schengener Durchführungsübereinkommen', in K. Ambos et al. (eds.), *Rechtshilferecht in Strafsachen*, 2nd edn., Munich: C.H. Beck, 2020, p. 971.

[69] Cf. Fahrner, *Handbuch Internationale Ermittlungen*, p. 65.

[70] K. Ambos, *European Criminal Law*, Cambridge: Cambridge University Press, 2018, pp. 412–3.

may detain the person pursued until the officials of the target State can take over (Art. 41(2)(b) CISA).[71] As in cases of cross-border surveillance, service weapons may be carried when crossing the border, but may only be used in self-defence (Art. 41(5)(e) CISA). It is up to the territorial (destination or target) State to declare (Art. 41(9) CISA) for which offences hot pursuit shall be permitted and define them (Art. 41(4) CISA) with a view to the list in Art. 41(4)(a) CISA or as extraditable offences (Art. 41(4)(b)).[72] The target State also determines any limitations in terms of space or time (Art. 41(3) CISA).

It follows that the scope of the rights of the pursuing State may vary considerably depending on the declarations made by the target State under Art. 41(9) CISA. For example, German police officers have a right of detention in the Netherlands insofar as the pursuit relates to an extraditable offence, in Belgium they have the right to detain for the first thirty minutes after crossing the border, whereas France does not grant German police officers this right at all.[73] This makes clear that there is no EU-wide common denominator and there still exist historical sensibilities.[74] The situation is further fragmented by some bilateral police treaties which go beyond Art. 41(1) CISA permitting cross-border pursuit not only of persons caught in the criminal act or on the run but also when the pursued person has evaded a dragnet control.[75]

13.3.1.3 Joint Investigation Teams

The use of JITs (as well as cross-border covert investigations) obviously differs from cross-border surveillance or hot pursuit in that such measures are not spontaneous but normally planned in advance. The Council's JITs Practical Guide defines a JIT as 'an international cooperation tool based on an agreement between competent authorities – both judicial

[71] Cf. Kubiciel, 'Schengener Durchführungsübereinkommen', p. 975.

[72] Cf. Fahrner, *Handbuch Internationale Ermittlungen*, p. 70.

[73] See the declarations pursuant to Art. 41(9) CISA of the Netherlands, Belgium and France reprinted (partially) in W. Schomburg and S. Gleß, 'Ausgewählte Erklärungen soweit für Deutschland und Österreich rechtshilferechtlich relevant', in W. Schomburg et al. (eds.), *Internationale Rechtshilfe in Strafsachen*, 4th edn., München: C.H. Beck, 2006, pp. 1457–8.

[74] Thus, for example, six years before Schengen, Anderson, *Policing the World*, p. 158 (with regard to bilateral police cooperation practices at the Franco-German border) opined that 'any presence of German police on French territory reawakens historic memories of the German annexation of Alsac-Lorraine from 1870–1918 and from 1940–45'.

[75] See Fahrner, *Handbuch Internationale Ermittlungen*, pp. 70–1.

(judges, prosecutors, investigative judges...) and law enforcement – of two or more States, established for a limited duration and for a specific purpose, to carry out criminal investigations in one or more of the involved States'.[76] The most concrete basis of a JIT is thus an agreement between the acting authorities in which the modalities of the operation are defined. The practical importance of the measure and the underlying agreement becomes manifest by the fact that the Council has provided a model agreement on the establishment of JITs.[77]

As far as the legal basis for JITs is concerned, Art. 3 EIO Directive explicitly states that the existing legal foundations should continue to be used.[78] This may be explained by the consideration that evidence obtained through a JIT is considered as having been obtained nationally and therefore there is, strictly speaking, no cross-border and mutual assistance issue in terms of the available evidence.[79] Further, JITs are agreed by consensus and not imposed by or an unilateral act of one party as happens under the principle of mutual recognition.[80] Be that as it may, in addition to Art. 13

[76] Council. Doc. 6128/1/17 REV 1, p. 4; also, see Meško, 'Police Cooperation in the European Union, Supported by Strengthening the EU Internal Security's External Dimension', 114.

[77] Council Resolution 2017/C 18/01) on a Model Agreement for Setting up a Joint Investigation Team (JIT), OJ C 18, 19.1.2017, p. 1.

[78] Art. 3 EIO Directive refers in this respect to Art. 13 EUMAC and the Council Framework Decision 2002/465/JHA of 13 June 2002 on JITs (OJ L 162, 20.6.2002, p. 1).

[79] In this vein, L. Wörner, 'Die Europäische Ermittlungsanordnung (RL EEA)', in K. Ambos, S. König and P. Rackow (eds.), *Rechtshilferecht in Strafsachen*, 2nd edn., Baden-Baden: Nomos, 2020, p. 1091; furthermore, see Council Doc. 9288/10 ADD 1, p. 5. Art. 13(10) EUMAC clarifies that evidence obtained in the course of a JIT is in principle admissible. For the related cases of cross-border surveillance and cross-border covert investigations, however, there are no corresponding provisions (apart from regulations on cross-border covert investigations in the German-Austrian and German-Dutch police treaties, which stipulate that the requested State can impose conditions on the use of evidence), so that the question of the admissibility of evidence remains unresolved (on this, see Rackow, 'Überlegungen zum EU-Rechtsrahmen grenzüberschreitender VE-Einsätze', (2013) 104 *Die Polizei*, pp. 311–2. Furthermore, see below fn. 86).

[80] See Council Doc. 9288/10 ADD 1, p. 5: 'However, some measures require specific rules which are better dealt with separately. This applies to the setting up of a JIT and the gathering of evidence within a JIT .... The creation of the team requires for example the signing of a complex agreement' furthermore, Art. 13(12) EUMAC and Art. 1(12) Council Framework Decision 2002/465/JHA provide scope for the involvement of investigators from non-member states. On the JIT consisting of several EU MS and Ukraine, investigating core crimes in ukraine since 25 March 2022, cf. https://www.eurojust.europa.eu/news/eurojust-supports-joint-investigation-team-alleged-core-international-crimes-ukraine, accessed 11 November 2022.

EUMAC and the Council Framework Decision 2002/465/JHA of 13 June 2002 on JITs,[81] the Council's model agreement proposes no fewer than seven possible legal bases (considered as a non-exhaustive list) to be used by competent authorities from EU States to establish a JIT.[82]

The relevant EU legal instruments allow for the formation of a JIT where, on the one hand, complex cross-border investigations have to be carried out and, on the other, interrelated investigations in several States have to be coordinated.[83] Each participating State appoints a JIT leader. This national JIT leader will be in charge if the group is operating in the territory of his/her State.[84] The other JIT members operate outside their own territory as so-called seconded members, who have the right to be present during investigations (unless the JIT leader decides otherwise). They can be tasked by the JIT leader, if both sides agree, to carry out certain investigative measures and are entitled to bring relevant information from their State into the group.[85] The core idea of the measure is, ultimately, to enable all sending States to use the information obtained by their members within the framework of the JIT (at least) for the purposes for which the JIT was formed.[86]

13.3.1.4 Cross-Border Covert Investigations

While all the measures analysed here affect individual rights and – given their cross-border nature – the sovereignty interests of the target State, the effect of cross-border covert personal investigations may,

[81] OJ L 162, 20.6.2002, p. 1.

[82] The following legal bases are mentioned: Art. 1 of the Agreement between the EU and the Republic of Iceland and the Kingdom of Norway on the application of certain provisions of the Convention of 29 May 2000 on Mutual Assistance in Criminal Matters between the Member States of the EU and the 2001 Protocol thereto of 29 December 2003 (OJ C 197, 12.7.2000, p. 3); Art. 5 of the Agreement on Mutual Legal Assistance between the EU and the USA (OJ L 181, 19.7.2003, p. 34); Art. 20 AP II EucMACM of 8 November 2011 (ETS 182); Art. 9(1)(c) of the UN Convention against Illicit Traffic in Narcotic Drugs and Psychotropic Substance (UNTS vol. 1582, p. 95); Art. 19 of the UN Convention against Transnational Organized Crime (UNTS vol. 2225, p. 209); Art. 49 of the UN Convention against Corruption (UNTS vol. 2349, p. 41); Art. 27 of the Police Cooperation Convention for South East Europe (www.pccseesecretariat.si/, accessed 4 March 2022).

[83] Council. Doc. 6128/1/17 REV 1, p. 6; also, see A. Klip, *European Criminal Law*, 4th edn., Cambridge et al.: Intersentia, 2021, p. 594.

[84] Council. Doc. 6128/1/17 REV 1, p. 8. [85] Council. Doc. 6128/1/17 REV 1, p. 9.

[86] See Art. 13(10)(a) EUMAC ('Information lawfully obtained by a member or seconded member while part of a joint investigation team which is not otherwise available to the competent authorities of the Member States concerned may be used for the following purposes: (a) for the purposes for which the team has been set up'); Art. 20(10)(a) AP II EuCMACM is largely identical.

arguably, be more intense.[87] In addition, the cross-border deployment of undercover police officers (not embedded into a JIT) requires clarity about the rights and duties of these undercover agents, not least in their own interest.[88] Art. 14 EUMAC, as the first EU legal basis, provides insofar that the requesting and requested MS can agree to assist each other in covert investigations (Art. 14(1) EUMAC), with the exact modalities of the deployment to be mutually agreed (Art. 14(2) EUMAC). A largely parallel provision is then contained in Art. 19 of the 2nd Additional Protocol to the 1959 CoE Mutual Assistance Convention of 8 November 2001.[89]

Remarkably, Art. 29 EIO Directive does not in any way create an obligation for the territorial (requested/executing) State, that is, this State can impede any (covert) investigative measure. Similar to the former standards, Art. 29(4) provides that, '[t]he duration of the covert investigation, the detailed conditions, and the legal status of the officers concerned during covert investigations shall be agreed between the issuing State and the executing State with due regard to their national laws and procedures'. In the event that such an agreement cannot be reached, Art. 29(3)(b) EIO Directive foresees an explicit ground for rejection[90] Thus, it is ultimately up to the competent authorities of the requested State to produce the rejection of the authorisation by making the negotiations on the undercover mission to fail or declare them as failed.[91] Although the EIO Directive is, at least formally, based on the principle of mutual recognition, Article 29 does not impose an obligation to comply with a request for assistance in undercover personal investigations if the conditions for an undercover operation in the requesting State are met.[92]

[87] In the context of covert personal investigations, the target persons are approached on a personal level, which has an independent quality compared to, for example interception of telecommunication. Cf. the case of British undercover investigators who allegedly had sexual relations with environmental activists for investigative purposes (www.theguardian.com/uk-news/2021/apr/20/police-spys-bosses-knew-activist-was-being-duped-into-sexual-relationship-court-told, accessed 4 March 2022).

[88] Cf. Fahrner, *Handbuch Internationale Ermittlungen*, p. 83.

[89] C. Schierholt, 'Art. 19 2. ZP-EuRhÜbk', in S. Gleß et al. (eds.), *Schomburg/Lagodny – Internationale Rechtshilfe in Strafsachen*, 6th edn., München: C.H. Beck, 2020, p. 986.

[90] 'In addition to the grounds for non-recognition and non-execution referred to in Article 11, the executing authority may refuse to execute an EIO referred to in paragraph 1, where: ... (b) it was not possible to reach an agreement on the arrangements for the covert investigations under paragraph 4'.

[91] Cf. BT-Drs. 18/9757, p. 69. [92] cf. already above main text with fn. 58.

Again, there may be more detailed regulations on cross-border covert investigations in bilateral police treaties, such as Art. 14 of the German-Dutch Treaty and Art. 17 of the Treaty between Germany and the Czech Republic.[93]

13.3.2 The Exchange of Information

The exchange of police information within the framework of the EU still takes place through various (informal) channels. The Commission's proposal to create a uniform European Information Exchange Model (EIXM)[94] has not been successful so far.[95] At any rate, the still relevant informal networks, such as the Police Working Group on Terrorism,[96] are now complemented by forms of automated exchange of information.[97] Insofar a distinction can be made between central databases and enabling access to databases of other MS.

13.3.2.1 Central Databases

The best-known central database to which the police forces of the MS have access is the Schengen Information System (SIS). It has been established in 1995 pursuant to Art. 92–119 CISA.[98] As early as 2006, the EU began to lay the legal foundation for the further development of the SIS into SIS II.[99] This explains why the SIS II, being a single database, is based on two legal acts that only entered into force in 2013: on the one hand, EC Regulation 1987/2006 as regards the areas of visa, asylum,

93 See Rackow, 'Überlegungen zum EU-Rechtsrahmen grenzüberschreitender VE-Einsätze', 306–7.

94 See Communication from the Commission to the European Parliament and the Council. Strengthening law enforcement cooperation in the EU: the European Information Exchange Model (EIXM), COM(2012) 735 final.

95 Aden, 'Europäische Rechtsgrundlagen und Institutionen des Polizeihandelns', p. 1663; H. Aden, 'Europäisierung der Polizeiarbeit', in C. Kopke and W. Kühnel (eds.), *Demokratie, Freiheit und Sicherheit*, Baden-Baden: Nomos, 2017, p. 245.

96 Aden, 'Europäische Rechtsgrundlagen und Institutionen des Polizeihandelns', p. 1662.

97 In addition, there is (of course) still the possibility of non-automated exchange of information by way of specific requests, in particular on the basis of the SFD (see below main text at fn. 117–115) or Art. 39 CISA, as far as Art. 39 CISA is still referred to by a bilateral police treaty (see Art. 12(1) and (3) SFD; on this cf. S. Trautmann, 'Rb-Informationsaustausch', in S. Gleß et al. (eds.), *Schomburg/Lagodny – Internationale Rechtshilfe in Strafsachen*, 6th edn., München: C.H. Beck, 2020, p. 1534).

98 K. Ambos, *European Criminal Law*, Cambridge: Cambridge University Press, 2018, p. 424.

99 Ibid., p. 426.

immigration and free movement of persons; on the other, Council Decision 2007/533/JHA (SIS II Decision) as to – of interest here – the area of police-judicial cooperation, formerly located in the Third Pillar.[100] The system contains 'alerts on persons and objects' (Art. 2(I) SIS II Decision, formerly Art. 92(3) CISA), inserted by the MS. The alerts relate to, inter alia, persons wanted for arrest for the purpose of extradition (Art. 26–31 SIS II Decision, formerly Art. 95 CISA), persons or vehicles for purposes of discreet surveillance or specific checks (Art. 36–37, formerly Art. 99 CISA) and data on objects sought for the purposes of seizure or use as evidence in criminal proceedings (Art. 38–9 SIS II Decision, formerly Art. 100 CISA).[101] In particular, SIS II has created the technical and legal possibilities to deposit photographs and fingerprints in the alerts (Art. 20(3)(e-f) SIS II Decision).[102] Apart from that, under SIS II an old problem of the previous system has been solved: Under Art. 95(2) CISA the State issuing an alert for the arrest of a person had to check whether the arrest was admissible under the law of all (!) MS. Given that this is not even feasible in bigger MS there was a high risk of unlawful arrests in view of the automated processes triggered by an alert.[103] Under the new regime, Art. 24(1) SIS II Decision provides that, in the case of an alert, the potential detention States shall consider whether the measure would be admissible under their respective laws.

To the extent that MS access the SIS database (and then act on their territory according to the alerts),[104] the SIS system can be compared, in structural terms, to police cooperation within the framework of Interpol. However, communication with the 'Interpol Global Communication System 24/7' takes place via the national contact points, in Germany,

[100] Cf. F. Meyer and S.D. Hüttemann, 'Internationale Fahndung nach Personen', (2016) 128 *ZStW*, 397; S. Gleß and T. Wahl, 'Das Schengener Informationssystem', in S. Gleß et al. (eds.), *Schomburg/Lagodny – Internationale Rechtshilfe in Strafsachen*, 6th edn., München: C.H. Beck, 2020, pp. 2026–7.

[101] Klip, *European Criminal Law*, p. 583.

[102] Meyer and Hüttemann, 'Internationale Fahndung nach Personen', (2016), 397, 398; S. Gleß and T. Wahl, 'Das Schengener Informationssystem', in S. Gleß et al. (eds.), *Schomburg/Lagodny – Internationale Rechtshilfe in Strafsachen*, 6th edn., München: C.H. Beck, 2020, p. 2029; K. Ambos, *European Criminal Law*, Cambridge: Cambridge University Press, 2018, p. 426.

[103] K. Ambos, *European Criminal Law*, Cambridge: Cambridge University Press, 2018, p. 424.

[104] The German Federal Police (Bundespolizei), for example, is entitled under § 34(1)(No. 1) BPolG (Gesetz über die Bundespolizei – Federal Police Act) to cross-check personal data collected during police controls with the SIS database.

for example via the BKA (Federal Criminal Police Office).[105] By contrast, under the SIS direct access is possible. This means (for Germany, for example) that the investigating police officer automatically triggers a SIS search through her request in the national search system and should receive the result within a short period,[106] a feature very much welcomed by law enforcement officials.[107] A further significant difference is, of course, that Interpol does not issue binding requests,[108] but the cooperation within the framework of SIS II imposes an obligation of the MS.[109]

As already indicated, the (essential) elements of the Prüm approach, initially created as a multilateral treaty, have been transferred into Union law – in a similar fashion as the Schengen acquis.[110] The importance of the Prüm approach in the information/data context is due to the fact that the 2005 Prüm Treaty as the first international instrument applied the principle of availability.[111] Its main rationale is to grant law enforcement

[105] See J. Ruthig, '§ 3 Internationale Zusammenarbeit', in W.-R. Schenke et al. (eds.), *Sicherheitsrecht des Bundes*, Munich: C.H. Beck, 2019, p. 426.

[106] See G. Dannecker, 'Art. 87 AEUV', in R. Streinz (ed.), *EUV/AEUV*, 3rd edn., Munich: C.H. Beck, 2018, p. 995; H. Aden, 'Police Information Sharing and Data Protection in the European Union before and after the Treaty of Lisbon', in H. Aden (ed.), *Police Cooperation in the European Union under the Treaty of Lisbon*, Baden-Baden: Nomos, 2015, p. 210.

[107] See, for example M. Tuffner, 'Das Schengener Informationssystem (SIS) – Ein Quantensprung der polizeilichen Fahndung in Europa', (2000) 2 *Kriminalistik*, 39 ('quantum leap').

[108] Nevertheless, Interpol's red notice alerts are often implemented automatically in the form of the arrest of the alerted person, which, given the fact that Interpol currently has 194 Member States, entails the risk of political instrumentalisation (cf. www.ejiltalk.org/echoes-of-kadi-reforms-to-internal-remedies-at-interpol/, accessed 4 March 2022). Freedomhouse sees Russia as 'perhaps the world's most prolific abuser of the Interpol notice system', responsible for a disproportionate number of alerts ('38%') (https://freedomhouse.org/report/transnational-repression/russia, accessed 4 March 2022). The recent appointment of former Inspector General of the Ministry of Interior in the United Arab Emirates Ahmed Nasser al-Raisi, against whom allegations of torture have been made, as Interpol president has been heavily criticised (cf. www.bbc.com/news/world-middle-east-59417409, accessed 4 March 2022). It appears that the Russian share of all public red notices increased by another 6% to 44% from 2021 to 3 March 2022 (see C. Grafton and S. Bailey, *EJIL: Talk!*, 4 March 2022, www.ejiltalk.org/does-interpol-have-a-role-to-play-in-the-conflict-in-ukraine/, accessed 4 March 2022 (discussing the possibility of removing Russia from Interpol and Interpol's General Assembly's apparent unwillingness to do so)).

[109] Meyer and Hüttemann, 'Internationale Fahndung nach Personen', 399.

[110] See Council Decision 2008/615/JHA of 23 June 2008 on the Stepping up of Cross-border Cooperation, particularly in Combating Terrorism and Cross-bordercrime, OJ L 210, 6.8.2008, p. 1.

[111] See Klip, *European Criminal Law*, p. 469.

authorities mutual access to information and data.[112] While the principle of availability follows the logic of mutual recognition in that it is based on mutual trust as a prerequisite of information exchange, it is (strictly understood) limited to obtaining or transmitting information that indeed is already existing. At any rate, if the law enforcement authorities of a MS have information, this information should also be available to the authorities of the other States without discrimination,[113] even if it is highly sensitive information. One may perceive this as a compelling interpretation of the non-discrimination principle.[114] Notwithstanding, under Prüm the principle of availability is understood broadly, reaching beyond data that already exists and is therefore already 'available'. Thus, Art. 7 of the so-called Prüm Decision[115] provides that, upon request by a MS, a – not yet existing (available) – DNA profile is to be obtained through the collection and analysis of a biological sample.[116] By contrast, Art. 9 (facilitating the direct automated access of the MS to all DNA databases within the EU) and Art. 12 (doing the same with regard to all fingerprint files and to the vehicle registers) are more in line with a strictly understood principle of availability.

[112] D. Kugelmann, 'Europäische Polizeiliche Kooperation', p. 924.

[113] Kugelmann, 'Europäische Polizeiliche Kooperation', pp. 924–5 ('diskriminierungsfreier Austausch von Informationen'); furthermore, see M. Böse, *Der Grundsatz der Verfügbarkeit von Informationen in der strafrechtlichen Zusammenarbeit der Europäischen Union*, Göttingen et al.: V & R Unipress, 2007, p. 47 ('Gedanke einer Gleichbehandlung').

[114] See, in particular, Aden, 'Europäisierung der Polizeiarbeit', p. 250, who rightly points to considerable differences between the police forces of the various EU States with regard to, among other things, their relationship with intelligence services, their working cultures and their susceptibility to corruption. Furthermore, see H. Satzger, *International and European Criminal Law*, 2nd edn., München et al.: C.H. Beck et al., 2018, p. 163 ('the principle of availability makes criminal prosecution more effective at the expense of suspect's rights'). Too descriptive Amicis, 'Horizontal Cooperation', p. 257 ('... principles, ... originally conceived with regard to goods and products, have found application over time to capitals, services, judicial decisions and intangible properties such as data and information collected by public authorities'.).

[115] Council Decision 2008/615/JHA of 23 June 2008 on the Stepping up of Cross-border cooperation, particularly in Combating Terrorism and Cross-border Crime, OJ L 210, 6.8.2008, p. 1.

[116] Amicis, 'Horizontal Cooperation', p. 257; N. Lauer, *Informationsrechtshilfe im Rahmen der polizeilichen und justiziellen Zusammenarbeit in Strafsachen*, Baden-Baden: Nomos, 2018, pp. 133–4; furthermore, see S. Gleß, 'TerrBekämpfungs-Beschluss', in S. Gleß et al. (eds.), *Schomburg/Lagodny – Internationale Rechtshilfe in Strafsachen*, 6th edn., München: C.H. Beck, 2020, pp. 1548.

13.3.2.2 The Swedish Framework Decision (SFD)

Last, but not least, the SFD has special significance for practical police work insofar as it provides for direct contacts between the police authorities.[117] This means that information no longer has to be transmitted via central offices, such as the BKA in Germany.[118] While the Prüm approach can be described as a sectoral one, the SFD follows a more general approach that is not limited to specific data. In line with a broad concept of availability, the SFD relates instead to 'any type of information or data which is held by law enforcement authorities' or 'any type of information or data which is held by public authorities or by private entities and which is available to law enforcement authorities without the taking of coercive measures' (Art. 2(d) SFD). It is explicitly clarified that no obligations are to be created 'to obtain any information or intelligence by means of coercive measures, defined in accordance with national law' (Art. 1(5) SFD). Art. 10 provides only limited '[r]easons to withhold information or intelligence'. In this context, it is particularly noteworthy that only a 'clear' disproportionality of a request gives a right of refusal.[119] Similar to the provision in Art. 39(5) CISA, Art. 1(2) SFD leaves room for other agreements among MS.[120]

13.4 Conclusion

It should have become clear that police cooperation in criminal matters within the EU still appears to be a rather fragmented and confusingly

[117] See Art. 6(1) SFD 'Exchange of information and intelligence under this Framework Decision may take place via existing channels for international law enforcement cooperation'.

[118] See Kubiciel, 'Schengener Durchführungsübereinkommen', p. 968 with regard to Art. 39(3) CISA, which as a rule provides for communication via the 'the central bodies responsible in each Contracting Party for international police cooperation'.

[119] Cf. Art. 10(1)(c) SFD: 'Without prejudice to Article 3(3), a competent law enforcement authority may refuse to provide information or intelligence only if there are factual reasons to assume that the provision of the information or intelligence would: ... (c) clearly be disproportionate or irrelevant with regard to the purposes for which it has been requested.' On this, see Lauer, *Informationsrechtshilfe im Rahmen der polizeilichen und justiziellen Zusammenarbeit in Strafsachen*, p. 119 (advocating a restrictive interpretation based on teleological considerations).

[120] 'This Framework Decision shall be without prejudice to bilateral or multilateral agreements or arrangements between Member States and third countries and to instruments of the European Union on mutual legal assistance or mutual recognition of decisions regarding criminal matters, including any conditions set by third countries concerning the use of information once supplied.'

regulated area. Alongside judicial cooperation, it seems almost a kind of special area of its own right and with its proper rules. From a policy perspective, it is fair to say that important steps towards this legal framework have been taken in reaction to established police practices.[121] From a more theoretical perspective, police cooperation appears to be less principle-based than its judicial counterpart. In this respect, it is somewhat unsurprising that Art. 87–89 TFEU – in contrast to Art. 82 TFEU – omit to invoke a kind of guiding principle such as that of mutual recognition. This lack of a principled approach, as compared for example to judicially dominated extradition, may be explained by the fact that criminal law enforcement typically takes place at rather early stages of criminal proceedings and pursues a pragmatic result-oriented approach,[122] which resists to be subjected to guiding principles.[123]

A similar picture emerges if one leaves the level of principles and takes a closer look at the concrete legal bases: while certain forms of investigative cross-border police activities are regulated in a quite detailed way (see again Art. 40, 41 CISA), the relevant legal bases in other areas discussed in this chapter (undercover investigations, JITs) merely form the basis or the framework for individual, case-related agreements of law enforcement official from different States with regard to concrete cases. This, too, can be explained with the great heterogeneity and dynamics of police investigative activities. This mode of cooperation, in turn, reminds us of the early forms of ad hoc cooperation essentially based on direct (personal) contacts.

Finally, as far as the area of information exchange is concerned, its dynamics is probably mainly due to the fact that the (guiding) principle of availability is less intensively and critically discussed than the principle of mutual recognition in the context of judicial cooperation in criminal matters. The result-oriented practice of police investigative activities

[121] See Spapens, 'Building Trust and More', p. 164 with reference to CISA (also see fn. 40): 'result of a combination of top-down initiatives, bottom-up pressure from practitioners who require specific tools'. Also, see Meško, 'Police Cooperation in the European Union, Supported by Strengthening the EU Internal Security's External Dimension', 110 ('constant process that develops proportionately with changes in the social environment in EU member states and beyond').

[122] See Aden, 'Europäisierung der Polizeiarbeit', p. 249 ('Orientierung weiter Teile der Zusammenarbeit an Logiken und Bedürfnissen der strafrechtlichen Ermittlung').

[123] Depending on the situation, a result desired by the police may be achieved by a database search or by complex cross-border undercover investigations.

seems to integrate the advances of IT technology with similar pragmatic ease in that, for example fingerprint technology has become a common instrument in the toolbox of police forces. At the same time, however, the considerable (qualitative) differences between the police authorities of EU MS[124] gives reason to question the extent to which the principle of availability really represents an appropriate basis for the exchange of police information. If this principle rather represents the theory than the practice of the daily police work,[125] we face an ambivalent situation, characterised by the combination of an old boys' mentality and the playing by somewhat formal rules with regard to the exchange of highly sensitive data. Be all this as it may, any descriptive and, in particular, any critical view of the practice of police cooperation in the EU needs to take into account its lines of development, its backgrounds and the particularities of cross-border repressive police activity.

Further Reading

Hartmut Aden (ed.) *Police cooperation in the European Union under the Treaty of Lisbon*, Baden-Baden: Nomos 2015.

Malcolm Anderson, *Policing the World*, Oxford: Clarendon 1989.

Cyrille Fijnaut, *A Peaceful Revolution. The Development of Police and Judicial Cooperation in the European Union*, Cambridge: Intersentia 2019.

Eva Oberloskamp, *Codename TREVI*, Oldenbourg: De Gruyter 2017.

Anne Weyemberg 'History of the Cooperation' in Roberto E. Kostoris (ed.) *Handbook of European Criminal Procedure*, Cham: Springer 2018, pp. 173–199.

[124] See above fn. 114. [125] Aden, 'Europäisierung der Polizeiarbeit', p. 250.

Part V

Institutions

Office de Lutte anti-fraude (OLAF) 14

Olivier Cahn

14.1 EU Anti-Fraud Policy – Administrative Investigations – EPPO

The European Union budget is mainly replenished by Member States' contributions and accessorily by resources accruing from VAT and customs duties. In 2020, it is set at 172,3 billion euros,[1] which allows the Union financing a wide range of projects and programmes within and outside its territory. The fraudulent misuse of these funds together with tax evasion impair the EU capacity to achieve its objectives; besides, it fuels organized crime[2] and affects citizens' confidence in the institutions. The difficulties faced by the Union in trying to curb these fraudulent activities are all the more considerable since, until the European Public Prosecutor[3] took office, it did not have the necessary law enforcement means of its own to fight them. Although the Treaty of Lisbon has substantially strengthened the Union's capacities in criminal law matters, such competence remains mainly in the hands of the Member States. Yet, to say the least, the Member States show an unequal culture of integrity in the use of public funds and rigour in the repression of their fraudulent use[4]; furthermore, EU programs often involve actors from various Member States and/or third countries.[5]

1 www.consilium.europa.eu/fr/policies/the-eu-budget/eu-annual-budget/2020-budget/.

2 P. Chassagne and K. Gjeloshaj Hysaj, 'La criminalité dans les Balkans', (2010) *Pouvoirs n°132 – Le crime organisé*, 127, at 129.

3 Council Regulation (EU) 2017/1939 of 12 October 2017 implementing enhanced cooperation on the establishment of the European Public Prosecutor's Office ('the EPPO'), OJ L 283, 31.10.2017, pp.1–71.

4 L. Kuhl, 'The European Public Prosecutor's Office – More Effective, Equivalent, and Independent Criminal Prosecution against Fraud?', (2017) *eucrim*, 135 at 138.

5 See OLAF, *Nineteenth Report of the European Anti-Fraud Office – 2018*, 2019, Executive summary.

As a consequence, the protection of its financial interests is a major and long-standing concern of the European Union.[6] As early as 1988, a task force, the 'Unit for the Coordination of Fraud Prevention' (UCLAF), integrated into the Secretariat-General of the European Commission, was set up to collaborate with the competent Member States' services in the fight against fraud involving European funds. Its means were substantially strengthened in 1993 and 1995. But in 1999, the *Cresson* scandal and the subsequent collective resignation of the *Santer* Commission highlighted UCLAF's weaknesses.[7] Therefore, OLAF was established by Commission Decision 1999/352/EC[8] and Regulations 1073/99 (EC)[9] and 1074/99 (Euratom)[10] as an independent investigative Commission agency. This legal basis remained valid after the entry into force of the Lisbon Treaty.[11] The Office was reorganised in 2006 to strengthen its operational capacities and improve its management. In 2011, the Commission launched a new strategy[12] to improve both the prevention and detection of fraud and to enhance fraud investigations in order to make them more efficient and deterrent and to increase the rate of the proceeds of crime's recovery. As a result, OLAF was reformed once again, weakening its legal basis which had already been undermined by the decisions handed down against it by the Court of Justice of the European Union in respect of some of its investigative practices.[13]

6 CJEU, *Commission* v. *Council*, C-209/97, Judgment, ECLI:EU:C:1999:559, 18 November 1999; M. Hofmann and S. Stoykov, 'OLAF – 20 Years of Protecting the Financial Interests of the EU', (2019) *eucrim*, 268.

7 V. Pujas, 'Les difficultés de l'OLAF pour s'imposer en tant qu'acteur légitime de la protection des intérêts économiques et financiers européens', (2006) 62 *Cultures & Conflits*, 107–127, para. 1.

8 1999/352/EC, ECSC, Euratom: Commission Decision of 28 April 1999 establishing the European Anti-fraud Office (OLAF), OJ L 136, 31.5.1999, pp. 20–22.

9 Regulation (EC) No 1073/1999 of the European Parliament and of the Council of 25 May 1999 concerning investigations conducted by the European Anti-Fraud Office (OLAF), OJ L 136, 31.5.1999, pp. 1–7.

10 Council Regulation (Euratom) No 1074/1999 of 25 May 1999 concerning investigations conducted by the European Anti-Fraud Office (OLAF), OJ L 136, 31.5.1999, pp. 8–14.

11 K. Ambos, *European Criminal Law*, Cambridge: Cambridge University Press, 2018, pp. 560–561.

12 Communication from the Commission to the European Parliament, the Council, the European Economic and Social Committee, and the Committee of the Regions and the Court of Auditors on the Commission anti-fraud strategy, 24.6.2011, COM(2011) 376 final.

13 See below, 14.3.1.5.

The implementation of a new legal instrument therefore appeared necessary. Thus, Regulation No 883/2013[14] (OLAF Regulation) was adopted which, slightly amended in 2015, now provides the legal basis for OLAF. However, the entry into operation of the European Public Prosecutor Office (EPPO),[15] the evaluation of Regulation 883/2013 carried out in 2017[16] and the reinforcement of the EU action against fraud affecting its financial interests[17] led the Commission to propose another reform of OLAF,[18] which after lengthy negotiations,[19] has led to the adoption of the Regulation No 2020/2223,[20] which amends Regulation No 883/2013 as regards cooperation with the EPPO and the effectiveness of OLAF's investigations.

OLAF is responsible for detecting suspected fraud against the EU budget, acts of corruption and serious misconducts within the EU institutions.[21] It carries out independent administrative investigations into fraud and corruption involving EU funds and on serious illegal activities detrimental to

[14] Regulation (EU, Euratom) No 883/2013 of the European Parliament and of the Council of 11 September 2013 concerning investigations conducted by the European Anti-Fraud Office (OLAF) and repealing Regulation (EC) No 1073/1999 of the European Parliament and of the Council and Council Regulation (Euratom) No 1074/1999, OJ L 248, 18.9.2013, pp. 1–22.

[15] Expected in 2021.

[16] Report from the Commission to the European Parliament and the Council, Evaluation of the application of Regulation (EU, EURATOM) No 883/2013 of the European Parliament and of the Council of 11 September 2013 concerning investigations conducted by the European Anti-Fraud Office (OLAF) and repealing Regulation (EC) No 1073/1999 of the European Parliament and of the Council and Council Regulation (Euratom) No 1074/1999, COM/2017/0589 final.

[17] Directive (UE) 2017/1371 of the European Parliament and of the Council of 5 July 2017 on the fight against fraud to the Union's financial interests by means of criminal law, OJ L 198, 28.7.2017, pp. 29–41; A. Juszczak and E. Sason, 'The Directive on the Fight against Fraud to the Union's Financial Interests by Means of Criminal Law (PFI Directive). Laying Down the Foundation for a Better Protection of the Union's Financial Interests', (2017) *eucrim*, 80–87.

[18] European Commission, Proposal for a Regulation of the European Parliament and of the Council amending Regulation (EU, Euratom) No 883/2013 concerning investigations conducted by the European Anti-Fraud Office (OLAF) as regards cooperation with the European Public Prosecutor's Office and the effectiveness of OLAF investigations, COM/2018/338 final.

[19] K. Bovend'Eerdt, 'The Commission Proposal Amending the OLAF Regulation', (2018) *eucrim*, 73–74.

[20] Regulation (EU, Euratom) No 2020/2223 of the European Parliament and of the Council of 23 December 2020 amending Regulation (EU, Euratom) No 883/2013, as regards cooperation with the European Public Prosecutor's Office and the effectiveness of the European Anti-Fraud Office investigations, OJ L 437, 28.12.2020, pp. 49–73.

[21] Art. 1(4) OLAF Reg.

the EU financial interests. Furthermore, OLAF is in charge of developing the European Commission anti-fraud policy[22] and of providing Member States and other EU partners, such as third countries bound by customs or financial international agreements with the EU, support in the implementation of EU related legislation. In 2019, the Commission adopted a new Anti-Fraud Strategy[23] which provides for the enhancement of OLAF's role to fulfill these purposes.[24]

OLAF enjoys financial and functional independence, which is enshrined in the case law of the European Court of Justice[25] and secured by its budgetary autonomy within the Commission's budget.[26] The 'dual function'[27] of the Office[28] is embodied in its institutional structure,[29] in the definition of its tasks and in the network of cooperations in which it operates.

14.2 Olaf's Institutional Structure

OLAF is headed by a Director General (DG), who is assisted by a deputy and four Directors. The Office's independence is furthermore safeguarded by

22 For example, OLAF is responsible for the preparation of legislative and regulatory initiatives of the Commission concerning the protection of the EU's financial interests against fraud and corruption and is involved in the drafting and negotiation of such legal instruments. It also contributes to the development and updating of the Commission anti-fraud strategies.

23 European Commission, *Communication from the Commission to the European Parliament, the Council, the European Economic and Social Committee, the Committee of the Regions and the Court of Auditors, Commission Anti-Fraud Strategy: enhanced action to protect the EU budget*, COM(2019) 196 final.

24 Art. 1(1), (2) and (4) OLAF Reg. See European Commission, *Action Plan accompanying the document Communication from the Commission to the European Parliament, the Council, the European Economic and Social Committee, the Committee of the Regions and the Court of Auditors, Commission Anti-Fraud Strategy: enhanced action to protect the EU budget*, 29.4.2019, SWD(2019) 170 final; Janda, M. and Panait, R. (2017), The OLAF Regulation – Evaluation and Future Steps, *eucrim*, 4, p.184.

25 ECJ, *Commission* v. *European Central Bank*, No. C-11/00, Judgment, ECLI:EU:C:2003:395, 10 July 2003, paras. 140–145 and CFI, *Viomichania Syskevasias Typopoiisis Kai Syntirisis Agrotikon Proïonton AE v. Commission*, No. T-334/02, Order, 2 December 2003, para. 39.

26 Art. 18 OLAF Reg.

27 J.A.E. Vervaele, 'The Shaping and Reshaping of Eurojust and OLAF. Investigative Judicial Powers in the European Judicial Area', (2008) *eucrim*, 184.

28 Ambos, *European Criminal Law*, p. 561.

29 M Hofmann and S. Stoykov, 'OLAF – 20 Years of Protecting the Financial Interests of the EU', (2019) *eucrim*, 268.

a Supervisory Committee (SC) and a Controller of procedural guarantees (CPG) has been established to ensure its activity complies with fundamental rights.

14.2.1 The Director General

The DG is appointed by the Commission, on a shortlist agreed by the European Parliament and the Council,[30] for a non-renewable seven-year term.[31] The recruitment procedure is supervised by the SC. He 'shall neither seek nor take instructions from any government or any institution, body, office or agency in the performance of his duties with regard to the opening and carrying-out of external and internal investigations or to the drafting of reports following such investigations'; if he considers his independence is threatened by the Commission, 'he shall immediately inform' the SC and consider bringing an action against the Commission before the Court of Justice.[32] The Commission's power to impose a disciplinary penalty on the DG is strictly regulated.[33]

The following provisions[34] specify the DG's functions. He 'shall report regularly to the European Parliament, the Council, the Commission and the Court of Auditors on the findings of investigations carried out by the Office, the action taken and the problems encountered'. He also determines each year, in accordance with the annual management plan and under supervision of the SC, 'the investigation policy priorities of the Office' (IPPs) and keeps regularly informed the SC of the Office's activities. Besides, the DG is expected to issue 'guidelines on investigation procedures for the staff of the Office' and to implement 'an internal advisory and control procedure' providing for a legality control of the respect of fundamental rights of the persons under investigation and of Member States' national laws.[35] The DG is furthermore vested with the power to initiate OLAF's investigations 'when there is a sufficient suspicion which may be based on information provided by any

[30] Art. 17(2) OLAF Reg. [31] Art. 17(1).

[32] Art. 17(3). On the scope of this requirement, see GC, *Dalli v. Commission*, No. T-399/17, 6 June 2019, paras. 211–212.

[33] Art. 17(9). [34] Art. 17(4)–(8).

[35] OLAF, *Guidelines on Investigation Procedures for OLAF Staff*, 1.10.2013, Ref. Ares(2013)3077837.

third party or on anonymous information, that there has been fraud, corruption or any other illegal activity affecting the financial interests of the Union' and without prejudice to EPPO's jurisdiction[36] and he 'shall direct the conduct of investigations'. The DG is furthermore responsible for the Final Reports drawn up by the Office at the end of these investigations.[37]

14.2.2 The Directorates

OLAF is structured around four directorates. Directorate A 'Expenditure' deals with direct expenditure and shared management investigations and internal investigations; Directorate B 'Revenue and International Operations' is in charge of customs and illicit trade operations and investigations and Directorate C 'Anti-Fraud Knowledge Centre' is in charge of anti-fraud/corruption strategies and analysis, intelligence and operational analysis, digital strategy and forensics issues. Directorate D 'General Affairs' is mainly in charge of the Office's legislation and anti-fraud programmes, of delivering legal advice and of managing the Document Management Centre of the Office.

OLAF's staff is composed of officers from the twenty-seven Members States, whose 'backgrounds stretch from investigative and legal expertise in financial crimes to digital forensics and auditing of EU projects'.[38] They bring to the Office their expertise of national anti-fraud legislation and proceedings. Nonetheless, OLAF is affected by a recurrent understaffing hardly consistent with the constant increase of its activities.[39]

14.2.3 The Supervisory Committee

OLAF's SC is composed of 'five independent members having experience in senior judicial or investigative functions or comparable functions relating to the areas of activity of the Office'. They are appointed 'by common accord of the European Parliament, the Council and the

[36] Art. 5(1). [37] See *infra*.

[38] OLAF, *Strategic plan 2016–2020*, available at https://ec.europa.eu/anti-fraud/sites/antifraud/files/olaf_sp_2016_2020_en.pdf.

[39] OLAF, *Management Plan 2019*, 20.12.2018, Ref. Ares(2018)6579174, Part. 2, A.

Commission' for a non renewable five years' mandate. Except on expiry of his term of office, a member of the SC can only be relieved of his duties on very restrictive grounds.[40] The Committee is supported by an independent secretariat provided by the Commission and has its own budget[41]; the Commission shall refrain from interfering with the monitoring functions of the SC. Like the DG, members of the SC shall, in the performance of their duties, 'neither seek nor take instructions from any government or any institution, body, office or agency'.[42]

The Committee is vested with the task to 'regularly monitor the implementation by the Office of its investigative function', especially as regards the protection of persons under investigation's rights and the duration of investigations. For this purpose, OLAF must keep the SC regularly informed of its activities.[43] The Committee is competent to address to the DG opinions and recommendations but is forbidden to interfere with the conduct of on-going investigations.[44] It shall publish an activity report at least once a year.[45]

In 2014, in order to enhance persons under investigation's procedural guarantees, the Commission proposed to establish a CPG, separate from the Committee, who should be a (former) magistrate and whose tasks would be to review complaints lodged by persons under investigation and to authorise OLAF to conduct certain investigative measures in respect of members of EU institutions.[46] The establishment of this new control organ is provided for in the Regulation 2020/2223.

14.2.4 The Controller of Procedural Guarantees

The CPG is appointed by the Commission for a non-renewable term of office of five years and is administratively attached to the SC. He/

[40] Art. 15(2), (3) and (5) OLAF Reg. [41] Art. 15(8). [42] Art. 15(7).

[43] Art. 15(1). On the scope of this requirement, see, for example, CFI, *Franchet and Byk v. Commission*, No. T-48/05, Judgment, ECLI:EU:T:2008:257, 8 July 2008, para.164.

[44] Art. 15(1). [45] Art. 15(9).

[46] Proposal for a Regulation of the European Parliament and of the Council amending Regulation (EU, Euratom) No 883/2013 as regards the establishment of a Controller of procedural guarantees, 11.6.2014 COM(2014) 340 final; see S. Manacorda, 'Le droit pénal de l'Union à l'heure de la Charte et du Parquet européen', (2013) 4 *RSC*, 48.

she exercices his/her functions 'in complete independence, including from the Office and from the Supervisory Committee, and shall neither seek nor take instructions from anyone in the performance of his or her duties'. The CPG is responsible, on the one hand, for monitoring 'the Office's compliance with procedural guarantees [...], as well as the rules applicable to investigations by the Office' and shall report to the SC on any systemic issue arising out of his/her assessments and, on the other hand, for handling complaints arising from the Office's activities.[47]

A complaints mechanism is thus established to allow a 'person concerned' to lodge a complaint with the Controller regarding the Office's compliance with procedural guarantees as well as on the grounds of an infringement of the rules applicable to investigations by the Office, in particular infringements of procedural requirements and fundamental rights. A complaint has no suspensive effect on OLAF's investigations. The Controller informs the DG 'immediately upon receipt of a complaint', and the Office must transmit him/her 'all information necessary [...] to assess whether the complaint is justified as well as information for the purpose of resolving the complaint and enabling the Controller to issue a recommendation'. The complaint is examined in an adversarial procedure, 'without interfering with the conduct of the investigation under way' and the CPG 'shall issue a recommendation on how to resolve the complaint without delay and in any event within two months of the Office informing the Controller of the action it has taken to resolve the complaint'. Besides, the DG may seek the opinion of the Controller on any matter related to procedural guarantees or fundamental rights[48]

14.3 Olaf's Tasks

As a shared competence with the Member States, the Commission is required by Article 325 of the Treaty on the Functioning of the European Union (TFEU) to counter fraud and any illegal activities affecting the financial interests of the Union. Article 317 TFEU requires it to set up a

[47] Art. 9a OLAF Reg. [48] Art. 9b.

framework to enable the effective prevention and detection of fraud and Article 36 of the Financial Regulation[49] requires the Commission to set up an effective and efficient internal control when implementing the EU budget.[50] OLAF 'draws its powers from those of the Commission'[51] and plays a leading role in the fulfillment of these duties. The Office's competence is twofold: it conducts administrative investigations into suspected frauds and contributes its expertise to help the Commission to develop anti-fraud policy and legislation.

14.3.1 Administrative Investigations

The Office's main task is to investigate acts detrimental to the financial interests of the Union. OLAF's jurisdiction covers all infringements against EU financial interests, that is fraud, corruption and other offences affecting these interests relating to EU expenditure and some areas of EU revenue but also suspicions of serious misconduct by EU staff and members of the EU institutions.[52] Thus, OLAF owes jurisdiction on misbehaviours perpetrated both within Member States' or third countries territories by beneficiaries of, or contributors to, EU budget and within the EU by its staff members. The scope of OLAF's investigative powers is broad.[53]

[49] Regulation (EU, Euratom) 2018/1046 of the European Parliament and of the Council of 18 July 2018 on the financial rules applicable to the general budget of the Union, amending Regulations (EU) No 1296/2013, (EU) No 1301/2013, (EU) No 1303/2013, (EU) No 1304/2013, (EU) No 1309/2013, (EU) No 1316/2013, (EU) No 223/2014, (EU) No 283/2014, and Decision No 541/2014/EU and repealing Regulation (EU, Euratom) No 966/2012, OJ L 193, 30.7.2018, 1.

[50] C.A. Makri and O. Marin, 'The Commission's New Anti-Fraud Strategy – Enhanced Action to Protect the EU Budget', (2019) *eucrim*, 219.

[51] Art. 1(1) OLAF Reg. See L. Kuhl, 'The Future of the European Union's Financial Interests Financial Criminal Law Investigations under the Lead of a European Prosecutor's Office', (2008) *eucrim*, 188.

[52] Hofmann and Stoykov, 'OLAF – 20 Years of Protecting the Financial Interests of the EU', 269.

[53] ECJ, *Commission v. European Central Bank*, No. C-11/00, Judgment, ECLI:EU:C:2003:395, 10 July 2003; GC, *Oikonomopoulos v. Commission*, No. T-483/13, Judgment, ECLI:EU:T:2016:421, 20 July 2016, paras. 144–147; CJEU, *Rothley v. Parliament*, No. T-17/00, Judgment, ECLI:EU:T:2002:39, 26 February 2002; GC, *Panzeri v. Parliament*, No. T-166/16, Judgment, ECLI:EU:T:2017:347, 18 May 2017; GC, *Le Pen v. Parliament*, No. T86/17, Judgment, 19 June 2018; GC, *Le Pen v. Parliament*, No. T-161/17, Judgment, ECLI:EU:T:2018:848, 28 November 2018.

To carry out its tasks, OLAF has been given operational capacities, that is investigative powers. K. Ambos points out that OLAF 'is an administrative authority and its activity thus does not, in principle, fall within the field of criminal procedure but rather represents preliminary investigative action of an administrative nature'.[54] As a consequence, OLAF is devoid of 'adjudicatory' or 'prosecutorial tasks' and its legal framework 'often refer back to national provisions'.[55] OLAF's investigations generally require further national judicial criminal proceedings in order to be able to implement freezing and confiscation powers,[56] to issue European investigation orders[57] or to enforce coercive measures. This reflects the 'hybrid' character of OLAF.[58]

OLAF may carry out internal investigations, that is administrative investigations within the European institutions, and external investigations, that is administrative investigations outside any European institution, either on the territory of a Member State or of a third country.

14.3.1.1 Provisions Common to Both Types of Investigations

OLAF has competence to implement the investigative powers available to the Commission[59] and Regulation No. 883/2013 further provides the Office with investigation prerogatives.

OLAF's selection procedure of cases is detailed in the *Management Plan* 2019.[60] The Office may receive information about suspected fraud and irregularities from a wide range of public and private sources, including whistleblowers who, after having reported fraud, corruption and any

[54] Ambos, *European Criminal Law*, p. 561; M. Wade, 'OLAF and the Push and Pull Factors of a European Criminal Justice System', (2008) *eucrim*, 128.

[55] M. Simonato, 'OLAF Investigations in a Multi-Level System. Legal Obstacles to Effective Enforcement, (2016) *eucrim*, 136.

[56] Council Framework Decision 2003/577/JHA of 22 July 2003 on the execution in the European Union of orders freezing property or evidence, OJ L 196, 2.8.2003, pp. 45–55 and Council Framework Decision 2006/783/JHA of 6 October 2006 on the application of the principle of mutual recognition to confiscation orders, OJ L 328, 24.11.2006, pp. 59–78.

[57] Directive 2014/41/EU of the European Parliament and of the Council of 3 April 2014 regarding the European Investigation Order in criminal matters, OJ L 130, 1.5.2014, pp. 1–36.

[58] R. Panait, 'Information Sharing between OLAF and National Judicial Authorities. The Advantages of a Supranational Structure and the Legislative Limitations Specific to a European Hybrid Body', (2015) *eucrim*, 64.

[59] For example, Council Regulation (EC) No 1225/2009 of 30 November 2009 on protection against dumped imports from countries not members of the European Community, OJ L 343, 22.12.2009, p. 51.

[60] Part 1, A.

other illegal activity affecting the financial interests of the Union, should be afforded the protection of Directive (EU) 2019/1937.[61] First, it must check its competence to investigate and determine whether available elements provide for a sufficient suspicion of the commission of an act within its jurisdiction.[62] To this end, OLAF owes prior to the opening of an investigation a 'right of access to any relevant information in databases' held by EU entities[63] in accordance with the principles of necessity and proportionality and within a time limit consistent with the requirement of 'a prompt assessment of the allegations'.[64] Once established, selectors, taking into account the IPPs,[65] proceed to the analysis of the criteria of proportionality, efficient use of investigative resources and expected reasonable duration of investigations.[66] In practice, this selection procedure leads OLAF to concentrate its activities on the most serious cases. In view of the Office's limited resources, and especially the impossibility for its agents to implement coercive investigative techniques required to fight criminal organisations or white-collar criminals, this option leads to a risk of counter-productivity of OLAF's intervention, which could alert fraudsters whereas its officers do not enjoy the adequate means of investigating their activities, at the risk of causing national law enforcement forces' investigators to be either unduly delayed or impeded in the performance of their duties.[67] Pursuant to Article 5 of OLAF Regulation,[68] the DG shall take, within a period of two months, the decision to open an investigation either 'on his own initiative' or upon request from a Member State or from an EU entity.[69]

[61] Directive (EU) 2019/1937 of the European Parliament and of the Council of 23 October 2019 on the protection of persons who report breaches of Union law, OJ, L305, 26.11.2019, p. 17; Art. 10(3a)–(3b) OLAF Reg.

[62] GC, *Dalli* v. *Commission*, No. T399–17, 6 June 2019, paras. 63–71; GC, *Oikonomopoulos* v. *Commission*, No. T-483/13, Judgment, ECLI:EU:T:2016:421, 20 July 2016, para.175.

[63] Meaning, here and after, 'the institutions, bodies, offices and agencies' of the EU.

[64] Art. 6 OLAF Reg.

[65] Based on the criteria set out un art. 5(1) OLAF Reg. See OLAF, *Management Plan* 2019, Annex.

[66] The due diligence principle means OLAF is under an obligation to act with diligence as soon as it becomes aware of facts that may constitute infringements resorting to its jurisdiction in order to assess whether an investigation should be opened and, if so, in the conduct of that investigation. See, for example CJEU, *Goetz* v. *Comité des Régions*, No. F-89/11, Judgment, 19 June 2013, para. 123.

[67] J. Gonzáles-Herrero Gonzáles and M. Madalina Butincu, 'The Collection of Evidence by OLAF and Its Transmission to the National Judicial Authorities', (2009) *eucrim*, 93.

[68] Art. 5(1). [69] Art. 5(2)–(3).

The decision not to open an investigation must be sufficiently reasoned. The DG then 'may without delay send any relevant information' to the EU entity or to the competent authorities of the Member State concerned 'for appropriate action to be taken'.[70]

If he takes the decision to open an investigation, the DG 'shall direct the conduct of investigations on the basis, where appropriate, of written instructions' and designate 'the staff of the Office' in charge of conducting 'under his direction' the investigation. Officers 'carry out their tasks on production of a written authorisation', issued by the DG,[71] and must carry out the investigations 'continuously over a period which must be proportionate to the circumstances and complexity of the case'[72] and in accordance with the principles of necessity and proportionality. When the investigation lasts more than twelve months, the DG must 'report to the Supervisory Committee' the reasons and the 'remedial measures envisaged'.[73] Officers are assisted by a legal advice unit and by the Investigation Support Directorate, which provides services to support both investigation and coordination activities. Member States' authorities, acting in accordance with their national law, and staff members of EU entities are expected to provide OLAF officers with the 'necessary assistance to enable [them] to fulfil their tasks effectively',[74] including through taking precautionary administrative measures.[75]

14.3.1.2 Internal Investigations

Article 4 of OLAF Regulation allows the Office to carry out 'internal investigations'. The Office must act 'in accordance with the conditions set out in this Regulation and in the decision' adopted by the entity concerned.[76] The scope of internal investigations is broader than those of external ones; their purpose is not only to find out offences but to investigate all 'serious matters relating to the discharge of professional duties constituting a dereliction of the obligations of EU officials liable to result in disciplinary

[70] Art. 5(5)–(6). [71] Art. 7(1)–(2). [72] Art. 7(5).

[73] Art. 7(8); on timeliness requirement, see CFI, *Franchet and Byk v. Commission*, No. T-48/05, Judgment, ECLI:EU:T:2008:257, 8 July 2008, paras. 272–274; GC, *Panzeri v. Parliament*, No. T-166/16, Judgment, ECLI:EU:T:2017:347, 18 May 2017, paras. 102–104.

[74] Art. 7(3) OLAF Reg. [75] Art. 7(6)–(7). [76] Art. 4(1).

or criminal proceedings, or an equivalent failure to discharge obligations on the part of Members of institutions and bodies'.[77]

When, the Office considers opening an internal investigation, it may inform the EU entity and the competent authorities of the Member State concerned and request them to 'inform the Office of any action taken' on the information's basis.[78] Then, OLAF has to inform the EU entities concerned by an investigation when it conducts 'an internal investigation on their premises or consult a document or request information held by them' but they are required to implement 'appropriate procedures and take necessary measures to ensure at all stages the confidentiality of internal investigations'.[79]

OLAF owes a 'right of immediate and unannounced access to any relevant information, including information in databases', held by EU entities 'and to their premises' and is 'empowered to inspect [their] accounts' and 'take a copy of [...] any document or the contents of any data medium' they hold. It may also 'request oral information, including through interviews, and written information' from any EU staff members or authorities.[80] Neither the consent of the person nor of the head of the entity concerned by the investigations is required. Furthermore, in accordance with the provisions of Regulation No 2185/96,[81] OLAF 'may carry out on-the-spot checks and inspections at the premises of economic operators in order to obtain access to information relevant to the matter under internal investigation'.[82]

The evaluation of OLAF Regulation carried out in 2017 enlighten shortcomings requiring improvements within the rules on internal investigations, mainly as regards the inspection of premises.[83]

14.3.1.3 External Investigations

When the Office considers the decision to open an external investigation, 'it may inform the competent authorities of the Member States concerned

[77] Hofmann and Stoykov, 'OLAF – 20 Years of Protecting the Financial Interests of the EU', 269.

[78] Art. 4(8) OLAF Reg. [79] Art. 4(4), (5) and (7). [80] Art. 4(2)(a)–(b).

[81] Council Regulation (Euratom, EC) No 2185/96 of 11 November 1996 concerning on-the-spot checks and inspections carried out by the Commission in order to protect the European Communities' financial interests against fraud and other irregularities, OJ L 292, 15.11.1996, pp. 2–5.

[82] Art. 4(3) OLAF Reg.

[83] Bovend'Eerdt, 'The Commission Proposal Amending the OLAF Regulation', 73.

and, where necessary, the competent Commission services'. The national authorities shall then 'ensure that appropriate action is taken, in which the Office may take part, in compliance with national law'.[84] The European Court stated that 'the investigations [...] carried out by OLAF form part of an environment marked by the application of national law, but that that law must in any event be replaced by Union law whenever the regulations so provide'.[85] M. Simonato emphasises that 'these regulations do not lay down an exhaustive EU-law-based procedure for autonomous investigations by OLAF, but rather refer to sectoral regulations [...] and to national law'.[86]

OLAF officers shall 'act, subject to the Union law applicable, in compliance with the rules and practices of the Member State concerned and with the procedural guarantees provided for in this Regulation'. Article 3(1) and (2) OLAF Regulation reads that, enforcing the powers conferred on the Commission by Regulation No 2988/95 and Regulation No 2185/96, the Office may 'carry out on-the-spot checks and inspections in the Member States and, in accordance with the cooperation and mutual assistance agreements and any other legal instrument in force, in third countries and on the premises of international organisations' and 'on economic operators' to establish whether an offence affecting the financial interests of the Union has been committed. The Court held that the power to carry out on-the-spot checks and inspections entails the power to schedule interviews with people involved in those operations.[87]

OLAF officers are not permitted to implement any law enforcement measures. At their request, 'the competent authority of the Member State concerned shall provide the staff of the Office with the assistance needed in order to carry out their tasks effectively' and ensure 'that the staff of the Office are allowed access, under the same terms and conditions as its competent authorities and in compliance with its national law, to all information and documents relating to the matter under investigation

[84] Art. 3(6).

[85] GC, *Sigma Orionis SA* v. *Commission*, No. T-48/16, Judgment, ECLI:EU:T:2018:245, 3 May 2018, paras. 78–82; see J. Tricot, 'Chronique de droit et de jurisprudence de l'Union européenne, (2018) *RSC*, 101.

[86] Simonato, 'OLAF Investigations in a Multi-Level System. Legal Obstacles to Effective Enforcement', 138.

[87] GC, *Oikonomopoulos v. Commission*, No. T-483/13, Judgment, ECLI:EU:T:2016:421, 20 July 2016, paras. 188–190.

which prove necessary in order for the on-the-spot checks and inspections to be carried out effectively and efficiently'.[88] For this purpose, Member States are required to designate an 'anti-fraud coordination service' (AFCOS), which must provide, obtain, or coordinate the assistance required by OLAF.[89] AFCOS should be able to provide or coordinate the necessary assistance to the Office to carry out its tasks effectively, before, during or at the end of an external or internal investigation. Moreover, OLAF has a margin of discretion in determining the information and documentation to which it considers it necessary to have access and to take copies of.[90] Finally, when carrying out an external investigation, the Office has access 'to any relevant information, including information in databases, held by' EU entities.[91]

Although extensive, investigative powers conferred to OLAF are not regarded as sufficient and shortcomings hamper the effectiveness of the Office's work. The subjection of OLAF's powers' enforceability to national laws leads to a 'jurisdictional fragmentation of OLAF's investigatory tools and competences'[92] which hinders the Office's efficiency. In its proposal to reform Regulation 883/2013, the Commission recommends 'to better equip OLAF with investigative tools' and suggests 'a number of targeted changes regarding access to bank account information, on-the-spot-checks and inspections, and VAT fraud'[93] or the improvement of the collaboration between OLAF and AFCOS.[94]

As a consequence, Regulation 2020/2223 clarifies the instances in which national law is to apply in the course of investigations by the Office and requires national authorities to implement the national enforcement legal tools for the benefit of OLAF officers in the same way and 'to the same conditions as those that apply to national administrative inspectors',[95] introduces a duty on the part of economic operators to cooperate with the Office, in accordance with their obligation under

[88] Art.3(3) OLAF Reg. [89] Art. 3(4).

[90] GC, *Vialto Consulting* v. *Commission*, No. T-617/17, Judgment, ECLI:EU:T:2019:446, 26 June 2019, para. 68.

[91] Art. 3(5).

[92] K. Bovend'Eerdt, Learning Lessons – Reflecting on Regulation 883/2013 through Comparative Analysis, (2017) *eucrim*, 191.

[93] Hofmann and Stoykov, 'OLAF – 20 Years of Protecting the Financial Interests of the EU', 271.

[94] Bovend'Eerdt, 'The Commission Proposal Amending the OLAF Regulation', 74.

[95] Art. 3(4).

Regulation (Euratom, EC) No 2185/96, and especially imposes on economic operators an obligation to answer factual questions and provide documents, even if that information may be used to establish against them or against another economic operator of the existence of illegal activity. The Office is furthermore granted the possibility to request access to information in privately owned devices used for work purposes and, to enable it to « follow the money trail in order to uncover the modus operandi typical of much fraudulent conduct »,[96] the Office is provided with the legal means to obtain bank account information relevant for its investigative activity held by credit institutions in a number of Member States through cooperation with and assistance by the national authorities as part of their general duty to assist the Office.

14.3.1.4 Final Report

On completion of an investigation, if no evidence of an offence has been found, the DG ends the investigation without further action and informs the person(s) concerned.[97] OLAF's decision does not prejudge the decision of the national authorities, which remain free to take legal action.[98]

When evidence of an offense has been found, the investigative unit may draw up a Final Report, under the authority of the DG, mentioning the legal basis of the investigation, the procedural measures implemented, the facts established and their *prima facie* legal characterisation and – if appropriate – an estimation of the financial damage induced by the infringement.[99] The report takes account of the national law of the Member State concerned so that it can constitute an admissible evidence in national administrative or judicial proceedings.[100] Having no mandatory legal effect, the Final Report is not adversarial to the person concerned[101] and OLAF is under no legal obligation whatsoever to disclose it to him before sending it to national authorities.[102] Accordingly,

96 Preamb. §.31. 97 Art. 11(7).

98 GC, *EKETA* v. *Commission*, No. T-166/17, Judgment, ECLI:EU:T:2019:26, 22 January 2019, paras. 184–185 and No. T-198/17, Judgment, ECLI:EU:T:2019:27, 22 January 2019, paras. 94–95.

99 Ambos, *European Criminal Law*, p. 562. 100 Art. 11(1)–(2) OLAF Reg.

101 GC, *Inox Mare v. Commission*, No. T-289/16, Order, ECLI:EU:T:2017:414, 21 June 2017, paras. 13, 22, 29, 42–43.

102 GC, *International Management Group v. Commission*, No. T110/15, Judgment, ECLI:EU:T:2016:322, 26 May 2016, paras. 66–68.

judicial protection against subsequent proceedings must be ensured at national level.[103] Nonetheless, reports drawn up by the Office constitute admissible evidence in administrative or judicial proceedings in the same way and under the same conditions as administrative reports drawn up by national administrative inspectors in judicial proceedings of a non-criminal nature before national and Union's courts as well as in administrative proceedings in Member States and in the case of national judicial proceedings of a criminal nature.[104]

If necessary, DG's recommandations are annexed to the Final Report. They can be of four different types: (i) financial recommandations, addressed to EU and Member States' authorities and intended to seek the recovery of the misused funds[105]; (ii) judicial recommandations, addressed to the national prosecution authorities, suggesting the institution of criminal proceedings[106]; (iii) disciplinary recommandations, addressed to EU authorities and (iv) administrative recommendations, addressed to EU authorities and aimed at pointing out the weaknesses in procedures or legislation. OLAF then monitors the way these recommendations are implemented and may request the national authorities to report on actions taken.[107]

The judicial follow-up of OLAF's recommendations is regarded as the 'Achilles heel' of the EU's protection of financial interests structure.[108] In theory, the principles of sincere cooperation and loyalty should ensure a uniform practice of all Member States; nonetheless, in accordance with the ECJ case law,[109] national authorities do not regard themselves

[103] GC, *Inox Mare* v. *Commission*, Order, ECLI:EU:T:2017:414, 21 June 2017, paras. 23, 26–27, 34–40; GC, *TE v. Commission*, No. T-392/17, Order, ECLI:EU:T:2018:459, 12 July 2018, para. 30.

[104] Art. 11(2)–(3) OLAF Reg.

[105] J.-P. Pétillon, 'Réussites et Défis de l'Office Européen de Lutte Antifraude', (2008) *eucrim*, 157; Hofmann and Stoykov, 'OLAF – 20 Years of Protecting the Financial Interests of the EU', 270.

[106] Art. 11(5) OLAF Reg. [107] Art. 11(6).

[108] A. Marletta, 'Interinstitutional Relationship of European Bodies in the Fight against Crimes Affecting the EU's Financial Interests. Past Experience and Future Models', (2016) *eucrim*, 143; K. Ligeti and M. Simonato, 'The European Public Prosecutor's Office: Towards a Truly European Prosecution Service?', (2013) 4 *NJECL* 8; M. Hofmann, 'Guest Editorial', (2017) *eucrim*, 161.

[109] CFI, *Comunidad Autónoma de Andalucía v. Commission*, No. T-29/03, Order, ECLI:EU:T:2004:235, 13 July 2004, T-29/03; CFI, *Tillack v. Commission*, No. T-29/03, Judgment, ECLI:EU:T:2006:292, 4 October 2006.

as bound by the recommendations.[110] This absence of mandatory legal effect[111] entails disparities in the treatment of cases transmitted by OLAF[112] as the adoption of sanctions remains within the exclusive discretionary competence of the national authorities.[113] Regulation 2020/2223 therefore provides that, in order to allow the Office to follow-up on the development of its cases, where the Office makes judicial recommendations to the national prosecution authorities of a Member State, Member States should, upon request of the Office, send the Office the final decision of the national court. Besides, the implementation of its prerogatives by the EPPO should help to correct, to some extent, this shortcoming.

14.3.1.5 Procedural Guarantees

K. Ambos emphasises that 'the current OLAF Regulation for the first time also contains a list of mandatory procedural guarantees', which he interprets as 'a response to widespread rights violations in the course of OLAF investigations'.[114] Probably, the integration of the Charter of fundamental rights[115] into EU primary law contributes to explain this development. Nonetheless, 'a continuous struggle regarding the legal character of the investigative powers of OLAF'[116] remains which gives rise to a substantial amount of litigations.[117] Investigations conducted by OLAF are indeed subject to an effective judicial control and the ECJ regularly states investigations conducted by the Office must respect the fundamental rights of

[110] Wade, 'OLAF and the Push and Pull Factors of a European Criminal Justice System', 128; see also L. Balogová, 'The Developments in the Case Law of the Community Courts with Regard to OLAF Investigations', (2008) *eucrim*, 144.

[111] GC, *Inox Mare* v. *Commission*, No. T-289/16, Order, ECLI:EU:T:2017:414, 21 June 2017; GC, *Remag Metallhandel and Jaschinsky v. Commission*, No. T-631/16, Judgment, ECLI:EU:T:2019:352, 23 May 2019.

[112] L. Kuhl and R. Panait, 'Les négociations pour un Parquet européen : un organe d'enquête et de poursuite européen pour la lutte antifraude dans l'Union européenne, ou un deuxième acteur de coordination judiciaire ?', (2017) *RSC*, para. 36.

[113] GC, *Remag Metallhandel and Jaschinsky v. Commission*, No. T-631/16, Judgment, ECLI:EU:T:2019:352, 23 May 2019, paras. 48–62.

[114] Ambos, *European Criminal Law*, pp. 560, 562.

[115] Charter of Fundamental Rights of the European Union, OJ C 326, 26.10.2012, pp. 391–407.

[116] Vervaele, 'The Shaping and Reshaping of Eurojust and OLAF. Investigative Judicial Powers in the European Judicial Area', 182.

[117] X. Groussot, and Z. Popov, 'What's Wrong with OLAF? Accountability, Due Process and Criminal Justice in European Anti-Fraud Policy', (2010) 47 *CMLR*, 605–643.

the person concerned.[118] The infringement by OLAF of these guarantees in the course of an investigation may give rise to liability and the claimant may obtain compensatory damages.[119]

OLAF is bound by the procedural guarantees of Regulation (EU, Euratom) No 883/2013 and Council Regulation (Euratom, EC) No 2185/96 and those contained in the Charter of Fundamental Rights of the European Union. Article 9 of OLAF Regulation rules the Office shall conduct the investigations 'objectively, impartially[120] and confidentially and in accordance with the principle of the presumption of innocence and with the procedural guarantees set out in this Article' and that it should seek out evidence of innocence as well as guilt.[121] The effective implementation of the procedural guarantees is to be monitored by the SC.

Persons under internal investigations must be informed as soon as possible, and OLAF is obliged to then record comments the person might make. The information may only be deferred on ground of an imperative requirements of absolute secrecy for the purposes of the investigation.[122] Persons under external investigation should be promptly informed of the investigation, provided that the information do not interfere with the investigation[123] and, in any event, not after information are sent to national judicial authorities.[124]

Persons under investigation and witnesses enjoy a right against self-incrimination. The Court stated that the burden of proof on the Commission implies that the obligation on an economic operator to provide information in its possession does not amount to an obligation to provide answers which might involve the admission of an infringement.[125]

118 CFI, *Santiago Gómez-Reino v. Commission*, No. T-215/02, Order, ECLI:EU:T:2003:352, 18 December 2003; GC, *Sigma Orionis v. Commission*, No. T-48/16, Judgment, ECLI:EU:T:2018:245, 3 May 2018, paras. 102–104.

119 V. Stojanovski, 'Procedural Rights of Persons under Investigation by OLAF', (2011) *eucrim*, 128 *et seq.*

120 CFI, *Camós Grau* v. *Commission*, No. T-309/03, Order, ECLI:EU:T:2006:110, 6 April 2006.

121 Art. 9(1).

122 CFI, *Nikolaou* v. *Commission*, No. T-259/03, Judgment, ECLI:EU:T:2007:254, 12 September 2007, para. 238.

123 GC, *Oikonomopoulos* v. *Commission*, No. T-483/13, Judgment, ECLI:EU:T:2016:421, 20 July 2016, para. 229–231.

124 CG, *De Esteban Alonso* v. *Commission*, No. T138–18, Judgment, ECLI:EU:T:2019:398, 11 June 2019.

125 CJEU, *Orkem* v. *Commission*, No. 374/87, Judgment, ECLI:EU:C:1989:387, 18 October 1989, paras. 34–35.

Except when the interview takes place in the context of on-the-spot checks and inspections, the interview of a person concerned is subjected to a prior ten working days' notice, except 'on duly reasoned grounds of urgency'; the notice period applicable to witnesses is of a minimum of twenty-four hours. The summons must inform the person concerned of their rights. Questioning of a witness shall be stopped when 'evidence emerges that [he] may be a person concerned'. Persons questioned may be assisted by a person of their choice. Minutes of the interview shall be drawn up and the interviewee may add observations and shall receive a copy of the record.[126] On the completion of the investigation, persons who may be referred by name in the report shall be informed about the closing of the investigation, given access to the relevant establishments[127] and invited to comment on facts concerning them.[128] Nonetheless, 'in duly justified cases where necessary to preserve the confidentiality of the investigation or an ongoing or future criminal investigation by the EPPO or a national judicial authority, the Director-General may, where appropriate after consulting the EPPO or the national judicial authority concerned, decide to defer the fulfilment of the obligation to invite the person concerned to comment'.[129] ECJ case law further admits the presumption of innocence is breached by infringement of the confidentiality of the investigations' rules,[130] especially when OLAF refers to persons under investigation as guilty of criminal offences trough leaks to the press.[131]

Finally, administrative investigations conducted by OLAF are subjected to strict data protection and confidentiality rules[132] and shared on a strict

126 Art. 9(2).

127 In *Franchet and Byk*, the Court stated that, with regard to the confidentiality of its mission and in order to protect the effectiveness of its investigations, OLAF is not obliged to grant access to the case file to the person concerned before the completion of the investigation (CFI, *Franchet and Byk v. Commission*, No. T-48/05, Judgment, ECLI:EU:T:2008:257, 8 July 2008, paras. 255–262); see, in the same vein, as regards external investigation, GC, *Oikonomopoulos v. Commission*, No. T-483/13, Judgment, ECLI:EU:T:2016:421, 20 July 2016, paras. 239–241 and GC, *Le Pen v. Parliament*, No. T86/17, Judgment, 19 June 2018, para. 84.

128 Art. 9(3)–(4). 129 Art. 9(4).

130 CST, *Giraudy v. Commission*, No. F-23/05, Judgment, ECLI:EU:F:2007:75, 2 May 2007.

131 CFI, *Franchet and Byk v. Commission*, No. T-48/05, Judgment, ECLI:EU:T:2008:257,8 July 2008, para. 210.

132 Art. 10 OLAF Reg. and Commission Decision (EU) 2018/1962 of 11 December 2018 laying down internal rules concerning the processing of personal data by the European Anti-Fraud Office (OLAF) in relation to the provision of information to data subjects and the restriction of certain of their rights in accordance with Art. 25 of Regulation (EU) 2018/1725 of the European Parliament and of the Council OJ L 315, 12.12.2018, pp. 41–46.

'need to know' basis.[133] In order to prevent litigations that may result from its investigators' 'varying traditions with respect to the processing of personal data', OLAF has appointed a Data Protection Officer in accordance with Article 43 of Regulation (EU) 2018/1725.[134]

14.3.2 Prevention

Besides its investigative activities, OLAF is involved in the Commission's development of preventive strategies and legislative initiatives[135] aimed at detecting or curbing illegal activities affecting the financial interests of the Union.

It is furthermore obliged to support, co-ordinate and enhance co-operations carried out by Member States' competent authorities.[136] The Office thus contributes to the operation of the Early Detection and Exclusion System (EDES) which is a database run by the Commission and aimed, within the limits set by the ECJ,[137] at identifying, flagging and/or excluding unreliable applicants from EU fundings.[138] The Office communicates its investigation results to the operators of the database, it is consulted before a flagging decision is made and may be consulted when a decision to exclude an economic operator is considered. Further, OLAF operates the Commission's Anti-Fraud Information System which gathers anti-fraud authorities from Member States, partner third countries and international organisations. This network supports mutual assistance in customs matters.[139] The Office also hosts and manages the Irregularities Management System (IMS) in which Member States fulfill their obligations to report to the Commission irregularities in expenditure detected in various sectorial policies of the Union. The purpose is

133 OLAF, *Strategic Plan 2016–2020*, above, Part 2, D.

134 Art. 10(4); L. Laudati, 'Data Protection at OLAF', (2013) *eucrim*, 15.

135 For example, OLAF was co-responsible with the Directorate General for Justice and Consumers for the legislative initiative that led to the adoption of the Directive on the Protection of EU's financial interests by means of criminal law (PIF Directive 2017).

136 For example, OLAF plays a leading role in the co-ordination of joint customs operations.

137 GC, *Planet AE Anonymi Etaireia Parochis Symvouleftikon Ypiresion v. Commission*, No. T-320/09, Judgment, ECLI:EU:T:2015:223, 22 April 2015.

138 OLAF, *Management Plan 2019* (above); art. 136(1) of the Financial Regulation.

139 OLAF, *Management Plan 2019* (above) and Council Regulation (EC) No 515/97 of 13 March 1997 on mutual assistance between the administrative authorities of the Member States and cooperation between the latter and the Commission to ensure the correct application of the law on customs and agricultural matters, OJ L 82, 22.3.1997, pp.1–16.

to reduce the deficit of knowledge of the cases of fraud detected in the European Union which results from the heterogeneity in the detection of fraud in the Member States.[140]

OLAF also manages the Hercule III programme[141] aimed at promoting activities of national and regional Member States' authorities in the field of the protection of EU's financial interests.[142] According to the 2018 Commission's proposal,[143] it is to be merged within the EU Anti-Fraud Programme. The Office further provides fraud prevention and detection trainings[144] to EU agencies and organises seminars for staff of Member States' authorities and joint-trainings gathering law enforcement forces officers from different Member States to enhance cross-border co-operations. Finally, it issues casebooks and guidance documents available to Commission's services, which highlight fraud indicators and *modus operandi* used by fraudsters, and provides national authorities with the skills it has developed in transnational fraud schemes analysis.

14.4 Olaf's Co-operations

M. Wade points out that 'OLAF's powers are clearly demarcated to leave it as an agency dependent upon good-will without the ability to act swiftly and independently one would usually expect from an investigative

140 Kuhl and Panait, 'Les négociations pour un Parquet européen : un organe d'enquête et de poursuite européen pour la lutte antifraude dans l'Union européenne, ou un deuxième acteur de coordination judiciaire?', § 31.

141 Regulation (EU) No 250/2014 of the European Parliament and of the Council of 26 February 2014 establishing a programme to promote activities in the field of the protection of the financial interests of the European Union (Hercule III programme) and repealing Decision No 804/2004/EC, OJ L 84, 20.3.2014, pp. 6–13.

142 For example, through providing grants to law enforcement authorities to purchase expensive investigation equipment.

143 COM/2018/386 final.

144 For example, OLAF organises seminars on a regular basis for anti-fraud coordination services (AFCOS) or Commission auditors and trainings on EU analytical tools – such as the Automated Monitoring Tool (AMT) made available to customs to detect undervaluation cases, evasion of anti-dumping duties or misdeclaration of the commodity – for members of national authorities involved in fighting fraud.

body'.[145] Vested only with administrative powers and no law enforcement prerogatives, OLAF's efficiency is subjected to its collaboration with law enforcement partners. Likewise, its investigations are likely to bring to light criminal or customs offences that require judicial action. On the other hand, the Office may contribute to investigations carried out by national authorities or other EU departments through facilitating and coordinating the gathering and exchange of information, particularly in complex transnational cases.[146]

All EU staff have an obligation of reporting possible 'illegal activity [...] detrimental to the interests of the EU, or of conduct relating to the discharge of professional duties which may constitute a serious failure to comply with the obligations of EU officials' to OLAF.[147] Besides, EU staff and, in accordance with their national law, Members States' authorities are expected to 'transmit to the Office any document or information they hold which relates to an ongoing investigation by the Office' and 'any other document or information considered pertinent which they hold relating to the fight against [...] any [...] illegal activity affecting the financial interests of the Union'.[148] Furthermore, the Office is aimed to become the privileged partner of the European Public Prosecutor, with whom cooperation is to be deployed on a daily basis, in support of or in addition to the activities of the public prosecutor's office; consequently, EU entities are expected to transmit to the Office a copy of their reports to the EPPO in accordance with Article 24 of Regulation (EU) 2017/1939.[149]

Therefore, OLAF's action is inserted into a vast network of cooperations based on administrative arrangements. Its stakeholders in the Member States and in third countries are the national law enforcement and customs authorities and the judicial authorities whereas within the EU institutions, there are mainly the Directorates General of the European Commission and the Commission itself.

[145] Wade, 'OLAF and the Push and Pull Factors of a European Criminal Justice System', 128.
[146] Hofmann and Stoykov, 'OLAF – 20 Years of Protecting the Financial Interests of the EU', 270.
[147] See, also, EP Decision concerning the terms and conditions for internal investigations in relation to the prevention of fraud, corruption and any illegal activity detrimental to the Communities' interests, OJ C 189, 7.7.2000, 210.
[148] Art. 8 OLAF Reg. [149] Art. 8(1).

14.4.1 Co-operation with Other EU Entities

OLAF's cooperation with other EU entities is primarily governed by an Interinstitutional Agreement of 25 May 1999[150] and by the provisions of Article 16 of OLAF Regulation. Law enforcement cooperation is, however, subject to specific provisions and arrangements.[151]

EU entities and, unless prevented by national law, the competent authorities of Member States shall, at the request of the Office or on their own initiative, transmit without delay to the Office any document or information they hold which either is necessary to assess the allegations or to apply the criteria for opening an investigation, or relates to an ongoing investigation by the Office together with any other information, documents or data considered pertinent which they hold, relating to the fight against fraud, corruption and any other illegal activity affecting the financial interests of the Union.[152]

Cooperation also takes place at the strategic level. Article 16(1) OLAF regulation, as amended by Regulation 2020/2223, reads: 'The European Parliament, the Council and the Commission shall once a year meet the Director-General for an exchange of views at political level to discuss the Office's policy relating to methods of preventing and combating fraud, corruption or any other illegal activity affecting the financial interests of the Union. The Supervisory Committee shall participate in the exchange of views. The European Chief Prosecutor shall be invited to attend the exchange of views. Representatives of the Court of Auditors, the EPPO, Eurojust and Europol may be invited to attend on an ad hoc basis upon request of the European Parliament, of the Council, of the Commission, of the Director-General or of the Supervisory Committee.'[153]

Article 13(1) provides that, 'within its mandate to protect the financial interests of the Union, the Office shall cooperate, as appropriate' with Eurojust and Europol.

[150] Interinstitutional Agreement of 25 May 1999 between the European Parliament, the Council of the European Union and the Commission of the European Communities concerning internal investigations by the European Anti-fraud Office (OLAF), OJ L 136, 31.05.1999, pp. 15–19.

[151] Art. 13(1) OLAF Reg. [152] Art. 8(2)–(3).

[153] Art. 16(2) specifies the subject matters and purposes of this exchange of views.

The cooperation with Eurojust is currently governed by a detailed Practical Agreement.[154] It is purposed 'to define [...] the modalities for a close co-operation between the Parties'[155] and provides for the establishment of bilateral 'teams' that shall meet on a regular basis to 'reinforce common strategies on cases', 'resolve practical problems in the co-operation' and 'support the development of priorities and strategies which are complementary'.[156] Direct cooperation is encouraged[157] and takes the shape of exchanges of 'Case Summaries' and exchanges of case-related and strategic information.[158] Moreover, the arrangement provides for crossed-participations to their respective operational meetings.[159]

The arrangement agreed with Europol[160] provides for the parties to exchange strategic and technical information, excluding personal data, 'when this is necessary to perform' their respective tasks,[161] to share technical tools and materials in the field of intelligence,[162] to consult each other on the production of their reports and, where possible, to produce common reports.[163] Article 21 of Regulation (EU) 2016/794 on Europol[164] completes this arrangement and fills some of its shortcomings.[165] The European Financial and Economic Crime Centre recently launched by Europol,[166] aimed at strengthening its ability to support law enforcement authorities in fighting economic and financial crime, may possibly lead to a further improvement of this cooperation. OLAF's *Management Plan 2019* already called for the conclusion of a 'revised working arrangement' to improve the collaboration between the two Offices.

[154] Practical Agreement on arrangements of cooperation between Eurojust and OLAF, OJ C 314/4, 9.12.2008.

[155] Pt. 2.1. [156] Pt. 3. [157] Pt. 4. [158] Pt. 5–7. [159] Pt. 9.

[160] Administrative arrangement between the European Police Office (Europol) and the European Anti-Fraud Office (OLAF), 8.4.2004, available at .

[161] Para. 2. [162] Para. 3. [163] Paras. 4–5.

[164] Regulation (EU) 2016/794 of the European Parliament and of the Council of 11 May 2016 on the European Union Agency for Law Enforcement Cooperation (Europol) and replacing and repealing Council Decisions 2009/371/JHA, 2009/934/JHA, 2009/935/JHA, 2009/936/JHA and 2009/968/JHA, OJ L 135, 24.5.2016, pp. 53–114.

[165] See, more specifically, art. 21(1) and (5).

[166] Europol launches the European Financial and Economic Crime Centre, 5.6.2020, available at www.europol.europa.eu/newsroom/news/europol-launches-european-financial-and-economic-crime-centre.

Besides, Regulation 2020/2223 amends Article 12 OLAF regulation to allow the Office to provide 'relevant information to the Eurofisc network established by Regulation (EU) No 904/2010' and Eurofisc coordinators to 'transmit relevant information from the Eurofisc network to the Office'.

The most significant expression of the operational collaboration between OLAF, Europol and Eurojust takes place under the JITs.[167]

Finally, according to Article 101 EPPO Regulation,[168] 'The EPPO shall establish and maintain a close relationship with OLAF based on mutual cooperation within their respective mandates and on information exchange' implying 'to ensure that all available means are used to protect the Union's financial interests through the complementarity and support by OLAF to the EPPO'. EPPO will be able to request OLAF to make some investigatory acts for the purpose of a criminal investigation it carries out and to request cooperation from OLAF to support and complement its activity.[169] OLAF's added value will consist in the identification and reporting of cases, the support provided to EPPO investigations through its operational and analytical tools and the conduct of 'complementary activities to ensure an administrative response to fraud'.[170] Besides, the continuation of OLAF's activities remains necessary as EPPO's jurisdiction does not extend to the Member States not involved in the enhanced cooperation nor to third countries[171] and as Article 22 of the EPPO Regulation limits its jurisdiction to situations involving €10 million and above at stake. OLAF will further 'keep its exclusive powers in the field of internal investigations and continue to proceed with coordinating the actions of the Member States' authorities'.[172]

[167] See point 5 of the 2004 Administrative Arrangement between Europol and OLAF; point 9 of the 2008 Practical Agreement between Eurojust and OLAF; and, more generally, Art. 6 of the 2009 Agreement between Eurojust and Europol; Marletta, 'Interinstitutional Relationship of European Bodies in the Fight against Crimes Affecting the EU's Financial Interests. Past Experience and Future Models', 142. See *infra*, Cooperation with Member States authorities.

[168] Art. 12(c)–(g) OLAF Reg. [169] Ambos, *European Criminal Law*, p. 579.

[170] Hofmann and Stoykov, 'OLAF – 20 Years of Protecting the Financial Interests of the EU', 271.

[171] A. Venegoni, 'The New Frontier of PFI Investigations. The EPPO and Its Relationship with OLAF', (2017) *eucrim*, 195.

[172] Kuhl, 'The European Public Prosecutor's Office – More Effective, Equivalent, and Independent Criminal Prosecution against Fraud?', 135 at 141; see also P. Klement, 'OLAF at the Gates of Criminal Law', (2017) *eucrim*, 198.

Regulation 2020/2223 defines the legal framework for future cooperation between OLAF and the EPPO.[173] According to its Preamble, the purposes are 'to strengthen the framework for the Office's investigations in order that the Office remains strong and fullyfunctioning and that it complements the EPPO's criminal law approach with administrative investigations, without changing the Office's mandate or powers' and 'to ensure the highest level of protection of the financial interests of the Union through synergies' between OLAF and the EPPO. Article 1 OLAF regulation is complemented with a paragraph 4a that reads: 'The Office shall establish and maintain a close relationship with the European Public Prosecutor's Office (EPPO) established in enhanced cooperation by Council Regulation (EU) 2017/1939. That relationship shall be based on mutual cooperation, information exchange, complementarity and the avoidance of duplication. It shall aim in particular to ensure that all available means are used to protect the financial interests of the Union through the complementarity of their respective mandates and the support provided by the Office to the EPPO.' The Office and the EPPO will specify the procedure and conditions for their cooperation in working arrangements that should establish practical arrangements for the exchange of information and complementary investigations. Furthermore, OLAF DG and the European Chief Prosecutor 'shall meet at least annually to discuss matters of common interest'.[174]

The Office should in principle not open an administrative investigation in parallel with an investigation conducted by the EPPO into the same facts.[175] Before starting an investigation, the Office should verify via the EPPO's case management system, whether the EPPO is conducting an investigation into the same facts. It is allowed to conduct a preliminary evaluation to ascertain allegations of criminal offenses but should conduct such an evaluation expeditiously and by means which do not risk jeopardising a possible future EPPO criminal investigation. Furthermore, the Office is, before or during an investigation, required to report to the EPPO without undue delay on any suspected

[173] Art. 2 Regulation 2020/2223 states the OLAF/EPPO cooperation provisions 'shall apply from a date to be determined in accordance with the second subparagraph of Article 120(2) of Regulation (EU) 2017/1939'.

[174] Art. 12g.

[175] The notion of 'same facts' should be considered, in light of the case law of the Court of Justice of the European Union (CJEU) on the *ne bis in idem* principle.

criminal conduct in respect of which the EPPO could exercise its competence. When, in the course of its investigation, a suspicion of a criminal offence arises, and the EPPO opens an investigation following its report, the Office should discontinue its investigation into the same facts, unless the EPPO orders the Office to carry it on.[176] However, when the EPPO decides not to conduct an investigation or will dismiss a case, it may, 'with a view to enabling the Office to consider appropriate administrative action in accordance with its mandate, provide relevant information to the Office'. Where the Office opens an investigation, it should conduct it, consulting the EPPO on an ongoing basis and if its administrative investigation reveals new facts unknown to the EPPO at the time of its decision to dismiss the case, OLAF DG will have to ask the EPPO to reopen an investigation.[177]

The Office is aimed to actively support the EPPO's investigations. Thus, the EPPO may request the Office to support or complement its criminal investigations through the exercise of powers under Regulation 883/2013. According to Article 12e 1., 'In the course of an investigation by the EPPO, and at the request of the EPPO [...], the Office shall, in accordance with its mandate, support or complement the EPPO's activity, in particular by: (a) providing information, analyses (including forensic analyses), expertise and operational support; (b) facilitating coordination of specific actions of the competent national administrative authorities and bodies of the Union; (c) conducting administrative investigations'. When providing support to the EPPO, the Office shall refrain from performing acts or measures that could jeopardise the investigation or prosecution. The supporting measures thus provided by the Office on request of the EPPO must be carried out in accordance with the procedural safeguards of Regulation (EU) 2017/1939 in order to protect the admissibility of evidence as well as fundamental rights. Furthermore, the EPPO may allow the Office to carry out a complementary administrative investigation before the conclusion of criminal proceedings initiated by the EPPO, with the purpose of facilitating the adoption of precautionary measures or of taking financial, disciplinary or administrative actions. To ensure effective coordination, cooperation and transparency, the Office and the EPPO should exchange information on an ongoing basis. In the absence of any EPPO's request, support

[176] Art. 12c. [177] Art. 12d.

or complementary investigations on the initiative of the Office are subjected to the prior consultation of the EPPO, which is able to object to the performance of any act likely to pertain to one of its investigations and the Office should then refrain from performing an action to which the EPPO has raised an objection.[178]

The launching of EPPO may somehow impair OLAF's capacities as members of its staff have already been seconded to EPPO whereas its involvement in preparatory steps for investigations that will be carried out by EPPO will notably increase its duty (Klement, p.198). Besides, the subordination of OLAF to EPPO could lead to litigation as it seems hardly consistent with the principle of independence of the Office.

14.4.2 Co-operation with Member States' Authorities

As a consequence of the limits of its own powers, it has been stated that OLAF is a 'prisoner of national laws'.[179] M. Janda and R. Panait emphasise: 'references to the national law of the Member State in which OLAF makes use of its competences are present in the OLAF Regulation at every stage of an investigation'.[180] On the other hand, 'The establishment of OLAF has conferred a new vertical dimension to EU law enforcement: a supranational body has been entrusted with operations across national borders in order to overcome the obstacles inherent to any domestic response to transnational offences.'[181]

The legal basis of the cooperation between OLAF and Member States' authorities is mainly to be found in OLAF Regulation[182] and in Article 15 of the PIF Directive.[183] Regulation 2020/2223 also amends Article 1 OLAF regulation by providing that 'competent authorities of the Member States [...] may establish administrative arrangements with the Office' which 'may concern, in particular, the transmission of information, the

[178] Art. 12e, 12f.

[179] K. Ligeti and M. Simonato, 'Multidisciplinary Investigations into Offences against the Financial Interests of the EU: A Quest for an Integrated Enforcement Concept', in F. Galli and A. Weyembergh, *Do Labels Still Matter? Blurring Boundaries between Administrative and Criminal Law. The Influence of the EU*, Brussels: Ed. de l'Université de Bruxelles, coll. Études européennes, 2014, p. 82.

[180] p. 184.

[181] Simonato, 'OLAF Investigations in a Multi-Level System. Legal Obstacles to Effective Enforcement, 136.

[182] Arts. 1(5) and 12(1), (2) and (4) OLAF Reg.

[183] Directive (EU) 2017/1371 (see above).

conduct of investigations and any follow-up action'. Article 7(3) reads: 'The competent authorities of Member States shall give the necessary assistance to enable the staff of the Office to fulfil their tasks in accordance with this Regulation effectively and without undue delay. When providing such assistance, the competent authorities of Member States shall act in accordance with any national procedural rules applicable to them' and assist the Office through implementing their enforcement capacities 'under the same conditions as those that apply to the national competent authorities'.

On these grounds, a regular cooperation with the competent national authorities, including at the prosecution stage, is part of OLAF's tasks to provide the Member States with technical and operational assistance. OLAF is mainly in charge of coordinating, through the AFCOS' network, Member States's authorities' activities in their fight against fraud and other offences falling within its jurisdiction, in particular as regards cross-border cooperation among Member States (coordination activities[184]). Regulation 2020/2223 specifies the relationship between OLAF and the AFCOS, which are aimed to 'facilitate effective cooperation and exchange of information, including information of an operational nature, with the Office' and to 'provide or coordinate the necessary assistance for the Office to carry out its tasks effectively'.[185] The Office may also request the opening of a national administrative investigation and take part to it, acting as 'a seconded expert or joint investigator, vested with the same powers as the national authorities' in a so-called 'mixed inspections'.[186] Besides, the Office may participate in joint investigation teams established in accordance with Union law and is entitled to exchange operational information acquired in that framework. When the Office participates in such joint investigation teams, it has a supporting capacity and takes the role of a partner subject to legal constraints that may exist in Union or national law.[187]

However, the commitment of Member States' administrative and judicial authorities to their duty to cooperate with OLAF is affected both by

[184] Art. 1(2), 3(4) and 12b OLAF Reg. [185] Art. 12a.

[186] Simonato, 'OLAF Investigations in a Multi-Level System. Legal Obstacles to Effective Enforcement,' 137.

[187] Art. 12b(4).

the diversity of services appointed as AFCOS in the different Member States[188] and by the disparities in national laws,[189] which involves a fragmentation in their level of cooperation.[190]

14.4.3 Co-operation with Third Countries' Authorities and International Organisations

EU competences carry an external dimension.[191] Rules governing the cooperation of the Office with third countries and international organisations – the so-called 'secondary territorial competence' of OLAF[192] – are provided for in Article 14 OLAF Regulation, which reads that, subjected to a coordination of its action with the competent Commission services and the European External Action Service, the Office may agree administrative arrangements with competent authorities in third countries and with international organisations. Furthermore, some provisions of specific pieces of legislation allow, at least implicitly, OLAF to engage in relations with third countries' authorities[193] and implement its powers outside the territory of the EU. The Financial Regulation[194] further oblige beneficiaries of EU funds to agree on OLAF's jurisdiction, to grant OLAF a national law basis allowing it to investigate on their territory and implement its powers and to cooperate in protecting the financial interests of the EU. Standard clauses establishing the competence of the Commission

[188] K. Bovend'Eerdt, Learning Lessons – Reflecting on Regulation 883/2013 through Comparative Analysis, (2017) *eucrim*, p. 190.

[189] Arts. 8(2) and 8(3) OLAF Reg.

[190] For example, the French Ministry of Justice prohibits the transmission to OLAF of material resulting from judicial proceedings arguing of the Office's status as an administrative investigation service (Interview with an officer of the French DNRED, 13.6.2020).

[191] CJEU, *Commission v. Council*, No. C-114/12, Judgment, 4 September 2014, para. 73.

[192] Panait, 'Information Sharing between OLAF and National Judicial Authorities. The Advantages of a Supranational Structure and the Legislative Limitations Specific to a European Hybrid Body', 65.

[193] For example, Council Regulation No 2185/96.

[194] Arts. 129(1), (2) and 220(5c) of Regulation (EU, Euratom) No 2018/1046 of the European Parliament and of the Council of 18 July 2018 on the financial rules applicable to the general budget of the Union, amending Regulations (EU) No 1296/2013, (EU) No 1301/2013, (EU) No 1303/2013, (EU) No 1304/2013, (EU) No 1309/2013, (EU) No 1316/2013, (EU) No 223/2014, (EU) No 283/2014, and Decision No 541/2014/EU and repealing Regulation (EU, Euratom) No 966/2012, *O.J.* L 193, 30.07.2018.

and OLAF to control the use recipients do of EU funds are thus inserted in EU international agreements with third countries. Besides, OLAF has currently agreed arrangements containing provisions on mutual administrative assistance in customs matters and/or anti-fraud measures in preferential tariff regimes with eighty-five third countries. Lastly, 'in the absence of such an agreement, the third country may provide its consent to OLAF's investigative activities de facto, when the competent authority agrees to OLAF's actions in a specific case'.[195]

On ground of these arrangements, the Office may carry out investigations and collect evidence of fraud on third countries territories. On completion of its investigations, when it reveals evidence that an offense has been committed, OLAF informs the European External Action Service of the outcomes of the investigation and transmits to the competent national authorities an 'Information Note' containing the elements of the Final Report pertinent to them.[196] If relevant, it may then transmit evidence thus collected to Member States national law enforcement authorities, which can include them in the proceedings initiated against their nationals, and to the Commission to allow it taking remedial actions.

Further Reading

Jan F. H. Inghelram, Legal *and Institutional Aspects of the European Anti-Fraud Office (OLAF),* Groningen: Europa Law Publishing 2011.

Constantin Stefanov, Simone White and Helen Xanthaki, *OLAF at the Crossroads: Action Against EU Fraud,* Oxford: Hart Publishing, 2011.

OLAF Annual Reports (https://ec.europa.eu/anti-fraud/about-us/reports/annual-olaf-reports_fr).

[195] C. Scharf-Kröner and J. Seyderhelm, 'OLAF Investigations Outside the European Union', (2019) *eucrim*, 211.

[196] Ibid., 213.

Europol 15

Katalin Ligeti and Fabio Giuffrida*

15.1 Introduction

The European Union Agency for Law Enforcement Cooperation (Europol) is the European Union's most important actor in the field of police cooperation. Sometimes misleadingly referred to as the 'European FBI',[1] Europol is competent to support and strengthen action by the Member States' (MS) law enforcement services, notably police, and their cooperation. Unlike the FBI, Europol does not have executive powers: Europol cannot arrest people nor conduct investigations on its own. As this chapter will demonstrate, however, Europol's contribution to the activities of national law enforcement authorities is at times so important that the boundaries between executive and non-executive powers seem to fade in practice.

The next sections provide a short overview of Europol's history and legal framework and examine its structure and competence. The analysis then moves on to the tasks of the Agency, including Europol's role in the so-called Policy Cycle, and its accountability. The final sections focus on the Agency's relations with its partners and the forthcoming revision of the Europol's legal framework.

15.2 History, Context and Legal Basis

Europol was established in the context of the former third pillar by means of a Convention, which was adopted in 1995 ('Europol

* The opinions expressed in this chapter by Fabio Giuffrida are personal opinions of the author and do not reflect those of the European Commission.

1 The idea of a 'European FBI' was launched by the German Chancellor Helmut Kohl between the 1980s and the 1990s (see C. Kaunert, 'Europol and EU Counterterrorism: International Security Actorness in the External Dimension', (2010) 33 *Stud. Confl. Terror.*, 652, 654). It is telling that 'Is Europol a European FBI?' is one of the Frequently Asked Questions on Europol's website – the answer being 'No. Europol has no executive powers' (see www.europol.europa.eu/faq/europol-european-fbi; all webpages mentioned in this contribution have been last accessed on 26 September 2021).

Convention'),[2] and replaced the former European Drugs Unit.[3] Due to some delays in the ratification process, the Convention entered into force only in 1998, with Europol starting its activities in 1999. At the time, Europol's mandate was more limited than it currently is, as Europol could support the coordination of national law enforcement authorities dealing with a few specific areas of crime listed in the Convention, notably terrorism and drug trafficking.[4] In the early 2000s, several Protocols amended the Europol Convention by extending its mandate and amending different aspects of Europol's structure and tasks.[5] The establishment of Europol and the start of its operations also triggered discussions on the need to create a similar body in the field of judicial cooperation, which led to the establishment of Europol's 'sister agency',[6] Eurojust (European Union Agency for Criminal Justice Cooperation). Established by means of a Council Decision adopted in 2002,[7] Eurojust is based in The Hague like Europol and is one of its key partners.

In parallel with the negotiations of the Constitutional Treaty that never entered into force, negotiations started also on a new instrument regulating Europol, which was eventually adopted in April 2009 and repealed the 1995 Convention ('2009 (Europol Council) Decision').[8] The 2009 Decision modernised Europol's tasks and functioning and, among others, changed its financial regime providing for its funding from the Union budget and not from the MS anymore.[9] A few months after the adoption of the 2009 Council Decision, the Treaty of Lisbon entered into force. Article 88 of the Treaty on the Functioning of the European Union (TFEU) provides that the European Parliament and the Council shall determine Europol's structure, operation and tasks by means of regulations.

[2] OJ C 316/2, 27.11.1995.

[3] On the developments that led to the creation of Europol see, among others, S. Hufnagel, *Policing Global Regions. The Legal Context of Transnational Law Enforcement Cooperation*, Abingdon, Oxon–New York, NY: Routledge, 2020, pp. 121–122.

[4] Art. 2(1) of the Europol Convention.

[5] Among the others, the 'Danish Protocol' (OJ C 2/3, 6.1.2004) provided for several changes to Europol's functioning, including on the exchange of information between Europol and national authorities (see the section on structure below).

[6] A. Weyembergh, I. Armada and C. Brière, 'The Inter-Agency Cooperation and Future Architecture of the EU Criminal Justice and Law Enforcement Area', Study for the LIBE Committee of the European Parliament, 2014, p. 11.

[7] OJ L 63/1, 6.3.2002. [8] OJ L 121/37, 15.5.2009.

[9] Art. 42 of the Europol Council Decision.

Article 88 TFEU clearly provides that the Agency does not have coercive powers.[10] The Treaties do not bestow upon Europol (as well as Eurojust)[11] the traditional coercive powers of national authorities but only those to support national law enforcement authorities and coordinate their activities. Nonetheless, as will be discussed in the sections below, Europol plays a pivotal role in the field of police cooperation and this was repeatedly acknowledged by the pre-Lisbon European Council's conclusions on the Area of Freedom, Security and Justice,[12] as well as by the most recent EU documents setting out the EU's agenda in the field of police cooperation. To name only one example, the EU Strategy to tackle Organised Crime 2021–2025 notes that 'Europol plays an important role as the EU criminal information hub, supporting police cooperation and information exchange'[13] and further describes the main features of such role.

Europol's activities are currently regulated by Regulation (EU) 2016/794 ('Europol Regulation'),[14] which the EU co-legislators adopted on the basis of Article 88 TFEU and entered into force on 1 May 2017. With this Regulation, Europol has been formally established as an 'agency' of the EU while before it was an 'office' of the Union.[15] In December 2020, the Commission tabled a proposal to revise the Europol Regulation,[16] which is still under negotiation, with the aim to ensure that the Agency's structure and powers keep pace with a fast-changing world.

[10] 'The application of coercive measures shall be the exclusive responsibility of the competent national authorities' (Art. 88(3) TFEU).

[11] Cf. Art. 85(2) TFEU.

[12] See European Council's Conclusions, Tampere, 1999, especially paras. 43–46; 'The Hague Programme: strengthening freedom, security and justice in the European Union', OJ C 53/1, 3.3.2005, especially para. 2.3; and 'The Stockholm Programme. An open and secure Europe serving and protecting citizens', OJ C 115/1, 4.5.2010, especially para. 4.3.1.

[13] COM(2021) 170 final, para. 1.2.

[14] Regulation (EU) 2016/794 of the European Parliament and of the Council of 11 May 2016 on the European Union Agency for Law Enforcement Cooperation (Europol) and replacing and repealing Council Decisions 2009/371/JHA, 2009/934/JHA, 2009/935/JHA, 2009/936/JHA and 2009/968/JHA, OJ L 135/53, 24.5.2016. Any further reference to Articles and Recitals should be understood as referring to Articles and Recitals of the Europol Regulation unless otherwise specified.

[15] Art. 1.

[16] Commission, Proposal for a Regulation of the European Parliament and of the Council amending Regulation (EU) 2016/794, as regards Europol's cooperation with private parties, the processing of personal data by Europol in support of criminal investigations, and Europol's role on research and innovation, COM(2020) 796 final. The Proposal is examined in a section further below.

Ireland opted in the Europol Regulation, while Denmark does not take part in it.[17] In April 2017, Denmark signed an Agreement with Europol to ensure that its non-participation in the Regulation does not impair its effective cooperation with the Agency.[18] Before the United Kingdom left the European Union, it participated in Europol as well and was one of the highest contributors to Europol and its databases.[19] The EU-UK Trade and Cooperation Agreement includes some provisions on the cooperation between Europol and UK authorities, which both parties are in the process of implementing.[20]

15.3 Structure

The two main organs of Europol are the Management Board and the Executive Director.[21] The Management Board is composed of one representative per MS and one representative of the Commission, each with voting right,[22] and takes most of its decisions by majority.[23] Unlike Eurojust, Europol does not have an Executive Board, that is, a body composed only of the representatives of some MS and the Commission which would streamline the Agency's decision-making process. When the Commission tabled its proposal for a Regulation on Europol in 2013, it suggested that the Management Board could establish an Executive Board,[24] yet the Council and the European Parliament opposed this proposal.

In addition to its competence on several matters related to the Agency's activities and functioning, including the adoption of the working programmes and the annual budget,[25] the Management Board is also competent to propose to the Council a shortlist of candidates

[17] Recitals 72 and 74.

[18] 'Agreement on Operational and Strategic Cooperation between the Kingdom of Denmark and the European Police Office', 29 April 2017, available at www.europol.europa.eu/publications-documents/agreement-operational-and-strategic-cooperation-between-kingdom-of-denmark-and-europol.

[19] V. Mitsilegas, 'European Criminal Law after Brexit', (2017) 28 *CLF*, 219, 240; see also the contribution (Chapter 18) by Mitsilegas in this volume.

[20] Arts. 564–579 of the Trade and Cooperation Agreement between the European Union and the European Atomic Energy Community, of the one part, and the United Kingdom of Great Britain and Northern Ireland, of the other part, OJ L 149/10, 30.4.2021.

[21] Art. 9. [22] Art. 10(1). [23] Art. 15(1).

[24] COM(2013) 173 final, Arts. 12(e), 21 and 22. [25] Art. 11(1).

for the post of Executive Director and Deputy Executive Directors,[26] who are eventually appointed by the Council.[27] The Director, whose mandate lasts four years (renewable once for another four-year term),[28] is responsible for Europol's day-to-day administration, implements the decisions taken by the Management Board and prepares a number of documents, including the draft work programmes, which are to be adopted by the Management Board.[29]

With a view to ensuring smooth cooperation between Europol and the MS, each MS is required to set up a Europol National Unit (ENU), which is defined the 'liaison body'[30] between the Agency and the national competent authorities. The heads of the national units (HENUs) shall meet on a regular basis to discuss and resolve problems that arise when such units cooperate with Europol.[31] The ENUs are located in the MS and are competent, among others, to ensure effective communication and cooperation of all relevant authorities with the Agency and supply it with the information necessary for Europol to fulfil its objectives.[32]

Such provision on the national units' task to share information with Europol was included also in the Europol Council Decision, yet it had a limited application in practice, in line with a well-known problem of police cooperation at the EU level – the occasional national authorities' reluctance to share information with Europol.[33] In order to streamline the cooperation between Europol and national units, the latter should designate at least one Europol Liaison Officer (ELO) to be posted at Europol.[34] The ELOs compose Europol's Liaison Bureaux, which assist in the exchange of information between Europol and their MS, as well as with the liaison officers of other MS or third countries when appropriate.

[26] Art. 11(1)(j). [27] Arts. 54(2) and 55. [28] Art. 54(3)–(6).

[29] Art. 16(5). [30] Art. 7(2) and (5). [31] Art. 7(9). [32] Respectively Art. 7(6)(b) and (a).

[33] See M. Fletcher, R. Lööf and B. Gilmore, *EU Criminal Law and Justice*, Cheltenham and Northampton, MA: Edward Elgar, 2008, p. 91; A. De Moor and G. Vermeulen, 'The Europol Council Decision: Transforming Europol into an Agency of the European Union', (2010) 47 *CMLR*, 1089, 1099; S. Gless, 'Europol', in V. Mitsilegas, M. Bergström and T. Konstadinides (eds.), *Research Handbook on EU Criminal Law*, Cheltenham and Northampton, MA: Edward Elgar, 2016, p. 459; C. Cocq and F. Galli, 'The Evolving Role of Europol in the Fight against Serious Crime: Current Challenges and Future Prospects', in S. Hufnagel and C. McCartney (eds.), *Trust in International Police and Justice Cooperation*, Oxford and Portland, Oregon: Hart, 2017, pp. 125–148.

[34] Art. 8(1).

While the 1995 Convention identified the ENUs as the only channel of communication between Europol and the national authorities, already in 2003 it became clear that a direct communication with such authorities was necessary for Europol to effectively perform its tasks. After the entry into force of the so-called 'Danish Protocol' that amended the Convention, Member States could therefore allow for direct contacts between Europol and national authorities.[35] As a testament to the MS' preference for a centralised model of communication, which arguably limits the encroachment of Europol on national law enforcement activities, the rule has not changed since then. National units remain the main and preferred channel of communication but, 'subject to conditions determined by the Member States, [...] the Member States may allow *direct contacts* between their competent authorities and Europol.'[36]

In sum, Europol has a hierarchical structure that, especially when compared to Eurojust, shows some intergovernmental features despite the 'communautarisation' of the Agency brought about by the Treaty of Lisbon and the 2016 Regulation. For instance, Europol's Director is elected by the Council, while Eurojust's President is chosen by the College of Eurojust and is not hierarchically superior to his or her colleagues in the College. The appointment of Europol's Executive Director was a controversial issue during the negotiations of the Regulation. While the Commission had proposed that the Management Board would appoint the Director from a list of candidates proposed by the Commission itself,[37] the European Parliament and the Council eventually opted for a procedure that reflects the 'still predominant intergovernmental nature of the agency'.[38] Eurojust has some national correspondents in each Member State as well but there is no provision in the Eurojust Regulation similar to the one in the Europol Regulation on the ENU as the main liaison body between the Agency and national authorities. Likewise, it is worth noting that, pursuant to the Europol Regulation, ELOs 'shall be instructed by their national units to represent the interests of the latter within Europol';[39] no similar rule, which reveals the MS' willingness to keep their influence over Europol's activities, is to be found in the Eurojust Regulation.

[35] Art. 1(3) of the Danish Protocol (OJ C 2/3, 6.1.2004).

[36] Art. 7(5) (emphasis added). [37] COM(2013) 173 final, Art. 56(2).

[38] V. Mitsilegas and F. Giuffrida, 'Bodies, Offices and Agencies', in V. Mitsilegas, *EU Criminal Law*, 2nd edn., London: Hart, in press.

[39] Art. 8(2).

15.4 Mission and Competence

Europol's mission is to support and strengthen action by competent authorities and their cooperation in preventing and combating 'serious crime affecting two or more Member States, terrorism and forms of crime which affect a common interest covered by a Union policy, as listed in Annex I.'[40] In addition, Europol is also competent for related criminal offences, that is, offences committed in order to facilitate or perpetrate – or procure the means of perpetrating – acts in respect of which Europol is primarily competent, as well as to ensure the impunity of persons committing those same acts.[41]

Annex I to the Europol Regulation lists forms of criminal conduct such as organised crime, drug trafficking, money laundering, computer crime, corruption and environmental crime. The list is largely similar to that of crimes for which Council Framework Decision 2002/584/JHA on the European arrest warrant[42] and other EU instruments of mutual recognition do not require the verification of double criminality and is identical to the list of crimes for which Eurojust is competent.[43]

The Annex refers to broad areas of crime (e.g., environmental crime, computer crime, etc.), which in turn may encompass different offences, and this may lead to some uncertainty in marking the precise boundaries of Europol's mandate. Furthermore, while the definitions and penalties of several of the offences listed in the Annex have been harmonised at the EU level, they are still different throughout the EU since it is ultimately for the national legislators to set out the rules on the definitions and sanctions of crimes. As a consequence, Europol's mandate may be interpreted in different ways in the EU,[44] although law enforcement authorities reportedly appreciate 'vague definitions that provide different options'.[45]

[40] Art. 3(1).

[41] Art. 3(2). See Mitsilegas and Giuffrida, 'Bodies, Offices and Agencies', in press, whereupon this section and the following four ones draw.

[42] OJ L 190/1, 18.7.2002.

[43] Cf. Annex I to Regulation (EU) 2018/1727, OJ L 295/138, 21.11.2018 ('Eurojust Regulation').

[44] De Moor and Vermeulen, 'The Europol Council Decision', 1098. Cf. also E. Disley et al., 'Evaluation of the implementation of the Europol Council Decision and of Europol's activities', Report for Europol Management Board, Rand Europe, 2012, p. 71 ('there was extensive discussion [...] as to whether Europol was competent to work on the riots which surrounded the G8 and G20 meetings, due to different definitions of terrorism and extremism').

[45] S. Hufnagel, 'Organized Crime', in V. Mitsilegas, M. Bergström and T. Konstadinides (eds.), *Research Handbook on EU Criminal Law*, Cheltenham and Northampton, MA: Edward Elgar, 2016, p. 363.

15.5 Tasks

Europol's tasks can be grouped into two categories: (i) data processing–related tasks, which are examined in Section 15.5.1 together with the main rules on data protection rights that set the boundaries of those tasks, and (ii) other tasks, which encompass both operational tasks and further ones related to the training of national authorities as well as gathering and spreading of knowledge and expertise. The Agency's role in the so-called Policy Cycle will be analysed in Section 15.5.3.

15.5.1 Data Processing–Related Tasks and Data Protection Safeguards

With regard to the analysis and exchange of information, Europol's core task is enshrined in Article 4(1)(a) of the Regulation, which requires the Agency to 'collect, store, process, analyse and exchange information, including criminal intelligence'.[46] Eurojust also manages SIENA (Secure Information Exchange Network Application), an online platform that facilitates the exchange of information among MS, EU bodies (including Europol), third countries, and international organisations.[47] Europol is committed to facilitating the information exchange among national authorities, and between them and other relevant actors (including Europol itself), and to analysing such information in order to prepare 'threat assessments, strategic and operational analyses and general situation reports'.[48]

As the latter provision shows, Europol is competent for both *strategic* analysis, which aims to support and develop a 'criminal policy that contributes to the efficient and effective prevention of, and the fight against, crime',[49] and *operational* analysis, which instead encompasses 'all methods and techniques by which information is collected, stored, processed and assessed with the aim of supporting criminal investigations'.[50] It follows that strategic analysis does not concern specific criminal investigations,

[46] Art. 4(1)(a). Other data processing–related tasks are listed in Art. 4(1)(e), (h), (j) and (k).

[47] Recital 24. See Disley et al., 'Evaluation of the Implementation of the Europol Council Decision and of Europol's Activities', p. 78. On the increase of operational message exchanges between national authorities and Europol after the setting up of SIENA in 2009, see Hufnagel, *Policing Global Regions. The Legal Context of Transnational Law Enforcement Cooperation*, pp. 81–82.

[48] Art. 4(1)(f). [49] Art. 2(b). [50] Art. 2(c).

while operational analysis is related to ongoing cases and can therefore lead Europol to unveil or collect relevant information that may be used by national law enforcement and prosecuting authorities in the context of a specific investigation, such as the location of the suspects or links among existing cases.

In order for Europol to perform its data processing–related tasks, the Agency relies on a computerised information system that has been subject to several reforms over the last years. In accordance with the Europol Convention and the Europol Council Decision, Europol had an IT system that was composed of the Europol Information System (EIS), analysis work files (AWFs) and index function.[51] Different rules regulated the data to be included and processed in the EIS, AWFs and the index. Duplication and overlaps, but also fragmentation of information, were the main risks following from such structure of the Europol's system,[52] which the Europol Regulation has considerably transformed by abolishing the previous internal components of Europol's information system (EIS, AWFs, index) with the aim to ensure a more flexible and integrated data management.[53] The main aim of the reform is that, once Europol receives a piece of information, it should be capable of analysing it without any obstacle linked to the specific and different rules governing the previous components of the Europol's system (EIS, AWFs, index).[54] The new information system therefore 'introduces, for the first time, one single data processing environment, instead of separated data systems, merging all three of the [previous] databases into one'.[55]

[51] Arts. 11–13 (EIS), 14 and 16 (AWFs) and 15 (index function) of the 2009 Europol Council Decision. See Disley et al., 'Evaluation of the implementation of the Europol Council Decision and of Europol's activities', p. 78.

[52] On the lack of flexibility resulting from data stored in different databases, see Disley et al., 'Evaluation of the implementation of the Europol Council Decision and of Europol's activities', pp. 80–84.

[53] See COM(2013) 173 final, 'Explanatory Memorandum', p. 8.

[54] Cf. D. Drewer and V. Miladinova, 'The BIG DATA Challenge: Impact and Opportunity of Large Quantities of Information Under the Europol Regulation' (2017) 33 *CLSR*, 298, 305.

[55] C. Blasi Casagran, 'The New Europol Legal Framework: Implications for EU Exchanges of Information in the Field of Law Enforcement', in M. O'Neill and K. Swinton (eds.), *Challenges and Critiques of the EU Internal Security Strategy: Rights, Power and Security*, Cambridge: Cambridge Scholars Publishing, 2017, p. 159. The author also adds that the Europol's information system now revolves around the purpose of processing, that is, 'different categories of data are collected and processed depending on the purpose' (ibid.).

There is however some continuity between the previous and current Europol's data processing regime. Before the Europol Regulation entered into force, operational analysis took place in the context of the 'focal points' within the AWFs. For instance, as Europol did not have a focal point on environmental crime until the end of 2017, it could not process and analyse personal data concerning environmental crimes, unless such crimes could be dealt with in the context of focal points devoted to other crimes (e.g., organised crime, if the environmental offences were committed by a criminal organisation).[56] Focal points have now been formally abolished and replaced with 'analysis projects', which represent the framework within which Europol's analysts can carry out a number of activities such as analysing 'information and intelligence, to obtain as much structured and concrete information as possible for law enforcement authorities to "hit" targets with'.[57] The Europol Regulation clarifies that, in principle, personal data may only be collected and processed for the purpose of the specified operational analysis project,[58] while it can be processed for the purposes of other analysis projects only under the specific and limited circumstances laid down in the Regulation.[59] In the absence of precise rules in the Regulation, one may wonder whether the Regulation has truly improved the Agency's processing activities in practice, since personal data can now be processed (mostly, if not only) in the context of 'analysis projects' in the same way as it could be processed only in the framework of 'focal points' before the entry into force of the Europol Regulation.

At any rate, such activities clearly encroach upon the individual's rights to privacy and data protection, which are enshrined in Articles 7 and 8 of the Charter of Fundamental Rights of the European Union. Since Europol is not subject to Directive (EU) 2016/680 (the 'Law Enforcement Directive'),[60] the Europol Regulation provides for a set of data protection rules that apply to Europol. Recital 39 of the Regulation lays down the key principle that should inspire the Agency's data processing activities, namely that any information that has 'clearly been obtained in obvious

[56] See V. Mitsilegas and F. Giuffrida, 'The Role of EU Agencies in Fighting Transnational Environmental Crime. New Challenges for Eurojust and Europol', (2017) 1 *BRP Trans.'l Crime*, 1, 92–95.

[57] 'European Analysis Projects', available at www.europol.europa.eu/crime-areas-trends/europol-analysis-projects.

[58] Art. 18(3)(b). [59] Ibid. [60] OJ L 119/89, 4.5.2016.

violation of human rights shall not be processed'.[61] Furthermore, Europol may carry out processing activities only in so far as necessary for the achievement of its objectives.[62] Among the several rules set out in the Regulation, Article 17 provides that Europol can only process information from MS, Union bodies, third countries, international organisations, private parties and private persons in accordance with the rules and procedures provided for in the Regulation itself.[63] Nonetheless, Europol may also retrieve and process information – including personal data – from publicly available sources and from Union, international and national information systems, if allowed by specific legal instruments.[64]

Furthermore, the Regulation provides that information can be processed only for the specific purposes of information processing activities mentioned in the Regulation itself (such as strategic and operational analyses or cross-checking with the aim of identifying links among cases)[65] and also clarifies that the entity that shares its information with Europol has the obligation to determine the purpose for which that information is to be processed by Europol ('purpose limitation').[66] While only the MS have the right to access and search all information provided to Europol for the purposes of cross-checking or strategic analysis,[67] Eurojust and the European Anti-Fraud Office (OLAF), as well as MS when information provided for operational analysis is concerned, have an indirect access on the basis of a hit/no-hit system.[68] This means that they can access Europol's system only to verify whether their information matches with information that is already in the Agency's system. In case of a match ('hit'), 'Europol shall initiate the procedure by which the information that generated the hit may be shared'.[69]

Several provisions of the Europol Regulation concern data protection safeguards.[70] They include, among others, rules on general data protection principles,[71] time limits for the storage and deletion of data,[72] data protection by design,[73] right of access of individuals to their personal data and right to rectification, erasure and restriction,[74] and responsibility in data protection matters, which lies with the MS for the information provided to Europol, and with the Agency for data it communicates to

[61] This is restated in Art. 23(9) on the Agency's relations with its partners (see Section 15.7).
[62] Art. 18. [63] Art. 17(1). [64] Art. 17(2) and (3), respectively. [65] Art. 18.
[66] Art. 19(1). [67] Art. 20(1).
[68] Arts. 20(2) (Member States) and 21 (Eurojust and OLAF). [69] Arts. 20(2) and 21(1).
[70] Arts. 28–46. [71] Art. 28. [72] Art. 31. [73] Art. 33. [74] Art. 36.

third parties or resulting from its analyses.[75] Furthermore, the Regulation requires each Member State to designate a national supervisory authority, which is competent to monitor independently, in accordance with its respective national law, 'the permissibility of the transfer, the retrieval and any communication to Europol of personal data by the Member State concerned, and [to examine] whether such transfer, retrieval or communication violates the rights of the data subjects concerned.'[76]

While national supervisory authorities operate in the MS, there are two further layers of safeguard at the EU level. First, Europol's Management Board appoints a Data Protection Officer (DPO), who is a member of Europol's staff acting independently in the performance of his or her duties[77] and has the task of ensuring the internal application of the Regulation to Europol's activities concerning the processing of data.[78] Second, the European Data Protection Supervisor (EDPS) monitors and ensures the application of the Regulation's provisions related to the protection of individuals' rights concerned by the processing of personal data by Europol,[79] and also advises such individuals, as well as Europol, on matters concerning personal data.[80]

15.5.2 Other Tasks: Operational and Knowledge-Related Activities

With regard to the Agency's 'operational' tasks, aside from those connected with the operational analysis examined above, they include tasks such as requesting national authorities to initiate a criminal investigation and to set up a joint investigation team (JIT),[81] which is an instrument of cooperation that is highly appreciated by practitioners.[82] Europol's request to initiate criminal investigations is not binding on national authorities. However, when they decide not to follow up on Europol's request, national authorities should motivate their refusal without undue

[75] Art. 38(2). [76] Art. 42(1). [77] Art. 41(1).
[78] See more in Art. 41(6). [79] Art. 43(1). [80] Ibid.
[81] Art. 5 regulates Europol's participation in JITs.
[82] See also Disley et al., 'Evaluation of the Implementation of the Europol Council Decision and of Europol's Activities', pp. 72–73; Hufnagel, *Policing Global Regions. The Legal Context of Transnational Law Enforcement Cooperation*, pp. 84ff. Europol can also, in accordance with Art. 5(4) and the conditions set out therein, process the information gathered by its officials in the context of JITs, with the consent and under the responsibility of the Member State that provided the information.

delay,[83] unless there are risks to jeopardise ongoing investigations or other overriding interests to take into account.[84]

The Regulation also tasks Europol with the coordination, organisation and implementation of investigative and operational actions 'to support and strengthen actions by the competent authorities of the MS, which are carried out: (i) jointly with the competent authorities of the MS; or (ii) in the context of joint investigation teams [...]'.[85] While such wording was not included in the Europol Council Decision, the Regulation has mostly codified the existing state of affairs rather than bestowing a new task upon the Agency, as Europol had already coordinated national investigations before the entry into force of the Regulation, especially in cases of terrorism, immigration, and cybercrime. Europol's operational support to national investigations can for instance lead to Europol sending some of its analysts on the ground who can even form 'a situation centre to coordinate a response to major security events and crises, [and] [create] a task force'.[86]

Finally, Europol has other tasks related to the training of national law enforcement authorities as well as the gathering of knowledge and expertise,[87] including the management of a secure online platform, the Europol Platform for Experts (EPE) where best practices, documentation, knowledge and non-personal data on crime can be shared.[88] Due to its unique position as the EU hub for intelligence sharing and data processing, Europol is in an ideal position to collect and spread knowledge on cross-border crimes and the best strategies to cope with them. Already before the entry into force of the Regulation, Europol had set up specialised units to deal with specific areas of crime: migrant smuggling (European Migrant Smuggling Centre, established in 2016), terrorism (European Counter Terrorism Centre, created in 2016 as well), and

[83] Art. 6(3). [84] Ibid. [85] Art. 4(1)(c).

[86] 'Europol Strategy 2016–2020', available at www.europol.europa.eu/publications-documents/europol-strategy-2016-2020, p. 16.

[87] See, for instance, Art. 4(1)(g) ('develop, share and promote specialist knowledge of crime prevention methods, investigative procedures and technical and forensic methods [...]') and (i) ('provide specialised training and assist Member States in organising training [...]').

[88] See 'Europol Platform for Experts (EPE)', available at www.europol.europa.eu/activities-services/services-support/information-exchange/europol-platform-for-experts. See also Disley et al, 'Evaluation of the implementation of the Europol Council Decision and of Europol's activities', Report for Europol Management Board, Rand Europe, 2012, p. 100.

notably cybercrime, to counter which Europol constituted the European Cybercrime Centre (EC3) in 2013.[89] In 2020, Europol set up the European Financial and Economic Crime Centre.

15.5.3 Europol's Role in the 'Policy Cycle-EMPACT'

Europol's commitment to producing documents known as 'threat assessments', which take stock of the existing state of affairs with regard to a given form of criminality and assess the threats they pose, has increased over the years. As mentioned above, the preparation of threat assessments and strategic analyses is one of Europol's tasks.[90] The IOCTAs (Internet Organised Crime Threat Assessments) and notably the SOCTAs (Serious and Organised Crime Threat Assessments) are the most known Europol's threat assessments.

The SOCTAs are key documents for the development of EU criminal policy as they represent the starting point of the four-step process known as 'Policy Cycle-EMPACT'[91] (EMPACT stands for 'European Multidisciplinary Platform Against Criminal Threats'). The Policy Cycle aims to counter the most important criminal threats 'in a coherent and methodological manner through optimum cooperation between the relevant services of the Member States, EU Institutions and EU Agencies as well as relevant third countries and organisations'.[92] The first Policy Cycle covered the years between 2011 and 2013, while fully fledged cycles followed for the periods 2014–2017, 2018–2021 and 2022–2025.[93]

Europol's SOCTAs set in motion the cycle as they single out the main criminal threats in Europe; on the basis of the SOCTA's main findings,

[89] Further information on these units can be found on the Europol's website. See also K. Ambos, *European Criminal Law*, Cambridge: Cambridge University Press, 2018, p. 564; S. Gless and T. Wahl, 'A Comparison of the Evolution and Pace of Police and Judicial Cooperation in Criminal Matters: A Race Between Europol and Eurojust?', in C. Brière and A. Weyembergh (eds.), *The Needed Balances in EU Criminal Law. Past, Present and Future*, Oxford and Portland, OR: Hart, 2018, p. 343.

[90] Art. 4(1)(f). See also Art. 4(3).

[91] See more in A. Gruszczak, 'The EU Criminal Intelligence Model', in J.B. Banach-Gutierrez and C. Harding (eds.), *EU Criminal Law and Policy. Values, Principles and Methods*, Abingdon, Oxon and New York: Routledge, 2017, pp. 149–167.

[92] Council conclusions on the creation and implementation of an EU policy cycle for organised and serious international crime, Justice and Home Affairs Council meeting, Brussels, 8–9 November 2010, para. 1.

[93] For the last Policy Cycle-EMPACT 2022–2025, see Council doc. 8665/21, 12 May 2021.

it is then for the Council to decide the EU priorities in the fight against serious and organised crime. Multi-annual strategic plans are prepared for each of them, and in their framework, operational action plans are implemented; on the basis of such action plans, national authorities take specific measures and actions, with Europol's support and coordination, to fight against the crimes identified as EU priorities. Once the cycle is over, an evaluation of the activities takes places and new priorities are decided for the next cycle. The cycle's overall objective is to ensure more effective reaction against the crimes that are considered as priorities at the EU level.

Europol's involvement in, and key contribution to the Policy Cycle-EMPACT is a testament to the Agency's increasing role in shaping EU and domestic criminal policies. Elevating a crime to an EU priority can indeed lead to the prioritisation of such crime and to the increase in the amount of resources allocated to the fight against it at the national and EU level. It is telling that, for instance, the first criterion that Eurojust takes into account when assessing whether a JIT should be funded by Eurojust (with EU money) is whether the JIT aims to investigate a crime that falls within the Policy Cycle's priorities.[94]

15.6 Accountability

Europol's accountability can be examined under different perspectives.[95] First, there are several rules concerning the Agency's accountability for its tasks connected with data processing activities, which have been discussed above. Second, with regard to the Executive Director, the Regulation provides that he or she is accountable to the Management Board,[96] which may propose the Council to extend the Director's term of office (for one more term of four years) or remove him or her.[97] In line with the still predominant intergovernmental logic that permeates Europol, the European Parliament plays a very limited role in this context. It can (but is not required to) give a non-binding opinion on the candidate selected by the

[94] 'Eurojust Single Programming Document 2020–2022', p. 70.

[95] On the monitoring of Europol, see Ambos, *European Criminal Law*, p. 564. On the multifaceted notion of 'accountability', especially vis-à-vis EU agencies, see M. Busuioc, *European Agencies. Law and Practices of Accountability*, Oxford: Oxford University Press, 2013, pp. 44–64.

[96] Art. 16(1). [97] Art. 54(4) and (7).

Council for the post of Executive Director before his or her appointment[98] and should only be informed (but has no decision making power) about the Director's removal by the Council.[99] Overall, the European Parliament's influence over Europol's activities – leaving aside the Parliament's role as co-responsible authority for the EU budget, from which Europol is financed – seems very limited if compared to the Council's influence.

There are even less provisions in the Europol Regulation on the accountability of the Management Board, which adopts several key decisions for Europol's functioning, and this arguably makes the known definition of Europol as 'perhaps the most controlled police agency in Europe'[100] now outdated. The Regulation only provides that the Board adopts and submits annual activity reports on Europol's activities to the European Parliament, the Council, the Commission, the Court of Auditors, and the national parliaments.[101] The Executive Director should also present the annual report to the European Parliament and the Council.[102]

Third, in line with Article 88(2) TFEU that requires the regulations on Europol to lay down also 'the procedures for scrutiny of Europol's activities by the European Parliament, together with national Parliaments', the Europol Regulation sets out some rules on the Joint Parliamentary Scrutiny Group (JPSG). Established in 2017, the JPSG politically monitors Europol's activities in fulfilling its mission, 'including as regards the impact of those activities on the fundamental rights and freedoms of natural persons'.[103] The JPSG should be consulted by the Management Board in relation to the multi-annual programming of Europol[104] and should receive several documents prepared by Europol, such as threat assessments and other strategic analyses and reports. The JPSG can in any case request access to other relevant documents necessary for the fulfilment of its tasks.[105]

While the establishment of the JPSG is a step forward in ensuring Europol's democratic accountability compared to the previous Europol's

98 Art. 54(2). 99 Art. 54(7).

100 C. Fijnaut, 'Police Co-operation and the Area of Freedom, Security and Justice', in N. Walker (ed.), *Europe's Area of Freedom, Security and Justice*, Oxford: Oxford University Press, 2004, p. 255.

101 Art. 11(1)(c). On the Management Board's accountability, see also Art. 50(2).

102 Recital 60.

103 Art. 51(2). On the JPSG, see more in Gless and Wahl, 'A Comparison of the Evolution and Pace of Police and Judicial Cooperation in Criminal Matters', pp. 352–353.

104 Art. 51(2)(c). 105 Art. 51(4).

regime,[106] and can ultimately strengthen the citizens' confidence in the EU and its bodies,[107] it remains to be seen how effective the JPSG can really be. It is a quite large group composed by up to four members of each national parliament and up to sixteen members of the European Parliament (that is, more than 120 persons),[108] which is supposed to meet in principle only twice a year.

Finally, with regard to the accountability in the strict sense of accountability before courts, the Court of Justice of the European Union (CJEU) is competent, on the hand, to give preliminary rulings on the validity and interpretation of the Europol Regulation and the Agency's acts. On the other hand, apart from a number of decisions it can take in cases such as those involving Europol's non-contractual liability or access to documents,[109] the Court is also competent to decide on Europol's liability in case an individual has suffered damage as result of an unlawful data processing operation, and therefore claims his or her right to receive compensation in accordance with Article 340 TFEU.[110]

In principle, the CJEU would also be competent to review the legality of Europol's acts pursuant to Article 263(4) TFEU. Nonetheless, since Europol cannot apply coercive measures, several of its acts such as the request to initiate investigations cannot be subject to the CJEU's judicial review upon request of the individual concerned (e.g., the suspect): most of Europol's acts do not bring about a 'distinct change in the [individual's] legal position',[111] which is the threshold set by the CJEU to review acts of EU bodies and agencies in accordance with Article 263(4) TFEU. The Court of Justice cannot review the coercive measures that national authorities

[106] Cf. M. Busuioc, D. Curtin and M. Groenleer, 'Agency Growth between Autonomy and Accountability: The European Police Office as a "Living Institution"' (2011) 18 *JEPP*, 848, 854–856.

[107] Meijers Committee, 'Note on the interparliamentary scrutiny of Europol', CM 1702, 1, 3. See also I. Cooper, 'A New Form of Democratic Oversight in the EU: The Joint Parliamentary Scrutiny Group for Europol' (2018) 10 *Perspectives on Federalism*, 185.

[108] 'Annex I To the Conclusions of the Conference of Speakers of EU Parliaments of 23–25 April in Bratislava as pertaining to the Europol JPSG'. See D. Fromage, 'The New Joint Parliamentary Scrutiny Group for Europol: Old Wine in New Bottles?', *TARN (The Academic Research Network Blog on EU Agencies & Institutional Innovation)*, 17 June 2017, available at https://tarn.maastrichtuniversity.nl/the-new-joint-parliamentary-scrutiny-group-for-europol-old-wine-in-new-bottles/.

[109] Arts. 49(4) and 65(3). [110] Art. 50(1).

[111] GC, *Tillack v. Commission*, No. T-193/04, Judgment, ECLI:EU:T:2006:292, 4 October 2006, para. 68.

adopt upon request or with the support of Europol either, in accordance with Article 276 TFEU. Some authors have therefore raised some concerns about the compliance of such regime with the EU human rights *acquis.*[112]

15.7 Relations with Third States and Other EU Bodies and Agencies

Europol's relations with partners within and beyond the EU are crucial to ensure the Agency can efficiently perform its tasks. The Regulation provides that Europol may establish and maintain cooperative relations with other EU bodies, third countries' authorities, international organisations and private parties.[113]

With regard to other EU bodies, it is Eurojust that is the main partner of Europol. In 2010, an agreement between Europol and Eurojust entered into force and it still regulates their relations with a view to increasing their effectiveness in fighting serious forms of international crime.[114] The agreement provides, inter alia, for regular consultations between the Director of Europol and the President of Eurojust (Article 3) and includes rules on the exchange of information between the two Agencies in the context of JITs (Article 6). The relations between the two agencies, which have been reportedly marred by tensions and mistrust especially in the 2000s,[115] go beyond the avenues of cooperation identified in the 2010 agreement and involve, for instance, the access by Eurojust to Europol's databases on the basis of a hit/no-hit system.[116]

As crimes affecting the Union's financial interests also fall within Europol's mandate, Europol needs to cooperate with both OLAF and the newly established European Public Prosecutor's Office (EPPO).[117] Europol recently concluded a new working arrangement with OLAF, which entered

[112] E. Guild et al., 'Implementation of the EU Charter of Fundamental Rights and its Impact on EU Home Affairs Agencies. Frontex, Europol and the European Asylum Support Office', Study for the LIBE Committee of the European Parliament, 2011, pp. 83–84.

[113] Art. 23(1).

[114] Art. 2 of the Agreement between Eurojust and Europol (2010), available at www.eurojust.europa.eu/agreement-between-eurojust-and-europol.

[115] See, among others, Weyembergh, Armada and Brière, 'The Inter-Agency Cooperation and Future Architecture of the EU Criminal Justice and Law Enforcement Area', pp. 19 and 22.

[116] See Section 15.5.1.

[117] On the EPPO, see the contribution (Chapter 17) by Allegrezza in this volume.

into force in October 2020. The arrangement lays down the foundation for the exchange of operational, tactical, classified, strategic and technical information between the two bodies, and, among others, sets out the rules for their participation in Joint Customs Operations and JITs (Article 4). Furthermore, as mentioned, OLAF can also access Europol's databases by means of a hit/no-hit system.

More recently, Europol concluded a working arrangement with the EPPO, which entered into force in January 2021.[118] Article 102(1) of Council Regulation (EU) 2017/1939 on the establishment of the EPPO ('EPPO Regulation')[119] provides that the EPPO shall establish and maintain a close relationship with Europol. The working arrangement regulates the appointment of a single contact point for the exchange of information (Article 5) as well as the possibility for both Europol and the EPPO to agree to the secondment of liaison officers or experts (Article 7). Article 102(2) of the EPPO Regulation also provides that the EPPO should be able to obtain from Europol, upon request, any relevant information held by the Agency, yet the supply of such information is subject to three conditions: it should concern a crime falling within the EPPO's competence and should be necessary and relevant for the EPPO's investigation. The same provision clarifies that the EPPO may ask for Europol's analytical support to a specific EPPO investigation; such support should therefore be limited to the 'personal, temporal and material scope'[120] of that investigation by the EPPO.

The Agency also cooperates with several other EU institutions, bodies or agencies, notably the European Border and Coast Guard Agency, known as Frontex, and the European Union Agency for Law Enforcement Training (CEPOL), with which the Commission had suggested Europol should be merged back in 2013.[121] With regard to non-EU partners,

[118] Working Arrangement establishing cooperative relations between the European Public Prosecutor's Office and the European Union Agency for Law Enforcement Cooperation (2021), available at www.europol.europa.eu/partners-agreements/working-arrangements.

[119] OJ L 283/1, 31.10.2017.

[120] D. Brodowski, 'Article 102: Relations with Europol', in H.-H. Herrnfeld, D. Brodowski and C. Burchard (eds.), *European Public Prosecutor's Office: Article-by-Article Commentary*, Baden-Baden, München, Oxford: Nomos, Beck, Hart, 2021, p. 616.

[121] COM(2013) 173 final. The Europol Parliament and the Council however rejected the merger between the two bodies. The full list of Europol's partners – EU bodies and institutions, third countries and international organisations – can be found on Europol's website at www.europol.europa.eu/partners-agreements.

Europol had signed – before the entry into force of the new Regulation – strategic agreements with five non-EU countries and two international organisations,[122] as well as operational agreements with seventeen non-EU countries[123] and Interpol. The main difference between strategic and operational agreements is that the former in principle do not allow for the exchange of personal data.

Before the Treaty of Lisbon, EU agencies such as Europol could themselves negotiate operational agreements with third countries which provided for, and regulated the exchange of personal data. The Treaty of Lisbon – and consequently the Europol Regulation – now bestows upon the Commission the power to negotiate, and on the Council that to conclude, such agreements, which must contain 'adequate safeguards with respect to the protection of privacy and fundamental rights and freedoms of individuals'.[124] On 20 December 2017, the Commission tabled eight Recommendations for Council decisions to authorise the opening of negotiations on international agreements between the EU and eight third countries that would allow the exchange of personal data between Europol and these countries' competent authorities.[125] A similar Recommendation was issued in 2019 with regard to an international agreement with New Zealand.[126] So far, none of these agreements has yet been concluded. While Europol cannot conclude operational agreements any longer, it can still sign working arrangements with its partners,[127] including EU bodies (the EPPO and OLAF for instance, as mentioned above) and third countries. Europol has so far concluded working arrangements with nine non-EU countries, including with the United Kingdom in September 2021.[128]

In line with Europol's nature and tasks, the exchange of information – and notably personal data – is at the heart of Europol's relations with its

[122] Brazil, China, Russia, Turkey and United Arab Emirates, and United Nations Office on Drugs and Crime and the World Customs Organisation, respectively.

[123] They include Australia, Switzerland and the USA.

[124] Art. 25(1)(b).

[125] COM(2017) 798 final (Jordan), COM(2017) 799 final (Turkey), COM(2017) 805 final (Lebanon), COM(2017) 806 final (Israel), COM(2017) 807 final (Tunisia), COM(2017) 808 final (Morocco), COM(2017) 809 final (Egypt) and COM(2017) 811 final (Algeria).

[126] COM(2019) 551 final.

[127] Art. 23(4).

[128] Working and Administrative Arrangement establishing cooperative relations between the competent authorities of the United Kingdom of Great Britain and Northern Ireland and the European Union Agency for Law Enforcement Cooperation.

partners. Article 24 of the Europol Regulation sets the framework for data exchange with EU bodies, while Articles 25–27 regulate the cooperation mechanisms with third countries and international organisations, private parties and private persons. Some general principles apply to all information exchanges, such as the above-mentioned prohibition of processing information 'clearly' obtained in 'obvious' violation of human rights[129] and the possibility for Europol to process personal data from partners only in so far as it is 'necessary and proportionate for the legitimate performance of its tasks'.[130]

Europol may exchange information with international partners when sufficient data protection safeguards are in place. Therefore, information exchange with third countries and international organisations can take place pursuant to the previously signed operational agreements (which remain valid),[131] but is also possible if the Commission has adopted an 'adequacy decision',[132] that is a decision finding that the country or international organisation in question ensures an adequate level of data protection.[133] Europol could also exchange personal data with an *ad hoc* authorisation by the Europol's Executive Director on a case-by-case basis and for exceptional reasons.[134]

Finally, exchange of information – including personal data – with private parties and private persons is subject to the strict conditions provided for by the Regulation.[135] Personal data from private persons and bodies should be processed if they are received via a qualified stakeholder such ENUs or a competent authority of a third country subject to an adequacy decision of the Commission, or with which an operational agreement has been signed by Europol (before the Lisbon Treaty) or by the Council (after Lisbon).[136] In any case, Europol should refrain from contacting private parties or private persons in order to retrieve personal data or information,[137] although in exceptional circumstances, Europol can still transfer personal data to private parties, even established outside the Union, but not to private persons.[138]

[129] Art. 23(9) and Recital 39.
[130] Art. 23(5). [131] Art. 25(1)(c) and (4). [132] Art. 26(1)(a).
[133] Recital 35. [134] Art. 25(5). [135] See Arts. 26 and 27. [136] Arts. 26(1) and 27(1).
[137] Arts. 26(9) and 27(4). [138] Art. 26(5) and (6) in combination with Art. 27(5).

15.8 The Proposal for a Revised Europol Regulation

On 9 December 2020, the Commission issued its Proposal for a Regulation amending the Europol Regulation (the 'Proposal').[139] The Proposal aims to strengthen Europol's mandate in light of 'evolving and increasingly complex security threats'[140] stemming from the technological developments, the continuous threat of terrorism and the COVID-19 outbreak. As explained by the Commission, the ever-fluctuating security landscape has led to a substantial change in the type of support 'Member States need and expect from Europol to keep citizens safe, in a way that was not foreseeable when the co-legislators negotiated the current Europol mandate.'[141] In May 2021, the European Parliament published its draft report on the Proposal and the Council agreed on a negotiating mandate one month later.[142] At the time of writing, negotiations are ongoing.

The Proposal first aims to modernise Europol's relations with its partners by amending the rules on the relations with private parties and third countries and introducing a new provision on the cooperation with the EPPO. As mentioned above, Europol may process personal data obtained from private parties only if they are received indirectly via specific intermediaries (e.g., ENUs). The Proposal seeks to allow Europol to *directly* receive personal data from private parties and inform such private parties of missing information and ask MS to request other private parties to share additional information if necessary.[143] The Proposal would also enable Europol to exchange personal data with private parties and process those personal data to prevent 'the dissemination of online content related to terrorism or violent extremism in crisis situations'.[144]

[139] COM(2020) 796 final. [140] Ibid., Explanatory Memorandum, pp. 1–2. [141] Ibid.

[142] European Parliament, 'Draft Report on the proposal for a regulation of the European Parliament and of the Council amending Regulation (EU) 2016/794, as regards Europol's cooperation with private parties, the processing of personal data by Europol in support of criminal investigations, and Europol's role on research and innovation', 10 May 2021, 2020/0349(COD); Council, 'Europol: Council agrees negotiating mandate on new rules to strengthen the role of the agency', Press release, 30 June 2021. For an overview of the negotiations within the Council, see Council, 'Progress report', Council doc. 9158/21, 28 May 2021.

[143] COM(2020) 796 final, Art. 1(12)(a) and (d). See Arts. 26(2) and 26(6a) and (6b) of the proposed revised Regulation.

[144] COM(2020) 796 final, Art. 1(13). See Art. 26a of the proposed revised Regulation.

This represents a 'considerable paradigm shift':[145] the Agency would have a much more proactive role than it currently has and would get information potentially even before national authorities are aware of such information, and irrespective of whether they would share it with the Agency.[146]

With regard to third countries, the section above explained that Europol's Executive Director may authorise the transfer of personal data to international partners on a case-by-case basis in exceptional circumstances. The Proposal allows the Executive Director to also authorise 'categories of transfers' of personal data.[147] However, as it is not entirely clear what the notion of 'categories of transfers' covers, this proposal may lead to extending the remit of such transfers 'from criminal investigations on specific suspects to surveillance activities in general, thus changing Europol's powers'.[148]

As far as the EPPO is concerned, the amendment of the Europol Regulation is necessary to align Europol's legal framework with the EPPO Regulation, which was adopted after the Europol Regulation entered into force. The Proposal suggests introducing in the Europol Regulation a new Article 20a, which will serve as a legal basis for Europol's relations with the EPPO[149] and largely reflects the wording of Article 102 of the EPPO Regulation.

Second, the Proposal tackles the issue of large datasets. As highlighted in the Impact Assessment accompanying the Commission's Proposal, '[d]ata collected in criminal investigations are increasing in size and becoming semantically more complex',[150] with an average investigation able to yield 'terabytes of data'.[151] However, MS often struggle to address this so-called big data challenge for a variety of reasons, including the lack of technical expertise and resources to process such data.[152] As a result, Europol increasingly receives from the MS 'large and unfiltered' datasets,[153] which the Agency is not always allowed to process in their entirety: Article 18(5) of the Regulation limits the processing of personal data to the categories of data subjects listed in Annex II of the Regulation;[154] hence,

[145] N. Vavoula and V. Mitsilegas, 'Strengthening Europol's Mandate. A Legal Assessment of the Commission's Proposal to Amend the Europol Regulation', Study for the LIBE Committee of the European Parliament, 2021, p. 30.

[146] Ibid.

[147] COM(2020) 796 final, Art. 1(11). See Art. 25(5) of the proposed revised Regulation.

[148] Vavoula and Mitsilegas, 'Strengthening Europol's Mandate. A Legal Assessment of the Commission's Proposal to Amend the Europol Regulation', p. 56.

[149] COM(2020) 796 final, Art. 1(8). [150] SWD(2020) 543 final, p. 23.

[151] Ibid. [152] Ibid. [153] Ibid., p. 25.

[154] They include, among others, suspects, convicted persons, witnesses and victims.

Europol cannot process personal data pertaining to other subjects. On 17 September 2020, however, the EDPS adopted a decision by which it concluded that 'there is a high likelihood that Europol continually processes personal data on individuals for whom it is not allowed to do so'.[155] In response to the EDPS' decision, the Commission's Proposal envisages the introduction of a new Article 18(5a) that will allow Europol to perform, for a maximum period of one year, a 'pre-analysis of personal data received with the sole purpose of determining whether such data falls into the categories of data subjects'[156] in respect of whom Europol is competent to perform its data processing tasks.

Third, the Proposal aims to strengthen Europol's role in steering innovation and research[157] and gives Europol the new task of proactively monitoring and contributing to research and innovation activities, supporting related activities of MS and implementing research and innovation activities, 'including the development, training, testing and validation of algorithms for the development of tools.'[158]

Fourth, another aspect of the Agency's powers that the Proposal intends to amend concerns the initiation of investigations. As discussed, Europol can request national authorities to start investigations on cross-border crime that falls within Europol's mandate. The Proposal enables Europol to make such requests in connection to a crime affecting a common interest covered by a Union policy[159] even where the crime concerned is *not* of a cross-border nature.[160] This suggested reform has met the opposition of several MS, which consider it disproportionate, and may not find its way through the final text.[161]

Finally, the Proposal aims to strengthen the safeguards surrounding Europol's activities, by enhancing both the Agency's data protection framework[162] and the parliamentary oversight of its activities, in

155 EDPS, 'Decision on the Own Initiative Inquiry on Europol's Big Data Challenge', 17 September 2020, para. 4.9.

156 COM(2020) 796 final, Art. 1(5)(d). See Art. 18(5a) of the proposed revised Regulation.

157 SWD(2020) 543 final, p. 31. See the changes envisaged in COM(2020) 796 final, Arts. 1(2)(a)(iv), 1(2)(d), 1(5)(a)(ii), 1(5)(b) and 1(19). See, respectively, Arts. 4(1)(t), 4(4a), 4(4b), 18(2)(e), 18(3a) and 33a of the proposed revised Regulation.

158 COM(2020) 796 final, Art. 1(2)(a)(iv). See Art. 4(1)(t) of the proposed revised Regulation.

159 COM(2020) 796 final, Art. 1(3). See Art. 6(1) of the proposed revised Regulation.

160 COM(2020) 796 final, Recital 14.

161 Vavoula and Mitsilegas, 'Strengthening Europol's Mandate. A Legal Assessment of the Commission's Proposal to Amend the Europol Regulation', p. 60.

162 For a detailed assessment of the proposed changes, see ibid., pp. 61–62.

particular with the introduction of additional reporting obligations from Europol to the JPSG.[163] However, the Proposal does not suggest any change in the JPSG's structure, which, as discussed above, will remain quite complex.

15.9 Conclusion

Europol is the most important EU actor in the field of police cooperation. Notably as the author of the document that sets off the Policy Cycle-EMPACT (SOCTA), it actively contributes to the shaping of EU criminal policy. Established in the mid-1990s with a limited mandate and strong intergovernmental features, the Agency has been subject to a process whereby its competence and tasks have been progressively but steadily extended and its nature (largely) 'communautarised'. Europol's added value is inextricably linked with its one-of-a-kind powers to exchange, process and analyse data at the EU level, which led some authors to refer to it as an 'enormous data processing agency rather than a law enforcing police office'.[164] Although Europol is prevented from taking coercive measures, its contribution to the fight against cross-border crime can hardly be underestimated. Europol's support, and especially its operational analyses and related data-processing activities, are at times so relevant for national investigations and prosecutions that the usual boundaries between 'coercive' and 'non-coercive' powers seem to fade in practice. After all, 'gathering and processing information, as Europol does, generates "knowledge" and produces "evidence", which by their very essence are no different from a traditional house search conducted by a police unit using its operational power'.[165] Europol's mission is by definition marked by the inherent tension between the goal to maximise the effectiveness of the Agency's activities and the need to do so without unduly encroaching upon the individual's fundamental rights, notably those connected with the rights to privacy and data protection.

[163] COM(2020) 796 final, Art. 1(37). See Art. 51(3) of the proposed revised Regulation. The Proposal would however not address the JPSG's structural weaknesses examined in the section on accountability.

[164] Gless, 'Europol', p. 465.

[165] Ibid., p. 464. See also A. Jonsson Cornell, 'EU Police Cooperation Post-Lisbon', in M. Bergström and A. Jonsson Cornell (eds.), *European Police and Criminal Law Co-operation*, Oxford and Portland, OR: Hart, 2014, p. 154.

Both challenges – enhancing Europol, and thus strengthening Europe's security, and ensuring adequate protection to fundamental rights – are likely to become always more complex in the years to come, due to the transnational, if not altogether global offline and online criminal threats that spread across the globe.

Further Reading

C. Blasi Casagran 'The New Europol Legal Framework: Implications for EU Exchanges of Information in the Field of Law Enforcement', in M. O'Neill and K. Swinton (eds.), *Challenges and Critiques of the EU Internal Security Strategy: Rights, Power and Security*, Cambridge: Cambridge Scholars Publishing, 2017.

D. Brodowski 'Article 102: Relations with Europol', in H.-H. Herrnfeld, D. Brodowski and C. Burchard (eds.), *European Public Prosecutor's Office: Article-by-Article Commentary*, Baden-Baden, München, Oxford: Nomos, Beck, Hart, 2021.

C. Cocq and F. Galli F., 'The Evolving Role of Europol in the Fight against Serious Crime: Current Challenges and Future Prospects', in S. Hufnagel and C. McCartney (eds.), *Trust in International Police and Justice Cooperation*, Oxford and Portland, OR: Hart, 2017.

I. Cooper, 'A New Form of Democratic Oversight in the EU: The Joint Parliamentary Scrutiny Group for Europol', (2018) 10 *Perspectives on Federalism*, 185.

S. Gless, 'Europol', in V. Mitsilegas, M. Bergström and T. Konstadinides (eds.), *Research Handbook on EU Criminal Law*, Cheltenham and Northampton, MA: Edward Elgar, 2016.

S. Gless and T. Wahl, 'A Comparison of the Evolution and Pace of Police and Judicial Cooperation in Criminal Matters: A Race between Europol and Eurojust?', in C. Brière and A. Weyembergh (eds.), *The Needed Balances in EU Criminal Law. Past, Present and Future*, Oxford and Portland, OR: Hart, 2018.

A. Gruszczak, 'The EU Criminal Intelligence Model', in J.B. Banach-Gutierrez and C. Harding (eds.), *EU Criminal Law and Policy. Values, Principles and Methods*, Abingdon, Oxon and New York: Routledge, 2017.

S. Hufnagel S., *Policing Global Regions. The Legal Context of Transnational Law Enforcement Cooperation*, Abingdon, Oxon–New York, NY: Routledge, 2020.

V. Mitsilegas and F. Giuffrida, 'Bodies, Offices and Agencies', in V. Mitsilegas, *EU Criminal Law*, 2nd edn., London: Hart, in press.

N. Vavoula and V. Mitsilegas, 'Strengthening Europol's Mandate. A Legal Assessment of the Commission's Proposal to Amend the Europol Regulation', Study for the LIBE Committee of the European Parliament, 2021.

Eurojust 16

Alejandro Hernández López and Francisco Jiménez-Villarejo Fernández

16.1 Background and Legal Basis

Eurojust is the European Union Agency for Criminal Justice Cooperation. It has legal personality and was set up to stimulate and to improve coordination and cooperation between competent judicial authorities of the Member States (MS), particularly in relation to serious organised crime.

The creation of Eurojust was first proposed in October 1999 during the Council summit in Tampere (Conclusion 46) with the aim of providing an answer to the need of a centralised unit for judicial cooperation in criminal matters which effectively supports national authorities when fighting cross-border organised crime while respecting the national *ius puniendi* and the different legal systems and traditions of the MS. In 2001, Eurojust started functioning as a provisional Unit (Pro-Eurojust)[1] and was finally established by the Council Decision 2002/187/JHA.[2] Eurojust's Decision has been amended twice by Council Decisions 2003/659/JHA[3] and 2009/426/JHA,[4] the latter being a reform which aimed to broaden its original powers.

The entry into force of the Lisbon Treaty foreseen the need to tackle a deeper reform to adapt Eurojust to the new requirements of primary law. Being one of the agencies of the AFSJ expressly mentioned in the Treaties (Article 85 TFEU), there was a need to adapt the above-mentioned legal framework to the new post-Lisbon scenario upgrading Eurojust legal basis to its revised mission and competences, strengthening and clarifying its mandate.

In this context, the Council's Stockholm Programme recommended exploring the possibilities offered by Arts. 85 and 86 TFEU in order to

[1] Council Decision 2000/799/JHA, OJ L 324, 21.12.2000.

[2] Council Decision 2002/187/JHA, OJ L 63, 6.3.2002.

[3] Council Decision 2003/659/JHA, OJ L 245, 29.9.2003.

[4] Council Decision 2009/426/JHA, OJ L 138, 4.6.2009.

enlarge Eurojust powers and facilitate the establishment of the European Public Prosecutor's Office (EPPO).[5] In July 2013, the Commission launched, in the same legislative package, two closely related legislative proposals,[6] linking the regulation of Eurojust to the establishment of the EPPO. Although both Proposals initially run in parallel, the lack of compromise among the MS in relation to the establishment of the EPPO delayed the adoption of the Eurojust Regulation.

After the adoption of the EPPO Regulation by means of enhanced cooperation, the preparations for the adoption of the Eurojust Regulation were intensified. During the Bulgarian Presidency, the Council, the European Parliament and the European Commission reached a provisional political agreement on the adoption of the new Regulation. The European Parliament approved the final text in October and the act was adopted by the Council in November 2018 as Regulation (EU) 2018/1727 of the European Parliament and of the Council on the European Union Agency for Criminal Justice Cooperation (Eurojust) (hereinafter, EJR),[7] replacing and repealing the Council Decision 2002/187/JHA.

16.2 Objectives, Scope of Application and Competences

16.2.1 Mission and Tasks

The current mission of Eurojust within the area of freedom, security and justice (AFSJ) is to stimulate and strengthen coordination between national judicial authorities of the MS, providing horizontal support to investigations and prosecutions within the EU. A brief reference to the tasks of Eurojust can be found in the first paragraph of Article 2 EJR, devoted to defining its mandate and its general scope of application.

While carrying out its tasks, Eurojust shall comply with any request issued from a competent national authority, taking into account any information provided by Union authorities, institutions, bodies, offices and agencies competent by virtue of the provisions adopted within the

[5] See Conclusion 3.1.1 *in fine* European Council, *Stockholm Programme – An Open and Secure Europe Serving and Protecting the Citizens*, OJ C115, 4.5.2010.

[6] See documents COM (2013) 534 final and COM (2013) 535 final, 17.07.2013.

[7] OJ L 295, 21.11.2018.

framework of the Treaties and any information collected by Eurojust itself.[8] Additionally, Eurojust shall facilitate the execution of requests for and decisions on judicial cooperation, including those based on instruments that give effect to the principle of mutual recognition.[9] The EJR also strengthens the decision-making and proactivity of Eurojust, allowing the exercise of some functions on its own initiative and not just at the request of other parties as a demand-driven organisation.[10] Furthermore, it provides for its intervention at the direct request of the EPPO.[11]

16.2.2 Scope of Application

Traditionally, all MS participated in Eurojust. However, after the date of application of the EJR, the scope of competence of Eurojust has been slightly modified.

First, Denmark, on the application of the special regime foreseen in the Protocol no. 22 to the Lisbon Treaty,[12] does not take part in the adoption of acts proposed pursuant to Title V of Part Three of the TFEU. Thus, the EJR does not apply to this Member State, which has led to the signing of an *ad hoc* cooperation agreement between this Member State and the agency before the 12 December 2019.[13] On the contrary, Ireland, on the application of the special regime established in the Protocol no. 21 to the Lisbon Treaty,[14] has decided to *opt-in* as a full-fledged member.

As regards to the situation of the United Kingdom, despite this State planning to take part in the Regulation regime on the basis of Article 4 of Protocol no. 21 to the Lisbon Treaty,[15] it finally does not participate due to Brexit. Actually, in 2020, the United Kingdom counted with a representative seconded at Eurojust, albeit she and the rest of the colleagues of the former UK Desk were not considered full-pledged Eurojust members but merely 'United Kingdom participants' who could stay in the Eurojust premises until the end of the transition period provided in the agreement on the withdrawal (31 December 2020).

[8] Art. 2(2)(a) EJR. [9] Art. 2(2)(b) EJR. [10] Art. 2(3) EJR.

[11] Art. 2(3) *in fine* EJR. [12] OJ C 202, 7.6.2016.

[13] www.eurojust.europa.eu/sites/default/files/InternationalAgreements/Eurojust-Denmark-2019-10-07_EN.pdf.

[14] OJ C 202, 7.6.2016.

[15] See Commission Decision (EU) 2019/1196, OJ L 187, 12.7.2019.

16.2.3 Material Scope of Competence

The EJR has designed a new and autonomous material scope of competence with respect to serious crimes that formally abandons the former 'cross-reference clause' to the material scope of competence of Europol. The new list of crimes which Eurojust is now competent for is provided in Annex I of the Regulation.[16] With this improved law-making technique, the European legislator also allows further updates in order to easily incorporate new crime trends.

The new list is more exhaustive, as it has specifically added new categories such as crimes against the financial interests of the EU (protection des intérêts financiers (PIF) previously included generically as fraud), and other crimes such as sexual abuse and sexual exploitation of women and children; insider dealing and financial market manipulation even when they are not committed by a criminal organization; environmental crime, including ship source pollution; and genocide, crimes against humanity and war crimes. The remit of competences of the agency is also enlarged to those crimes related to the criminal offences listed in Annex I.[17]

As regards to PIF crimes, a list of exceptions to the horizontal competence of Eurojust has been introduced as a consequence of the establishment of the EPPO.[18] Once this new body started the investigative and prosecutorial functions described on Article 120(2) Regulation (EU) 2017/1939,[19] Eurojust, in principle, should not exercise any competence for crimes falling under EPPO's remit of competences.[20] In this sense, it shall be remembered that the EPPO has been established through an enhanced cooperation that currently comprises twenty-two MS. Therefore, the abstention of Eurojust shall only be expected in relation to PIF crimes committed in those MS that are already participating in the EPPO, while Eurojust would keep its competence in relation to those offences committed in the rest of the MS upon the request of their authorities or under a

16 Art. 3(1) in relation with Annex I EJR. 17 Art. 3(4) EJR. 18 Art. 3(2) EJR.

19 OJ L 283, 31.10.2017.

20 EPPO's material scope of competence is established in Art. 22 of the Regulation (EU) 2017/1939, which refers to the PIF Directive (EU) 2017/1371, OJ L 198, 28.7.2017. In order to clarify what is to be understood as PIF crime competence of the EPPO, Eurojust has internally proposed a working definition to clarify the exercise of its functions. Notwithstanding, the Commission has already proposed to the European Council an initiative to extend the competences of the EPPO to cross-border terrorist crimes. See COM (2018) 641 final, 12.09.2018.

request issued by the EPPO itself. Notwithstanding, Eurojust will retain its horizontal competence regarding PIF crimes on those cases involving MS participating in the EPPO whenever the EPPO has no competence over those crimes or has decided to not exercise it.

Article 3(2) *in fine* EJR foresees the obligation to mutually consult and cooperate with the EPPO and the MS involved in order to facilitate the exercise of the competences of Eurojust envisaged in Article 3(2). This obligation to cooperate is also established in a EPPO Regulation mirror provision, albeit the practical arrangements of the exercise of these competences shall be ruled by a future working agreement (Article 47(3) EJR). In this sense, Article 4(1)(e) EJR includes among the operational functions of Eurojust to 'cooperate closely with the EPPO on matters relating to its competence'.

Additionally, Article 3(3) EJR includes a flexible clause that allows its assistance to forms of crime other than those listed in Annex I. In fact, Eurojust may potentially assist with judicial assistance requests and mutual recognition instruments in general terms, no matter the crime allegedly committed. This formula permits to adapt to the different interpretations of the crime categories listed in Annex I and the seriousness of the criminal offence as key parameters that would fix the material scope of competence of Eurojust, bearing in mind that full harmonization of substantive criminal law does not exist in the Union nor with respect to the definition of crimes nor to the penalties envisaged for them.[21]

Likewise, Eurojust may also assist with investigations and prosecutions that only affect that Member State and a third country. In those cases, a cooperation agreement or arrangement establishing cooperation should be in place or at least, that there is an essential interest in providing such assistance in the specific case as assessed and approved by the College of Eurojust.[22]

Finally, at the request of a competent authority of a Member State or the Commission, Eurojust may continue assisting investigations and prosecutions that only affect that Member State whenever the given case

[21] Actually, the formula used shall equally allow to have a wider approach in relation to the material scope of competence when national authorities request Eurojust assistance, provided that the Annex I includes offences that may have different *nome iuris* in the different national legal systems, allowing Eurojust to always intervene when the issues at stake deserved international judicial cooperation.

[22] Art. 3(5) EJR.

would have an impact at EU level. However, before acting at the request of the Commission, Eurojust shall always consult the competent authority of the Member State concerned.[23]

16.3 Structure

16.3.1 National Members

16.3.1.1 Status of the National Member

National members are the cornerstone of the operational functions of Eurojust. They are part of the structure of Eurojust as representatives of the MS, head of each national delegation and members of the College.[24] The EJR builds Eurojust governance in a manner that the administrative burden on national members is reduced to a minimum, so that they can fully focus on Eurojust's operational and judicial work.[25] The national member comprise the National Desk along with a deputy and an assistant, appointed to support the national member in the exercise of his powers through delegation and proper distribution of existing case-related workload, without prejudice to the possibility of acting on his behalf or substituting him when legally provided.

Regarding the new judicial status of the national members, the key pre-conditions they should meet in advance (as well as the deputies) is to be a judge or a prosecutor or, at least, to be a representative of a judicial authority. Therefore, a police officer of equivalent competence could no longer be appointed as provided by the repealed Eurojust Council Decision. This has been substituted by the term 'representative of a judicial authority', in our view most appropriate but to be duly interpreted by the CJEU. The EJR definitely strengthens the judicial profile of the national member's new status, as well as the judicial nature of their powers, stepping out from the previous intergovernmental nuance and clearly opting for a judicial statute of magistrate, in order to protect and take the maximum advantage of the judicial powers granted. The new formula does not leave any doubt with respect to the necessary judicial nature that must have the national members, and it is strengthened by

[23] Art. 3(6) EJR. [24] Art. 6 EJR.
[25] As provided by Recitals 9 and 15 EJR.

the specific references made in the preamble of the EJR to their functional independence.[26] Therefore, the EJR provides a statute of magistrate and guarantees the independence of the national members when exercising its operational functions.

The national member shall have his regular place of work at the Eurojust Headquarters in The Hague. On the contrary, as a general rule, the deputies and assistants shall be exempted from that requirement.[27] However, the College may request the Member State to assign the deputy or assistant or both to work at the seat of Eurojust for a specified period whether there is an operational need. In this case, the Member State involved must comply with this request without undue delay.[28]

The mandate of the national members has also been modified by the EJR, replacing the open clause of four years minimum provided in the former Eurojust Decision by a new mandate of five years only renewable once.[29] So, a uniform five years' term of office has been set up in line with the mandate of discretionary positions of prosecutors and judges at national level, deepening the judicial profile of this post and trying to avoid the current disturbing identification with the executive.

16.3.1.2 Powers of National Members

National members are granted with a series of powers that can be exercised by their own or in concurrence with the national judicial authorities.

Generally speaking, albeit the EJR has not added new minimum powers, it is true that Article 8 EJR strengthens the role of national members by legitimizing them to directly contact and exchange information not only with any competent national authority but also with any other competent body, office or agency of the Union, including the EPPO, or with any other competent international authority, in accordance with the international commitments of each Member State.

One of the main advantages that offers the new EJR over this matter lies in its direct effect and no need for transposition, which theoretically permits a homogeneous recognition of powers to all national

[26] Recitals 16 and 62 EJR. [27] Art. 7(2) EJR.

[28] Art. 7(2) *in fine* EJR. It is important to note that the EJR does not seem to contemplate the option to reject this request from the College, since the word used in the different language versions of the Regulation does not actually leave room to a negative answer from the Member States.

[29] Art. 7(5) EJR. This provision also applies to the deputies of the national member.

members from the date of application of the Regulation, which should reduce the pre-existing asymmetric implementation of powers to the minimum expression.[30] Hence, the minimum ordinary powers that may be exercised autonomously by the national members must be identified with those enshrined in Article 8(1) of the EJR. This provision must be read along with Article 8(2) EJR, a new open clause that allows MS to grant additional powers to their national members. However, what kind of powers and to what extend they can be granted are not specified in Article 8(2) so it is not possible to determine at this moment what could be the actual scope of this provision, nor to assess whether it can lead, paradoxically, to an asymmetric recognition of powers.[31]

With regard to the powers that national members must exercise in accordance with their national judicial authorities and according to their national law, they could be resumed into two different scenarios, although widely formulated, both stated in Article 8(3) EJR:

(1) Issue or execute any request for mutual legal assistance or mutual recognition. This implies a proactive action from the national member that is not limited to the modification, addition or complementation of any existing request or decision but also could be extended to the issuing of a new request, order or certificate, which definitely underlines the necessity for national members to be judicial authorities in active service, in line with the recent case law of the CJEU.[32]
(2) Order, request or execute investigative measures, as provided for in Directive 2014/41/EU. In this way, the EJR foresees an active role for

[30] Precisely, the harmonising of powers of the national members has been one the main issues of the functioning of Eurojust since its establishment. In this sense, the EJR shall replace the different national laws currently in force, a consequence that was already pointed out by K. Ambos, *European Criminal Law*, Cambridge: Cambridge University Press, 2018, p. 570.

[31] There is no specific mechanism provided in the EJR to monitor the level of compliance with Art. 8(2) but a generic obligation by the Member States to notify the Commission and the College of Eurojust any additional powers granted on the basis of the abovementioned provision, but the rationale behind this provision does not seem to go beyond a mere information duty.

[32] Regarding to the concept of 'issuing judicial authority' within the EAW Decision, see CJEU, *OG and PI*, Joined cases Nos. C-508/18 and C-82/19 PPU, Judgment, ECLI:EU:C:2019:456, 17 May 2019; *NJ*, No. C-489/19 PPU, Judgment, ECLI:EU:C:2019:849, 9 October 2019; *JR* and *YC*, Joined cases Nos. C-566/19 PPU and C-626/19 PPU, Judgment, ECLI:EU:C:2019:1077, 12 December 2019; *XD*, No. C-625/19 PPU, Judgment, ECLI:EU:C:2019:1078, 12 December 2019; *ZB*, No. C-627/19 PPU, Judgment, ECLI:EU:C:2019:1079, 12 December 2019.

the national members when there is a need to issue and execute a European Investigation Order (EIO).[33]

Actually, the powers mentioned above shall not be exercised by the national member itself, but by the competent national judicial authority. In this sense, the involvement of the national member will be typically limited to the proposal and the support in the execution of the requested investigative measures. Notwithstanding, in urgent (or rather emergency) cases where it is not possible to identify or to contact the competent national authority in a timely manner, national members shall be competent to autonomously take these measures referred to in Article 8(3) EJR provided that they inform the competent national authority as soon as possible.[34]

Nevertheless, bearing in mind that not all domestic legislations permit to grant national members an autonomous exercise of the competences described above, the EJR preserves an alternative regime, which consists in granting every national member the power to submit a proposal to their competent national authorities to carry out these measures where the exercise of these powers by the national member would be in conflict with their constitutional rules or fundamental aspects of their national criminal justice system. According to the EJR,[35] the latter occurs where the exercise of these powers would be in conflict with the division of powers between the police, prosecutors and judges; or the functional division of tasks between prosecution authorities; or the federal structure of the Member State concerned. This proposal must be handled without undue delay by the competent national authority,[36] which does not really preclude a discretionary dismissal.

Therefore, it is necessary to distinguish between the judicial functions (which are inherent to the international cooperation tasks) and the pure jurisdictional function. This distinction is enshrined in Article 85(2) TFEU, which provides that, with regard to the intervention of Eurojust, 'formal acts of judicial procedure shall be carried out by the competent national officials'. This means that those powers are to be exercised in accordance with national law and subject to judicial revision as 'the courts of Member States should be competent to review those measures', in accordance with the requirements and procedures laid down by national law as stated in

[33] Regarding the concept of 'issuing judicial authority' within the OEI Directive, see CJEU, *A and Others*, No. C-584/19, Judgment, ECLI:EU:C:2020:1002, 8 December 2020.

[34] Art. 8(4) EJR. [35] Art. 8(5) (b) EJR. [36] Art. 8(6) EJR.

Recital 15 *in fine* of the EJR Preamble. This judicial review, which was not envisaged in the repealed Council Decision, provides a solid judicial character to the powers granted to the national member.

For the proper exercise of their powers, national members should have access to or at least be able to obtain information contained in the national criminal records, register of arrested persons, investigation registers, DNA registers and other registers of public authorities in their Member State where it is necessary to fulfil their tasks.[37]

16.3.2 The College of Eurojust

The College of Eurojust is comprised of all national members. Within this body, all participant MS are equally represented, as every national member has one vote.[38] Nevertheless, when the College purely exercises management functions, a representative of the Commission will be invited to attend the meetings, who shall be the same person that represents the Commission in the Executive Board of Eurojust, a new body established by the EJR devoted to management functions.[39]

The College is represented by the president of Eurojust or, in their behalf, by one of the vice presidents, positions covered by national members in active service.[40] The president and the vice presidents are elected by the national members in active service by secret ballot,[41] for a term of office of four years renewable once. The appointment of a national member as president or vice president shall automatically extend their term of office to ensure that they can fulfil their additional functions properly.[42] Furthermore,

37 Art. 9 EJR.

38 Art. 14(2) EJR; Art. 6(8) Eurojust Rules of Procedure (2020), OJ L 50, 24.2.2020. The deputy and, in its absence, the assistant abled to act on behalf of the national member, shall be entitled to exercise the right to vote.

39 The intention of the European legislator is to rationalise the decision-making procedure in Eurojust's governance (Recital 18 EJR), reducing to the minimum the administrative burden on national members to allow them to focus on the operational work. For that purpose, the EJR clarifies the functions of the national members, the College and the Administrative Director and creates an Executive Board (Recital 17 EJR). The EJR includes a non-exhaustive list of tasks that are specifically granted to the College (Art. 5), and/or the Executive Board (Art. 16), and/or the Administrative Director (Art. 18).

40 The Powers of the president and the vice presidents of Eurojust are established in Art. 11(2) EJR and further developed by Art. 1 of the Eurojust rules of procedure (2020).

41 The election system of the president and the two vice presidents of Eurojust is established in Art. 11(1) EJR and in Art. 3 of the Eurojust rules of procedure (2020).

42 Art. 11(5) EJR.

when a national member is elected as president of Eurojust, the EJR permits the Member State concerned to second a new person to reinforce the National Desk for the duration of the president's mandate,[43] and where it is the case, they are entitled to apply for a compensation in the form of a reimbursement, financed by Eurojust's budget, of part of the costs occasioned.[44]

Regarding the voting rules of the College, the EJR provides that 'unless stated otherwise, and where a consensus cannot be reached, the College shall take its decisions by a majority of its members'.[45] This provision should be completed with the Eurojust Rules of Procedure, recently amended to include the possibility of a telematic vote system in the context of convened videoconference College meetings due to the COVID-19 pandemic.[46] According to these provisions, the College must always seek for unanimity in its decisions and, only in those cases when consensus is not possible, simple majority of its members will be sufficient unless the EJR or the Rules of Procedure requires a larger majority for specific acts.[47]

16.3.3 National Coordination System and the OCC

16.3.3.1 Eurojust National Coordination System

The Eurojust National Coordination System (ENCS) is a structure that was introduced by the Council Decision 2009/426/JHA.[48] The ENCS is comprised by one or more national correspondents for Eurojust, appointed by each Member State; a national correspondent for Eurojust for terrorism matters[49]; the national correspondent for the European Judicial Network (EJN) in criminal matters and up to three other contact points of the EJN[50]; and the national members or contact points of the network

[43] Art. 11(7) EJR.

[44] Art. 11(7) § 2° and Art. 12 EJR, implemented by the Council Implementing Decision (EU) 2019/2251, OJ L 336, 30.12.2019.

[45] Art. 14(1) EJR.

[46] See Arts. 6 to 8 Eurojust rules of procedure (2020). Due to the COVID-19 pandemic, the College of Eurojust approved on 24 July 2020 an amendment of the rules of procedure to allow electronic voting.

[47] For example, adopting the annual work programme requires a decision taken by majority of two-thirds of its members, see Art. 5(2)(e) EJR.

[48] Although it is true that the national correspondents were envisaged in the original text of the Decision (Art. 12), primarily in terrorism matters, their appointment was not mandatory and their powers were not equal to those currently granted to the ENCS.

[49] In accordance with Art. 2(2) Council Decision 2005/671/JHA, OJ L 253, 29.9.2005.

[50] In accordance with Art. 2(2) and (3) of the Council Decision 2008/976/JHA, OJ L 348, 24.12.2008.

for JITs and of the networks referred to in Article 12(2) of the former Decision and the current Article 20(3) EJR. The EJR has extended the ENCS, now including any national correspondents for issues relating the competence of the EPPO.[51] Moreover, a new open 'melting pot' clause has been included,[52] which allows to incorporate, where applicable, any other relevant judicial authority not expressly provided by the EJR. All ENCS correspondents shall retain their position and status under national law during their term of office.[53]

The main task of the ENCS is to coordinate the work of the different members to assure that the Eurojust Case Management System (CMS) receives information in an efficient and reliable manner. Therefore, the ENCS must be understood as a coordinating, facilitating and supporting structure for the establishment of direct contact between national judicial authorities and national members.[54] In this sense, national members must be informed of all meetings of their ENCS where casework-related issues are to be discussed and may attend such meetings when he deemed necessary.[55]

16.3.3.2 On-Call Coordination Mechanism

Also introduced by the amendment of the Eurojust Decision adopted in 2008,[56] the on-call coordination (OCC) mechanism is a practical tool that is always available and operational to receive and process urgent requests from national authorities. The *raison d'être* of this system is the need for a special 'on-call' service at the National Desks that ensures an immediate response and assistance of Eurojust beyond the working hours for urgent cases and matters.

The OCC is comprised of a unique contact point for Eurojust and of a representative per Member State. The representatives acting in the OCC shall be unconditionally ready to assist 24/7 around the clock and

51 Art. 20(3)(b) EJR. 52 Art. 23(3)(f) EJR.

53 Art. 12(3) Decision 2002/187/JHA (consolidated version); Art. 20(4) EJR.

54 As an example of this coordination task, we can mention the distribution of cases between Eurojust and the EJN, in accordance with Art. 48(1)(d) EJR in connection with Art. 20(7)(b), which permits to use the ENCS to determine whether a request for assistance should be examined by Eurojust or by the EJN.

55 Art. 20(6) EJR. The COVID-19 pandemic has shown that semestral, sectorial or thematic meetings between the members of the ENCS and the national member may combine presential attendance and the use of technical means such as video conference.

56 Art. 5(a) Decision 2002/187/JHA (consolidated version).

must intervene effectively and without any delay when executing a time-sensitive request from their national authorities.[57] The OCC representative function could be alternated by various persons of the National Desk but subject to the condition that an expert is always effectively providing this service. The representative may be either the national member, their deputy, an assistant entitled to replace the national member or, as specifically provided by the EJR, a Seconded National Expert (SNE).[58]

In practice, the OCC will attend any person who calls for this service externally in the language/s of his Member State.[59] The call will be forwarded to the representative of the National Desk on duty service for the OCC at that moment. Article 19 EJR does not provide that the national authority demanding this service could directly contact the representative of the Member State in which the urgent measures must be taken into effect. Thus, the connection should be only established with the representative of its National Desk on duty at the OCC.

16.4 Operational Functions of Eurojust

The operational functions of Eurojust could be exercised through one or more of the national members concerned or by the College.

Generally speaking, the EJR has strengthened the proactive role of the national members, allowing them to directly establish contact and exchange information not only with any competent national authority but also with any competent body, office or agency of the Union, including the EPPO, or with any competent international authority, in accordance with the international commitments of each Member State.

In the same way, they could carry out their tasks based on 'any information collected by Eurojust itself'.[60] This major change in the exercise of the essential coordination function of Eurojust adapts to the existing needs, reality and possibilities and entails a marked reinforce of their operational and analytic capacities. In this sense, national members are

[57] Art. 19(3) EJR. [58] Art. 19(2) EJR.

[59] Access to the OCC is restricted to judges, public prosecutors and police officers. These persons may access to the service from any MS by directly calling to an international free telephone number or, if they are located in a third State, by calling to a special Dutch telephone number.

[60] Art. 2(2)(a) *in fine* EJR.

backed by Europol as a source of *notitia criminis*, as well as rely on the support provided by the Operations Department of Eurojust.

The functions granted by the EJR to the national members are detailed in Article 5(1), which forwards to the functions granted in Article 4(1) and (2) EJR. Article 4(1) lists a sort of general functions (e.g., assist judicial authorities in ensuring the best possible coordination of investigations), whilst Article 4(2) refers to the most specific ones (e.g., ask the competent authorities to undertake an investigation or prosecution of certain acts or to set up a JIT).

The EJR grants the College of Eurojust the same functions granted to the national members. Hence, the College shall be also able to exercise both general and specific functions detailed in Article 4(1) and (2) EJR, where the case involves investigations or prosecutions that have repercussions at EU level or that might affect other MS at the request of one or more of the national members concerned.[61]

The College has been additionally granted with some exclusive competences, provided by Article 5(2)(b) EJR, which forwards to Article 4(3)–(5). These include:

(1) To provide Europol with opinions based on analyses carried out by this agency and supply logistical support, including translation, interpretation and the organisation of coordination meetings (Article 4(3) EJR).
(2) The prevention and settlement of conflicts of jurisdiction. In those cases, when two or more Member States cannot reach an agreement on which of them should undertake an investigation or prosecution after a recommendation has been issued by a national member, the College shall issue a written opinion on the case (Article 4(4) EJR).
(3) Recurrent refusals or difficulties concerning the execution of requests for and decisions on, judicial cooperation, despite of the previous mediation of national members concerned. In this case, the College shall also issue a written opinion on the case at the request of a competent authority, or on its own initiative (Article 4(5) EJR).

The functions that could lead to a written opinion of the College provided by Article 4(4) and (5) EJR could seem, at a first glance, a reproduction of Article 7(2) and (3) of the repealed Eurojust Council Decision. However, the EJR provisions, unlike the former Decision, fails to rule out the binding nature of these written opinions. In this regard, Article 4(6)

[61] See Art. 5(2)(a)(i) and (ii) EJR. In practice, these cases are the exceptions.

EJR only provides that the competent national authorities may refuse to comply with such requests if doing so would harm essential national security interests, would jeopardise the success of an ongoing investigation or would jeopardise the safety of an individual. These exceptional grounds are deliberately ambiguous and its concurrence only may be properly valued by the competent national judicial authority. Actually, Recital 14 of the EJR Preamble does clarify that the written opinions of Eurojust are still of a non-binding nature though should be responded timely and a good-ground. Consequently, despite its non-binding nature, the national authorities must always respond to Eurojust and explicit the exceptional grounds applied when opposing its written opinions, albeit Eurojust cannot exercise any kind of control over the national decision.

16.5 Relations with Other EU Bodies, Agencies and Institutions

16.5.1 Relations with the EJN and Other Networks

Eurojust gets support from its administrative structure and resources, even shares the staff and hosts the Council Networks' Secretariats at Eurojust headquarters in The Hague, always respecting their identity, autonomy and functional activities.

In accordance with Article 48(2) EJR, the Network secretariats (EJN, JITs network and genocide network)[62] shall form part of the staff of Eurojust. Nevertheless, those secretariats shall function as separate units and may draw on the administrative resources of Eurojust which are necessary for carrying out their tasks.

As a consequence of the administrative internal reorganization of Eurojust, as of the first of January 2019, the secretariats of the networks were incorporated to the Operations Department of Eurojust, which allows to establish closer relations between them and guarantees the alignment with the agency's strategy and the coordination to be ensured.

Likewise, within Eurojust, the Board on Relations with Partners is the College's substructure in charge of the relationship between the Council Networks hosted at Eurojust. The interaction between the networks and Eurojust is supported and backed up by the specific contact points appointed within this Board.

[62] More information at: www.eurojust.europa.eu/judicial-cooperation/practitioner-networks.

There is a particular and privileged relationship between Eurojust and the EJN. Considering the long track record of the EJN, in accordance with Article 85(1) TFEU, Article 48(1) EJR provides that they shall maintain privileged relations with each other. These relations are not built up in the abstract but developed on a daily basis between national members and EJN contact points. Furthermore, some national members are also EJN contact points and the national correspondents for Eurojust. This provision also ensures that both may make use of the ENCS when determining whether cases should be dealt with by the EJN or Eurojust. Precisely, one of the main issues at the EU level around the relationship between Eurojust and the EJN is to distinguish between the different levels of assistance to be provided. With the aim to establish a guidance for practitioners, Eurojust and the EJN have published a joint paper on this issue.[63]

Looking forward, Article 48(2) EJR envisages the support of Eurojust to the secretariat of any relevant network or European body involved in judicial cooperation in criminal matters, what is already being considered with respect to the European Judicial Cybercrime Network (EJCN).

16.5.2 Relations with Europol

The relationship between Europol and Eurojust is particularly important for the daily functioning of both EU agencies.

The EJR provides that both agencies shall maintain a close relationship based on cooperation to the extent relevant to performing their tasks and achieving their objectives.[64] The EJR also provides the main guidelines of this relationship, despite Europol and Eurojust have already signed several agreements on cooperation.[65] All these provisions must be completed with the mutual provisions established in Europol's Regulation.[66]

At the operational level and in relation with the exchange of information, the EJR establishes that Eurojust shall mandatorily enable Europol, within the limits of its mandate, to indirectly access the information

[63] www.eurojust.europa.eu/sites/default/files/Publications/Reports/EJN-EJ-paper-on-judicial-cooperation-in-criminal-matters_2018-01_EN.pdf.

[64] Art. 49(5) EJR.

[65] www.eurojust.europa.eu/sites/default/files/InternationalAgreements/Eurojust-Europol-2010-01-01-EN.pdf; www.eurojust.europa.eu/sites/default/files/InternationalAgreements/MoU-EJ-EP-on-JITs-funding_2018-06-01_EN.pdf.

[66] Art. 21 Regulation (EU) 2016/794, OJ L 135, 24.5.2016.

provided to Eurojust.[67] This 'indirect access' consists in allowing Europol to know whether specific information introduced in the system is registered in the databases. Thus, this search shall be performed only for the purposes to determine whether the information available at Europol matches with information processed at Eurojust (hit). In the case of a hit, Eurojust must initiate a procedure by which the information that generated the hit may be shared with Europol. However, before allowing this kind of hit/no hit searches, Eurojust must obtain from Europol precise information on which staff members have been authorised to perform such searches.[68]

If during information processing activities in respect of an individual investigation, Eurojust or a Member State detects the need for coordination, cooperation or support in accordance with Europol's mandate, Eurojust must notify Europol of this circumstance and initiate the procedure for sharing the information.[69] In order to increase the security when exchanging information and to avoid reluctance and mistrust between the national authorities when providing information to Eurojust, the EJR obliges Europol to respect any restriction or access to use, no matter if it was given in general or specific terms, that has been implied by a Member State, Union body, office, agency or third country or international organisation that provided the information.[70]

16.5.3 Relations with the EPPO

Before assessing what is the nature and intensity of the relationship that must apply between Eurojust and the EPPO, it is necessary to recall that Article 86 TFEU states that the Council may establish the EPPO from Eurojust. However, after the formal adoption of both regulations, this statement cannot be taken literally. The European legislator, aware of the doctrinal discussion created around the meaning of Article 86 TFEU, has introduced its own interpretation of the primary law, stating in the recitals of the EPPO Regulation (EPPOReg) that 'in accordance with Article 86 TFEU, the EPPO should be established from Eurojust. This implies that this Regulation should establish a close relationship between them based on mutual cooperation'.[71] Therefore, on the nature of the relationship between Eurojust and the EPPO, so far it is only clear that it must be close and based on mutual cooperation.

[67] Art. 49(1) EJR. [68] Art. 49(3) EJR. [69] Art. 49(5) EJR. [70] Art. 49(6) EJR.

[71] Recital 10 Regulation (EU) 2017/1939. This statement is also reproduced in Art. 100(1) Regulation (EU) 2017/1939, and mutually provided by Art. 50(1) EJR.

Accordingly, the EPPO may be invited to participate in the meetings of the College of Eurojust.[72] In operational matters, the EPPO may associate Eurojust with its activities inviting the agency or its national members to provide support in the transmission of its decisions or requests of mutual legal assistance, including its execution, to those MS that do not participate in the EPPO or to third countries.[73] For this purpose, Eurojust shall deal with these requests without undue delay and, where appropriate, as if they had been received from a national authority.[74] Where necessary, Eurojust may make use of the ENCS as well as its relations with third countries, including its liaison magistrates, to support cooperation with the EPPO.[75] Mutually, Eurojust may request the EPPO to provide support and associate with its activities regarding cross-border cases in those situations falling under its scope of application.[76]

In relation with the exchange of operational information, Eurojust and the EPPO are able to exchange information, including personal data, on their investigations in relevant cases related to the competence of the EPPO.[77] Furthermore, both shall have indirect access to each other's case management systems through a hit/no-hit system[78] similar to the system established for the search of information between the databases of Eurojust and Europol described above.[79]

At the institutional and administrative levels, the EPPOReg establishes, in first place, that the EPPO shall cooperate with Eurojust and rely on its support.[80] Such institutional and administrative assistance comes in many forms according to the wording of both regulations.

The institutional influence of Eurojust is manifested, primarily, in the election of the European Chief Prosecutor, since former national members of Eurojust are part of the selection panel.[81] The European Chief Prosecutor shall meet on a regular basis with the President of Eurojust to discuss matters of common concern[82] and may participate in the meetings of the Executive Board of Eurojust, without the right to vote. The EPPO shall also

72 Art. 13(3) EJR. 73 See Art. 100(2) Regulation (EU) 2017/1939.
74 Art. 50(2) EJR. 75 Art. 50(3) EJR. 76 Art. 50(4) (b) EJR.
77 Art. 50(4)(a) EJR; Art. 100(2)(a) Regulation (EU) 2017/1939.
78 Art. 50(5) EJR; Art. 100(3) Regulation (EU) 2017/1939.
79 See Art. 50(5) *in fine* EJR; Art. 100(3) *in fine* Regulation (EU) 2017/1939.
80 See Art. 3(3) Regulation (EU) 2017/1939.
81 See Art. 14(3) Regulation (EU) 2017/1939. Accordingly, a former national member has been part of the selection panel for the appointment of the first European Chief Prosecutor, see Council Decision (EU) 2018/1275, OJ L 238, 21.9.2018.
82 Art. 100(1) *in fine* Regulation (EU) 2017/1939, and Art. 50(1) *in fine* EJR.

participate in the draft of the annual and multi-annual programming of Eurojust but, on paper, its participation seems to be limited to receiving the previous draft elaborated by the Administrative Director.[83]

At administrative level, the EPPO may count with the assistance and administrative resources of Eurojust, as well as the agency may provide services of common interest to the EPPO.[84] However, both Regulations remain silent regarding the extent to which this assistance should be provided, a silence that is in contrast with the thoroughness with which the Commission's proposal for regulation pursued this matter.[85] In any case, both instruments look forward to a future arrangement on these matters.[86]

16.5.4 Relations with Other Bodies and Agencies of the EU

In the search for a better mutual understanding with other bodies acting in the AFSJ, Eurojust maintains and has subscribed agreements with other European bodies and agencies throughout its existence. As the agreements concluded with other bodies are limited to non-operational matters, the impact of these relationships in terms of the development of Eurojust remit of competences is lower than the existing relations with the EJN, Europol and the foreseen relations with the EPPO previously analysed. Saying that, Eurojust has signed agreements under the legal formula of Memorandums of understanding (MoU) with the following European bodies and agencies: OLAF, Frontex, eu-LISA, FRA, EUIPO, EMCDDA, CEPOL and the EJTN.

16.6 Relations with the EU Institutions

16.6.1 European Commission

The relationship between Eurojust and the Commission was initially developed by the provisions laid down within the Eurojust Decision,[87] the former Eurojust Rules of Procedure,[88] and two *ad hoc* MoUs.[89] All

[83] Art. 15(1) EJR.
[84] Art. 100(4) Regulation (EU) 2017/1939, and Art. 50(6) EJR.
[85] See Art. 42(7) Proposal for a Regulation COM (2013) 535 final.
[86] Art. 100(4) *in fine* Regulation (EU) 2017/1939 and Art. 50(6) *in fine* EJR.
[87] In particular, Art. 11 Decision 2002/187/JHA (consolidated version).
[88] Arts. 10 (3), 19 (3) and 21 Eurojust Rules of Procedure (2002), OJ C 286, 22.11.2002.
[89] www.eurojust.europa.eu/memorandum-understanding-between-european-commission-and-eurojust.

these provisions specified and defined the nature of the association of the Commission with the work of Eurojust, which was circumscribed to general issues, to the exchange of non-operational information and to the administrative and financial control.

After the application of the EJR, the Commission has a permanent representative in the new Executive Board of Eurojust in charge of the administrative management of the agency.[90] It can attend to and also request a meeting of the College to discuss the administrative tasks[91] and shall actively participate in the drafting of the annual and multi-annual programming of Eurojust.[92]

The Commission also still participates in the drafting of Eurojust's budget and exercises financial control functions over the agency.[93] In relation with this matter, in accordance with Article 12(1) EJR, the Commission proposed to the Council the mechanism for compensating the Member State whose national member is elected President of Eurojust.

As have been previously said, the Commission still have the power to request Eurojust's assistance in investigations and prosecutions that only affect one Member State but which have repercussions at EU level, but this power is expressly conditioned to the position adopted by the competent authority, which can oppose to this request.[94]

16.6.2 Council

The incidence of this EU institution in the daily work of Eurojust has been enormous through history. First, Article 26(1)(d) of the former Decision expressly provided the duty to establish and maintain a cooperative relationship with the Council, particularly, with the Joint Situation Centre, later succeeded by the EU Intelligence and Situation Centre (EU INTCEN) which currently forms part of the European External Action Service (EEAS)[95] and has an important role in the fight against international terrorism. Consequently, Eurojust signed an agreement on cooperation with the EEAS.[96]

After the application of the EJR, the relations between Eurojust and the Council have been tempered because of the adaptation of the

90 Art. 16(4) EJR. 91 Art. 13(2) EJR.
92 Art. 15 EJR. 93 Arts. 61, 63 and 64 EJR. 94 Art. 3(6) *in fine* EJR.
95 Council Decision 2010/427/EU, OJ L 201, 3.8.2010.
96 www.eurojust.europa.eu/letter-understanding-cooperation-between-eurojust-and-eeas.

functioning of the agency to the new institutional reality under the Lisbon Treaty. In fact, the Council has no longer the competence to request Eurojust's opinion on all proposed legislative acts related to judicial cooperation in criminal matters and police cooperation, an initiative that is now restricted to the Commission and to the MS.[97] Furthermore, the Council shall now share with the European Parliament most of the control functions.[98]

16.6.3 European Parliament and the Role of the National Parliaments

Inversely to the case of the Council, the influence of the European Parliament in the daily work of Eurojust has been traditionally limited due to the restricted role that this European institution had under the former Third Pillar. For that reason, the Eurojust Decision only envisaged a limited intervention of the European Parliament in the annual evaluation of the activities of Eurojust.

The EJR has foreseen a strengthened role of the European Parliament and the national parliaments of the MS in the evaluation of Eurojust's activities, in accordance with Article 85(1) *in fine* TFEU. As a result, the European Parliament and the national parliaments shall participate in the evaluation of Eurojust's activities and of the liaison magistrates seconded by Eurojust in third States,[99] which includes the annual appearing of the President of Eurojust for a joint evaluation within an interparliamentary committee meeting. Likewise, Eurojust shall transmit the results of the studies and strategic projects elaborated or commissioned by Eurojust, the annual and multi-annual programming, the working arrangements concluded with third parties and the annual report of the European Data Protection Supervisor (EPDS) on his supervisory activities in relation to Eurojust.[100] In this sense, Recital 62 of the EJR Preamble clearly states that the joint supervision 'should fully respect Eurojust's independence as regards actions to be taken in specific operational cases and as regards the obligation of discretion and confidentiality'.

[97] Art. 68 EJR.

[98] For example, the annual evaluation of the activities of Eurojust, see Art. 67 EJR.

[99] Arts. 67(1) and 53(6) EJR. [100] Art. 67(4) EJR.

16.6.4 Court of Justice of the European Union

Once more, due to the restrictions of the former Third Pillar, the Eurojust Decision did not establish any explicit reference or provision devoted to the relationship between Eurojust and the Luxembourg Court.

The EJR has amended this situation, establishing the jurisdiction of the CJEU to rule, in accordance with Article 340 TFEU, for unauthorised or incorrect processing of data,[101] in which case particulars may request a compensation for non-contractual damages provided by Article 268 TFEU. At the same time, national courts still have competence to rule on those cases where the incorrect processing of data was carried out by MS.[102] The judicial control of the CJEU provided by the EJR is completed with its intervention in specific aspects of the contractual liability of Eurojust[103] and in the decisions taken by Eurojust on public access of documents.[104]

16.7 Relations with Third Countries and International Organisations

In accordance with Chapter IV of the EJR, Section III, titled 'international cooperation', Eurojust may establish and maintain cooperation with authorities of third countries and international organisations. In this sense, Eurojust has the responsibility to elaborate, in agreement with the Commission, a four-year strategic programming identifying the third countries and international organisations flagged as priority, based on its operational needs.[105] However, from the application of the EJR and in accordance with Article 218 TFEU, Eurojust does no longer have the capacity to negotiate and conclude international cooperation agreements autonomously, which allow to transmit operational personal data to third countries in a standardised manner.

[101] Arts. 44 and 46 EJR. [102] Art. 46(3) EJR. [103] Art. 78(2) EJR.

[104] Art. 74(3) EJR, in connection with Arts. 228 and 263 TFEU and Art. 8 Regulation (CE) No. 1049/2001, OJ L 145, 31.5.2001.

[105] In fact, the first four-year cooperation strategy was adopted by the College in November 2019 based on a report of the Board on relations with Partners, which contained a list of third countries and international organizations with which there is an international need for cooperation. This document was sent to the Commission, remaining vested in the Council the final election of the countries and organisations in accordance with the operational requirements and external judicial cooperation needs of the agency.

On the other hand, Eurojust may conclude working agreements, in accordance with Article 47(3) EJR, but they cannot be the basis for allowing the exchange of personal data and shall not bind the Union or its MS. Thus, in the absence of an international cooperation agreement, as a general rule, the transmission of operational personal data on a regular and standardised basis to any authority of a third country would require an adequacy decision from the Commission,[106] provided that the third country concerned has a standard of protection of personal data that allows to do so.

The adequacy decisions have not been subject to discussion and might be worth exploring. In case of an adequacy decision, Eurojust could conclude a working agreement in order to set out modalities to implement them.[107] Those countries that have developed data protection rules in line with the EU regulation on this matter and which have strong mechanisms of cooperation with other data protection agencies of the EU, may proactively address the Commission showing their interest in activating and participating in an adequacy procedure. Furthermore, ongoing EU-funded cooperation programmes supported by Eurojust such as EuroMed Justice[108] or EL PAcCTO[109] may be an ideal platform to explore these evaluations.

The working agreements with third countries may serve as a basis to the exchange of strategic information, for the appointment of contact points and for seconding liaison magistrates.[110] Liaison magistrates shall stimulate and smooth the judicial cooperation in criminal matters, including the development of direct contacts with the competent national authorities of the host country, and they should have the power to exchange with them operational personal data where an agreement on cooperation previously exists.[111] After the replacement of the Joint Supervisory Body (JSB), their activities are supervised by the EDPS.[112]

Additionally, the EJR envisages two more options for the transference of operational personal data with third countries, but with a more restrictive approach and on a case-by-case basis: through appropriate safeguards[113] and in specific cases under exceptional circumstances.[114] Notwithstanding, these two options must be interpreted in a restrictive

[106] Art. 57 EJR. [107] Art. 56(3) EJR. [108] www.euromed-justice.eu.
[109] www.elpaccto.eu. [110] Art. 53(1) EJR. [111] Art. 53(2) EJR.
[112] Art. 53(6) EJR. [113] Art. 58 EJR. [114] Art. 59 EJR.

way,[115] and should not permit frequent, massive and structural transfers of personal data, or large-scale transfers of data but should be limited to data strictly necessary.

Eurojust is also authorized to maintain relations with international bodies and organisations to the extend it is necessary to perform its tasks.[116] For the time being, Eurojust has concluded this kind of agreements with the office of the prosecutor of the ICC, Iber-Red, UNODC and INTERPOL.

16.8 Final Remarks

Indeed twenty years ago, few politicians, scholars or prosecutors all over Europe could have even imagined that Eurojust would exist and, much less, that it would support in 2020 about 8,800 cross-border investigations, or open 4,200 cases, organize 468 coordination meetings or participate in 262 JITs in a single year.[117] However, Eurojust is a reality whose figures clearly reflect its growing success, showing up that ambitious projects in the field of criminal justice are far from being a window-dressing exercise, but possible and feasible.

Once its different identity from the European Public Prosecutor's Office has been legally clarified, Eurojust should find its core purpose in its judicial dimension and in the need to preserve the functional independence of its national members, who are at the same time the cornerstone of its structure. Indeed, the administrative and management structure of Eurojust has been instrumentally designed to allow the national members to perform their tasks more effectively, fully respect fundamental rights and freedoms, while safeguarding its independence in the exercise of their operational functions and judicial powers without any interference from the national executives or even from the Eurojust administration itself. Without prejudice to its configuration as an EU agency, the handling and processing of cases by the national members – as well as the judges and prosecutors working with the national members at the National Desks – should be prioritized and preserved, in order to avoid any instruction from the executive or any interference or impact from

115 See Recital 52 EJR. 116 Art. 52 EJR.

117 Statistics available at: www.eurojust.europa.eu/ar2020.

the Eurojust management bodies, the Commission and the European and national Parliament's joint evaluation. This is particularly relevant, if we take into account the judicial nature of its operational activity deployed within the AFSJ, in order to definitely improve mutual trust between judicial authorities, amounting to an extension, functionally speaking, of the national judicial systems, and particularly relevant nowadays for the primacy of the rule of law in the EU (in line with the Commission's report of 30 September 2020).[118]

Looking forward, Eurojust's modernization challenges are reflected in the Commission's final report on Cross-border Digital Criminal Justice published in September 2020.[119] Specifically, twenty-first century judicial cooperation standards would require secure communication channels between Eurojust and national judicial authorities, namely, a new CMS, a new JIT's platform for the exchange of information and evidence, a fully functional centralised database with information on convictions of third-country nationals and stateless persons (ECRIS-TCN), and improvements in the functioning of the Counter-terrorism Judicial Register (hosted at Eurojust since September 2019). Likewise, effective access between Eurojust CMS and those of Europol, the EPPO, and information exchange channels with Frontex and OLAF, as provided for in mirror provisions of the relevant Regulations. Indirect access to information between agencies will profoundly change the way Eurojust will operate in the future, as it will allow parallel investigations to be identified much more frequently and in a systematic or automated way.

The exceptional situation we are going through during the COVID-19 pandemic has highlighted the vulnerabilities of European judicial systems but also Eurojust's resilience and adaptability by promoting digitized solutions and extensive use of email communications and videoconferencing meetings to deliver a prompt and efficient response to any international cooperation needs. A good example of this is the compilation of the impact of COVID-19 on international judicial cooperation coordinated by Eurojust together with the EJN.[120] Undoubtedly, Eurojust, as an

[118] First annual report issued by the Commission on the state of the rule of law in the EU. Document COM (2020) 580 final, 30.09.2020.

[119] COM Directorate-General for Justice and Consumers, *Cross-Border Digital Criminal Justice. Final Report*, 2020.

[120] www.eurojust.europa.eu/sites/default/files/2021-02/st06178.en21.pdf.

agency that operational work is based on the exchange and communication of secure and encrypted data, requires not only investments for its technological renewal but also legal reforms that would provide a clear basis for this purpose. Furthermore, in the field of cooperation with third countries, the international cooperation agreements to be concluded by the EU institutions following Eurojust's four-year external strategy will allow this agency to become in the near future increasingly international and open to the rest of the world.

Further Reading

C. Brière, 'Cooperation of Europol and Eurojust with External Partners in the Fight against Crime: A Legal Appraisal', in H.C.H. Hofmann, E. Vos, and M. Chamon, *The External Dimension of EU Agencies and Bodies*, Cheltenham: Edward Elgar Publishing, 2019, pp. 59–77.

M. Coninsx, 'Eurojust', in V. Mitsilegas, and M. Bergström (eds.), *Research Handbook on EU Criminal Law*, Cheltenham: Edward Elgar Publishing, 2016, 441–456.

V. Covolo, 'From Europol to Eurojust: Towards a European Public Prosecutor', (2012) 7 *eucrim*, 83–88.

G. De Amicis, and R. Kostoris, 'Vertical Cooperation', in P. Kostoris (ed.), *Handbook of European Criminal Procedure*, Cham: Springer, 2018, 223–234.

A. Hernández López, *El papel de Eurojust en la resolución de conflictos de jurisdicción penal en la Unión Europea. Propuestas legislativas*, Cizur Menor: Thomson Reuters Aranzadi, 2020, 35–147.

M. Luchtman, and J.A.E. Vervaele, 'European Agencies for Criminal Justice and Shared Enforcement (Eurojust and the European Public Prosecutor's Office)', (2014) 10 *Utrecht L. Rev.*, 132–150.

A. Suominen, 'The Past, Present and the Future of Eurojust', (2009 15 *Maastricht J. Eur. Comp. L.*, 217–234.

A. Weyembergh, 'An Overall Analysis of the Proposal for a Regulation on Eurojust', (2013) 4 *eucrim*, 129–130.

The European Public Prosecutor's Office (EPPO) 17

A Milestone for the EU Integration Process

Silvia Allegrezza

17.1 Introduction

The new European Public Prosecutor Office (EPPO) was introduced by Regulation 2017/1939 (RegEPPO) and became operative on 1 June 2021, when national authorities of the twenty-two participating EU Member States (MS)[1] transmitted more than 2,000 cases. Coronation of the European criminal justice project, the EPPO is the outcome of a 'rocky road'[2] of more than two decades of political and doctrinal debate.[3] Approved only thanks to the enhanced cooperation mechanism,[4] this new supranational body has been conferred with investigative and prosecutorial powers throughout the territory of the participating MS, albeit with the limited scope of investigating the crimes affecting the European financial interests as defined by Directive 2017/1371.[5] Despite this limited material scope, the creation of this new supranational body with executive powers proves to be problematic to many in terms of subsidiarity and

[1] All the Member States of the European Union participated to the initiative except for Denmark and Ireland having opted out from the area of freedom, security and justice (AFSJ), and Hungary, Poland and Sweden having decided so far not to join. Working arrangements with these five non-participating MS are being established to define how the EPPO will cooperate with them.

[2] Described in these terms in V. Mitsilegas, *EU Criminal Law after Lisbon: Rights, Trust and the Transformation of Justice in Europe*, Oxford: Hart Publishing, 2016, p. 83.

[3] See L. Bachmaier Winter (ed.), *The European Public Prosecutor's Office. The Challenges Ahead*, Cham: Springer, 2018.

[4] The Lisbon Treaty constituted a turning point in the political debate around EPPO, with the introduction of the enhanced cooperation mechanism under Art. 86 TFEU. In the absence of unanimity, a group of at least nine MS may establish an enhanced cooperation procedure under Articles 20(2) and 329(1) TEU.

[5] Directive (EU) 2017/1371 of the European Parliament and of the Council of 5 July 2017 on the fight against fraud to the Union's financial interests by means of criminal law, [2017] OJ 2017 L 198/29. See V. Mitsilegas, 'European Prosecution between Cooperation and Integration: The European Public Prosecutor's Office and the Rule of Law', (2021) 28–2 *Maastricht J. Eur. Comp. Law*, 245, 246.

proportionality,[6] where others saw its added value as a milestone of the EU integration process as it extends direct enforcement to the sensitive field of criminal justice.[7] Given the strong reluctance of some participating MS to accept the Commission's original proposal of an exclusive competence of the EU, the EPPO Regulation finally opted for a model of a 'priority' competence, with a right of evocation for the EPPO.[8]

The foundation of the EPPO relies on a basic but revolutionary idea: a separation between the prosecutorial powers – concentrated at the EU level – and the adjudicatory powers – remaining at the national level in the hands of national courts. This idea of biphasic criminal proceedings was originally elaborated by a group of academics[9] and then filtered into the Treaties. This structure, in which prosecutorial powers have been dissociated from the *ius dicere* and attributed to a common European prosecutor (EP), is described in Article 86 TFEU. The original design was aimed at overcoming the visceral opposition and political veto against a fully fledged EU criminal justice system, implying the establishment of a common European criminal court. However, the choice – or more correctly, the political compromise – of combining the European investigation and prosecution with the national adjudication has considerable consequences: the EPPO is governed by a complex legal framework requiring to adapt to different legal traditions of the EU MS.[10]

[6] P. Asp, *The Procedural Criminal Law Cooperation of the EU – Towards an Area of Freedom, Security & Justice – Part 2*, Stokholm: Jure, 2016, p. 203; K. Ambos, *European Criminal Law*, Cambridge: Cambridge University Press, 2018, p. 575.

[7] J. Monar, 'Eurojust and the European Public Prosecutor Perspective: From Cooperation to Integration in EU Criminal Justice?', (2013)14 *European Politics and Society*, 340. C. Gómez-Jara, 'European Federal Criminal Law: What Can Europe Learn from the US System of Federal Criminal Law to Solve Its Sovereign Debt Crisis?', 3 (2013) *EuCLR*, 170, 171 ff.; T. Rafaraci, 'Brief Notes on the European Public Prosecutor's Office: Ideas, Project and Fulfilment', in T. Rafaraci and R. Belfiore (eds.), *European Criminal Justice. Fundamental Rights, Transnational Proceedings and the European Public Prosecutor's Office*, Cham: Springer, 2019, 157, 158.

[8] V. Mitsilegas and F. Giuffrida, 'Raising the Bar? Thoughts on the Establishment of the European Public Prosecutor's Office', (2017) *CEPS Research Report* www.ceps.eu/system/files/PI%202017-39%20Mitsilegas_Giuffrida_0.pdf. Kai Ambos considers it a shared competence with national prosecution authorities, see Ambos, *European Criminal Law*, p. 576.

[9] See M. Delmas-Marty and J.A.E. Vervaele, *The Implementation of the Corpus Juris in the Member States – Penal Provisions for the Protection of European Finances*, Cambridge: Intersentia, 2001.

[10] See *infra*, para. 9.

The complex structure is detailed by Regulation 2017/1939, completed by Internal Rules of Procedures (IRoP) governing the EPPO operations,[11] and by the applicable national laws, aiming to identify the competent MS (Art. 5 RegEPPO).

17.2 Statute and Architectural Design of the EPPO

The EPPO is defined as a body of the Union having legal personality (Article 3 RegEPPO), enjoying full independence, and accountable only to the European Parliament, the Council and the Commission for its general activities (Article 6 RegEPPO).[12] The EPPO shall act in the interest of the Union and 'neither seek nor take instructions from any person external to the EPPO, any MS of the European Union or any institution, body, office or agency of the Union.'[13] Against this background, the concept of independence as applied to the EPPO combines a traditional concept of non-interference by European or national authorities with 'the interest of the Union as a whole' which it is called to protect disregarding private interests from companies, individuals or States.[14]

In its original proposal presented in 2013, the Commission envisaged a vertical model, with a European Public Prosecutor, his Deputies and the supporting staff at the core of the European Office and European Delegated Prosecutors (EDPs) in the MS.[15] Four years of political negotiations led to a considerable shift in terms of minor centralisation, more collegial procedures and reduced hierarchy between the EU and the national level. In particular, the initial centralised structure was revised to include a decentralised[16] and less-hierarchically organised office following the blueprint of Eurojust. When the Greek Presidency decided

[11] Internal rules of procedure of the European Public Prosecutor's Office (2021/C 22/03).

[12] A duty to report annually is established by Art. 7 RegEPPO.

[13] Art. 6(1) RegEPPO. [14] Ibid., 4.

[15] See L. Erkelens, A. Meij and M. Pawlik (eds.), *The European Public Prosecutor's Office: An Extended Arm or a Two-Headed Dragon?*, The Hague: TMC Asser Press, 2014.

[16] S. Ruggeri, 'Criminal Investigations, Interference with Fundamental Rights and Fair Trial Safeguards in the Proceedings of the European Public Prosecutor's Office. A Human Rights Law Perspective', in L. Bachmaier Winter (ed.), *The European Public Prosecutor's Office. The Challenges Ahead*, Cham: Springer, 2018, 201, 203 ff.; A. Martínez Santos, 'The Status of Independence of the European Public Prosecutor's Office and Its Guarantees', in L. Bachmaier Winter (ed.), *The European Public Prosecutor's Office. The Challenges Ahead*, Cham: Springer, 2018, 1 ff.

to introduce collegial organs in the EPPO structure – an amendment, which the following Presidencies retained – the light, hierarchical structure at the central level was replaced by a more articulated construct in which only coordination was centralised, whereas enforcement was conferred to national delegated prosecutors. In its final setting, the EPPO appears as an indivisible supranational body operating as one single Office with a decentralised structure[17] (Art. 8(1) and (2) RegEPPO). The current organigram is composed by a 'double-layered design'[18]: a central level – including the College, the Permanent Chambers (PCs), the European Chief Prosecutor (ECP), the Deputy ECPs, the EPs and the Administrative Director – combined with a decentralised level, composed by EDPs located in the participating MS (Art. 8 RegEPPO).

The *College* of the EPPO is conceived as a collective organ consisting of the ECP and one EP per participating MS. Its main functions are to overview the EPPO's activities and adopt decisions on strategic matters and general issues arising from individual cases (except procedural decisions), ensuring coherence, efficiency and consistency in the prosecution policy (Art. 9 RegEPPO). To this aim, all the PCs are required to report annually on their activity to the College. A clear example of this pivotal function of the College are the IRoP adopted in October 2020 and the Operational Guidelines on investigation, evocation policy and referral adopted by the Decision of the College of 21 April 2021.[19]

The role to adopt operational decisions in individual cases is conferred to the *Permanent Chambers*, each one composed by three members from different MS and different legal traditions: the ECP (or one of her Deputies or an EP appointed as Chair) with two additional EPs as permanent Members.[20] Moreover, the EP supervising an investigation or prosecution in an individual case takes part in the deliberations and decision-making of the PC in that individual case.[21] So far, the EPPO has

[17] See I. Maschl-Clausen, 'The Permanent Chambers at the Heart of the EPPO's Decision-Making', (2021) *eucrim*, 55, 56; C. Burchard, 'Article 8', in H.-H. Herrnfeld, D. Brodowski and C. Burchard (eds.), *European Public Prosecutor's Office: EPPO*, Baden Baden: Nomos, 2021, pp. 41 ff.

[18] M. Panzavolta, 'Choosing the National Forum in Proceedings Conducted by the EPPO: Who Is to Decide?', in L. Bachmaier Winter (ed.), *The European Public Prosecutor's Office. The Challenges Ahead*, Cham: Springer, 2018, 59, 64.

[19] Decision of the College 029/2021.

[20] Art. 10(1) RegEPPO.

[21] Art. 10(9) RegEPPO allows the supervising EP to participate but with no right to vote on 'decisions on delegation or withdrawal of delegation in accordance with Article 10(7), on

established fifteen PCs.[22] The equal distribution of the cases among the Chambers is granted by the EPPO's Case Management System (CMS), a system of random allocation as established by the IRoP. The operational decision-making power of a PC consists of monitoring and directing the investigations and prosecutions conducted by the EDPs and coordinating these operations in cross-border cases alongside implementing the general and strategic decisions taken by the College. The PC decides whether to bring a case to judgment or to dismiss it, whether to apply a simplified prosecution procedure or to refer it to the national authorities or, finally, to reopen an investigation (Art. 10 RegEPPO). Some specific powers to instruct the EDP directly or via the supervising EP – on whether to initiate an investigation or to evoke a case; or on allocation or reallocation of cases, or for the approval of the EP decision to conduct the investigation himself or herself in accordance with Art. 28(4) RegEPPO – are all linked to the hierarchical structure of the organ.

Some of the above-mentioned decisions can be delegated to the EP supervising an investigation or a prosecution in accordance with Art. 12(1) RegEPPO. The latter is identified as the EP of the same MS as the EDP handling the case. The knowledge of the national legal framework and practice will enable the supervising EP to know what actions are most appropriate and efficient in that given state. The EPs are called to play several roles within the EPPO machinery: they compose the College, sit as permanent members of the different Chambers and supervise all the cases of their MS of origin. The supervisory role entails presenting summaries of the cases under their supervision and, where applicable, proposals for decisions to be taken by the Chamber, based on draft decisions prepared by the EDP.

The *European Delegated Prosecutors* represent the very heart of the entire mechanism. They are national prosecutors – at least two for each participating MS[23] – who are supposed to work under a 'double-hat' as part of both their national judicial system and the EPPO. EDPs can continue working on national cases to the extent that this does not prevent them

allocation and reallocation [...] and on bringing a case to judgment [...]where more than one Member State has jurisdiction for the case[...]'.

[22] Art. 2(1) of College Decision 015/2020.

[23] The amount of EDPs per country varies greatly: two for many smaller participating MS to five for France, seven for Spain, eleven for Germany and fifteen for Italy; see www.eppo.europa.eu/en/news/european-delegated-prosecutors-overview-country.

from fulfilling their obligations under RegEPPO (Art. 13(3)). The double-hat model ensures both coherent (through central and hierarchical decision-making) and effective prosecutorial action (through local law enforcement, the proximity of the EDPs to the field work of the investigation, and direct access to the national resources and law enforcement agencies).[24] The EDPs 'shall act on behalf of the EPPO in their respective Member States and shall have the same powers as national prosecutors in respect of investigations, prosecutions and bringing cases to judgment' in addition to the specific powers and status conferred by the Regulation (Art. 13 RegEPPO). They are responsible for the investigations and prosecutions of all the cases allocated to them, required however to follow the direction and instructions of the PC as well as the instructions from the supervising EP, aiming to coordinate the EPPO operations and overcome potential obstacles at national level. They enjoy a wider freedom in their responsibility for bringing a case to judgment; in particular, they can present trial pleas, participate in taking evidence and exercise the available remedies in accordance with the applicable national law (Art. 13 RegEPPO).

The complex articulation of organs and powers shows the real distance of the final setting from the original EPPO concept.[25] The now existing, heavier structure raises questions as to whether the current EPPO is in line with the Commission's original intent of reducing complexity, with respect to both institutional complexity and normative source complexity.[26]

17.3 The Material Scope (ratione materiae) of the EPPO

Art. 4 RegEPPO clarifies the material scope and procedural limits of the EPPO: it shall be responsible for 'investigating, prosecuting, and bringing to judgment the perpetrators of, and accomplices to, criminal offences

[24] K. Ligeti, 'The European Public Prosecutor's Office: Which Model?', in A. Klip (ed.), *Substantive Criminal Law of the European Union*, Apeldorn: Maklu, 2011, 51, 51 ff.

[25] A light, hierarchical model that turns into a collegial decentralised model composed by nation-based investigative authorities, short lines of communication and the power of the head office to give instructions in individual cases, thought to be the ideal setting for effectively fighting fraud against the Union's financial interests.

[26] See S. Allegrezza and A. Mosna, 'Cross-Border Criminal Evidence and the Future European Public Prosecutor. One Step Back on Mutual Recognition?', in L. Bachmaier Winter (ed.), *The European Public Prosecutor's Office. The Challenges Ahead*, Cham: Springer, 2018, pp. 143, 143 ff.

affecting the financial interests of the Union which are provided for in Directive (EU) 2017/1371' (the so-called PIF Directive).[27] At the beginning of its activities, the EPPO received the reports of PIF offences committed after 20 November 2017 related to passive and active corruption, fraud in respect of revenues and expenditure, misappropriation, subsidy abuse that damages or is likely to damage the Union's financial interests, and money laundering of property derived from PIF offences, including inchoate offences (incitement, aiding and abetting and attempt to commit PIF offences).

The extension of the EPPO's material competence to the offences regarding participation in a criminal organisation having one of the PIF offences as the main focus might imply a significant increase of the EPPO power.[28] The April 2021 Guidelines seem to suggest a very cautious approach, limiting its competence to cases of organised crime having a major European impact and where the separation of proceedings will be detrimental to the investigation.[29] With reference to money laundering, the EPPO is competent only for crimes involving property derived from PIF offences and it should act only when there is a preponderant EU interest in terms of damages, reputation or repercussions.[30]

The EPPO 'ancillary competence', including 'any other criminal offence that is inextricably linked' to criminal conducts that fall within the scope of the EPPO (Article 22(2) and (3) RegEPPO), is controversial. This vague notion has potentially the power to centralise the competence on any offence having a strong connection with the respective PIF offence and may compromise *de facto* the political choice to establish a common prosecutorial office with limited competence, reducing the legitimacy of the EU intervention.[31] According to Recital 54 of the

[27] Directive 2017/1371 of 5 July 2017 on the fight against fraud to the Union's financial interests by means of criminal law on the choice of a Directive as the legal basis for the EPPO competence and its consequences on the rule of law, see J.A.E. Vervaele, 'The Material Scope of the Competence of the European Public Prosecutor's Office: A Harmonised National Patchwork?' (2015) *CSDPE*, 13, available at http://dirittopenaleeuropeo.it/wp-content/uploads/2015/10/Vervaele-2014-15.pdf. See also P. Asp, *The Substantive Criminal Law Competence of the EU*, Stockholm: Stokholm Universitet, 2012; K. Ligeti, 'Approximation of Substantive Criminal Law and the Establishment of the European Public Prosecutor's Office', in F. Galli and A. Weyembergh (eds.), *Approximation of Substantive Criminal Law in the EU*, Bruxelles: Editions ULB, 2013, pp. 73–84.

[28] Articles 22(2) and 22(3) of Regulation (EU) 2017/1939.

[29] Decision 029/2021, 6.

[30] Ibid.

[31] J. Öberg, 'The European Public Prosecutor: Quintessential Supranational Criminal Law?', (2021) 28(2) *Maastricht J. Eur. Comp. Law*, 164, 170.

Regulation's Preamble, the notion of 'inextricably linked offence' refers to the identity of the material facts in the sense of the existence of a set of concrete circumstances that are inextricably linked together in time and space, as established by the case law on *ne bis in idem* principle.[32] However, this analogy is unconvincing given that this principle involves by definition an assessment with regard to the existence of the same fact, whereas the ancillary EPPO competence refers to criminal offences other than PIF offences.[33] A better definition is offered by Recital 56, echoing the definition of the EUROPOL Regulation, where an 'inextricably linked offence' should be considered in light of the jurisprudence of the CJEU as the one that has been committed for the main purpose of creating the conditions to commit the PIF offence, such as offences strictly aimed at ensuring the material or legal means to commit them or to ensure the related profit or product. However, Art. 22 RegEPPO serves the interest of justice in that a single prosecuting office carries out investigations on crimes that are closely interwoven.[34] In any other case, ancillary competence is actionable only when the inextricably linked offence is 'preponderant, in terms of the seriousness of the offence concerned, as reflected in the maximum sanctions that could be imposed' (Recital 55 RegEPPO).

Some clarifications are offered by the April 2021 Guidelines, according to which two or more offences should be considered as inextricably linked when 'both offences were committed by means of the same material activity and driven by the same intent; or the set of facts composing those offences was carried out as parts of the execution of the same criminal plan in order to achieve the same common goal; or the specific unlawful conduct composing one of the offences is linked in time, in space and by subject matter to the other, making up an inseparable whole; or the facts subjacent to those offences are interlinked in a way that a separate investigation, prosecution or adjudication of the offences

[32] See Ambos, *European Criminal Law*, p. 577.

[33] F. Giuffrida, 'The European Public Prosecutor's Office: King without Kingdom?', (2017) *CEPS Research Report*, 10–11; A. Nieto Martin and M. Munoz de Morales Romero, 'The Office of the European Public Prosecutor and Related Offences: Deconstructing the Problem', in P. Asp (ed.), *The European Public Prosecutor Office – Legal and Criminal Policy Perspective*, Stockholm: Stiftelsen Skrifter utgivna av Juridiska Fakulteren vid Stockholms Universitet, 2015, pp. 120, 120 ff.

[34] Mitsilegas and Giuffrida, 'Raising the Bar? Thoughts on the Establishment of the European Public Prosecutor's Office', 9.

in different proceedings would artificially split up the series of events that form the natural process of action'.[35]

A strong indication coming from the CJEU's take in the *Taricco* case[36] led to the extension of the EPPO's competence to VAT frauds that are connected with the territory of two or more MS and involve a total damage of at least €10 million. The two mentioned requirements – total damage and cross-border nature of VAT fraud – show a very limited willingness of Member States to lose their control over the matter.[37] Damage assessment shall take into consideration the actual and the potential loss to the EU resources or assets and the value of the contract, in procurement-related cases, when the conduct did not cause an actual material loss (Decision 029/2021, 5).

As already mentioned, the Regulation as finally approved abandoned the EPPO exclusive competence on PIF offences, opting for a *sui generis* shared competence model: the EPPO can evoke the case if national investigations have already been opened[38] and refer it back to national authorities, aiming at handling the case at the most appropriate level.[39]

Special rules are set to mitigate the absolute prevalence of the EPPO competence over national authorities, enforceable when the EPPO is 'better placed' to investigate the case. While aiming to safeguard a fair distribution between the European and the national level, the EPPO can retain only cases having repercussions at Union level or where the suspects are officials or other servants of the Union or when the PIF offence has caused a damage inferior to 10,000 euros. The EPPO shall also refrain from exercising its competence when other inextricably linked offences are punished with more severe penalties than the PIF offence or their impact on other victims

[35] Decision of the College of the European Public Prosecutor's Office of 21 April 2021 adopting operational guidelines on investigation, evocation policy and referral of cases (College Decision 029/2021, 6).

[36] CJEU, *Taricco and Others* [GC], No. C-105/14, Judgment, ECLI:EU:C:2015:555, 8 September 2015. See S. Allegrezza, 'On Legality in Criminal Matters between Primacy of EU Law and National Constitutional Traditions. A Study of the Taricco Saga', in V. Mitsilegas, A. di Martino and L. Mancano (eds.), *The Court of Justice and European Criminal Law*, Oxford: Hart 2019,165, 165 ff. On the debate on PIF offences as including VAT revenues, see K. Ligeti, 'The European Public Prosecutor Office', in V. Mitsilegas, M. Bergström and T. Konstantinides (eds.), *Research Handbook on EU Criminal Law*, Cheltenham: Edward Elgar 2016, 480, 490–491.

[37] Mitsilegas and Giuffrida, 'Raising the Bar? Thoughts on the Establishment of the European Public Prosecutor's Office,' 9.

[38] See *infra*, para. 4. [39] See *infra*, para. 7.

is higher than the one on the EU financial interests. The vagueness of these criteria can only be solved on a case-by-case basis. In case of disagreement on distribution of competence between the EPPO and the national prosecution authorities, the decision is attributed to the national authority. For this purpose, every participating MS shall specify the national authority which will decide on the attribution of competence.[40]

As for territorial and personal competence, the EPPO will investigate the PIF offences committed in whole or in part within the territory of one or several MS participating to the initiative.[41] The EPPO is competent for externally committed offences only if the author is a national of a participating MS or a member of EU staff, provided that the respective MS has jurisdiction for such offences when committed outside its territory (Article 23 RegEPPO).

17.4 The Interplay between the European and the National Level: Duty to Report, Power of Evocation and Opening of the Investigation

Normative and operative powers of the EPPO and its national ramifications are defined by a constant double reference to national and European rules.

The EPPO shall investigate, prosecute and exercise prosecutorial functions in the competent courts of the MS, until the case has been finally disposed of. The opening of the investigation and the 'final disposition of the case' represent the beginning and the end of the EPPO's competence. All the EPPO activities should be governed by the rule of law, proportionality and impartiality, seeking 'all relevant evidence whether inculpatory or exculpatory' without undue delay (Art. 5 RegEPPO).

The EPPO can exercise its competence by initiating an investigation where there are reasonable grounds to believe that an offence within its competence has been committed. The case is assigned to a PC, a supervising EP and a handling EDP. The shared competence system sets a specific priority for the EP. Consequently, the competent national authorities shall refrain from exercising their own competence in respect of the same criminal conduct.

40 H.-H. Herrnfeld, 'Article 23', in H.-H. Herrnfeld, D. Brodowski and C. Burchard (eds.), *European Public Prosecutor's Office: EPPO*, Baden Baden: Nomos, 2021, pp. 171, 171 ff.

41 Ibid., p. 173.

All EU and national law enforcement agencies of participating MS shall without undue delay report to the EPPO any criminal conduct falling within its material scope, this *reporting duty* being applicable even after an investigation has been opened at the national level (Art. 24(1) and (2) RegEPPO). To this aim, MS are free to identify which agencies are to be considered as 'national competent authorities'.

Upon receipt of the information, the EPPO might decide whether to exercise its right of *power of evocation*[42] no later than five days after notification from the national authorities. Pending the EPPO decision on the evocation, national authorities shall refrain from taking any decision that may have the effect of precluding the EPPO's decision and they shall also cooperate adopting any urgent measures necessary to ensure effective investigation and prosecution. The right of evocation may be exercised directly by an EDP, autonomously or upon indication of the competent PC, 'provided that the national investigation has not already been finalised and that an indictment has not been submitted to a court'.[43] However, an evocation concerning a PIF offence already under investigation at the national level erodes the sovereignty of the national State to the extent that the latter cannot investigate the case any longer regardless of its ability or willingness to do so.[44] The power of evocation should not be understood as a public reprimand for the State concerned for a lack of initiative, but rather as a way to protect the residual spirit of centralisation of the EPPO.[45]

In case of conflict between the national authorities that estimate that the EPPO could not exercise its competence, the latter can apply Art. 27(3) RegEPPO by analogy and informs the competent national authority accordingly. If the national authority maintains its position that the EPPO is not competent, we are faced with a 'positive competence conflict'. While

42 See Art. 27 RegEPPO. 43 Idem.

44 H. Satzger, 'The European Public Prosecutor's Office and Its Coordination with the National Public Prosecutor's Office: The Model of Complementarity', in L. Bachmaier Winter (ed.), *The European Public Prosecutor's Office. The Challenges Ahead*, Cham: Springer, 2018, 52.

45 See College Decision 029/2021, 4: the communication received in accordance with Article 24(1) RegEPPO is aimed at triggering a decision of the EPPO on whether to exercise its competence by initiating an investigation; hence, it shall be addressed only to the EPPO. 'Primary and exclusive' reporting to the EPPO will 'prevent interference with the prerogatives of the EPPO [...] and would prevent the risk of parallel investigations and their [...] consequences, as well as a serious glitch to the mechanism of exchange of information [...]'.

the Regulation does not contain any procedure on how to raise the conflict, according to the April 2021 Guidelines, 'the EPPO shall comply with the rules established by the national Law regarding the resolution of conflicts of competence and address the authority specified by the concerning MS as the appropriate to decide on the attribution of competence'.[46]

17.5 Applicable National Law

One of the most crucial – and controversial – part of the entire EPPO regulation is represented by the rules identifying which EDP shall initiate the investigation and, consequently, under what national law. The issues at stake are enormous: the entire design of organs, powers and controls is left to this crucial choice, as the applicable national law transforms a European investigation and prosecution into a national criminal proceeding. European rules are so basic and the system designed by the Regulation so immature and incomplete that there is no chance for it to survive without the recourse to national law.[47]

The final version of the Regulation rejected the – already cautious – concept of European territoriality, where the participating MS are composing a 'single legal area'.[48] Sovereign prerogatives have found their way back especially in cross-border investigations[49] where the borders are amplified by the distinction between the handling EDP and the assisting EDP.[50]

As a general rule, the investigation shall be initiated and handled by a EDP from the participating MS 'where the focus of the criminal activity is, or if several connected offences within the competences of the EPPO have been committed, the MS where the bulk of the offences has been committed' (Art. 26 RegEPPO).

46 Decision 029/2021, 9.

47 Giuffrida, 'The European Public Prosecutor's Office', 11.

48 V. Mitsilegas, 'The European Prosecutor's Office Facing National Legal Diversity', in C. Nowak (ed.), *The European Public Prosecutor's Office and National Authorities*, Milano: Wolters Kluwer-Cedam, 2016, 11, 20; Martínez Santos, 'The Status of Independence of the European Public Prosecutor's Office and Its Guarantees', 1, 4; Panzavolta, 'Choosing the National Forum in Proceedings Conducted by the EPPO', 59, 71; K. Ligeti, 'The European Public Prosecutor Office', in V. Mitsilegas, M. Bergström and T. Konstantinides (eds.), *Research Handbook on EU Criminal Law*, Cheltenham: Edward Elgar 2016, 480, 498.

49 See *infra*, para. 6.

50 The assisting EDP supports the handling EDP in case of cross-border investigations.

The *locus commissi delicti* – described in a questionable way as 'the focus of the criminal activity' – represents the main parameter and the additional ones, listed in an order of priority, are the place of the habitual residence of the suspect, the nationality of the latter or the place where the main financial damage has occurred. Nevertheless, the uncertainty of those concepts remains and raises a plethora of concerns in legal literature.[51] Vague and puzzling notions, such as 'focus of the activity' and 'bulk of the offences' (does it imply an arithmetical approach or emphasise the seriousness of the main offence?), fail to provide the necessary legal certainty.[52] The decision on which EDP is going to handle the investigation is taken by the PC and based on a draft decision prepared by the EDP who received the information from national authorities. The defence has no say despite the significant implication of such a choice on the general setting of defence rights.[53]

Judicial control over this decision is entirely left to national authorities that can hardly perform a proper supervision of the forum choice that is supranational in nature, resting above the prerogatives of a single national sovereignty.[54] When the choice of forum intervenes at the very beginning of the investigation, the decision can be revisited by the PC after consultation with the EP and the EDPs concerned until the decision to prosecute (or to drop the case) has been taken. This reallocation of the case to another EDP of a different MS, or the decision to merge or split the cases, might be adopted when they are 'in the general interest of justice' (Art. 26(5) RegEPPO) and taking in 'due account of the current state of the investigations' (Art. 26(6) RegEPPO).

17.6 The Investigative Powers in National and Cross-Border Cases

The power to investigate follows this multi-layered structure of the Office, involving European and national authorities linked by the duty of loyal cooperation and the quest for efficiency. The EPPO model envisages a

[51] Giuffrida, 'The European Public Prosecutor's Office', 11; Panzavolta, 'Choosing the National Forum in Proceedings Conducted by the EPPO', in 59, 74 ff.

[52] Panzavolta, 'Choosing the National Forum in Proceedings Conducted by the EPPO', 59, 79.

[53] See *infra*, para. 10.

[54] Panzavolta, 'Choosing the National Forum in Proceedings Conducted by the EPPO', 59, 80.

centralised investigative power exercised by decentralised bodies – the EDPs – located in the competent participating MS or in a different participating one where the evidence is located. As we will see, the lack of common rules and the pivotal role played by both the *lex fori* and the *lex loci*, makes the EPPO prisoner of national laws.[55]

Art. 28 RegEPPO confers investigative powers to the handling EDP under the control of the PC and of the supervising EP. The EDP can undertake investigative and other measures individually, or instruct the competent authorities in their MS. When necessary, national authorities shall take urgent measures in accordance with national law to ensure effective investigations, even where not specifically acting under an instruction given by the handling EDP but informing the latter on the results without undue delay.

The complex chain of command implies a constant duty for the handling EDP to report to the supervising EP and to the PC on any significant development via the CMS. The Chamber also has the power to reallocate the case to another EDP of the same MS when the first cannot perform his duties or has failed to follow the instructions. When required by the seriousness of the case or by the involvement of EU staff, the supervising EP can be authorised by the PC to conduct the investigations personally or give instructions to the national authorities. Even though the current design goes beyond a traditional intergovernmental system, since the authorities that request and provide the cooperation are integrated into the same supranational structure,[56] this constant hierarchical control is meant to account for the stronger centralisation as originally proposed. However, given the absence of a harmonised criminal procedure applicable to all EPPO proceedings, its capacity to ensure a higher efficiency than the previous system of coordination of transnational inquiries remains in doubt.[57]

A composite set of investigative measures is available to the EDPs under Art. 30 RegEPPO, incorporating a few common investigative powers to be complemented by measures provided for by the applicable national law.

55 K. Ligeti (ed.), *Toward a Public Prosecutor for the European Union*, Oxford: Hart Publishing, 2013, 19.

56 L. Bachmaier Winter, 'Cross-Border Investigations under the EPPO Proceedings and the Quest for Balance', in L. Bachmaier Winter (ed.), *The European Public Prosecutor's Office. The Challenges Ahead*, Cham: Springer, 2018, 117, 121.

57 D. Negri, 'Best Practices and Operational Models in Financial-Economic Investigations in Europe in View of the EPPO', in A. Bernardi and D. Negri (eds.), *Investigating European Fraud in the EU Member States*, Oxford: Hart Publishing, 2017, 149, 152.

The harmonization is limited to these minimum investigative measures,[58] cut down from originally twenty-one to just six: searches of premises, production orders of objects or data, freezing orders, interceptions of communications and track and trace of technical means, including controlled deliveries. The participating MS shall provide for those measures '[a]t least in cases where the offence subject to investigation is punishable by a maximum penalty of at least four years of imprisonment' (Article 30 RegEPPO).

In addition to these common investigative measures, Art. 30(4) RegEPPO confers upon the EDPs the power 'to request or to order any other measures in their MS that are available to prosecutors under national law in similar national cases'. The reference to the multitude of EDPs instead of to the EPPO indicates the collegial nature and intergovernmental structure of the new body.

The rules governing cross-border investigations confirm the change in approach.

Art. 31 RegEPPO establishes a system of cooperation between the EDPs of the different MS in cross-border investigations. The terminology echoes a network of traditional mutual legal assistance: references to the 'handling European Delegated Prosecutor', the 'assisting European Delegated Prosecutor' and their obligation to 'act in close cooperation' speak to a system in which plural actors carry out a bunch of investigative activities that will affect the coherence of evidence on which the final assessment will be based. Ultimately, the EPPO Regulation establishes that, in cross-border cases, the handling EDP might need to undertake an investigatory measure in a different country. In such a case, they must first decide on the necessity of the measure according to their own law but then refer the matter to the national EDP of the country where the measure needs to be carried out. While the original proposal's rules on evidence relied on the *locus regit actum* principle, the final Regulation adopted a different, more complex system. A combined reading of Art. 31 and 32 RegEPPO suggests that the choice of an investigation measure and its application must comply with both the procedural rules of the MS of the handling EDP and the national law of the assisting EDP. In concreto, this obliges to respect both the rules of the *lex fori* and the *lex loci*.

[58] Allegrezza and Mosna, 'Cross-Border Evidence and the Future European Public Prosecutor. One Step Back on Mutual Recognition?', 152.

When required by the law of the MS of the handling EDP or by the law of the assisting EDP, they should apply for judicial authorisation according to their national law (Article 31(3) RegEPPO). When the latter is required in both MS involved, it must be clearly specified in which MS such authorisation must be obtained, assuming that there must only be one authorisation. The wording of Article 31 RegEPPO seems to give prevalence to the law of the assisting EDP. In the absence of harmonising rules on the matter, national law will determine whether, and under which modalities, such judicial authorisation is necessary for the execution of the respective investigative measure. However, as it is unclear to what extent the courts of the assisiting EDP MS can verify the requested measure under their national law, the question is now pending before the CJEU (footnote: CJEU, *G.K. and others, No.* C-281/22, 25 April 2022) as there is no explicit time limit for the obtention of such authorisation, investigations could be significantly delayed. The competent PC may invoque Article 31(7) if the assigned measure is not undertaken within the time limit set out in the assignment or within a reasonable time, despite the lack of provisions on concrete deadlines.

Once the decision of adopting a measure in a MS other than the handling EDP's MS has been taken, the assisting EDP is entitled to evaluate its form and content. The measures must however not be executed should the assisting EDP have doubts. Rather, as there are no grounds for refusal,[59] they must inform their supervising EP and consult with the handling EDP in order to resolve the matter bilaterally, when considering that the assignment is incomplete or contains a manifest relevant error, or the measure cannot be undertaken within the time limit set out in the assignment for justified and objective reasons, or an alternative but less intrusive measure would achieve the same results, or, lastly, the assigned measure does not exist or would not be available in a similar domestic case (Art. 31(5) RegEPPO). It is therefore evident that the broad and imprecise formulation, particularly in subparagraph (a), is likely to give rise to an unlimited range of cases in which the assignment, if not refused at the outset, could be put on hold by the assisting EDP. Such mechanism seems inconsistent with the general trend in EU legislation in simplifying and accelerating cooperation in cross-border criminal matters.[60]

[59] Bachmaier Winter, 'Cross-Border Investigations under the EPPO Proceedings and the Quest for Balance', 117, 122.

[60] Allegrezza and Mosna, 'Cross-Border Evidence and the Future European Public Prosecutor. One Step Back on Mutual Recognition?', 152.

The EPPO may also rely on other instruments of cross-border investigations, in particular on the European Investigation Order (EIO); this is especially relevant when the assigned measure does not exist in a purely domestic setting but would be available in a cross-border situation covered by legal instruments on mutual recognition (Article 31(6) RegEPPO). However, the possibility to have recourse to other tools of mutual recognition 'should not replace the specific rules on cross-border investigations under this Regulation' (Recital 73 RegEPPO), meaning that the channels of communication foreseen in the EPPO are to be applied with preference to other mutual recognition instruments,[61] but the latter will be relevant especially for investigations to be carried out in non-participating MS.

17.7 The Closing of the Investigation

When the EPPO's investigation is completed, the handling EDP prepares a motivated draft decision to be submitted to the supervising EP and to the PC to which the final decision is conferred. Several outcomes are possible: the PC can refer the case to national authorities, dismiss it, or prosecute the case before a national court; or choose a simplified prosecution procedure (Article 35 RegEPPO).

The PC can follow this suggestion or undertake its own review of the case file before taking a final decision or giving further instructions to the EDP. The EPPO enjoys a certain margin of discretion, when deciding whether to drop a case or transfer it to the national authorities, yet 'this discretion is not unlimited'.[62] The final Regulation adopted the principle of legality with regard to the decision to prosecute – when enough evidence supports it – and providing for a scrutiny of a dismissal aimed at avoiding arbitrary decisions merely based on discretion[63] (Recital 66 RegEPPO).

As for the deferral[64] to the national level – where the investigation reveals that the investigated facts do not constitute a criminal offence within the EPPO's competence or the specific conditions defining the transnational dimension of the offence are no longer met, the competent PC shall 'refer

[61] Bachmaier Winter, 'Cross-Border Investigations under the EPPO Proceedings and the Quest for Balance', 117, 123.

[62] M. Caianiello, 'The Decision to Drop the Case: Res Iudicata or Transfer of Competence?', in L. Bachmaier Winter (ed.), *The European Public Prosecutor's Office. The Challenges Ahead*, Cham: Springer, 2018, pp. 103, 104.

[63] Ibid., p. 104. [64] Ambos, *European Criminal Law*, p. 577.

the case [...] to the competent national authorities' (Article 34 RegEPPO). With its April 2021 Guidelines, the College offered specific criteria the PC should follow in referring the case to the national authorities.[65] The sensitiveness of such a decision is witnessed by the hierarchical control exercised by the ECP to whom the PC shall communicate within three days any referral to national authorities. If the latter do not accept the case, the EPPO maintains its competence. When the national authorities accept the case and decide to open an investigation, the EPPO shall transfer the entire file and 'refrain from taking further investigative or prosecutorial measures and close the case' (Art. 34(7) RegEPPO). Thereafter, the EPPO shall inform the relevant institutions, bodies, offices and agencies of the Union, as well as, where appropriate under national law, suspects or accused persons and the crime victims. Scholars observed that uncertainty might arise for example when the EPPO defers the case to national authorities and then makes use of its right to evocation given that this power persists as long as an indictment has not been submitted to a court (Art. 27(7) RegEPPO).[66]

Art. 39 RegEPPO indicates on which grounds the handling EDP can propose the dismissal of the case to the PC, being the organ in charge of the final decision. These grounds, complemented by the applicable national law, refer to the death of the suspect or winding up of a legal person, the insanity of the suspect or accused person, an amnesty or an immunity granted, the expiry of the national statutory limitation to prosecute, the final disposal of the case in relation to the same acts and, lastly, the lack of relevant evidence. In every case in which the EPPO is sharing its competence with the MS, the PC shall dismiss the case only after consultations with the national authorities (Art. 39(3) RegEPPO), the Regulation imposing a consultation at national level over the dismissal decision.[67] An official notification of the dismissal is given to the competent national authorities, all relevant Union bodies, as well as, where appropriate under national law, to the suspects and victims. The dismissed cases may also be referred to OLAF or to the competent national administrative or judicial authorities for recovery – of assets presumably – or a different administrative follow-up (Art. 39(4) RegEPPO). After dismissal, the PC can reopen the case on the basis of new facts unknown at the time of the decision.

65 See Decision 029/2021, 16–17.

66 Crit. Caianiello, 'The Decision to Drop the Case: Res Iudicata or Transfer of Competence?', 103, 108.

67 Ibid., p. 109.

When recommending to prosecute a case, the handling EDP motivates the grounds of the decision and the choice of appropriate forum. Even though the final decision is attributed to the PC, the EDP's recommendation has strong legal implications: if they propose to prosecute a case, the PC cannot dismiss the case – showing a sort of *favor persecutionis* – and has to take a decision within twenty-one days; if no decision is taken, the EDP's proposal 'shall be deemed to be accepted' (Art. 35(1) and (2) RegEPPO).

The PC has an ample margin of discretion: upon the proposal of the handling EDP, the PC can merge more cases related to the same person if they fall under the jurisdiction of the same MS. As for the choice of forum, if more than one MS has jurisdiction over the case, the PC 'shall in principle decide to bring the case to prosecution in the MS of the handling EDP' (Art. 36(3) RegEPPO). A different solution can bring the case to a different MS 'if there are sufficiently justified grounds to do so' in accordance with the criteria set out in Art. 26(4) and (5). The rule-exception relationship is meant to avoid forum shopping,[68] a risk highlighted in literature.[69]

However, the PC may, considering the report provided in accordance with Art. 35(1), decide to bring the case to prosecution in a different MS and instruct an EDP of that MS accordingly. Once the choice of forum is made, the competent national court in that MS is to be determined pursuant to the applicable national law. From that moment on, all relevant decisions and procedures are determined by national law, including the right to appeal. If the handling EDP decides to lodge an appeal, their decision has to be validated by the PC (Art. 36(7) RegEPPO).

Simplified procedures, when applicable according to national law, can be required by the EDP as an alternative form of prosecution. Mainly, this option includes those forms of negotiated justice aiming 'at the final disposal of a case on the basis of terms agreed between the suspect and the prosecutorial authorities' (Art. 40(1) RegEPPO). Where applicable, the handling EDP may propose to the competent PC to apply that procedure in accordance with the conditions provided for in national law. The decision is taken by the PC based on the seriousness of the offence, the damage caused, the willingness of the suspected offender to repair

[68] Ambos, *European Criminal Law*, p. 578.

[69] Mitsilegas and Giuffrida, 'Raising the Bar? Thoughts on the Establishment of the European Public Prosecutor's Office', 7; A. Damaskou, 'The European Public Prosecutor's Office: A Ground-Breaking New Institution of the EU Legal Order', (2015) 6 *NJECL*, 143; Mitsilegas, *EU Criminal Law after Lisbon*, p. 93.

the damage caused by the illegal conduct and the fact that the use of the procedure would be in accordance with the general objectives and basic principles of the EPPO.

17.8 Admissibility of Evidence

Trial rules are determined by national law and assessed by national courts, including the admissibility of evidence. For which no common rules are given in the Regulation nor in general EU law. The sole provision states that the admissibility of evidence should not be denied 'on the mere ground that [it] was gathered in another Member State or in accordance with the law of another Member State' (Article 37 RegEPPO), mirroring the *lex loci* and *lox fori* criteria on cross-border investigations.

At any rate, Art. 37 represents a change of perspective compared to the Commission Proposal. The latter set out as a general rule the admissibility of evidence presented by the EPPO, which could nonetheless be refuted only in exceptional cases. On the contrary, Art. 37(1) introduces a simple non-discrimination clause on 'foreign' evidence admissibility, a minimal regulatory imperative,[70] leaving it entirely to the national law and courts to solve any dispute on the legality of evidence. Thus, it represents no real advancement compared to previous cooperation systems: there are no strict exclusionary rules on evidence,[71] thus confirming the *lex fori* rule[72] and perpetuating the differences between more admissibility-friendly and more admissibility-adverse criminal procedures of the MS.[73] It is worthwhile noting that the mere reference to 'another Member State' in Art. 37(1) RegEPPO seems to extend the rule to evidence collected in all participating and non-participating EU MS.[74]

Article 37(2) RegEPPO, according to which 'the power of the trial court to freely assess the evidence presented by the defendant or the prosecutors of the EPPO shall not be affected by this Regulation' appears more cryptic. As the first paragraph focuses only on admissibility, the European

[70] Allegrezza and Mosna, 'Cross-Border Evidence and the Future European Public Prosecutor. One Step Back on Mutual Recognition?', pp. 141, 159 ff.

[71] Ibid., 159.

[72] Ambos, *European Criminal Law*, p. 578.

[73] Burchard, 'Article 37', p. 346.

[74] See ibid., p. 349, for a different opinion.

legislator, apparently, felt the need to clarify that the free evidence assessment in trial is in no way affected by the establishment of the EPPO, be it with regard to cross-border or just domestic evidence. Even though the wording of paragraph 2 refers exclusively to the assessment at trial, it seems reasonable to understand it more broadly, including any assessment of evidentiary, also with regard to pre-trial decisions on detention.[75]

As to exclusionary rules – on which the Regulation is silent – an interpretative guideline can be found in Recital 80, suggesting that evidence admission must respect the fairness of the procedure and the suspects and accused person's rights under the Charter of Fundamental Rights of the European Union (CFREU) and Article 6 Treaty on European Union (TEU). Recital 80 also confirms the prevalence of national law on evidence, stating that 'nothing in this Regulation may be interpreted as prohibiting the courts from applying the fundamental principles of national law on fairness of the procedure that they apply in their national systems, including in common law systems'. Additionally, a range of rights is identified which, in case of breach, could form the basis for a (further) exclusion of evidence, going beyond Art. 37. By referring to the CFREU and explicitly to fundamental rights under the ECHR, the catalogue of relevant principles and rights is indeed very broad. However, the mere reference to an entire list of rights does not guarantee the adequate protection of the fairness of the evidence admission procedure. Those rights are explicitly meant to identify and protect minimum standards and the related case law shows no automatism between the breach of fundamental rights and the duty for the Court to exclude tainted evidence. The complex relationship between a rights violation and the ensuing exclusion of affected evidence does not offer a clear guidance for judges given that the ECtHR focuses on the 'fairness as a whole'.[76]

17.9 Judicial Control over Activities Carried Out by the EPPO

The judicial control of the EPPO's activities is to be undertaken by an intricate control system in which national courts and the CJEU play different roles. Art. 86 TFEU mentions the need for a specific legal framework,

[75] Ibid., p. 352.

[76] S. Trechsel, *Human Rights in Criminal Proceedings*, Oxford: Oxford University Press, 2005, p. 86 ff.

requiring the future Regulation to determine the rules applicable to the judicial review of procedural measures. A rich doctrinal debate[77] focused on the political and legal opportunity of limiting the CJEU's competence with reference to an EU organ and on the need of a centralised control over the EPPO's activities with a view to increase harmonisation of criminal procedural rules.[78] The Commission adopted a minimalistic approach to the CJEU's jurisdiction, largely excluding a centralised (EU) judicial review of the EPPO.[79] This limitation was obtained by a sort of legal *escamotage*: when performing its functions, the EPPO would be considered as a national authority for the purpose of judicial review. The academic criticism[80] and the concerns of the EU Parliament were partially taken up in the final Regulation introducing a minimum level of centralised control by the CJEU.

As a general rule, Art. 42 RegEPPO affirms that '[p]rocedural acts of the EPPO [...] intended to produce legal effects *vis-à-vis* third parties' – as well as the 'failures of the EPPO to adopt procedural acts' – shall be subject to review by the competent national courts in accordance with their national law coherently with the general legal setting of EPPO operations.[81] Without such a rule, Article 263 TFEU would confer the entire review to the CJEU for the simple fact that the EPPO is an organ of the Union. However, the complexity of the EU legal system and the overarching role of the Court as defined by the Treaties made it necessary to explicitly provide for a European level of control. To this aim, Art. 42 RegEPPO identifies a set of situations in which the CJEU has exclusive competence. Some of them are uncontroversial – disputes relating

[77] H.-H. Herrnfeld, 'Article 42', in H.-H. Herrnfeld, D. Brodowski and C. Burchard (eds.), *European Public Prosecutor's Office: EPPO*, Baden Baden: Nomos, 2021, 405 ff; W. Van Ballegooij, 'European Public Prosecutor's Office – A View on the State of Play and Perspectives from the European Parliament', in W. Geelhoed, L.H. Erkelens and A. Meij, (eds.), *Shifting Perspectives on the European Public Prosecutor's Office*, The Hague: Asser Press, 2018, pp. 27 ff., 35.

[78] See G. Giudicelli-Delage, S. Manacorda and J. Tricot (eds.), *Le contrôle judiciaire du parquet européen. Nécessité, modèles, enjeux*, Paris: Société de législation comparé, 2015.

[79] Mitsilegas, 'European Prosecution between Cooperation and Integration: The European Public Prosecutor's Office and the Rule of Law', 245, 260.

[80] J. Tricot, 'Le contrôle juridictionnel du parquet européen dans les projets législatifs. Observations critiques sur la proposition du règlement portant création du parquet européen', in G. Giudicelli-Delage, S. Manacorda and J. Tricot (eds.), *Le contrôle judiciaire du parquet européen*, pp. 155 ff.

[81] Rafaraci, 'Brief Notes on the European Public Prosecutor's Office', pp. 157, 160.

to compensation for damage caused by the EPPO, disputes concerning arbitration clauses contained in contracts concluded by the EPPO and disputes concerning staff-related matters – even when they have a high political value, such as the CJEU jurisdiction on the dismissal of the ECP or EPs (Art. 42(7)) RegEPPO. The CJEU maintains its power, in accordance with Art. 267 TFEU, to give preliminary rulings concerning the validity of the Regulation and of procedural acts of the EPPO when the question of validity is raised 'directly on the basis of Union law' (Art. 42(2)(a)). The CJEU is in charge of solving any conflict of competence between the EPPO and the competent national authorities (Art 42(2)(c)). It has been correctly observed that the rule seems to have no substance as the interpretation of Art 22 and 25 RegEPPO would have already been covered by the possibility to ask for a preliminary ruling.[82]

A very special power conferred to the CJEU, in accordance with Art 263(4) TFEU, concerns the review of the EPPO's decision to dismiss a case when contested directly on the basis of Union law since this is the only 'procedural act' of the EPPO not supervised by national courts (Art 42(3) RegEPPO). It is noteworthy that Art 42 RegEPPO does not cover all potential judicial review issues, being limited to the EPPO activities and excluding – for example – judicial authorisations of coercive measures.[83]

17.10 Multilevel Protection of Defence Rights

The Regulation offers three different levels of the protection of defence rights. The first level refers to the European constitutional framework of criminal justice, in particular to the rights of suspects and accused persons under the CFREU, such as the right to a fair trial and the rights of the defence.

A second level of protection refers to the right to enjoy a minimum level of protection of procedural rights as provided for by Union law, including the directives on procedural rights, as implemented by national law. Thereby, a list of minimum rights is explicitly mentioned: the rights to interpretation and translation (Directive 2010/64/EU), information and access to the case materials (Directive 2012/13/EU), access to a lawyer

[82] Herrnfeld, 'Article 42', p. 432. [83] Ibid., p. 403.

and to communicate with and have third persons informed in the event of detention (Directive 2013/48/EU), the right to remain silent and to be presumed innocent (Directive 2016/343/EU) and the right to legal aid (Directive 2016/1919/EU) (Article 41(2) RegEPPO).

At the third level, Art. 41(3) provides that suspects and accused persons and 'other persons involved in the proceedings' must be given 'all the procedural rights available to them under the applicable national law'. 'Other persons involved in the proceedings' includes witnesses, victims, persons for which an EAW has been issued, persons affected by mutual legal assistance measures and of course their lawyers.[84] This has met with criticism since it equates the EPPO to national prosecutorial bodies, ignoring the impact its particular status might have on the balance of powers that lie at the very heart of any criminal proceedings. First and foremost, the Regulation 'calls for an equivalent standard compared to national prosecutions but does not set out an equivalent standard throughout the Union'.[85]

Art. 41 RegEPPO does not introduce any additional rights or defensive powers protecting the suspect or accused facing such a powerful counterpart. There are at least three additional risks for defence rights in EPPO investigations: first, the legal and organisational complexity due to the structure of the Office, increasing the need for qualified legal advice; second, the potential Union-wide publicity and related reputational damage; third, the more substantial need for a transnational defence given that investigation and trial take place in different *fora*[86] or, especially in cross-border cases, using evidence collected by a variety of national rules whose admissibility can be contested only with reference to a patchwork of national laws. The lack of standardisation and specific strengthening of the position of the suspect or the accused person under the EPPO Regulation could be criticised not only with regard to the principles of

[84] D. Brodowski, 'Article 41', in H.-H. Herrnfeld, D. Brodowski and C. Burchard (eds.), *European Public Prosecutor's Office: EPPO*, Baden Baden: Nomos, 2021, p. 398.

[85] Ibid., p. 383; M. Kaiafa-Gbandi, 'The Establishment of an EPPO and the Rights of Suspects and Defendants: Reflections upon the Commission's Proposal and the Council's Amendments', in P. Asp (ed.), *The European Public Prosecutor Office – Legal and Criminal Policy Perspective*, Stockholm: Stiftelsen Skrifter utgivna av Juridiska Fakulteren vid Stockholms Universitet, 2015, pp. 234 ff.

[86] Brodowski, 'Article 41', p. 386.

fair trial and equality of arms[87] but also with regard to potential difficulties in the assessment of the legality of the evidence collected abroad.

The simple referral, in Art. 41 RegEPPO, to general principles and fundamental rights as enshrined in the CFREU, to a plain catalogue of defence rights and to the applicable national law, without contemplating any additional harmonisation of defence rights, might not suffice to solve the natural imbalance between the prosecution and the defence and effectively guarantee a homogeneous protection standard in the MS participating in the EPPO. The Regulation seems to ignore the structural differences among MS in shaping the concrete exercise of defence rights, especially in the pre-trial stage, even after the implementation of the Roadmap Directives.[88]

17.11 Conclusions

The new supranational EU Prosecutor is governed by a multi-level, complex and at first sight rather bureaucratic system of powers and balances involving several levels. It breaches the traditional jurisdictional link between the *accusatio* and the *ius dicere* (adjudication), offering an unprecedented combination of European and national law, submitted to a multi-level judicial review. However, the renunciation to a single legal area and the choice of a minimum level of harmonisation led to a substantial failure of a signification move from cooperation to integration, leaving the final judgment on the real innovation of the EPPO with regard to the entire system of European criminal justice to practice.

The initially centralised structure has been transformed in a complicate chain of command that exalts collegiality but seems to have left behind the paramount quest of efficiency. Nevertheless, the EU's history has taught us that the Union has the capacity – when political obstacles can

[87] Bachmaier Winter, 'Cross-Border Investigations under the EPPO Proceedings and the Quest for Balance', pp. 117, 120; T. Wahl, 'The European Public Prosecutor's Office and the Fragmentation of Defence Rights', in K. Ligeti, M. João Antunes and F. Giuffrida (eds.), *The European Public Prosecutor's Office at Launch*, Milano: Wolters Kluwer, 2020, pp. 85 ff.; A. Weyembergh and C. Brière, *Towards a European Public Prosecutor's Office*. Study for the LIBE Committee, Brussels: European Union, 2016, p. 35; available at www.europarl.europa.eu/RegData/etudes/STUD/2016/571399/IPOL_STU(2016)571399_EN.pdf.

[88] S. Allegrezza and V. Covolo (eds.), *Effective Defence Rights in Criminal Proceedings. A European and Comparative Study on Judicial Remedies*, Milano: Cedam – Wolters Kluwer, 2018.

be overcome – to transform imperfect organs into an integration engine, conferring upon the practice the power to solve conflicts and to remedy original flaws. So the hope remains that this process will be shaped by a large judicial dialogue in which the very special nature of criminal law and the need to integrate the rich national traditions on procedural safeguards and evidence law are brought together to a healthy mix.

Further Reading

P. Asp (ed.), *The European Public Prosecutor's Office – Legal and Criminal Policy Perspectives*, Stockholm: Stiftelsen Skrifter utgivna av Juridiska Fakulteren vid Stockholms Universitet, 2015.

L. Bachmaier Winter (ed.), *The European Public Prosecutor's Office. The Challenges Ahead*, Cham: Springer, 2018.

M. Delmas-Marty and J.A.E. Vervaele, *The Implementation of the Corpus Juris in the Member States, Vol. I*, Cambridge: Intersentia, 2000.

W. Geelhoed, L.H. Erkelens and A. Meij (eds.), *Shifting Perspectives on the European Public Prosecutor's Office*, The Hague: Asser Press, 2018.

G. Grasso, R. Sicurella, G. Illuminati and S. Allegrezza (eds.), *Le sfide dell'attuazione di una Procura europea: definizione di regole comuni e loro impatto sugli ordinamenti interni*, Milano: Giuffrè, 2013.

H.-H. Herrnfeld, D. Brodowski and C. Burchard (eds.), *European Public Prosecutor's Office: EPPO*, Baden Baden: Nomos, 2021.

K. Ligeti (ed.), *Toward a Public Prosecutor for the European Union*, Oxford: Hart Publishing, 2013.

K. Ligeti, M.J. Antunes and F. Giuffrida (eds.), *The European Public Prosecutor's Office at Launch*, Milano: Wolters Kluwer, 2020.

V. Mitsilegas and F. Giuffrida, 'Raising the Bar? Thoughts on the Establishment of the European Public Prosecutor's Office', (2017) *CEPS Research Report* www.ceps.eu/system/files/PI%202017-39%20Mitsilegas_Giuffrida_0.pdf (accessed 3 March 2022).

Part VI

Perspectives

18 Brexit and European Criminal Law

Valsamis Mitsilegas

18.1 Introduction

Brexit has presented a major change in European Criminal Law.[1] Notwithstanding the complicated constitutional position of the United Kingdom in the field of criminal justice, structured around a series of 'opt-outs',[2] the United Kingdom played an active, and at times leading, role in the strategic development and in the implementation of the enforcement aspects of the EU Criminal Law *acquis* as an EU Member State.[3] With the UK now having withdrawn from the EU and upon the end of the transitional post-Brexit period, relations between the UK and the EU in the field of criminal justice are now governed by the UK–EU Trade and Co-operation Agreement (TCA) which entered into force on 1 May 2021.[4] Criminal justice cooperation is covered by a separate part in the Agreement, Part III on law enforcement and judicial cooperation in criminal matters. Part III is supplemented by a series of Annexes developing further implementing, definitional or technical provisions. It is also accompanied by a series of notifications by the UK and the EU on behalf of the Member States (MS)[5] (and by the EU separately).[6]

The aim of this chapter is to analyse the key provisions of the TCA concerning judicial co-operation in criminal matters, in order to evaluate the extent to which EU–UK co-operation after Brexit can replicate, and

[1] This contribution is based on the extended chapter on 'European Criminal Law after Brexit' in V. Mitsilegas, *EU Criminal Law*, 2nd edn., Oxford and Portland, OR: Hart, 2022.

[2] V. Mitsilegas, 'The Uneasy Relationship between the United Kingdom and European Criminal Law. From Opt-Outs to Brexit?', (2016) 6 *EuCLR*, 517–536.

[3] V. Mitsilegas, 'European Criminal Law after Brexit', (2017) 28 *CLF*, 219–250.

[4] https://eur-lex.europa.eu/legal-content/EN/TXT/PDF/?uri=CELEX:22021A0430(01)&from=EN.

[5] https://eur-lex.europa.eu/legal-content/EN/TXT/HTML/?uri=OJ:C:2021:117I:FULL&from=EN.

[6] https://eur-lex.europa.eu/legal-content/EN/TXT/HTML/?uri=CELEX:22020X1231(02)&from=EN.

to what extent, the pre-Brexit status quo. The analysis will highlight the varied areas of ambition in the field of judicial cooperation and analyse the parameters of cooperation within the broader institutional and constitutional framework underpinning the position of the United Kingdom as a third country.

18.2 Surrender and the Arrest Warrant

The TCA aims to provide a high-degree continuity with the previously applicable European arrest warrant (EAW) system. The pre-Brexit terminology of 'surrender' of an 'arrest warrant' is maintained in the text, the heading of Title VII is 'surrender', the basis of the system is a 'surrender decision'[7] and the objective of UK–EU cooperation is to base extradition on a mechanism of surrender pursuant to an arrest warrant.[8] Title VII on surrender replaces the corresponding provisions of the following conventions applicable in the field of extradition in relations between the United Kingdom, on the one side, and MS, on the other side: (a) the European Convention on Extradition (EuCExt), done at Paris on 13 December 1957, and its additional protocols (APs); and (b) the European Convention on the Suppression of Terrorism (EuCTerr), as far as extradition is concerned.[9] Title VII is applicable in respect of EAWs issued in accordance with Council Framework Decision 2002/584/JHA by a State before the end of the transition period where the requested person has not been arrested for the purpose of its execution before the end of the transition period.[10]

Cooperation remains judicial. The 'Arrest Warrant' for the purposes of the TCA means a judicial decision issued by a State with a view to the arrest and surrender by another State of a requested person, for the purposes of conducting a criminal prosecution or executing a custodial sentence or detention order.[11] 'Judicial authority' means an authority that is, under domestic law, a judge, a court or a public prosecutor – a public prosecutor is considered a judicial authority only to the extent that domestic law so provides.[12] The Court of Justice of the European Union (CJEU) has held that, for the purposes of the EAW, the issuing

[7] Art. 613. [8] Art. 596. [9] Art. 629(1). [10] Art. 632.
[11] Art. 598(a). [12] Art. 598(b).

authority (including public prosecutors) must be capable of exercising its responsibilities objectively without being exposed to the risk that its decision-making power be subject to external directions or instructions in particular from the executive, such as that it is beyond doubt that the decision to issue an EAW lies with that authority and not, ultimately, with the executive.[13]

Cooperation continues to take place in similar terms to the EAW in a number of respects. In terms of scope of cooperation, an arrest warrant may be issued for acts punishable by the law of the issuing State by a custodial sentence or a detention order for a maximum period of at least twelve months or, where a sentence has been passed or a detention order has been made, for sentences or detention orders of at least four months.[14] Cooperation takes place on the basis of specific elements introduced in a form.[15] Cooperation is intended to be swift – the TCA has introduced cooperation, similar deadlines with the EAW. Mirroring Article 17 of the EAW FD, the TCA sets out strict time limits for the decision to execute the arrest warrant.[16] The latter must be dealt with and executed as a matter of urgency[17] – in cases where the requested person consents to surrender, the final decision on the execution of the arrest warrant must be taken within ten days after the consent was given;[18] in other cases, the final decision on the execution of the arrest warrant shall be taken within sixty days after the arrest of the requested person, a deadline that can be extended by a further thirty days where this is not possible.[19] The TCA further mirrors the EAW FD (Article 23) in the provision on time limits for surrender[20]

The TCA includes a number of grounds to refuse to execute an Arrest Warrant. As with the EAW system, mandatory grounds for non-execution are initially limited to age; amnesty, and *ne bis in idem*.[21] There are a number of grounds for optional non-execution, in a provision that includes details on the treatment of in absentia hearings.[22] The TCA

[13] The key ruling is CJEU, *OG and PI*, Nos. C-508/18 and C-82/19 PPU, Judgment, ECLI:EU:C:2019:456, 27 May 2019, para. 73; thereto K. Ambos, 'The German Public Prosecutor as (no) Judicial Authority within the Meaning of the European Arrest Warrant: A Case Note on the CJEU's Judgment in OG (C-508/18) and PI (C 82/19 PPU)', (2019) 10 *NJECL*, 399–407. For an analysis of the CJEU case law on the topic, see V. Mitsilegas, *EU Criminal Law*, 2nd edn., Oxford and Portland, OR: Hart, 2022, Chapter 4.

[14] Art. 599. [15] Art. 606 – form contained in Annex 43. [16] Art. 615.

[17] Art. 615(1). [18] Art. 615(2). [19] Art. 615(3) and (4). [20] Art. 621.

[21] Art. 600. [22] Art. 601.

includes a detailed provision on guarantees to be given by the issuing State in particular cases.[23] The provision incorporates the case law of the CJEU[24] in requiring guarantees if there are substantial grounds for believing that there is a real risk to the protection of the fundamental rights of the requested person, the executing judicial authority may require, as appropriate, additional guarantees as to the treatment of the requested person after the person's surrender before it decides whether to execute the arrest warrant.[25] The TCA contains a general provision on the rights of a requested person, outlining rights of information, translation and interpretation and access to a lawyer[26] – however this provision is much less detailed than the series of EU Directives on procedural rights in criminal proceedings. In addition to these safeguards, surrender will not occur on the basis of a series of grounds related to non-compliance with the proportionality principle, the non-existence of dual criminality, the occurrence of political offences and the existence of a nationality exception.

All these elements constitute a departure from cooperation under the EAW model. If the executing judicial authority finds the information communicated by the issuing State to be insufficient to allow it to decide on surrender, it must request that the necessary supplementary information. This is in particular with respect to Article 597 [Principle of proportionality], Articles 600 [Grounds for mandatory non-execution of the arrest warrant] to 602 [Political offence exception], Article 604 [Guarantees to be given by the issuing State in particular cases] and Article 606 [Content and form of the arrest warrant], be furnished as a matter of urgency and may fix a time limit for the receipt thereof, taking into account the need to observe the time limits provided for in Article 615.[27]

Respect for the principle of proportionality underpins the TCA surrender system: cooperation through the arrest warrant shall be necessary and proportionate, taking into account the rights of the requested person and the interests of the victims, and having regard to the seriousness of the act, the likely penalty that would be imposed and the possibility of a State taking measures less coercive than the surrender of the requested

[23] Art. 604.

[24] See, in particular, CJEU, *Aranyosi and Căldăraru*, Nos. C-404/15 and C-659/15 PPU, Judgment, ECLI:EU:C:2016:198, 5 April 2016.

[25] Art. 601(c). [26] Art. 609. [27] Art. 613(2).

person particularly with a view to avoiding unnecessarily long periods of pre-trial detention.[28] Non-compliance with the proportionality principle may constitute a ground of refusal to recognise and execute an arrest warrant.[29]

The TCA introduces a political offence exception to surrender.[30] In principle, it is provided that the execution of an arrest warrant may not be refused on the grounds that the offence may be regarded by the executing State as a political offence, as an offence connected with a political offence or as an offence inspired by political motives.[31] However, the UK and the Union, acting on behalf of any of its MS, may each notify the Specialised Committee on Law Enforcement and Judicial Cooperation that paragraph 1 will be applied only in relation to terrorist offences, and in particular : (a) the offences referred to in Articles 1 and 2 EuCTerr; (b) offences of conspiracy or association to commit one or more of the offences referred to in Articles 1 and 2 of the EuCTerr, if those offences of conspiracy or association correspond to the description of behaviour referred to in Article 599 of this Agreement; and (c) terrorism as defined in ANNEX 45 to the TCA.[32] Where an arrest warrant has been issued by a State having made a notification as referred to in paragraph 2 or by a State on behalf of which such a notification has been made, the State executing the arrest warrant may apply reciprocity.[33]

The TCA further contains a provision on the verification of dual criminality. It states that in principle surrender is subject to the condition that the acts for which the arrest warrant has been issued constitute an offence under the law of the executing State, whatever the constituent elements or however it is described.[34] There are two exceptions to the requirement to verify the existence of dual criminality. The first concerns offences, where behaviour is punishable by deprivation of liberty or a detention order of a maximum period of at least twelve months, referred to in Articles 1 and 2 of the EuCTerr, or in relation to illicit trafficking in narcotic drugs and psychotropic substances, or murder, grievous bodily injury, kidnapping, illegal restraint, hostage-taking or rape, even where that person does not take part in the actual execution of the offence or offences concerned – such contribution must be intentional and made with the knowledge that the participation will contribute

[28] Art. 597. [29] Art. 597(1). [30] Art. 602. [31] Art. 602(1). [32] Art. 602(2).
[33] Art. 602(3). On the EU notification, see 2021/C 117 I/01. [34] Art. 599(2).

to the achievement of the group's criminal activities[35] and terrorism as defined in Annex 45 of the TCA.[36] The second exception concerns the re-introduction of the exceptions to the verification of the existence of dual criminality in a manner similar to the model established by the EAW FD – however this exception required notification by both the UK and the Union, acting on behalf of any of its MS, to the Specialised Committee on Law Enforcement and Judicial Cooperation that, on the basis of reciprocity, the condition of dual criminality referred to in paragraph 2 will not be applied.[37] The EU has made such a notification on behalf of a number of MS.[38]

According to the TCA, the execution of an arrest warrant may not be refused on the grounds that the requested person is a national of the executing State.[39] However, the text contains significant inroads to the end of the bar of surrendering own nationals introduced by the EAW FD. The UK and the Union, acting on behalf of any of its MS, may each notify the Specialised Committee on Law Enforcement and Judicial Cooperation that that State's own nationals will not be surrendered or that the surrender of their own nationals will be authorised only under certain specified conditions. The notification shall be based on reasons related to the fundamental principles or practice of the domestic legal order of the UK or the State on behalf of which a notification was made. In such a case, the Union, on behalf of any of its MS or the UK, as the case may be, may notify the Specialised Committee on Law Enforcement and Judicial Cooperation within a reasonable time after the receipt of the other Party's notification that the executing judicial authorities of the Member State or the UK, as the case may be, may refuse to surrender its nationals to that State or that surrender will be authorised only under certain specified conditions.[40]

In case of refusal to surrender on nationality grounds, executing states must consider instituting proceedings against its own nationals which are commensurate with the subject matter of the arrest warrant, having taken into account the views of the issuing State. In circumstances where a judicial authority decides not to institute such proceedings, the victim of

[35] Art. 599(3)(a). [36] Art. 599(3)(b). [37] Art. 599(4).

[38] At the time of writing: *Belgium, Ireland, Greece, Spain, France, Italy, Cyprus, Lithuania, Luxembourg, Hungary, The Netherlands, Austria, Poland, Portugal, Romania.*

[39] Art. 603(1). [40] Art. 603(2).

the offence on which the arrest warrant is based must be able to receive information on the decision in accordance with the applicable domestic law.[41] Where a State's competent authorities institute proceedings against its own national in accordance with paragraph 3, that State must ensure that its competent authorities are able to take appropriate measures to assist the victims and witnesses in circumstances where they are residents of another State, particularly with regard to the way in which the proceedings are conducted.[42] A detailed notification has been submitted with a number of EU MS declaring that whey will no longer surrender their own nationals.[43]

However, these deadlines may be frustrated in practice by the fact that the UK as a third country no longer has direct access to real-time EAW-related alerts inserted in the second-generation Schengen Information System (SIS II). The operational gap resulting from the lack of UK access to SIS II after Brexit has been highlighted by UK law enforcement authorities – with the UK Government attempting to mitigate this loss by using the Interpol I-24/7 system for alerts.[44] The challenges of replacing SIS with Interpol are two-fold. From an operational/political perspective, it may prove an uphill struggle to persuade the authorities of EU MS to duplicate work by inserting alerts in both SIS II and Interpol systems.[45] From a fundamental rights point of view, reliance on Interpol may prove to be controversial in view of the challenging human rights record of a number of its members and reports of abuse of the Interpol Red Notice alerts system.[46] While the provisions of the TCA are marked by the clear ambition of replicating the pre-Brexit EAW system to the extent possible, the constitutional position of the UK as a third country after Brexit (leading to its exclusion from EU databases and the re-introduction of bars to surrender by a number of EU MS) as well as the need to persuade,

[41] Art. 603(3). [42] Art. 603(4).

[43] At the time of writing: *Germany, Greece, France, Croatia, Latvia, Poland, Slovenia, Slovakia, Finland, Sweden. France will also not surrender a person who was a French national when the act was committed.*

[44] Northern Ireland Affairs Committee, *Cross-Border Co-operation on Policing, Security and Criminal Justice after Brexit* (4th Report, session 2019–21, HC Paper 766), para. 59.

[45] House of Lords, European Union Committee *Beyond Brexit; Policing, Law Enforcement and Security* (25th Report, session 2019–21, HL Paper 250), para. 86.

[46] For a critical view of Interpol governance and the misuse of Interpol Red Notices, see House of Commons Foreign Affairs Committee, *In the Room: The UK's Role in Multilateral Diplomacy* First Report of Session 2021–22, para. 119.

politically, overstretched authorities in EU MS to grant equal priority to UK cooperation requests compared to requests received by their counterparts in EU MS under the EAW, under tight deadlines, pose key challenges to the effectiveness of the new EU–UK cooperation on surrender.

18.3 Mutual Legal Assistance

The general provisions on mutual legal assistance are contained in Title VIII. The latter does not replace but merely supplements and facilitates the application between the UK and EU MS of the 1959 European Convention on Mutual Assistance in Criminal Matters (EuCMACM) and its AP of 1978.[47] A competent authority for the purposes of this Title is any authority that is competent to send or receive requests for mutual assistance in accordance with the provisions of the European Mutual Assistance Convention and its Protocols and as defined by States in their respective declarations addressed to the Secretary General of the Council of Europe. 'Competent authority' also includes Union bodies notified in accordance with point (c) of Article 690(7).[48] The EU has notified the UK that the European Public Prosecutor's Office (EPPO) will be deemed as 'competent authority' for the purposes of Title VIII.[49] In addition to the channels of communication provided for under the European Mutual Assistance Convention and its Protocols, if direct transmission is provided for under their respective provisions, requests for mutual assistance may also be transmitted directly by public prosecutors in the UK to competent authorities of the MS.[50] In addition to the channels of communication provided for under the European Mutual Assistance Convention and its Protocols, in urgent cases, any request for mutual assistance, as well as spontaneous information, may be transmitted via Europol or Eurojust, in line with the provisions in the respective Titles of the TCA.[51]

Mutual assistance will be based on a standard form, which has not been developed yet but will be established by the Specialised Committee on Law Enforcement and Judicial Cooperation.[52] Time limits for the execution of requests are not as ambitious as the ones in the European

[47] Art. 633(1). [48] Art. 634.

[49] EU-UK Trade and Cooperation Agreement – Notification by the Union- 31.12.2020-L 444/1486, section A(1).

[50] Art. 641(1). [51] Art. 641(1). [52] Art. 635.

Investigation Order (EIO) Directive. The requested State must decide whether to execute the request for mutual assistance as soon as possible and in any event no later than forty-five days after the receipt of the request[53] – compared to the 30-day limit set out in Article 12(3) of the EIO Directive. The TCA does not include the EIO commitment for the decision on execution to be taken and for investigative measures to be carried out with the same celerity and priority as for a similar domestic case (Article 12(1) EIO). The TCA mirrors the EIO by stating that a request for mutual assistance must be executed as soon as possible and in any event no later than ninety days after the decision authorising the request[54] and that if it is indicated in the request for mutual assistance that, due to procedural deadlines, the seriousness of the offence or other particularly urgent circumstances, a shorter time limit is necessary, or if it is indicated in the request that a measure for mutual assistance is to be carried out on a specific date, the requested State shall take as full account as possible of that requirement.[55]

The text of the TCA mirrors the EIO Directive in introducing a proportionality test at the stage of issuing a request. The competent authority of the requesting State may only make a request for mutual assistance if it is satisfied that the following conditions are met: (a) the request is necessary and proportionate for the purpose of the proceedings, taking into account the rights of the suspected or accused person and (b) the investigative measure or investigative measures indicated in the request could have been ordered under the same conditions in a similar domestic case.[56]

Wherever possible, the competent authority of the requested State must consider recourse to an investigative measure other than the measure indicated in the request for mutual assistance if: (a) the investigative measure indicated in the request does not exist under the law of the requested State; or (b) the investigative measure indicated in the request would not be available in a similar domestic case.[57] The competent authority of the requested State may also have recourse to an investigative measure other than the measure indicated in the request for mutual assistance if the investigative measure selected by the competent authority of the requested State would achieve the same result by less intrusive means than the investigative measure indicated in the request.[58] However, the

[53] Art. 640(1). [54] Art. 640(2). [55] Art. 640(3). [56] Art. 636.
[57] Art. 637(2). [58] Art. 637(3).

following investigative measures must always be available under the law of the requested State: (a) the obtaining of information contained in databases held by police or judicial authorities which is directly accessible by the competent authority of the requested State in the framework of criminal proceedings; (b) the hearing of a witness, expert, victim, suspected or accused person or third party in the territory of the requested State; (c) any non-coercive investigative measure as defined under the law of the requested State; and (d) the identification of persons holding a subscription to a specified phone number or IP address.[59]

The text of the TCA reverts back to the European Mutual Assistance Convention and its Protocols on the grounds for refusal to execute a request for mutual legal assistance (which include political and fiscal offence exceptions and *ordre public* grounds) and adds to this list *ne bis in idem,* in cases where the person in respect of whom the assistance is requested and who is subject to criminal investigations, prosecutions or other proceedings, including judicial proceedings, in the requesting State, has been finally judged by another State in respect of the same acts, provided that, if a penalty has been imposed, it has been enforced, is in the process of being enforced or can no longer be enforced under the law of the sentencing State.[60] The TCA allows for the establishment of joint investigation teams (JITs) but states that the relationship between MS within the JIT must be governed by Union law, notwithstanding the legal basis referred to in the Agreement on the setting up of the JIT.[61]

Overall, mutual legal assistance is a field where the TCA has demonstrated a markedly lower level of ambition in comparison to surrender, which means that cooperation may be significantly slower. This relative lack of ambition may be explained perhaps by the view that the traditional system of MLA will be gradually replaced by cooperation (including public–private partnerships) in the field of digital evidence, where the EU is in the process of developing internal rules and in negotiating an agreement with the United States after the Cloud Act, and where the UK has already concluded such an agreement with the United States.[62] Mitigations in the TCA include the introduction of specific provisions on the exchange of criminal records.

[59] Art. 637(2). [60] Art. 639. [61] Art. 642.

[62] On the EU proposals on digital evidence and their relationship with the Cloud Act, see inter alia K. Ligeti and G. Robinson, 'Sword, Shield and Cloud: Toward a European System of Public-Private Orders for Electronic Evidence in Criminal Matters?', in V. Mitsilegas and

18.4 Criminal Records

Part III of the TCA contains a specific title on the exchange of criminal record information whose objective is to enable the exchange between EU Members States and the UK, of information extracted from the criminal record.[63] Title IX takes precedence over the Title on Mutual Assistance.[64] The provisions of Title IX *supplement* Articles 13 and 22(2) EuCMACM and its AP of 17 March 1978 and 8 November 2001 and *replace* Article 22(1) EuCMACM, as supplemented by Article 4 of its AP of 17 March 1978.[65] In the relations between an EU Member State, on the one side, and the UK, on the other side, each one must waive the right to rely on its reservations to Article 13 EuCMACM and to Article 4 of its AP of 17 March 1978.[66]

Article 645 provides for the designation of central authorities which will be competent for the exchange of criminal record information. The UK has notified The Chief Constable of Hampshire Constabulary, ACRO, as the central authority. Central authorities must communicate criminal record information to each other at least once per month ((Article 646(2)) – in EU law, the FD on the exchange of criminal records calls for the communication of such information as soon as possible (Article 4 of FD 2009/315/JHA). Replies to requests for information must be transmitted by the central authority as soon as possible and in any event within twenty working days from the date the request was received[67] – this is a longer deadline to the EU system that requires in principle transmission of information within ten working days (Article 8 of FD 2009/315/JHA). The TCA requires for specific information to be included when replying to requests made for the purposes of recruitment for professional or organised voluntary activities involving direct and regular contacts with children.[68] The exchange between States of information extracted from the criminal record will take place electronically in accordance with the technical and procedural specifications laid down in ANNEX 44.[69] While the UK is no longer a member of the European Criminal Records Information System (ECRIS), the infrastructure developed pre-Brexit can form the basis for the electronic communications channel under the TCA.

N. Vavoula (eds.), *Surveillance and Privacy in the Digital Age. European, Transatlantic and Global Perspectives*, Oxford and Portland, OR: Hart, 2021, pp. 27–70.

[63] Art. 643(1). [64] Art. 633(2). [65] Art. 643(2). [66] Art. 643(3).

[67] Art. 649(1). [68] Art. 649(3). [69] Art. 650.

18.5 Confiscation

The TCA contains a Title on anti-money laundering and counter terrorist financing devoted largely to preventive measures[70] as well as detailed provisions on UK–EU cooperation on freezing and confiscation.[71] The objective of the confiscation Title is to provide for cooperation between the UK, on the one side, and the MS, on the other side, to the widest extent possible for the purposes of investigations and proceedings aimed at the freezing of property with a view to subsequent confiscation thereof and investigations and proceedings aimed at the confiscation of property within the framework of proceedings in criminal matters.[72] The Title contains specific provisions on bank information[73] as well as provisions on the obligation to take and on the execution of provisional measures.[74] Title XI also contains a detailed provision on the obligation to confiscate.[75] Value-based confiscation is envisaged.[76] Moreover, the scope of cooperation extends to non-criminal proceedings: a state must cooperate to the widest extent possible under its domestic law with a State requesting the execution of measures equivalent to confiscation of property, where the request has not been issued in the framework of proceedings in criminal matters, in so far as such measures are ordered by a judicial authority of the requesting State in relation to a criminal offence, provided that it has been established that the property constitutes proceeds or: (a) other property into which the proceeds have been transformed or converted; (b) property acquired from legitimate sources, if proceeds have been intermingled, in whole or in part, with such property, up to the assessed value of the intermingled proceeds; or (c) income or other benefit derived from the proceeds, from property into which proceeds of crime have been transformed or converted or from property with which the proceeds of crime have been intermingled, up to the assessed value of the intermingled proceeds, in the same manner and to the same extent as proceeds.[77]

The provisions of this Title apply in place of the 'international cooperation' Chapters of the Council of Europe Convention on Laundering, Search, Seizure and Confiscation of the Proceeds from Crime and on

70 Title X on Anti-Money Laundering. 71 Title XI on Confiscation. 72 Art. 656(1).
73 Arts. 659–661. 74 Arts. 663 and 664. 75 Art. 665.
76 Art. 665(3). 77 Art. 665(5).

the Financing of Terrorism, done at Warsaw on 16 May 2005 ('the 2005 Convention') and the Convention on Laundering, Search, Seizure and Confiscation of the Proceeds from Crime, done at Strasbourg on 8 November 1990 ('the 1990 Convention'). Article 657 [Definitions] of this Agreement replaces the corresponding definitions in Article 1 of the 2005 Convention and Article 1 of the 1990 Convention. The provisions of this Title do not affect the States' obligations under the other provisions of the 2005 Convention and the 1990 Convention.[78]

Cooperation will take place on the basis of a standard form provided in the Annexes to the TCA.[79] The deadlines are similar to the EU Regulation on the mutual recognition of confiscation orders: the requested State must take the decision on the execution of the confiscation order without delay, and, without prejudice to paragraph 8 of this Article, no later than forty-five days after receiving the request.[80] Provisional measures must be taken within ninety-six hours of receiving the request.[81] The requested state must ensure that the requests coming from another State to identify, trace, freeze or seize the proceeds and instrumentalities receive the same priority as those made in the framework of domestic procedures.[82]

Investigative assistance and provisional measures must be carried out as permitted by and in accordance with the domestic law of the requested State. Where the request concerning one of these measures specifies formalities or procedures that are necessary under the domestic law of the requesting State, even if unfamiliar to the requested State, the latter must comply with such requests to the extent that the action sought is not contrary to the fundamental principles of its domestic law.[83] When requesting confiscation, investigative assistance and provisional measures for the purposes of confiscation, the requesting State shall ensure that the principles of necessity and proportionality are respected.[84]

Cooperation may be refused if (a) the requested State considers that executing the request would be contrary to the principle of *ne bis in idem*; or (b) the offence to which the request relates does not constitute an offence under the domestic law of the requested State if committed within its jurisdiction; however, this ground for refusal applies to cooperation under Articles 658 [Obligation to assist] to 663 [Spontaneous information] only in so far as the assistance sought involves coercive

[78] Art. 656(6). [79] Art. 679 and Annex 46. [80] Art. 665(7). [81] Art. 663(4).
[82] Art. 656(4). [83] Art. 656(3). [84] Art. 656(5).

action.[85] The UK and the Union, acting on behalf of any of its MS, may each notify the Specialised Committee on Law Enforcement and Judicial Cooperation that, on the basis of reciprocity, the condition of double criminality referred to in point (b) of paragraph 1 of this Article will not be applied provided that the offence giving rise to the request is: (a) one of the offences listed in Article 599(4) [Scope], as defined by the law of the requesting State; and (b) punishable by the requesting State by a custodial sentence or a detention order for a maximum period of at least three years.[86] The EU has notified, on behalf of the following MS, that, on the basis of reciprocity, the condition of double criminality will not be applied: Belgium, Ireland, Greece, Spain, France, Italy, Latvia, Lithuania, Austria, Poland and Portugal.

Cooperation under Articles 658 [Obligation to assist] to 663 [Spontaneous information], in so far as the assistance sought involves coercive action, and under Articles 663 [Obligation to take provisional measures] and 664 [Execution of provisional measures] may also be refused if the measures sought could not be taken under the domestic law of the requested State for the purposes of investigations or proceedings in a similar domestic case.[87] Where the domestic law of the requested State so requires, cooperation under Articles 658 [Obligation to assist] to 663 [Spontaneous information], in so far as the assistance sought involves coercive action, and under 663 [Obligation to take provisional measures] and 664 [Execution of provisional measures] may also be refused if the measures sought or any other measures having similar effects would not be permitted under the domestic law of the requesting State, or, as regards the competent authorities of the requesting State, if the request is not authorised by a judicial authority acting in relation to criminal offences.[88]

Cooperation under Articles 665 [Obligation to confiscate] to 669 [Imprisonment in default] may also be refused if: (a) under the domestic law of the requested State, confiscation is not provided for in respect of the type of offence to which the request relates; (b) without prejudice to the obligation pursuant to Article 665(3) [Obligation to confiscate], it would be contrary to the principles of the domestic law of the requested State concerning the limits of confiscation in respect of the relationship between an offence and: (i) an economic advantage that might be qualified

[85] Art. 670(1). [86] Art. 670(2). [87] Art. 670(3). [88] Art. 670(4).

as its proceeds; or (ii) property that might be qualified as its instrumentalities; (c) under the domestic law of the requested State, confiscation may no longer be imposed or enforced because of the lapse of time; (d) without prejudice to Article 665 (5) and (6) [Obligation to confiscate], the request does not relate to a previous conviction, or a decision of a judicial nature or a statement in such a decision that an offence or several offences have been committed, on the basis of which the confiscation has been ordered or is sought; (e) confiscation is either not enforceable in the requesting State or it is still subject to ordinary means of appeal; or (f) the request relates to a confiscation order resulting from a decision rendered in absentia of the person against whom the order was issued and, in the opinion of the requested State, the proceedings conducted by the requesting State leading to such decision did not satisfy the minimum rights of defence recognised as due to everyone against whom a criminal charge is made.[89]

For the purposes of point (f) of Article 670(5), a decision is not considered to have been rendered in absentia if: (a) it has been confirmed or pronounced after opposition by the person concerned or (b) it has been rendered on appeal, provided that the appeal was lodged by the person concerned.[90] When considering, for the purposes of point (f) of Article 670(5) whether the minimum rights of defence have been satisfied, the requested State shall take into account the fact that the person concerned has deliberately sought to evade justice or the fact that that person, having had the possibility of lodging a legal remedy against the decision made in absentia, elected not to do so. The same applies where the person concerned, having been duly served with the summons to appear, elected not to do so nor to ask for adjournment.[91]

States must not invoke a series of facts as a ground to refuse to cooperate.[92] States must not invoke bank secrecy as a ground to refuse any cooperation under this Title. Where its domestic law so requires, a requested State may require that a request for cooperation which would involve the lifting of bank secrecy be authorised by a judicial authority acting in relation to criminal offences.[93]

Where there are substantial grounds for believing that the execution of a freezing or confiscation order would entail a real risk for the protection of fundamental rights, the requested State shall, before it decides on the execution of the freezing or confiscation order, consult the requesting

[89] Art. 670(5). [90] Art. 670(6). [91] Art. 670(7). [92] Art. 670(9). [93] Art. 670(8).

State and may require any necessary information to be provided.[94] Each State must ensure that persons affected by measures under Articles 663 [Obligation to take provisional measures] to 666 [Execution of confiscation] have effective legal remedies in order to preserve their rights. The substantive reasons for requested measures under Articles 663 to 666 must not be challenged before a court in the requested State.[95]

Each State must designate a central authority to be responsible for sending and answering requests made under Title XI, the execution of such requests or their transmission to the authorities competent for their execution.[96] The EU may designate a Union body which may, in addition to the competent authorities of the MS, make and, if appropriate, execute requests under this Title. Any such request is to be treated for the purposes of this Title as a request by a Member State. The Union may also designate that Union body as the central authority responsible for the purpose of sending and answering requests made under this Title by, or to, that body.[97] Central authorities will communicate directly with one another.[98] In urgent cases, requests or communications may be sent directly by the judicial authorities of the requesting State to judicial authorities of the requested State. In such cases, a copy must be sent at the same time to the central authority of the requested State through the central authority of the requesting State.[99] The EU has notified the UK that the EPPO, in the exercise of its competences as provided for by Articles 22, 23 and 25 of Council Regulation (EU) 2017/1939, will be deemed to be a competent authority for the purpose of making and, if appropriate, executing freezing requests made under Title XI, as well as a central authority for the purpose of sending and answering to such requests. Requests will be sent to the Central Office of the EPPO.[100] The UK has designated the Home Office as the Central Authority for the purposes of the sending, answering and execution of requests, or the transmission of such requests to the authorities competent for their execution, related to the freezing and confiscation of property.[101]

94 Art. 671. 95 Art. 689(2). 96 Art. 676(1). 97 Art. 676(2).
98 Art. 677(1). 99 Art. 677(2).
100 *EU-UK Trade and Cooperation Agreement – Notification by the Union* – 31.12.2020-OJ L 444/1486.
101 *Competent authorities designated by the United Kingdom under* Part Three *of the Agreement: Law Enforcement and Judicial Cooperation in Criminal Matters* (2021/C 117 I/02), OJ CI 117/11, 6.4.2021.

18.6 Bodies, Offices and Agencies

Part III of the TCA contains provisions on UK cooperation with Eurojust[102] which aims to provide for a number of avenues of cooperation taking into account the position of the UK as a third country. Cooperation between the UK and Eurojust will continue in the form of the appointment of liaison officers (UK Liaison Prosecutor to Eurojust[103] – a Eurojust Liaison Magistrate in the UK[104]) in the form of the establishment of contact points.[105] and in the form of cooperation with a wide range of UK authorities. The UK competent authorities for cooperation with Eurojust are the International Justice and Organised Crime Division at the CPS, the Crown Office & Procurator Fiscal Service, the Public Prosecution Service Northern Ireland and any other UK public body that is responsible for investigating and/or prosecuting criminal conduct or that acts as a central authority in any jurisdiction of the UK. The centrality of cooperation with the UK for Eurojust will lead to a broader re-think of Eurojust's internal legal framework with regard to the role and powers of liaison officers of third states and exchange of information with third states – and may lead to the revision of internal EU law *acquis* – and in particular the Eurojust Regulation – in order to facilitate cooperation with third countries. In this manner, Brexit may act as a trigger for internal EU law reform.

The TCA does not refer expressly to cooperation with the EPPO. However, as seen above, the EU has designated the EPPO as a competent authority in cooperation on mutual legal assistance and confiscation. Moreover, according to its Regulation, the EPPO is granted competence for offences committed by a national of a participating EU Member State, provided that the Member State has extraterritorial jurisdiction over these offences; and for offences committed extraterritorially by a person who is subject to EU Staff Regulations or Conditions of Employment provided that the Member State has extraterritorial jurisdiction (EPPO Regulation, Article 22(b) and (c)). The TCA constitutes an Agreement of cooperation between the UK and the EPPO under Article 104(3) of the EPPO Regulation on EPPO relations with third countries. Its rules on mutual legal assistance and cooperation on freezing and confiscation are applicable to the EPPO following the notification by the EU that the EPPO constitutes a competent authority for

[102] Title VI. [103] Art. 585. [104] Art. 586. [105] Art. 584.

the purpose of these Titles. Here it can be seen that Brexit has provided an opportunity for the EU to strengthen its external relations profile and its place as a global actor in criminal matters. The TCA is a laboratory where for the first time EU agencies assume a central, operational role in external relations in the field of judicial cooperation in criminal matters.

18.7 Benchmarks, Governance and Dispute Resolution

A key question for the future of EU–UK relations in European Criminal Law involves the substance and the monitoring of the constitutional benchmarks underpinning such cooperation. Part III of the TCA contains a specific provision on the protection of human rights and fundamental freedoms in the field of law enforcement and judicial cooperation in criminal matters.[106] Cooperation is based on the Parties' and MS' longstanding respect for democracy, the rule of law and the protection of fundamental rights and freedoms of individuals, including as set out in the Universal Declaration of Human Rights and in the European Convention on Human Rights (ECHR), and on the importance of giving effect to the rights and freedoms in that Convention domestically.[107] Respect for and enforcement of the ECHR is thus key for cooperation under the TCA. The CJEU has already confirmed the importance of the UK being party to the ECHR for post-Brexit cooperation.[108] The EU may terminate Part III if the UK denounces the ECHR.[109] Part III may also be suspended in the event of serious and systemic deficiencies within one Party as regards the protection of fundamental rights or the principle of the rule of law.[110] The same applies in the event of serious and systemic deficiencies within one Party as regards the protection of personal data, including where those deficiencies have led to a relevant adequacy decision ceasing to apply.[111] Part III includes detailed provisions on the data protection benchmarks applicable to cooperation.[112]

In terms of monitoring, the TCA has introduced a multi-level political system of governance and dispute resolution. A key role in the field of criminal justice is envisaged for the Specialised Committee on Law Enforcement and Judicial Cooperation established in Part I of the TCA.[113] Specialised

[106] Art. 524. [107] Art. 524(1).
[108] CJEU, Minister for Justice and Equality v. RO, No. C-327/18 PPU, Judgment, ECLI:EU:C:2018:644, 7 August 2018.
[109] Art. 692(2). [110] Art. 693(1). [111] Art. 693(2). [112] Art. 525. [113] Art. 8(1)(r).

Committee's powers include monitoring and reviewing the implementation and ensure the proper functioning of the TCA, adopting decisions, including amendments, and recommendations and providing a forum for consultations as part of the dispute resolution process.[114] Part III of the TCA contains a specific Title on dispute settlement (Title XIII) which has exclusivity.[115] It contains provisions on consultations,[116] on a mutually agreed solution[117] and on suspension[118] envisaging a role for the Specialised Committee on Law Enforcement and Judicial Cooperation throughout the process.

The Agreement contains no reference to the CJEU for the purposes of dispute resolution. However, the Court will remain relevant in the implementation of the TCA. It has jurisdiction to rule on aspects of the functioning of the TCA, including on the adoption of data protection adequacy Decisions by the European Commission. It will continue to receive preliminary references from courts of EU MS regarding the operation and the implementation of the TCA (for instance, on questions on the compatibility of the execution of Arrest Warrants or Mutual Legal Assistance requests received by UK authorities with EU law). The CJEU will further continue to develop the EU benchmarks applicable in the field of criminal justice via ongoing and evolving interpretation. The Court's role in defining the EU *acquis* is central, as EU MS are under a duty to comply with EU law in their external relations.

18.8 Conclusion

From the analysis of the TCA, the impact of Brexit on the future EU–UK criminal justice cooperation can be viewed from two different perspectives. Those who see the glass as 'half-full', can point out to the high level of ambition of the parties to replicate to the extent possible the pre-Brexit status quo in key areas including surrender, the exchange of criminal records, confiscation and cooperation with EU bodies and agencies. Those who view the glass as 'half-empty' will point out the fact that constitutional and institutional constraints underpin these areas of high ambition, the fact that key areas such as mutual legal assistance are marked by a lower level of ambition, and the fact that there are areas where the UK is entirely excluded by EU law (most notably in access to EU databases such

[114] Art. 8(4). [115] Art. 697. [116] Art. 698.
[117] Art. 699. [118] Art. 700.

as SIS II); in addition, that there are a number of areas where the TCA is silent and where relations revert to a purely intergovernmental level (in the vast majority of areas covered by the EU mutual recognition *acquis*).

It remains to be seen how the TCA will be received by those who will deal with it on the ground from an operational and from a legal perspective. From an operational perspective, it remains to be seen whether authorities in EU MS will continue to treat requests from their UK counterparts as a matter of priority. From a legal perspective, it remains to be seen how the provisions of the TCA will be interpreted and monitored, and how national authorities (for instance those asked to execute Arrest Warrants) will deal with concerns regarding non-compliance with fundamental rights. Notwithstanding the silence in the TCA, the role of the CJEU will remain important in this context. It remains also to be seen whether the TCA will survive changes in the development of the EU criminal justice *acquis* (and whether the UK will align its law with the evolving *acquis*) and changes in internal UK law (especially concerning a potential change in the constitutional position of the ECHR in the UK).

While the impact of Brexit on the position of the UK vis-à-vis the EU has been inevitably the focus of much of analysis thus far, this chapter has also attempted to demonstrate that Brexit and the TCA will also have an impact on internal EU law and on the strengthening of the EU as a global actor in criminal matters. The designation by the EU of the EPPO as an authority for the purposes of the operation of a number of judicial cooperation elements in the TCA is a key example of this trend, which may transcend Brexit and lead to the EU emerging with a strong external representation at the global level.

Further Reading

K. Ambos and S. Bock, 'Brexit and the European Criminal Justice System – An Introduction', (2017) 28 *CLF*, 191–217.

House of Lords, European Union Committee *Beyond Brexit; Policing, Law Enforcement and Security* (25th Report, session 2019–21, HL Paper 250).

V. Mitsilegas, 'The Uneasy Relationship between the United Kingdom and European Criminal Law. From Opt-Outs to Brexit?', (2016) 6 *CLR*, 517–536.

A. Oehmichen and W. Schomburg (eds.), 'Special Issue: EU-UK Cooperation in Criminal Matters'. (2021) 12 *NJECL*, 184–297.

A. Weyembergh, 'Consequences of Brexit for European Union Criminal Law', (2017) 8 *NJECL*, 284–299.

19 Rethinking European Criminal Law

Frank Meyer

19.1 Introduction

Chapters promising to rethink entire fields of law are prone to disappoint. That the assigned subject is particularly complex and interwoven with many other policy areas is not helpful either. There is also little momentum for a comprehensive self-reflection after Brexit. EU and member states' (MS) bodies wish to carry on and not get bogged down in yet another grand project. Interest in rethinking, even understood modestly as reassessing foundations, institutional design and aims of European Criminal Law (ECL), therefore appears to be limited. Communication from European institutions and member state governments suggest that rethinking is not a priority of ECL policy. The evolution of ECL is grinding on along a prescribed path. Substantive ECL contends itself with consolidation (of legislative instruments), minor adjustments and pet projects, whereas procedural ECL is preoccupied with the implementation of mutual recognition and the functioning of EU agencies and information systems. Ground-breaking innovations in e-Evidence are under negotiation, but by and large the EU machinery churns out new action plans, proposals, and legal instruments that look like little surprising products of the Lisbon Treaty. However, the Lisbon Treaty also calls on the Union to 'offer its citizens an Area of Freedom, Security and Justice (AFSJ) without internal frontiers, in which the free movement of persons is ensured in conjunction with appropriate measures with respect to external border controls, asylum, immigration and the prevention and combating of crime', Art. 3 para. 2 TEU.

One may therefore take stock after more than a decade and ask the innocent question whether ECL is on the right track. To do so, one would initially need to answer what contribution Art. 3 para. 2 TEU, which promises an AFSJ, expects from ECL to achieve its objectives. The AFSJ comprises a broad range of law-making powers (from judicial cooperation in civil matters to immigration policy) with their own specific subsets of preconditions and functional justifications. Many of them seem to live a life of their own with the AFSJ being little else than a provider of competences and rhetorical ploy. If we accept that the creators of Art. 3 para. 2 TEU did not assume that any legal exercise of one of these competences would automatically serve its ulterior goal and that the authority to define what is necessary to achieve an AFSJ is not entirely left to the discretion of the competent law-making bodies one is left to wonder what guidance and restrictions result from the concept and objective of the AFSJ. Alas, this approach might not yield deeper insights or clarity. When the notion of the AFSJ was introduced, some learned observers pointed out that the true beauty of this new creature lay in its obscurity and flexibility.[1] It offered intuitive appeal and vivid connotations of commonality and transnationality without predetermining the path of future activities, let alone requiring that such activities serve supranational objectives. One would have expected that this situation changes over time in lockstep with further integration of cooperation and its conversion into an aim of the Union stricto sensu. Yet, intensification and consolidation have not spawned a common and comprehensive vision as to what shall be offered to EU citizens. Notwithstanding influential programmatic fragments such as mutual recognition, the concept of the AFSJ has not cultivated a normatively prescriptive core. In comparison with the single market, the lack of conceptual integration and depth is startling.[2]

To make matters worse, the three supposedly interlinked notions of freedom, security and justice oftentimes seem to pull in different directions or even contradict each other.[3] If there is a movement towards deeper integration of these vectors at all, it is rather a subordination dominated by the so-called securitization of EU law.[4] Fragmentation caused by a Europe of multiple speeds (or rather, multiple depths) and lacklustre implementation have further exacerbated the situation. The AFSJ remains

[1] J. Monar, 'Der Raum der Freiheit, der Sicherheit und des Rechts' in A. von Bogdandy and J. Bast (eds.), *Europäisches Verfassungsrecht*, Berlin: Springer, 2009, pp. 749, 755–6, 763.

[2] F. Meyer, '§ 43 Verfahren der strafrechtlichen Zusammenarbeit', in S. Leible and J. Terhechte (eds.), *Enzyklopädie Europarecht*, Vol. 3, 2nd edn., Baden-Baden et al.: Nomos et al., 2021, mn. 17.

[3] See also E. Popa, 'A Game of Chance – The Future of the AFSJ', (2018) *eucrim*, 42, 45.

[4] M. Fichera, 'Sketches of a Theory of Europe as an Area of Freedom, Security and Justice', in M. Fletcher, E. Herlin-Karnell, and C. Matera (eds.), *The European Union as an Area of Freedom, Security and Justice*, London: Routledge, 2017, pp. 34, 38; V. Mitsilegas, 'European Criminal Law and the Dangerous Citizen', (2018) 25 *Maastricht J. Eur. Comp. L.*, 733, 748; on notions of security and its development; V. Mitsilegas, 'Security versus Justice: The Individualisation of Security and the Erosion of Citizenship and Fundamental

a ramshackle compound of related policy areas without a masterplan and well-conceived structural design.[5] It presents itself as a bundle of legal domains with separate policies, separate operating and substantive principles, separate strands of jurisprudence and human rights doctrines that nonetheless magically contribute to a common AFSJ.

Scholars have tried to describe pathways to align the three notions in the direction of the common objective as a way forward. They have, for instance, raised the question, whether there is an integrating EU Criminal Policy or what a theory of Europe as an AFSJ could look like.[6] Others proposed a citizenship turn in ECL[7] or called for a human rights focus.[8] Irrespective of their different focus and methodologies all those intellectually inspiring contributions might have been in vain as they followed a vision that was never meant to be. The inherent tensions could render more coherence and uniformity in this area unattainable. It, hence, might neither be possible nor productive to better align the notions of freedom, security and justice and their trajectories. A more modest approach that proposes a shifting of perspectives for the interpretation and application of ECL competences might be more advisable. This chapter argues that ECL in its present state suffers

Rights', in B. Hudson and S. Ugelvik (eds.), *Justice and Security in the 21st Century: Risks, Rights and the Rule of Law*, London: Routledge, 2012, pp. 199, 200 f. The conceptualisation of punishment, which is increasingly driven by the notion of dangerousness, is a case in point, see I. Wieczorek, 'Punishment, Deprivation of Liberty and the Europeanization of Criminal Justice', (2018) 25 *Maastricht J. Eur. Comp. L.*, 651; L. Mancano, 'Punishment and Rights in European Union Citizenship: Persons or Criminals?', (2018) 24 *ELJ*, 10.

[5] N. Walker, 'In Search of the Area of Freedom, Security and Justice: A Constitutional Odyssey', in N. Walker (ed.), *Europe's Area of Freedom, Security, and Justice*, Oxford et al.: Oxford University Press, 2004, pp. 3, 5: No comprehensive broad policy theme; S. Coutts, 'The Lisbon Treaty and the Area of Freedom, Security and Justice as an Area of Legal Integration', (2011) 7 *CYELP*, 87, 91 f.

[6] A. Weyembergh and I. Wieczorek, 'Is There an EU Criminal Policy?', in R. Colson and S. Field (eds.), *EU Criminal Justice and The Challenges of Diversity: Legal Cultures in the Area of Freedom, Security and Justice*, Cambridge: Cambridge University Press, 2016, pp. 44 f.; Fichera, 'Sketches of a Theory of Europe as an Area of Freedom, Security and Justice', p. 34.

[7] M. Wade, 'True EU Citizenship as a Precursor to Genuine Criminal Justice in Europe: An Analysis of EU Citizenship as It Relates to a Sustainable Area of Freedom, Security and Justice', (2020) 31 *CLF*, 291, 294 f., 300 f.; S. Coutts, *Citizenship, Crime and Community in the European Union*, Oxford: Hart, 2019: transnational-supranational dimension of citizenship; F. Meyer, 'Das Strafrecht im Raum der Freiheit, der Sicherheit und des Rechts', (2011) 46 *EuR*, 169.

[8] S. Hüttemann, *Principles and Perspectives of European Criminal Procedure*, Florence: European University Institute, 2012, pp. 195 f., 213.

from two lacunae which result from an uninspired reading of Art. 3 para. 2 TEU and Art. 67 TFEU. These articles very broadly define the AFSJ as a key objective of the Union and spell out some mid-range policy goals and pertinent instruments. Yet, in practice, the implementation of this objective disregards the broader constitutional framework and evolution.

First, scholars and practitioners have not paid enough attention to the supranationality of the AFSJ. The area in which freedom, security and justice evolve and link up is a common area of supranational nature; that is, a transnational sphere, hovering above and transcending national borders created by the Union in the pursuit of common (rather than overlapping national) interests. Ignoring this fact makes actors on all levels of government (national and supranational) overlook that the laws adopted and applied under this title are supranational norms serving supranational interests. Indeed, activating and shaping ECL at the union level remains a top-down operation with a strong focus on state interests. Political thinking is at least partly stuck in an intergovernmental world. And it does not stop there. The awareness of supranationality and its implications is lacking at each step of the enforcement process too, from prosecutorial discretion to sentencing.[9] In the same vein, those norms are supposed to serve citizens, who in this specific context are to be understood as citizens of the Union. Taking their perspective would entail seriously considering what these very citizens need and expect from the AFSJ in their capacity as citizens of the Union. Lawmakers must not lose sight of whose interests they are to serve, in particular with respect to the laws that they pass and the way they construe and use Articles 82 and 83 TFEU. Unfortunately, citizens primarily play a rhetorical role as potential beneficiaries of a more secure and protective Union. Even so, all MS primarily have an eye on the needs of their citizens in this regard. The 'EU citizen' remains an abstract artefact in the discourse. Yet, as an expression of EU public authority, ECL must be authorized, accountable and exercised with respect to its constituents to preserve its legitimacy. Even under a theory of dual democratic legitimacy,[10] this would demand a huge shift of attention towards the supranational strand of democratic power. Illuminating the democratic basis of the *ius puniendi* enshrined in Art. 83 TFEU should also prompt

9 F. Meyer, 'Europäisches Wirtschaftsstrafrecht (Teil 2)', (2017) 36 *wistra*, 249, 254.

10 Anchoring the legitimacy of the Union in the national demoi and EU citizens in their supranational capacity.

legislative bodies to develop a more proactive view and recognize their general constitutional obligation to fulfil the normative promises of the Charter of fundamental rights (CFREU) vis-à-vis the Union's citizens.

Second, Article 67 para. 1 TFEU demands respect for fundamental rights and the different legal systems and traditions of the MS. While the protection of fundamental rights and especially data protection has surely improved in recent years, it does not correlate with the pioneering transition of cooperation towards a common multilevel enforcement system that comprises and interlocks highly innovative forms and structures of cooperation, joint investigation and adjudication. In comparison, procedural safeguards and fundamental rights standards lag far behind. That policy- and lawmakers struggle with the catch-up process does not surprise bearing in mind that the AFSJ lacks an integrated supranational criminal justice system. States and national law enforcement agencies continue to be the key players. The AFSJ has not yet evolved into a single legal area. It comprises twenty-seven criminal justice systems and does not envision the establishment of a centralized supranational criminal justice layer, but merely supranational actors. Stopping short of integration, the interconnections and interactions between the systems have been transformed profoundly, nonetheless. And it remains an unsolved key challenge for the future to size up these highly enhanced and sophisticated forms of multilevel cooperation and enforcement. For it is only on such solid groundwork that adequate safeguards can be discussed.

This chapter will address both distortions in turn. It hopes to alert its readers to the scope and variety of issues that are affected by these lacunae. Through brief sketches the consequences and opportunities of a reorientation will be presented. The chapter suggests a series of remedies from policymaking to doctrinal innovations to stimulate further debate. It will not culminate in sweeping propositions of major overhauls but stake out a gradual and granular response.

19.2 Substantive Criminal Law

19.2.1 The Imbalance of the AFSJ

Policymakers did not get it all wrong. The notion of freedom as encapsulated in Art. 67 TFEU is typically understood to be preoccupied with the intra-area use and effectuation of fundamental freedoms of EU citizens without impeding borders. In comparison with the single market, the AFSJ therefore similarly and correctly starts out with the idea to bolster freedom of movement.[11] Its effective, unimpeded exercise requires guarantees of security as much as the single market requires removal of territorial regulatory obstacles to the free movement of goods and services and common rules that ensure efficiency and fairness. But while the commitment to a functioning single market has drawn in more and more policy areas and underlying economic, social, and environmental questions, the AFSJ has moved away from fostering the freedoms and rights of EU citizens (perhaps except for judicial cooperation in civil matters) in the direction of a security area much less focused on transnational freedoms of supranational citizens and the rules established in their name and interest. The supranationality and transnational scope that matter to the MS are those of legislative competences and threats, respectively.[12] Much less interest is expressed for the enforcement of the substantive, harmonized EU laws of these very citizens with whose authority the EU has produced these very norms; let alone for basic social norms or the protection of fundamental rights! It unsurprisingly falls to the EU Commission to float new ideas such as focussing on environmental crimes or gender-based violence. However, the Commission for its part attributes significant added value to fighting serious organised crime because 'if people can trust that their rights are respected, in all EU countries, if they are suspected or accused of a crime, they are more likely to use their right to live, work or study in another EU country'.[13] It is this 'security link' which is holding back evolution. The Security wing of the AFSJ is focussed on keeping others out of the Area (as symbolized by enhanced functions of the Schengen Information System (SIS II), requiring authorization before entry with ETIAS (European Travel Information and Authorization System) or the exponential growth of Frontex after the refugee crisis), monitoring dangerous people (using the SIS II or sifting through Passenger Name Records), or reining in and controlling dangerous side-effects of these

11 See also M. Fichera, 'Criminal Law beyond the State: The European Model', (2013) 19 *ELJ*, 174, 177.

12 The AFSJ comprises very different forms and rationales of criminal law; F. Meyer, 'Eine Geologie des Strafrechts', (2011) 123 *ZStW*, 1.

13 EU Commission, *EU Criminal Justice Strategy: Objectives of a Common Strategy.*

very freedoms. I will continue to refer to the latter as Schengen pedigree, which – in a nutshell – established a strong link between the conceptualisation and justification of EU criminal law and the protection of fundamental freedoms. And much less than expressing condemnation of crimes as supranational public wrongs and professing the necessity to speak with one voice in this respect, the approximation of national criminal provisions and upper sentencing ranges still primarily seeks to enable effective mutual legal assistance and extradition or shut down safe havens.[14]

Much greater reluctance prevails when it comes to the protection of important interests and provisions of EU law. MS have habitually tended to squeeze such matters into a serious transnational crime paradigm instead of using Art. 83 para. 2 TFEU, which authorizes criminal legislation to enforce harmonized EU law; e.g., environmental protection, EU budget. This stance obscures the fact that ECL, if viewed in the context of the TFEU, is a cross-policy area and supposed to play a vital role in a coherent supranational cross-policy enforcement approach. ECL, hence, needs to be brought in line with the level of integration and enforcement interests in other policy areas. Furthermore, these 'enforcement crimes' are probably the most natural examples of supranational criminal law as they embody the *ius puniendi* of the EU and its commitment to protect the democratic will of EU citizens. Shackles in the conceptualisation of ECL resulting from the 'security link' and Schengen pedigree must, hence, be cast off. These notions do not fit enforcement-oriented crimes. Admittedly, the emancipation process has already begun, albeit grudgingly. But ECL should not restrain its ambitions to harmonized EU law. Other areas of crime might be just as fundamentally important to protect core values and legal foundations of the EU (including laws protecting the functioning of its institutions).

A change of perspective thus calls for two initial steps. Legislative action and policy initiatives need to overcome the Schengen pedigree and sever the security link between criminal law and freedom of movement. Second, ECL needs to move beyond mobility-related crime. The concept of freedom in the AFSJ promises more than safe travel

[14] *Coutts* rightly criticizes that the communicative and ethical function of criminal law is overlooked or disregarded in the policy discourse surrounding criminal law, Coutts, *Citizenship, Crime and Community in the European Union*, pp. 164 f.

and establishment. According to Art. 67 para. 3 TFEU, the Union shall endeavour to ensure a high level of security through measures to prevent and combat crime, racism and xenophobia, and through measures for coordination and cooperation between police and judicial authorities and other competent authorities, as well as through the mutual recognition of judgments in criminal matters and, if necessary, through the approximation of criminal laws. From a fundamental rights point of view, 'high level of security' can be construed as to include the enjoyment of individual rights in the entire AFSJ. Providing a robust legal framework to this end is a key function of modern states. In treaty areas governed and to be nurtured by the EU, this duty falls to the Union's legislative bodies. A strong supranational, fundamental-rights-based vision of the AFSJ calls for commitment against a multitude of ills: racial discrimination, violence against women, hate crimes, harassment of LGBTI communities, attacks on the freedom of speech and press, attacks on the rule of law and on democratic institutions, business conduct violating human rights,[15] environmental degradation and socially corrosive tax practices. The high level of security that Art. 67 para. 3 alludes to presupposes a sociocultural and legal safe space. One might even say that European democracy and the rule of law can only thrive on such a solid normative foundation.[16]

Positive obligations to fulfil are well established in international human rights law.[17] The jurisprudence of the ECtHR has become increasingly assertive in recent years. In a growing number of landmark decisions, the

15 A. Nieto, 'Towards a European Economic Criminal Law of Human Rights', (2021) 11 *EuCLR*, 6, 35.

16 In a similar vein, v. Bogdandy/Spieker argued in a recent article to use ECL to defend EU values enshrined in Art. 2 TEU, in particular the rule of law, with criminal sanctions. They suggest that flagrant breaches of the rule of law by judges (which would include ignoring ECJ precedent and obstructing preliminary referrals) be prosecuted as perversion of the course of justice (*Rechtsbeugung*); A. von Bogdandy and L. Spieker, 'Reverse Solange 2.0: Die Durchsetzung europäischer Werte und die unions- und strafrechtliche Verantwortung nationaler Richter', (2020) 55 *EuR*, 301–331; M. Wade, 'True EU Citizenship as a Precursor to Genuine Criminal Justice in Europe', 291, 313–4, 327, resorts to a more comprehensive concept of EU citizenship to postulate a stronger focus of legislation on benefitting citizens.

17 F. Mégret, Nature of Obligations, in D. Moeckli, S. Shah, and S. Sivakumaran (eds.), *International Human Rights Law,* 3rd edn., Oxford: Oxford University Press, 2018, pp. 86, 98; K. Ambos, 'Ius puniendi and Constitution: A Comparative (Canadian-German) Perspective', (2020) 14 *ICL Journal*, 253, 271.

court has called on the contracting parties to criminalize, de-criminalize, prosecute or cooperate. The CJEU, by contrast, has shown reluctance as it is the job of the legislative branch (and the MS as the architects of the treaties) to respond to constitutional obligations to provide a safe environment with robust legal frameworks, including criminal law to address matters of European concern. This view is in line with the separation of powers at the supranational level of the Union.

Fulfilment of these normative expectations necessitates enlisting the supranational level of government. So far, the supranational DNA of ECL (and of the CFREU more generally) has not been sufficiently translated into policies and structures. Potential critics and supporters of this vision might agree that the TFEU does not confer a competence to respond to constitutional claims to guarantee certain standards, even if they were legitimate. The present structure of criminal law competences stands in the way of a more proactive implementation of ECL.[18] The so-called Passerelle[19] built into Art. 83 para. 3 TFEU is too static, narrow, and not focused on the people who live in the EU while Art. 83 para. 2 TFEU is highly limited in its focus on effective enforcement of harmonized EU laws. One may argue, though, that a reorientation of focus would be possible even within these structures. Art. 83 para. 1 is broad enough for a richer, more citizen-oriented interpretation of competences derived from positive obligations to suppress serious transnational crime in the interest of the CFREU. An analogous argument could be raised with respect to the interpretation of the 'essentiality' threshold in Art. 83 para. 2 TFEU, at least when compliance with positive EU law is at stake. Furthermore, the EU could reanimate this competence in a two-step process. Other policy areas provide the EU with ample opportunity to write basic values and rights into law, for instance Corporate Social Responsibility standards including sustainability and sourcing. Should it become necessary to underscore the magnitude of transgressions or to

[18] See also in this context on the tensions between primary and secondary EU law; I. Wieczorek, *The Legitimacy of EU Criminal Law*, Oxford: Hart, 2020.

[19] Passerelle clauses are mechanisms for introducing narrowly circumscribed changes to TEU or TFEU built into these very treaties in certain limited areas in very specific, predefined forms. They embody exceptions to the standard process of treaty-making for reasons of efficiency and flexibility but retain a strict consent requirement which squares with their treaty-changing character.

react to rampant non-compliance, the adoption of new ECL provisions would be a permissible option.[20]

Still, these competences do not allow for a coherent evolution of ECL. Especially the Passerelle of Art. 83 para. 3 is left to the whims of the MS and creates a bottleneck for legal evolution. Unanimity is a poor proxy for supranational necessity. Where expansive interpretation of existing competences and the Passerelle clause do not open themselves up to the promotion of supranational rights and values, treaty change is the only, although least likely, way forward to align obligations and competences.

If the road to EU legislation remains blocked for this reason, EU bodies should consider an alternative route. At the very least, if MS were to dismiss a more proactive interpretation of their competences, the division of labour with the Council of Europe (CoE) in pan-European criminal matters should be invigorated and structured.

19.2.2 Interaction with the Council of Europe

As of now, cooperation and consultation take place at multiple levels but not in a visibly coherent fashion. Most importantly, a common understanding of joint responsibility for the well-being of Europeans grounded in rights and values enshrined in the ECHR and the CFREU apparently exists among the competent subcommittees and directorates but awaits stronger conceptualisation at the organisational level. EU and CoE should engage in a much more coherent fashion to preserve pan-European core values. For the EU, this mandate is even stronger as, unlike the ECHR, the CFREU guarantees fundamental rights in transnational and supranational contexts. This character entails obligations on the part of EU institutions and MS to activate their powers, if necessary, in the external dimension of the AFSJ and reach out to other actors whose authority and agenda might be vital for the effective enjoyment and strengthening of the rights and values of EU citizens and residents. The EU might therefore find itself in the awkward position to need to rely on the CoE to provide for more fundamental norms. Even worse and more fundamental to the constitutional self-conception of the EU, a lack of competences and viable instruments threatens to undermine the standing of the CFREU itself.

20 A. Nieto, 'Towards a European Economic Criminal Law of Human Rights', (2021) 11 *EuCLR*, 6, 25 f., 35.

19.2.3 External Dimension of the AFSJ

Finally, the pursuit of the objectives of the AFSJ might require engaging with the outside world beyond the CoE. While EU bodies have already turned to the external dimension of the area in security matters (examples include exchange of e-evidence, PNR data or Frontex cooperation with third states' border patrols and coastal guards),[21] they have largely refrained from adopting a more positive and proactive stance to throw their weight behind the promotion of basic EU values and norms. Setting global standards may sometimes be the best or only way forward to advance the (supranational) interests behind EU norms and preserve their integrity against international pressures. The EU, perhaps to its own surprise, has emerged as international standard-setter in some areas, most notably data protection.[22] The GDPR does not need to become a one-hit wonder. The EU shows interest to pull off this trick in other security-related areas as well, namely Anti-Money Laundering (AML), supply chain responsibility[23] and Artificial Intelligence (AI).[24] It may be worth considering whether the EU should step up its efforts and show similar dedication in matters more directly linked to rights and freedoms guaranteed in the CFREU as those highlighted above. The EU could turn the attractiveness of its single market into an instrument to promote values und standards beyond Art. 83 TFEU. However, in contrast to data protection or AML, the EU would not be able to pass unitary regulations towards which others could orientate their activities. It would need to content itself with soft law which will lessen its impact and gravitational force.

[21] J. Vervaele, 'European Criminal Justice in the European and Global Context', (2019) 10 *NJECL*, 7, 13.

[22] For another example in the field of MLA standards and fundamental rights, see A. Weyembergh and I. Wieczorek, 'Norm Diffusion as a Tool to Uphold and Promote EU Values and Interests: A Case Study on the EU Japan Mutual Legal Assistance Agreement', (2020) 11 *NJECL*, 439–466.

[23] Proposal for a Directive of the European Parliament and of the Council on Corporate Sustainability Due Diligence and amending Directive (EU) 2019/1937, COM/2022/71 final; A. Nieto, 'Towards a European Economic Criminal Law of Human Rights', (2021) 11 *EuCLR*, 6, 24 f. The EU could turn the economic attractiveness of the single market and its capability to promulgate comparatively unitary regulations into an instrument to promote values und standards beyond; see also L. Staffler, 'Nationales, Europäisches und Internationales Unternehmensstrafrecht', in R. Soyer (ed.), *Handbuch Unternehmensstrafrecht*, Wien: MANZ, 2020, Chap. 20, mn. 92.

[24] EU Commission, *Proposal for a Regulation of the European Parliament and of the Council laying down harmonised rules on Artificial Intelligence (Artificial Intelligence Act) and amending certain Union legislative acts*, COM/2021/206 final.

19.2.4 Interim Conclusion: Towards Normative Supranationality

Rethinking ECL starts with raising self-awareness of the AFSJ's supranationality and its normative implications. The constitutional dimension of ECL must be stressed and not brushed over. Academic discourse and political debates need to reflect that ECL crimes constitute supranational public wrongs. Legislation and policy plans must be justified to this end. Irrespective of the general need for a supranational turn in ECL, the structures of the AFSJ, which relies on domestic laws and courts for the implementation and enforcement of rules adopted under its auspices, require moderation. National traditions and culture must be considered in this process as required by Art. 67 TFEU itself. Determining the scope and limits of supranationalisation is a matter of case-by-case and country-by-country analysis. It will take further carefully designed studies to develop a common principled approach to discern how much uniformity is indispensable and how much national variety and diversity warranted.

These tensions concern legislative implementation as well as application. Interestingly, it is here where the greatest potential for further supranationalisation of ECL is hidden. It has been pointed out that the EU has only prescriptive jurisdiction (to introduce and define criminal provisions) but lacks adjudicative jurisdiction to enforce,[25] which seems to be an important limitation. Where criminal law wields its sword and communicates directly with citizens, the EU is absent. At first sight, the non-existence of EU criminal courts appears to vitiate whatever communicative force EU legislation might possess. The centre stage belongs to national lawyers and national law. Yet, this view is not entirely accurate. While there are no EU criminal courts stricto sensu, domestic criminal courts are supposed to act on behalf of the EU (so-called indirect enforcement) any time they decide cases that involve EU laws, including criminal provisions that have been implemented or assimilated following EU criminal legislation or EU constitutional principles.[26] That the EU must content itself with indirect criminalisation competences does not negate the Union's supranational *ius puniendi*. While Art. 83 paras. 1 or 2 TFEU do not regulate an efficient joint exercise of national jurisdictions to prescribe, they nevertheless, as we have seen, legitimately lay claim to

[25] I. Wieczorek, 'Book Review', (2020) 59 *Howard JCJ*, pp. 532, 534.

[26] Meyer, 'Europäisches Wirtschaftsstrafrecht (Teil 1)', (2017) 36 *wistra*, 209, 210; 'Europäisches Wirtschaftsstrafrecht (Teil 2)', (2017) 36 *wistra*, 249, 250.

a supranational power to criminalize and punish. That this dimension is often disregarded or not understood at the national level does not mean that it does not exist. It is exactly this kind of rethinking that needs to sink in, both at the level of legislation and adjudication.

As regards the latter, national actors still do not show sufficient and coherent awareness of the supranational origin of implementing criminal provisions and its implications. As I have analysed in more detail elsewhere,[27] national courts are cogs in the machinery of supranational enforcement. It falls to national courts to reconcile supranational obligations of effective enforcement and national particularities. That the application of ECL in national courts has not sparked the evolution of a proto-common law with transnationally agreed idiosyncratic doctrines, concepts and methods poses a serious obstacle in that process. And that EU bodies do not sufficiently contemplate what level of stringency, detail, comprehensiveness or flexibility of rulemaking is required to achieve regulatory objectives does not help either. These theoretical and instrumental lacunae breed tensions between supranational expectations and established national practices and theories, if national actors are aware of the supranational necessities at all.

Nevertheless, EU-induced criminal provisions are to be interpreted and applied in conformity with primary and secondary EU law.[28] As a general requirement of EU law, the effet utile of EU obligations must be ensured in the implementation process.[29] The duty of sincere cooperation (Art. 4 para. 3 TEU) demands that MS' agencies follow the principle of effective enforcement. Beyond utility, within the scope of application of the CFREU (Art. 51 CFREU), they are also to respect and protect fundamental rights in this context, which is not a one-dimensional duty as fundamental rights might restrict,[30] strengthen or even trigger the principle of effectiveness.

[27] Meyer, 'Europäisches Wirtschaftsstrafrecht (Teil 2)', (2017) 36 *wistra*, 249, 254.

[28] Interpretation in conformity with directives and other EU legal sources; CJEU, *von Colson and Kamann*, No. 14/83, Judgment, ECLI:EU:C:1984:153, 10 April 1984, para. 26; CJEU, *Adeneler and Others*, No. C-212/04, Judgment, ECLI:EU:C:2006:443, 4 July 2006; M. Heger, '§ 5 Einwirkungen des Europarechts auf das nationales Strafrecht', in M. Böse (ed.), *Enzyklopädie Europarecht*, Vol. 11, 2nd edn., Baden-Baden et al.: Nomos et al., 2021, § 5 mn. 103 f.

[29] P. Craig and G. De Búrca, *EU Law*, 6th edn., Oxford: Oxford University Press, 2015, p. 231 f.

[30] CJEU, *M.A.S. and M.B.*, No. C-42/17, Judgment, ECLI:EU:C:2017:936, 5 December 2017, paras. 52 f.

These requirements have far-reaching consequences for a multitude of substantive and procedural decisions throughout the criminal process. Provided that functional equivalence (incl. effectiveness) is guaranteed, MS retain the choice of means to attain Union goals.[31] It is quite unfortunate in this regard that EU jurisprudence or case law have not produced a sufficiently profound understanding of functional equivalence and effectiveness in criminal justice. It has not been settled whether these requirements attach to each individual case[32] or refer to all national cases in aggregate.[33] This hampers the pursuit of ECL's objective and epitomizes an obvious starting point for normative supranationalism in practice.

Potential fields of application are numerous. The duty of loyal cooperation might compel countries to cooperate with one another and go to great lengths in order to make transnational law enforcement work.[34] The principle of effectiveness has also been invoked to limit judicial and prosecutorial discretion[35] or to disapply national regulations[36] or precedents which create excessive or insurmountable barriers for loyal

[31] CJEU, *von Colson and Kamann,* No. 14/83, Judgment, ECLI:EU:C:1984:153, 10 April 1984, para. 15; A. Klip, *European Criminal Law*, 4th edn., Cambridge et al.: Intersentia, 2021, p. 90; Craig and De Búrca, *EU Law,* 6th edn., Oxford: Oxford University Press, 2015, p. 243.

[32] In CJEU, *Commission v. Greece*, No. C-68/88, Judgment, ECLI:EU:C:1989:339, 21 September 1989, para. 22; and CJEU, *Taricco and Others,* No. C-105/14, Judgment, ECLI:EU:C:2015:555, 8 September 2015, para. 51: Provisions of EU primary law impose on member states a precise obligation as to the result to be achieved, the ECJ seems to focus on results and legality obligations in individual cases. On the other hand, the ECJ also expressed in *Taricco* that the shortfall in effectiveness must concern a 'considerable number of cases', para. 47.

[33] Klip, *European Criminal Law*, pp. 82–84; CJEU, *Taricco and Others,* No. C-105/14, *Opinion of Advocate General Kokott,* ECLI:EU:C:2015:293, 30 April 2015, para. 124: realistic prospect to conduct proceedings in the permissible time span. Between micro- and meta-level perspectives, the latter would be the only practically feasible option without denying the general duty to consider and apply EU principles in each case.

[34] As the ECtHR has expressed recently, EU MS might be obliged to use mutual recognition instruments resolutely to prevent impunity and live up to their collective duties to investigate serious crimes against individuals under their jurisdiction; ECtHR, *Romeo Castaño,* Appl. No. 8351/17, Judgment, 9 July 2019.

[35] CJEU, *Alcan*, No. C-24/95, Judgment, ECLI:EU:C:1997:163, 20 March 1997; *Commission v. France,* No. C-265/95, Judgment, 9 December 1997, paras. 31 f., 65 f.; *Spain v. Council,* No. C-9/89, Judgment, ECLI:EU:C:1990:141, 27 March 1990, para. 31.

[36] CJEU, *Taricco and Others,* No. C-105/14, Judgment, ECLI:EU:C:2015:555, 8 September 2015: Statutes of limitation inapplicable; additional liability requirements which render EU minimum standards ineffective are impermissible; B. Hecker, *Europäisches Strafrecht*, 6th edn., Berlin: Springer, 2021, § 7 mn. 34–6.

enforcement.[37] In the most well-known example of the Greek Maize, the ECJ introduced a trio of sanctioning requirements ordering MS to impose sanctions that are at the same time dissuasive, effective and proportionate and equivalent to those imposed in similar national cases.[38] In other matters, the influence of EU law might be more subtle but still demands tweaking national doctrines and modifying domestic decision-making standards.[39] The EPPO will showcase how supranational objectives and obligations impact the investigative phase, charging decisions or dismissals and even the convictions and sentences sought by the prosecutor. Its activities will almost inevitably draw attention to these questions.

In the daily life of law enforcement and adjudication, the limits of measurability will be reached rather quickly though.[40] It is hence quite unclear what variations and divergencies stay within the boundaries of functional equivalence and loyal cooperation. Both national and supranational actors are called upon to improve this situation which is harmful for ECL objectives and national legal traditions. Introducing normative supranationalism as leitmotiv offers a way forward to strike the right balance. That will involve that already in the legislative process EU bodies would need to assess where and what approximation is due to achieve the aspired aims. Consistency across policy areas is another aspect to be borne in mind.[41] Exploratory memoranda and implementation monitoring should also reflect EU legal principles and a level of detail and clarity that reminds MS' agencies of their responsibility but also stakes out their leeway in decision-making accurately.

[37] CJEU, *Simmenthal II*, No. 106/77, Judgment, ECLI:EU:C:1978:49, 9 March 1978; *Commission v. Italy*, No. Case 104/86, Judgment, ECLI:EU:C:1978:49, 24 March 1988, para. 12.

[38] CJEU, *Commission v. Greece*, No. C-68/88, Judgment, ECLI:EU:C:1989:339, 21 September 1989, para. 23.

[39] Compare F. Meyer, 'Article 83', in H. v. d. Groeben, J. Schwarze, and A. Hatje, *Europäisches Unionsrecht*, 7th edn., Baden-Baden: Nomos, 2015, mn. 4, 60.

[40] With respect to the approximation of elements belonging to the general part of criminal law, C.-F. Stuckenberg, '§ 10 Allgemeiner Teil eines Europäischen Strafrechts', in M. Böse (ed.), *Enzyklopädie Europarecht*, Vol. 11, 2nd edn., Baden-Baden et al.: Nomos et al., 2021, mn. 70.

[41] A policy-by-policy approach obscures the bigger picture and has allowed remarkably incoherent standards to emerge in ECL; sentencing ranges and factors are but one example, F. Zimmermann, 'Strafrechtliche Sanktionen und das Recht der Europäischen Union: eine Bestandsaufnahme', in H. Satzger (ed.), *Harmonisierung strafrechtlicher Sanktionen in der Europäischen Union*, Baden-Baden: Nomos, 2020, pp. 577, 593 f., 603 f.

19.2.5 Results

The present situation is at odds with the very promise of the TEU. Rethinking starts with considering what constitutional elements and perspectives are missing in substantive criminal law and cooperation in criminal matters. Without this theoretical reckoning, ECL consequentially lacks critical perspective as to whether the EU, first, has sufficient powers to satisfy these expectations and, second, if secondary law instruments pay sufficient attention to such needs and obligations. This chapter hopes to advance this debate. But substantive criminal law is not the only area in dire need of fresh thinking. Judicial cooperation in criminal matters has not merely undergone dramatic changes but witnessed a gradual formation of new structures and types of transnational cooperation that have neither historical precedent nor national counterparts.

19.3 Procedural Rights and Safeguards

The highly enhanced and sophisticated forms of multilevel cooperation and enforcement in the AFSJ await further exploration from the vantage point of procedural rights. It is not denied that considerable progress has been made in the context of mutual recognition. Data protection framework, Roadmap directives,[42] victims' rights and the new generation of mutual recognition instruments (with the remarkable exception of the confiscation regulation) mark significant steps ahead. The Roadmap directives, in particular, have tried to smooth out frictions that hampered cooperation and fix some of the most serious shortcomings, yet always with a view to facilitating mutual recognition.

It is submitted, however, that a more thorough, comprehensive and principled analysis is due. One cannot help the impression that MS and courts turn a blind eye or obfuscate structures und consequences of novel modes of cooperation in the AFSJ. Cumulative, indirect or transnational effects are ignored or not perceived as legally relevant. If not directly legally binding, the (autonomy-diminishing) influence of coordinating powers, comply-or-explain mechanisms, as well as multilaterally planned and orchestrated operations is flatly denied despite their factual

[42] See Chapter 10 by M. Böse in this volume.

and normative impact. In a similar line of thinking, joint operation and complex interactions are broken down into tiny bits (step-by-step or measure-by-measure) and split up along institutional lines and national borders. The result is a particularisation of infringements and legal protection within otherwise integrated, cross-border (and perhaps multilevel) law enforcement operations. This practice creates an almost dramatic asymmetry. The targets of law enforcement activities are potentially exposed to concerted measures by multiple agencies in multiple countries irrespective of national borders while their legal defence work, rights and legal remedies are usually locked in separate national criminal justice systems.[43] And whereas judicial decisions against the defendant are to be enforced vertically and transnationally, decisions in his favour (with few exceptions like *ne bis in idem*, Art. 50 CFREU[44]) do not enjoy reverse mutual recognition.

The prevailing nonchalance is difficult to defend under the CFREU. The CFREU is a fully integrated, comprehensive EU bill of rights. It represents the primary check that citizens rely on vis-à-vis the exercise of EU power and must as such be developed and interpreted with a view to the specific types of public authority that can be found within the EU's legal system. From the standpoint of individuals, the vision of the single legal area has already become a reality in this regard. Whether as a potential security risk or as a defendant, they are exposed to a wide variety of cooperation mechanisms that may affect their rights not only in manifold and multiple ways but also in many countries (frequently at the same time) based on competences in the TFEU. Yet, EU and MS have not discharged their corresponding duties to respect, protect and fulfil in lockstep with this evolution. They have not lived up to the promise of Art. 67 TFEU, according to which all AFSJ activities will respect fundamental rights. In light of the new dangers, effective fundamental rights protection demands that

[43] Important exceptions are Art. 1 para. 3 Directive 2014/41/EU (the issuing of a European Investigation Order may be requested by a suspected or accused person, or by a lawyer on his behalf, within the framework of applicable defence rights in conformity with national criminal procedure) and Art. 5 Directive 2016/1919/EU (legal aid in the issuing MS for requested persons in European arrest warrant (EAW) proceedings in the executing MS). Alas, these improvements are still imperfect. Instead of imposing binding transnational standards, EU law tends to leave considerable discretion to MS in terms of to whether and how they implement such rights within their own national proceedings. This may result in these rights not being granted at all.

[44] See Chapter 10 by M. Böse in this volume.

the new mechanisms and structures be dissected in greater detail and adequate safeguards discussed based on such solid groundwork. Alas, the AFSJ still lacks doctrinal tools and theoretical concepts to come to terms with these types of cooperation. One of the main reasons explaining this blind spot might be that these activities are not perceived as expressions of supranational public authority. Of course, the AFSJ was not conceived of as an integrated criminal justice system, nor have the criminal justice systems of its twenty-seven MS been merged into a single legal area. But the AFSJ was envisioned, and should hence be reconsidered, as an integrated transnational and multilevel criminal justice enforcement structure. As was explained above, national criminal justice actors play an important role in the indirect enforcement of EU law. Legal actions of domestic agencies that find their basis and justification in Union law are emanations of supranational public authority. EU public authority is not the exclusive domain of direct enforcement and EU agencies in the strict sense. Rather, interactions between several MS, EU agencies and facilities on these grounds should be seen and assessed as joint, transnational measures. Even in areas of criminal law, which fall outside the substantive scope of ECL (Art. 83 TFEU), EU MS help implement supranational objectives, namely the establishment of an AFSJ, wherever their agencies resort to competences, instruments and infrastructure predicated on EU competences in judicial cooperation and law enforcement (Art. 82 f. TFEU) when cooperating with each other. Such measures should equally be perceived as an, at least implicit and parallel, exercise of EU public authority.[45] Either way, the EU has a residual responsibility by virtue of the CFREU to ensure FR compliance. Especially courts should take proactive responsibility for the integration of the AFSJ (*positive Integrationsverantwortung*) and set about substantiating FR standards under these new circumstances.

Rethinking should therefore address new concepts capable of capturing the phenomenology and essence of cooperation modes and structures. It appears that many courts and agencies are stuck in a legal world shaped by the methodology and doctrines of the ECtHR. In terms of substance, the minimum guarantees of the ECHR are part and parcel of the CFREU. But they are incapable of processing transnational and supranational

[45] For a similar view on their supranational dimension, see Wade, 'True EU Citizenship as a Precursor to Genuine Criminal Justice in Europe', (2020) 31 *CLF*, 291, 335, 339.

interactions. The CFREU goes much further. Consequently, the key future challenge lies in identifying and implementing sufficient safeguards that fit the design and impact of AFSJ cooperation. Perhaps, the most demanding operation will be the transformation of domestic fundamental rights standards and doctrines to multilevel settings. The CJEU has a pivotal role to play in this process. But responsibility does not rest on the shoulders of the Luxembourg court alone. MS courts, which review EU-related cases at the national level, must become more engaged as well. They are the natural starting point for a pluralistic multi-layered dialogue between national and European courts about the interpretation and co-creation of fundamental rights and safeguards within the general framework of the CFREU.[46]

Presumably, there are inherent limits to this approach. Idiosyncratic, complex structures in the AFSJ might call for new concepts of infringement and modes of shared and multilevel accountability (encompassing and tying together supranational and national co-actors from different jurisdictions in accordance with their involvement). The ECtHR has displayed great reluctance to formulate joint or cumulative responsibilities between MS, although this may be exactly what structures of EU enforcement demand. In the same vein, concepts like cumulative or additive infringement (meaning that a series or multitude of actions is measured on the whole and not compartmentalised) are little known outside small academic circles. As a corollary, legal remedies are falling short of effective protection as they are limited to isolated direct infringements by individual agencies. Except for incipient efforts in data protection law, a comprehensive transnational fundamental rights review is nowhere to be found. Yet, all actors involved must answer for the totality and subtleties of their interactions congruous with their respective contributions and responsibilities with respect to the rights of the persons affected.

The EU will need to break new ground in this respect. First proposals have been formulated in earlier works.[47] At this point, it may suffice to summarize that three basic idiosyncratic types of cooperation

[46] In the context of the EAW, V. Mitsilegas, 'Judicial Dialogue, Legal Pluralism and Mutual Trust in Europe's Area of Criminal Justice', (2021) 46 *E.L. Rev.*, 579, 604.

[47] Meyer, '§ 43 Verfahren der strafrechtlichen Zusammenarbeit', mn. 154 f.; F. Meyer, 'Strafe ohne Staat? Zukunftskonzepte für ein transnationales Strafrecht', (2018) *ZIS*, 68, 71; regarding shared enforcement and controlling EU agencies M. Scholten, M. Maggetti, and E. Versluis, 'Political and Judicial Accountability in Shared Enforcement in the EU', in M. Scholten and M. Luchtman (eds.), *Law Enforcement by EU Authorities: Implications*

stand out: first, a mutual recognition-based structure, which gives MS quasi-vertical access to each other's criminal justice systems to enforce or substitute national law enforcement measures (*Vollstreckungs- und Substitutionsverbund*)[48]; second, a massive data-sharing network of multiple centralised, but mostly de-centralised (increasingly interoperable), partly crosslinked information systems (*Informationsverbund*) that provide access to reams of data propelled by the principles of availability and necessity, stretching purpose limitation to breaking point;[49] and third, a composite system of prosecution (*Verbundverfolgung*), in which national and supranational agencies are mutually complementing and interconnecting their respective activities across borders and between national and supranational levels, with its characteristic cumulation, hybridisation (that is, the uncontrolled merging of procedural fragments, competences and instruments from the different legal orders that are involved) and joint coordination of investigative powers and operational capacities.[50] In light of the since recently operative EPPO and the proposed direct access to e-evidence, one is tempted to add a fourth type of law enforcement that is no longer bothered by national borders and clunky MLA proceedings, namely genuine transnational operations in a single legal area.

Potential cures include additional concepts and strings of accountability, novel doctrines of infringement capable of processing the essence of what happens to the fundamental rights of persons concerned across the AFSJ, comprehensive legal protection against multilevel enforcement but also careful reflection of additional rights and safeguards to restore equality of arms and offer meaningful transnational protection of substantive guarantees.[51]

A reasonable starting and anchor point would be to conceive of persons who are affected by law enforcement measures within the legal framework of the AFSJ as transnational legal subjects (*transnationale*

for Political and Judicial Accountability, Cheltenham: Edward Elgar, 2017, pp. 353, 354 f.; M. Scholten, M. Maggetti, and Y. Papadopoulos, 'Towards a Comprehensive System of Controls for EU Agencies' in M. Scholten and A. Brenninkmeijer (eds.), *Controlling EU Agencies: The Rule of Law in a Multi-Jurisdictional Legal Order*, Cheltenham: Edward Elgar, 2020, pp. 312, 314.

48 Meyer, '§ 43 Verfahren der strafrechtlichen Zusammenarbeit', mn. 140.

49 Ibid., mn. 144.

50 Ibid., mn. 146 f.

51 With respect to legal protection, see Meyer, '§ 44 Rechtsschutz im europäischen Strafrecht', mn. 47 f.

Prozesssubjekte).[52] This approach is inherently holistic and asks what process is due procedurally and substantively to those individuals and legal persons. It is a general principle of law and well established in the case law of the ECtHR that 'the rules of criminal procedure must be laid down by law' (*nullum judicium sine lege*). It 'imposes certain specific requirements regarding the conduct of proceedings, with a view to guaranteeing a fair trial, which entails respect for equality of arms'. The Court further observed that 'the primary purpose of procedural rules is to protect the defendant against any abuse of authority, and it is therefore the defence which is the most likely to suffer from omissions and lack of clarity in such rules'.[53] Where public authority is exercised in transnational or multilevel structures and normative frameworks such as the AFSJ, this primary purpose applies with comparable force. Admittedly, this idea needs further theorisation to explain and conceptualise the legal position of legal subjects in transnational proceedings with a view to the ultimate purpose and structure of these proceedings. This exploration overlaps nicely with the general imperative to survey the AFSJ de novo. On the downside, apart from the theoretical challenge, this approach has manifest institutional obstacles to overcome. The implementation of future findings will be confronted with limitations of the TFEU. As the CFREU does not create new competences, the courts will be left to their own devices. Doctrinal innovations and explorations of the scope of the CFREU are methodologically possible and constitutionally permissible. But the principle of conferred powers inhibits the capacity of the EU's legislative bodies to find an appropriate competence to fulfil their positive obligations as required by the principle of nullum judicium sine lege. Once again, the TFEU does not empower EU lawmakers to introduce procedural safeguards and substantive requirements commensurate with the types of public authority that the TFEU authorizes.

[52] Meyer, '§ 43 Verfahren der strafrechtlichen Zusammenarbeit', mn. 129, 155. This approach extends traditional criminal procedure theory into a multileveled supranational system. It puts the defendant at the centre of its reasoning. Citizenship-based theories overlook that nationality and democratic membership matter with respect to the legislative adoption of legitimating procedures, but much less as regards their application in the criminal process that affects nationals and foreigners alike; in a similar direction, see L. Gröning, 'Security, Justice and the Criminal Justice System' in B. Hudson and S. Ugelvik (eds.), *Justice and Security in the 21st Century: Risks, Rights and the Rule of Law*, London: Routledge, 2012, pp. 134, 150–1, who advocates a system perspective in EU criminal law that centres on individual autonomy in the multilevel system context of the EU.

[53] ECtHR, *Coëme and Others v. Belgium*, Appl. Nos. 32492/96, 32547/96, 32548/96, 33209/96 and 33210/96, Judgment, 22 June 2000, para. 102, in fine.

A further blind spot is the protection of fundamental freedoms and rights in the external dimension. The *Petruhhin* case and its progeny[54] have created much confusion and exposed serious theoretical shortcomings. In *Petruhhin*, the ECJ held that an Estonian national accused of drug trafficking sought by Russia and arrested in Latvia is discriminated against based on nationality under Latvian law as it prohibits extradition of its own nationals to third states without offering similar protection to EU citizens.[55] To avert a discriminatory infringements of the freedom of movement, the ECJ requires the requested MS contact the home state to find out whether that state would consider issuing an EAW to try its citizen in its own courts. Yet, the court stopped short of introducing any legal duties on the part of requested or home state to make such transfer work.

One may applaud the outcomes of this innovative ruling or bemoan its ill-considered practical ramifications.[56] But first and foremost, the EU struggles with the key question what legal implications follow from offering its citizens an AFSJ dedicated to fundamental freedoms and rights, particularly in the external dimension vis-à-vis third states.[57] At the moment, some decisions tend towards expanding the transnational protection of safeguards anchored in fundamental freedoms. Yet, the approach remains unprincipled. The pivotal question would be how much protection the CFREU should afford to persons residing in the EU in the external dimension of the CFREU irrespective of the contingencies of national constitutional privileges for nationals or existing treaty relations. With respect to substantive core rights or fair trial, the *Soering* doctrine of the ECtHR and the *Kadi* jurisprudence of the ECJ provide reliable answers.[58] As regards freedom of movement and residence or citizenship, the answer is much less clear.

The ECJ has held that is not incompatible with Art. 18 and Art. 21 TFEU to draw distinctions based on a rule of constitutional law, between

54 CJEU, *Petruhhin*, No. C-182/15, Judgment, ECLI:EU:C:2016:630, 6 September 2016; *Pisciotti*, No. C-191/16, Judgment, ECLI:EU:C:2018:222, 10 April 2018.

55 In the *Pisciotti* case, this privilege was conferred by a bilateral extradition treaty.

56 CJEU, *BY*, No. C-398/19, Opinion of Advocate General Hogan, ECLI:EU:C:2020:748, 24 September 2020, paras. 42 ff.

57 The Interpol red notice case before the CJEU represents a telling example, CJEU, *WS v. Bundesrepublik Deutschland*, No. C-505/19, Judgment, ECLI:EU:C:2021:376, 12 May 2021; see also recently CJEU, *Generalstaatsanwaltschaft München and ne bis in idem*, No. C-435/22 PPU, Judgment, ECLI:EU:C:2022:852, 28 October 2022: extradition of a third-country national to the USA and ne bis in idem.

58 ECtHR, *Soering*, Appl. No. 14038/88, Judgment, 7 July 1989; CJEU, *Yassin Abdullah Kadi and Al Barakaat International Foundation*, Joined Cases Nos. C-401/05 P and C-415/05 P, Judgment, ECLI:EU:C:2008:461, 3 September 2008.

nationals and the nationals of other MS in extradition cases provided this infringement of the freedom of movement is justified under Art. 52 CFREU. The court identifies the avoidance of impunity as compelling legal aim but adds that extradition is only proportionate if no less severe option is available, namely, representative jurisdiction or surrender to home country. The ECJ stressed in Case C-398/19 (BY – Generalstaatsanwaltschaft Berlin) on 17 December 2020 that the justification of nationality-based discrimination would therefore turn on the question whether the requested Member Stare is able to adopt a course of action which would be less prejudicial to the exercise of the concerned citizen's right to free movement and residence, by considering that he or she should be surrendered to the member state of which he or she is a national rather than extradited to the third state that is requesting extradition.[59]

It remains a mystery why the effective protection of such fundamental guarantees is left to discretion, happenstance, or sheer luck. The ECJ adopts a purely procedural approach. The test has no substantive protective core. If the protection of fundamental freedoms matters so much that it would justify rejecting requests even in the absence of any other tested ground for refusal, then a constitutional duty to fulfil should arise and require EU and MS to adjust their laws so as to ensure that lesser means exist to fend off extradition to third states. A possible rationale would be to treat persons entitled to freedom of movement and residence in a holistic way and afford them the same level of protection anywhere in the AFSJ (in particular vis-à-vis third countries). The AFSJ would have to be envisioned as a unified zone of free movement which (analogous to the special regime for nationals in the EAW) lays claim to adjudicating crimes of its residents itself or at least demands retransfer after conviction for the execution of the sentence in order to justify such a far-reaching protection which would amount to claiming jurisdictional priority based on an EU-wide active personality principle. At present, by contrast, potential protection for the freedom is contingent on whether the requested member state privileges its own nationals. If not, the discrimination argument falls apart and the *Petruhhin* test does not apply. If, on the other hand, a member state discriminates against non-nationals, its permissibility can hardly hinge on satisfying procedural information requirements alone. Furthermore, it is theoretically unclear why effective protection

[59] CJEU, *BY*, No. C-398/19, Judgment, ECLI:EU:C:2020:1032, 17 December 2020.

against the effects of nationality-based discrimination should depend on the autonomous decision of a given home country whether it wants to do something or not.

These inconsistencies have not led the ECJ to reconsider its judgment. The court holds firm to its initial decision not to demand effective substantive protection. *Petruhhin* is a haphazard and half-hearted effort to potentially soften the effects of nationality-based discrimination (in tension with international duties to prevent impunity). Knowing that the EU and most MS lack the means to provide substantive protection based on fundamental freedoms might have motivated the court to adopt this conceptually and substantively unsound approach as the least bad option. Yet, for the future, the discussion must focus on whether and why residents in the AFSJ deserve special protection grounded in their fundamental freedoms and, if the answer is in the affirmative the legal framework including EU agreements with third states needs to be changed accordingly. If, however, there are no good reasons for enhanced external protection, then *Petruhhin* should be discarded altogether.[60]

19.4 Final Observations

Rethinking ECL is a thankless task and doomed to either fail or to be ridiculed for academic naivety. In spite of that, this chapter unabashedly proposes to adopt fresh perspectives in two major areas. It first suggests a stronger emphasis on the notion of normative supranationality and its implications in substantive criminal law. Academic discourse and political and legislative debates need to better reflect the constitutional dimension of ECL as definitions and expressions of supranational public wrongs. ECL crimes and action plans must not only be justified in this normative dimension but also implemented and applied in conformity with supranational requirements. National legal practice appears to dramatically fall short of this bare necessity.

Present political and legislative discourse also tends to oversimplify the legal situation in the AFSJ with its tremendous variety of types and

[60] The extraterritorial application of the CFREU and the ECHR would continue to provide robust protection against extradition to rogue states and notorious human rights abusers.

variations of cooperation and integrated interactions and composite structures. This nonchalance results in insufficient interpretation and application of the CFREU. Doctrinal and theoretical lacunae must be addressed to live up to the promise of the AFSJ and to the obligations under the CFREU. For the time being, procedural safeguards and fundamental rights standards lag far behind. The conceptual and doctrinal tools identified in this chapter in line with the CFREU could serve as starting points for an intellectually stimulating debate on ensuring respect for fundamental rights in the AFSJ.

Further Reading

C. Brière/A. Weyembergh (eds.), *The Needed Balances in EU Criminal Law – Past, Present and Future*, Hart Publishing 2018.

S. Coutts, *Citizenship, Crime and Community in the European Union*, Hart Publishing 2019.

L. Mancano, *The European Union and Deprivation of Liberty – A Legislative and Judicial Analysis from the Perspective of the Individual*, Hart Publishing 2019.

V. Mitsilegas, A. di Martino, L. Mancano (eds.), *The Court of Justice and European Criminal Law – Leading Cases in a Contextual Analysis*, Hart Publishing 2019.

I. Wieczorek, *The Legitimacy of EU Criminal Law*, Oxford: Hart, 2020.

General Bibliography

Amati, E. et al., *Introduzione al diritto penale internazionale*, 4th edn., Turin: Giappichelli 2020.

Ambos, K., *European Criminal Law*, Cambridge: Cambridge University Press, 2018.

Boister, N., *An Introduction to Transnational Criminal Law*, 2nd edn., Oxford: Oxford University Press, 2018.

Harris, D. et al., *Law of the European Convention on Human Rights*, 4th edn., Oxford: Oxford University Press 2018.

Klip, A., *European Criminal Law: An Integrative Approach*, 4th edn., Cambridge, Antwerp, Chicago: Intersentia, 2021.

Mitsilegas, V., *EU Criminal Law*, Oxford and Portland, OR: Hart Publishing, 2009.

Mitsilegas, V., *EU Criminal Law after Lisbon*, Oxford and Portland, OR: Hart Publishing, 2016.

Mitsilegas, V., Bergström, M., and Konstadinides, T., *Research Handbook on EU Criminal Law*, Cheltenham: Edward Elgar Publishing, 2016.

Muñoz de Morales Romero, M., *Derecho Penal Europeo*, Valencia: Tirant lo Blanch, 2020.

Satzger, H., *European and International Criminal Law*, 2nd edn., München, Oxford, Portland, Baden-Baden: C. H. Beck, Hart Publishing, Nomos, 2018.

Index

For EU product safety concerns, contact us at Calle de José Abascal, 56–1°, 28003 Madrid, Spain or eugpsr@cambridge.org.

www.ingramcontent.com/pod-product-compliance
Lightning Source LLC
LaVergne TN
LVHW052016200926
848481LV00005B/1507

* 9 7 8 1 1 0 8 7 9 9 7 9 9 *